CW01666454

good NON RETIREMENT GUIDE 2003

good NON RETIREMENT GUIDE 2003

17th EDITION

rosemary brown

ENTERPRISE DYNAMICS

KOGAN PAGE

This edition published in 2003

120 Pentonville Road
London N1 9JN
www.kogan-page.co.uk

British Library Cataloguing in Publication Data

A CIP record for this book is available from the British Library.

ISBN 0 7494 3935 1

Typeset by Saxon Graphics Ltd, Derby.
Printed and bound in Great Britain by Bell & Bain Ltd, Glasgow.

Contents

Introduction

Retirement has rarely, if ever, been as much in the news.

Week in, week out, a new sorry story has hit the headlines. Investment savings down in value... the closure of final salary schemes... annuities at an almost historic low... the misery of savers trapped in Equitable Life... suggestions to raise the State retirement age to 70... bank and building society accounts paying negative interest...

In all my years of editing the Guide, I can't remember a time when as many people have asked me what point there is in saving for a pension or in trying to plan prudently for the future. Most of those I spoke to feel let down by employers, let down by financial advisers, let down by the government and enraged that promise, after promise, seems to have been broken.

There are few words of consolation that one can say to victims like Ted, who is two years off retirement and is now due to receive only a fraction of his expected pension, because the bulk of the fund will be eaten up in paying the benefits of earlier retirees. Equally, one can only feel deeply sorry for those like George, whose pension in payment has suddenly been cut by the best part of £2,000 a year because the money is no longer there to pay him the full amount.

The plunge in shares values and increased life expectancy account for some of the damage but are by no means the only cause.

If employers must share some of the blame for past pension holidays, a far greater part is due to the financial services industry and more especially to government who not only raided pension schemes to the tune of £5 billion a year in Gordon Brown's first budget but whose plethora of new initiatives (second state pension, stakeholder pension, the replacement of PEPs and TESSAs by ISAs, the minimum income guarantee and means-tested credits, which variously come in the form of tax relief or cash benefits) have added immeasurably to the complexity of financial planning for retirement.

The new pension credit, designed to reward those with modest savings, is due to be introduced next October. Yet how many people are likely to benefit when already, either through ignorance or pride, many of the neediest pensioners are failing to claim the minimum income guarantee to which they are entitled?

Instead of an ever-changing kaleidoscope of new schemes, what is urgently needed is a bonfire of half the means-tested benefits and, in their place, a single improved state pension. At the same time, many of the existing rules and regulations are in urgent need of reform.

Unfortunately, the pensions green paper, which was expected in November is now only due to be published after we go to press. Hopefully, we shall see it addressing our readers' main grievances.

There is deep and growing resentment about the requirement to buy an annuity which, with interest rates as low as they are, are forcing many people into a reduced standard of living for the remainder of their lives. There is also a strong case for changing the rules to allow the transfer of investment-linked annuities to a different provider, especially in instances when pensions in payments have actually been cut. The FSA has been flagging up the Open Market Option to advise people when buying an annuity of their right to shop around. It is surely only logical that individuals should have the same freedom when their existing annuity is losing them hundreds, if not thousands, of pounds a year.

It is also high time to review the regulations that prevent people from working part-time for a company that has started to pay their pension. On the one hand, employers are being urged to recruit and retain older workers, with presumably part of the aim being to enable them to save more for the future. Yet on the other hand, due to the existing final salary rules, employees lucky enough to have an employer willing to allow them to ease gradually into retirement, risk ending up with a reduced pension.

With the millions of pounds that financial services companies have had to pay in compensation, it has to be hoped that we have finally seen an end to the many mis-selling scandals. What we have not yet seen, however, is a wholesale improvement in the quality of their sales literature. While some have made commendable efforts to clarify the nature of their products and explain the risks in plain English, I still all too often pick up leaflets that read like double dutch or where the terms and conditions are in minute type that is virtually impossible to read without a magnifying glass.

However, if others are to blame for some of the current woes, almost all of us could do more to improve our own finances.

Like millions of others, I could get better interest rates by switching my account to one of the banks or building societies offering more competitive rates on-line. Many non-taxpayers could save themselves even more money by requesting to have their interest paid gross, instead of having tax deducted for which they are not due. Even higher rate taxpayers could make savings by sheltering up to £3,000 a year in a mini-cash ISA, with the advantage that all interest is tax-free.

Literally hundreds of thousands of people are going without by not claiming benefits to which they are entitled. In particular, many of the neediest pensioners are impoverishing themselves by several pounds a week by failing to claim the Minimum Income Guarantee.

Empty-nesters could make up to £4,250 a year tax free by taking in a lodger. Many married couples could also cut their tax by transferring some of their money to a lower or non-tax-paying spouse.

Despite the recent financial gloom, there are nevertheless several good news items. State pensions are due to rise in April and, with the launch of the Pension Credit next autumn, those with small savings should be able to keep more of their money. Also, because of the government's need to issue new gilts, annuity rates should begin to show some improvement over the coming year.

A further cause for cheer is that the contribution of older carers has, at last, been recognised and carers aged 65 and over are now equally entitled to claim the Invalid Care Allowance.

Although still some way off, age discrimination will become illegal in 2006. The directive, however, is already beginning to have its desired effect with more and more companies looking favourably on employing mature workers.

If some people want nothing better than to continue in work, for others the whole pleasure of retirement is to look forward to a new way of life. A chance to travel, take up a new sport, get an allotment, join a choir, go to art classes, become a beekeeper... the Guide includes a vast choice of ideas that you might enjoy. Also, if you have ever wondered about becoming more involved in the community or spending a few hours a week doing voluntary work, you will find dozens of organisations that would welcome you with open arms.

With so many opportunities, and more, perhaps it is hardly surprising that many retired people say they have never been as busy in their life. But then, the funny thing about retirement is that, whatever you start planning, activities suddenly snowball as you discover all the exciting possibilities.

Hopefully the Guide will give you plenty of ideas, as well as other practical tips, to help make retirement everything you wish for – and more.

As always, I owe a big thank you to the many hundreds of people who have generously given their time to provide information. While it is impossible to mention everyone by name, I am particularly indebted to the Inland Revenue and other government departments for their invaluable assistance in helping to keep me up-to-date with the various changes and new developments.

I am also most grateful to our publishers, Kogan Page, for their continued enthusiasm and support. Lastly, and right at the top of my list, my very special thanks to my wonderful PA, Jean, and also to Annette: Jean, who despite producing a baby son this year, has been her usual marvel of efficiency and Annette for valiantly holding the fort during Jean's maternity leave. They have both done a fantastic job and I could never have managed without them.

Finally, to all our readers, my very best wishes for many years of happiness and fulfillment.

Rosemary Brown
November 2002

Stop Press

Budget changes to remember

- The personal allowance for the 2003–04 tax year, for those aged under 65, has been frozen and will remain at the present (2002–03) figure of £4,615.
- Age-related personal allowances are being raised as normal and will be increased to £6,610 for those aged 65 to 74 and to £6,720 for those aged 75 and older. The new income limit to qualify for the full age allowance goes up by £400 to £18,300.
- The minimum married couple's allowance is being raised to £2,150 in April 2003. Less well-off married couples under 75 will get £5,565, while those aged 75 and over will receive £5,635. As with age-related personal allowance, the income limit to qualify for more than the minimum is being increased to £18,300. In all cases, as before, the allowance is restricted to 10 per cent tax relief.
- National Insurance contributions are being increased by 1 per cent in April 2003, with the starting point for both employers' and employees' contributions remaining at £89 a week. The extra means that employers will have to pay 12.8 per cent on all earnings above the £89 threshold. Employee rates will increase from 10 to 11 per cent on all earnings between the £89 threshold and the upper earnings limit of £595; additionally 1 per cent will be payable on all earnings above the upper limit. Class 4 contributions for the self-employed are being raised from 7 to 8 per cent on earnings between £4,615 and £30,940, plus 1 per cent payable on all earnings over £30,940.
- The new pension credit to reward pensioners with modest savings is due to be introduced in October 2003. It will benefit single pensioners with incomes of up to £139 a week and couples with incomes of up to £200. A single pensioner with income of £110 a week will receive a top-up of £11.60. Couples with income of £170 a week will get £13.50 extra.
- Working Families Tax Credit, Disabled Person's Tax Credit and the Children's Tax Credit are all being abolished in April 2003 and are being replaced by a Working Tax Credit (WTC) and Child Tax Credit (CTC). The major changes are that WTC will extend support to include low paid individuals, irrespective of whether they have children or a disability. In the case of CTC, eligibility will be based on the combined income of the parents as opposed to, as now, automatically excluding most families where either parent is a higher-rate taxpayer. Parents with a joint income of up to £58,000 will qualify.

New benefit up-ratings from April 2003

Highlights include:

- The basic pension for a single person goes up to £77.45 a week and to £123.80 for couples.
- The Minimum Income Guarantee is being increased next April from £98.15 to £102.10 for single pensioners and from £149.80 to £155.80 for couples.
- The basic rate of long term Incapacity Benefit will rise to £72.15 a week.
- Attendance Allowance is increased to £38.30 at the lower rate and to £57.20 at the higher rate.
- Jobseeker's Allowance rises to £54.65 for single adults over 25 and to £85.75 for couples. There are additional premiums for carers, those with dependent children and for people with disabilities.
- The new care component figures for Disability Living Allowance will be: highest £57.20; middle £38.30; lowest £15.15. The new mobility components will be: higher £39.95; lower £15.15.
- The basic rate of Severe Disablement Allowance will rise to £43.60 a week.
- The carer premium, which applies to income-related benefits, will rise to £25.10 weekly from April 2003.
- Bereavement benefits, as from April 2003, will be as follows: the lump sum bereavement benefit remains at £2,000; the standard bereavement allowance, paid to widowed persons aged between 55 and 59 inclusive, increases to £77.45; the age-related allowance rates, payable to younger widowed persons, vary according to age from £23.24 for 45 year olds to £72.03 for those aged 54. The widowed parent's allowance rises in April to £77.45.

Other highlight points

- The previous age limit for entitlement to Invalid Care Allowance has been removed and carers aged 65 and over are now equally entitled to claim. The allowance, currently £42.45 a week, will rise in April 2003 to £43.15. It will also be renamed Carer's Allowance.
- Free flu jabs are available on the NHS this winter (2002–2003) for all persons aged 65 plus.
- The capital limit for receiving help with the cost of residential or nursing home care is expected to be raised from £19,000 to £19,500 in April 2003. People with

assets below £12,000 (currently £11,750) will not have their capital taken into account.

- Some help for small businesses. The VAT flat rate scheme will be extended from April 2003 to include businesses with an annual turnover of up to £150,000 (excl. VAT). Eligibility for the Small Firms Loan Guarantee Scheme will also be extended in April.

- Retirement relief, allowable to owner-managers selling all or part of their business on retirement, is being withdrawn on 5 April 2003. Those selling before this date should be able to claim 100 per cent tax relief on the first £50,000 of capital gain, with a further exemption of one-half of gains between £50,001 and £200,000.

- SERPS benefits for surviving spouses are in process of being halved over the present decade. The first cut, to 90 per cent, came in October 2002 and lasts until October 2004 when the benefits will be further reduced to 80 per cent. Importantly, anyone over State pension age on 5 October 2002 is exempt from any cuts and will keep the right to pass on their SERPS benefits in full to a bereaved spouse. Equally, any younger widowed person who had already inherited their late spouse's SERPS entitlement before 6 October 2002 will continue to receive the full amount.

1 Looking Forward to Retirement

Just as there are some people who become engaged within three hours of meeting and live happily ever after, there are others who without any apparent planning enjoy a totally fulfilled retirement, clearly relishing everything it has to offer.

But for most of us life does not work like that. Important events require some preparation if we are to make the most of them and arguably this is more true of retirement than of any other stage.

A majority of people retiring today are fitter, more skilled and better off financially than any previous generation. Also, thanks to increased longevity, a great many of us can realistically look forward to 25 years or more of active life ahead. As a result, planning the future has become even more critically important. The *Good non-Retirement Guide* is not designed to offer you a ready-made philosophy or a few rose-tinted blueprints on the theme 'Life Begins in Middle Age'. Its sole aim is to set you thinking along constructive lines, to indicate what is possible, to advise on the best sources of information and to help you avoid the pitfalls that can trap the unwary.

Key concerns are likely to be the question of money and how you will occupy your time. Others may well include: where you live, how best to keep fit, the effect of your retirement on close personal relationships and perhaps new responsibilities such as the care of elderly parents.

You do not need to be an accountant to know that once you stop earning your income will drop. However, if you complete the Budget Planner (see pages 138–143), you may be pleasantly surprised to find that the difference is far less than you had feared. On the plus side, you will be saving on travel and other work-related expenses as well as enjoying a welcome reduction in tax.

As with all questions affecting retirement, it is sensible if possible to plan ahead. Assess your likely savings including the lump sum from your pension and any insurance policies you may have. Then draw up a plan as to how you can maximise their value. Should you invest your money in a building society, ISA, unit trust, stocks and shares or government securities? Does it make sense to buy an annuity?

What are the tax angles for someone in your position? Should you consider consulting a good accountant, stockbroker or other professional adviser? If you are unsure of the answers, then the Investment and Financial Advisers chapters (chapters 5 and 6) may help to clarify your thinking.

Your retirement income may well depend on whether you start a new career, especially if – as has happened to many thousands of people – you were made redundant with no immediate job prospects on offer. While we are not pretending that starting afresh is easy, a great many men and women do in fact find rewarding work, including some who are well into their sixties. While some individuals turn their talents to something entirely new, others go freelance or become consultants in their existing area of expertise. Chapter 11, Looking for Paid Work, may give you some useful leads.

An increasing number of people are taking the heady step of starting their own business. This is not a decision to be entered into lightly. The risks are legion and most budding entrepreneurs find that they have never worked as hard in their lives. In the early days at least, being your own boss means sacrificing your social life, forgoing a salary and traipsing out in the rain to post your own letters. Moreover, if you are married, then unless your partner is solidly behind you there are liable to be domestic tensions – especially if you run the business from home. Against this, many who take the plunge derive enormous satisfaction from building up a family enterprise. If you are seriously flirting with the idea Chapter 10, Starting Your Own Business, provides a lot of the detail you will need to know.

A worthwhile alternative to becoming a business tycoon is to devote your energies to voluntary work. There are literally scores of opportunities for retired people to make a valuable contribution within their own community. You might visit the elderly in their own homes, drive patients to hospital, run a holiday playscheme, help out in your Citizens' Advice Bureau or become a Samaritan. Other ideas which might appeal are conservation work or playing a more active role in politics by joining your local party association. Whether you can only spare the occasional day or are prepared to help on a regular basis Chapter 12, Voluntary Work, lists a fund of suggestions you might like to consider.

A prime requirement, whether you are thinking of paid or unpaid work, or for that matter simply planning to devote more time to your hobbies, is to remain fit and healthy. Good health is the most valuable possession we have. Without it, energy is lacking, activities are restricted and the fun goes out of life. No amount of money can compensate for being bed-ridden or a semi-invalid.

While anyone can be unfortunate enough to be struck down by an unexpected illness, your future good health is largely in your own hands. The reason why the seventies are so often dogged by aches and pains is that sufficient care has not been taken during the fifties and sixties.

As well as all the obvious advice about not smoking, becoming too fat or drinking to excess, there is the important question of exercise. While you could of course do press-ups and go for walks, you will probably have a much better time if you join the new keep-fit brigade.

There are opportunities around the country for almost every kind of sport, with 50-plus beginners especially welcome. Additionally, dancing, yoga, keep-fit-to-music and relaxation classes are readily available through most local authorities as well as being offered by the many specialist bodies listed in both the Health and Leisure Activities chapters.

The only problem is likely to be fitting everything in. The choice of organised leisure pursuits is little short of staggering. If you have ever wanted to learn about computers, take a degree, join a choir, become proficient in a craft, play competitive

Scrabble, start coin collecting or become a beekeeper, you will find an organisation that caters for your enthusiasm.

The type of activities you enjoy could be an important consideration in choosing where you will live. Because we are conditioned to thinking of retirement as a time for settling into a new home, many people up sticks without perhaps giving enough thought to such essentials as proximity to family and friends and whether a different area would provide the same scope for pursuing their interests.

A fairly common mistake is for people to retire to a place where they once spent an idyllic holiday, perhaps 15 or 20 years previously with only a minimum of further investigation. Resorts that are glorious in mid-summer can be bleak and damp in winter as well as pretty dull when the tourist season is over. Equally, many people sell their house and move somewhere smaller without taking account of the fact that when they are spending more time at home they may actually want more space, rather than less. This is particularly true of anyone planning to work from home or who has a hobby such as carpentry which requires a separate workroom.

While moving may be the right solution, especially if you want to realise some capital to boost your retirement income, there are plenty of ways of adapting a house to make it more convenient and labour-saving. Likewise, you may be able to cut the running costs, for example with insulation. These and other possibilities, including taking in a lodger and creating a granny flat, are explored in Chapter 8, Your Home.

On the subject of granny flats, if you are caring for elderly parents there may come a time when a little bit of outside help could make all the difference. The range of organisations that can provide you with back-up is far more extensive than is generally realised. For single women especially, who may feel that they have to give up a career, knowing what facilities are available could prove a veritable godsend.

While there may be pressure if a parent, however much loved, requires an undue amount of attention, a more commonplace problem is the effect of retirement on a couple's relationship. Many husbands are puzzled, and sometimes hurt, by their wife's attitude to the event. For years she has been complaining 'I never see anything of you darling' and 'Why can't you spend a little more time with the family?' – so naturally he expects her to be delighted to have him at home. But according to some husbands, the enthusiasm may seem less than whole-hearted. As one recently retired 62-year-old put it: "I had hardly had a chance to enjoy a couple of days pottering in the garden for the first time in years, when my wife was nagging me to go out and find something to do. She was the one who wanted me to take early retirement. Now she is wishing that I was back at work."

The reverse situation can also apply, especially if the wife had a high-powered career. Although in general the evidence suggests that it is usually the man's retirement that provokes most friction, this may change as more of today's working wives turn sixty and find themselves facing the same need to make difficult adjustments.

Either way, the point is that after years of seeing relatively little of each other, retirement suddenly creates the possibility of much more togetherness. Put in blunt terms, many wives grumble that having a husband at home during the day means an extra meal to cook and inevitable disruption to their normal routine. And while this may not apply in an 'equal opportunity' marriage, where the domestic jobs are shared equally between husband and wife, in a majority of households women still do the lion's share of the cooking and cleaning. So, if he stays in bed longer in the morning, the chores will be finished later which can be an irritation. But an even greater cause for resentment is that she may feel guilty about meeting her friends or pursuing her usual weekday activities unless her partner is also busy.

If she is still at work, the situation can be even more fraught as, apart from the extra housework, she may find her loyalties uncomfortably divided. Furthermore, quite irrationally, some retired husbands begin to harbour dire suspicions about their wives' working colleagues, imagining romantic entanglements that had never crossed their mind before.

Sometimes too, retired people subconsciously label themselves as 'old' and start denying themselves and their partner the pleasures of a happily fulfilled sex life. It is difficult to know whether this is more ludicrous or tragic. As studies in many parts of the world show, the sexual satisfaction of both partners continues in a high proportion of cases long after the age of seventy and often well into the eighties. Moreover, according to recent medical research, an active sex life in middle age can positively help to promote good health and longer life expectancy. A welcome book which discusses the subject frankly is *The Relate Guide to Loving in Later Life*, by Marge Thoburn and Suzie Powling, price £9.99.

Usually, problems that coincide with retirement can be fairly simply overcome by willingness to discuss them frankly and to work out a solution that suits both partners. The situation is very much easier today than even ten years ago when male/female roles were far more stereotyped and many couples felt that they had to conform to a set pattern for the sake of convention.

Many non-marrieds equally find that adjusting to retirement is not always that easy. Relatives may impose new pressures once you are no longer at work. Likewise, close friendships sometimes alter when one friend retires – and not the other. Additionally, many single people admit that they had not realised before how much they relied on their job for companionship and sometimes, even for part of their weekend social life.

Pre-retirement courses

Talking to other people to find out how they plan to tackle the challenges as well as the opportunities of retirement can be immensely helpful. Many companies recognise this need by providing pre-retirement courses. If you are unlucky enough to be in a firm where this is not offered, or if you are self-employed, there are a number of organisations to which you can turn for advice and help.

Before deciding on a particular course, it is worthwhile giving a little thought to the best time to go and the subjects which the counselling should cover. The traditional view is that the ideal time is somewhere between one or two years before you are due to retire. While this is probably true for most people, it is also important to remember that preparing for retirement really has to be a staged process. Some financial decisions, such as those affecting company or personal pension planning, need to be taken as early as possible. Others, such as whether to move house, can probably only be made much later.

The basic subjects that the best courses address are: finance, health, activity, leisure, housing and the adjustments which will need to be made by both you and your family when you retire.

The crucial test however is not the amount of factual information that is contained but the extent to which the course helps to focus and stimulate your own thoughts on the various issues and to lead to discussion with your partner and others in the same situation.

The following is a list of the best known courses available to individuals enrolling independently of company sponsorship.

The Pre-Retirement Association of Great Britain & Northern Ireland, 9 Chesham Road, Guildford, Surrey GU1 3LS. T:01483 301170. The PRA, the national body for retirement counselling, runs Positive Change Management Ltd. which offers both company courses and those for individuals who are not sponsored by their employer. These courses are independent, free from commercial bias and partners are encouraged to attend. They are held in Central London, Slough, Guildford, Reigate and Leeds; cost (2002) is £263 per person, or £418 per couple (excluding VAT), for a two-day course.

Some affiliated local organisations of the PRA arrange their own pre-retirement courses, often in collaboration with other educational authorities. For further details, contact the PRA at the Guildford address above.

Time of Your Life, 78 Capel Road, East Barnet, Herts EN4 8JF. T:020 8449 4506. Five-day mid-life and retirement planning holiday courses are run during the spring at Torquay Leisure Hotels. Price is about £260 which includes full board, accommodation, all course activities and evening entertainment.

The Retirement Trust, 19 Borough High Street, London Bridge, London SE1 9SE. T:020 7378 9708. Runs pre-retirement seminars, lasting a day, once a month in Central London. Topics covered include money matters, health and keeping active in the third age. Price, including lunch, is £150 per person or £225 per couple.

Scottish Pre-Retirement Council, Alexandra House, 204 Bath Street, Glasgow G2 4HL. T:0141 332 9427. Runs courses in all areas of Scotland. These are normally held over three days and cost (2002) about £60.

Greater London Association for Pre-Retirement, 32 Westbourne Park Villas, London W2 5EA. T:020 7221 3020. Runs two-day non-residential courses in Central London during February, April, June and October. Subjects covered are leisure, health, money matters and state benefits. Cost for two days, including lunch and book pack, is £120 (£105 for GLAP members).

Adult Education Centres

See local telephone directory under your local council listing. A growing number of Adult Education Centres run both day and evening courses. Standards vary but you should be able to get a good idea of the approach from the syllabus.

Workers' Educational Association, Temple House, 17 Victoria Park Square, Bethnal Green, London E2 9PB. T:020 8983 1515. Many of the 650 branches of the WEA run local courses. Check your telephone directory for the nearest branch or contact the London HQ for further information.

Universities. A number of universities run retirement planning courses. These are typically held once or twice a year and are normally arranged by the Department of Extra-Mural Studies.

Commercial organisations

The following organisations offer an attractive mix of courses with, hopefully, something to suit almost everyone. Some are residential; others, day courses. Several are specifically for senior executives and one is especially for women.

Chase de Vere Investments, Eastcheap Court, 11 Philpot Lane, London EC3M 8AE. T:020 7618 0207. Chase de Vere offers a two-day programme for professional people and senior executives, 'Planning for Retirement', which by dovetailing personal development with financial planning is designed to help participants get the most out of retirement. The seminars which are held in various locations around the country cost £300 per person; £500 per couple. One-day seminars for female groups, 'Women – Independence in Retirement', are also available, priced at £150 per person including lunch. All prices are exclusive of VAT. For programme details, contact Jackie Francis at the above address.

Millstream, South Harting, Petersfield, Hants GU31 5NS. T:01730 825711. Millstream specialises in providing courses for senior executives designed to help them adjust to the changes on leaving their main employment. These are held regularly in the exclusive setting of the Royal Yacht Squadron in the castle at Cowes. Small numbers make for a sympathetic approach and the participation of partners is encouraged. Topics covered over the 2 1/2 days include personal adjustments, health considerations, finance (totally independent) and new opportunities. Expert speakers are available throughout for one-to-one discussion; and a follow-up service is provided. Accommodation, meals, drinks, full notes and a number of books are included in the fees which (2002 prices) are £3,400 per participant or couple, excluding VAT.

New Life Retirement Services Ltd., 58 Park Road, Chandler's Ford, Eastleigh, Hants SO53 2ES. T:01983 730390. Two-day non-residential courses are held quarterly in Southampton and also in other parts of the country where there is sufficient interest. The programme covers money matters, housing, leisure and health. Cost, including course literature and refreshments, is £120 per person; £185 per couple.

Prudential Retirement Counselling Service, Abbey Gate, 57–75 Kings Road, Reading, Berks RG1 3AB. T:0118 949 4314. Pre-retirement, mid-career and financial planning seminars are offered on an open basis to individuals and their partners every month at a variety of locations around the country. Topics include: state and company pension benefits, financial planning, health, long-term care, relationships, moving house, opportunities for further work and leisure pursuits. All financial advice sessions are conducted by independent financial advisers. The price for a two-day non-residential programme inclusive of literature and luncheon is £260 per person, plus VAT. Exclusive residential seminars for senior executives are held in Surrey and the Cotswolds; price is £540 plus VAT per person. For further information, contact Victoria Wilkinson or Wladek Koch (Retirement Counselling Manager) at the above address.

Retirement Counselling Service, Apex House, Chiltern Avenue, Amersham, Bucks HP6 5AE. T:01494 433553. The Retirement Counselling Service runs over 40 open seminars a year including some specifically for executives. Two-day residential courses cost £395; senior manager/executive courses held in the Cotswolds and Lake District cost £590 and £690 respectively. A reduction is made for partners. All prices are exclusive of VAT. For further information, contact Derek Wildey.

Chapter 14 also contains the names of one or two organisations that run pre-retirement courses as part of their holiday programme.

New focus for the retired

Over the years, a number of organisations have been formed to represent the interests of retired people and to give them a more powerful voice in putting forward their views on issues that affect their lives at both national and local levels. Three of the best known, which in addition to their campaigning role arrange a variety of social and other events, are listed below.

Age Resource, 1268 London Road, Norbury, London SW16 4ER. T:020 8765 7610. Age Resource is part of Age Concern's Activage Unit. It promotes positive ageing by proving that over-50s are not just capable of leading active and fulfilling lives but that they also have a positive contribution to make to their community. Among other activities, it holds a week of 'virtual' events in its Internet chat cafe; and also operates a growing nationwide network of Age Resource Desks that offer Internet and e-mail taster sessions together with information about local opportunities for leisure, voluntary work and further learning. For information, contact the above address.

ARP/O50, 5th Floor, Windsor House, 1270 London Road, London SW16 4DH. T:020 8764 3344. The Association of Retired and Persons Over Fifty is a social and campaigning membership organisation for the 50 plus age group in the UK. A hundred and ninety-five Friendship Centres around the country offer a varied programme of social events and take a keen interest in local and national issues. There are three free 24-hour emergency helplines (legal, tax and domestic). Among other facilities, members receive a bi-monthly magazine and have access to a range of shopping, travel and insurance discounts. Membership costs £23 a year (£32 per couple) by direct debit.

National Pensioners Convention, 9 Arkwright Road, London NW3 6AB. T:020 7431 9820. The NPC is an umbrella group for pensioner associations throughout the country, which collectively have a membership of around a million retired people. While each group is autonomous and so organises its own programme of events, a main aim of affiliated organisations is to act as a pressure group to improve facilities and opportunities for older people, including in particular a substantial improvement in the basic State pension and better community care for older people. For further information and addresses of local groups, contact the NPC at the address above.

2 Money in General

For most people approaching retirement, the major concern is money. Some individuals have no worries; they have planned the event for years, made maximum pension contributions, carefully invested their savings, covered themselves and family in insurance policies, budgeted ahead and can even gleefully tell you about the exotic round-the-world trip they intend to take just as soon as their new life begins.

But for a majority of people, however, it is not like that. After years of hardly giving a thought to their pension, panic suddenly sets in as they consider the prospect of no longer drawing a regular salary. The fact that most of their friends who have already retired seem to manage pretty well is of little comfort. Even quite wealthy individuals confess to conjuring up images of going cold and hungry.

Happily, the reality is far rosier than many people imagine. For a start, those retiring today are better off financially than any previous generation. Equally to the point, the spectre of drastic economies that haunts so many men and women is often the result of their having only the haziest idea as to their likely income and expenditure.

Doing the sums

Knowing the facts is the first priority. To make a proper assessment, you need to draw up several lists:

- Expected sources of income on retirement
- Unavoidable outgoings
- Normal additional spending (including holidays and other luxuries).

Stage two, you need to consider a number of options under the following headings:

- Possible ways of boosting your retirement income
- Spending now for saving later
- Cherished plans, if affordable.

Most difficult of all, you will require a third list of variables and unknowns which, while impossible to estimate accurately, must as a matter of prudence be taken into account in any long-term budget planning. The two most important are tax and inflation. A survey of retired people by MORI revealed that nearly half of those questioned said that they had not made sufficient allowance for inflation. Two-thirds of the total cited heating and fuel bills in particular as being more expensive than they had anticipated. Additionally, there are all the possible emergency situations, such as your health, for which, if this ever were to become a problem, you might want to make special provision. Your life expectancy is another consideration, as is that of your partner and any dependants.

Ideally, you should start thinking about at least some of these points, especially those that relate to your pension and to any savings or investment plans, five or even ten years before you retire. When doing the sums, aim to be realistic. Many people make the mistake of basing their calculations on their current commitments and expenditure, without properly realising that some of their requirements will change. To get the figures into perspective, it is a good idea to imagine yourself already retired. The good news is that, while some items will probably take a heftier slice of your budget, others will certainly be cheaper or no longer cost you anything at all.

Possible savings and extra outgoings are discussed below. The most practical way of examining the list is to tick off the items in each column that you expect definitely to apply and, where possible, to write down the expenditure involved in the adjacent box (see Budget Planner, pages 138–143). While inevitably this will be a somewhat rough-and-ready exercise – and obviously there will be gaps – the closer you are to retirement, the more worthwhile it will be.

Possible savings

Going out to work generally involves a fair number of expenses. When you leave your job, you will probably save at least several pounds a week. Items for which you will no longer have to pay include: your travelling costs to work, bought lunches, special clothes; plus all the out-of-pocket incidentals such as drinks with colleagues, trade magazines and collections for presents or the Christmas party.

You will not have to pay any more national insurance contributions and, unless you choose to invest in a private plan, your pension payments will also cease. Additionally, when you retire, you may be in a lower tax bracket.

At the same time you may have reached the stage when your children are now independent, your mortgage is substantially paid off and you have stopped subscribing to a life assurance policy. Moreover, one of the gratifying aspects of attaining state retirement age is that you become eligible for a variety of benefits, for example: concessionary travel, free national health service prescriptions, cheaper theatre and cinema tickets (usually matinees), reduced entrance charges for exhibitions and a wide choice of special holiday offers. Some benefits apply to both men and women from age 60.

Another point worth remembering is that many insurance companies give discounts to mature drivers. In some instances, discounts apply to those aged 50; other companies restrict eligibility to those aged 55 or even 60. Normally, but again this varies, the scheme is terminated when the policy holder reaches 75. Most companies, but not all, extend the cover to a spouse or other named person with a good driving record. At time of writing, average discounts for people over 50 ranged from 10 to 15 per cent with considerable extra savings for drivers with a five-year claim free record.

Best advice is first approach your existing insurance company and ask what terms they will give you. If these appear dullish, it could pay to shop around. Among those that offer special rates for mature drivers are: Axa Direct, Zurich Insurance, Eagle

Star, Direct Line, Saga Services and Age Concern Insurance Services. It is also worth surfing the Internet, as a growing number of insurers give discounts to those buying a policy online.

Extra outgoings

There is no escaping the fact that when you retire some of your expenses will be heavier than at present.

Firstly, you will probably be spending more time at home, so items like heating and lighting are liable to be costlier.

If you received any perks with your job, such as a company car or health insurance, then unless you have a very generous employer these will have to come out of your own pocket in future. Equally, any business entertaining you enjoyed will largely cease, so any free lunches and the like will have to be paid for instead from the domestic housekeeping.

Another very important consideration is your extra leisure. With more time available, you will understandably be tempted to spend more on outings, your hobbies and on longer holidays from home. To avoid having to stint yourself, these need to be budgeted for in advance. Most people say that in an ideal world they would assume to be spending roughly double on entertainment of all kinds, compared with when they were working. Even voluntary activity is not without its hidden expenses, for example: more use of the telephone, petrol costs, raffle tickets, support of fund-raising occasions and so on.

Looking ahead, as you get older you may want more home comforts. Likewise, you may have to pay other people to do some of the jobs, such as the decorating, that you previously managed yourself.

Anticipating the areas of additional expenditure is not to be pessimistic. On the contrary, it is the surest way of avoiding future money worries. Moreover, when you have sat down and worked out your retirement income in detail, you may even be pleasantly surprised.

Expected sources of income on retirement

Your list will include at least some of the following. Once you have added up the figures in the budget planner, you will have to deduct income tax to arrive at the net spending amount available to you.

- State basic pension
- State graduated pension
- SERPS
- Second State pension
- Occupational pension
- Personal pension
- Stakeholder pension
- State benefits

Additionally, you may receive income or a capital sum from some of the following:

- Company share option scheme
- Investments (stocks and shares, building society etc.)
- Bank deposit account
- Endowment policy
- Sale of business or personal assets
- Other existing income (from a trust, property, family business)
- Interest from a National Savings and Investments bond or certificate

You might also be in receipt of income from an annuity. However, since at this stage you will be unlikely to have purchased one, this really belongs in the category of investment decisions.

Unavoidable outgoings

One person's priority is another person's luxury – and vice versa. For this reason, the divide between 'unavoidable' and 'normal additional spending' (see section following) is fraught with obvious difficulty. For example, readers who do not possess a pet would never include pet food among the essentials, whereas a dog or cat owner unquestionably would.

Almost everyone will want to juggle some of the items between the two lists; or add their own particular commitments or special enthusiasms, omitted by us.

Our suggestions are simply intended as memory joggers – and emphatically not as a guide to what should, or should not, constitute a luxury. What matters is the basic principle behind the exercise. If at some stage budgeting choices have to be made, decisions will be very much easier if you already know: your total outgoings, what you are spending on each individually and those you variously rate as important or marginal.

Whatever your own essentials, some of the following items will certainly feature on your list of unavoidable expenses:

- Food
- Rent or mortgage repayments
- Council tax
- Repair and maintenance costs
- Heating
- Lighting and other energy
- Telephone
- Postage (incl. Christmas cards)
- TV licence/rental
- Household insurance
- Clothes
- Domestic cleaning products
- Laundry, cleaners' bills, shoe repair
- Miscellaneous services, e.g. plumber, window cleaner
- Car, including licence, petrol, AA, etc.
- Other transport
- Regular savings and life assurance
- HP/other loan repayments
- Outgoings on health

Normal additional expenditure

This may well include:

- Gifts

- Holidays
- Newspapers/books
- Drink
- Cigarettes/tobacco
- Hairdressing
- Toiletries/cosmetics
- Entertainment (hobbies, outings, video purchase/rental, home entertaining etc.)
- Miscellaneous subscriptions/membership fees
- Charitable donations
- Expenditure on pets
- Garden purchases
- Other

Work out the figures against these lists. Then in order to compare your expenditure against likely income, jot them down on the Budget Planner (see pages 138–143).

Possible ways of boosting your retirement income

Other than luck – winning the lottery or coming into a legacy – there are three main possibilities for providing you with extra money: your home, work and investment skill.

Your home

Your home offers several different options.

Moving somewhere smaller. You could sell your present home, move into smaller accommodation and end up with the double bonus of pocketing a lump sum and reducing your running costs.

Leaving aside such considerations as whether you would still be able to have your grandchildren to stay and looking at the matter strictly in financial terms, it is as well to realise from the outset that the cash difference on the exchange – in other words, your profit – will invariably be less than you expect. What with removal charges and lawyers' fees, moving home is a very expensive business.

Additionally, you will probably have some decorating expenses and there is bound to be a period of overlap when you will be paying two lots of telephone rental, extra electricity bills and so on.

This is not to say that moving may not be an excellent decision; simply that, if money is the main criterion, you need to be thoroughly realistic when calculating the gains.

A particular point to be aware of is that, if you buy a new home before selling your existing one, you could be faced by a bridging loan problem, which despite relatively low interest rates could soon eat into any profits you hope to realise on the exchange. Ideally, you should try to dovetail selling and buying at the same time. If this is not possible (and it usually isn't), the golden advice must be to sell first rather than risk lumbering yourself with the expense of having to borrow for several months or possibly longer.

If you do decide to move, you might consider transferring an existing mortgage to your new property or getting a new one, even if you could afford to buy the property outright. Too old? Not at all. Today mortgages are commonly available to people over retirement age. However, there may be good reasons why a mortgage would not be sensible for you. Among other factors (as if any of us needs reminding) mortgage interest relief no longer exists. You will need to do the sums carefully to see whether there is any real gain. If in doubt, consult an accountant or solicitor who will help you work out the various after-tax and other angles.

Taking in lodgers. If your children have left home and you have more space than you need, you could consider taking in lodgers, either as paying guests or, if your property lends itself to the creation of a separate flatlet, in a tenancy capacity.

When assessing the financial rewards, it is wise to assume that there will be times when the accommodation is empty – so you will not be receiving any rent. The good news is that you may be able to keep more of any earnings you make.

Until 1992, any money you received in rent was counted as part of your taxable income. Today, however, people letting out rooms in their home can claim tax relief of up to £4,250 a year. Any excess rental over £4,250 will be assessed for tax in the normal way. The relief only applies to accommodation that is 'part of your main home', so if you are thinking of creating a separate flatlet, you will need to take care that this qualifies and that it is not at risk of being assessed as a commercial let. Since the dividing line is somewhat hazy, check with your architect or other professional adviser that he/she fully understands the technical requirements.

Raising money on your home. A third option is to part-sell your home either for a capital sum or regular payments, under an equity-release scheme, and continue to live in it for as long as you wish. Sounds wonderful? There are both attractions and drawbacks which need to be considered carefully and you would be strongly advised to discuss the matter with your solicitor.

All these possibilities are explored in greater detail in Chapter 8, 'Your Home'. If you think any of the ideas sound interesting, see sections as follows: 'Moving to a new home', 'Letting rooms in your home' and 'Raising money on your home'.

Work

If you would like to continue working, arguably the easiest solution if your employer is agreeable is for you to remain where you are and to defer your pension. See 'Deferring your pension', page 28 in Chapter 3. Alternatively, as many people do, you may look on retirement as the opportunity for a job switch (with perhaps a reduction in hours) or the chance you have always wanted of setting up on your own. When assessing your budget plans, it is as well to err on the cautious side as regards the additional income you will be likely to earn as – although this has been improving – many so called 'retirement jobs' are notoriously badly paid.

If, instead of paid work, you are thinking of becoming self-employed or setting up a business, you will not only have the start-up costs but, as you are probably well aware, very few new enterprises make a profit during the first two or three years.

On the other hand – again, just looking at the economics – while you are working, you will not be spending money on entertainment. Also, particularly if you are self-employed or own a business, there may be certain tax advantages as well as possible scope for improving your pension. Lastly, of course, you may be one of the lucky ones for whom work after retirement really pays. Quite apart from the money, work can be thoroughly enjoyable and rewarding in its own right. For ideas and information, see chapters: 11, Looking for Paid Work and 10, Starting Your Own Business.

Investment

Contrary to what some people believe, you do not need to be very rich; nor for that matter is it too late to start thinking about investing once you are over the age of 55.

As you will see from Chapter 5, investment can take many different forms and among the list of different options there should be something to suit almost everyone. Although you may consider this to be specialist reading, we do suggest that you at least look at it, since maximising your income in retirement could make all the difference between being able to enjoy life or worrying about money.

Spending now for saving later

Although you may normally take the view that there is never a best time for spending money, retirement planning is different in that sooner or later you will need, or want, to make certain purchases – or pay off outstanding commitments, such as a mortgage. Most people's basic list – at least to think about – under this heading includes one or more of the following:

- Expenditure on their home
- The purchase of a car
- The termination of HP or other credit arrangement

Additionally, there may be a number of general domestic or luxury items which you had been promising yourself for some time and the only question is one of actual timing, i.e. determining the right moment to buy. Typical examples might include: a microwave, gardening equipment, a video recorder, a home computer, hobby materials and so on.

To help you decide whether a policy of 'spending now' is sensible, or possibly self-indulgent, there are two very simple questions you should ask:

- Can I afford it more easily now – or in the future?
- By paying now rather than waiting, shall I be saving money in the long run?

True, the issue may be complicated by tax and other considerations but for most choices this very basic analysis helps greatly to clarify the financial arguments on both sides.

Home improvements. If you plan to stay where you are, the likelihood is that at some point you will want to make some changes or improvements: install central heating, insulate the loft, modernise the kitchen or perhaps convert part of the house to a granny flat for an elderly parent who is becoming too frail to live alone.

Conventional wisdom has it that any significant expenditure on your home is best undertaken several years prior to retirement. However, in our experience the matter is less clear-cut and what is right for some is not the solution for others.

As with many other important decisions, the question largely depends on individual circumstances. Some people find it easier, and more reassuring, to pay major household bills while they are still earning. Others specifically plan to use part of the lump sum from their pension to create a dream home.

To arrive at the answer that makes best financial sense, present commitments have to be weighed against likely future expenditure (together with what money you will have available). Equally, as with insulation for example, you will need to work out what long-term savings you could effect by taking the plunge now. There is also the safety aspect: if you have bad lighting or dangerously worn carpet on part of the staircase, waiting for a few years to tackle the problem because it is all part of the grand plan could prove very false economy indeed.

Another very important consideration is how certain you are that you intend to stay in your present home. Investing a fortune and then upping sticks a couple of years later is generally a recipe for being out of pocket. Despite what one or two people may have told you, it is very unusual to recoup all your expenditure by reaping a vast profit when you come to sell.

Though it involves a few minutes' paperwork, a worthwhile exercise is to jot down your own personal list of pros and cons, under the headings: 'spending now' and 'spending later'. If still in doubt, then waiting is normally the more prudent course.

Purchasing a car. There could be two good reasons for buying a new car ahead of your retirement. One is that you have a company car that you are about to lose. The other is that your existing vehicle is on the old side and is beginning (or will probably soon start) to give you trouble. If either of these apply, then it probably makes sense to buy a replacement while you are still feeling relatively flush.

However, on the principle of 'look before you leap', company car owners should first check whether they might be entitled to purchase their present car on favourable terms: many employers are quite happy to allow this. Also, dreary though the suggestion sounds, if economies look like being the order of the day, two-car families might assess whether, come retirement when perhaps husband and wife will be doing more things together, two cars are really such an essential as before.

Paying off HP and similar. In general, this is a good idea since delay is unlikely to save you any money – and may in fact actually cost you more. The only precaution is to check the small print of your agreement, to ensure that there is no penalty for early repayment.

A further exception to the rule could be your mortgage. An accountant would advise you; or, if you are thinking of moving (and the issue is really whether to transfer an existing mortgage – or possibly acquire a new one), include this among the points to raise with your solicitor.

Cherished plans, if affordable

The Budget Planner (pages 138–143) may help you to work out whether the various luxuries and plans of which nearly all of us dream could be affordable or are destined to remain as fantasies.

Fun as it might be to imagine what a 'top twenty' list might include, there would be little real purpose in discussing the practicalities, or otherwise, of going on a cruise, owning a race horse, installing a swimming pool, buying a caravan or whatever, since not only – even among married couples – would there be wide variations in choice but more particularly, since normal budget wisdom does not apply, any advice would risk being grossly misleading. This does not mean that you should promptly forget the whole idea of noting items which come into this category; but that, as this is such a very personal decision area, only you can really make the assessments.

As a general point, however, if you plan your finances with a specific objective in view, you may find that against expectations a notion that first seemed impossible is actually affordable. Or possibly, when you really think about the choices, some of your earlier priorities will seem less important.

Money – if you become redundant

Much of the information in the earlier part of the chapter is equally valid whether you become redundant or retire in the normal way. However, there are several key points with regard to money which it could be to your advantage to check.

You may be entitled to statutory redundancy pay. Your employer is obliged to pay the legal minimum, which is calculated on your age, length of service and weekly pay. To qualify, you will need to have worked for the organisation for at least two years. The maximum weekly pay taken into account is £250 a week (this figure is revised annually, normally around February to reflect any changes in the Retail Prices Index). For further information, see booklet PL 808 *Redundancy Payments*, available from Jobcentres; or by post from the DTI Publications Orderline, T:0870 150 2500).

Ex-gratia payment. Many employers are prepared to be more generous. The Inland Revenue allows individuals to receive up to £30,000 in redundancy pay/benefits, free of tax, provided this is not one of the terms and conditions included in their contract of employment. Amounts over this are taxed under the PAYE system, so there could be an advantage in requesting that some of the payment be made into your pension scheme. For tax relief to apply, this must be before your departure.

Benefits that are not part of your pay. Redundancy may mean the loss of several valuable benefits, e.g. a company car, life assurance, health insurance. Your employer may let you keep your car as part of your pay-off and might be willing to extend any health/other insurance cover for a few months after you leave. Some insurance companies allow preferential rates to individuals who were previously insured with them under a company scheme.

You could be owed back holiday entitlement for which you should be paid.

Your mortgage. Your mortgage lender should be notified as soon as possible and might agree to a more flexible repayment system. Check whether your mortgage package includes insurance against redundancy. If you have a very low income, you may be able to obtain income support (IS) to help with your mortgage costs. If your mortgage was taken out before 2 October 1995, IS would be obtainable after 8 weeks. If it was taken out after 2 October 1995, you would normally have to wait for about nine months.

Other creditors/debts. Any creditors whom you may have difficulty in paying (electricity, gas, a bank overdraft) should be informed soonest in the hope of agreeing easy payment terms. There could be an argument for paying off credit card bills immediately, even if this means using some of your redundancy pay.

Thanks to a fairly recent new regulation, people who have taken out insurance to cover debts in the event of unemployment no longer have the money taken into account in calculating their eligibility for income-related benefits, provided the money is actually used to pay off past debts. Previously, this only applied if the money was paid direct to a creditor, as opposed to being received by the individual.

Company pension. Company pension scheme members normally have several choices. See section 'early leavers' in Chapter 3, Pensions, page 41.

Jobseeker's allowance (JSA). Even if you are hoping to get another job very soon, you should sign on without delay, since as well as the allowance itself (£53.95 a week) your national insurance contributions will be credited to you. This is important to protect your State pension. To qualify for JSA: you would need to be under State pension age and must either have paid sufficient class 1 contributions or have a low income. You must also be both available for and actively seeking work. For further details, see leaflet JSA L5 *Jobseeker's Allowance: Helping You Back to Work*, available from any social security office or Jobcentre.

Redundancy helpline. Can answer queries on all aspects of redundancy. Dial free: 0500 848489.

Money left unclaimed

Many people lose track of their financial assets, either because they have forgotten about them or because they do not know how to contact the relevant organisation that owes them money. If you think this could apply to you, the Unclaimed Assets Register might be able to help. The products they cover include: life policies, personal and occupational pensions, unit trusts and dividends. There is a small search fee, ranging from £15 to £25, which is payable whether or not they are successful. For further information, contact the **Unclaimed Assets Register Ltd.**, 8 Devonshire Square, Cutlers Gardens, London EC2M 4PL. T:0870 241 1713.

Cheques act 1992

Over the past few years, there has been growing concern about the number of cheques being stolen in the post. The risks have been somewhat reduced thanks to the 1992 Cheques Act which shifts responsibility to the banks provided all safeguards have been taken.

If you write the words 'Account Payee Only' between the crossings on the cheque, you can be certain that the cheque can only be banked by the person to whom you made it out. Most banks have altered their cheque books accordingly. If your cheques still say 'or order', cross these words out and initial the amendment.

Covenants

Making a deed of covenant used to be a popular and tax-efficient way of both giving to charity and for grandparents to help pay towards their grandchildren's education. To all effects and purposes covenants of both types have been abolished. However, covenants existing at the time of their abolition – 1998 for covenants drawn up for the benefit of an individual and April 2000 for charitable donations – are not affected and can continue as before until their expiry.

Charitable Giving

Charitable giving got a major boost in the March 2000 Budget as a result of a package of new tax reliefs, including the possibility of giving quoted stocks and shares to a charity free of both income tax and capital gains tax. (For more information contact CAF's shareline on T: 01732 520338). Additionally, both the Payroll Giving Scheme and Gift Aid have been amended to enable more generous donations to be given with the benefit of tax relief.

Payroll Giving Scheme. This scheme allows anyone paying PAYE, either through their earnings or their pension, to give any amount, free of tax, to the charities of their choice. The money is taken out of your pre-taxed income, so if you choose to give £10 a month, it will only cost you £7.80 in real terms as a basic rate taxpayer or £6 as a higher rate taxpayer.

You will, however, need to know whether your employer/former employer or pension paying organisation has or will be introducing the scheme before you can take part.

As part of the campaign to get people giving to charity, the government has pledged to add an extra 10 per cent to all donations made through payroll giving for the three years from April 2000 to April 2003.

For further information, contact your employer/former employer, or write to: **CAF (Charities Aid Foundation)** for details of its own scheme, Give As You Earn, at Kings Hill, West Malling, Kent ME19 4TA. T:01732 520000.

Gift Aid. This scheme allows individuals to make regular or one-off donations to charity with the benefit of tax relief. The charity will be entitled to claim repayment of the base rate tax from the Inland Revenue which, if you give £100, would mean the charity receiving in total £128.

CAF Charity Account. CAF operates an account scheme which can be used for Gift Aid and Give As You Earn. The donations, together with any reclaimed tax, are paid into a CAF account from which the donor distributes funds to charities of his or her choice, either by voucher or CharityCard, CAF's special debit card.

CAF can also help you set up a charitable trust as well as a new legacy account, should you wish to leave money to a charity in your will but then later want to add to, or alter, the list of charities you wish to benefit.

For further information contact CAF at the West Malling address.

Extra income

There are a great many State benefits and allowances available to give special help to people in need. Definition of need covers a very wide range and applies, among others, to problems connected with: health, housing, care of an elderly or disabled relative, as well as widowhood and problems encountered by the frail elderly who for example may require extra heating during the winter.

While many of these benefits are 'means-tested', in other words are only given to people whose income is below a certain level, some – such as disability living allowance – are not dependent on how poor or how wealthy you are. Moreover, even when 'means-testing' is a factor, for some of the benefits income levels are nothing like as low as many people imagine. Because this information is not widely enough known, many individuals including in particular nearly a million pensioners are not claiming help to which they are entitled and for which in many cases they have actually paid through their national insurance contributions.

The main benefits and allowances are listed in their appropriate chapters: for example, housing benefit appears in Chapter 8, Your Home; invalid care allowance is briefly described in Chapter 15, Caring for Elderly Parents.

A number of voluntary organisations also provide assistance to individuals: sometimes in cash or sometimes with facilities, such as special equipment for disabled people. Details are given in the relevant chapters.

For further advice and information, contact your local social services department or citizens' advice bureau. Another very useful source of help is your local Age Concern group.

The national addresses of these organisations are as follows:

Department for Work and Pensions: Richmond House, 79 Whitehall, London SW1A 2NS. T:020 7210 3000.

Department of Health, Social Services and Public Safety, Castle Building, Stormont Estate, Belfast BT4 3SG. T:028 9052 0500.

National Association of Citizens' Advice Bureaux, 115–123 Pentonville Road, London N1 9LZ. T:020 7833 2181.

Age Concern

England, Astral House, 1268 London Road, London SW16 4ER. T:020 8765 7200.
Northern Ireland, 3 Lower Crescent, Belfast BT7 1NR. T:028 9024 5729.
Scotland, 113 Rose Street, Edinburgh EH2 3DT. T:0131 220 3345.
Cymru, 4th Floor, 1 Cathedral Road, Cardiff CF11 9SD. T:029 2037 1566.

where's your pension now?
...we can help!
Millions of people join occupational pension schemes run by their employer. But what happens to your pension when you change jobs or leave? Employers can change their name, move address, be taken over or simply close down. If you have lost touch with your former pension scheme, you may miss out on your pension rights when you retire.
The Pension Schemes Registry (part of the Occupational Pensions Regulatory Authority) provides a free tracing service to anyone who has lost contact with a pension scheme. We cannot tell you if you are entitled to a pension, but we can supply up-to-date contact names for you to write to and find out. You can either:
• phone us on 0191 225 6316 for a tracing request form;
• visit our website at www.opra.gov.uk and fill in the tracing request form online; or
• write to us at Pension Schemes Registry, PO Box 1NN, Newcastle upon Tyne NE99 1NN giving details of the employer(s) you have worked for and the period(s) you were employed.

3 Pensions

At time of writing, you could hardly pick up a paper without reading about some fresh concern to do with pensions. While it is undeniable that the downturn in the stock market has hit both employers' schemes and self-employed pensions alike, what is often not mentioned is that pensions are a long-term investment and what goes down in a bad patch normally goes up a year or two later. (Take negative equity and today's housing boom!).

This is not to minimise the concerns of those whose pension scheme has suddenly been changed from a final salary one to money purchase, nor those of the many other individuals who have been told that they need to make bigger contributions to maintain the value of their fund – although in both cases, the situation may not be as bad as they feared.

The essential point is, however, that despite the current gloom, next to your home, your pension is still almost certainly your most valuable asset. It is therefore important to check where you stand – and what you can best do – to ensure that when you retire you receive the maximum benefit.

State pensions

You can get a pension if you are a man of 65 or a woman of 60, provided you have paid (or been credited with) sufficient national insurance contributions.

In time, the age of women will alter as the Government has published plans to equalise State pension age for men and women at 65. The change will be phased in over ten years, beginning in 2010. This will affect younger women only. Those born before 6 April 1950 have no need to alter their retirement plans.

Your right to a State pension

Your right to a State pension depends on your (or your spouse's) national insurance contributions. Most people have to pay contributions into the national insurance scheme while they are working.

If you are an employee, your employer will have automatically deducted Class 1 contributions from your salary, provided your earnings were above a certain limit (currently £89 a week).

If you are self-employed, you will have been paying a flat-rate Class 2 contribution every week and possibly the earnings-related Class 4 contributions as well.

You may also have paid Class 3 voluntary contributions at some point in your life in order to maintain your contributions record.

If you are over pension age (65 for men and 60 for women) you do not pay national insurance contributions.

There may have been times during your working life when you have not, either knowingly or unwittingly, paid national insurance contributions. If you have not paid sufficient NI contributions to qualify for a full rate basic pension you may be entitled to a reduced rate of pension. However, your NI contributions record will have been maintained in the following circumstances:

If you have lived or worked outside Great Britain. If you have lived in Northern Ireland or the Isle of Man, any contributions paid there will count towards your pension.

The same should also apply in most cases if you have lived or worked in a European Union country or any country whose social security is linked to Britain's by a reciprocal arrangement. However, there have sometimes been problems with certain countries so, if you have any doubts, you should enquire what your position is at your social security office.

If you have received Home Responsibilities Protection (HRP). If you have not worked regularly at some time since 1978, because you have had to stay at home to care for either a child or a sick or elderly person, you may have protected your right to a pension by claiming HRP. This benefit allows you to deduct the years when you were required to give up work from the normal qualifying period for a basic pension and so, in effect, shorten the number of years when you would otherwise have been required to make contributions.

There are two important points to note. Firstly, if you are a woman and were claiming child benefit, HRP would have been credited to you automatically, whereas a man staying at home to care for a child would have needed to arrange the transfer of child benefit to himself. Secondly, HRP is only available for complete tax years in which earnings were less than 52 times the lower earnings limit.

While HRP can be claimed by both sexes, it predictably applies more frequently to women. For more information, see 'Pensions for women' at the end of the chapter or obtain form CF 411 *Home Responsibilities Protection – How to Protect your State Retirement Pension*, available from any social security office.

If you have been in any of the following situations, you will have been credited with contributions (instead of having to pay them):

- If you were sick or unemployed (provided you sent in sick notes to your social security office, signed on at the Unemployment Benefit office or have been in receipt of jobseeker's allowance);
- If you were a man aged 60–64 and not working;
- If you were entitled to maternity allowance, invalid care allowance or unemployability supplement;
- If you were taking an approved course of training;

- When you left education but had not yet started working;
- If since April 2000, your earnings have fallen between what are known as the lower earnings limit and the primary threshold, i.e. (2002/03) between £75 and £89 a week.

Married women and widows who do not qualify for a basic pension in their own right may be entitled to a basic pension on their husband's contributions at about 60 per cent of the level to which he is entitled (see 'Pensions for women' at the end of the chapter).

Since the introduction of independent taxation, husband and wife are assessed separately for tax. As a result, a married woman is now entitled to have her section of the joint pension (currently £45.20) offset against her own personal allowance – instead of being counted as part of her husband's taxable income. For many pensioner couples, this should mean a reduction in their tax liability.

Reduced rate contributions note. Many women retiring today may have paid a reduced rate contribution under a scheme which was abolished in 1978. Women who were already paying a reduced rate contribution were however allowed to continue doing so. These reduced rate contributions **do not count** towards your pension and you will not have had any contributions credited to you.

If you are still some years away from retirement, it could be to your advantage to cancel the reduced rate option, as by doing so you may be able to build up a wider range of benefits without paying anything extra. This applies if you are currently (2002/03) earning between £75 and £89 a week, i.e. between the lower earnings limit and the primary threshold. If you are earning above the primary threshold (i.e. £89), to get the same extra benefits you would have to start paying extra contributions. For advice, contact your local tax office.

How your pension is worked out

Your total pension can come from three main sources: the basic pension, the additional pension and the graduated pension.

Anyone wanting to work out what they are due can write to their social security office for a 'pension forecast'. This is normally expressed in percentage terms so, for instance, someone with full contributions will get 100 per cent of pension. You can also get a forecast of the additional earnings related pension to which you are entitled. To obtain a forecast complete Form BR 19.

It is worth getting an early estimate of what your pension will be, as it may be possible to improve your national insurance contribution record by making additional Class 3 voluntary contributions. These can, however, only be paid for six years in arrears, so this concession may not help if you think about it too late.

Basic pension

The full basic pension for a man or woman (April 2002/03) is £75.50 a week, £120.70 for a married couple (unless your spouse is entitled to more than the £45.20 spouse's addition on his/her own contributions, in which case you will receive more). Pensions are uprated in April each year. Up-to-date rates are contained in leaflet GL23 *Social Security Benefit Rates*, obtainable from social security offices and main post offices.

All pensions are taxable other than one or two special categories, such as war widows and the victims of Nazism. If, however, your basic pension is your only source of income, you will not have to worry as the amount you receive is below the income tax threshold.

The rate of basic pension depends on your record of NI contributions over your working life. To get the full rate you must have paid (or been credited with) NI contributions for roughly nine-tenths of your working life, although widows can also be entitled to a full basic pension on their husband's contributions. If you are divorced, you may be able to use your former spouse's contributions to improve your own pension entitlement, provided that you have not remarried before reaching pension age.

Your working life, for this purpose, is normally considered to be 44 years for a woman and 49 years for a man (i.e. age 16 until pension age), but it may be less if you were of working age but not in insurable employment when the National Insurance Scheme started in 1948.

Reduced rate pension

If you do not have full contributions but have maintained your contributions record for between a quarter and nine-tenths of your working life, you may get a pension at a reduced rate. The amount is calculated according to the number of years for which you have paid contributions. However, to get any basic pension you must satisfy two conditions. Firstly, you must actually have paid enough full rate contributions in any one tax year, from 6 April 1975, for that year to count as a qualifying year; or have paid 50 flat rate contributions, in any one year, before 6 April 1975. Secondly, your total contributions must be enough to have entitled you to at least 25 per cent of the full basic rate.

Additional pension: SERPS

SERPS, the additional State pension scheme, was discontinued by the government in April 2002 and has been replaced by a new additional scheme, called the Second State Pension.

Those formerly contracted into SERPS will not suffer any loss, as they will still keep the benefit of any contributions made. Equally, of course, those already in receipt of a SERPS pension will continue to receive their payments as normal.

If you paid into the scheme, you probably know that the amount of additional pension you will get depends on your earnings above an annually adjusted 'lower earnings limit' for each complete tax year since April 1978. The current maximum amount to which you could be entitled is £134.35 a week.

If you have not already done so, it would be sensible to apply for a statement of your savings in SERPS by completing Form BR 19 *Pension Forecast Application Form*, obtainable from any social security office. Full details and examples of how SERPS is worked out can be found in leaflet NP 46 *A Guide to Retirement Pensions*, available from social security offices.

In practical terms, the fact that SERPS has been discontinued may make very little difference to your plans. You can remain in the additional State pension scheme, i.e., the Second State Pension. Or as before, if you think you can do better by making independent provision, you can invest instead in either a personal pension or stakeholder pension. For details, see 'Personal Pensions Schemes' and 'Stakeholder Pensions', pages 48 and 57.

SERPS benefits for surviving spouses. As was announced some time ago, SERPS benefits are due to be halved over the coming years. The cut is not happening in one fell swoop but instead is being gradually phased in between October 2002 and October 2010. Additionally, anyone over State pension age on 5 October 2002 will be exempt from any cuts and will keep the right to pass on their SERPS pension in full to a bereaved spouse, however many years away this may be. Equally, any younger widow or widower who had already inherited their late spouse's SERPS entitlement before 6 October 2002 will not be affected and will continue to receive the full amount. The DWP table below shows how the cuts apply to those reaching State pension age between October 2002 and 2010. For further information, see leaflet *Inheritance of SERPS – Important Information for Married People*, available from any social security office; or call the helpline on T:0845 600 6116; textphone: 0845 6012 1913.

% SERPS passing to surviving spouse	Date when contributor reaches State pension age
100%	5.10.2002 or earlier
90%	6.10.2002 – 5.10.2004
80%	6.10.2004 – 5.10.2006
70%	6.10.2006 – 5.10.2008
60%	6.10.2008 – 5.10.2010
50%	6.10.2010 or later

Second State Pension (S2P)

If you were previously contributing to SERPS, you are unlikely to notice very much difference. Your future additional pension will continue to be worked out on earnings on which you have paid class 1 contributions as an employee.

Class 1 contributions are paid (or credited) as a percentage of earnings, currently (2002/03) between £75 and £585 a week.

In time this may change as, a few years from now, the pension payments are planned to become flat-rate instead of earnings-related.

The main beneficiaries of the S2P will be: (1) people earning up to around £10,800 who will be able to save towards a much better pension and (2) some carers and people with a long-term illness or disability who will receive credits, equivalent to their earning £10,800, for periods when due to their caring responsibilities or health they are unable to work.

Others likely to gain are employees with earnings up to about £24,600 who should be able to look forward to a more generous additional pension than with SERPS.

The Second State Pension is not applicable to the self-employed for whom the alternative pension choices are either a stakeholder or personal pension. See pages 57 and 48.

If you are a member of a contracted-out occupational pension scheme, you are legally entitled to: either a pension which must be broadly the same, or better, than you would have got under the State scheme; or to what are known as protected rights (i.e. your and your employer's compulsory contributions to your pension together with their accumulated investment growth).

Graduated pension

This pension existed between April 1961 and April 1975. The amount you receive depends on the graduated NI contributions you paid during that period. Anyone over 18 and earning more than £9 a week at that time will probably be entitled to a small graduated pension. This includes married women and widows with reduced contribution liability. A widow or widower whose spouse dies when they are both over pension age can inherit half of the graduated pension based on their late spouse's contributions.

Ways to increase your pension

Deferring your pension. Your pension may be increased if you delay claiming it and instead continue working after normal retirement age. This applies between the ages of 65 and 70 for a man and from 60 to 65 for a woman. For every year that you defer retirement, approximately another 7.5 per cent a year will be added to your pension. This extra pension is paid either when you claim your pension or when you reach 70 (65), regardless of whether you have retired from work or not. Your social security office could help you work out the figures to see if deferment would be worthwhile.

An exception to the age rule sometimes applies in the case of a married woman over 65 whose pension is based on her husband's contributions. Her pension can continue to increase until such time as her husband gets his pension or reaches the age of 70, whichever is sooner.

Good news for younger people is that from 2010, i.e. the start date for the phasing-in of equal pension ages, the amount earned by deferring your pension will be increased to 10 per cent a year. Also, the present limit of five years' deferral will be abolished.

Warning. If you plan to defer your pension, you should also defer any graduated pension to which you may be entitled – or you risk losing the increases you would otherwise obtain.

Increases for dependants. Your basic pension may be increased if you are supporting a dependent spouse or children. Most typically, this applies in respect of a non-working wife (or one whose earnings are very low) who is under 60 when her husband retires. However, this also applies for a retired wife supporting a husband dependent by reason of invalidity. The current rates are £45.20 a week for a spouse, £9.65 for the first child and £11.35 each for any other dependent children. The definition of dependent child is one for whom you are receiving child benefit. See leaflet GL23 *Social Security Benefit Rates*, obtainable from any social security office.

Age addition. Your pension will be automatically increased once you reach 80. The current rate is 25p a week.

Income support

If you have an inadequate income, you may qualify for Income Support. There are special premiums (i.e. additions) for lone parents, disabled people, carers and pensioners.

A condition of entitlement is that you should not have capital, including savings, of more than £8,000. To qualify for maximum income support, the capital limit is £3,000. For every £250 of capital over £3,000, individuals are deemed to be getting £1 a week income – so the actual amount of benefit will be reduced accordingly.

A big advantage is that people entitled to income support receive full help with their rent and should also not have any council tax to pay. See 'Housing benefit' and 'Council tax benefit', in Chapter 7.

If your only source of income is your basic State pension, you are likely to be entitled to income support.

N.B. All pensioners are guaranteed at least a minimum income, known as **Minimum Income Guarantee (MIG)**. For single pensioners, this is £98.15 a week; for couples, the amount is £149.80. In April 2003, the rates are being increased to a guaranteed minimum of £100 for a single pensioner and to £154 for a couple. These totals exclude mortgage interest and disregarded income, for example, attendance allowance.

A further helpful point is that the capital limits are more generous than those applicable to standard income support. Instead of the normal £3,000 and £8,000 limits, people aged 60 and over can have capital of up to £6,000 to qualify for maximum support; or up to £12,000 to be eligible for partial support.

Those not receiving their full entitlement should be contacted by a personal adviser to help ensure they receive the money. If you do not hear from a personal adviser and your income is below £12,000, contact your social security office or ring the Minimum Income Guarantee Claimline on T:0800 028 1111.

Social fund. If you are faced with an exceptional expense you find difficult to pay, you may be able to obtain a Budgeting or Crisis Loan, or Funeral Payment, from the Social Fund. Ask at your social security office.

Working after you start getting your pension

This used to be a problem for many people as a result of the Earnings Rule. At the time, men between the ages of 65 and 69 and women between the ages of 60 and 64 who earned more than £75 a week had their basic State pension reduced. Happily, this does not apply any more and today there is no longer any limit to the amount pensioners can earn.

Early retirement and your pension

Because so many people retire early, there is a widespread belief that it is possible to get an early pension. While the information is correct as regards a growing number of employers' occupational pension schemes, it does not apply to the basic State pension. If you take early retirement before the age of 60, it may be necessary for you to pay voluntary Class 3 national insurance contributions in order to protect your contributions record for pension purposes. If you are a man over 60, however, you will automatically get contribution credits from the tax year in which you reach 60.

How you get a pension

You should claim your pension a few months before you reach State pension age. The Department for Work and Pensions (DWP) should send you a claim form (BR 1) at the proper time but if this does not arrive, it is your responsibility to contact them. Remember they will send the claim form to the last recorded address they hold for you, so if you have moved and not informed them do make sure they have your new address. You should apply for the form about four months before you are due to retire. Or, if you prefer, instead of using a claim form you can ring the National Tele-Claim service on T:0845 300 1084 and give your details over the 'phone.

After you claim, you are told in writing exactly how much pension you will get. You will also be told what to do if you disagree with the decision. The information you are given should include the name and address of the organisation responsible for paying you any guaranteed extra pension (i.e. the equivalent of what you would have received from the additional State pension).

How your pension can be paid

If you live in the UK, you can choose to have your pension paid either by credit transfer or in order book form.

Credit transfer. This method gives you the choice of having your pension paid direct into a bank or National Giro account; or, alternatively, into an investment account with either the National Savings and Investments Bank or with most building societies. Payment will be made in arrears every four weeks, or quarterly, whichever you prefer.

Order book. You receive a book of orders (or pension book) which you can cash at a post office of your choice. Each order is your pension entitlement for one week and is valid for 12 weeks after the date shown on the voucher. If it is difficult for you to get to the post office, the coloured pages in the book explain how someone else can draw the payment for you.

Other situations. If your pension is £2 a week or less, it will normally be paid once a year in arrears by a crossed order which you can pay into a bank or building society account. Payment is made each year shortly before Christmas.

Pensions can be paid to an overseas address, if you are going abroad for six months or more. For further details see leaflets NI 38 *Social Security Abroad*, obtainable from Inland Revenue (NI Contributions) offices and GL 29 *Going Abroad and Social Security Benefits*, obtainable from social security offices.

If you are in hospital, your pension can still be paid to you. You will receive a reduced amount if you are in hospital for more than six weeks. N.B. From April 2003, your pension will only start to be reduced if you stay in hospital for thirteen weeks or longer. Leaflet GL 12 *Going Into Hospital?* (obtainable from any social security office) provides full information.

Christmas bonus

Pensioners usually get a small tax-free bonus shortly before Christmas each year. The amount and due date will be announced in advance. For the last few years the sum has been £10. The bonus is combined with your normal pension payment for the first week in December, so if you have not received it by the end of that month ask at your social security office.

Advice

If you have any queries or think you may not be obtaining your full pension entitlement, you should contact your social security office as soon as possible. If you think a mistake has been made, you have the right to appeal and can insist on your claim being heard by an independent Social Security Tribunal.

Before doing so, you would be strongly advised to consult a solicitor at the Citizens' Advice Bureau or the Welfare Advice Unit of your social security office. Some areas have special Tribunal Representation Units to assist people to make claims at Social Security Tribunals.

If you are writing to your social security office with a query you should quote either your national insurance number (or your spouse's) or your pension number if you have already started receiving your pension.

For further information about pensions, see leaflets RM1 *Retirement*, booklet NP 46 *A Guide to Retirement Pensions*, obtainable from any social security office; and PM2 *You and State Pensions*, obtainable by calling the Pensions Info-Line on T:0845 731 3233.

Private pensions

The importance of persuading individuals to save for their own pension instead of just relying on the State has been recognised by successive governments. Encouragement has been made through tax incentives, so that pension savings are now one of the most tax effective investments available.

- You get income tax relief on contributions at your highest tax rate.
- The pension fund is totally exempt from income tax and capital gains tax, providing excellent growth prospects for your money.

- Part of the pension can be taken as a cash sum when you retire and that too is tax free.

Private pension schemes fall into two broad categories: those arranged by employers, e.g. company pension schemes, and those you can arrange for yourself.

Company pension schemes

About 10.6 million people, roughly half the employed population, are now participating in company schemes. While these can vary considerably, the following basic features apply to all of them.

Pension fund. Pension contributions go into a pension fund which is quite separate from your employer's company. It is set up under trust and run by trustees, appointed from management and from pension scheme members. It is the job of the trustees to manage the fund and its investments and to ensure that the benefit promises are kept.

Payments into the fund. Your scheme may or may not ask for a contribution from you. For this reason, schemes are known as 'contributory' or 'non-contributory'. If (as is normally the case) you are required to make a contribution, this will be deducted from your pay before you receive it.

Your employer's contributions to the scheme represent the money he is setting aside for your pension and other benefits. In some schemes the amount is calculated as a fixed percentage of your earnings. In others the scheme actuary would estimate the amount that your employer needs to pay to ensure your (and other members') benefits in the future.

Benefits from the scheme. All pension scheme members should be given a booklet describing how the scheme works, what benefits it provides and other information including the address of the Pensions Ombudsman. If you do not receive one, you should ask the person in the company responsible for the pension scheme – this is often the personnel manager – to supply you with a booklet. You can also ask to see a copy of the trust deed as well as the latest annual report and audited accounts.

The key benefits applicable to most pension schemes include:

- A pension due at whatever age is specified by the scheme, usually somewhere between 60 and 65 (although many companies offer early retirement provision)
- Death benefit (sometimes known as lump sum life assurance), paid out if you die before retirement age
- A widow/widower's pension paid for life no matter when you die.

Benefit limits. The Inland Revenue sets limits on pension benefits which members of company schemes can receive. The main ones are:

- The maximum pension you are allowed is two-thirds of your final pay (excluding State pension)

- If you die, the pension can be passed on to someone else but no one beneficiary can receive more than two-thirds
- The tax-free lump sum, if you choose to take it, cannot be more than one and a half times salary. (If you take a lump sum, this will reduce the amount you receive in pension each year.)

The above figures are governed by a 'cap', currently based on £97,200 earnings a year. In other words, the maximum figure allowed for two-thirds of final salary is £64,800 a year; and the maximum tax-free lump sum allowed is £145,800.

The measure is not as draconian as it sounds. Firstly, of course, because it only affects high earners, i.e. those earning more than £97,200 a year. Secondly, because the £97,200 limit is not a static figure but is regularly revalued in line with price increases. Finally, the ruling only applies to members of schemes, set up after 13 March 1989, and to new employees joining existing schemes from 1 June 1989. Members of an established company scheme at the time of the 1989 Budget, who remain in the same scheme – or who change schemes within the same group of associated employers – are not affected by the change.

Types of scheme

Most employers' schemes are of the final salary or money purchase type. Other types that exist are average earnings and flat rate schemes.

Final salary scheme. Your pension is calculated as a proportion of your final pay, which could mean literally the last year you work or for example (and this is a requirement for controlling directors and those earning over £100,000) the average of three consecutive years during the last ten.

The amount you receive depends on two factors: the number of years you have worked for the organisation plus the fraction of final pay on which the scheme is based, typically 1/60th or 1/80th. So if you have worked 30 years for a company that has 1/60th pension scheme, you will receive 30/60ths of your final pay – in other words, half.

Final pay schemes can be contracted into or out of the additional State pension scheme. If a scheme is contracted out, it must provide a pension that is broadly equal to, or better than, its State equivalent.

Money purchase scheme. Unlike final salary schemes, the amount of pension you receive is not based on a fixed formula but (within Inland Revenue limits) is dependent on the investment performance of the fund into which your own and your employer's contributions on your behalf have been paid.

Although there is an element of risk with money purchase schemes, in that no one can forecast with certainty how well or badly a pension fund might do, in practice most trustees act very conservatively.

Different schemes have different ways of determining how members' pension entitlements are calculated. You should enquire what the rules are and additionally, to give you a better idea of what size pension you might realistically expect, you could ask for some practical examples – say, over the last five years – of retired individuals in a similar earnings bracket to your own.

An important feature of money purchase schemes is that the bulk of the fund must be used to purchase an annuity that will provide you with a guaranteed income for life. (See 'Compulsory purchase annuities', page 37).

N.B. The tax regime for contributions to money purchase schemes has been changed to bring it in line with stakeholder pensions. The important difference is that, whereas previously contributions were linked to earnings, you can now contribute £3,600 a year regardless of how much, or little, you earn. Those wishing to contribute more are still able to do so. For further information, see 'Stakeholder pensions', page 57.

Group Personal Pension Scheme. Employers sometimes arrange group schemes for employees wishing to build up a personal pension. They are usually more advantageous than individual personal pensions because employers normally make contributions of 3 per cent (or more) into all participants' pension fund. Also, because of the group savings, the charges tend to be lower than for individually administered schemes. All personal pensions, whether group or individual, are a form of money purchase scheme.

Contracted Out Mixed Benefit Scheme (COMBS). This is a mixed scheme which combines elements of salary-related and money purchase schemes.

Average earnings scheme. As its name implies, this is based on your average earnings over the total period of time that you are participating in the scheme. Every year, an amount goes into the scheme on your behalf, calculated in accordance with your level of earnings. As your salary increases, so too do your potential benefits. Each year, your 'profits' from the scheme are worked out from a formal table and the total of all these annual sums constitutes your pension.

Flat rate pension scheme. Your level of pay is not a factor. Instead, the same flat rate applies to everyone, multiplied by the number of years in which they have been participants of the scheme. So, for example, if the flat rate is £500 a year of pension and you have been a member of the scheme for 20 years, your pension will be £10,000 a year.

Additional or other schemes. There may be one scheme that applies to everyone in the organisation or there may be a variety of schemes for different grades of employee. For example, there may be a works scheme and a staff scheme operating side by side. It is also quite common for there to be a special pension scheme for executives and directors.

Executive pension plans

These are individual pension plans arranged by an employer for the benefit of some or all executives above a certain grade. In some companies, executive pension plans only apply to directors; in others, they may also include senior and middle management.

Equally, there may be a separate policy for each individual or a master policy, covering everyone in the scheme.

One of the attractions of executive pension plans is their potential flexibility. They can be tailored to cater for differing retirement ages as well as for varying contribution levels, which explains why some organisations are able to offer early retirement on very attractive terms.

Historically, executive pension plans are of the money purchase type. Because they are provided by the employer, the maximum benefit allowed is two-thirds of final salary; and, as from the 1989 Budget, the same rules apply as for final salary schemes. Normally, one of the following four types of investment policy is used: with profits, unit linked, deposit administration and non-profit.

These are described in the section on page 55, 'Personal pension schemes'. See also 'Top-up schemes' on page 36.

Possible changes to your scheme

Unfortunately, many employers have recently been closing their final salary schemes to new entrants and, even in a few cases, discontinuing them for existing members – replacing them instead with money purchase schemes.

While there is no pretending that money purchase schemes are as good as final salary ones, you will almost certainly be better off remaining in you employer's scheme than leaving it in favour of, say, a personal pension.

Your employer will still be making contributions into the scheme on your behalf, which very few employers do in the case of personal pensions and additionally you will not have any management charges to pay which, if you had a PP, would come out of your own fund.

Also, if you fear that your pension will be insufficient, you have two possible ways of helping to improve it: you can make AVC contributions (see page 39) and/or you can invest in a stakeholder scheme.

Focus on high earners

Several changes in the tax treatment of pensions with particular implications for high earners were introduced in both the 1987 and 1989 Budgets. The measures, except for the rule regarding accelerated accrual rates, are unlikely to affect anyone who has been in a pension scheme prior to March 1987 and remains with the same employer. Individuals on current salaries of £97,200 or more who are thinking of changing jobs and either joining a new scheme or transferring their existing pension to one will need to weigh up the financial consequences.

Maximum tax free lump sum. Prior to the 1987 Budget, the only restriction that applied was that the maximum was set at one and a half times salary. For the vast majority of individuals this is still the case and they have no need to be concerned about the changes described below.

In the 1987 Budget, a ceiling of £150,000 was imposed on the amount that individuals could take in the form of a tax-free lump sum on retirement. The new rule only affected those on earnings of more than £100,000 who actually joined a new pension scheme after 17 March 1987.

In the 1989 Budget, the Chancellor brought in a new ceiling limit of £90,000, based on earnings of £60,000 to be revalued in line with price increases. The 2002/03 ceiling limit is £145,800, based on earnings of £97,200.

As with the 1987 change, this latest rule only affects members of new schemes (set up after 13 March 1989) or new members joining established schemes after 1 June 1989. Members of an existing scheme prior to these dates who remain with the same employer should not be adversely affected by the change.

Accelerated accrual rates. Some schemes allow individuals to enjoy an enhanced accrual scale to qualify for full pension benefits after an agreed minimum number of years service. According to government regulations, the minimum period of service must be at least 20 years.

Definition of 'final salary' for high earners. Up until the 1987 Budget, individuals could base their final salary for pension purposes on any one of their last five years' earnings. In March 1987 a new rule was introduced, whereby anyone with earnings of more than £100,000 who joined a new pension scheme was required to base their final salary assessment on their average earnings over any three consecutive years over the last ten.

Two additional changes (also only relevant to joining a new scheme) were brought in at the same time. Firstly, gains from share options in the final year of employment were no longer allowed in the calculation of final salary. Secondly, individuals who were controlling directors were no longer permitted to resign just before retirement to boost their salary but instead had to use the three year average method of calculation.

These rules still apply with one important difference. Instead of £100,000 being the ceiling limit for tax relief purposes, the maximum final salary allowed is now £97,200 (2002/03). As already stated, the change only affects those joining new pension schemes set up after 13 March 1989 or new members joining existing schemes after 1 June 1989.

Top-up schemes. Employers can still set up 'top-up' pension schemes to provide additional benefits above the new ceiling but such schemes are now taxable. If given any choice in the matter, you should know that funded-in-advance schemes, including FURBS (funded unapproved retirement benefit schemes), offer greater security but are not tax-efficient, as the employee has to make contributions out of his net income. Also lump sums received from offshore FURBS set up after 30 November 1993 are now taxed at an employee's marginal rate; or more precisely, tax is charged on the difference between the amount the employee receives and the contributions to the scheme. The CGT changes in the 1998 Budget (in particular the abolition of indexation and bed and breakfasting) have also removed many of the previous advantages, as has the fact that since April 1999 FURBS have been liable for NI contributions.

Unfunded 'top-up' schemes, i.e. where the employer does not fund the top-up benefits but simply promises to pay them at retirement, are more tax-efficient but offer less security as you would be dependent on your employer keeping his promise. In the event of a take-over especially, there would be no guarantees.

As a result of FURBS having lost some of their attractions, some companies have set up a new type of unfunded scheme, known as SUURBS (Secured, Unfunded, Unapproved Retirement Benefits Scheme), which is backed by charged assets. Should you be offered this type of scheme, it might be sensible to check with an accountant to ensure you understand any technicalities you might need to know.

Compulsory purchase annuities

Everyone with a personal pension, Section 226 policy, retirement annuity, contracted-out company money purchase scheme (COMPS) or AVC arrangement must by law purchase an annuity.

An annuity is an insurance product which, in exchange for the money invested, guarantees an income for life. You have the choice of using the whole of your accumulated pension fund; or you can first take all, or part, of your tax-free lump sum. If you take your lump sum, this will reduce the size of your annuity and the amount of annual income you receive.

Other important factors that can affect your annuity 'earnings' include: what add-on options you may choose; the timing when you buy your annuity; and the choice of provider to whom you go.

A further consideration could be your life expectancy. Some providers offer annuities which pay enhanced rates to people suffering from ill health or who have been regular smokers for some years.

Add-on options. The most typical options that you will be offered include: a spouse's pension; annual increases which may either be fixed at, say, 3 or 5 per cent or may be linked to retail price inflation; a return of some of the capital (either in the form of a lump sum or in annual payments over five or ten years) should you die unexpectedly early. Wise as such options usually are to protect your and your dependants' long-term security, there will almost invariably be some additional cost which, if you were to go for all the possible extras, could reduce the annual income by around 50 per cent.

Timing. Until fairly recently, most people – except those with personal pensions and members of small self-administered schemes – had no choice in the matter. The rule was that they had to purchase an annuity on retirement. Today, however, thanks to a change in the regulations, everyone with a money purchase scheme including those with a free-standing AVC (FSAVC) can choose when they wish to purchase an annuity between the ages of 50 and 75.

The two key factors when it comes to a question of timing are what age you are when you purchase an annuity and what the level of interest rates are at the time. As a general rule, the older you are and the higher the level of interest rates, the bigger the annual income you will receive.

If you choose to wait, you have what is known as the **income withdrawal option** or **drawdown** as it is sometimes called. This allows you to take your tax-free lump sum, any time from age 50 to 75, and to withdraw a limited income from the fund (i.e. the maximum permitted is broadly equal to the annuity your fund could have provided) during the deferral period. The rest of the money has to remain in the fund where it can continue to be invested and grow tax-free. In case of death, the fund may pass to the surviving spouse who can either continue with the income withdrawal option or purchase an annuity. Alternatively, the fund can be paid out to the surviving spouse (or to the estate of the deceased) as a lump sum, minus a 35 per cent tax charge.

Attractive as this sounds, income withdrawal is not a decision to be entered into lightly.

While the big gain of the withdrawal option is that it allows individuals both to delay purchase of an annuity until interest rates are favourable and obtain their lump sum and an income in the mean time, there are also very considerable risks. In particular: the stock market could fall, reducing the capital value of your pension fund; interest rates could be even less favourable when you eventually need to purchase an annuity; commission rates are usually high compared to those for conventional annuities and there could also be substantial administration charges to pay; additionally, some plans are more tax-efficient than others. Not only is independent financial advice very strongly recommended if you are considering deferring the purchase of an annuity, but many experts advise that the income withdrawal option is not suitable for anyone with less than £200,000 in their pension fund (some put the figures as high as £250,000).

An alternative to drawdown, for those who have no need to take their tax-free lump sum upfront, is **phased retirement**. It is, however, not available to people in an employer's scheme but only to those with personal pensions.

The scheme works broadly as follows. In effect, your pension fund is divided into slices – say 500 – and each year you can withdraw a number of these to purchase an annuity, while at the same time take up to 25 per cent of the money as tax-free income. The remainder of your money stays in the fund and can continue to be invested.

As well as allowing you greater control over your annuity purchase (since, as opposed to just one, you would be buying a series of smaller annuities), one of the major advantages of phased retirement is that all money left in your pension fund on death can be passed on to your spouse, or other beneficiaries, free of tax.

However, as with drawdown, there are risks as well as advantages and expert advice is strongly recommended.

Choice of provider. Whether you intend to buy a normal retirement annuity, a 'draw-down pension plan' as described above or one of the newer with-profits or unit-linked annuities, this is one area above all where expert independent advice is essential. Annuity rates offered by life companies vary by as much as 25 per cent and the difference between the best and worst choice could affect your income by hundreds of pounds a year or more.

There is no obligation to buy your annuity from the company that has been managing your pension plan. Indeed, the best people for pension plans are not usually the most competitive for annuities and while there may be attractions in remaining with the same company (some offer loyalty bonuses), your decision will need to be based on the best all-round terms you can get at the time of purchase. **But** once you have made a choice, it is extremely difficult to switch.

You can take advice from an independent financial adviser, from a pensions consultant or from one of the several companies that specialise in tracking annuity rates.

The Annuity Bureau, for example, monitors the rates on a daily basis and will track the optimum rate that best suits your particular circumstances. The fee for this is £50 plus VAT. If you would like them to do so, they can also arrange the purchase and deal with the paperwork. For copy of a free guide *You and Your Annuity* and further information, contact: **The Annuity Bureau**, The Tower, 11 York Road, London SE1 7NX. T:020 7902 2300. Their associate, **The Drawdown Bureau**, provides advice, information and a free guide on income drawdown and phased retirement schemes. T:020 7401 2040.

Another annuity specialist that offers similar services is: **Annuity Direct**, 32 Scrutton Street, London EC2A 4RQ. T:020 7684 5000. A free guide with information about with profit/investment-linked annuities and drawdown is available by telephoning Freephone: 0500 506575.

Additional voluntary contributions (AVCs)

If, as you approach retirement, you become aware that you are not going to have a big enough pension to live as comfortably as you would like, you might seriously consider the possibility of making additional voluntary contributions. AVCs are a very attractive way of making extra savings for retirement for two special reasons. Firstly, AVCs – as well as the growth of the plan – enjoy full tax relief, so for basic rate taxpayers the Inland Revenue is in effect paying £22 of every £100 invested. A further key advantage for many people is that AVCs allow you to purchase 'added years', to make up any shortfall in your entitlement to benefit under a company scheme.

There should be no difficulty in purchasing AVCs, since all occupational schemes are required by law to provide AVC facilities.

However, as you are probably aware, an option, known as 'free-standing AVCs', is also on offer. As the name implies, these are not linked to a company scheme but can be purchased independently from: insurance companies, building societies, banks, unit trusts, friendly societies and independent financial advisers.

Individuals can, if they wish, contribute both to company AVCs and to a free-standing plan or plans. Although the rules only allow the purchase of one new free-standing AVC policy a year, it is possible to purchase a different policy every year, so building up a spread of investments.

The total of all your AVCs plus other contributions to the pension plan is not allowed to exceed 15 per cent of your earnings. In the event of over-funding occurring, whether from a free-standing or company AVC, the surplus will simply be refunded to you in cash, minus the tax relief involved.

Individuals paying less than £2,400 a year in free-standing AVCs will not normally need to involve their employer but just have to certify that they are not paying more than 15 per cent of their earnings in total contributions. Where larger amounts are concerned, the employer will need to become involved but this should not deter you if you believe that the purchase of free-standing AVCs is in your best long-term interest.

Rule changes. Over the years, there have been several rule changes of which you should be aware.

- The £97,200 final salary limit applies to AVCs in the same way as to other earnings. It goes without saying that it is not £97,200 in respect of each but the total earnings' figure which must not exceed £97,200.
- Previously, individuals had to make a commitment to pay regular contributions for a period of at least five years. This requirement has been abolished and (provided the actual scheme rules permit) both the amount and timing of payments can be varied to suit members according to their personal circumstances.
- Prior to 8 April 1987, AVC plans could be used towards funding an individual's lump sum. Under today's rules, the contributions can only be used for boosting the actual pension itself. These arrangements, however, only affect AVCs that were applied for after the April 1987 deadline. AVCs already entered into, are exempt from the 'no commutation' rule.
- Thanks to new regulations announced in July 1999, AVC benefits – which previously could only be taken at the same time as the other main benefits from an occupational pension scheme – can now be taken at any time between ages 50 and 75 (or earlier if an individual is forced to leave employment due to incapacity). If you choose to draw your AVC benefits before you retire then, provided the scheme rules allow it, they must be taken in the form of income drawdown (see page 37). While helpful if you need the extra money, you should realise that unless you have built up a considerable AVC fund, you are unlikely to receive all that much income.

Transfers from Personal Pension Schemes. Personal pension scheme members who enter pensionable employment can, if they wish, transfer their PP to an FSAVC scheme. Under the rules which came into effect in March 1997, they will still be entitled to take up to 25 per cent of their fund as a tax-free lump sum.

Choosing an AVC plan. A number of recent reports have suggested that the claims made for AVCs often fall well short of the mark. The main criticisms are variously (a) the poor performance of some AVC schemes and (b) the high charges which in extreme cases have left investors with a negative return. By contrast, the best schemes can yield excellent value and for many individuals can be one of the most effective ways of increasing their security in retirement.

Happily, spotting the duds has become very much easier thanks to a number of strict regulations. For a start, all scheme providers (i.e. both company AVC and FSAVC schemes) must give prospective investors 'key features' information, including in particular details of the charges. Secondly, anyone advising you about the purchase of FSAVCs must at very least explain the basic differences between the FSAVCs being recommended and the AVCs offered by your employer's scheme.

Independent Financial Advisers must go further and give you an analysis of the specific differences to help you decide which type of scheme – or possible alternative type of investment – would be in your best financial interest. When discussing the options, a particular question you might ask is whether it would be more sensible for you to invest in an Individual Savings Account (ISA) which, unlike AVCs, is not affected (until April 2004) by the recent abolition of dividend tax credit.

As general wisdom, the charges are likely to be lower with a collective AVC scheme offered by an employer than for free-standing contracts. Also, some employers match members' contributions to a company AVC scheme with extra contributions to the occupational scheme. Against this, if the performance is pedestrian or if there are early retirement penalties, you might still be better off with FSAVCs.

As with any other important investment decision, you would be well advised to take your time, do some basic research into the track record of any policies you might be considering (specialist publications such as *Money Management* provide a good starting point) and on no account sign any document without first being absolutely certain that you fully understand all the terms and conditions.

Finally, if you are already subscribing to company AVCs, before investing in a new plan check on your present level of contributions and the benefits that these are expected to yield. Your company pension adviser should be only too happy to answer any questions.

Compensation for mis-sold FSAVCs. Despite the 'key features' information and other safeguards governing the sale of FSAVCs, there is evidence to suggest that thousands of people may have been mis-sold an FSAVC when they would have done better joining their employer's AVC scheme.

A review was set up by the FSA to identify those individuals and, where appropriate, to compensate them for any loss. The target date for completion was the end of 2002, by when all outstanding compensation offers should have been made. If you have any concerns, or queries, contact the FSA's Consumer Helpline on T: 0845 606 1234.

Compensation for mis-sold FSAVCs is exempt from tax.

Early leavers

In the past early leavers tended to do very badly, due to the heavy financial penalties of withdrawing from a scheme in mid-term. In recent years, however, the Government has introduced new rules which help considerably.

For example, employers can now pay full pension, without actuarial reduction, at any age between 50 and 70, provided an employee has completed 20 years' service with the organisation. Companies are under no obligation to do so but, for those people lucky enough to work for an organisation that has amended its pension scheme rules accordingly, this provision could make an immense difference to the financial position of early retirees. It has to be said, however, that most employers still apply actuarial reductions (although these are sometimes waived in special cases such as redundancy) so, if you are thinking of taking early retirement it is advisable to work out very carefully how this might affect your pension.

Another important change concerns what are known as your **preserved rights** – in other words, your financial rights with regard to your pension. Previously you were entitled to these rights only if you had been in an employer's scheme for at least five years. Today, the qualifying period is two years.

If you leave earlier, although there is no obligation, the scheme would usually return the contributions you have paid. But, as you will realise, the amount of money involved is not likely to be very large. There are three choices available to people with preserved rights who leave a company to switch jobs.

Leaving the pension with the scheme. You remain a member of the scheme and receive a pension at the scheme's normal retirement age. If the scheme is a final salary one, the value would probably be calculated on 1/60th (or 1/80th) of your earnings at the time of your leaving and the number of years you have worked for the company. Whereas previously most pensions got frozen, today company schemes are obliged to increase the accrued pension rights by 5 per cent a year or the rate of inflation, whichever is lower. Another advantage of remaining in the scheme is that you keep any benefits – such as a widow's pension and possibly others – that are already included. Also, once you start receiving your pension, you would be entitled to any extra increases that may be given.

In the case of money purchase schemes, your accumulated assets would normally remain invested in the fund, hopefully growing every year to buy you a bigger pension on retirement. You would also be entitled to any benefit that the scheme provided under the rules.

Taking your pension to a new scheme. You do not have to make an immediate decision. You can transfer your pension scheme at any time, provided you do so over a year before you retire. If you wish to switch to a new scheme, this could either be to another company scheme, a personal pension or to a stakeholder pension. Personal and stakeholder pensions are described a couple of pages further along, so if you are interested in taking advantage of either of these options you should read the section carefully. Here, we explain the various possibilities if you wish to join a scheme run by your new employer.

Early leavers now have the right to move their pension – or more precisely, its transfer value – to a new employer's scheme willing to accept it. The transfer value is the cash value of your current pension rights. Calculating this, however, can be problematic and early leavers are often at a disadvantage compared with those who remain in the scheme. For example, if the job change has meant a salary increase, the new scheme will probably be more expensive to buy into as the likelihood is that it will be earnings-related. Any added years will also be calculated in relation to your new salary, so these too will be more expensive.

Your new employer might appear to place a disconcertingly low valuation on your old company pension rights. However, even if 10 years' worth of rights from an old company pension scheme are commuted to no more than two years' worth in your new one, it could still be worth accepting, particularly if your new job is likely to produce rapid pay rises. As your pension will quite likely be based on the size of your salary when you retire, the two years' worth of added rights could still be worth a tidy amount. When doing the sums high earners will, however, need to take account of the £97,200 cap (see page 33) which applies to anyone joining a new pension scheme.

Joining a new employer's scheme does not necessarily oblige you to transfer your previous benefits. In some circumstances, there may be very good arguments for leaving your existing benefits with your former scheme and joining your new employer's scheme from scratch for the remaining years that you are working. Since you could be at risk of giving up more than you stand to gain by transferring your benefits to a new scheme, expert advice is strongly recommended.

Taking your pension to an insurance company. If neither of the two previous options appeal, or your new company will not accept your old pension value into its own scheme, you can go independent and have the transfer value of your pension invested by a life company into a personal scheme – normally either a Section 32 buy-out or a personal pension. After deducting its charges, the life company would invest the balance of the money in the fund, or funds, of your choice.

Advice. Deciding on your best option is not easy, so before taking action you should at least consult your company pension scheme manager to give you an assessment of the likely value of your pension if you leave it in the scheme. As a result of the improved revaluation changes, explained earlier, this option could be considerably more attractive than it would have been a few years ago. A further point to bear in mind is that your present company scheme may include valuable extras, such as a spouse's pension, life cover and attractive early retirement terms in the event of ill-health.

If you are planning to switch, you will need to decide between a Section 32 buy-out, a personal pension or a stakeholder pension. Although for a majority of employees a personal or stakeholder pension is usually likely to offer a higher return, there are certain limitations and the accepted wisdom seems to be that the older the employee and the larger the transfer value, the more attractive a section 32 buy-out becomes. Because this is a complex area – and making the wrong decision could prove expensive – independent expert advice is very strongly recommended. Particularly if a large sum of money is involved, it could pay you to get the advice of a pension consultant. For a list of those operating in your area, write to the **Society of Pension Consultants**, St. Bartholomew House, 92 Fleet Street, London EC4Y 1DG.

Useful reading

Leaflet PM4 *You and Personal Pensions*, obtainable by calling the Pensions Info-Line on T:0845 731 3233.

Stakeholder Pensions and Decision Trees, obtainable from the Financial Services Authority, T:0845 606 1234.

Becoming self-employed

If, as opposed to switching jobs, you leave paid employment to start your own enterprise, you are allowed to transfer your accumulated pension rights into a new fund. You may have a choice of three options.

The more obvious solution is to invest your money with an insurance company, as mentioned above, or to take either a personal or stakeholder pension.

Alternatively, if you expect to be in a high earning bracket, you might consider setting up a limited company, even if you are the only salaried employee, rather than launching the same business as a self-employed individual. The company could set up a self-administered pension scheme with attractive loan-back facilities plus other advantages.

However, there are various pros and cons that will need to be weighed up carefully depending on your age, the transfer value of your earlier pension and the anticipated annual amount available for investing in your new scheme. This is rather a complex area, so before taking any action you are strongly advised to consult an accountant.

A third possibility which might be more attractive if you are fairly close to normal retirement age is to leave your pension in your former employer's scheme. See page 42 'Leaving the pension with the scheme'.

Minimum retirement age

At the present time, many pension schemes allow you to take early retirement and draw your pension from the age of 50. As you may have read in the press, the government is considering proposals to raise the minimum age by five years to 55. The proposals envisage phasing in the change over 10 years, starting in 2010, to coincide with the process of phasing in the equalisation of the State pension age for men and women. Individuals born before April 1950 would not be affected and, provided their scheme rules allow it, can still if they wish (and can afford to do so!) retire from age 50.

Questions on your pension scheme

Most people find it very difficult to understand how their pension scheme works. However, your pension may be worth a lot of money and, especially as you approach retirement, it is important that you should know the main essentials, including any options that may still be available to you.

If you have a query (however daft it may seem) or if you are concerned in some way about your pension, you should approach whoever is responsible for the scheme in your organisation. If the company is large, there may be a special person to look after the scheme on a day-to-day basis: this could be the pensions manager or, quite often, it is someone in the personnel department. In a smaller company, the pension scheme may be looked after by the company secretary or managing director.

The sort of questions you might ask will vary according to circumstance, such as: before you join the scheme, if you are thinking of changing jobs, if you are hoping to retire early and so on. You will probably think of plenty of additional points of your own. The questions listed are simply an indication of some of the key information you may require in order to plan sensibly ahead.

Before you join the scheme

- As a basic point, you should enquire whether the scheme is contracted in or out of the additional State pension scheme and, if it is contracted in, what will happen once the Second State Pension (S2P) which has replaced SERPS switches from being earnings-related to flat-rate.
- What are the criteria for eligibility to become a member of the scheme? For example, there may be different conditions for different grades of staff. There may be an age ceiling for new entrants. Sometimes too, although this is becoming less common, there is a minimum period of service required before you can join. (N.B. Exclusion of part-timers **on grounds of sex** has become unlawful under the sex discrimination legislation).
- Over the past few years, many companies have set up contracted-out money purchase schemes – or COMPS, as they are known for short – which operate on a different principle from final salary schemes. You should enquire what type of scheme it is that you would be joining and if it is a money purchase one, how in particular members' entitlements are calculated. (See 'Money purchase scheme' and 'Contracted-out mixed benefit scheme' pages 33 and 34).
- If it is a final salary scheme, is it based on 1/60th, 1/80th or other fraction?
- If the scheme is a group personal pension scheme, ask what extra contributions, if any, the employer makes (3 per cent is a fairly normal figure).
- If it is a final salary scheme, what is the exact definition of 'final salary'? This could be very important if the organisation offers phased retirement or the opportunity of a sponsorship in the voluntary sector and, as some employers do, adjusts your remuneration to take account of a shorter working week or less onerous responsibilities.
- Another point, if it is a final salary scheme, is whether pension increases (over and above the statutory increases) are given and, if so, whether these are guaranteed or discretionary? Since April 1997, schemes must by law, give annual increases of at least 5 per cent or the rate of inflation, whichever is lower.
- Is anything deducted from the scheme to allow for the State pension?
- At what age is the pension normally paid?
- Is there a widow/widower's pension and does it get contractual increases?

If you want to leave the organisation to change jobs

- Can you have a refund of contributions if you were to leave within two years?

- How much will your deferred pension be worth?
- Should you wish to move the transfer value to another scheme, how long would you have to wait from the date of your request? (This should normally be within three to six months).

If you leave for other reasons

- What happens if you become ill – or die – before pension age?
- What are the arrangements if you want to retire early? Most schemes allow you to do this if you are within about 10 years of normal retirement age but your pension may be reduced accordingly. Many schemes, in fact, operate a sliding scale of benefits with more generous terms offered to those who retire later rather than earlier. The flexi-age retirement provision is unlikely to help you if you move to a new job, since it only applies to employees of 20 years' standing.

If you stay until normal retirement age

- What will your pension be on your present salary? And what would it be assuming your salary increases by, say, 5 or 10 per cent before you eventually retire?
- What spouse's pension will be paid? Can a pension be paid to other dependants?
- Similarly, can a pension be paid to a partner, male or female?
- What happens if you continue working with the organisation after retirement age? Normally, any contributions you are making to the scheme will cease to be required and your pension (which will not be paid until you retire) will be increased to compensate for its deferment. Whereas previously, however, by deferring their pension individuals could boost the amount above their two-thirds earnings, under a 1989 Budget change this is no longer allowed. However, existing members of a scheme prior to the change taking effect (i.e. 1 June 1989) are not affected and are still entitled to defer their pension under the old rules, provided their employer is agreeable.
- What are the arrangements if you retire from the organisation as a salaried employee but become a retained consultant or contractor?

What to do before retirement

In addition to understanding your current pension scheme, you may also need to chase up any previous schemes of which you were a member. This is well worth pursuing as you could be owed money from one or more schemes, which will all add to your pension on retirement day.

You may be able to get the information from your previous employer/s. Or, if you have difficulty in locating them – perhaps because the company has been taken over – contact the Occupational Pensions Regulatory Authority (OPRA), which manages a pensions registry and tracing service to assist individuals who need help in tracing their pension rights. All occupational and personal pension schemes including free-standing AVC (FSAVC) schemes are required to register. Applicants can either write to the Registrar giving as much essential detail about the scheme as possible; or alternatively can request a trace application form (PR4) to complete. This is a free service. The address to write to is: **Pension Schemes Registry**, PO Box 1NN, Newcastle upon Tyne NE99 1NN. T:0191 225 6316.

Other help and advice

If you have any queries or problems to do with your pension, in addition to the Registry there are three main sources of help available to you. These are: the trustees or managers of your pension scheme; OPAS; the Pensions Ombudsman.

Trustees or managers. These are the first people to contact if you do not properly understand your benefit entitlements or if you are unhappy about some point to do with your pension. The pensions manager (or other person responsible for pensions) should give you their names and tell you how they can be reached.

OPAS, the Pensions Advisory Service. This is an independent voluntary organisation with a network of 500 advisers throughout the UK. OPAS can give free help and advice, other than financial advice, on all matters to do with any type of pension scheme – except State schemes. The service is available to any member of the public who either has a specific query or who just needs general information.

OPAS operates a local call rate helpline: T:0845 601 2923. Or, if you prefer, you can write to: **OPAS**, the Pensions Advisory Service, 11 Belgrave Road, London SW1V 1RB.

Pensions Ombudsman. You would normally only approach the Ombudsman if neither the pension scheme trustees nor OPAS are able to solve your problem.

The Ombudsman can investigate: (1) complaints of maladministration by the trustees or managers of a pension scheme or by an employer; (2) disputes of fact or law with the trustees, managers or an employer.

He cannot, however, investigate: complaints about mis-selling of pension schemes; a complaint that is already subject to court proceedings; one that is about a State social security benefit or a dispute that is more appropriate for investigation by another regulatory body. There is also a time limit for lodging complaints which is normally within three years of the act, or failure to act, about which you are complaining.

Provided the problem comes within the Ombudsman's orbit, he will look into all the facts for you and will inform you of his decision, together with his reasons. There is no charge for the Ombudsman's service. The address to write to is: **The Pensions Ombudsman**, 11 Belgrave Road, London SW1V 1RB. T:020 7834 9144. This is the same address (but different telephone number) as OPAS.

If you have a **personal pension**, contact the **Financial Ombudsman Service (FOS)**, South Quay Plaza, 183 Marsh Wall, London E14 9SR. T:0845 080 1800. It is possible you may be referred to the Pensions Ombudsman above but if so, you will be informed very quickly.

Protection for pension scheme members

Since the mid-nineties a raft of new measures have been brought into law which significantly improve protection for pension scheme members.

Among the most welcome is the requirement for early leavers to have their entire frozen pension uprated and not just, as had been the case, benefits earned after 1995.

Additionally, all company pension schemes are now required to index the whole of pensions in payment, excepting AVCs, in line with prices up to 5 per cent a year. Indexation only applies to pensions rights earned after 6 April 1997.

New rules have also been introduced to protect pension scheme members in the event of a company take-over or proposed bulk transfer arrangement.

A further welcome reform is that in the event of a scheme in deficit being wound up, the deficiency becomes a debt on the employer which the trustees can pursue. As an additional safeguard, self-investment by occupational pension funds is now restricted to 5 per cent.

The regulatory system has also become much more stringent, the Occupational Pensions Regulatory Authority (OPRA) has wide-ranging powers to investigate the way schemes are run and to impose sanctions on those that break the law. Among its powers, it has the final authority to determine whether schemes that are in surplus over the Inland Revenue limit (105 per cent) have complied with the law and acted fairly towards members before allowing any money to be returned to the company. The rules oblige the pension scheme trustees to tell members how they intend to distribute the surplus and if the members believe that they would be getting less than their statutory entitlement, they can refer the decision to OPRA to investigate.

Other recent measures include a right for members to appoint up to a third of the trustees and the establishment of a compensation scheme, chaired by the Pensions Ombudsman, available as a last resort to cover losses in the event of fraud.

During 2002, several of the provisions were further strengthened. Chief among these were (1) that all schemes (subject to existing exemptions) should have at least one-third member-nominated trustees, (2) that OPRA be given greater powers to hasten the winding-up process in the event of an occupational scheme becoming insolvent and (3) that pension schemes be required to give members better information as to their likely future entitlement.

Personal pension schemes

The self-employed have long been able to make their own pension arrangements. Since July 1988, this option is now available to all. Everyone – whether self-employed or working for an employer – has the choice of continuing as they are or of switching instead to a personal pension or stakeholder pension. In this section we concentrate exclusively on personal pensions. For information about stakeholder pensions, see page 57.

Although, in general, individuals who have reached their fiftieth birthday are less likely to be tempted than younger people to leave a company scheme for a personal pension or to alter their current self-employed arrangements, if you are thinking of starting your own business, if you are moving to a new job or if you are ineligible to join your company pension scheme, one of the options described below may offer you an attractive solution.

Choices for the self-employed

Personal pensions are largely modelled on the old-style self-employed pensions – with one or two important differences, including in particular the age at which you can retire. As from July 1988, however, the rules for self-employed pensions were also altered to bring them in line with personal pensions. This will not affect anyone who was already contributing to a pension plan prior to July 1988 unless, that is, they actually wish to change.

Differences between Section 226 policies and personal pensions. If you have an existing Section 226 policy (or retirement annuity contract, as it is sometimes also called), then, as you will know, it is an insurance policy designed to invest money for your retirement. It will probably have been sold to you by an insurance broker or insurance company salesman and, at time of buying, you will have had a choice of four different types of investment policy: with profits, unit linked, deposit administration and non-profit policy.

Under Inland Revenue rules, you are allowed to invest, up to 17.5 per cent of your relevant earnings tax free in the policy (with higher limits, rising to 27.5 per cent, if you are over 60). In accordance with the terms of the contract, you can choose to retire at any time after the age of 60, when the policy will buy you a regular pension plus the option of taking part of the money as a tax free lump sum.

However, as stated a few paragraphs higher, the rules for self-employed pension plans have been altered to bring them in line with other personal pensions. Section 226 policies have been abolished and are no longer available for purchase. In consequence, individuals who wish or need to make their own arrangements will have to buy either a new style personal pension (PP) or a Stakeholder pension.

In practical terms, this change is unlikely to affect many people. For a start, anyone with an existing Section 226 policy has no need, unless they wish to alter their arrangements, to do anything at all. They can continue contributing to the policy on exactly the same terms and conditions as before.

As general wisdom, the view in the pensions industry is that for most people with an existing Section 226 policy there would be little point in changing – and for high earners, in particular, it could be positively detrimental. However, as with most decisions there are advantages and disadvantages on either side and it is important that you should at least know what the choices are.

There are four main differences between Section 226 policies and personal pensions. These concern: the age of retirement, the method of calculating the lump sum, allowable contributions into the plan and the possible size of your pension allowed for tax relief.

- **Age of retirement**. Under a Section 226 policy, retirement cannot be taken before the age of 60. With a personal pension, you can retire at any time between 50 and 75.
- **Method of calculating the lump sum**. Under Section 226 contracts, this is expressed as three times the residual annuity paid. The PP rules define the amount as 25 per cent (or a quarter) of the total fund excluding your protected rights.
- **Allowable contributions**. A Section 226 policy limits you to a maximum of 27.5 per cent of your earnings. For personal pensions, individuals over the age of 50 can contribute up to 30 per cent, rising (depending on their age) to a maximum of 40 per cent.
- **Size of pension**. For high earners, the £97,200 cap is probably the strongest argument for hanging on to an existing Section 226 policy, since such policies are not affected by the earnings' cap. A personal pension on the other hand would stand to be affected.

For those who might be interested in switching, perhaps because a major aim is to retire before age 60, you should know that whereas at one time insurance companies were virtually the only outlet for buying individual pension plans, today these are also available from banks, building societies, unit trusts, friendly societies and independent financial advisers (IFAs).

For further information, see leaflet PM5 *Pensions for the Self-employed* obtainable by phoning the Pensions Info-Line on 0845 731 3233.

Personal pensions for employees

A main aim behind personal pensions is to give people working for an employer the same freedom as the self-employed to make their own independent pension arrangements, should they wish to do so.

Before making any decision, a basic point to understand is that nearly everyone who pays NI contributions as an employee is already contributing towards an additional pension: either to the Second State Pension; or to a contracted-out company pension scheme.

You have the right to take a personal pension (PP) in place of the Second State Pension; or alternatively in place of your employer's scheme (whether this is contracted-in or out).

To judge whether a personal pension is a good idea, you need to understand the advantages and possible limitations of your present arrangements compared with the attractions – but also risks – of a PP.

If you are a member of a good contracted-out final salary scheme – or have the opportunity of joining one – it is very unlikely that a PP would be in your best interest. If, however, your employer does not have a pension scheme, if you are ineligible to join, if the scheme is contracted-into the State scheme or if you think you could do better for yourself than your current scheme, then a PP could be worth considering.

A main advantage of a personal pension is that if you change jobs you can take it with you without penalty. There are attractive tax relief benefits. You will have real choice as to how your pension payments are invested. If you have built up a big enough fund, you can retire at any age between 50 and 75. Also, if you change your mind after having taken a personal pension, you can switch back into the State scheme; or, if the scheme rules allow it, you can transfer your payments into a company contracted-out scheme.

The big potential drawback of a personal pension, particularly for an older person, is that it may not offer you such attractive benefits as your present scheme. For a start, most employers do not make extra contributions to a personal pension so, other than your rebate from the Second State Pension (S2P) (see 'Minimum contributions' below), all the investment towards your pension will need to come out of your earnings. You may also lose out on valuable extra benefits that are often included in an employer's scheme, e.g.: a pension before normal age were you to become ill; protection for your dependants should you die; attractive early retirement terms if you were made redundant; any increases in pension payments that the scheme may give to help offset inflation.

A further problem could be the sheer plethora of choice when selecting a pension plan. Not only is there a variety of different types of investments (see next section) but you can obtain a personal pension from any of the following: insurance companies, banks, building societies, unit trusts, friendly societies and independent financial advisers (IFAs). It may also be possible to join a Group Personal Pension Scheme, arranged by your employer.

Knowing what to choose, assessing one policy against another, weighing up the risk factor as well as trying to estimate what this will mean in terms of your standard of living after you retire could be a bit of a gamble even for a financial expert.

Although as a breed pension providers act very conservatively, no-one can forecast with total confidence how well or otherwise any particular investment will do. So while it is possible that you could do better with a personal pension, unlike a final salary scheme or the Second State Pension where you should have the certainty of a guaranteed figure, you would not know the value of your pension until you come to retire. The amount would depend on: how much money you had paid in, how well it had been invested and how good an annuity you were able to buy (see 'Compulsory purchase annuities', page 37).

Before taking a decision, a first essential is to understand how personal pensions work.

Starting date. You can decide to start a personal pension at any time you want and then, in order to receive all the minimum contributions that will be paid into your pension plan, backdate it to the start of the tax year on 6 April. The formalities involved are very easy.

Contributions into your pension plan. There are three possible ways (previously four, see 'special incentive payments') of building up savings in your pension plan.

- **Minimum contributions**. These will be paid into your new scheme automatically. They are worked out according to the level of national insurance contributions that both you and your employer are required to pay by law. Instead of going into either the Second State Pension or a contracted-out company pension scheme, they will be paid directly into your personal pension plan at the end of the income tax year to which they relate.

The older you are, the bigger the contribution rebate. Whereas previously there was a fixed percentage for all personal pension members (with those over 30 receiving an extra 1 per cent), since April 1997 contribution rebates are calculated on an age-related basis, starting at 3.8 per cent for people aged 15 (on the last day of the preceding tax year) and rising in stages to 9 per cent for those aged 48 and over.

You will also be entitled to tax relief, at the basic rate, on your share of the contracted-out rebate (currently 1.6 per cent).

- **Extra contributions made by you**. You can make extra contributions into your pension plan. If you do so, you will not only build up more savings for your retirement but you also enjoy full tax relief on these contributions.

A further advantage is that you will have more flexibility as to when you can retire. If only the minimum contributions are paid, you will have to wait until the normal State retirement age. If you make extra contributions, you can use them to retire whenever you like between 50 and 75.

There are **Inland Revenue rules** as to the amount you can invest, which (but see N.B. below) varies according to your age. Additionally, for the purposes of tax relief, the £97,200 cap (2002/03), applies to all new personal pensions taken out since the 1989 Budget.

- If you are aged 35 or under, you can pay up to 17.5 per cent of your earnings into a personal pension.
- If you are between the ages of 36 and 45, the maximum is 20 per cent.
- If you are between the ages of 46 and 50, the amount is 25 per cent.
- If you are between the ages of 51 and 55, you can pay 30 per cent.
- If you are between the ages of 56 and 60, the maximum is 35 per cent.
- If you are over 60, you are allowed to invest up to 40 per cent of your earnings.

Ages are calculated at the beginning of the tax year.

N.B. While the above age/earnings link for PP contributions still normally applies, the rules were amended in April 2001 to bring the tax regime for personal pensions (and other money purchase schemes) in line with that of stakeholder pensions. The important result of this change is that you can now make contributions of up to £3,600 a year regardless of your age or how much, or little, you earn. Those wanting to contribute more than £3,600 will still be able to do so under the existing PP rules above. For further information, see 'Stakeholder pensions' page 57.

- **Voluntary contributions by your employer**. Your employer might decide that he wishes to help you improve your pension by making contributions over and above the statutory national insurance contributions into your pension plan. If you are considering leaving a company pension scheme, this could be one of the questions you should ask as a means of comparing the value of a personal pension against your existing scheme. The Inland Revenue limits described above include any contributions made by your employer, so the total must therefore not exceed the allowed amount.
- **Special Incentive Payments**. An extra 2 per cent payment was given by the government as part of the launch of personal pensions. These payments have now ceased. Anyone who previously received them can look forward to enjoying the benefit when they retire.

Carry forward/carry back facility. Until recently, those with personal pensions could variously carry forward, or carry back, unused tax relief on contributions to their pension plan. Sadly, the carry forward facility was abolished in April 2001. Exceptionally those with retirement annuity plans are not affected by the new rules and can still carry forward any unused tax relief on pension contributions for up to six years.

Not all flexibility is lost. The **carry back** facility, which remains unchanged, allows you to 'relate back' personal pension premiums. This means that a premium paid during a tax year is treated as if it had been paid during the previous tax year; or the tax year before that, if there were no relevant earnings in the previous year. So if a premium is paid before 6 April 2003, it may be treated as having been paid during 2000/01.

N.B. Higher contributions needed in future. As most people with an existing PP will be aware, as a result of a technical tax change – i.e. the abolition of ACT – anyone with a PP will need to make bigger contributions than previously to ensure a decent pension. While this will especially affect younger people, if you are still some way off retirement and haven't already done so, you should speak to your pension adviser to check what extra you should be paying to compensate for the removal of the dividend tax credit. The recent downturn in the Stock Market may also have caused some shortfall so, even if you are fairly close to retirement, you would still be advised to check with your pension adviser whether ideally you should be increasing your contributions.

Your pension receipts. As with all money purchase schemes, the amount of pension you eventually receive will depend on two main factors: the size of the fund you have been able to build up and the fund's investment performance. As general wisdom, the longer you have been saving towards a personal pension and the bigger the total contributions paid, the larger your pension will stand to be. You have a great deal of choice in the matter but there are also certain rules designed to protect you.

A basic rule concerns what are known as your **protected rights**. These are the minimum contributions (including the value of the extra 2 per cent introductory payment) and tax relief you may have received – together with their accumulated investment growth.

Your protected rights can only be invested in a single contract, in contrast to your/your employer's extra or voluntary contributions which can be invested in as many different personal plans as you please.

A further point is that your protected rights must be used to purchase the annuity which will pay for your annual pension when you retire; they cannot be used as a contribution towards your lump sum.

Your lump sum derives from the extra contributions that you and perhaps also your employer have made including (as from the 1989 Budget) the value of dependants' benefits. You can take up to 25 per cent (or a quarter) of this part of the fund. The remainder will be added to your protected rights to purchase a better annuity. (See 'Compulsory purchase annuities', page 37).

Choosing a pension plan. Personal pensions are offered by insurance companies, building societies, unit trusts, friendly societies and IFAs. Before you make up your mind, you should aim to look at a variety of plans. Furthermore, you should not hesitate to ask as many questions as you want about any points that are unclear or any technical term that you do not fully understand – including in particular any questions you may have about the level of charges.

Understanding the figures has become very much easier over the past few years. Today, not only are all life and pension policy providers required to state their charges in writing but they must also disclose any salesman's commission – stated in cash terms – in advance of any contract being signed.

These together with other essential 'consumer' information about the policy should be included in what is called the 'key features' document. Advisers must now also state in writing their reasons for any recommendations to you.

Because choosing both the right type of investment and the particular institution with which you are likely to feel happiest is such an important decision, even after you have chosen a scheme you will have a **14-day cooling off period** that gives you a chance to change your mind.

Is a personal pension a wise decision? This is a question that only you, or an adviser who knows your personal circumstances, can answer. As a general rule, if you are in a good company pension scheme the advice is to stay there. This is especially likely to apply if the scheme is a final salary one as, since the abolition of dividend tax credits in the July 1997 budget, people with personal pensions will need to invest more to make up for the 20 per cent tax that their pension fund can no longer reclaim on the dividend income.

However, remaining in their employer's scheme may not be the best choice for everyone and those for whom a personal pension might be an advantage are likely to be in the category: under 45 (under 40 for women), high flyer, mobile worker in the sense of being likely to switch jobs and well-off older people who are not covered by company arrangements. Those for whom opting out is likely to be least advised are older people in a good company or public sector pension scheme.

The key issue is how your existing pension arrangements compare with the alternatives. You will therefore need to know what the value of your pension would be if you stay in the additional State pension scheme or in your company scheme, whichever is applicable.

For information about the value of your State scheme rights, complete BR 19 *Pension Forecast Application Form* obtainable from your social security office.

In the case of an employer's scheme, ask the pensions department or the person responsible for pensions (this could be the personnel manager or company secretary) to provide you with full information about your pension and future benefits, including details of death and disability cover.

Other points you will need to consider include: what type of investment policy would suit you; what size contributions (within Inland Revenue allowed limits) you could realistically afford; and what, after deduction of administrative and other charges, your plan might be worth when you come to retire. This is not to say that taking a personal pension is either a right or a wrong decision. Simply that you need to be aware of all the various factors before opting out of your present arrangements. Since the sums are often very complex, if you are thinking of making a change you would be strongly advised to consult an independent pensions specialist.

Useful reading

Leaflets PM1 *Don't Leave Your Pension to Chance*, PM3 *You and Occupational Pensions*, PM4 *You and Personal Pensions* and PM5 *Pensions for the Self-Employed*, obtainable by ringing Pensions Info-Line on T:0845 731 3233.

Inland Revenue leaflet IR 78 *Personal Pensions*, obtainable from any tax office.

Stakeholder Pensions and Decision Trees; *Personal Pensions Mis-selling* and *FSA Guide to Pensions*, obtainable free from the FSA, T:0845 606 1234.

Types of investment policy

There are four different types of investment policy: with-profits, unit-linked, deposit administration and non-profit policies. Brief descriptions of each follow.

With-profits policies. These are one of the safest types of pension investments. They guarantee you a known minimum cash fund and/or pension on your retirement and, while the guaranteed amount is not usually very high, bonuses are added at regular intervals, according to how the investments in the fund perform. Additionally, a terminal (or final) bonus is given when the pension policy matures. Over the past couple of years most terminal bonuses have been lower than those paid in the late eighties, reflecting a reduction in interest rates and a patchy performance by equities. However, an important feature is that once bonuses are given, they cannot later be withdrawn or put at risk due to some speculative investment.

Unit-linked policies. These are less safe than with-profits policies but they offer the attraction of potentially higher investment returns. Unit-linked policies by and large have performed fairly well over the last decade and have consequently been growing in popularity. However, as illustrated by the recent stock market volatility there is always the risk that they might not continue to perform as well in the future and, if there were a further down-turn, the size of your pension could obviously be affected. For this reason, many advisers recommend that their clients swap their unit-linked policies to the with-profits type about five years before they retire, provided market conditions are favourable at the time.

The decision as to what is best will very much depend on timing. Clearly if the stock market is depressed, then cashing in equity based contracts before you need could lose you money, unless of course your adviser takes the view that the stock market is likely to plunge even further. Another factor that will need to be taken into account is the prevailing level of interest rates, since these affect annuity rates.

Deposit administration policies. These lie somewhere between with-profits and unit-linked policies in terms of their risk/reward ratio. They operate rather like bank deposit accounts, where the interest rate is credited at regular intervals.

Non-profit policies. These have lost favour in recent years. Although they provide a guaranteed pension payment, the return on investment is usually very low. As a rule, they tend only to be recommended for people starting a plan within five years of their retirement.

Choosing the right policy. This is one area where it really pays to shop around. Great care is needed when choosing the organisation to invest your pension savings. Once you have committed yourself to a policy, you will not usually be able to move your money without considerable financial penalty.

As a general rule, it is sensible to select a large, well-known company that has been in the market for a long time. Before deciding, you should compare several companies' investment track records. What you should look for is evidence of good, consistent results over a period of 10 to 20 years.

An important point to be aware of is that insurance and other financial companies may give illustrative projections of their investment performance. Projections, however, even when based on a company's own figures – including their charges – (as since 1995 they now have to be), are not the same as guarantees and if, in the event, the results are disappointing you are most unlikely to have any claim.

Information about the administrative and other charges you will have to pay is one of the essential questions you should ask when discussing a personal pension. Until recently, many people did not realise how much they were paying in commission, since this was usually obscured. Today, however, anyone selling personal pensions is required to disclose their commission in advance, stated in cash terms. Normally, the best arrangement to keep the cost down is to pay a series of single premiums at one go or as a 'single recurring premium' contract.

A further point to check is whether the pension plan includes a waiver-of-premium option to ensure that your contributions continue to be paid, should you suffer a long-term illness. Particular questions to ask are: how much extra it will cost; what conditions you must satisfy before payment is made; and whether the insurance is related to your own job – or instead, only covers you against being unable to do any type of work.

You should aim at very least to talk to two or three financial institutions or independent financial advisers (IFAs) and make it clear to all of them that you are doing so. If you need further advice – and particularly if a large sum of money is involved – there could be a strong argument for consulting an independent pension consultant or IFA who charges fees rather than earns commission. For further information see Chapter 6, Financial Advisers. You might also like to read the section on investor protection at the end of Chapter 5.

Another possibility, not previously mentioned, is to set up your own Self-Invested Personal Pension (SIPP). As the name implies, these are do-it-yourself schemes which among other assets can include directly held shares and even commercial property. Their big advantage is that they offer greater flexibility than ordinary pensions but, against this, the administration costs are far higher. Such schemes are only suitable for fairly sophisticated investors who can afford to pay £10,000 or more a year into their plan.

Complaints. If you have a complaint about advice you have received in relation to your personal pension, contact the Financial Ombudsman Service (FOS). For further information, see 'Financial Advisers' chapter, page 137.

Stakeholder pensions

Stakeholder pensions were launched in April 2001 with the aim of encouraging more people to begin saving towards a pension. While essentially targeted at those earning between £10,800 and £24,600, most other people, except individuals in final salary schemes whose earnings are over £30,000, can if they wish start, or switch to, a stakeholder pension.

Stakeholders are very similar to personal pensions but with the advantage that they are required to meet specified government standards, including limiting maximum annual charges (excluding financial advice) to 1 per cent.

Whereas until very recently pension contributions were always linked to earnings, a major change is that anyone with a stakeholder scheme can invest up to £3,600 a year, regardless of how much or how little they earn – or even if they have no earnings at all. A husband or wife could make contributions for a non-earning partner. Those wishing to contribute more than £3,600 can do so but the same age/percentage-of-earnings rules will apply as those governing personal pensions (see page 52).

All contributions paid will be net of basic rate tax with the pension provider reclaiming the tax from the Inland Revenue. Higher rate taxpayers will need to reclaim the excess tax through the self-assessment system. N.B. Because of the tax relief, the actual cost of a contribution worth £3,600 is £2,808. For higher rate taxpayers, the cost is £2,160. Higher rate taxpayers, however, can only claim the excess relief if the stakeholder scheme is in their own name, rather than that of a partner or other person.

Among other welcome features, savers can stop, start or alter payments without penalty. Those contributing over £3,600 who become unemployed or stop work and who, therefore, might have lost out because of the age/earnings link applicable to higher contributions, are allowed to continue paying in the same amounts as before for up to five years.

Although not many people are expected to do so, you could contribute to both a stakeholder pension and to a personal, or other, money purchase pension, provided the total of your annual contributions does not exceed £3,600; or, in the case of higher contributions, is within the limit allowed under the personal pension rules. People with a final salary scheme can also contribute to a stakeholder pension provided their earnings are not above £30,000. Equally, those (typically early retirees) who are already drawing an occupational pension can, if they wish, start contributing to a stakeholder pension. A good reason for doing so might be to take advantage of an immediate, or series of immediate, self-vesting pensions.

As with personal pensions, stakeholder pensions can be taken at any age between 50 and 75.

How to obtain. Stakeholder pensions are available from banks, post offices, insurance companies and other financial institutions. Although the basic charges may not be very different between one provider and another, you are nevertheless strongly advised to investigate at least two or three plans and ask for much the same sort of information as you would if you were considering a personal pension.

This is even more important if you are actually thinking of switching from a PP to a stakeholder pension or, as is possible, having a stakeholder as well as a PP.

Advantages and drawbacks. As general wisdom, many experts are of the view that if you are happy with your present arrangements, you might be best staying as you are. Though stakeholders are usually cheaper, you could face penalties if you terminate your existing scheme early. Equally, if you are thinking of switching from an employer's money purchase scheme, you will lose the extra contributions that your employer is making on your behalf.

Against this, the flexibility you would get with a stakeholder to alter or stop payments without penalty is attractive, as is the fact that regardless of your former earnings you can continue paying into a stakeholder for an extra five years after you stop work.

Since weighing up the pros and cons of making a change is not easy, you are strongly recommended to get expert advice. Or if you have a particular query, ring the OPAS helpline on T:0845 601 2923. (OPAS cannot, however, give financial advice.)

Useful reading. *Stakeholder Pensions: Your Guide*, obtainable by ringing the DWP Orderline on T:0845 731 3233.

Opting Back into the State scheme

If you are over 54, as a man, or over 49 as a woman, you may have been told by a financial adviser that, rather than continue with your personal pension, you might be better off switching into the second state pension (S2P). One reason you may have been given is that the rebates paid to those who have contracted out of the state scheme are insufficient in the light of increased longevity and the expected return on equity investments. Another reason, quite simply, could be that your present fund is unlikely to yield you as good a pension as S2P.

The advice is most likely to be pertinent if you have average, or modest, earnings. However, if you can afford to do so, there is nothing to stop you from contracting back into the state scheme and also having a personal pension.

Before you decide, check that your adviser has taken account of all the factors. Particular points you might want to discuss include: (1) the likely value of your pension if (a) you stay as you are (b) contract back into the state scheme (c) contribute to both S2P and a personal pension; (2) what contributions you would need (or be advised) to make in each of the above situations; (3) whether there would be a penalty if you stopped paying into your personal pension and (4) how easy it would be to restart the plan should a PP be more advantageous when the second state pension changes from being earnings-related to flat-rate, as the government has planned to happen in the next few years.

Another point to take into account could be your financial adviser's charges, as these will come out of the fund that you are building towards your pension. As guidance, many PP managers have recently reduced their fees to around 1 per cent – in line with the norm (excluding financial advice) for stakeholder pensions.

Individual Pension Accounts (IPAs)

IPAs were launched in April 2001, at the same time as stakeholder pensions. They are not another new type of pension scheme but a means of enabling those with stakeholder pensions, personal pensions and other types of money purchase scheme to have more personal control over their pension investments by allowing them to direct their contributions into equity funds, via unit trusts, OEICs and investment trusts. IPAs are subject to the same tax rules as traditional pension investments but have the advantage that if you change jobs, take a break from work or wish to move your IPA to a new pension scheme, your IPA investments will not incur the usual penalty or transfer charges.

IPAs are expected to be of most benefit to those with stakeholder pensions as well as other moderate earners including part-timers and those doing contract or freelance work.

A lump sum?

Members of company pension schemes and people with individual pension policies are allowed to take a lump sum of money tax free when they retire. The greatest amount normally permitted is one-and-a-half times your average final salary up to a ceiling of £145,800 (or higher if your pension plan pre-dates the 1989 Budget).

Taking a lump sum reduces the pension you receive but, on the other hand if you invest the money wisely, you could end up with a higher income. Alternatively of course, as many people do, you could use the capital for a worthwhile project such as improving your home; or, if you were planning to give something to your grandchildren, this could be an opportune time to settle it on them. Lifetime gifts (in contrast to money left in a will) will normally escape the taxman. The first priority, however, is to ensure that you will have enough income for your own needs.

If you take a lump sum, the amount by which your pension will be reduced is mainly determined by your age. The younger you are, the smaller the reduction. Another consideration is your tax status. Since the lump sum is tax free, as a general rule the higher your top rate of tax after retirement, the greater the advantage in opting for a lump sum. Your life expectancy can also be an important factor. The shorter this is, the more sense it makes to take the lump sum, rather than deny yourself for a longer-term pension that you will not be around to enjoy. If you come from a long line of octogenarians, then clearly you will need to work out the sums on the basis of the next 20 years or longer.

Contrary to what some people believe, it is not 'an all or nothing' decision. You have considerable flexibility and can choose between: not taking a lump sum, taking the maximum amount allowed or taking a portion of it only (whatever sum you decide).

Often the deciding factor when choosing whether to take a lump sum is the problem of investing it. If you have never had to think of it before, the prospect of what to do with several thousand pounds can seem a very daunting challenge. It could be prudent to 'invest' some of it in getting good financial advice.

Before consulting an expert, it would be helpful to both of you if you could work out – at least in very general terms – what your financial priorities are. The sort of questions your adviser will ask are: whether you are investing for income now or capital growth in the future; whether you need to go for absolute security with every penny you have or whether you can afford slightly more risky investments in the hope of making more money in the long run; what other sources of income you have, or might expect to receive.

As is normal conservative practice, you will probably find that you will be recommended to spread your lump sum across a mixture of investments. Depending on your circumstances, these might be long or short term investments; income or capital producing; or quite likely, a combination of all of them.

An outline of the different types of investment is given in Chapter 5.

Pension rights if you continue to work after retirement age

When you reach normal retirement age, you will usually stop making contributions into your company pension scheme, even if you decide to carry on working. Your employer, of course, would have to agree to your continuing to work, which he is under no compulsion to do. Indeed, some organisations have fixed rules about retirement age and do not allow any exceptions.

If, however, you are allowed to remain, you probably have three options:

- You can continue working, draw your company pension and put some of your earnings into a separate scheme. Once you are over 60, the Inland Revenue allows you to invest up to 40 per cent of your earnings tax free into a pension plan.

Provided you joined your current scheme before 13 March 1989 (or an existing scheme where you were employed before 1 June 1989) you also have the following choices:

- You can leave your pension in the fund where it will continue to earn interest until you retire. In most private schemes, you can expect to receive an extra 9 per cent for every year that you delay retirement. If you continue working, say for an additional five years, your pension will then be 45 per cent higher than if you had started taking it at the normal age. You will also have been earning a salary meanwhile, so you are likely to be considerably better off as a result.
- You can leave your pension in the fund, as described above, and additionally contribute to a personal or stakeholder pension, provided your contributions do not exceed the allowed Inland Revenue limit.

Equal pension age

Employers are required to treat men and women equally with regard to retirement and pension issues. This means that by law they must have a common retirement age that applies equally to both sexes. Similarly, they must also have a common pension age and pension schemes must offer the same benefits to their male and female members.

In time the State pension age will also be equalised for men and women at 65. The change will be phased in over ten years, starting in 2010. Because this is such a long way off, it will only affect younger women. Any woman born before 6 April 1950 will have no need to alter her retirement plans.

Divorce

Until recently, a long-standing grievance of many divorcees (ex-wives especially) was that the courts did not normally take pension benefits into account when deciding the financial arrangements between the couple. Although since the mid-nineties the courts had powers to 'earmark' pension assets and/or to direct pension schemes to make maintenance payments to the other spouse, neither option was especially popular as an ex-wife had to wait until her former husband retired before she could receive any benefit. A further drawback in the case of 'earmarking' was that if the pension scheme member died, his (her) ex-spouse might not receive anything at all.

To help overcome these problems, a new provision known as pension-sharing has now been made legally available in respect of divorce or annulment proceedings commenced on or after 1 December 2000. While a main advantage of pension sharing is that it allows a clean break on divorce, many experts believe that it may well have the effect of so diminishing the husband's (or wife's) retirement fund that he may not have sufficient left to rebuild an adequate pension. The situation could equally apply the other way round. Though women are expected to benefit most from pension sharing, the legislation could allow ex-husbands to have a share in their former wife's pension rights.

If sadly you are in the throes of a divorce, the question of pension sharing could be a subject to raise with your solicitor. But however much in favour he/she may be, in the final analysis it is up to the court to decide on what they see as the fairest arrangement – and pension sharing is only one of the several options available to them.

Part-timers

Thanks in large part to the sex discrimination legislation being extended to include access to pension schemes, many part-timers who were previously excluded can now join their employer's occupational pension scheme as of right – or may even be able to claim retrospective membership for the years they were 'unlawfully excluded'.

Their claim can only be back-dated to 1976 or, if later, to the start date of their employment and must be made (at absolute latest) within six months of leaving their job.

Part-timers who wish to claim must apply to an Employment Tribunal and, as a condition of receiving any back-dated benefits due, must pay contributions in respect of those years. Although it is perhaps stating the obvious, successful appeals are not automatic as the issue will be judged solely on grounds of sex-discrimination (and not on exclusion for other reasons).

Pensions for women

Women who have worked all their adult lives and paid full Class 1 contributions should get a full basic pension in their own right at the age of 60. The current amount is £75.50 a week. This is up-rated each year in April.

Women who have only worked for part of their adult lives may not have enough contributions to get a full basic pension on their own record. Instead, they may receive a reduced pension or one based on their husband's contributions; or one topping up the other. A wife entitled to a reduced pension on her own contributions can claim it at 60, regardless of whether or not her husband is receiving his pension.

Married women who have never worked are also entitled to a pension on their husband's contributions. In money terms, the value is about 60 per cent of the level of basic pension to which their husband is entitled. There are several important conditions, however.

Firstly, women can only receive a pension based on their husband's contributions if he himself is in receipt of a basic pension. He will have to have reached 65 and must have retired. Additionally, the wife herself must be over 60 to qualify.

If she is still under 60 when her husband claims his State pension and does not work or her earnings do not exceed £53.95, he should be able to obtain a supplement of around £45.20 to his pension, on the grounds of having a wife to support. If the couple are living apart, the earnings limit for the wife is £45.20. Your social security office will be able to advise.

In contrast, if a wife has had her sixtieth birthday but her husband has not yet reached 65 (or has decided to defer his retirement), she must wait until her husband retires to receive her share of the married couple's pension.

An important point to note is that since the introduction of independent taxation, a married woman is entitled to have her section of the joint pension offset against her own personal allowance instead of it being counted as part of her husband's taxable income. For many pensioner couples, this should have the happy result of reducing their tax liability.

If a wife who formerly worked is over 60 and retired but cannot yet get a basic pension on either her own or her husband's contributions, she may be able to qualify for an additional or graduated pension based on her own contributions. These are described a little further on.

But first a word about two other important matters: reduced rate contributions and Home Responsibilities Protection.

Reduced rate contribution

Many women retiring today have paid a reduced rate of NI contribution, also known as 'the small stamp'. This option was given to working wives in 1948 and withdrawn in 1978 but women who had already chosen to pay the reduced rate were allowed to continue, provided they did not take more than a two-year break from employment after 1978. If you have never paid anything but reduced rate contributions, you are not entitled to a basic pension in your own right but instead must rely on your husband's contributions for the married couple's pension.

Home Responsibilities Protection (HRP)

Men and women, whether single or married who have been unable to work regularly because they have had to stay at home to care for children and/or a disabled or elderly person may be able to safeguard their pension by claiming Home Responsibilities Protection. This is a very important benefit, especially for the many single women in their fifties who are sacrificing their career to look after an elderly parent. This measure was introduced in 1978 and protection only applies therefore from this date. The person you are caring for must come into one of the following categories:

- A child under 16 for whom you are getting child benefit
- Someone whom you are looking after regularly for at least 35 hours a week, who is in receipt of attendance allowance, constant attendance allowance or disability living allowance

- Someone – for example, an elderly person – for whom you have been caring at home and in consequence have been getting income support (or supplementary benefit in the past)
- A combination of the above situations.

A married woman or widow cannot get HRP for any tax year in which she was only liable to pay reduced rate national insurance contributions. HRP can only be given for complete tax years (6 April to 5 April), so if you simply gave up work for a few weeks in order to help out, you would be unlikely to qualify. Additionally, HRP cannot be used to reduce your total working life to below 20 years. To obtain a claim form, you should ask your social security office for form CF 411.

Since 1978, anyone in receipt of child benefit, supplementary benefit or income support who is caring for someone in one of the eligible categories listed above is automatically credited with HRP. All other claimants should obtain form CF 411 from their social security office.

Graduated pension

This scheme operated between April 1961 and April 1975. Anyone earning over £9 a week and over age 18 at the time would probably have paid graduated contributions and be due a pension. You can only get a graduated pension based on your own personal contributions. However, the pension from the graduated scheme is likely to be small. Further, women were penalised because their pension was calculated at a less favourable rate than for men on account of their longer life expectancy.

Additional pension

The additional State pension scheme started with SERPS in 1978. As mentioned earlier, SERPS was discontinued by the government in April 2002 and has been replaced by a similar scheme called the Second State Pension (S2P). See pages 26 to 28.

Women in contracted-out pension schemes are entitled either to a pension which is broadly equal to, or better than, its State equivalent; or to what are known as protected rights (i.e. their and their employer's compulsory contributions together with their accumulated investment growth).

Divorced wives

If you have a full basic pension in your own right, this will not be affected by divorce. However if, as applies to many women, despite having worked for a good number of years you have made insufficient contributions to qualify for a full pension, you should contact your social security office, quoting your pension number and national insurance number. It is possible that you may be able to obtain the full single person's pension, based on your ex-husband's contributions.

Your right to use your ex-husband's contributions to improve or provide you with a pension depends on your age and/or whether you remarry before the age of 60. As a general rule, you can use your ex-husband's contributions towards your pension for the years you were married (i.e. until the date of the decree absolute). After that, you are expected to pay your own contributions until you are 60 unless you remarry.

If you are over 60 when you divorce, then whether you remarry or not, you can rely on your ex-husband's contributions. If you remarry before the age of 60, then you cease absolutely being dependent on your former husband and instead, your pension will be based on your new husband's contribution record.

N.B. The same rules apply in reverse. Although it happens less frequently, a divorced man can rely on his former wife's contribution record during the years they were married to improve his basic pension.

For further information, ask your social security office for leaflet CA10, *National Insurance for Divorced Women*. You should also read leaflet NP 46 *A Guide to Retirement Pensions.*

A divorced wife might have some claim to her former husband's occupational pension benefits. See section headed 'Divorce', page 61 and also 'Pension sharing' below.

Pension sharing. As previously mentioned, provisions to enable the court to share occupational/personal pension rights at the time of divorce or annulment came into law on 1 December 2000. The legislation now equally applies to the additional State pension. Sharing, however, is only one option for dealing with pension rights and would not necessarily apply in all cases.

Separated wives

Even if you have not lived together for several years, from a national insurance point of view you are still considered to be married. The normal pension rules apply including, of course, the fact that, if you have to depend on your husband's contributions, you will not be able to get a pension until he is both 65 and in receipt of his own pension.

If you are not entitled to a State pension in your own right, you will receive the dependant's rate of benefit, i.e. about 60 per cent of the full rate (or less if your husband is not entitled to a full pension). In such a case, you can apply for income support to top up your income.

Once you are 60, you can personally draw the wife's pension of £45.20 a week, without reference to your husband.

If you are under 60 but your husband has reached 65 and is retired, he may be able to claim a dependency addition of £45.20 for you, provided he pays it to you or is maintaining you to an equivalent amount. He will not be able to claim dependency addition if you are earning more than £45.20 a week.

If your husband dies, you may be entitled to bereavement benefits in the same way as other widows. If there is a possibility that he may have died but that you have not been informed, you can check by writing to or visiting The Family Records Centre, where the indexes of registered deaths are filed. The address is: Office for National Statistics, **The Family Records Centre**, 1 Myddelton Street, London EC1R 1UW. T:0870 243 7788.

Widows

There are three important benefits to which widows may be entitled: bereavement benefit, bereavement allowance and widowed parent's allowance. All are largely modelled on the former widows' benefits (widow's payment, widow's pension, widowed mother's allowance), with the important difference that all are now also applicable to widowed men. To claim the benefits, fill in Form BB 1, obtainable from any social security office. You will also be given a questionnaire (BD 8) by the Registrar. It is important that you complete this, as it acts as a trigger to help speed up payment of your benefits. For more information, see leaflet *The New Bereavement Benefits*, obtainable by ringing the Pensions Info-line on T:0845 731 3233. N.B. Widows who were already in receipt of the widow's pension before it was replaced by bereavement allowance in April 2001 are not affected by the change and will continue to receive their pension as normal.

Bereavement benefit. This has replaced what used to be known as widow's payment. It is a tax-free lump sum of £2,000, paid as soon as a woman (man) is widowed provided that: (1) her husband had paid sufficient NI contributions (2) she is under state retirement age; or (3) if she is over 60, her husband had not been entitled to retirement pension. Her claim will not be affected if she is already receiving a State pension, provided this is based on her own contributions. (In the case of a widower, the male state retirement age (65) applies and receipt is dependent on his wife's NI contributions.)

Bereavement allowance. This has replaced the widow's pension. As stated earlier, women already in receipt of widow's pension before 6 April 2001 are not affected and will continue to receive their pension as normal.

The new bereavement allowance is for those aged between 45 and State pension age who do not receive widowed parent's allowance. It is payable for 52 weeks and, as with widow's pension before, there are various levels of payment: the full rate and age-related bereavement allowance. Receipt in all cases is dependent on sufficient NI contributions having been paid.

Full-rate bereavement allowance is paid to widows (also widowers) between the ages of 55 and 59 inclusive. The weekly amount is £75.50, which is the same as the current pension for a single person.

Age-related bereavement allowance is for younger widows/widowers, who do not qualify for the full rate. It is payable to widowed persons, who are aged between 45 and 54 inclusive when their partner dies. Rates depend on age and vary from £22.65 for 45 year olds to £70.22 for those aged 54.

Bereavement allowance is normally paid automatically once you have sent off your completed form BB 1, so if for any reason you do not receive it you should enquire at your social security office. In the event of your being ineligible, due to insufficient NI contributions having been paid, you may still be entitled to receive income support, housing benefit or a grant or loan from the social fund. Your social security office will advise you.

As applies to widow's pension, widows who remarry, or live with a man as his wife, cease to receive bereavement allowance.

Widowed parent's allowance. This is paid to widowed parents with at least one child for whom they receive child benefit. The current value (2002/03) is £75.50 a week. The allowance is usually paid automatically. If for some reason, although eligible, you do not receive the money, you should inform your social security office.

Retirement pension. Once a widow reaches 60, she would normally receive a State pension based on her own and/or her late husband's contributions.

If at the time of death the couple were already receiving the State retirement pension, the widow will continue to receive her share. An important point to remember is that a widow may be able to use her late husband's NI contributions to boost the amount she receives.

Other important points. Separate from the basic pension, a widow may also receive money from her late husband's occupational pension, whether contracted in or out of the State scheme. She may also get half of any of his graduated pension.

War widows and widowers. Until recently war widows who remarried or cohabited lost their war widow's pension, unless either the cohabitation ceased or they became single again as a result of the death of their new husband, divorce or legal separation, in which circumstances their war widow's pension was restored.

After years of campaigning by many groups, at last the rules have been changed and war widows can now keep their pension for life. The new rules also include men and war widowers equally can keep a late spouse's pension for life.

Useful reading

Guide *Pensions and Women*, obtainable by ringing the Pensions Info-Line on T:0845 731 3233.

FSA *Guide to Saving for Retirement – Reviewing Your Plans*; obtainable by ringing T:0845 606 1234.

4 Tax

Unfortunately, much as we should like to leave this out, the taxman never seems to retire!

Unless you are on a very low income, you will almost certainly be paying income tax and possibly one or two other varieties of tax as well. Paradoxically, however, although over the years you may have been contributing many thousands of pounds to the Inland Revenue, in practice you may have had very little direct contact with the tax system.

The accounts department will have automatically deducted – and accounted for – the PAYE on your earnings as a salaried employee. So unless you have been self-employed or have had other money, not connected with your job, you may never really have needed to give the question very much thought.

Come retirement, even though for most people the issues are not particularly complex, a little basic knowledge can be invaluable. Firstly, it will help you to calculate how much money (after deduction of tax) you will have available to spend: the equivalent, if you like, of your take-home pay. At a more sophisticated level, understanding the broad principles could help you save money, by not paying more in taxation than you need.

The purpose of this chapter, however, is not to suggest clever ways of reducing your liability – although in fact almost everyone has a certain amount of scope to do so without in any way cheating on the system. Apart from some general points, listed here (as well as scattered elsewhere in the book where especially relevant, such as in Chapter 10, Starting Your Own Business), giving tax planning advice is the job for a specialist; and moreover one who is fully conversant with your financial affairs, so that he can advise in the light of your own particular circumstances.

If you are lucky enough to be fairly wealthy or if some of the points mentioned in connection with recent Budget changes give you genuine cause to wonder whether you are taking advantage of the concessions available to you, you should talk to an accountant.

The aim here is simply to remind you of the basics and to draw your attention to some of the new provisions that could have a bearing on your immediate or longer term plans.

Income tax

This is calculated on all (or nearly all) your income, after deduction of your personal allowance; and, in the case of older married people, of the married couple's allowance.

The reason for saying 'nearly all' is that some income you may receive is tax free: types of income on which you do not have to pay tax are listed a little further on.

Most income, however, counts and you will be assessed for income tax on: your pension, interest you receive from most types of savings, dividends from investments, any earnings (even if these are only from casual work) plus rent from any lodgers, if the amount you receive exceeds £4,250 a year. Many social security benefits are also taxable.

The tax year runs from 6 April to 5 April the following year, so the amount of tax you pay in any one year is calculated on the income you receive (or are deemed to have received) between these two dates.

There are three different rates of income tax: the 10 per cent rate which applies to the first £1,920 of your taxable income; the 22 per cent basic rate tax which applies to the next slice of taxable income between £1,921 and £29,900; and the 40 per cent higher rate tax which is levied on all taxable income over £29,900.

All income tax payers will pay the 10 per cent rate on their first £1,920 of taxable income. Or put another way, for every £100 of your income that counts for income tax purposes up to £1,920, you have to pay £10 to the Exchequer – and are allowed to keep the remaining £90. If you are a basic rate taxpayer, the amount you have to pay the Exchequer increases (after the first £1,920) to £22; and if you are a higher rate taxpayer, it goes up to £40 for every £100 of your taxable income over £29,900.

The different rates sometimes change or, as in the 1999 Budget, a new rate may be introduced. Any changes, whether reductions or increases, are invariably announced in the Budget.

Tax allowances

Personal allowance

Income tax is not levied on every last penny of your money. There is a certain amount you are allowed to retain before income tax becomes applicable. This is known as your personal allowance. Therefore, when calculating how much tax you will have to pay in any one year, you should first deduct from your total income the amount represented by your personal allowance (plus any additional or other tax allowance to which you may be entitled, see sections following). If your income is no higher than your personal allowance (or total of these allowances), you will not have to pay any income tax.

Calculating your personal allowance used to be fairly complicated, as there were all sorts of variations according to whether individuals were married or single and whether only one partner, or both husband and wife, worked. Happily, since the introduction of independent taxation the system has become very much easier to understand.

Today everyone receives the same basic personal allowance, regardless of whether they are male, female, married or single; and regardless of whether any income they have comes from earnings, an investment, their pension or other source.

- The basic personal allowance (2002/03) is £4,615.

People aged 65 and over may be entitled to a higher personal allowance than the basic, by virtue of their age. Those aged 75 and above may receive even more generous treatment.

The full amount is only given to people whose income does not exceed £17,900. People with higher incomes may still receive some age-related allowance but this is gradually withdrawn by £1 for every £2 of income above the (£17,900) income limit. People with incomes above a certain level do not receive any age allowance. This ceiling is known as the upper limit. But however large your income, your personal allowance can never be reduced below the basic personal allowance.

For those aged 65 (or due to reach 65 before 5 April 2003) to 74:

- personal allowance is increased to £6,100
- the upper limit is £20,870.

For those aged 75 (or due to reach 75 before 5 April 2003) and older:

- personal allowance is increased to £6,370.
- the upper limit is £21,410.

N.B. Extra allowance linked to age is normally given automatically. If you are not receiving it but believe you should be doing so, you should write to your local tax office (see under Inland Revenue in the telephone directory) stating your age and, if married, that of your partner. If you have been missing out, you may be able to claim back anything you have lost for up to six years and should receive a tax rebate. The amounts have been altered several times since 1996/97, so any rebate would only apply to allowances that would have been due to you at the time.

2003–04 Tax Year. The Chancellor has given advance notice of the personal allowances for the April 2003–04 tax year. The personal allowance for those aged under 65 will be frozen at the present figure of £4,615. The age-related allowance for those aged 65–74 will be increased to £6,610; for those aged 75 and older, it will be raised to £6,740.

Married couple's allowance

Married couple's allowance was abolished, except for older couples, at the start of the April 2000/01 tax year.

Those still entitled to receive the allowance are (1) couples where at least one of the partners was born before 6 April 1935 and (2) older newly-weds, provided that one of the partners is aged 65 or more at the time of the marriage and that their date of birth was before 6 April 1935. In both cases, to be eligible, a couple must live together, i.e. as opposed to being separated.

Similar to (age-related) personal allowance, couples whose income is below a set ceiling (known as the upper limit) are entitled to a higher allowance. This used to be known as age-related married couple's allowance because it always only applied to couples where either husband or wife was aged at least 65. This is still the case, except that for couples where neither partner has yet had a 75th birthday income rather than age is now the only consideration.

When either partner reaches 75, the allowance is increased but, as before, only couples whose income is below the upper (income) limit receive any extra.

A further point to note is that unlike the old basic married couple's allowance which could be shared equally between the spouses or transferred in whole to the wife, the age/income related addition always goes to the husband.

The current (2002/03) married couple's allowance, together with the income limits for the higher allowance, are as follows:

- The minimum married couple's allowance is £2,110.
- The higher income-related allowance for couples where both partners are under 75 is £5,465. The income limit to receive the full amount is £17,900. The upper limit is £24,610.
- When the husband or wife reaches 75, the allowance is increased to £5,535. The income limit stays at £17,900 but the upper limit is increased to £24,750.

N.B. Three important points you should know:

- Married couple's allowance is restricted to 10 per cent tax relief.
- The increases based on age/income are normally given automatically. If couples are not receiving any extra but believe they should be, the husband should write to their local tax office stating their ages. If there has been a mistake, he will be given a rebate.
- A widowed partner, where the couple at time of death were entitled to married couple's allowance, can claim any unused portion of the allowance in the year they became widowed.

Registered blind people can claim an allowance of £1,480 a year. If both husband and wife are registered as blind, they can each claim the allowance. It is called the Blind Person's Allowance.

If you think you would be eligible, you should write to your local tax office (see under Inland Revenue in the telephone directory) with full relevant details of your situation. If you were entitled to receive the allowance earlier but for some reason missed out on doing so, you may be able to obtain a tax rebate.

Useful reading

For more detailed information about tax allowances, see the following Inland Revenue leaflets obtainable free from any tax office (see under Inland Revenue in the telephone directory).

- IR 90 *Tax Allowances and Reliefs*
- IR 121 *Income Tax and Pensioners*

Tax relief

Separate from any personal allowances, you can obtain tax relief on the following:

- A covenant for the benefit of a charity; or donation under the Gift Aid Scheme.
- Contributions to occupational pensions, self-employed pension plans and other personal pensions.
- Some maintenance payments, if you are divorced or separated and were aged 65 or older at 5 April 2000.

Mortgage interest relief. As most home-owners will know, mortgage interest relief was withdrawn on 6 April 2000. The only purpose for which relief is still available is in respect of loans secured on an older person's home to purchase a life annuity. However, to qualify the loan must have been taken out (or at least processed and confirmed in writing) by 9 March 1999.

Borrowers in this situation can continue to benefit from the relief for the duration of their loan.

As before, the relief remains at 10 per cent on the first £30,000 of loan.

Self-employed and other personal pension plans. The rules are not the same for all types of pension plan. In particular, there are important differences between personal pensions and retirement annuity contracts. According to your age, you can pay the following amounts into a **personal pension (PP)** scheme and obtain tax relief:

- if you are aged 35 or under, 17.5 per cent of your earnings (up to a ceiling of £97,200)
- between the ages of 36 and 45, 20 per cent of your earnings
- between the ages of 46 and 50, 25 per cent
- between the ages of 51 and 55, 30 per cent
- between the ages of 56 and 60, 35 per cent
- ages 61 and over, 40 per cent

N.B. You can make contributions of up to £3,600 a year to a Personal Pension (PP), regardless of your age or earnings. If you wish to contribute more, you can do so under the rules described just above.

If you choose to take out a **stakeholder pension**, as with PPs, you can make contributions of up to £3,600 each tax year irrespective of your earnings (and even if you earn nothing at all). Contributions above £3,600 are subject to the same age and earnings-related limits as personal pensions, with the added advantage that contributions can continue for 5 years after earnings have ceased. You pay the contributions net of basic rate tax and your pension provider will then reclaim the tax from the Inland Revenue.

Personal pension schemes started before 1 July 1988 are known as **retirement annuity contracts**. You can pay the following amounts into a retirement annuity and obtain tax relief (unlike PPs, there is no ceiling on earnings):

- if you are aged 50 or under, 17.5 per cent of your earnings

- between the ages of 51 and 55, 20 per cent
- between the ages of 56 and 60, 22.5 per cent
- ages 61 and over, 27.5 per cent.

Ages are calculated at the beginning of the tax year.

N.B. The £97,200 ceiling on earnings applies to all age groups although in practice, since it is only relevant to high earners, it is more likely to affect senior people. The ceiling only applies to people (with a self-employed/other personal pension plan) who contribute to a personal pension (PP) scheme or stakeholder pension. It does not affect those who contribute to a retirement annuity contract.

The ceiling also applies to people who joined an occupational pension scheme set up since 14 March 1989; or who joined any occupational scheme from 1 June 1989.

Maintenance payments. Tax relief for maintenance payments was withdrawn on 6 April 2000.

Individuals in receipt of maintenance payments are not affected and will continue to receive their money free of income tax. Those who had to pay tax under the pre-March 1988 rules now also receive their payments free of tax.

Most individuals paying maintenance, however, face higher tax bills. This applies especially to those who set up arrangements before the March 1988 budget. While previously they got tax relief at their highest rate, since 6 April 2000 when maintenance relief was withdrawn, they no longer get any relief at all. An exception has been made in cases where one, or both, of the divorced/separated spouses was aged 65 or over at 5 April 2000. Those paying maintenance are still able to claim tax relief – but only at the 1999/00 standard rate of 10 per cent.

Tax credits

At time of writing, there are three tax credits that could be of possible interest: the Working Families Tax Credit (WFTC), the Disabled Person's Tax Credit (DPTC) and the Children's Tax Credit. If you are in receipt of any of these, you will know that they are providing you with extra income: either by topping up your earnings, or in the case of Children's Tax Credit, by giving you extra tax relief.

Come April 2003 the present system is due to be overhauled, with the existing three tax credits being replaced by two new ones: the Working Tax Credit and the Child Tax Credit.

To understand the changes and how these could affect you – or how you might benefit in the future – it helps to start by knowing how the present tax credits work. The knowledge might even help you claim some extra income for the remaining few weeks that the existing credits last!

Both the **Working Families Tax Credit (WFTC)** and the **Disabled Person's Tax Credit (DPTC)** are payments given to individuals who, despite working at least 16 hours a week, only have a modest income and limited savings.

An essential condition to receive the Working Families Tax Credit is that the family, or lone parent, must have at least one child in full-time education, aged under 19, living with them.

The Disabled Person's Tax Credit is only given to individuals on low income with an illness or disability to help them return to work.

Each credit consists of a basic credit plus a number of possible extras, variously for children and also a further supplement if the earner works at least a 30-hour week. However, because the credits are means-tested, the amount actually payable depends on the family's, or disabled person's, net income.

Most recipients get the money in their pay packet. However the self-employed receive the payment direct from the Inland Revenue, as can a non-earning partner (i.e. if a couple so chooses) in the case of WFTC.

Application forms can be obtained from post offices, job centres, social security offices, Citizens' Advice Bureaux and Inland Revenue Tax Enquiry Centres. Or for further information, telephone the following helplines: Working Families Tax Credit helpline T:0845 609 5000; Textphone: 0845 606 6668 (open 7.30 a.m. – 6.30 p.m. Monday – Friday). Disabled Person's Tax Credit helpline T:0845 605 5858. Textphone: 0845 608 8844. (Open 7.30 a.m. – 6.30 p.m. Monday – Friday).

The **Children's Tax Credit** is not a payment as such but a tax relief, which reduces the amount of tax payable by a family, or lone parent, with at least one child under 16 who lives with them for all or part of the year.

The credit is worth up to £529 a year but is clawed back progressively for higher-rate taxpayers who lose the relief completely if their annual income reaches £42,450. The rule applies if either one of the parents is a higher-rate taxpayer.

There is also a baby bonus, increasing the relief to £1,049 for the first year of the baby's life. The income cut-off point from the baby bonus is £50,250.

An important point, applicable to both Children's Tax Credit and the baby bonus, is that because the credit is given as a tax allowance, the relief cannot exceed a family's tax bill, so those on low incomes may not get the full amount. However, they may be eligible for the Working Families Tax Credit, described above.

To obtain the Children's Tax Credit application form, ring T:0845 300 1036. Or for further information, see booklet CTCR/1 *Children's Tax Credit*, obtainable from any tax office.

As mentioned earlier, the three tax credits are shortly due to go in their present form and are being replaced on 6 April 2003 by a new Working Tax Credit and Child Tax Credit. A number of people who do not benefit from any of the existing tax credits will be able to do so from April 2003 as a result of the changes.

Working Tax Credit (WTC) is an earnings top-up given to low income individuals to make work pay. It replaces what are in effect the **adult-related elements** of Working Families Tax Credit, Disabled Person's Tax Credit and the New Deal 50+ Employment Credit. The major change is that WTC will extend support to those aged 25 plus, who work at least 30 hours a week, irrespective of whether they have children or a disability. As before, most recipients will get the money in their pay packet, with the self-employed receiving it direct from the Inland Revenue.

Child Tax Credit (CTC) is a payment that will be given to most families or lone parents with one or more children under 16 (or under 19 in full-time education). It will streamline the present varied systems of support for children by merging the existing Children's Tax Credit with the **child-related elements** of Income Support, Jobseeker's Allowance, Working Families Tax Credit and Disabled Person's Tax Credit. Many families will gain by less form-filling and more generous help towards bringing up their children.

There are several important differences between CTC and the existing Children's Tax Credit. Firstly, eligibility will be based on the combined income of the parents as opposed to, as now, automatically excluding most families where either parent is a higher-rate taxpayer. Although (in common with Children's Tax Credit) it will be progressively clawed back from the better off, the credit will only be lost completely when the parents' joint income reaches £58,175 a year.

The money will be paid direct to the main carer (normally the mother) rather than through the pay packet – and regardless of whether either parent has a job. As a result, certain groups such as students who are currently excluded from receipt of Children's Tax Credit will be eligible to benefit from CTC.

How to claim. If you are currently in receipt of the Working Families Tax Credit, Disabled Person's Tax Credit or Children's Tax Credit, you should have had a letter from the Inland Revenue inviting you to apply for one, or both, of the new tax credits. If you have not already put in your application, you should do so as soon as possible in order to ensure that you do not miss out on the new payments from April 2003.

If to date, you have not been getting any tax credits but believe you might be eligible for the new Working Tax Credit and/or Child Tax Credit you should be able to pick up an application form from any Inland Revenue Enquiry centre. Or for information, contact the relevant Helpline. WTC: 0845 609 5000; CTC: 0845 605 5858.

Come October 2003, a new **Pensioner Credit** is being introduced designed to give those with modest savings extra relief against tax. It is expected to benefit single people with incomes of up to £135 a week and couples with incomes up to £200.

Tax-free income

Some income you may receive is entirely free of tax. It is not taxed at source. You do not have to deduct it from your income, as in the case of personal allowances. Nor do you have to go through the formality of claiming relief on it.

If you receive any of the following, you can forget about the tax angle altogether – at least as regards these particular items:

- Disability living allowance
- Industrial injuries disablement pension

- Income support (in some circumstances, e.g. when the recipient is also getting jobseeker's allowance, income support benefit would be taxable)
- Housing benefit
- Council tax benefit
- Any extra which may be added to your State pension if you support children under 16
- All pensions paid to war widows (plus any additions for children)
- Pensions paid to victims of Nazism
- Certain disablement pensions from the armed forces, police, fire brigade and merchant navy
- Annuities paid to the holders of certain gallantry awards
- £10 Christmas bonus (paid to pensioners)
- National Savings Premium Bond prizes
- SAYE bonuses
- Winnings on the football pools and on other forms of betting
- Rental income of up to £4,250 a year from letting out rooms in your home
- Winter fuel payment (paid to pensioners)
- Income received from certain insurance policies (mortgage payment protection, permanent health insurance, creditor insurance for loans and utility bills, various approved long term care policies) if the recipient is sick, disabled or unemployed at the time the benefits become payable.
- All income received from savings in an ISA (Individual Savings Account).

Other tax-free money

The following are not income, in the sense that they are more likely to be 'one off' rather than regular payments. However, as with the above list they are tax free:

- Virtually all gifts (in certain circumstances you could have to pay tax if the gift is above £3,000 or if, as may occasionally be the case, the money from the donor has not been previously taxed).
- Redundancy payment, or a golden handshake in lieu of notice, up to the value of £30,000.
- Lump sum commuted from a pension with (2002/03) a maximum figure of £145,800 allowed. Existing members of pension schemes set up prior to the 1989 Budget or who joined established schemes before 1 June 1989 may not be affected by the rule and may be entitled to a higher tax-free lump sum.
- A matured endowment policy.
- Accumulated interest from a Tax Exempt Special Savings Account (TESSA) held for five years.
- Dividends on investments held in a Personal Equity Plan (PEP).
- Compensation money paid to people who were mis-sold personal pensions.
- Compensation paid to those who were mis-sold free standing AVCs (FSAVCs). To qualify for exemption from tax, the money must be paid as a lump sum as opposed to in annual payments.

Income tax on savings

Until recently, all income from savings was taxed at a normal rate of 20 per cent and at 40 per cent for higher rate taxpayers.

Perversely, the 10 per cent starting rate of tax was not applicable to savings income such as bank and building society interest but instead only applied to earned and pension income. In consequence many less well off people, including in particular thousands of pensioners, were paying more tax than they would otherwise have been due.

Happily in the March 2000 budget, the Chancellor extended the 10p starting rate of income tax to include savings income. This means that any income – whether from earnings, a pension or savings – now qualifies towards the 10p starting rate of tax. For 2002/03, this is on the first £1,920 of taxable income.

If you largely rely on your savings income and so believe you are among those who are or have been paying excess tax, you can reclaim this from the Inland Revenue. For advice on what to do, call the Taxback helpline on T:0845 077 6543 (calls charged at local rates). You might also find it useful to see 'Reclaiming tax overpaid', page 78.

Income tax on other investments

For most investments on which you are likely to receive dividends, basic rate tax will already have been deducted before the money is paid to you.

If you are a basic rate taxpayer, the money you receive will be yours in its entirety and you will not have to worry about making deductions for tax.

If you pay tax at the higher rate, you will have to pay some additional tax and should allow for this in your budgeting.

Exceptionally, there are one or two types of investment where the money is paid to you gross – without the basic rate tax deducted. These include National Savings and Investments income bonds, capital bonds, the NS&I Investment Account – and all gilt interest. (People who prefer to receive gilt interest net can opt to do so.) As with higher rate taxpayers, you will need to save sufficient money to pay the tax on the due date.

Avoiding paying excess tax on savings income

Banks and building societies automatically deduct the normal 20 per cent rate of tax from interest before it is paid to savers. As a result most working people, except higher rate taxpayers, can keep all their savings without having to worry about paying additional tax.

While convenient for the majority, a problem is that some 4 million people on low incomes – including in particular many women and pensioners – are unwittingly paying more tax than they need.

Those most affected are non-taxpayers (anyone whose taxable income is less than their allowances) who, although not liable for tax, are having it taken from their income before they receive the money.

Non-taxpayers can stop this happening quite simply by requesting their bank and/or building society to pay any interest owing to them gross, without deduction of tax at source.

If applicable, all you need do is to request form R85 from the institution in question or Inland Revenue Enquiry Centre, which you will then need to complete. If you have more than one bank or building society account, you will need a separate form for each account. Forms are also included in booklet IR 110 *A Guide for People with Savings*, obtainable from any tax office or from your bank/building society; or by telephoning the IR helpline on T:0845 077 6543.

People who have filled in an R85 should automatically receive their interest gross. If your form was not completed in time for this to happen, you can reclaim the tax from your tax office after the end of the tax year in April.

Reclaiming tax overpaid

If you are a non-taxpayer and have not yet completed an R85 form (or forms), you are very likely to be eligible to claim a tax rebate.

However, as stated earlier, this may also apply if you only pay tax at the 10 per cent starting rate; or if, since becoming retired, most of your income now comes from either taxed investments or bank/building society interest.

If any of these circumstances apply and you believe that the probability is that you could be due a refund, best advice is to ring the special **Taxback Helpline** on T:0845 077 6543 who will send you a copy of *A Guide for People with Savings*, together with a claim form and, if relevant, copies of form R85 for you to complete and give to your bank/building society.

Mistakes by the Inland Revenue

The Inland Revenue sometimes also makes mistakes. Normally, if they have charged you insufficient tax and later discover the error, they will send you a supplementary demand requesting the balance owing. However, under a provision known as the 'Official Error Concession', if the mistake was due to the Inland Revenue's failure 'to make proper and timely use' of information it received it is possible that you may be excused the arrears. For this to be likely, you would need to convince the IR that you could reasonably have believed that your tax affairs were in order. Additionally, the IR itself would need to have been tardy in notifying you of the arrears: i.e. this would normally mean more than 12 months after the end of the tax year in which the IR received the information indicating that more tax was due.

Under-charging is not the only type of error. It is equally possible that you may have been over-charged and either do not owe as much as has been stated or, not having spotted the mistake, paid more than you needed to previously. In time the Inland Revenue may notice the error and send you a refund. But equally, they may not. So if you have reason to think your tax bill looks wrong, check it carefully. Then, if you think there has been a mistake, write to your tax office explaining why you think the amount is too high. If a large sum is involved it could well be worth asking an accountant to help you.

As part of the Citizen's Charter, the Inland Revenue has appointed an independent Adjudicator to examine taxpayers' complaints about their dealings with the Revenue and, if considered valid, to determine what action would be fair.

Complaints appropriate to the Adjudicator are mainly limited to the way the Inland Revenue has handled someone's tax affairs, for example: excessive delay, errors, discourtesy or how discretion has been exercised. In deciding fair treatment, the Adjudicator has power to recommend the waiving of a payment or even the award of compensation if, as a result of error by the Inland Revenue, the complainant had incurred professional fees or other expenses.

Before approaching the Adjudicator, taxpayers will be expected to have tried resolving the matter with their local tax office or, if this fails, with the Regional Office.

For further information, see IR booklet, Code of Practice 1, *Mistakes by the Inland Revenue*, available from tax offices. Or contact the Adjudicator's Office for information about referring a complaint. The address is: **The Adjudicator's Office**, 3rd Floor, Haymarket House, 28 Haymarket, London SW1Y 4SP. T:020 7930 2292.

Tax rebates

When you retire, you may be due for a tax rebate. If you are, this would normally be paid automatically, especially if you are getting a pension from your last employer. The matter could conceivably be overlooked: either if (instead of from your last employer), you are due to get a pension from an earlier employer; or if you will only be receiving a State pension – and not a company pension in addition.

In either case, you should ask your employer for a P45 Form. Then, either send it – care of your earlier employer – to the pension fund trustees; or, in the event of your only receiving a State pension, send it to the tax office together with details of your age and the date you retired. Ask your employer for the address of the tax office to which you should write. If the repayment is made to you more than a year after the end of the year for which the repayment is due – and is more than £25 – the Inland Revenue will automatically pay you (tax free!) interest. The Revenue call this 'Repayment Supplement'.

Post-war credits

Post-war credits are extra tax that people had to pay in addition to their income tax between April 1941 and April 1946. The extra tax was treated as a credit to be repaid after the war. People who paid credits were given certificates showing the amount actually paid.

Repayment started in 1946, initially only to men aged 65 or over and to women aged 60 or over, but the conditions for claiming varied over the years until 1972 when it was announced that there would be a 'general release' and that all credits were to be repaid without any further restrictions. In 1972 people who could produce at least one of their post-war credit certificates were invited to claim.

In cases where the original credit holder has died without claiming repayment and the Post War Credit certificate is still available, repayment can be made to the next of kin or personal representative of the estate.

Interest is payable on all claims at a composite rate of 38 per cent. The interest is exempt from income tax.

All claims should be sent to the **Special Post-War Credit Claim Centre** at: Inland Revenue, HM Inspector of Taxes – PWC Centre V, TY Glas, Llanishen, Cardiff CF4 5TX.

Capital gains tax (CGT)

You may have to pay capital gains tax if you make a profit (or to use the proper term, gain) on the sale of a capital asset, for example: stocks and shares, jewellery, any property that is not your main home and other items of value.

CGT only applies to the actual gain you make, so if you buy shares to the value of £25,000 and sell them later for £35,000 the taxman will only be interested in the £10,000 profit you have made.

Not all your gains are taxable. There is **an exemption limit of £7,700 (2002/03) a year**: so if during the year your total gains amount to £14,500, tax would only be levied on £6,800.

Additionally, **certain items are exempt from capital gains tax**; others, such as the sale of a family business, may get special treatment. Details are given a little further on.

A very important point for married couples to know is that as a result of independent taxation each partner now enjoys his/her own annual exemption of £7,700 instead of, as before, their gains being aggregated (i.e. added together) for tax purposes. This means in effect that, provided both partners are taking advantage of their full exemption limit, a couple can make gains of £15,400 a year free of capital gains tax. However, it is not possible to use the losses of one spouse to cover the gains of the other.

Transfers between husband and wife remain tax free, although any income arising from such a gift will of course be taxed. Income would normally be treated as the recipient's for tax purposes.

Gains are variously taxed at: the 10p starting rate, a 20 per cent basic rate or at 40 per cent for higher rate taxpayers; or a mixture of rates, i.e. in instances where a gain, or gains, pushes part of an individual's income into a higher rate bracket.

Prior to the March 1998 budget, there were two perfectly legal ways for individuals to reduce their capital gains tax liability. The one was known as 'bed and breakfasting'; the other was indexation. Sadly, both no longer apply.

Bed and breakfasting was the term used for selling shares one day and repurchasing them the following day, in order to reduce the tax charge on a subsequent sale or to generate a loss which could be offset against other gains. This practice is no longer allowed. Under the rules which came in in 1998, the minimum period for selling and buying back the same share must be 31 days.

Indexation has also been withdrawn. This means, in effect that inflation is no longer taken into account in calculating a chargeable gain. Assets acquired before 1 April 1998 continued to be given an allowance for indexation up until the end of the 1997–98 tax year (5 April 1998), at which point all indexation ceased and has now been replaced by a taper – with diminishing tax rates for longer held assets.

Taper relief. The top rate of capital gains tax remains at 40 per cent as before but reduces in stages, after the first three years, down to an effective 24 per cent tax on assets held for 10 years or longer (i.e. after 6 April 1998). For basic rate taxpayers, CGT reduces in stages, after the first three years, from 20 per cent to an effective 13.8 per cent.

Assets acquired before 17 March 1998 get a bonus year on the taper, so qualifying them for the bottom rates of tax (variously 24 and 13.8 per cent) after 9 years, i.e. from April 2007.

Assets transferred between spouses do not lose any taper relief as, come their disposal, this is based on the combined period of holding by both spouses.

Business assets. Prior to the March 2000 budget, tax on gains from business assets similarly reduced over 10 years but on a more generous scale, with an effective bottom rate of 10 per cent tax (5.75 per cent for basic rate taxpayers). As with other assets, business assets acquired prior to March 1998 enjoyed a bonus year on the taper.

To qualify, however, full-time employees had to own at least 5 per cent of their company's shares; other investors were required to hold at least 25 per cent of the shares.

A number of major changes were made in the March 2000 budget. The holding period for maximum taper relief (i.e. 10 per cent rate of CGT) was reduced from 10 years to 4 years. Importantly for those who had made investments prior to the Budget, the new 4 year taper applied to shares held from 6 April 1998 provided these were not sold before the new rules came into effect on 6 April 2000.

Since April 2002, the holding period for maximum taper relief has been further reduced to 2 years. Investors selling business assets after only one year will also see their CGT cut, i.e. to 20 per cent as opposed to the previous 35 per cent.

Shares that qualify as business assets include: (1) all shares held by anyone in unquoted companies (shares traded on the Alternative Investment Market count as unquoted); (2) all shares held by employees, including part-timers, in quoted trading companies; (3) all shares held by employees in non-trading close companies provided the individual, and/or close members of the family, do not have a material interest of more than 10 per cent of the voting rights of the company; (4) shareholdings of at least 5 per cent, held by outside investors in quoted companies.

Free of capital gains tax

The following assets are not subject to capital gains tax and do not count towards the £7,700 gains you are allowed to make:

- Your main home (but, see note below)
- Your car
- Personal belongings up to the value of £6,000 each
- Proceeds of a life assurance policy (in most circumstances)
- Profits on UK Government stocks
- National Savings Certificates
- SAYE contracts
- Building society mortgage cash backs
- Futures and options in gilts and qualifying corporate bonds
- Personal Equity Plan (PEP) scheme
- Gains from assets held in Individual Savings Account (ISA)
- Premium Bond winnings
- Football pool and other bettings winnings
- Gifts to registered charities
- Small part disposals of land (limited to 5 per cent of the total holding, with a maximum value of £20,000)
- Gains on the disposal of qualifying shares in a Venture Capital Trust or within the Enterprise Investment Scheme, provided these have been held for the necessary holding period (see below).

The **Enterprise Investment Scheme (EIS)** allows individuals exemption from capital gains tax plus income tax relief at 20 per cent on investments of up to £150,000 a year. Formerly, to benefit, investors needed to hold the shares for a minimum of 5 years. While this still remains the case for some existing EIS shares, new shares acquired after 5 April 2000 need only be held for a minimum period of 3 years. Losses qualify for income tax or capital gains tax relief. Also, an investor can become a paid director, provided he/she was not previously connected with the company. For further information, including possible roll-over relief advantage, see Inland Revenue booklet IR 137.

N.B. The rules on companies qualifying for EIS relief were tightened up in the 1998 budget. The following, all property-related activities, are now excluded: farming and market gardening; forestry and timber production; property development; operating or managing hotels, guest houses, nursing homes or residential care homes. Individuals who had already subscribed to shares in such companies before the new rules were first announced in the July 1997 Budget are not affected.

Three further changes have been made to the rules over the past few years: (1) the gross asset limit for a company to qualify from the Scheme has been raised to £15m before an investment and £16m after an investment; (2) the proportion of money that must be invested within 12 months (for a qualifying business activity) has been reduced from the full 100 per cent amount to 80 per cent; (3) previously companies raising money needed to remain unquoted for at least 3 years if investors were not to lose their tax relief. This rule has now been scrapped provided that the company was unquoted at the time of the share issue and that no arrangements existed for it to cease to be an unquoted company.

Your home. Your main home is usually exempt from capital gains tax. However, there are certain 'ifs and buts' which could be important.

If you convert part of your home into an office or into self-contained accommodation on which you charge rent, that part of your home which is deemed to be a 'business' may be separately assessed – and CGT may be payable when you come to sell it. (CGT would not apply, if you simply take in a lodger who is treated as family, in the sense of sharing your kitchen or bathroom).

If you physically vacate some or all of your home and let it for profit – perhaps because you have decided to live permanently with a friend – under tax law, the property would be treated as an investment and subject to certain exemptions would be assessed for CGT when it was sold.

Part of the argument hinges on owner occupation. If you are not living in the property (or a part of it which you have let out for rent), then the house – or that section of it – is no longer considered to be your main home. People who are liable for CGT in these circumstances can apply for special relief of up to £40,000.

If you leave your home to someone else who later decides to sell it, then he/she may be liable for CGT when the property is sold (although only on the gain since the date of death). There may also be inheritance tax implications, so if you are thinking of leaving or giving your home to someone, you are strongly advised to consult a solicitor or accountant.

If you own two homes, only one of them is exempt from CGT, namely the one you designate as your 'main residence'. An exception was sometimes allowed if a second home was occupied by a dependent relative, who lived in it rent free.

This concession was abolished as from 6 April 1988. However, anyone who had a dependent relative living in a second home before that date will continue to enjoy capital gains tax relief. BUT the relief only applies while the dependant is actually inhabiting the property. If he/she moves to more sheltered accommodation and you keep the property as an investment, it will be assessed for capital gains tax purposes from the date of your relative's departure.

Selling a family business. If you sell all or part of your business when you retire, then provided this is before 6 April 2003, you may not have to pay tax on the first £50,000 of capital gain with a further exemption allowed of one-half of gains between £50,001 and £200,000.

To get maximum relief, you must be aged 50 or older and when selling shares must have owned at least 5 per cent of the company, either as a working director or employee for 10 years. In general, only trading businesses are eligible. If you are forced to retire early through ill health, the age rules may be applied less stringently.

N.B. Unfortunately, retirement relief is being withdrawn on 5 April 2003, so if you plan to sell your business after this date you will no longer be able to benefit. However, thanks to the new minimum holding period, most owner-managers should be able to take advantage of CGT taper relief (see page 81) to reduce their tax liability.

Another possible option are Venture Capital Reliefs, applicable to both the Enterprise Investment Scheme and Venture Capital Trusts.

Investors – including entrepreneur owner/directors with gains arising from the sale of shares in their own companies – can defer paying CGT and in many cases can also obtain income tax relief at 20 per cent on investments of up to £150,000 a year, provided gains are re-invested in either a VCT or in qualifying unquoted companies within three years.

In recent years, some of the rules have been altered to create a unified system of venture capital reliefs.

The key changes that potential investors should note are: (1) that the amount that can be invested is now £150,000 (previously £100,000); (2) that the amount an individual may invest in shares issued in the first half of the tax year and qualify for income tax relief for the previous year is now £25,000 (previously £15,000); (3) that qualifying companies are limited to £15 million of gross assets before an investment (£16 million after an investment and (4) that companies with property-backed assets, such as farming and nursing homes, no longer qualify as eligible trading companies.

Since this is a very complex field, before either retiring or selling shares, you are strongly recommended to seek professional advice.

Selling shares for gain should not be confused with giving part of your family business to the next generation, which was made easier a few years back under the inheritance tax rules. However, the advice about seeking professional help still applies, especially since all disposals including gifts may be liable for CGT.

Useful reading
For further information about capital gains tax, see leaflet CGT 1 *Capital Gains Tax: An Introduction*, available from any tax office.

Inheritance tax

Inheritance tax (IHT) applies to money and/or gifts with a capital value passed on at time of death (or sometimes before).

The first £250,000 of an individual's estate is tax free. Amounts over this are taxed at a single rate of 40 per cent. However, before any tax is calculated, there are a number of exemptions and other concessions of which perhaps the most important is that there is no tax on gifts or inheritances between spouses.

Additionally, most family-owned farms and businesses are exempted from IHT; as are most life-time gifts, provided certain important conditions are met.

There is no immediate tax on lifetime gifts between individuals. The gifts become wholly exempt if the donor survives for seven years. When the donor dies, any gifts made within the previous seven years become chargeable and their value is added to that of the estate. The total is then taxed on the excess over £250,000.

Chargeable gifts benefit first towards the £250,000 exemption, starting with the earliest gifts and continuing in the order in which they were given. Any unused balance of the £250,000 threshold goes towards the remaining estate.

Taper relief – in other words, a tapering rate of tax according to how close to the seven year limit the death of the donor occurred – reduces the amount of inheritance tax payable on lifetime gifts. Gifts made within three years of death do not qualify for any relief and the tax will have to be paid in full. For gifts made more than three years before death, the rates are as follows:

- Death between 3 and 4 years of gift, IHT reduced by 20%
- Death between 4 and 5 years of gift, IHT reduced by 40%
- Death between 5 and 6 years of gift, IHT reduced by 60%
- Death between 6 and 7 years of gift, IHT reduced by 80%

A previous loophole, whereby it was possible for a donor to give away a house, or land, as a lifetime gift but continue to enjoy the benefit of it, has now been closed. Unless the benefit is negligible or the donor is effectively forced to occupy the house/land due to unexpected hardship arising after the gift, the asset will continue to be regarded as their property under the IHT rules, until the benefit to them ceases.

Gifts or money up to the value of £3,000 can also be given annually free of tax, regardless of the particular date they were given. Additionally, it is possible to make small gifts to any number of individuals free of tax, provided the amount to each does not exceed £250.

Quite apart from IHT, capital gains tax may have to be paid on any asset you left to a beneficiary, or as part of your estate, which is subsequently sold. The Inland Revenue treats such assets as having been acquired at the date of death and at their prevailing market value at the time. By the same token, CGT will have to be paid on any gain that has built up on an asset you gave away during your lifetime and which is subsequently sold. Not surprisingly perhaps, tax specialists say that there are legitimate ways of minimising the liability.

Another important consideration that should not be overlooked is the need to make a will. The rules of intestacy are very rigid and neglecting to make a proper will can have serious consequences for those whom you might wish to benefit. For further information, see 'Making a will', (pages 430).

Likewise, if you have already written a will, it is strongly recommended that you have this checked by a professional adviser to ensure that you do not give money unnecessarily to the taxman.

For further information about inheritance tax, see booklets *An Introduction to Inheritance Tax* (IHT 3), *Inheritance Tax on Lifetime Gifts* (IHT 2) and *Alterations to an Inheritance Following a Death* (IHT 8), obtainable from any tax office.

IHT Relief for Businesses. Most small businesses have been largely exempt from inheritance tax for a number of years. In the 1995 Budget, the Chancellor went even further in protecting family-owned concerns from break-up by extending 100 per cent business relief to all shares in qualifying unquoted companies that have been held for at least two years. The rules for the transfer of agricultural assets have also been eased to abolish previous anomalies. For further information, see IR booklet *Inheritance Tax on Businesses, Farms and Woodlands* (IHT 17).

Independent taxation

The introduction of independent taxation in April 1990 affects nearly all married couples. As well as allowing married women privacy over their own financial affairs, another major gain is that many couples – especially retired people – are better off financially.

In contrast to the old system, whereby a married woman's income was treated as belonging to her husband for taxation purposes, both husband and wife are now taxed independently on their own income. Each has their own personal allowance and rate band; and each pays their own tax and receives their own tax rebates.

Moreover, independent taxation applies equally to the age-related additions and both husband and wife are now eligible for their own higher tax allowance from the age of 65 (and more generous still after age 75).

A further important point for many couples is that independent taxation does not simply apply to income tax but applies equally to both capital gains tax and inheritance tax. As a result, both husband and wife enjoy their own capital gains tax exemption (£7,700 in the 2002/03 tax year) and their own exemption from inheritance tax (£250,000 in the 2002/03 tax year). Property left to a surviving spouse remains, as before, free of inheritance tax.

N.B. The new Child Tax Credit is one area where independent taxation could be said not to apply, as eligibility is based on the combined income of the parents.

Value added tax (VAT)

Unless you are thinking of starting a business or already run one, you do not require any special information about VAT. You pay it automatically on most goods and services, at the flat rate of 17.5 per cent. As a general rule, if you purchase a tangible object, it will be included in the price. For most services, including restaurant bills, it is itemised separately. N.B. Exceptionally, VAT on both domestic fuel and the installation of energy-saving materials is only 5 per cent. The 5 per cent rate also applies to children's car seats and to central heating systems, grant-funded by government, to help less well-off pensioners and other needy households.

Small firms that are not registered for VAT naturally do not charge it. However, even for very small enterprises, there may be definite advantages in registering. If you are planning to become self-employed or start a business after you retire, you should read the VAT section, in Chapter 10, Starting Your Own Business.

Other expenditure taxes

Similar to VAT, these are simply added to your bill and do not need to be declared on any tax return.

Insurance Premium Tax (IPT)

Tax is 5 per cent and applies to premiums paid on all general insurance, **except** travel insurance and insurance bought as part of a package, e.g. when included with a warranty. In both these cases, the IPT is 17.5 per cent.

Air passenger duty
Except for flights from airports in the Scottish Highlands and Islands, where the duty has been abolished, passengers are charged £5 duty on economy fares, and £10 duty on business and first-class fares, on flights within the UK and to other destinations within the European Economic Area (EEA). The same £5 and £10 charges also apply to Switzerland and to the thirteen countries applying for membership of the European Union. The duty on economy air fares to all other destinations is £20; £40 on business and first class fares.

Corporation tax

This is a business tax and unless you are involved in running a company, there is nothing you need to know. If you are already engaged in running a small business, you will probably hardly need reminding that the standard small companies' rate of corporation tax was cut in the 2002 Budget from 20 to 19 per cent and that the former 10 per cent rate for companies with taxable profits of £10,000 or less has been reduced to zero. The standard rate for larger companies remains, as before, at 30 per cent.

The lower and upper limits for the application of marginal relief are unchanged and remain variously at: £10,001 and £50,000; and £300,001 and £1,500,000.

Useful reading
Zurich Tax Handbook published by Financial Times Management. Available from Pearson Education, Edinburgh Gate, Harlow, Essex CM20 2JE. T:01279 623928. Price £29.99 plus £3 p&p.

Your Taxes and Savings (2002/03) – published by Age Concern. Price £5.99 plus £1.95 p&p. From Age Concern Books, PO Box 232, Newton Abbot, Devon TQ12 4XQ. T:0870 442 2044.

Inland Revenue leaflets which could be helpful, especially if you are interested in the possibility of becoming self-employed or starting your own business include:

- CWL 1 *Starting Your Own Business*
- NE 1 *First Steps as a New Employer*
- IR 56/NI 39 *Employed or Self-Employed?*

Self-assessment

If you are one of the 9 million people who needs to complete a tax return, you will probably be all too familiar with self-assessment.

The tax return forms are sent out in April. If you have not already done so (and time is now running very short) the details you need to enter on the form you received in April 2002 are those relating to the 2001/02 tax year. The details you need to enter on the form you receive in April 2003 are those relating to the 2002/03 tax year.

Even if you have never had a tax return, so are unlikely to be directly affected by self-assessment unless your circumstances change, all taxpayers now have a legal obligation to keep records of all their different sources of income and capital gains. These include:

- details of your earnings plus any bonus, expenses and benefits in kind you received
- bank and building society interest
- dividend vouchers and/or other documentation showing gains from investments
- pension payments, i.e. both State and occupational/private pension
- misc. income, such as freelance earnings, maintenance payments, taxable social security benefits
- payments against which you claim tax relief (e.g. charitable donations, contributions to a personal pension).

The Inland Revenue advises that you are obliged to keep these records for 22 months after the end of the tax year to which they relate.

If you are self-employed or a partner in a business, as well as the above list, you also need to keep records of all your business earnings and expenses, together with sales invoices and receipts. All records (both personal and business) need to be kept for 5 years after the fixed filing date.

Those most likely to be affected by the self-assessment system include: anyone who normally receives a tax return, higher rate taxpayers, company directors, the self-employed and partners in a business.

If your only income is from your salary from which tax is deducted at source you will not have to worry about self-assessment. If, however, you have other income that is not fully taxed under PAYE (e.g. possibly benefits in kind or expenses payments) or that is not fully taxed at source, you need to notify the Inland Revenue within six months of the end of the tax year and you may need to fill in a tax return.

The same may be true when you retire. Even though you may not think of yourself as wealthy, if your financial affairs change as they sometimes do on retirement (e.g. if you become self-employed or receive income that has not already been fully taxed), it is your responsibility to inform the Inland Revenue and, depending on the amount of money involved, you may need to complete a tax return.

Until recently, many thousands of people with incomes of just over £500, that had not been taxed at source, received a self-assessment form. However, thanks to a change in the rules, some 400,000 people – including an estimated 200,000 pensioners – have been taken out of self-assessment and no longer receive a form to complete. Instead, income of up to £2,500 is dealt with where possible through the PAYE system.

A very important point for anyone who might be feeling worried to know is that **self-calculation is optional**. If you think the calculations are too complicated or that you might be at risk of making a mistake, the Inland Revenue will continue as before to do the sums for you.

Those choosing to calculate the tax themselves will have until 31 January following the end of the tax year to send in their tax return. Those wishing the Revenue to work out the amount of tax due will need to submit their returns by the earlier date of 30 September. The dates are important, as there is an automatic penalty of £100 if your tax return arrives after 31 January. For further information, see booklets SABK3 *Self-Assessment – A Guide to Keeping Records for the Self-employed*; SABK4 *Self-Assessment – A General Guide to Keeping Records*; SABK6 *Self-Assessment – Penalties for Late Tax Returns*; SABK7 *Self-Assessment – Surcharges for Late Payment of Tax* and SABK8 *Self-Assessment – Your Guide*, all obtainable free from any tax office. You can also call the Self-Assessment Leaflet Line on T:0845 900 0444.

Retiring abroad

The stories are legion of people who retired abroad in the expectation of being able to afford a higher standard of living and who returned home a few years later, thoroughly disillusioned. As with other important decisions, this is an area where homework really pays!

Holiday memories of dinner for two complete with bottle of wine for the princely sum of a tenner are, alas, no guide to the cost of actually living in a country – especially if the holiday in question took place five years ago or more. While some services may be cheaper, others may be very much more expensive; and the same goes for any goods you buy in the shops. In particular, if you want to purchase British brands, you can expect to pay considerably more than you do at home. It is crucial to investigate property prices as well as, of course, the cost of health care. As anyone who has ever needed a doctor or dentist abroad knows, the term 'free health service' does not always mean what it says.

While these and similar points are perhaps obvious, a vital question that is often overlooked are the taxation effects of living overseas.

Taxation abroad

Tax rates vary from one country to another: a prime example being VAT, which in some parts of Europe at the time of writing is over 20 per cent on certain items. Additionally, many countries levy taxes that happily do not apply to Britain. Wealth tax exists in quite a few parts of the world. Estate duty between husbands and wives is also fairly widespread.

There are all sorts of property taxes, different from our own, which – however described – are variously assessable as income or capital. Sometimes a special tax is imposed on foreign residents. Some countries charge income tax on an individual's worldwide income, with none of the (by British standards) normal exemptions allowed.

Even so-called tax havens may fail to live up to their privileged reputation. While admittedly not actual taxation, many impose all sorts of conditions on foreigners, effectively excluding all but the super-rich. The terms may vary but could include any, or all, of the following. Only property above a minimum (and pretty exorbitant) price may be purchased. You might have to produce evidence of a sky-high annual income. You may be required to invest in a local business. Or, insultingly, you could be requested to deposit a sum with the government to cover you against repatriation costs, should the necessity arise.

Perhaps even more alarming, many hundreds of Britons in Spain have been landed with vast bills because, unbeknown to them, the developers from whom they purchased their home had taken out a mortgage against the property and then subsequently gone out of business, leaving the British owners with the debt plus interest and legal fees. Although new laws have been introduced in Spain to protect the buyer, it appears that these are not being applied as rigorously as they might.

Apart from the essential of getting first class legal advice when buying property overseas, if you are thinking of retiring abroad the golden rule must be to investigate the situation thoroughly before you take an irrevocable step, such as selling your home.

However, if many people blithely ignore the 'nasties' that may await them overseas, an even more common mistake is to misunderstand their UK tax liabilities after their departure.

Your UK tax position if you retire overseas

Many intending emigrants cheerfully imagine that once they have settled themselves in a dream villa overseas, they are safely out of the clutches of the UK taxman. This is not so, however. You first have to acquire **non-resident status**. If you have severed all your ties, including selling your home, to take up a permanent job overseas, this is normally granted fairly quickly.

But for most retirees, acquiring unconditional non-resident status can take up to three years. The purpose is to check that you are not just having a prolonged holiday but are actually living as a resident abroad. During the check period, the Inland Revenue may allow you conditional non-resident status; and if they are satisfied, full status will be granted retrospectively.

Rules. The rules for non-residency are pretty stringent. You are not allowed:

- to spend more than 182 days in the UK in any one tax year or
- to spend more than an average of 90 days per year in the UK over a maximum of four tax years.

Even if you are not resident in the UK, some of your income may still be liable for UK taxation.

Income tax

- All overseas income is exempt from UK tax liability
- Income deriving from a UK source is, however, normally liable for UK tax. This includes any director's or consultant's fees you may still be receiving, as well as more obvious income.

- An exception may be made if the country in which you have taken up residency has a double tax agreement with the United Kingdom (see below). If this is the case, you may be taxed on the income in your new residence – and not in the UK.
- Additionally, interest paid on certain British Government securities is not subject to tax.
- Non-residents may be able to arrange for their interest on a British bank deposit or building society account to be paid gross.
- Some former colonial pensions are also exempted.

Double tax agreement. A person who is a resident of a country with which the UK has a double taxation agreement may be entitled to exemption or partial relief from UK income tax on certain kinds of income from UK sources and may also be exempt from UK tax on the disposal of assets. The conditions of exemption or relief vary from agreement to agreement. It may be a condition of the relief that the income is subject to tax in the other country. N.B. If, as sometimes happens, the foreign tax authority later makes an adjustment and the income ceases to be taxed in that country, you have an obligation under the self-assessment rules to notify the Inland Revenue.

Capital gains tax

- This is only charged if you are resident or ordinarily resident in the UK; so if you are in the position of being able to realise a gain, it is advisable to wait until you acquire non-resident status. However to escape CGT, you must wait to dispose of any assets until after the tax year of your departure and must remain non-resident (and not ordinarily resident) in the UK for five full tax years after your departure.
- Different rules apply to gains made from the disposal of assets in a UK company. These are subject to normal CGT.

Inheritance tax

- You only escape tax if (a) you were domiciled overseas for all of the immediate three years prior to death (b) you were resident overseas for more than three tax years in your final twenty years of life and (c) if all your assets were overseas. Even if you have been resident overseas for many years, if you do not have an overseas domicile, you will have to pay IHT at the same rates, as if you lived in the UK.

Domicile. Broadly speaking you are domiciled in the country in which you have your permanent home. Domicile is distinct from nationality or residence. A person may be resident in more than one country but at any given time he/she can only be domiciled in one.

If you are resident in a country and intend to spend the rest of your days there, it could be sensible to decide to change your domicile. If, however, you are resident but there is a chance that you might move, the country where you are living would not qualify as your domicile. This is a complicated area, where professional advice is recommended if you are contemplating a change.

UK pensions paid abroad

- Any queries about your pension should be addressed to the International Payments Office, Room TB 218, International Pensions Centre, Tyneview Park, Newcastle upon Tyne NE98 1BA. T:0191 218 7777.
- Technically your State pension could be subject to income tax, as it derives from the UK. In practice, if this is your only source of UK income, tax would be unlikely to be charged.
- If you have an occupational pension, UK tax will normally be charged on the total of the two amounts.
- Both State and occupational pensions may be paid to any country. If you are planning to retire to Australia, Canada, New Zealand or South Africa, you would be advised to check on the up-to-date position regarding any annual increases you would expect to receive to your pension. Some people have found the level of their pension 'frozen' at the date they left Britain, while others have been liable for unexpected tax overseas.
- If the country where you are living has a double tax agreement with the UK, as previously explained your income may be taxed there – and not in Great Britain. Britain now has a double tax agreement with most countries. For further information, check the position with your local tax office.
- If your pension is taxed in the UK, you will be able to claim your personal allowance as an offset. A married man living with his wife may also be able to claim the married couple's allowance, if by virtue of their age they would still be eligible to receive it (see 'Married couple's allowance', page 70).

Health care overseas. People retiring to another EC country before State retirement age can apply to DWP Overseas Contributions for a form E106 which will entitle them to State health care in that country on the same basis as local people.

An E106 is only valid for a maximum of 2 1/2 years, after which it is usually necessary to take out private insurance cover until State retirement age is reached. Thereafter, UK pensioners can request the International Pensions Centre at Newcastle (see under 'Pensions' above) for a form E121, entitling them and their dependants to State health care as provided by the country in which they are living.

Useful reading

Residents and Non Residents – Liability to Tax in the UK (IR 20), available from any tax office.

Leaflet SA 29 *Your Social Security Insurance, Benefits and Health Care Rights in the European Community* contains essential information about what to do if you retire to another EC country. Available from any social security local office.

The Daily Telegraph Guide to Living Abroad by Michael Furnell and Philip Jones, published by Kogan Page, £9.99.

5 Investment

Investment is a subject for everyone. One of your single most important aims must be to make your existing money work for you so you will be more comfortable in the years ahead. The younger you start planning the better. If you are already 65 or over, there is still plenty you can do.

Many articles written on the subject of financial planning for retirement concentrate almost exclusively on ways of boosting your immediate income to compensate for your loss of earnings. Frankly, this is very misleading and short-sighted advice. An equally if not even more critical consideration must be to safeguard your long-term security, even if this means some minor sacrifice to your current standard of living.

The likelihood is that you will live for 20 years or longer after you retire and your partner may live longer still. Your investment strategy must therefore be aimed not just for your sixties but also for your eighties, or even your nineties.

Inflation is another essential factor that must be taken into account. People on fixed incomes are the hardest hit when inflation rises and, as happened in the 1970s, many even quite wealthy people were drastically impoverished as a result of their savings being slashed in value.

Even low inflation, as we have today, takes its toll to an alarming extent. For example, if you have an after tax income of £11,000 a year and inflation averages 4 per cent for the next decade, your spending power will be reduced to £7,520. If it averages 6 per cent, it will have dropped still further to £6,580. And if it averages 10 per cent, you will end up with a miserable £4,170 in purchasing power terms.

Sources of investable funds

You do not need to be in the director league to have money for investment. Possible sources of quite significant capital include:

- Commuted lump sum from your pension. The maximum you are allowed to take is one-and-a-half times your final earnings, with a ceiling of £145,800. (Members of existing pension schemes joined prior to the 1989 Budget are allowed a higher tax free lump sum, provided this does not exceed one-and-a-half times final earnings). There is no tax to pay when you receive the money.
- Insurance policies, designed to mature around your retirement. These are normally tax free.
- Profits on your home, if you sell it and move to smaller, less expensive accommodation. Provided this is your main home, there is no capital gains tax to pay.

- Redundancy money, golden handshake or other farewell gift from your employer. You are allowed £30,000 redundancy money free of tax. The same is usually true of other severance pay up to £30,000 but there can be tax if, however worded, your employment contract indicates that these are deferred earnings.
- Sale of SAYE and other share option schemes. The tax rules vary according to the type of scheme, the date the options were acquired and how long the shares have been held before disposal.

General investment strategy

Investments differ in their aims, tax treatment and the amount of risk involved. One or two categories are only suitable for the very rich, who can afford to take more significant risks. Others, such as certain types of National Savings, are only really suitable for those on a very low income.

These two groups apart, the aim for most people should be to acquire a balanced portfolio: in other words, a mix of investments variously designed to provide some income to supplement your pension and also some capital appreciation to maintain your standard of living long term.

Except for annuities, National Savings and Investments and property, which have sections to themselves, the different types of investment are listed by groups, as follows:

- Variable interest accounts
- Equities
- Fixed interest securities
- Long-term lock-ups

As a general strategy, it is a good idea to aim to choose at least one type of investment from each group.

Annuities

Definition. A normal life annuity is a very simple investment to understand. You pay a capital sum to an insurance company and in return are guaranteed a fixed income for life. The money is paid to you at fixed intervals and will remain exactly the same year in, year out. Payments are calculated according to life expectancy tables and for this reason an annuity may not really be a suitable investment for anyone under 70. Other than your age, the key factor affecting the amount you will receive in payments is the level of interest rates at the time you buy: the higher these are, the more you will receive.

An annuity would probably give you more immediate income than any other form of investment. But whether you actually get good value depends on how long you live. When you die, your capital will be gone and there will be no more payments. So if you die a short while after signing the contract, it will represent very bad value indeed. On the other hand, if you live a very long time, you may more than recoup your original capital.

As a precaution against early death, it is possible to take out a capital protected annuity, an annuity which includes a guaranteed payment period or an annuity which transfers to your partner for the duration of his/her life. Any of these options will reduce the annuity income you receive but could be worth considering if your primary concern is to give your partner (or other beneficiaries) added security.

The difference between the three choices is briefly as follows. **Capital protected annuities** pay out any balance left from your original investment after deduction of the annuity payments paid to date. **Annuities with a guarantee period** are normal life annuities with the important difference that if you die before the end of the guaranteed period, the payments for the remaining years (of the guaranteed period) will go to your partner or other beneficiary. **Annuities incorporating a spouse's benefit** pay out the annuity income to you during your lifetime and will then pass to your partner for the remainder of his/her life.

There are also other types of annuity, such as capital and income plans (or temporary annuities, as they are sometimes called) which pay you a small income, say, for a 10-year period, at the end of which your capital is returned. These are sometimes taken out, as a kind of holding operation, by people who are too young to obtain sufficiently attractive terms on a normal life annuity. You have to assess whether you could get a better return from another fixed interest security. There are also: index-linked annuities, increasing annuities, unit-linked annuities, with-profits annuities, annuity growth accounts and annuity care plans which offer an annuity income with inbuilt protection against the cost of long term care provision.

Annuities, such as those described above, which you choose to buy as a purely optional purchase should not be confused with **pension-linked annuities** which are a required purchase for people with personal pensions (including Section 226 policies or retirement annuities) or with other types of money purchase pension plans. For further information about compulsory purchase annuities, see chapter 3 'Pensions'.

Tax. Income tax on optional annuities is relatively low, as part of the income is allowed as a return on capital which is not taxable. Pension-linked annuities are fully taxable.

How to obtain. You can buy an annuity either direct from an insurance company or via an intermediary, such as an independent financial adviser (IFA). But shop around, since as mentioned above the payments vary considerably. To find an IFA, contact: **IFA Promotion Ltd**., 17–19 Emery Road, Brislington, Bristol BS4 5PX. T:0117 971 1177.

Assessment. Safe. Attractive if you live to a ripe old age. But highly vulnerable to inflation. Sacrifice of capital that might otherwise benefit successors.

National Savings and Investments

NS&I is one of the biggest savings institutions in the country. It is guaranteed by the government and all investments are backed by the Crown.

It is extremely easy to invest in National Savings and Investments, as all you need do is go to the post office for information or telephone the NS&I Customer Enquiries on T:0845 964 5000 or Textphone: 0800 056 0585 (lines open 24 hours, 7 days a week); all calls are charged at local rates.

Most types of investment offered by NS&I are broadly similar to those provided by banks and other financial bodies. So rather than explain in detail the exact terms and conditions of, say, an NS&I Investment Account, it is easier to suggest that you pick up the relevant booklet at the post office counter; or telephone the above number.

National Savings and Investments Certificates, of which there are two types – Fixed Interest and Index-linked – are free of tax. Although in most cases they do not pay a particularly high rate of interest, any investment that is tax free is of potential interest especially to higher rate taxpayers.

A long-standing feature of National Savings and Investments has been that non-taxpayers enjoyed the benefit of income receipts being paid gross, without deduction of tax. Since the abolition of composite rate tax, this now also applies to bank and building society interest. The one advantage, however, that NS&I still offers non-taxpayers is that there is no need for them to complete an Inland Revenue form to receive their money in full, as this is automatic.

The main investments offered by National Savings and Investments are:

- **Ordinary Account**. Pays a fairly low rate of variable interest. You can invest between £10 and £10,000. The first £70 of interest each year is free of tax (£140 for joint holdings). Ask for booklet X760 at your post office.
- **Investment Account**. Pays quite an attractive rate of interest which increases with larger investments. You can invest between £20 and £100,000. Interest is taxable but paid in full without deduction of tax at source. Ask for booklet X761.
- **Income Bonds**. Pay fairly attractive rate of interest, increasing with larger investments. Interest is taxable, but paid in full without deduction of tax at source. You can invest between £500 and £1 million. Ask for booklet X767.
- **64th (current) Issue of Fixed Interest Savings Certificates**. Offers an attractive rate of interest that is tax free. You can invest from £100 to £10,000. For maximum benefit, you must hold the certificates for five years. Ask for booklet X762.
- **Index-linked Savings Certificates (23rd issue)**. You can invest from £100 to £10,000. There is a fixed rate of interest (at time of writing 1.6 per cent) plus the increase in the Retail Prices Index; to obtain this rate, certificates must be retained for five years. Interest is tax free. You can buy additional certificates if you wish to reinvest earlier certificates held for at least five years. Ask for booklet X763.
- **2-Year Tax Free Certificates**. Both fixed interest and index-linked savings certificates are now available for 2-year terms. As with the 5-year certificates, you can invest from £100 to £10,000. You can hold the 2-year versions in addition to any 5-year certificates you have.
- **Capital Bonds Series 7**. These offer a guaranteed interest rate, providing you do not withdraw your money before five years. The one big drawback is that tax on the

interest has to be paid annually – with higher bills every year as the interest grows – until you actually receive any money. However, for non-taxpayers especially, it offers an attractive investment as well perhaps as an ideal gift for grandparents to give children. Minimum purchase is £100 and Capital Bonds can be bought over the counter at post offices. Ask for booklet NSA768.

- **Children's Bonus Bond**. Bonds are sold in multiples of £25 and the maximum purchase per child in the current Issue 4 is £1,000. Both interest and bonus, which will be paid after five years, are free of income tax and need not be declared to the Inland Revenue. Interested parents and grandparents should ask for booklet X769 at their local post office.
- **Fixed-Rate Savings Bond**. These are lump sum investments that earn guaranteed rates of interest over set periods of time: variously 1 year, 3 years and 5 years. You can decide whether to have your interest paid out or reinvested into your bond, either on a monthly or annual basis, or at the end of the term. Either way the interest is taxable and is paid net of tax. The minimum investment is £500; the maximum, £1 million. As for booklet NSA 777
- **5-Year Pensioners Guaranteed Income Bond**. A special bond for savers aged over 60, offering a guaranteed rate of interest per annum for five years. The income is paid monthly and, helpful to non-taxpayers, is paid gross. Minimum purchase is £500; the maximum, £1 million. Ask for booklet X773.
- **1-Year and 2-Year Pensioners Guaranteed Income Bond**. Similar to the above 5-year pensioners bond, with the important difference that to obtain full value the money is only locked up for 1 or 2 years respectively.

National Savings and Investments also offers a TESSA ISA and a cash mini ISA with a government approved CATmark.

Complaints. No reader has yet complained to us about their dealings with National Savings and Investments. However, for information, disputes which cannot be resolved with the Director of Savings can be referred to the independent adjudicator. The address to write to is: Secretary to **The Adjudicator for National Savings and Investments**, PO Box 2252, London W14 8SS.

Property

With the recent increase in property values, many individuals are being tempted into taking out a second mortgage or getting a loan, with the idea of buying-to-let. While this could be a good investment, equally you could soon find yourself out of pocket, lumbered with expenses and inadequate income to cover the cost.

Even before you get your first tenant, there will be lawyer's fees to pay and you will probably need to spend some money decorating and furnishing the property.

Regular outgoings will include: interest on your loan, insurance and whatever repairs, or maintenance, are necessary to keep the property in good condition. If you use an agent to find a tenant, there will be commission to pay for the duration of the let and possibly a managing agent's fees as well, if you want to avoid the hassle of collecting the rent and dealing with any problems yourself.

Unless you are extremely lucky, there will also be periods when the property will be unlet and, in order to attract a tenant, you may need to settle for less rent than you hoped.

If rather than provide extra income now, the real objective is to have an appreciating asset that you can sell on retirement, you need to be thoroughly realistic about the various 'unknowns' that could upset your plans.

Interest rates could (and probably will) rise, making the repayment of your loan more expensive. Property prices could drop in, what most experts agree, is an overvalued market; so, rather than make a profit, you could make a loss. Also, as anyone who has tried to sell a property knows, there's many a slip when it comes to timing; so if you are likely to need the money around a particular date, such as retirement, you may find yourself at least temporarily hard-pressed. In the meantime, you will have lost the interest on the money you originally invested and, although this may, or may not, apply in the future, historically equities have outperformed property as an investment.

An over-pessimistic view? Possibly so but at the present time even mortgage lenders are concerned about the number of people at risk of over-committing themselves without properly calculating the consequences. If you have the money and are in the lucky position of being able to afford to wait until the next property boom, then investing in property might pay handsomely. However, as with any other major investment, you need to weigh up the pros and cons carefully before taking the plunge.

Variable interest accounts

Few people who rely on interest from their savings to provide them with extra income in their retirement will need reminding that interest rates can go down as well as up. In the early nineties, many savers found their income slashed by around a third and, while to some extent this was partly mitigated by the drop in inflation, many older people especially were sorely out of pocket. This is not to say that variable interest accounts should necessarily be avoided (when interest rates were high, they provided one of the best homes for many people's money); but it is essential to understand how such accounts work – together with their advantages and drawbacks.

Recent changes. Over the past few years, most banks and building societies have introduced interest-bearing current accounts. Although an improvement on the standard current account, these do not qualify in anyone's language as a vehicle for investment and, as the banks themselves would be the first to agree, are not a suitable place for anyone to keep large savings for more than a short time. If you are tempted to switch to an interest-bearing current account, you should check very carefully what charges apply if you dip into overdraft. Likewise, you should enquire whether you are being offered 'tiered rates' – those paying the top rate of interest applicable on all your funds; or the less attractive 'banded rates' – those with two levels of interest, with a lower amount paid on, say, the first £500 or £1,000 and the higher rate only on funds above that amount.

A further point to investigate is whether there is a fixed monthly or other charge. This can sometimes change at fairly short notice. You should check your monthly statement carefully and consider moving your account if you are dissatisfied.

While it is perhaps stating the obvious, you should also keep an eye on what rate of interest you are being paid – and compare it to the rates being offered by other savings institutions. According to a recent survey some savings accounts pay sub-inflation rates so, far from increasing their savings, some customers are actually losing money in real terms. To complicate matters, banks and building societies frequently introduce new accounts with introductory bonuses which are then slashed in value after a few months. While keeping track may be fairly time-consuming, at least comparing the rates offered by different savings institutions has become very much easier, as all advertisements for savings products must now quote the Annual Equivalent Rate (AER). Unlike the former variety of ways of expressing interest rates, the AER provides a true comparison taking into account the frequency of interest payments and whether or not interest is compounded.

Finally, you should know about ISAs – or to give them their full name, Individual Savings Accounts – which were launched in April 1999 as a replacement for TESSAs and PEPs (see a couple of pages over).

Definition. Other than the interest-bearing current accounts described above, these are all savings, or deposit, accounts (share accounts in building societies) of one form or another, arranged with banks, building societies, the National Savings and Investments Bank and with some financial institutions that operate such accounts jointly with banks. They include among others: basic deposit accounts, high interest accounts and fixed term deposit accounts.

Your money collects interest while it is on deposit, which may be automatically credited to your account or for which you may receive a regular cheque. Some institutions pay interest annually, others – on some or all of their accounts – will pay it monthly. If you have a preference, this is a point to check. The rate of interest will vary, up or down, according to the level of national interest rates. While you may get a poor return on your money if interest rates drop, your savings will nearly always be safe as you are not taking any kind of investment risk. Moreover, provided you deal with an authorised bank, up to £2,000 of your money will be 100 per cent protected under the Financial Services Compensation Scheme. A further £33,000 will be 90 per cent protected, making a maximum repayment of £31,700.

Access. Access to your money depends on the type of account you choose: you may have a cheque book and withdraw your money when you want; you may have to give a week's notice or slightly longer; or if you enter into a term account, you will have to leave your money deposited for the agreed specified period. In general, accounts where a slightly longer period of notice is required earn a better rate of interest.

Sum deposited. It is not usually sensible to consider a deposit account unless you have a minimum of £100. For certain types of account, the minimum investment could be anything from £500 to about £5,000. The terms tend to vary according to how keen the institutions are, at a given time, to attract small investors.

Tax. With the exception of TESSAs and cash ISAs, (see page 101) which are tax-free, and of the National Savings and Investments Bank, where interest is paid gross, tax is deducted at source – so you can spend the money without worrying about the tax implications. However, you must enter the interest on your tax return; and if you are a higher rate taxpayer, you will of course have additional liability.

Since the start of the April 1996–97 tax year, basic rate taxpayers have enjoyed a reduction in tax on their bank and building society interest. Instead of paying the full basic rate, the amount charged is only 20 per cent. Higher rate taxpayers continue, as before, to pay 40 per cent. Non-taxpayers can arrange to have their interest paid in full by completing a certificate which enables the financial institution to pay the interest gross. For further information see 'Avoiding paying excess tax on savings income' and 'Reclaiming tax overpaid', pages 77–78.

N.B. Until recently, people who would normally only have paid tax at the 10p starting rate were at a major disadvantage as the 10 per cent rate only applied to earned and pension income – and not to savings income such as bank and building society interest. As a result, although not basic rate taxpayers, many less well off people were still charged the full 20 per cent rate on their savings income. Happily this injustice has now been put right and the 10 per cent rate now equally applies to savings income. If you largely rely on your savings income and believe you are or have been paying excess tax you can reclaim this from the Inland Revenue. For further information, see 'Income tax on savings' and 'Reclaiming tax overpaid' pages 77–78.

Choosing a deposit account

There are two main areas of choice: the type of deposit account and where to invest your money. The relative attractions of the different types of account and of the institutions themselves can vary, according to the terms being offered at the time. Generally speaking, however, the basic points are as follows:

Basic deposit account. This attracts a relatively low rate of interest. But it is both easy to set up and very flexible, as you can add small or large savings when you like and can usually withdraw your money without any notice. It is a much better option than simply leaving your money in a current account and is an excellent temporary home for your cash if you are saving short term for, say, a holiday. However, it is not recommended as a long-term savings plan.

High interest deposit account. Your money earns a higher rate of interest than it would on an ordinary deposit account. However, to open a high interest account you will need to deposit a minimum sum, which could be of the order of £500 to £1,000. While you can always add to this amount, if your basic deposit drops below the required minimum, your money will immediately stop earning the higher interest rate. If you require an overdraft facility, a high interest deposit account is worse than useless.

Fixed term deposit account. You deposit your money for an agreed period of time, which can vary from a few months to over a year. In return for this commitment, you will normally be paid a superior rate of interest.

As with high interest accounts, there is a minimum investment: roughly £1,500 to £10,000. If you need to withdraw your money before the end of the agreed term, there are usually hefty penalties. Before entering into a term account, you need to be sure that you can afford to leave the money on deposit.

Additionally, you will need to take a view about interest rates: if they are generally low, your money may be better invested elsewhere.

A further important point is that you should keep a note of the date when the agreement expires. As a rule, your money will no longer earn preferential rates after the term has come to an end (unless of course you renew the agreement). The bank or other institution may not notify you in advance and may, quite legitimately, simply credit you with the normal interest rates after the contract's expiry.

Equity linked deposit account. Offers a potentially better rate of return, as the interest is calculated in line with the growth in the stock market. Should the market fall, you may lose the interest but your capital remains protected. The minimum investment varies from about £500 to £5,000 and the money must remain deposited for 5 years. As with any investment, it is important to ensure that you fully understand all the terms and conditions – and if anything is unclear, that you ask to have the point explained to you properly in simple language.

Tax Exempt Special Savings Account (TESSA). TESSAs were withdrawn on 6 April 1999 with the launch of the new Individual Savings Account (ISA). However, although it is no longer possible to open a TESSA account, anyone with an existing TESSA at the time of their withdrawal can continue to pay into it under the old rules for its full five-year life without this counting against their annual subscription limit to an ISA. The capital from a maturing TESSA can then be transferred into an ISA.

NB. If you are continuing to make payments into your TESSA, you might be advised to check what interest rates you are being paid. Some savers have found that these have been disproportionately slashed and that, even taking into account the fact that the interest would be tax-free on the maturity of their TESSA, their money would be better invested elsewhere.

ISA Savings. Except for people in the happy position of having a maturing TESSA, who are allowed more, the maximum amount you are allowed to save in cash form (as opposed to stocks and shares and life assurance) in an ISA is £3,000 a year.

As with TESSAs, all interest earned is tax free. A further possible attraction is that savings held in an ISA are not 'locked up' but can be withdrawn at any time. (For further information about ISAs, see page 111.)

Information. For banks, enquire direct at your nearest high street branch. There will be leaflets available, describing the different accounts in detail. Or if you have any questions, you can ask to see your bank manager. You can also investigate the other banks to see whether they offer better terms.

For building societies, enquire at any building society branch or, better still, pop into several as the terms and conditions may vary quite widely.

The **Building Societies Association** at 3 Savile Row, London W1S 3PB offers a free range of helpful leaflets and information sheets, including: *Taxation of Building Society Interest*; *Individual Savings Accounts and Building Societies;* and *Why We Need Building Societies*; *A Directory of Members*, giving head office addresses and telephone numbers, is also available.

The safety of your investment. No ordinary investor in a UK building society has lost a penny of his or her savings in living memory. Investors are protected by the legislative framework in which societies operate and also by the high standard of prudent management. Additionally, in common with bank customers, their money (up to a maximum of £31,700) is protected under the Financial Services Compensation Scheme. Further details about the scheme are explained in the BSA information sheet, obtainable from the above address.

Complaints. If you have a complaint against a bank or building society, you can appeal to the Financial Ombudsman Service (FOS) to investigate the matter, provided that the complaint has already been taken through the particular institution's own internal disputes procedure and the matter is within the scope of the Ombudsman Scheme. Generally speaking, the FOS can investigate complaints about the way a bank or building society has handled some matter relating to its services to customers. The address to contact is: **Financial Ombudsman Service**, South Quay Plaza, 183 Marsh Wall, London E14 9SR. T:0845 080 1800. See also 'Complaints', page 121.

Other accounts

A growing number of unit trusts and other financial institutions now offer interest bearing accounts that are very similar to those run by banks and building societies. If you have a complaint, the Financial Ombudsman Service (see above) may be able to help. As before, you will first need to go through the institution's own internal disputes procedure.

Fixed interest securities

In contrast to variable interest accounts, fixed interest securities offer a fixed rate of interest which you are paid, regardless of what happens to interest rates generally. If you buy when the fixed rate is high and interest rates fall, you will nevertheless continue to be paid interest at the high rate specified in the contract note. However, if interest rates rise above the level when you bought, you will not benefit from the increase. As a generalisation, these securities give high income but only modest, if any, capital appreciation.

The list includes: high interest gilts, permanent interest bearing shares, local authority bonds and stock exchange loans, debentures and preference shares.

Corporate loans, debentures and preference shares

Definition. Companies use fixed interest loan, debenture and preference shares as one of the ways of raising money for expansion. Unlike ordinary shares, bonds and debentures pay a fixed guaranteed rate of interest, usually six monthly, but do not entitle the holder to share in the profits or to vote at the annual general meeting. By contrast, preference shares pay a fixed rate of dividend but this is not always guaranteed.

All are bought and sold on the Stock Exchange and, similar to gilts, their price rises and falls with the market view of future interest rates.

As with other shares, they are backed by the assets of the company and are therefore secure unless the company actually fails. But while your interest payments are virtually guaranteed, you could make a loss when you sell the shares – but equally, of course, a profit.

In theory, you could buy today and sell tomorrow. However, generally speaking it is inadvisable to purchase these shares other than as a long-term holding.

There will be stockbrokers' commission to pay and there is normally about a 3-day delay between selling and receiving the money, i.e. provided that the relevant certificates and transfer deeds are immediately available. Otherwise settlement may well take about 10 days.

To find a stockbroker, see Chapter 6, Financial Advisers.

Tax. Income tax on your interest is deducted at source. If you make a profit, there could be liability for capital gains tax.

Assessment. Normally pay better interest than gilts – but a more risky investment. There is a chance of a windfall in the event of a takeover. Only really suitable for experienced investors. Specified corporate bonds and preference shares are allowable for ISAs and enjoy the normal (ISA) tax advantages (see page 111).

Gilt-edged securities

Definition. Usually known as 'gilts', these are stocks issued by the Government which guarantees both the interest payable and the repayment price which is promised on a given date.

The maturity date varies and can be anything from a few months to 20 years or longer. Accordingly, stocks are variously known as: short-dated, medium-dated and long-dated. A further category is undated. Additionally, there are index-linked gilts.

Prices for gilts are quoted per £100 of nominal stock. For example, a stock may be quoted as: 10 per cent Treasury Stock 2004, 99½ – 100. In plain English, this means the following:

- 10 per cent represents the interest you will be paid. The rate is fixed and will not vary, whatever happens to interest rates generally. You will receive the interest payment twice yearly, 5 per cent each time.

- You are buying Treasury Stock.
- The maturity date is 2004.
- To buy the stock, you will have to pay £100.25p (i.e. 100¼).
- If you want to sell the stock, the market price you will get is £99.50p (i.e. 99½).

In addition, when buying or selling, regard has to be given to the accrued interest which will have to be added to or subtracted from the price quoted.

Gilts are complicated by the fact that you can either retain them until their maturity date, in which case the Government will return the capital in full. Or you can sell them on the Stock Exchange at market value. This accounts for the different buying and selling prices that may be quoted.

Prices are affected by current interest rates. If interest rates are at 4 per cent, a gilt with a guaranteed interest payment of 9 per cent is a very attractive buy so the price will rise. Conversely, if interest rates are 9 per cent, a guaranteed interest payment of 4 per cent is a poor proposition, so there will not be many buyers and the price will drop. Because gilts are so closely tied to interest rates, the price can fluctuate daily, often by quite big jumps.

Index-linked gilts, while operating on the same broad principle, are different in effect. They are designed to shield investors against inflation: they pay very low interest but are redeemable at a higher price than the initial purchase price, as their value is geared to the cost of living. They are most valuable when inflation is high but are even more sensitive than other gilts to optimum timing when buying or selling.

Tax. Before April 1998 income tax was normally deducted at source, except in the case of gilts bought on the National Savings Stock Register (NSSR), where the interest was paid gross. Today however, gilt interest from whatever source is paid gross. Gross payment does not mean that you avoid paying tax, simply that you must allow for a future tax bill before spending the money. Recipients who prefer to receive the money net of tax can request for this to be arranged.

A particular attraction of gilts is that no capital gains tax is charged on any profit you may have made. But equally no relief is allowed for loss.

How to buy. You can buy gilts through banks, building societies, a stockbroker or financial intermediary. Or you can get a form at the post office and purchase gilts through the Bank of England, who have taken over the postal gilts buying and selling service from the National Savings Stock Register. In all cases, you will be charged commission. Prices of gilts are published every day in all the quality newspapers under the heading 'British Funds'.

You may also find it helpful to see section headed 'Bonds' on page 119.

A booklet *Investing in Gilts*, together with purchase forms, is obtainable from: The Chief Registrar, **Bank of England**, Southgate House, Southgate Street, Gloucester GL1 1UW. Freephone: 0800 818614.

Assessment. Gilts normally pay reasonably good interest and offer excellent security, in that they are backed by the Government. You can sell at very short notice and the stock is normally accepted by banks as security for loans, if you want to run an overdraft.

However, gilts are not a game for amateurs as, if you buy or sell at the wrong time, you could lose money; and if you hold your stock to redemption, inflation could take its toll on your original investment. Index-linked gilts, which overcome the inflation problem, are generally speaking a better investment for higher rate taxpayers – not least because the interest paid is very low.

Gilt plans. This is a technique for linking the purchase of gilt-edged securities and with-profit life insurance policies to provide security of capital and income over a 10 to 20-year period. It is a popular investment for the commuted lump sum taken on retirement. These plans are normally obtainable from financial intermediaries, who should be authorised by the FSA.

Permanent interest bearing shares (PIBS)

These are a form of investment offered by some building societies to financial institutions and private investors, as a means of raising share capital.

They have several features in common with gilts, as follows. They pay a fixed rate of interest which is set at the date of issue: this is likely to be on the high side when interest rates generally are low and on the low side when interest rates are high. The interest is usually paid twice yearly and – again, similar to gilts – there is no stamp duty to pay, nor capital gains tax on profits.

Despite the fact that PIBS are issued by building societies, they are very different from normal building society investments and have generally been rated as being in the high risk category. Anyone thinking of investing their money should seek professional advice. To buy the shares, you would need to go to a stockbroker or financial adviser.

Equities

These are all stocks and shares, purchased in different ways and involving varying degrees of risk. They are designed to achieve capital appreciation as well as give you some regular income. Most allow you to get your money out within a week. In the past, equities were by and large only considered suitable for a privileged minority. Today, the number of shareholders is estimated to have soared to around 15 million people. One reason is that equities can be excellent money-spinners. Another is that over the last few years, investment has become very much easier, largely as a result of the increase in the number of Internet and telephone share dealing facilities.

As many will know to their cost from the recent market volatility, equities are always risky. But for those who believe in caution, the gamble can be substantially reduced by avoiding obviously speculative investments and by choosing a spread of investments, rather than putting all your eggs in one basket. Equities include: ordinary shares, unit trusts, OEICs and ISAs.

Unit trusts and OEICs

Definition. Unit trusts and OEICs (open-ended investment companies, a modern equivalent of unit trusts) offer an alternative to buying shares on the Stock Exchange. Your money is pooled in a fund, run by professional managers, who invest the proceeds in a wide range of shares and other securities. The advantages are that: it is usually less risky than buying individual shares; it is very simple to understand; you get professional management and there are no day-to-day decisions to make. Additionally, every fund is required by law to have a trustee (called a depository in the case of OEICs) to protect investors' interests.

Over the last twenty years, the number and variety of funds has increased dramatically. Some specialise in producing high income; some, in maximising capital gains; others are mixed funds, aiming to combine both virtues. Some of the newer funds concentrate on particular sectors, such as: gilts, corporate bonds, European, North American, Far Eastern or other overseas markets. One of the more recent new-comers are index-tracker funds which track the performance of major stock market indices.

There are also cash funds which invest in the money markets and offer rates of return comparable to those of building society postal accounts.

The minimum investment in some of the more popular funds is £500; in others, it can be as high as £10,000. Many funds allow you to purchase units (shares in an OEIC) for smaller amounts, typically £50, on a regular monthly savings plan.

There is often a front-end fee of around 5 per cent but this varies, however, from group to group and from fund to fund. Certain management companies have recently abolished the front-end fee, although in a few cases this has been replaced with an exit charge when the units are sold.

Investors' contributions to the fund are divided into units (shares in OEICs) in proportion to the amount they have invested. As with ordinary shares, you can sell all or some of your investment by telling the fund manager that you wish to do so. The price you will receive is called 'the bid price'. The price at which you buy a unit is called 'the offer price'. OEICs have a corporate structure and, instead of purchasing units with a bid/offer spread, investors buy and sell shares at a single mid-market price. These prices are published daily in the financial pages of the quality newspapers.

How to obtain. Units and shares can be purchased from banks, building societies, insurance companies, stockbrokers or specialist investment fund providers, either directly or via independent financial advisers. Some firms advertise in the national press and financial magazines and also, increasingly, on the Internet. Some have their own salesforces. Many of the larger firms may use all these methods.

You may be asked to complete a form – stating how much you want to invest in which particular fund – and then return it to the company with your cheque. Alternatively, you may be able to deal over the telephone or Internet.

For a list of unit trusts and OEICs, you can look in the *Financial Times*. Alternatively, write to the **Unit Trust Information Service** at 65 Kingsway, London WC2B 6TD; or call the Information Service on T:020 8207 1361 to obtain a copy of *The Directory*. There is also a range of booklets, obtainable from the Information Service, including: *The Handbook: Saving and Investment In Unit Trusts;* and factsheets on ISAs, OEICs, ethical investment, unit trusts and tax, monthly savings and savings for children.

Tables comparing the performance of the various funds are published in specialist magazines, such as *Money Management, Money Observer* and *What Investment*.

With over 2,000 funds from which to choose, it is important to get professional advice. You can ask an independent adviser, your bank, an accountant or solicitor. For further information see Chapter 6, Financial Advisers.

Tax. Units and shares invested through an ISA have special advantages (see ISAs, page 111). Otherwise, tax treatment is identical to ordinary shares (see next section).

Assessment. An ideal method for smaller investors to buy stocks and shares: both less risky and easier. This applies especially to tracker funds, which have the added advantage that charges are normally very low. Some of the more specialist funds are also suitable for those with a significant investment portfolio.

Complaints. Complaints about unit trusts and OEICs are handled by the Financial Ombudsman Service (FOS). It has power to order awards of up to £100,000.

Before approaching the FOS, you must first try to resolve the problem with the management company direct via their internal complaints procedure. If you remain dissatisfied, the company should advise you of your right to refer the matter to the FOS. Whether they inform you or not, the address to contact is: **Financial Ombudsman Service**, South Quay Plaza, 183 Marsh Wall, London E14 9SR. T:0845 080 1800.

Ordinary shares listed on the Stock Exchange

Definition. Public companies issue shares as a method of raising money. When you buy shares and become a shareholder in a company, you own a small part of the business and are entitled to participate in its profits through a dividend which is normally paid six monthly.

Dividends go up and down according to how well the company is doing and it is possible that in a bad year no dividends at all will be paid. However, in good years, dividends can increase very substantially.

The money you invest is unsecured. This means that, quite apart from any dividends, your capital could be slashed in value – or if the company goes bankrupt, you could lose the lot. Against this, if the company performs well you could substantially increase your wealth.

The value of a company's shares is decided by the stock market. Thousands of large and small investors are taking a view on each company's prospects and this creates the market price. The price of a share can fluctuate daily and this will affect both how much you have to pay, if you want to buy; and how much you will make (or lose), if you want to sell.

To find out more about becoming an investor you can contact the **London Stock Exchange**, Public Information Department, Old Broad Street, London EC2N 1HP (T:020 7797 1372) for a list of brokers in your region who would be willing to deal for you (see Chapter 6, Financial Advisers).

Alternatively, you can go to the securities department of your bank – or to one of the 112 authorised share shops – who will place the order for you.

Another option which has become increasingly popular are telephone share dealing services, which offer an easy, low-cost way of buying and selling shares over the 'phone. A possible drawback is that most share lines operate an execution-only service – i.e. they accept instructions but do not give advice – which is fine if you know exactly what shares you want to purchase or sell but not so good if you want investment help. However, as part of the service, some share lines are happy to provide factual information. Increasingly too, analysts' buy/sell recommendations are being published on the Internet.

Indeed, use of the Internet is growing at an explosive rate and over the past couple of years a number of firms have introduced Internet share-dealing services, allowing investors to purchase shares online with, among other benefits, the advantage of speedier execution.

Whether you use a stockbroker, a share shop, a telephone share dealing service or the Internet, you will be charged both commission and stamp duty which is 1/2 per cent. Unless you use a nominee account (see below), you will be issued with a share certificate which you or your financial adviser must keep, as you will have to produce it when you wish to sell all or part of your holding.

It is likely, when approaching a stockbroker or other share-dealing service, that you will be asked to deposit money for your investment up-front or advised that you should use a nominee account. This is because of the introduction of several new systems, designed to speed up – and streamline – the share-dealing process. The first, which came in in 1995, was the rolling settlement system which cut the time for settling transactions from ten days to the present three days. An even bigger innovation was the launch of Crest, which is an electronic share-dealing system that is expected to do away with the need for paper share certificates by holding the information on computer files.

No one is forced to use the electronic system. Paper shares are still valid and there is also no compulsion to switch to a nominee account. However, people without one are likely to have to pay more for transactions now that the transition to Crest has been completed – and they will also have to keep their own tax and dividend-payments records.

A further turn of the screw has come with the introduction of yet another new system, known as Sets. At present, usage is largely limited to the 100 biggest companies quoted on the FTSE index but many stockbrokers expect that in time the system will be expanded to cover a wider sector of companies – and that one of the consequences will be that nominee accounts will become all but compulsory to obtain normal settlement.

The big disadvantage of a nominee account is that it usually means missing out on some shareholder rights, such as receipt of the annual report and access to various benefits – including shareholders' perks.

The number of companies offering perks has been increasing over the past few years. Most come in the form of discounts on goods and services including reduced price travel, vouchers for clothes, concessionary prices on hotel and restaurant bills and many others. Among the 2002 crop were 50 per cent off the price of a fitted kitchen, a 15 per cent discount on purchases from a well-known chain store and £500 discount on every £25,000 spent towards the purchase of a house. In some companies, to be eligible a minimum shareholding is required and/or retention of the shares for a minimum period. Enjoyable as such perks are, it goes without saying that investors should only buy stocks if the share is worthwhile in its own right. A cheaper holiday is no bargain if the price of obtaining it is a dud investment!

There are two types of share both quoted on the Stock Exchange that are potentially suitable for small investors. These are investment trusts and convertible loan stocks. Other possibilities, but only for those who can afford more risky investments, are warrants and zero coupon loan stocks.

Investment trusts are companies just like Tesco's and Dixons but, instead of making products to sell, they invest in the shares of other companies, providing a spread of risk. You can buy investment trusts through a saving and investment scheme (offering monthly savings, lump sum investment and dividend re-investment) which is simple and cheap. There are over 300 different trusts from which to choose.

For a free information pack on investment trusts, saving schemes and ISAs, write to **The Association of Investment Trust Companies**, Durrant House, 8–13 Chiswell Street, London EC1Y 4YY.

Convertible loan stocks give you a fixed guaranteed income for a certain length of time and offer you the opportunity to convert them into ordinary shares. While capital appreciation prospects are lower, the advantage of convertible loans is that they usually provide significantly higher income than ordinary dividends. They are also allowable for ISAs.

Zero coupon loan stocks. These stocks provide no income during their life but pay an enhanced capital sum on maturity. They would normally only be recommended for higher rate taxpayers and professional advice is strongly recommended.

Warrants are issued by companies or investment trusts to existing shareholders either at launch or by way of an additional bonus. Each warrant carries the right of the shareholder to purchase additional shares at a pre-determined price on specific dates in the future. As such, warrants will command their own price on the stockmarket. These are a high-risk investment and professional advice is essential.

Tax. The standard rate of tax on income from share dividends (including unit trust distributions) is 20 per cent, with higher rate taxpayers required to pay 40 per cent. Quite apart from income tax, if during the year you make profits by selling shares that in total exceed £7,700, you would be liable for capital gains tax.

Changes in the taxation of share dividends. Until a few years ago, companies paid advanced corporation tax (ACT) and investors enjoyed the benefit of a 20 per cent tax credit on their dividends from shares. However, all that has now changed. ACT was abolished on 6 April 1999, as were tax credits – with the exception of those applying to dividends held in PEPs and ISAs. These tax credits have now been halved in value to 10 per cent and are due to be abolished altogether in April 2004.

Although most people investing in shares will not have to pay any more tax, their dividend income will be reduced. Non-taxpayers, including many pensioners, have been especially badly hit as they can no longer reclaim any tax credit direct.

Assessment. Although dividend payments generally start low, in good companies they are likely to increase over the years and so provide a first class hedge against inflation. The best equities are an excellent investment. In others, you can lose all your money. Good advice is critical as this is a high risk/high reward market.

Personal equity plan

PEPs have ceased to be available since 6 April 1999, when they were withdrawn by the government to be replaced by Individual Savings Accounts (ISAs). However, although it is no longer possible to acquire a PEP, anyone with an existing PEP (or number of PEPs) before their withdrawal can retain it under the old rules and continue to enjoy the same tax advantages as before. Individuals can, if they wish, also subscribe to an ISA – see below.

For those who may have forgotten the detail, PEPs allow you to buy shares in a range of investments including corporate bonds and investment trusts, with the advantage that all income and gains are tax free. The money has to be invested through an authorised manager, for example: a bank, building society or financial intermediary.

Since April 2001, PEPs have been made more flexible as a result of the government aligning the rules with those of ISAs. The main changes are: (1) there is no longer a distinction between general and single company PEPs, so investors who wish to do so can merge the two (2) investors are now able to invest in the listed shares of companies anywhere in the world and (3) investors can now transfer part of a PEP to another PEP manager and not just the whole PEP as before.

Tax. PEPs are free of both income tax and capital gains tax. Capital gains tax losses incurred on other investments cannot be offset against PEP profits (and vice versa). N.B. The dividend tax credit, which was one of the attractions of PEPs, was reduced from 20 to 10 per cent as from 6 April 1999 and will cease to be repayable from April 2004.

Assessment. The tax advantages are attractive, although the halving of dividend tax credits has removed some of the shine. Also, no shares are without risk and even corporate bond PEPs are not totally risk-free as capital values could fall. If you are worried about the present volatility on the stock market, you might want to discuss with your PEP manager whether it would be wise to change some of your investments or keep a larger percentage in cash. While probably remaining worthwhile for higher rate taxpayers, the charges could be a critical factor in deciding whether a PEP is still the best place for your money.

Individual Savings Account (ISA)

Definition. ISAs are the new savings accounts which the government launched on 6 April 1999 as a replacement for PEPs and TESSAs. They contain many of the same advantages in that all income and gains generated in the account are tax free.

As with PEPs and TESSAs, there is a subscription limit – with the maximum annual amount you can put into an ISA being £7,000. This was to have been reduced to £5,000 a couple of years ago but thanks to a late change is now to remain at £7,000 until April 2006.

An ISA can contain any, or all, of the following:

- up to £3,000 in cash;
- up to £1,000 in life assurance;
- stocks and shares.

The £3,000 cash element can include National Savings, bank and building society accounts and also supermarket savings accounts.

There are two types of ISA: a maxi ISA and a mini ISA. It is important to understand the difference because, once you have made a choice, you cannot change your mind. The essential point is that with a maxi ISA you can invest more, or all, of your money in shares, whereas with a mini ISA you are limited to a maximum of £3,000.

You are not obliged (as is required with TESSAs) to keep savings/investments in the account for a fixed period but instead can make withdrawals at any time. However, once you have subscribed the maximum in a year, you will not be allowed to put in any more, regardless of how much is withdrawn.

All money held in an ISA – whether cash, life assurance or stocks and shares – must be administered by an authorised manager, or managers. If you choose to have a maxi ISA, the whole of your ISA must be with a single manager. In the case of a mini ISA, you could subscribe to separate mini ISAs for cash savings, life assurance and stocks and shares with different managers.

As a further safeguard, the government has introduced a voluntary benchmark guaranteeing that the ISA being offered meets approved standards with regard to cost, access, terms and conditions. The sign to look for is called a CATmark.

Tax. ISAs are completely free of all income tax and capital gains tax. However, you should be aware that a 20 per cent charge is levied on all interest accruing from non-invested money held in an ISA that is not specifically a cash ISA.

Assessment. ISAs offer a simple, flexible way of starting, or improving, a savings plan. The tax advantages are attractive, although will become rather less so when tax credits are finally abolished in 2004. Although the CATmark should be helpful as a guarantee of standards, investment in stocks and shares (which is not essential but over the years has proved the best way of making savings grow) always carries some element of risk.

Useful reading

The FSA Guide to Individual Savings Accounts, available free from the FSA, T:0845 606 1234.

Investment clubs

A number of readers have asked us about investment clubs. These typically consist of a group of 10 to 15 members, who each invest about £30 a month. They meet regularly to decide how best to invest their collective portfolio. Some clubs make money; others, that are less wised up, sadly lose it. ProShare, which operates for over 10,000 affiliated clubs, has published a guide to setting up and running an investment club. Price £29.50 (£25 to *Good non-Retirement Guide* readers), from: **ProShare**, Centurion House, 24 Monument Street, London EC3R 8AQ. T:020 7220 1750. Please quote Guide as reference when ordering, to obtain the £4.50 discount.

Small businesses

Many people invest in a small business more as a way of providing themselves with a retirement interest than to make money. Although if you are lucky it is possible to achieve both, there is no escaping the fact that investing in small firms is highly risky. Quite apart from the fact that about one in three fails, you may have a problem in realising any profits you make, as – unlike companies listed on the Stock Exchange – most small business shares do not have a ready market.

If despite the warnings the idea of becoming a business angel still appeals, you should know about the recent changes made to the Enterprise Investment Scheme (EIS), which offers investors attractive tax relief benefits. See page 82.

Another possibility are **Venture Capital Trusts**. These are investment vehicles (similar to investment trusts), aimed at encouraging more investment in smaller companies. To qualify as a VCT, at least 70 per cent of a Trust's investments must be in unlisted companies and the VCT itself must be quoted on the Stock Exchange. In theory at least, it is less risky than investing directly in just one or two enterprises, which could both fail.

People investing in VCTs will be exempt both: from income tax on their dividends and from capital gains tax on disposal of their shares for investments of up to £100,000 a year provided the shares are held for at least three years (5 years prior to 6 April 2000).

New subscribers will also receive roll-over relief on any gains used to invest in the VCT, as well as up-front income tax relief of 20 per cent.

Since June 1999, the rules have been relaxed to enable VCTs and individual investors to retain their investment in growing companies without risk of losing their tax relief, as was the case before. This applies: (1) where a VCT's shareholding in a company is exchanged for shares in a new holding company in preparation for a stock market flotation and (2) where a VCT exercises conversion rights in qualifying convertible shares or securities it holds as investments. Extra safeguards were introduced in the March 2000 budget to protect investors from risk of losing their tax relief in the event of the company, in which an investment had been made, going into receivership.

For a list of VCTs, currently open, visit the **BVCA's** website, see website index page 446.

Long-term lock-ups

Certain types of investment, mostly offered by insurance companies, provide fairly high guaranteed growth in exchange for your undertaking to leave a lump sum with them or to pay regular premiums for a fixed period, usually 5 years or longer. The list includes: life assurance policies, investment bonds and some types of National Savings certificates.

Life assurance policies

Definition. Life assurance can provide you with one of two main benefits: it can either provide your successors with money when you die or it can be used as a savings plan to provide you with a lump sum (or income) on a fixed date.

In the past, it was very much an 'either – or' situation: you chose whichever type of policy suited you and the insurance company paid out accordingly. In recent years, however, both types of scheme have become more flexible and many policies allow you to incorporate features of the other. This can have great advantages from the point of view of enabling you 'to have your cake and eat it'. But the result is that some of the definitions appear a bit contradictory.

There are three basic types of life assurance: whole life policies, term policies and endowment policies.

Whole life policies are designed to pay out on your death. In its most straightforward form, the scheme works as follows: you pay a premium every year and, when you die, your beneficiaries receive the money.

As with an ordinary household policy, the insurance only holds good if you continue the payments. If one year you did not pay and were to die, the policy could be void and your successors would receive nothing.

Term policies involve a definite commitment. As opposed to paying premiums every year, you elect to make regular payments for an agreed period: for example, until such time as your children have completed their education, say eight years.

If you die during this period, your family will be paid the agreed sum in full. If you die after the end of the term (when you have stopped making payments), your family will normally receive nothing.

Most policies, whether term or otherwise, pay the money in lump sum form. Under term assurance, it is possible, however, to arrange for the benefit to be paid out as regular income. This is known as **family income benefit**. The income payments will cease at the end of the insured term.

There is a fairly widespread view that term and whole life policies, while eminently sensible for people in their thirties or forties, are not really suitable for older people, since: on the one hand death is at some stage inevitable; while on the other, when children grow up, there is less requirement to provide for their security.

Additionally, many people argue that when income is tight, as it often is on retirement, this is one expense that can cheerfully be dropped. While generally true, the thinking could nevertheless prove short-sighted. A major problem for many widows is that, when their husband dies, part of his pension dies with him – leaving them with a significantly reduced income. A lump sum or regular income plan could make all the difference in helping to bridge the gap. Alternatively – and for some this could be a more attractive option – whole life or term can be converted into an endowment policy.

Endowment policies are essentially a savings plan. You sign a contract to pay regular premiums over a number of years and in exchange receive a lump sum on a specific date.

Most endowment policies are written for periods, varying from 10 to 25 years. Once you have committed yourself, you have to go on paying every year (as with term assurance). There are heavy penalties if, after having paid for a number of years, you decide that you no longer wish to continue. According to the terms of the policy, you may receive a token lump sum based on the premiums you have paid; or you may receive nothing at all. This is especially likely to apply if you withdraw during the early years. (However, see heading 'Alternatives to surrendering a policy' on page 116).

An important feature of endowment policies is that they are linked in with death cover. If you die before the policy matures, the remaining payments are excused and your successors will be paid a lump sum on your death.

Endowment policies have long been a popular way of making extra financial provision for retirement. They combine the advantages of guaranteeing you a lump sum, with a built-in life assurance proviso. The amount of money you stand to receive, however, can vary hugely, depending on the charges and how generous a bonus the insurance company feels it can afford on the policy's maturity. Over the past year or so, pay-outs have been considerably lower than their earlier projections might have suggested. Aim to compare at least three policies before choosing.

Options. Both whole life policies and endowment policies offer two basic options: with profits or without profits. Very briefly the difference is as follows:

Without profits. This is sometimes known as 'guaranteed sum assured'. What it means is that the insurance company guarantees you a specific fixed sum (provided of course you meet the various terms and conditions). You know the amount in advance and this is the sum you – or your successors – will be paid.

With profits. You are paid a guaranteed fixed sum plus an addition, based on the profits that the insurance company has made, by investing your annual or monthly payments. The basic premiums are higher and, by definition, the profits element is not known in advance. If the insurance company has invested your money wisely, a 'with profits' policy provides a useful hedge against inflation. If its investment policy is mediocre, you could have paid higher premiums for very little extra return.

Unit linked. This is a refinement of the 'with profits' policy, in that the investment element of the policy is linked in with a unit trust.

Other basics. Premiums can normally be paid monthly or annually, as you prefer. Size of premium varies enormously, depending on: the type of policy you choose and the amount of cover you want. Also, of course, some insurance companies are more competitive than others. As very general guidance, £35-£50 a month would probably be a normal starting figure. Again as a generalisation, higher premiums tend to give better value as relatively less of your contribution is swallowed up in administrative costs.

As a condition of insuring you, some policies require that you have a medical check. This is more likely to apply if very large sums are involved. More usually, all that is required is that you fill in and sign a declaration of health. It is very important that this should be honestly completed: if you make a claim on your policy and it is subsequently discovered that you gave misleading information, your policy could be declared void and the insurance company could refuse to pay.

Many insurance companies offer a better deal if you are a non-smoker. Some also offer more generous terms if you are teetotal. Women generally pay less than men of the same age because of their longer life expectancy.

How to obtain. Policies are usually available through banks, insurance companies, independent financial advisers (IFAs) and building societies. The biggest problem for most people is the sheer volume of choice. Another difficulty can be understanding the small print: terms and conditions which sound very similar may obscure important differences which could affect your benefit.

An accountant could advise you in general terms, whether you are being offered a good deal or otherwise. However, if it is a question of choosing a specific policy best suited to your requirements, it is usually advisable to consult an IFA. For help in finding an IFA in your area, contact: **IFA Promotion Ltd.**, 17–19 Emery Road, Brislington, Bristol BS4 5PX. T:0117 971 1177. See also Chapter 6, Financial Advisers.

As general wisdom, before buying a policy it is sensible to check whether the person selling it to you is an independent financial adviser, or a tied agent who is restricted to selling his/her company's (or institution's) own products. You need not feel in the slightest bit embarrassed to ask the individual concerned since this is a question that most people dealing in financial services expect and are happy to answer (as well as being required to do so by law). Indeed, in the light of the problems of Equitable Life, you cannot afford to be too careful.

Disclosure rules. Under the disclosure rules, which came into force during 1995, salesmen must give clients certain essential information before a contract is signed. Although the requirements vary according to different types of products, they normally include a 'key features' document (explaining the product, the risk factors, charges, benefits, surrender value if the policy is terminated early, tax treatment and salesman's commission/remuneration) and a 'suitability' letter, explaining why a particular product/policy is recommended. For further information, see 'Investor protection', page 120.

The **Association of British Insurers (ABI)** has a number of useful information sheets on life insurance. Contact ABI, 51 Gresham Street, London EC2V 7HQ.

Tax. Under current legislation, the proceeds of a qualifying policy – whether taken as a lump sum or in regular income payments (as in the case of Family Income Benefit) – are free of all tax.

Assessment. Life assurance is normally a sensible investment, whether the aim is to provide death cover or the benefits of a lump sum to boost your retirement income. It has the merit of being very attractive from a tax angle and additionally certain policies provide good capital appreciation – although a point to be aware of is that recent bonuses have tended to be considerably lower than their projected amount. However, you are locked into a long-term commitment. So, even more than most areas, choosing the right policy is very important. Shop around, take advice and, above all, do not sign anything unless you are absolutely certain that you understand every last dot and comma.

Complaints. Complaints about life assurance products, including alleged mis-selling, are handled by the Financial Ombudsman Service (FOS). Before approaching the FOS, you would first need to try to resolve a dispute with the company direct. For further information, contact the: **Financial Ombudsman Service**, South Quay Plaza, 183 Marsh Wall, London E14 9SR. T:0845 080 1800. See also 'Complaints', page 121.

Alternatives to surrendering a policy

As already mentioned, there are heavy penalties if you surrender an endowment policy before its maturity. Some people however, either because they can no longer afford the payments or for some other reason, wish to terminate the agreement – regardless of any losses they may make/or investment gains they sacrifice.

Instead of simply surrendering the policy to the insurance company, people in this situation have two alternative options, both of which stand to yield them a higher return than surrender. The one is to sell the policy by auction; the other to sell it to a market-maker.

Probably the best known specialist auctioneer in this field is Foster & Cranfield. They hold weekly auctions in London, and twice a month outside London, and suggest to clients a reserve price, which by definition would be higher than the surrender value – otherwise they would not accept it on their books. They charge a £50 registration fee plus commission, which is a third of the excess (they make at auction) above the surrender value quoted. While auctioneers can never guarantee a sale, auctioning a policy is a very low risk gamble, since if the policy fails to reach its reserve it can still be surrendered in the normal way. Furthermore, if the policy does not sell at auction, the £50 registration fee would not be payable. For further information, contact: **Foster & Cranfield**, 20 Britton Street, London EC1M 5NQ. T:020 7608 1941.

If rather than auction a policy, you prefer to sell it outright, Beale Dobie & Co. Ltd. may be able to help you. They deal in with-profits endowment and whole life policies (not unit linked) and say, that to be of interest to them, the policy; must have run at least five years of its life; have a surrender value of more than £1,500; and must be with a leading life office. Provided these conditions are met, they can often make a cash offer which, if accepted by the vendor, would be paid in the same time-scale as surrender. As with Foster & Cranfield, they would not make an offer unless that offer exceeded the surrender value. For further information, and free copy of *'Cashing in an Endowment Policy? The Beale Dobie Guide to Selling for More'*, contact: **Beale Dobie & Co. Ltd.**, Fullbridge Mill, Maldon, Essex CM9 5FN. T:01621 851133.

For those looking for investment possibilities, second-hand policies could be worth investigating. Known as Traded Endowment Policies (TEPs), they offer the combination of a low risk investment with a good potential return. As a result of recent growth in the market, there is now a wide range of individual policies and a number of specialist funds managed by financial institutions.

A full list of appropriate financial institutions and authorised dealers that either auction or buy and sell mid-term policies is obtainable from the **Association of Policy Market Makers**. They can also arrange for suitable policies to be valued by three market makers, free of charge. T:020 7739 3949.

Bonds

You may have read that as you near retirement you should increasingly be moving your investments from equities into bonds. The reason for this advice is that, while bonds generally offer less opportunity for capital growth, they tend to be lower risk as they are less exposed to stock market volatility and also have the advantage of producing a regular guaranteed income.

Although normally recommended as sensible, a particular problem at time of writing is that, as a result of the recent downturn in the Stock Market, you are likely to make a loss by selling some of your shares now whereas, possibly if you wait, they might recover (although equally of course they might further decline).

A bigger problem is that there are different types of bonds, with varying degrees of risk, which it is important you should understand.

The three main types are: government bonds, called gilt-edged securities or 'gilts'; corporate bonds and investment bonds.

Gilts, which are explained earlier in the chapter (see page 103), are the least risky as they are secured by the government which guarantees both the interest payable and the return of your capital in full if you hold the stocks until their maturity.

Corporate bonds are fairly similar except that, as opposed to loaning your money to the government, you are lending it to a large company or taking out a debenture. The risk is higher because, although you would normally only be recommended to buy a corporate bond from a highly rated company, there is always the possibility that the company could fail and might not be able to make the payments promised.

In general, the higher the guaranteed interest payments, the less totally secure the company in question.

While gilts and corporate bonds are normally recommended for cautious investors, investment bonds (described below) are different in that they offer potentially much higher rewards but also carry a much higher degree of risk.

Because even gilts can be influenced by timing and other factors, if you are thinking of buying bonds expert advice is very strongly recommended.

Investment bonds

Definition. This is the method of investing a lump sum with an insurance company, in the hope of receiving a much larger sum back at a specific date – normally a few years later.

All bonds offer life assurance cover as part of the deal.

A particular feature of some bonds is that the managers have wide discretion to invest your money in almost any type of security. The risk/reward ratio is, therefore, very high.

While bonds can achieve significant capital appreciation, you can also lose a high percentage of your investment. An exception are guaranteed equity bonds which, while linked to the performance of the FTSE 100 or other stock market index, guarantee to protect your capital if shares fall. However, while your capital will always be returned in full at the end of the fixed term (usually 5 years), a point not always appreciated is that, should markets fall, far from making any return on your investment you will have lost money in real terms: firstly, because your capital will have fallen in value, once inflation is taken into account; also, because you will have lost out on any interest that your money could have earned had it been on deposit.

All bond proceeds are free of basic rate tax but higher rate tax is payable. However, the higher rate taxpayer can withdraw up to 5 per cent of his/her initial investment each year and defer the higher rate tax liability for 20 years or until the bond is cashed in full – whichever is earlier.

Equally, although there is no capital gains tax on redemption of a bond (or on switching between funds), some CGT may be payable by the fund itself which could affect its investment performance.

Companies normally charge a front-end fee of around 6 per cent plus a small annual management fee, usually not related to performance.

Some financial institutions – banks, unit trusts, and others – offer investment bonds through their insurance subsidiaries. Accordingly, almost any type of financial adviser will have some knowledge of this area.

The performance of existing bonds is monitored each month in *Money Management* and other specialist magazines.

Tax. Tax treatment is very complicated, as it is influenced by your marginal income tax rate in the year of encashment. For this reason, it is generally best to buy a bond when you are working and plan to cash it after retirement. N.B. If you hold a policy with personal portfolio bonds, you should speak to your financial adviser or insurance company as there have been some recent changes to the tax regulations.

Assessment. This investment is more likely to be attractive to the sophisticated investor with high earnings in the years before retirement.

Other investment points

In recent years there has been a considerable increase in the number of alternative investments to those which can only be purchased on a recognised investment exchange (such as the Stock Exchange). These include traded options and sponsored securities, some but by no means all of which are also traded on the Stock Exchange.

Under the Financial Services Act (1986), firms which make markets in shares of this type have to be authorised by the Financial Services Authority (FSA) – see 'Investor protection' below – and have to obey the same stringent conduct of business rules as other authorised companies. In addition, they have to abide by special rules for those transactions which take place outside a recognised investment exchange.

It is important to realise that investments of this kind tend to be more risky than those traded on recognised exchanges. Not only are the companies in whose shares you invest more likely to fail, but also you should remember that if the shares are traded by only one market maker, you may not be able to sell them if the market maker goes out of business or ceases to trade in that particular stock. Advertisements for shares which may not be easily marketable have to include a statement to this effect. Equally where an adviser recommends such an investment he is obliged to make you aware of the difficulties you may face should you wish to sell.

While these safeguards help to clarify the nature of such investments, it is nevertheless still important for you to be careful in investing your money and to assess the degree of risk you are prepared to bear before committing yourself.

Useful reading

Fair Shares by Simon Rose. A layman's guide to buying and selling stocks. Mercury. Price £12.99.

Investor protection

Over the past few years, we have heard a great deal about investor protection.

There is now a set of stringent rules on businesses offering investment services and also a powerful new regulatory body, the Financial Services Authority (FSA), which is charged by Parliament with responsibility for ensuring that firms are 'fit and proper' to operate in the investment field and for monitoring their activities on an ongoing basis.

The main effects of these safeguards are as follows:

- Investment businesses (including accountants or solicitors giving investment advice) are not at liberty to operate without authorisation or exemption from the FSA. Operating without such authorisation (or exemption) is a criminal offence.
- Under the polarisation rules, businesses may either provide advice on their own in-house investment plans (unit trusts, insurance policies and so on) or they must act as independent financial advisers (IFAs). The dual intention is: (1) to enable customers to know the status of an adviser, and (2) to ensure that those who call themselves independent financial advisers, or intermediaries, can legitimately offer 'best advice' by virtue of being free of commercial bias. (Exceptionally, the polarisation rules do not apply to stakeholder pensions which, in certain circumstances, can be sold through another company's representatives).
- Investment businesses must adhere to a proper complaints procedure with provision for customers to receive fair redress, where appropriate.
- Unsolicited visits and telephone calls to sell investments are for the most part banned. Where these are allowed for package products (such as unit trusts and life assurance), should a sale result the customer will have a 14-day 'cooling-off period' (or a 7-day 'right to withdraw' period if the packaged product is held within an ISA and the sale follows advice from the firm.) The cooling-off period is to give the customer time to explore other options before deciding whether to cancel the contract or not.
- There is also the requirement for disclosure of the following information to consumers: a financial adviser's remuneration including commission (expressed in cash terms); and the company's costs and expenses, also expressed in cash terms, to enable investors to make inter-company comparisons.

Additionally, certain 'key features' must be provided to investors, including: information on the penalties of early surrender, easier identification of intermediary status and the provision of a 'suitability' letter explaining the rationale on which recommendations are based.

A new single regulatory authority

Finding out whether investment businesses are authorised or not and checking up on what information they are required to disclose has recently become very much easier. As a result of the Financial Services Markets Act 2000, all the former self-regulating organisations (including the PIA, IMRO and SFA) have now been merged under the Financial Services Authority with the purpose of improving investor protection and of providing a single contact point for enquiries. The address, should you need to contact the FSA, is: **Financial Services Authority**, 25 The North Colonnade, Canary Wharf, London E14 5HS. T:0845 606 1234 (calls charged at local rate).

A Single Ombudsman Scheme

Since December 2001, there is now also a single statutory Financial Ombudsman Service (FOS). This has replaced the various former schemes which used to deal with complaints about financial services and provides a 'one-stop shop' for dissatisfied consumers. The schemes concerned are: Banking Ombudsman, Building Societies Ombudsman, Insurance Ombudsman, Personal Insurance Arbitration Service, PIA Ombudsman, Investment Ombudsman, SFA Complaints Bureau (and Arbitration Schemes) and FSA Complaints Unit.

A welcome result of there being a single ombudsman scheme is that the FOS covers complaints across almost the entire range of financial services and products – from banking services, endowment mortgages and personal pensions to household insurance and stocks and shares. The list equally includes unit trusts and OEICs, life assurance and FSAVCs. A further advantage is that the FOS applies a single set of rules to all complaints.

Complaints

If you have a complaint against an authorised firm, in the first instance you should take it up with the firm concerned: you may be able to resolve the matter at this level, since all authorised firms are obliged to have a proper complaints-handling procedure.

The Financial Ombudsman Service advises that the best approach is to start by contacting the person you originally dealt with and, if you 'phone, to keep a written note of all telephone calls. If complaining by letter, it helps to set out the facts in logical order, to stick to what is relevant and to include important details such as customer, policy or account numbers. You should also keep a copy of all letters both for your own record purposes and also as useful evidence should you need to take the matter further.

If having gone through the firm's complaints procedure or if after eight weeks you are still dissatisfied, you can approach the Financial Ombudsman Service who will investigate the matter on your behalf and if they find your complaint is justified may require the firm to pay compensation which, depending on your losses, could be up to £100,000.

If you disagree with the Ombudsman's decision, this does not affect your right to go to court should you wish to do so.

For further information, contact the **Financial Ombudsman Service (FOS)**, South Quay Plaza, 183 Marsh Wall, London E14 9SR. T:0845 080 1800.

Warning

Although the investor protection legislation should improve standards and help to rid the financial services industry of cowboy operators, as the Financial Services

Authority writes in its published guide: 'All investment carries some degree of risk, whether relating to business or general economic conditions. The existence of the FSA no more removes the need for investors to pay attention to where they place their money than the existence of the highway code removes the need to look before crossing the road.'

The existence of the FSA does at least, however, enable you to check on the credentials of anyone purporting to be a financial adviser or trying to persuade you to invest your money in an insurance policy, bond, unit or investment trust, equity, futures contract or similar. If either they or the organisation they represent are not authorised by the FSA, you are very strongly recommended to leave well alone. You can check whether a firm is authorised by ringing the FSA's Central Register on T:0845 606 1234.

Useful reading

Investors Compensation Scheme: How We Handle Your Claim for Compensation and *FSA Guide to Financial Advice*; available free from the Financial Services Authority (FSA), T:0845 606 1234.

6 Financial Advisers

If there is one golden rule when it comes to money matters, it must be: when in doubt, ask. This applies as much if it is a term with which you are unfamiliar, as whether you are wondering how best to invest your savings.

When thinking ahead to retirement planning, it is especially important to get as much advice as possible. Nearly everyone has a certain amount of leeway in budgeting for the future and the difference between an unwise choice and a sensible one could very significantly affect your standard of living.

While a great deal of unnecessary mystique seems to pervade the financial services sector, questions to do with money are often genuinely more complex than they at first appear.

There may be important tax angles to consider. Phrases commonly used in conversation may, when written into a formal document, have legal implications of which you are unaware. The jargon is apt to be confusing: for example, the term 'bond' has a variety of different meanings. Another problem is the volume of propaganda. There are plenty of enticing advertisements seeming to offer the moon which, if you were to take them at face value without being totally sure that you understood the commitment, could prove a sorry mistake.

Moreover, whereas most professional advisers are extremely sound, not everyone who proffers advice is qualified to do so. Before parting with your money, it is essential to ensure that you are dealing with a registered member of a recognised institution.

Checking has become easier. Under the Financial Services Act, not only are those claiming to be specialists required to register with their appropriate professional body and obey its code of conduct but, as a further safeguard, the institutions themselves must comply with the regulations of the Financial Services Authority, i.e. the government watchdog concerned (see 'Investor protection' page 120).

Even if you have never done so before, there is no cause to feel hesitant about approaching financial advisers. Nor should you feel that because you have asked for advice, you are morally obliged to use a particular individual's services. Indeed, when it comes to investment decisions, you are strongly recommended to shop around in order to compare the many different options on offer.

As someone who may shortly be retiring, you are seen as a very attractive potential client especially if you are a member of a pension scheme with a sizeable commuted lump sum to invest.

However, before making contact, it is generally a good idea to try to sort out your priorities, for example: whether you are looking for capital growth or whether your main objective is to increase your income. Also, if you have any special plans such as helping your grandchildren or if you need several thousand pounds to improve your home, these too should be thought through in advance as they could affect the advice you receive.

A further reason for doing some advance thinking is that, whereas certain types of advisers – for example, insurance brokers – do not specifically charge you for their time, others such as accountants and solicitors charge fees by the hour. Drinking coffee in their office and musing aloud about the future delights of retirement may be a pleasant way of spending the afternoon but it can also work out to be pretty costly!

Choosing an adviser

When choosing an adviser, there are usually four main considerations: respectability, suitability, price and convenience.

Where your money is concerned, you cannot afford to take unnecessary risks. Merely establishing that an individual is a member of a recognised institution, while a basic safeguard, is insufficient recommendation if you want to be assured of dealing with someone who will personally suit you. The principle applies as much with friends, as with complete strangers.

If you are thinking of using a particular adviser whom you do not already know in a professional capacity, you should certainly check on their reputation and, ideally, talk to some of their existing clients. No one who is any good will object to your asking for references. On the contrary, most will be delighted if this means that the relationship will be founded on a basis of greater trust and confidence.

However, quite apart from their general competence, enlisting professional help is very much a question of 'horses for courses'. Just as you would hardly consult a divorce lawyer if you were planning to buy a house, so too in the financial field most practitioners have different areas of expertise. It is, therefore, important to establish that your adviser has the particular capability you require.

This issue is less of a consideration if you choose a sizeable firm, with at least four or five partners, since the likelihood is that between them they will be able to offer a mix of skills. But it can be a problem with the one or two-man band who, though outstanding generalists, may lack the specialist knowledge if you require sophisticated advice in, say, tax planning or investment strategy.

Although some people enjoy bobbing up to London to consult their solicitor, or whoever, generally speaking it makes more sense to choose a firm that is reasonably accessible.

If you live in a part of the country, where the choice of financial advisers is limited, you can approach one of the organisations listed on the following pages that maintain a register of members and will be pleased to send you local names and addresses. Alternatively, and this is often the best way, you might find someone who would suit you through personal recommendation.

Finally, you should be aware that some specialist advisers are in the business of selling; or at least stand to gain some financial advantage from persuading you that the investments they market are best for you. In some cases, the commissions are publicly known. In others, they tend to be disguised. Also some brokers and dealers are tied agents for a specific company, so under the Financial Services Act regulations can only promote their own in-house products. To know where you stand, you should ask any agent whom he represents and if it is a single company or group, however excellent the prospect sounds, you should aim to investigate at least two or three other propositions before signing on the dotted line.

Accountants

Accountants are specialists in matters concerning taxation. If there is scope to do so, they can advise on ways of reducing your tax liability and can assess the various tax effects of different types of investment you may be considering. Likewise, they can help you with the preparation of tax returns and if you are thinking of becoming self-employed or starting your own business, they will be able to assist you with some of the practicalities – such as registering for VAT and establishing a system of business accounts.

Additionally, they may be able to advise in a general way about pensions and your proposed investment strategy. Most accountants, however, do not claim to be experts in these fields and may refer their clients to stockbrokers or other advisers for these more specialised services.

If you need help in locating a suitable accountant, any of the following should be able to assist:

Institute of Chartered Accountants in England and Wales, PO Box 433, Chartered Accountants' Hall, Moorgate Place, London EC2P 2BJ.

Institute of Chartered Accountants of Scotland, CA House, 21 Haymarket Yards, Edinburgh EH12 5BH.

Institute of Chartered Accountants in Ireland, Chartered Accountants House, 87–89 Pembroke Road, Ballsbridge, Dublin 4.

Association of Chartered Certified Accountants, 29 Lincoln's Inn Fields, London WC2A 3EE.

Complaints. Anyone with a complaint against an accountant can write to the Secretary of the Institute's Investigating Committee who, if the complaint is valid, will refer the matter to the Disciplinary Committee.

Banks

Most people need no introduction to the clearing banks since, if they have a bank account, they are probably being regularly bombarded with literature. Yet despite this, many customers do not actually realise what a comprehensive service their bank provides.

In addition to the normal account facilities, all the major high street banks offer (either direct or through one of their specialised subsidiaries) investment, insurance and tax planning services, as well as advice on drawing up a will, together with a variety of special arrangements for small businesses.

While some of their services are excellent and while approaching your bank manager is also a convenient solution, especially if you are not very well up on stockbrokers and the like, the banks have tended to be criticised in the past for their rather pedestrian investment advice.

Again as a generalisation, most of their specialist services are not particularly cheap and for certain functions, such as the administration of estates, their fees could be higher than a solicitor's. Also, you should be aware that the banks run their own unit trusts and insurance broking divisions and may direct their clients to these.

Indeed, whereas a few years ago some clients may not have realised that the bank might be recommending one of its own unit trusts, today there can be no such confusion. Under the Financial Services Authority (FSA) rules on polarisation, banks are obliged to give 'best advice' and to make it clear whether they are acting as a general broker offering everyone's policies – or whether, by contrast, they are promoting their own in-house products.

Brief information follows on the main clearing banks but there also are other more specialised banks such as Williams and Glynn, Coutts, Hoares and overseas banks that are all part of the UK clearing system and can offer a very good service. The addresses given are those of the head office.

Abbey National Plc, 215–229 Baker Street, London NW1 6XL. Abbey National offers a range of savings, mortgage, pension, current account, medical and other insurance products plus loans for such items as home improvements, a car or money to finance a holiday.

A broad range of savings accounts paying tiered rates of interest are also available. These include: both branch-based and postal instant access accounts; also fixed and variable rate savings bonds, including a retirement income bond for the over 55s. There is also a range of ISAs.

Full details of all Abbey National services can be obtained from any high street branch or by calling Abbey National Direct on T:0800 555100.

Barclays Bank Plc, 54 Lombard Street, London EC3P 3AH. Barclays Bank offers customers a range of accounts to suit a variety of personal savings requirements. Additionally, a number of financial planning services are available through Barclays Bank subsidiary companies. These include: Personal Investment Advice, Investment Management, Stockbroking, Unit Trusts, Personal Taxation, Wills and Trusts.

You can either write to the above address or apply through your local branch of Barclays Bank.

HSBC Personal Financial Services, Poultry, London EC2P 2BX. HSBC Personal Financial Services offers a comprehensive choice of financial products ranging from

OEICS and ISAs to life assurance, which are selected according to a customer's requirements by a personal financial planning manager.

HSBC Private Clients offers a discretionary Investment Management and Estate Planning Service to clients who prefer to have a local specialist to look after their affairs on a regular basis. Clients would typically have over £100,000 to invest. The Estate Planning Service includes preparation of a will, drawing up trusts and administering customers' estates.

Any HSBC branch can arrange a meeting if you would like to discuss these services.

Lloyds TSB Group, 71 Lombard Street, London EC3P 3BS. Lloyds TSB offers a wide range of financial services, including: current and savings accounts; health and home insurance; investment management; and also life assurance, through Scottish Widows.

As well as the classic account which offers all the normal current account facilities and the Gold Service, which among other facilities includes free travel insurance, there is Private Banking which is a comprehensive wealth management service tailored to individual requirements for customers with £100,000 or more of liquid assets. Details of all these services, as well as life assurance and investment products, are available at all Lloyds TSB branches.

The branches can also give information about health and home insurance; or to discuss your requirements, telephone the following numbers: (health) 01633 818200; (home insurance) Freephone 0800 750750.

NatWest, 135 Bishopsgate, London EC2M 3UR. NatWest Financial Planning Managers can advise on a wide range of banking and financial planning services for retirement, including unit trusts and ISAs. To make an appointment, contact your local NatWest branch or call free on T:0800 255200 between 8 a.m. and 8 p.m. weekdays, or 9 a.m. to 6 p.m. Saturdays.

Royal Bank of Scotland, 42 St Andrew Square, Edinburgh EH2 2YE. The Royal Bank of Scotland offers a comprehensive range of current accounts and savings products.

The Bank's Private Trust and Taxation Department offers free advice on making a will, although the usual legal fees are applicable if you proceed. This is available to customers and non-customers and you should write to The Royal Bank of Scotland, Freepost, PO Box 31, Edinburgh EH2 0BG. You can also write to this address or approach your local branch manager for a personal tax service or for help with completing a self-assessment tax return. The service is charged according to the complexity of the work involved.

Royal Scottish Assurance, the Royal Bank of Scotland's life assurance, pensions and investment company, offers a full financial planning service free of charge. Financial planning consultants can also recommend ISAs and unit trusts provided by the Royal Bank of Scotland Unit Trust Managers.

Further information is available from any branch of the Bank.

New high street and other banking services. As the many lucky people who received windfalls will know, since 1997 several building societies have converted to banks, including: The Halifax, Woolwich, Alliance & Leicester, Bristol & West, Bradford & Bingley and Northern Rock. Full information about their services should be obtainable from your local branch.

Although not banks in the full sense of the word, as they only provide a limited range of services, a growing number of life insurance subsidiaries and supermarkets offer savings accounts, with in some cases discounts on purchases or other special offers available to customers.

Among other recent trends, there has been an explosion of both telephone and Internet banking services, many of which at time of writing were offering very competitive interest rates.

Complaints

If you have a complaint about a banking matter, you must first try to resolve the issue with the bank, or building society, concerned. If you remain dissatisfied, you can contact the Financial Ombudsman Service (FOS).

The FOS can handle complaints on most aspects of personal banking, including bank credit cards and other matters normally transacted through bank and building society branches, as well as maladministration or undue delays by banks dealing with wills and trusts. However, except where there has been maladministration, the Ombudsman's powers do not extend to commercial decisions by a bank or building society on the grant of an overdraft or loan.

In addition to the above, the FOS can also investigate complaints about life assurance and other investment products sold by banks and building societies.

The service is free and the FOS is empowered to award compensation of up to £100,000. For further information, contact the **Financial Ombudsman Service (FOS)**, South Quay Plaza, 183 Marsh Wall, London E14 9SR. T:0845 080 1800.

Insurance brokers

The insurance business covers a very wide range from straightforward policies – such as motor or household insurance – to the rather more complex areas, including life assurance and pensions. Quite apart from the confusion of the enormous choice of policies available and the importance of ensuring that you understand the conditions laid down in the small print, a further difficulty is the number of different categories of people – agents, salesmen, brokers, independent financial advisers – who may try to sell you insurance.

Although many people think of brokers and independent financial advisers (IFAs) as doing much the same job, IFAs specialise in advising on products and policies with some investment content, whereas brokers primarily deal with the more straightforward type of insurance, e.g. motor, medical, household and holiday insurance. (Some brokers are also authorised to give investment advice.) In this section we concentrate on insurance brokers, with IFAs in the section following.

Unless you are already dealing with an insurance company whose advice you value, as a general rule you would be advised to consult an insurance broker. A broker should be able to help you choose the policies that are best suited to you, help you determine how much cover you require and explain any technical terms contained in the documents. He can also assist with any claims and advise you when renewals are necessary. An essential point to check before proceeding is that the firm the broker represents is regulated (other than for anything to do with investment) by the General Insurance Standards Council, which operates a code of conduct. (In 2004, the Financial Services Authority will be responsible for regulation).

Although a condition of registration is that a broker must deal with a multiplicity of insurers and therefore be in a position to offer a comprehensive choice of policies, most companies pay insurance brokers on a commission basis; so, despite the code of conduct which emphasises that the customer's interest is paramount, it is possible that you could be offered advice that is not totally unbiased. If you are worried about this, you are perfectly entitled to ask a broker how much commission he is receiving.

Generally speaking, you are safer to use a larger brokerage with an established reputation. Also, before you take out a policy, it is advisable to consult several brokers in order to get a better feel for the market. The **British Insurance Brokers Association**, which represents nearly 2,200 insurance broking businesses, can put you in touch with a member broker in your area.

Complaints

If you have a complaint against an insurance broker you could contact the General Insurance Standards Council. They will investigate the matter and, if they think your complaint is justified, will seek to get redress for you. You should write to the **General Insurance Standards Council**, 110 Cannon Street, London EC4N 6EU. T:0845 601 2857.

Also useful to know about is the Association of British Insurers. It represents 438 companies (as opposed to Lloyd's syndicates or brokers), providing all types of insurance from life assurance and pensions to household, motor and other forms of general insurance. About 90 per cent of the worldwide business done by British insurance companies is handled by members of ABI.

The Association publishes a wide range of information sheets and will, if you are in dispute with one of its member companies, ensure that your complaint is dealt with at top level. Contact: **Association of British Insurers** (ABI), 51 Gresham Street, London EC2V 7HQ. T:020 7600 3333.

There is also the Financial Ombudsman Service which, as well as helping private policy holders, can also take up the cudgels on behalf of small businesses that have an insurance dispute. However, the Ombudsman is powerless to act if legal proceedings have been started.

The Ombudsman has power to make awards up to £100,000 and while he can advise or adjudicate on most issues, some matters such as third party claims are outside his scope.

You must contact the Ombudsman within six months of the insurance company's final decision on the dispute, giving the details as briefly as possible. There is no charge for the service. You may accept or reject the Ombudsman's decision. If you reject it, your right to take legal action is not affected. If you want help, you should contact the: **Financial Ombudsman Service**, South Quay Plaza, 183 Marsh Wall, London E14 9SR. T:0845 080 1800.

Independent Financial Advisers (IFAs)

IFAs can advise you across the whole spectrum of investment policies and products: endowment policies, personal pensions, life assurance, permanent health insurance, critical illness cover, unit trusts, PEPs and other forms of personal investment such as, for example, mortgages.

Their job is to help you work out whether the type of policy you have in mind would be most suitable and where, depending on your circumstances and objectives, you could obtain best value for money. In other words, they would act as your personal adviser and handle all the arrangements for you.

In order to be able to offer 'best advice', an IFA needs to try to ensure that you would not be at risk of over-committing yourself or taking some other risk that might jeopardise your security. He/she will, therefore, need an understanding of your existing financial circumstances (and future expectations) including, for example: your earnings, employment prospects and any other types of investment you might already have. Your adviser will of course also need to understand what your major aims are, e.g.: to boost your long term retirement income, to provide money for dependants should you unexpectedly die, to help meet the costs should you develop a critical illness, to start a savings plan that will mature around the time of your retirement or to try to invest your money for capital appreciation.

In turn, you should also ask your adviser a number of questions including – as a first essential – by whom they are regulated. This should normally be the FSA but could be one of a small number of Designated Professional Bodies, who themselves are answerable to the FSA. If you have any doubts, you can check by ringing the FSA's Central Register on T:0845 606 1234.

As well as enquire about any technical terms or other points in the sales literature which are not crystal clear, you should also ask: what charges are involved; what commission, if any, your adviser will be getting; whether it is possible you could lose money; how soon surrender values will equal premiums paid; and why, in particular, you are being recommended to buy the policy or investment in question. Your adviser should provide you with a 'key features document' and a 'suitability letter', explaining all these points but, if for some reason you do not receive them or if there is anything you do not understand, you should not hesitate to ask.

While commission is still the norm, over the past four or five years a growing number of financial advisers have switched from commission to offering a fee-based service, rather in the manner of an accountant or solicitor. This means, of course, that clients are charged an up-front fee. But against this, they are not forfeiting the often very much larger sum – deducted from their investment – that the IFA would have received. Because of the way some insurance companies operate, fee-charging advisers may still receive the commission in the first instance but will then – depending on the client's preference – either rebate it back to them in cash or (and this could be more sensible) re-invest it on their behalf in the product.

Until recently, the big difficulty for someone wanting to consult a fee-charging adviser was discovering those who actually offered such a service. However, the search should now be very much easier thanks to The Money Management National Register of Fee-based Advisers. Anyone wanting a list of names should write to the Register and will receive back (free of charge) details of at least six local advisers for them to investigate.

The address is: **The Money Management National Register of Fee-based Advisers**, Freepost 22 (SW1565), London W1E 1BR. Hotline T:0870 013 1925.

Another organisation that will be happy to send you names and addresses of local IFAs is: **IFA Promotion Ltd.**, 17–19 Emery Road, Brislington, Bristol BS4 5PX. T:0800 085 3250.

Complaints

If you have a complaint about an IFA, the most likely organisation to be able to help is the Financial Ombudsman Service (FOS).

Before approaching the ombudsman service, you must first try to settle the dispute with the company or adviser direct. If this fails, the Ombudsman will investigate your complaint and if he finds the complaint justified can award compensation of up to £100,000, including a small sum for distress and inconvenience. Although he has very wide powers and can adjudicate on such matters as mis-selling or allegations of 'churning' a policy, he cannot intervene over an actuarial dispute. Nor will he be able to assist if legal proceedings have been started.

For further information, write to the **Financial Ombudsman Service**, South Quay Plaza, 183 Marsh Wall, London E14 9SR. T:0845 080 1800.

Other pension advisers

If you have a query to do with your pension, there are other organisations – or professional advisers – who may be able to assist.

Individuals in paid employment

If you are (or have been) in salaried employment and are a member of an occupational pension scheme, the normal person to ask is your company's personnel manager or pensions adviser – or via them, the pension fund trustees.

Alternatively, if you have a problem with your pension you could approach your union, since this is an area where most unions are particularly active and well informed.

If you are in need of specific help, a source to try could be OPAS. It has a network of 500 volunteer advisers who can give free help and advice on all matters to do with any type of pension scheme, except State pensions. OPAS operates a local call rate helpline, T:0845 601 2923. Or write to **OPAS**, the Pensions Advisory Service, 11 Belgrave Road, London SW1V 1RB.

As with most other sectors, there is now also a Pensions Ombudsman. You would normally only approach the Ombudsman if neither the pension scheme trustees nor OPAS are able to solve your problem.

Also, as with all ombudsmen, he can only investigate matters that come within his orbit. These are: (1) complaints of maladministration by the trustees or managers of a pension scheme or by an employer; (2) disputes of fact or law with the trustees, managers or an employer. He cannot, however, investigate: complaints about mis-selling of pension schemes; a complaint that is already subject to court proceedings; one that is about a State social security benefit; or a dispute that is more appropriate for investigation by another regulatory body.

You can write direct to: **The Pensions Ombudsman**, 11 Belgrave Road, London SW1V 1RB. T:020 7834 9144. (N.B. Unlike many of the other ombudsman services, the Pensions Ombudsman has not become part of the single statutory Financial Ombudsman Service and will continue to remain as a separate scheme.)

Another source of help is the pensions registry and tracing service, managed by the Occupational Pensions Regulatory Authority (OPRA), which assists individuals in need of help to trace their pension rights. Like the Ombudsman, there is no charge for the service. For further information, write to: **Pension Schemes Registry**, PO Box 1NN, Newcastle upon Tyne NE99 1NN. T:0191 225 6316.

If, although in paid employment, you have a personal pension rather than an occupational pension and are in dispute with the insurance company or your financial adviser, you should contact the **Financial Ombudsman Service** (see page 137).

Two other organisations which, while they do not advise on individual cases, are interested in matters of principle and broader issues affecting the pensions debate. These are:

National Association of Pension Funds, NIOC House, 4 Victoria Street, London SW1H 0NX. T:020 7808 1300.

Occupational Pensions Regulatory Authority (OPRA), Invicta House, Trafalgar Place, Brighton BN1 4DW. T:01273 627600. OPRA is the independent regulator, set up under the Pensions Act 1995 to ensure that the interests of occupational pension scheme members are properly protected. As well as its main regulatory role, it also manages the Pension Schemes Registry, described above.

Self-employed or running a company

If you are self-employed and want to make pension arrangements, you would probably approach an insurance company or independent financial adviser; or possibly your bank, a building society, unit trust or friendly society. However, in certain circumstances you might be better off to pay for the services of an authorised pension consultant.

The roles are fairly similar. In general, however, pension consultants would normally only be used by employers and by individuals with significant self-employment income.

There are two ways in which the services of a pension consultant are paid for: either in commission or in fees paid directly by the client to the consultant. The position as regards commission is that if advice given by the consultant results in money being invested in an institution, that institution will often pay a commission to the consultant, which may mean that there will be no direct charge to the individual. Fees need no explanation, as they are charged on broadly the same basis as any other professional fees. In order to know where you stand, it is a good idea to enquire from the outset how the consultant will expect to be paid – by you or in commission – and if a fee is involved, what this is likely to be.

Although apparently expensive, the best consultants are independent specialists who can give very valuable advice. Many of them will be members of the Society of Pension Consultants. If you would like a list of local members or other information, contact: The Secretary, **Society of Pension Consultants**, St Bartholomew House, 92 Fleet Street, London EC4Y 1DG. T:020 7353 1688.

For information about other independent financial advisers who can help with pensions – and also what to do in the event of a complaint – see IFAs, page 130.

Solicitors

Solicitors are professional advisers on subjects to do with the law or on matters that could have legal implications. They can assist with: the purchase or rental of property; drawing up a will; if you are charged with a criminal offence; or if you are sued in a civil matter.

Additionally, their advice can be invaluable in vetting any important document before you sign it, for example: an employment contract, the purchase of a business, a trading arrangement or other form of contract, where either you or the other party is giving an undertaking of some kind.

A solicitor can also help with the legal formalities of setting up a business; trusts; guardianship arrangements or other agreement, where the intention is to make it binding. Likewise, a solicitor would normally be the first person to consult if you were thinking of suing an individual or commercial organisation.

If you do not have a solicitor (or if your solicitor does not have the knowledge to advise on, say, a business matter), often the best way of finding a suitable lawyer is through the recommendation of a friend or other professional adviser, such as an accountant.

If you need a solicitor specifically about a business or professional matter, organisations such as chambers of commerce, small business associations, your professional institute or trade union may be able to put you in touch with someone in your area who has relevant experience.

Another solution would be to contact the **Law Society Records Department** on T:0870 606 6575 who will give you three names of solicitors in your area.

A further resource of possible interest is SIFA (Solicitors for Independent Financial Advice). This is a network of law firms, offering financial as well as legal services, with the aim of providing clients with a 'one-stop shop' when making important financial decisions. It maintains a nationwide register and will send enquirers details of up to six local firms according to whether the type of help needed is to do with investments, pension planning, wills or choosing a long term care policy. For further information, contact **SIFA**, 10 East Street, Epsom, Surrey KT17 1HH. T:01372 721172.

Community Legal Service Funding

The Legal Aid Board was replaced by a new body called the Legal Services Commission in April 2000. If you need a legal services solicitor (or want to find out if you are eligible for financial assistance), the place to go is a solicitor's office or advice centre. Ask for leaflet *The Community Legal Service*, which will tell you about the types of legal advice and help which are available. There is a more detailed leaflet called *A Practical Guide to Community Legal Service Funding by the Legal Services Commission*. You can ask an adviser to go through this with you to help you work out if you are eligible. Leaflets about the services are also obtainable from many libraries or from the **LSC Leaflet Line**, St. Ives Direct, Enterprise Way, Edenbridge, Kent TN8 6HF. T:0845 300 0343.

Also useful to know about is the *CLS Directory* which, among other information, lists solicitors who do community legal service work. Copies should be available at most libraries or call the Directory Line on T:0845 608 112; minicom: 0845 609 6677.

Complaints

All solicitors are required by the Law Society to have their own in-house complaints procedure. If you are unhappy about the service you have received, you should try to resolve the matter with the firm through their complaints-handling partner.

If you still feel aggrieved you can approach the Office for the Supervision of Solicitors (OSS) which is an independent arm of the Law Society, responsible for handling complaints against solicitors.

The OSS can investigate such complaints as: failure to reply to letters; delay in dealing with your case; overcharging (see below); wrongly retaining your papers; dishonesty and deception. It can also deal with complaints which allege 'inadequate professional service (IPS)', that is to say the carrying out of work by your solicitor to an unacceptably low standard, and is able to award compensation up to £5,000, as well as reduce bills and recommend other action.

The Office for the Supervision of Solicitors (OSS) cannot, however, give legal advice or tell a solicitor how to handle a case; nor can it investigate claims of professional negligence. The difference between inadequate professional service (IPS) and negligence is that IPS relates to substandard work, whereas negligence is a mistake by your solicitor which has lost you money or caused some other loss for which you may be entitled to financial redress.

If you believe you have a complaint of negligence, The Office for the Supervision of Solicitors will help you either by putting you in touch with a solicitor specialising in negligence claims or by referring you to the solicitor's insurers. If it arranges an appointment for you with a negligence panellist, the panel solicitor will see you free of charge for up to an hour and advise you as to your best course of action.

If you believe that you have been overcharged, you should ask to be sent the booklet *Can We Help?*, which explains the procedure for getting your bill checked, the various time limits involved and the circumstances in which you might be successful in getting the fee reduced.

You can ring the OSS Helpline on T:0845 608 6565 for practical assistance if you are having problems with your solicitor. Alternatively, if you prefer, you can write to: **The Office for the Supervision of Solicitors**, Victoria Court, 8 Dormer Place, Leamington Spa CV32 5AE and request a copy of the complaint form.

If you are still not satisfied, you can approach the **Legal Services Ombudsman** at Sunlight House, Quay Street, Manchester M3 3JZ. T:0161 839 7262.

General queries. For queries of a more general nature, you should approach: **The Law Society**, 113 Chancery Lane, London WC2A 1PL. T:020 7242 1222.

For those in Scotland and Northern Ireland. If you live in Scotland or Northern Ireland, The Office for the Supervision of Solicitors will not be able to help you. Instead you should contact the Law Society at the relevant address, as follows:

The Law Society of Scotland, The Law Society's Hall, 26 Drumsheugh Gardens, Edinburgh EH3 7YR. T:0131 226 7411.

The Law Society of Northern Ireland, Law Society House, 98 Victoria Street, Belfast BT1 3JZ. T:028 9023 1614.

Stockbrokers

Stockbrokers buy and sell shares quoted on the main market of the London Stock Exchange and on the Alternative Investment Market (AIM), which trades mainly in the shares of young and growing companies. Investments can be made in UK and international equities, bonds, investment trusts and gilts (government stocks).

As well as trading for clients, stockbrokers can advise on the prospects of different companies, help individuals choose the best type of investment according to their financial situation and can also provide a wide range of other financial services including tax planning.

According to your temperament and expertise, you can either give a stockbroker partial or total discretion – or insist that he consults you on every deal. Some people know exactly what investments they wish to make and only want their stockbroker to carry out the transactions for them. Accordingly, a number of stockbroking firms have introduced 'execution-only' services, through which they buy and sell shares for you, without offering any investment advice. This is often considerably cheaper than a full stockbroking service. Also, execution-only services generally do not have any minimum investment criteria.

Other people do not want to have to keep such a close eye on their money. Instead, they agree a set of guidelines and then leave their stockbroker to make all the investment decisions, just reporting afterwards what has been done. This is known as a 'discretionary service'.

As a half-way house between execution-only and discretionary, there is also an 'advisory' service in which the stockbroker will offer you advice and information but leave you to make the actual investment decisions.

As a result of these different options, it is difficult to be very specific about the cost of using a stockbroker. While some now charge fees in the same way as, say, a solicitor, as a general rule stockbrokers make their living by charging commission on every transaction. Until fairly recently, there was a standard scale rate, varying from 1/2 per cent to 1.65 per cent according to the size of the order but today this no longer applies, so you will need to enquire what the terms and conditions are before committing yourself, as these can vary quite considerably between one firm and another.

Many people still believe that it is pointless to go to a stockbroker unless you have at least £50,000 to invest. This is no longer true. A growing number of provincial stockbrokers are happy to deal for private investors with sums from about £5,000. Additionally, nearly all major stockbrokers now run unit trusts and, because through these they are investing collectively for their clients, welcome quite modest investors with around £2,000.

Also good news is that stockbrokers are becoming more accessible. Some firms have formed themselves into national networks, giving them the ability to extend their range of services. Others have been opening share shops in the high streets or linking with banks and building societies to provide convenient retail outlets, where you can buy and sell shares and discuss your investments.

There are several ways of finding a stockbroker: you can approach an individual through recommendation; you can ask the **London Stock Exchange** (Old Broad Street, London EC2N 1HP, T:020 7797 1000) to send you their *Regional Brokers List*; or you can write to APCIMS (The Association of Private Client Investment Managers and Stockbrokers) for a free directory of stockbrokers and investment managers, together with details of their services. The address is: **APCIMS**, 112 Middlesex Street, London E1 7HY. T:020 7247 7080. APCIMS also has an online directory, which is searchable by region and type of service.

Alternatively, if you are more interested in investment trusts, you can write to the **Association of Investment Trust Companies**, Durrant House, 8–13 Chiswell Street, London EC1Y 4YY, T:020 7282 5555, for their information pack.

You might also like to contact ProShare. As well as give general information over the telephone, it produces a wide range of factsheets and booklets, many of which are specially written for first-time investors. To obtain copies, write to: **ProShare**, Centurion House, 24 Monument Street, London EC3R 8AQ. T:020 7220 1730.

Complaints
If you have a complaint about a stockbroker or other member of the former Securities and Futures Authority (SFA), you should put this in writing to the compliance officer of the stockbroking firm involved. If the matter is not satisfactorily resolved, you can then contact the Financial Ombudsman Service (FOS) which will investigate your complaint and, if the ombudsman considers this justified, can award compensation.

The address for the FOS is: **Financial Ombudsman Service**, South Quay Plaza, 183 Marsh Wall, London E14 9SR. T:0845 080 1800.

A note of warning. Despite the safeguards of the Financial Services Act, when it comes to investment – or to financial advisers – there are no cast iron guarantees. Under the investor protection legislation, all practitioners and/or businesses they represent offering investment or similar services must be authorised by the Financial Services Authority (FSA) or, in certain cases, by a small number of Designated Professional Bodies who themselves are answerable to the FSA.

A basic question, therefore, to ask anyone offering investment advice or products is: are you registered and by whom? The information is easy to check by telephoning the FSA's Central Register on T:0845 606 1234.

For further information, see 'Investor protection' at the end of Chapter 5, Investment.

Useful reading
Share Ownership for All and *A Guide to the London Stock Exchange – What You Need to Know*; available free by telephoning the London Stock Exchange Public Information Line, T:020 7797 1372.

FSA Guide to Financial Advice and *Investors Compensation Scheme: How We Handle Your Claim for Compensation*, free from the Financial Services Authority (FSA), T:0845 606 1234.

Financial Ombudsman Service (FOS)

Prior to December 2001, there were a variety of financial ombudsmen schemes and complaints handling organisations, each dealing with different aspects of the financial services market. In order to create a more unified system, these have now been merged into a single Financial Ombudsman Service.

A welcome advantage is that there is now a single contact point for dissatisfied customers as the FOS covers complaints across almost the entire range of financial services including: banks, building societies, unit trusts, OEICS, insurance companies and independent financial advisers (IFAs).

The service is free and the FOS is empowered to award compensation of up to £100,000. However, before contacting the FOS, you must first try to resolve your complaint with the organisation concerned. Also, the ombudsman is powerless to act if legal proceedings have been started. For further information, contact the **Financial Ombudsman Service** at the following address: South Quay Plaza, 183 Marsh Wall, London E14 9SR. T:0845 080 1800.

7 Budget Planner

Whether you are about to retire tomorrow or not for several years, completing the following Budget Planner (even if there are a great many gaps) is well worth the effort.

If retirement is imminent, then hopefully doing the arithmetic in detail will not only reassure you but will enable you to plan your future life with the confidence of really knowing how you stand financially. Moreover, even at this stage, there are probably a variety of options available to you and just examining the figures you have written down will highlight the areas of greatest flexibility.

An imaginative tip, given to us by one of the retirement magazines, is to start living on your retirement income some six months before you retire. Not only will you see if your budget estimates are broadly correct but since most people err on the cautious side when they first retire, you will have the added bonus of all the extra money you will have saved.

If retirement is still some years ahead, there will be both more unknowns and more opportunities. When assessing the figures, you should take account of your future earnings; and perhaps more to the point, since your pension may well be based on it, what your final salary is likely to be. Also, though it may mean stinting a bit now, you should consider whether you should be paying AVCs and/or making other investments.

Imprecise as they will be, the Budget Planner estimates you have made in the various income/expenditure columns should indicate whether, unless you take action now, you could be at risk of having to make serious adjustments in your standard of living.

To be on the safe side, you must assume some increase in inflation. Equally, everyone should budget for a nest egg, to pay for any emergencies or special events – perhaps a family wedding – that may come along.

1. Possible savings when you retire

Item	*Est. Monthly Savings*
National insurance contributions	....
Pension payments	....
Travel expenses to work	....
Bought lunches	....
Incidentals at work, e.g. drinks with colleagues, collections for presents	....
Special work clothes	....
Concessionary travel	....
Free NHS prescriptions	....
Free eyes tests	....
Mature drivers' insurance policy	....
Retired householders' insurance policy	....
Life assurance payments and/ or possible endowment policy premiums	....
Other	....
TOTAL	....

N.B. You should also take into account reduced running costs, if you move to a smaller home; any expenses for dependent children that may cease; plus other costs, e.g. mortgage payments, that may end around the time you retire. Also the fact that you may be in a lower tax bracket.

2. Possible extra outgoings when you retire

Items	*Est. Monthly Cost*
Extra heating/lighting bills	....
Extra spending on hobbies and other entertainment	....
Replacement of company car	....
Private health care insurance	....
Longer, or more frequent, holidays	....
Life/permanent health insurance	....
Cost of substituting other perks, e.g. expense account lunches	....
Out-of-pocket expenses for voluntary work activity	....
Other	....
TOTAL	....

N.B. Looking ahead, you will need to make provision for any extra home comforts you might want; and also, at some point, of having to pay other people to do some of the jobs that you normally manage yourself. If you intend to make regular donations to a charity or perhaps help with your grandchildren's education, these too should be included on the list. The same applies to any new private pension or savings plan that you might want to invest in to boost your long term retirement income.

Note on table 3

Many people have difficulty understanding the tax system and you should certainly take professional advice if you are in any doubt at all.

However, if you fill in the following table carefully, it should give you a pretty good idea of your income after retirement and enable you to make at least provisional plans.

Remember too that you may have one or two capital sums to invest, such as:

- the commuted lump sum from your pension
- money from an endowment policy
- gains from the sale of company shares (SAYE or other share option scheme)
- profits from the sale of your home or other asset
- money from an inheritance.

3. Expected sources of income on retirement

A. *Income Received Before Tax*

State basic pension	....
Graduated pension	....
SERPS	....
Occupational pension(s)	....
Stakeholder or personal pension	....
State benefits	....
Investments and savings plans paid gross (e.g. gilts, National Savings)	....
Casual or other pre-tax earnings	....
Total	....
Less Personal Tax Allowance and possibly also Married Couple's Allowance	....
The 10 per cent rate tax on the first £1,920 of taxable income	....
Basic Rate Tax	....
TOTAL A	....

B. *Income Received After Tax*

Dividends (unit trusts, shares, etc.)	....
Bank deposit account	....
Building society interest	....
Annuity income	....
Other (incl. earnings subject to PAYE)	....
TOTAL B	....
TOTAL A + TOTAL B	....
Less Higher rate tax (if any)	....
Plus Other tax-free receipts, e.g. some State benefits income from a matured TESSA, PEP plan, ISA	....
Investment Bond withdrawals etc.	....
Other	....
TOTAL NET INCOME	....

4. Unavoidable outgoings

Items	*Est. Monthly Cost*
Food	....
Rent or mortgage repayments	....
Council tax	....
Repair and maintenance costs	....
Heating	....
Lighting and other energy	....
Telephone/mobile	....
Postage (incl. Christmas cards)	....
TV licence/rental	....
Household insurance	....
Clothes	....
Laundry, cleaner's bills, shoe repair	....
Domestic cleaning products	....
Misc. services, e.g. plumber, window cleaner	....
Car (incl. licence, petrol etc.)	....
Other transport	....
Regular savings/life assurance	....
HP/other loan repayments	....
Outgoings on health	....
Other	....
TOTAL	....

N.B. Before adding up the total, you should look at the 'Normal Additional Expenditure' list, as you may well want to juggle some of the items between the two.

5. Normal additional expenditure

Items	*Est. Monthly Cost*
Gifts	....
Holidays	....
Newspapers/books/videos	....
Drink	....
Cigarettes/tobacco	....
Hairdressing	....
Toiletries/cosmetics	....
Entertainment (hobbies, outings,home entertaining etc.)	....
Misc. subscriptions/membership fees	....
Charitable donations	....
Expenditure on pets	....
Garden purchases	....
Other	....
TOTAL	....

N.B. For some items, such as holidays and gifts, you may tend to think in annual expenditure terms. However, for the purpose of comparing monthly income versus outgoings, it is probably easier if you itemise all the expenditure in the same fashion. Moreover, if you need to save for a special event such as your holiday, it helps if you get into the habit of putting so much aside every month (or even weekly).

8 Your Home

One of the most important decisions to be taken as you approach retirement is where you will live. To many people, one of the biggest attractions is the pleasure of moving home. No longer tied to an area within easy commuting distance of work, they can indulge their cherished dreams of a wisteria-covered cottage in the Cotswolds or a white-washed villa in some remote Spanish resort. While this could turn out to be everything they hoped for, and more, many people rush full steam ahead without any real assessment of the pros and cons.

It is normally sensible at least to examine the other options, even if you end up rejecting them. An obvious possibility is to stay where you are and perhaps adapt your present home to make it more suitable for your requirements. You might move in to live with family or friends. Or looking further ahead, you could consider buying or renting some form of purpose-built retirement accommodation.

Before you come to any definite decision, first ask yourself a few down-to-earth questions. What are your main priorities? To be closer to your family? To have a smaller, more manageable home that will be easier to run – and less expensive? To realise some capital in order to provide you with extra money for your retirement? To live in a specific town or village, which you know you like and where you have plenty of friends? Or to enjoy the security of being in accommodation that offers some of the facilities you may want as you become older, such as a resident caretaker and the option of having some of your meals catered?

Whatever choice you make is bound to have its advantages and drawbacks but, if you weigh these up, you will be far less likely to take a decision which – while attractive in the short term – you may later regret.

Staying put

While there may be plenty of arguments for moving there are probably just as many for staying where you are. Moving house can be a traumatic experience at the best of times and even more so as you become older, when emotional ties are harder to break and precious possessions more painful to part with, as is usually the necessity especially when moving somewhere smaller.

Although ideally you may want to remain where you are, you may feel that your home is really too large or inconvenient for you to manage in the future. However, before you heave your last sigh of regret and put it on the market, it is worth considering whether there are ways of adapting it to provide what you want. If your house is too big, you might think about re-using the space in a better way. Would it be possible, for example, to turn a bedroom into a small upstairs study? Or perhaps you could convert a spare room into a separate workroom for hobbies and get rid of the clutter from the main living area? Equally, have you thought about letting one or two rooms? As well as solving the problem of wasted space, it would also bring in some extra income.

A few judicious home improvements invested in now could make the world of difference in terms of comfort and practicality. Many of us carry on for years with inefficient heating systems that could be improved relatively easily and cheaply. Stairs need not necessarily be a problem, even when you are very much older, thanks to the various types of stair lifts now on the market. Even so, a few basic facilities installed on the ground floor could save your legs in years to come. Similarly, gardens can be endlessly replanned to suit changing requirements: for example, extending the areas of lawn or paving could spare you hours of exhausting weeding.

For some people, the problem is not so much the size or convenience of their home as the fact that they are unable to buy the freehold, or extend the lease, and so fear for their long term security. At last there is some hope. The 1993 Leasehold Reform – Housing and Urban Development Act extends the right of enfranchisement to thousands of flat leaseholders, variously by giving them the collective right to buy the freehold of their building and the individual right to extend their leases at a market price.

Among other requirements to enfranchise, your flat must be held under a lease that was originally granted for more than 21 years and at least two-thirds of the eligible tenants must also wish to buy the freehold. Before proceeding, you would be advised to obtain a professional valuation as a first step to establishing a fair price to which the landlord will be entitled. 'Fair price' is made up of the open market value of the building, at least half the marriage value plus possible compensation to the landlord for any severance or other losses. If you have a dwindling lease but do not wish to enfranchise, the more straightforward purchase of a 90-year lease extension might be a better option. For further information see booklet *Leasehold Flats: Your Right to Buy the Freehold of Your Building or Renew Your Lease*, available from Citizens' Advice Bureaux or ODPM Free Literature, PO Box 236, Wetherby LS23 7NB. T:0870 122 6236.

If, as applies to many people, you want protection from a greedy landlord but do not want to buy the freehold or extend your lease, you will be glad to know that the 1996 Housing Act has strengthened leaseholders' rights. Among other gains, where leaseholders believe that their service charges are unreasonable, they have the right to ask a Leasehold Valuation Tribunal, rather than a court, to determine what charge is reasonable. This includes work which has been proposed but not yet started. Also, where there are serious problems with the management of a building, tenants can ask the Tribunal to appoint a new manager. Importantly, Leasehold Valuation Tribunals are less formal than a court and avoid the risk of potentially unknown costs associated with court proceedings. For further information, obtain leaflets *Long Leaseholders: Your Rights and Responsibilities* and *Applying to a Leasehold Valuation Tribunal*, available from Citizens' Advice Bureaux or ODPM Free Literature at the address above.

More good news is that the Commonhold and Leasehold Reform Act 2002 will further improve leaseholders' rights. Come May 2003, when all the new leasehold provisions should have been phased in, the Act will: introduce a new right to manage your property without having to prove fault on the part of the landlord; make buying the freehold or an extended lease of a flat easier; strengthen leaseholders' rights against unreasonable service charges and provide further protection for the holding of leaseholders' monies; make lease variations easier to obtain and will also prevent landlords from taking any action for unpaid ground rent unless this has first been demanded in writing. Further information about these new provisions can be obtained from the OPDM, Leasehold Reform Branch, Zone 2/J6, Eland House, Bressenden Place, London SW1E 5DU. T:020 7944 3462.

Free advice on any of these issues is available from **LEASE** – the Leasehold Advisory Service, 70–74 City Road, London EC1Y 2BJ. T:020 7490 9580.

Moving to a new home

If you do decide to move, the sooner you start looking for your new home the better. There is no point in delaying the search until you retire and then rushing round expecting to find your dream house in a matter of weeks. With time to spare, you will have a far greater choice of properties and are less likely to indulge in any panic buying.

While a smaller house will almost certainly be easier and cheaper to run, make sure that it is not so small that you are going to feel cramped. Remember that when you are both at home, you may need more room to avoid getting on top of each other. Also if your family lives in another part of the country, you may wish to have them and your grandchildren to stay. Conversely, beware of taking on commitments such as a huge garden. While this might be a great source of enjoyment when you are in your sixties, it could prove a burden as you become older.

If you are thinking of moving out of the neighbourhood, there are other factors to be taken into account such as: access to shops and social activities, proximity to friends and relatives, availability of public transport and even health and social support services. While these may not seem particularly important now, they could become so in the future. Couples who retire to a seemingly 'idyllic' spot often return quite quickly. New friends are not always easy to make. So-called 'retirement areas' can mean that you are cut off from a normal cross-section of society and health services are likely to be over-taxed.

After a hard week's wheeling and dealing it is tempting to wax lyrical about exchanging the rat race for a life of rustic solitude. While retiring to the country can be glorious, city dwellers should, however, bear in mind some of the less attractive sides of rural living. Noise, for example low flying aircraft and church bells, can be an unexpected irritant. If you are not used to it, living near a silage pit or farm can also be an unpleasant experience. Prices in village shops are often higher than in city supermarkets and bus services tend to be more infrequent.

Finally, would a small village or seaside resort offer sufficient scope to pursue your interests once the initial flurry of activity is over? Even if you think you know an area well, check it out properly before coming to a final decision. If possible take a self-catering let for a couple of months, preferably out of season when rents are low and the weather is bad. A good idea is to limit your daily spending to your likely retirement income rather than splurge as most of us do on holiday.

This is even more pertinent if you are thinking of moving abroad, where additional difficulties can include learning the language, lower standards of health care and the danger of losing contact with your friends. Another problem for ex-patriates could be a change in the political climate, resulting perhaps on the one hand in your not being so welcome in your adopted country and on the other, in a drop in the purchasing power of your pension. For more information on the financial implications of living overseas, see section 'Retiring Abroad', pages 89–92.

Counting the cost

Moving house can be an expensive exercise. It is estimated that the cost is between 5 and 10 per cent of the value of a new home, once you have totted up such extras as search fees, removal charges, insurance, stamp duty, VAT, legal fees and estate agents' commission. If you plan any repairs, alterations or decorations, the figure will be considerably higher. On the other hand, if you move to smaller or cheaper accommodation you will be able to release money for other uses.

A useful annual survey detailing the latest costs of all the unavoidables when moving house is prepared by Woolwich Plc based on information from solicitors, estate agents, surveyors and removal firms in 50 towns and cities. For a free copy, contact: **Woolwich Press Office**, 54 Lombard Street, London EC3P 3AH.

A good tip to remember is that stamp duty, which applies to nearly all properties costing more than £60,000, see exception below, is not levied on fitments such as carpets and curtains. If you are considering a purchase which includes some of these, try to negotiate a separate price for them. Exceptionally, properties costing up to £150,000 in certain depressed areas of the country are exempt from stamp duty.

While on the subject of stamp duty, as you may know, there is now a higher rate duty on property purchases over £250,000. This was increased in the March 2000 budget, from to 2.5 to 3 per cent on properties costing over £250,000 and to 4 per cent on those costing above £500,000.

When buying a new home, especially an older property, it is essential to have a full building (structural) survey done before committing yourself. This will cost in the region of £400 for a small terraced house but is worth every penny. In particular, it will provide you with a comeback in law should things go wrong. A valuation report, while cheaper, is more superficial and may fail to detect flaws which could give you trouble and expense in the future.

If you are buying a newly built house, there are now a number of safeguards against structural defects. Most mortgagors will only lend on new homes with a National House Building Council (NHBC) insurance or its equivalent. The NHBC operates a

10-year warranty scheme under which the builder will remedy most defects which appear in the first two years. For the next eight years, it provides insurance against a number of structural defects. For more information, T: 01494 735363.

Many of the problems of buying or selling a house could be eased in time thanks to a logbook called *The House Diary*, which has been devised by the Northern Consortium of Housing Authorities in association with the Building Centre Trust.

Its purpose is to help owners record all the vital information about their property including such technical areas as the foundations and the roof loading, as well as more everyday concerns such as the location of the gas and electricity meters, the essentials of the central heating system and the position of water stopcocks. As well as being of help to both buyers and sellers, the information could also prove invaluable to owners planning a conversion or extension to their home.

The *House Diary* which costs £1 is available from the **Northern Consortium of Housing Authorities**, Webster's Ropery, Ropery Road, Deptford Terrace, Deptford, Sunderland, Tyne & Wear SR4 6DJ. T:0191 566 1000.

Also helpful to home-buyers, H.M. Land Registry allows members of the public to seek information direct about the 18 or so million properties held on its register. There is a small charge for the service, details of which are explained in Leaflet No. 15 *The Open Register – A Guide to Information Held by the Land Registry and How to Obtain It*. To request a free copy, write to **HM Land Registry**, Lincoln's Inn Fields, London WC2A 3PH; or call T:020 7917 8888 and ask for Customer Information Centre.

Another welcome change is that, thanks to the 1990 Courts and Legal Services Act, conveyancing has become more competitive with banks, building societies, insurance companies and other bodies (as well of course as solicitors) now allowed to offer these services.

Bridging loans

Finally a word about bridging loans which for some unlucky people can end up costing them literally thousands of pounds. Tempting as it may be to buy before you sell, unless you have the money available to finance the cost of two homes – including possibly two mortgages – you need to do your sums very carefully indeed.

To give you an idea of the sort of costs involved, banks usually charge 2 points or more over base rate plus an arrangement or administration fee on top. In other words, if bank rate is 6 per cent, the interest charged on a £100,000 loan works out at £666 a month; or £3,996 if it takes you six months to sell. Although by shopping around the building societies you may get somewhat better terms, you don't need to be a mathematician to work out that if your home is on the market for more than a very short while, the payments can escalate alarmingly.

As an alternative to bridging loans, some of the major institutional estate agents operate chain-breaking schemes and may offer to buy your property at a discount: normally around 10 or 12 per cent less than the market price. In some circumstances this could be worthwhile but a lot of money is involved, so this is not a decision to be taken lightly.

Estate agents

Finding your dream house may prove harder than you think. The grapevine can be effective, so pass the word around about what you are looking for. The property advertisements, especially in local newspapers, may also be worth scanning. Additionally, you could contact a good estate agent in the area to which you want to move.

The National Association of Estate Agents (NAEA), Arbon House, 21 Jury Street, Warwick CV34 4EH. T:01926 496800, runs a service called Homelink, bringing together over 850 agency branches throughout Europe and the UK. Your nearest member of Homelink can get details of houses for sale from a Homelink member in your target area. For names of member agents, telephone the Homelink Hotline: 01926 410785.

Some building societies, banks and insurance companies have created large chains of estate agents and many of these maintain systems for full exchange of information between their branches nationwide. These include: Your Move, Bradford & Bingley Estate Agents, Halifax and Legal and General.

All these, together with most other large groups as well as many independent estate agents, have introduced a Code of Practice and also formed an Ombudsman Scheme to provide an independent review service for buyers or sellers of UK residential property in the event of a complaint. The Ombudsman is empowered to make awards of up to £25,000. However, complaints must be reported to the company within 12 months of the incident and to the Ombudsman within 6 months of receiving the member agency's final letter. As with most ombudsman schemes, action can only be taken against firms that are actually members of the scheme. The Ombudsman also cannot intervene in disputes over surveys and the letting of property. Copies of the *Consumer Guide*, the Code of Practice and other information can be obtained from Member Agencies or by contacting the Ombudsman at the following address: **The Ombudsman for Estate Agents**, Beckett House, 4 Bridge Street, Salisbury, Wiltshire SP1 2LX. T:01722 333306.

A further welcome move to improve standards is the 1993 Property Misdescriptions Act which prohibits estate agents and property developers from making misleading, or inflated, claims about a property, site or related matter.

If you want to contact qualified local agents, the **Royal Institution of Chartered Surveyors**, 12 Great George Street, Parliament Square, London SW1P 3AD, T: 0870 333 1600 can provide names and addresses of chartered surveyors who are estate agents. Contact their Customer Services Department at the address above.

If you are thinking of retiring abroad, beware of unscrupulous property developers who it is thought have swindled hundreds of Britons, many of them retired people, in Mediterranean tourist resorts. In particular, don't be rushed into a purchase you may later regret by fast-talking salesmen; and ensure that all documents are thoroughly checked by an independent lawyer before you sign anything. Visit the property first and find out what other developments, if any, are planned in the vicinity.

Removals

Transporting your worldly goods from A to B is an exhausting business. Professional help can remove many of the headaches if carried out by a reputable firm. Not only will they heave all the heavy furniture around for you, but they will also wrap your china and ornaments safely in packing cases which they provide as part of the service.

Costs can vary considerably depending on the type and size of furniture, the distance over which it is being moved and other factors including insurance and seasonal troughs and peaks. Obviously, valuable antiques will cost more to pack and transport than standard modern furniture. It pays to shop around and get at least three written quotes from different removal firms. Some may be able to help reduce costs by arranging part or return loads. It is also worth asking whether the firm has a 'low price day', as rates are often cheaper at the start of the week. Remember, however, that the cheapest quote is not necessarily the best. Find out exactly what you are paying for and whether the price includes packing and insurance.

A useful organisation to contact is: **British Association of Removers**, 3 Churchill Court, 58 Station Road, North Harrow HA2 7SA. T:020 8861 3331.

They will send you a free leaflet advising you what to do when you move house and a list of approved removal firms. (Please enclose sae).

Moving in with family or friends

This may be accommodation such as a self-contained flat or actually living together as part of the family. It may be possible to get a renovation grant from your local council to help with any conversion costs. Ask about the availability of such grants before any work is started.

There are many advantages to such an arrangement. While you are active, you can contribute to the household. Should you become frail or ill, help will be at hand.

Living together can also be fraught with problems, however. You only need to think back to any bachelor flat-sharing days to be reminded of the countless petty arguments – over washing up, noise or bills – that can develop if you are not careful. As a general precaution, try to work out in advance any potential problems or you may have a month of honeymoon and years of regret. Questions worth considering include: whether you will share any meals, social life or transport; whether you will contribute in any practical ways, like baby-sitting, shopping, cleaning or looking after the house during the family's holidays; also, whether you can keep a pet and have friends to stay.

Money is also a common source of dispute. Decide whether you will have your own telephone or whether you will share one. If you will be paying rent, make it a formal arrangement exactly as if you were a normal tenant. You must agree a set figure: what it will cover, how it will be assessed in future and how it will be paid, i.e. weekly, monthly, cash or standing order. If you make a contribution towards the cost of any conversion work, work out beforehand how you would be reimbursed should the arrangement have to be terminated for one reason or another.

Living with family or friends is generally an informal arrangement. However, it is worth having a word with your solicitor or local housing advice centre about how it might affect your rights and obligations as either landlord or tenant. In particular, you should take advice before embarking on any construction work, such as a self-contained 'granny flat', which might affect the property's exemption from capital gains tax in the future.

Sharing with friends

Yet another possibility is to share your own home with one or two friends. For some, this can be a perfect solution but the same pitfalls as living with your family apply, so work out the arrangements carefully beforehand. Legal advice is an absolute 'must' in these circumstances. Your solicitor or housing advice centre will be able to explain any important points that could affect you, as will your building society or bank should you be considering actually buying a property together.

Retirement housing and sheltered accommodation

The term 'retirement' or 'sheltered accommodation' covers a wide variety of housing but generally means property with a resident warden/caretaker, an emergency alarm system, optional meals and some communal facilities such as living rooms, garden and laundry. Guest accommodation and visiting services such as hairdressers and chiropodists are sometimes also available. A number of companies offer extra care and nursing facilities in some of their developments.

Designed to bridge the gap between the family home and residential care, such housing offers continued independence for the fit and active within a secure environment. Much of it is owned and run by local authorities, housing associations and charities. However, there are an increasing number of well-designed, high quality private developments of 'retirement homes' now on the market, for sale or rent, at prices to suit most pockets.

Many of the more attractive properties – and among the most expensive – are in converted country houses of architectural or historic merit or in newly developed 'villages' and 'courtyard' schemes. As a general rule, you have to be over 55 when you buy property of this kind. While you may not wish to move into this type of accommodation just now, if the idea interests you in the long term it is worth planning ahead as there are often very long waiting lists.

Full details on the various types of sheltered accommodation, together with a price guide and some addresses, are given in Chapter 15, Caring for Elderly Parents.

Other options

Boarding houses

At least 30,000 people live in privately-run premises such as boarding houses, guest houses, hotels or hostels at which they have accommodation, meals and some services, but not nursing care.

If you are attracted to this idea, make sure you are dealing with a reputable establishment. Following evidence that many retired people were being 'ripped off' by their landlords, anyone offering this type of accommodation to four or more people must now register with the local Social Services Department.

Caravan or mobile home

Many retired people consider living in a caravan or mobile home which they keep either in a relative's garden or on an established site, possibly at the seaside or in the country. You may already own one as a holiday home which you are considering turning into more permanent accommodation. If you want to live in a caravan on your own or other private land, you should contact your local authority for information about any planning permission or site licensing requirements that may apply.

If, on the other hand, you want to keep it on an established site, make absolutely sure that the site owner has all the necessary permissions. You should check this with the Planning and Environmental Health Department of the local authority. It should be noted that many site owners will not accept prospective residents' own mobile home, but require them to buy one from the site or from an outgoing resident.

The rights of owners of residential mobile home sites and of residents who own their mobile home but rent their pitch from a site owner are set out in the Mobile Homes Act 1983.

Find out what conditions the site owner attaches to any agreement (by law he must provide a written statement setting out such terms as the services provided, charges and maintenance of the site). You should also check your statutory rights (which should be included in the written statement) in particular regarding security of tenure and resale. Under the Act, residents have the right to sell their unit to a person approved by the site owner, who will be entitled to up to 10 per cent commission on the sale price.

In the event of a dispute, either party is free to go to court; or, with the agreement of both sides, to arbitration. If following a sale the resident is unhappy with the terms of the written agreement, appeal to the court must be within six months of the written terms being received.

It should also be noted that ordinary caravans are not always suitable as long-term accommodation for the over-sixties. They can be damp as well as cramped and what may have been an enjoyable adventure on holiday may soon pall when it is your only option.

Modern residential park homes have the advantage of being more spacious and sturdier but, though usually cheaper than a house of equivalent size, are nevertheless a major expense. Moreover, the law regarding such purchases is complex and legal advice is very strongly recommended before entering into a commitment to purchase a home.

If you do decide to go ahead with the plan, you might like to obtain a copy of *Mobile Homes, A Guide for Residents and Site Owners*, a free booklet, available from your housing department.

Self-build

Some 25,000 people a year are now building their own homes and with typical cost savings estimated at between 25 and 40 per cent, the number has been growing. New building methods have been developed which defy the assumption that you need to be a fit young man to undertake such a project and both women and elderly people have successfully become self-builders. No prior building experience is necessary, although this of course helps.

Further good news is that in response to the demand some building societies offer self-build mortgages to enable borrowers to finance the purchase of land plus construction costs.

However, as with any mortgage, it is essential to make sure that you are not in danger of over-committing yourself. Not so very long ago, hundreds of people lost their sites because, due to falling land prices, the size of their loan exceeded the value of the property – and by law building societies cannot make secured loans that are more than 100 per cent of the valuation. Although this is less of a problem today, thanks to the upturn in the property market, there is no cast-iron guarantee that prices will not slump again at some time in the future. After all, not many people in the late eighties imagined that negative equity could become an issue!

Most self-builders work in groups and/or employ sub-contractors for some of the more specialised work, but individuals who wish to build on their own can make arrangements with an architect or company which sells standard plans and building kits.

A useful organisation to contact is the **Walter Segal Self Build Trust**, 15 High Street, Belford, Northumberland NE70 7NG. T:01668 213544. This is a charitable trust, named after the architect who pioneered a practical post-and-beam timber frame method of construction particularly appropriate for self-builders with no previous building skills. The Trust provides free advice and information on self-build methods, the costs involved and the financial options available. They can also supply a useful publication *Out of the Woods: Ecological Designs for Timber Frame Housing*. Price £13.50 plus £1.50 p&p.

Another helpful resource is the **Plotfinder Database** which provides information about available building sites. Telephone the hotline on T:0906 557 5400 (calls cost £1 per minute).

Centre for Alternative Technology, Machynlleth, Powys, Wales SY20 9AZ. T:01654 705950. Displays featuring energy-efficient housing can be seen at the Centre. Plans are available for the Walter Segal method of self-build. For other publications and a mail-order catalogue of environment-friendly products, write to the address above. Entrance fee for visiting the Centre is £7; £5 for retired people.

Making your home more practical

It is sensible to set about any home improvement plans earlier rather than later. For one thing, these are often easier to afford when you are still earning a regular salary.

For another, any building work is tiresome and most people find it easier to put up with the mess when they are not living among it 24 hours a day. Thirdly, if you start early, you will enjoy the benefit that much sooner.

A perhaps unnecessary point to mention is that when embarking on changes a specific aim should be to make your home as economic, labour-saving and convenient as possible. A reason for saying this is that many people become so involved with the decorative aspects that they forget to think about some of the longer-term practicalities which, at next to no extra cost, could have been incorporated along with the other work.

Insulation

When you retire, you may be at home more during the day so are likely to be using your heating more intensively. One of the best ways of reducing the bills is to get your house properly insulated. Heat escapes from a building in four main ways: through the roof, walls, floor and through loose-fitting doors and windows. Insulation can not only cut the heat loss dramatically but will usually more than pay for itself within four or five years.

Loft insulation. As much as 25 per cent of heat in a house escapes through the loft. The answer is to put a layer of insulating material, ideally 250mm thick, between and across the roof joists. You might be able to lay this yourself. The materials are readily available from builders merchants. If you prefer to employ a specialist contractor, contact the **National Association of Loft Insulation Contractors**, PO Box 12, Haslemere, Surrey GU27 3AH. T:01428 654011 for a list of their members. Your local Age Concern group or volunteer bureau may also be able to help.

Doors and windows. A further 25 per cent of heat escapes through single-glazed windows, half of which could be saved through double-glazing. There are two main types: sealed units and secondary sashes (that can be removed in the summer). Compared with other forms of insulation, double glazing is expensive; however, it does have the advantage of reducing noise levels. As a result of new building regulations, which came into effect in April 2002, any replacement doors and windows installed after that date have to comply with strict thermal performance standards and the work will need to be done by an installer who is registered under the new FENSA scheme. To be on the safe side, contact the **Glass and Glazing Federation**, 44–48 Borough High Street, London SE1 1XB. T:020 7403 7177.

Effective draught-proofing saves heat loss as well as keeping out cold blasts of air. It is also relatively cheap and easy to install. Compression seals, mounted by a variety of methods and supplied in strip form, are the simplest and most cost-effective way to fill the gap between the fixed and moving edges of doors and windows. For draught-proofing older sliding sash windows and doors, wiper seals, fixed with rust-proof pins and screws, need to be used. For very loose fitting frames, gap fillers that can be squeezed from a tube provide a more efficient seal between frame and surround, but this is normally work for a specialist.

If you do fit draught seals, make sure you leave a space for a small amount of air to get through, or you may get problems with condensation. If the house is not well ventilated, you should put in a vapour check to slow down the leakage of moisture into the walls and ceiling. For advice on durable products and contractors, contact the **Draught Proofing Advisory Association**, PO Box 12, Haslemere, Surrey GU27 3AH. T:01428 654011.

Heat loss can also be considerably reduced through hanging heavy curtains (both lined and interlined) over windows and doors. Make sure all curtains cover the window sill or rest on the floor. It is better to have them too long than too short.

Wall insulation. More heat is lost through the walls than perhaps anywhere else in the house: it can be as much as 50 per cent. If your house has cavity walls – and most houses built after 1930 do – then cavity wall insulation should be considered. This involves injecting mineral wool (rock wool or glass wool), polystyrene beads or foam into the cavity through holes drilled in the outside wall.

It is work for a specialist and therefore quite expensive, costing from around £500 for a terraced house up to £725 plus for a detached house. Against this, you could expect a typical saving of around 25 per cent off your heating bill each year so that, in most cases, the initial outlay should be recovered in about four years. Make sure that the firm you use is registered with a reputable organisation, such as the British Standards Institution, or can show a current Agrément Certificate for the system and is approved by the BBA. If using a foam fill, the material should comply with British Standard BS 5617 and the installation with BS 5618.

Solid wall insulation can be considerably more expensive, but well worth while, providing similar savings of around 25 per cent off your annual heating bill. Again, this is work for a specialist and involves applying an insulating material to the outside of the wall, plus rendering or cladding.

For further information and addresses of registered contractors, contact:

British Board of Agrement, PO Box 195, Bucknalls Lane, Garston, Herts WD25 9BA. T:01923 665300.

British Standards Institution, 389 Chiswick High Road, London W4 4AL. T:020 8996 9000.

Cavity Foam Bureau, PO Box 79, Oldbury, Warley, West Midlands B69 4PW. T:0121 544 4949. All installers that belong to the Cavity Foam Bureau are registered with the BSI.

Eurisol UK Ltd., 3 CIGA House, Vimy Court, Vimy Road, Leighton Buzzard, Beds LU7 1FG. T:01525 385886.

Expanded Polystyrene Cavity Insulation Association, c/o Polypearl, 52–56 Oswald Road, Scunthorpe DN15 7PQ. T:01724 847 844.

Insulated Render & Cladding Association Ltd, PO Box 12, Haslemere, Surrey GU27 3AH. T:01428 654011 – for solid or defective walls.

National Cavity Insulation Association, PO Box 12, Haslemere, Surrey GU27 3AH. T:01428 654011.

Floor insulation. Up to 15 per cent of heat loss can be saved through filling the cracks or gaps in the floorboards and skirting. If you can take up your floorboards, rock wool or glass wool rolls can be extremely effective when fixed underneath the joists. Filling spaces with papier mache or plastic wool will also help especially if a good felt or rubber underlay is then laid under the carpet. Be careful, however, that you do not block up the underfloor ventilation which is necessary to protect floor timbers from dampness and rot. Solid concrete floors can be covered with cork tiles or carpet and felt or rubber underlay.

Hot water cylinder insulation. If your hot water cylinder has no insulation, it could be costing you several pounds a week in wasted heat. An insulating jacket around your hot water cylinder will cut wastage by three-quarters. Most hot water tanks now come ready supplied with insulation. If not, the jacket should be at least 80mm thick and will cost around £25. Jackets come in various sizes, so measure your cylinder before buying. Only purchase one that carries BSI's Kitemark and BS 5615.

Grants

Recipients of income support, housing benefit or council tax benefit – as well as other groups including elderly, infirm and disabled people – may be able to get help with insulation costs by applying for Home Repair Assistance. To be eligible, you must normally either be an owner occupier or a private sector tenant (this includes tenants of housing associations and those who have no formal tenancy but a right to live in the property for at least five years). Mobile homes and houseboats may also be eligible but in all cases, the property must be your only or main residence.

Payment of the grant is at the discretion of your local council. It can cover either the cost of labour if a contractor is used and/or the cost of materials, including: loft or floor insulation, draught proofing or the lagging of water tanks and pipes. The maximum amount that can be awarded is £5,000 for each application. It is important that you should not start on any work before your application has been approved.

For further information and an application form, you should contact the Environmental Health or Housing Department of your local council. It is possible that they may recommend that you apply instead for a Renovation Grant. They may also point out that Home Repair Assistance can be used for other home improvement purposes. For further information on both points, see section 'Improvement and Repair Grants' on page 161.

In addition to the above, there is also the government funded Warm Front Team Grant scheme which provides grants of up to £2,500 for home insulation and heating measures as well as energy efficiency advice. The grants are mainly targeted at low income householders – including people who are disabled, chronically sick or over 60 – who own or privately rent their home. The part of the scheme aimed at people over 60 is known as Warm Front Plus. Slightly different schemes apply in Scotland, Wales and Northern Ireland. For further information contact: **EAGA Partnership Ltd.**, EAGA House, Archbold Terrace, Newcastle upon Tyne NE2 1DB; or telephone freephone 0800 952 0600.

Heating

It may be possible to save money by using different fuels or by heating parts of your house off different systems. This could apply especially if some rooms are only occasionally used. Your local gas and electricity offices can advise on heating systems, running costs and energy conservation, as well as heating and hot water appliances. In particular, you might usefully enquire about Economy 7 electricity which provides cheaper rate supplies at night.

Your local office of the **Solid Fuel Association** (see telephone directory) will also give free advice and information on all aspects of solid fuel heating, including appliances and installation.

If you are in London, a visit to the **Building Centre**, 26 Store Street, London WC1E 7BT, T:020 7692 4000, could save you a lot of leg work. It has a very wide range of appliances on display with experts on hand to give information.

Shopping note. Many people get rushed into expensive purchases on the promise of cheaper energy bills. A point to remember when comparing, say, gas with electricity is that fuel prices are volatile and relative cost advantages are not always maintained. If you have an otherwise adequate system, it could be false economy to exchange it for the sake of a small saving in current heating costs.

Buying and installing heating equipment. When buying equipment, check that it has been approved by the appropriate standards approvals board.

For electrical equipment, the letters to look for are BEAB (British Electro-technicals Approvals Board) or CCA (Cenelec Certification Agreement), which is the European Community equivalent.

For gas appliances, look for the CE mark which denotes that appliances meet the requirements of the Gas Appliance (Safety) Regulations Act 1995. Domestic solid fuel appliances should be approved by the Solid Fuel Appliances Approval Scheme (see sales literature).

When looking for contractors to install your equipment, check that they are enrolled with the relevant inspection council or are members of the relevant trade association. Electricians should be approved by the **National Inspection Council for Electrical Installation Contracting**, Vintage House, 37 Albert Embankment, London SE1 7UJ. T:020 7564 2323. All approved contractors are covered for technical work by the NICEIC Complaints Procedure and Guarantee of Standards Scheme and undertake to work to British Standard 7671. Any sub-standard work must be put right at no extra cost to the consumer. Names and addresses of local approved contractors can be found in the NICEIC Roll of Approved Contractors, kept in local libraries and some CABs, or can be obtained from NICEIC direct or by visiting their website.

An alternative source for finding a reputable electrician is the **Electrical Contractors' Association**, 34 Palace Court, London W2 4HY. T:020 7313 4800. Their members, all of whom have to be qualified, work to national wiring regulations and a published ECA Code of Fair Trading. There is also a Work Bond which guarantees that, in the event of a contractor becoming insolvent, the work will be completed by another approved electrician at the originally quoted price subject to the conditions of the scheme.

Gas appliances should only be installed by a CORGI (Council for Registered Gas Installers) registered installer. Registration is now compulsory by law. As a further safeguard, all registered gas installers carry a CORGI ID card with their photo, types of gas work they are competent to do, their employer's trading title and the CORGI logo. The address is: **Council for Registered Gas Installers**, 1 Elmwood, Chineham Business Park, Crockford Lane, Basingstoke, Hants RG24 8WG. T:01256 372200.

Additionally, members of the Heating and Ventilating Contractors' Association can advise on all types of central heating. All domestic installation work done by member companies is covered by a free one-year guarantee. There is also an optional extended warranty scheme. For further information contact the **Heating and Ventilating Contractors' Association**, ESCA House, 34 Palace Court, London W2 4JG. T:020 7313 4900; or call the Home Heating Linkline (all calls charged at local rate) on T:0345 581158.

Grants. If you are disabled or on a low income you may be eligible for a grant to assist with improving the heating system to your home. See 'Improvement and repair' on pages 161–164.

Tips for reducing your energy bills

Energy can be saved in lots of small ways. Taken together, they could amount to quite a large cut in your heating bills. You may find some of the following ideas worth considering:

- Set your central heating timer and thermostat to suit the weather. A saving of half an hour or one degree can be substantial. For example, reducing the temperature by 1 degree Centigrade could cut your heating bills by up to ten per cent.
- A separate thermostat on your hot water cylinder set at around 60 degrees Centigrade will enable you to keep hot water for taps at a lower temperature than for the heating system.
- If you run your hot water off an immersion heater, have a time-switch fitted attached to an Economy 7 meter so that the water is heated at the cheap rate overnight. An override switch will enable you to top up the heat during the day if necessary.
- Showers are more economical than baths as well as being easier to use when you become older.

- Reflective foil sheets put behind your radiators help to reduce heat loss through the walls.
- Switch off, or reduce, the heating in rooms not being used and close doors.
- Low energy light bulbs can save several pounds a year.
- If you have an open fire, a vast amount of heat tends to be lost up the chimney. A wood-burning stove can help reduce heat loss as well as maximise the amount of heat you get from your wood or solid fuel in other ways. If you dislike the idea of losing the look of an open fire, there are now a number of appliances on the market that are open fronted and fit flush with the fireplace opening. Contact your local office of the Solid Fuel Association for further information. If you decide to block up a fireplace, don't forget to fit an air vent to allow some ventilation.
- Some small cooking appliances can save energy in comparison with a full-sized cooker. An electric casserole or slow cooker uses only a fraction more energy than a light bulb and is economical for single households. Similarly, an electric frying pan or multi-cooker can be a sensible alternative for people living on their own. Pressure cookers and microwave ovens can save fuel and time.
- Defrosting fridges and freezers regularly reduces running costs.
- Finally, it is a good idea to get in the habit of reading your electricity and gas meters regularly. This will help you keep track of likely bills.

You might like to take advantage of one of the British Gas. Payment options which allows customers to spread their gas or electricity payments over the year in fixed monthly or quarterly instalments, based on an estimate of their annual consumption. Estimates are periodically adjusted up or down, depending on actual meter readings. Price reductions are offered to customers paying by monthly direct debit or to those who pay within ten days of the date shown on the bill. For further details, call British Gas (see your gas or electricity bill for telephone number). Many other suppliers have similar budget plans.

Useful reading

For a free *Energy Efficiency Action Pack*, telephone the Energy Efficiency Hotline on T:0845 727 7200.

Be More Energy Efficient and other useful guides. British Gas publishes a number of guides, describing their many services, including several specifically aimed at older, disabled or chronically sick customers. Information includes advice on safety checks, services for visually impaired people, energy saving tips and other practical help. Available free by calling British Gas.

Other useful addresses

OFGEM, 9 Millbank, London SW1P 3GE. T:020 7901 7000. **OFGEM Scotland,** Regent's Court, 70 West Regent Street, Glasgow G2 2QZ. T:0141 331 2678. OFGEM is the regulator for the gas and electricity industry. Its main functions from a consumer point of view are: to promote competition between suppliers; to regulate the monopoly parts of the industry by setting price controls and standards of service; and to encourage companies to develop easy-payment terms for vulnerable and elderly customers.

Energywatch, T:08459 060708. This is the statutory body representing gas and electricity consumers' interests in England, Scotland and Wales.

If you have a query or problem about gas, electricity or a gas or electrical appliance which you cannot resolve with the supplier or with the appliance retailer, you can approach your regional Energywatch office. These are located in: Birmingham, Bournemouth, Cardiff, Glasgow, London, Manchester and Newcastle. For address and telephone number, see the back of your gas or electricity bill or contact Energywatch at the above number.

Useful reading

Free factsheet *Help With Heating*, available from Age Concern, Freepost (SWB 30375), Ashburton, Devon TQ13 7ZZ; or ring free T:0800 009966.

Improvement and repair

Building work is notoriously expensive and can be a major deterrent to doing some of the alterations to your home that may be necessary. Before abandoning the idea, it is worth investigating whether you could take advantage of some of the various grants available.

A bank loan may be the simplest way of raising funds for most repairs and improvements.

Many banks and building societies are prepared to offer interest-only mortgages to older people to cover essential repairs and improvements.

If you are unlucky enough to discover dry rot or the like in your home, there is little you can do but try to ensure that the builder you employ does not do a botched job. Unfortunately, insurance cover does not usually extend to damage to your house caused by normal wear and tear, woodworm, rot, insects and vermin.

If your house does need structural repairs, contact the Royal Institution of Chartered Surveyors (see 'Useful Addresses' a couple of pages over). They will be able to advise you on your legal position as well as point you in the direction of reputable chartered surveyors.

Improvement and repair grants

Improvements and structural repairs, especially to older houses, may qualify for grants from the local council. Other than for certain mandatory items applicable to Disabled Facilities Grant, all grants are discretionary. There are five types of grant as follows.

Renovation grant. There are seven main eventualities where application for a grant might be successful: (1) to bring a property up to a standard of fitness for human habitation; (2) for works to comply with a statutory repairs notice served on the owner;

(3) to replace or repair rotten or defective parts of the structure including, for example, doors, windows, walls, an ineffective damp-proof course or unsatisfactory wiring; (4) for home insulation or other energy-saving work; (5) to provide heating facilities; (6) for the provision of satisfactory internal arrangements such as improvement of a very steep or winding staircase; (7) for conversions, such as the creation of a self-contained flat.

All claims for grant are at the discretion of the council. Applicants are means-tested and different tests apply according to whether the applicant is an owner-occupier or tenant or whether he/she is a landlord. An individual's resources are also taken into account in determining the actual amount of grant, so even if you are eligible you could be required to contribute to the cost of the works.

The property must have been built or converted at least 10 years before the date of application for grant. Second homes do not qualify.

Common parts grant. This is for the improvement or repair of the common parts of a building containing one or more flats. Items that normally count as common parts include the roof, lift, staircase and entrance lobby. Grant is discretionary and can be applied for either by a landlord and/or by at least three-quarters of the occupying tenants. Tenants' financial resources are taken into account and (where applicable) the property must have been converted at least 10 years previously.

HMO grant. This can only be applied for by a landlord and is for the improvement of Houses in Multiple Occupation (e.g. a house converted into bedsits); or for the conversion of a property for HMO use.

Disabled facilities grant. This is designed to adapt or provide facilities for a home (including the common parts where applicable) to make it more suitable for occupation by a disabled person. It can cover a wide range of improvements to enable someone with a disability to manage more independently including, for example: adaptations to make the accommodation safe for a disabled occupant; work to facilitate access either to the property itself or to the main rooms; the provision of suitable bathroom or kitchen facilities; the adaptation of heating or lighting controls; improvement of the heating system.

Provided the applicant is eligible, a mandatory grant of up to £25,000 may be available for all the above (councils may use their discretion to award more). Discretionary grant is also available for a variety of other works where these would make a home suitable for a disabled person.

The individual must be registered (or registrable) as disabled and, as with other grants, there is a means test. The council will want to check that the proposed work is reasonable and practicable according to the age/condition of the property and the local social services department will need to be satisfied that the works are necessary and appropriate to meet the individual's needs. The grant can either be applied for by the disabled person or by a joint owner/tenant or landlord, on their behalf. For further information, contact the Environmental Health or Grants Department.

Eligibility for all the above grants depends on the validity of the proposed work and on the applicant's resources, taking into account their income and any savings over £6,000 (savings below this amount are ignored). There are different calculations according to whether an applicant is an owner-occupier or tenant – or whether he/she is a landlord.

Home repair assistance. HRA can help pay for small but essential works of repair, improvement or adaptation to your home, including works to make it suitable for an elderly or disabled person to come to live with you permanently.

Payment of the grant is at the discretion of your local council. Eligibility is restricted to those who are elderly, infirm or disabled or who are in receipt of one of the following benefits: income support, housing benefit, income-based jobseeker's allowance, council tax benefit, working families tax credit, disabled person's tax credit or (after April 2003) working tax credit. Applicants must normally either be an owner occupier or private sector tenant (this includes tenants of housing associations) and the property itself (which could be a mobile home or houseboat) must be their only, or main, residence.

People with a right to live in the dwelling for more than five years may be eligible if they have lived there for three years prior to making the application.

Maximum grant is £5,000 per application.

How to apply. Contact the Home Improvement Section or the Environmental Health Department of your local council for an application form. Other applications, such as planning permission, may also be necessary; or, in the case of flats, you may need to apply jointly with other tenants.

Before making an application, you should read the House Renovation Grants booklet (available from the council) which explains the various requirements in detail and also suggests sources such as your Citizens' Advice Bureau and local Home Improvement Agency that can help you assess your likelihood of qualifying and advise you of any preliminary steps (such as getting estimates) you need to take. Even if they are highly optimistic of your chances of obtaining a grant, **do not start work until approval has been given to your grant application, as you will not be eligible for a grant once works have started**.

Community care grant. Income support recipients may be able to obtain a community care grant from the Social Fund to help with repairs. For further information, see leaflet GL18 *Help from the Social Fund*, obtainable from any social security office.

Other help for disabled people. Your local authority may be able to help with the provision of certain special facilities such as a stair lift, telephone installations or a ramp to replace steps. Apply to your local Social Services Department and, if you encounter any difficulties, ask for further help either from your local Disability Group, local Age Concern Group or from **RADAR (Royal Association for Disability and Rehabilitation)**, 12 City Forum, 250 City Road, London EC1V 8AF, T:020 7250 3222; Minicom: 020 7250 4119.

Useful reading

House Renovation Grants, Home Repair Assistance and Disabled Facilities Grant, obtainable from: ODPM Free Literature, PO Box 236, Wetherby, West Yorkshire LS23 7NB. T:0870 122 6236.

Useful addresses

Association of Building Engineers, Lutyens House, Billing Brook Road, Weston Favell, Northampton NN3 8NW. T:01604 404121. Can supply names of qualified building engineers/surveyors.

Association of Master Upholsterers & Soft Furnishers Ltd, Francis Vaughan House, 102a Commercial Street, Newport, S. Wales NP20 1LU. T:01633 215454. Has a list of over 700 approved members throughout the country who specialise in all forms of upholstery including curtains and soft furnishings. Names of those operating in your area can be obtained from the Chief Executive.

The British Wood Preserving and Damp-Proofing Association (BWPDA), 1 Gleneagles House, Vernon Gate, South Street, Derby DE1 1UP. T:01332 225100. The Association has over 220 remedial treatment member companies throughout the UK and will advise on anything to do with wood preservation and damp-proofing in the home.

The Building Centre, 26 Store Street, London WC1E 7BT. T:020 7692 4000. Helpline (premium rate): 09065 161136. The Centre has displays of building products, heating appliances, kitchen layouts and other exhibits and can give information about building problems. It has manufacturers' lists and other free literature you can take away and there is also a well-stocked bookshop covering all aspects of building and home improvement. Open Monday to Friday, 9.30 a.m. to 6 p.m.; Saturday, 10 a.m. to 4 p.m.

Federation of Master Builders (FMB), Gordon Fisher House, 14–15 Great James Street, London WC1N 3DP. T:020 7242 7583. Lists of members are available from regional offices. A Warranty Scheme, which insures work in progress and gives up to ten years' guarantee on completion of work, is available from some of its members.

Guild of Master Craftsmen, Castle Place, 166 High Street, Lewes, East Sussex BN7 1XU. T:01273 478449. Can supply names of all types of specialist craftsmen including, for example, carpenters, joiners, ceramic workers and restorers.

Institute of Plumbing, 64 Station Lane, Hornchurch, Essex RM12 6NB. T:01708 472791. Can provide a list of professional plumbers; sae appreciated.

APHC (Association of Plumbing & Heating Contractors), 14–15 Ensign Business Centre, Westwood Way, Coventry CV4 8JA. T:024 7647 0626. Maintains a national register of licensed members who offer a 2-year guarantee against defective workmanship.

The Scottish and Northern Ireland Plumbing Employers' Federation (SNIPEF), 2 Walker Street, Edinburgh EH3 7LB. T:0131 225 2255. SNIPEF is the national trade association for all types of firms involved in plumbing and domestic heating in Scotland and Northern Ireland. It has almost 1,000 member firms and operates a Code of Fair Trading and Guarantee of Work Scheme. Lists of local members are available on request.

Royal Institute of British Architects, 66 Portland Place, London W1B 1AD. T:020 7580 5533. The RIBA has a free Clients' Service which, however small your building project, will recommend up to three suitable architects. It can also supply you with useful leaflets giving advice on working with an architect.

Royal Institution of Chartered Surveyors, The RICS Customer Services Department, Surveyor Court, Westwood Way, Coventry CV4 8JE. T:0870 333 1600. The RICS will nominate qualified surveyors in your area who can be recognised by the initials MRICS or FRICS after their name. It also publishes a number of useful leaflets.

Useful reading

Older Home Owners – Financial Help With Repairs and Adaptations, free factsheet from Age Concern, Freepost (SWB 30375), Ashburton, Devon TQ13 7ZZ. A separate Scottish version is available.

Home improvement agencies

Home Improvement Agencies (sometimes known as Staying Put or Care & Repair agencies) work with older or disabled people to help them remain in their own homes by providing advice and assistance on repairs, improvements and adaptations. They also advise on the availability of funding and welfare benefits, obtain prices, recommend reliable builders and inspect the completed job. Your Citizen's Advice Bureau should know about local schemes. Or you could contact Anchor Trust which has 'Staying Put' agencies across England: **Anchor Trust**, Anchor Staying Put, Burnbank House, Balliol Business Park, Benton Lane, Longbenton, Newcastle Upon Tyne NE12 8EW. T: 0191 270 6067.

Safety in the home

Accidents in the home account for 40 per cent of all fatal accidents, resulting in nearly 5,000 deaths a year. Seventy per cent of these victims are over retirement age and nearly 80 per cent of deaths are caused by falls. A further 3 million people need medical treatment. The vast majority of accidents are caused by carelessness or by obvious danger spots in the home that for the most part could very easily be made safer. Tragically, it is all too often the little things that we keep meaning to attend to but never quite get round to doing that prove fatal.

Steps and stairs should be well lit with light switches at both the top and bottom. Frayed carpet is notoriously easy to trip on and, on staircases especially, should be repaired or replaced as soon as possible. All stairs should have a hand rail along the wall to provide extra support – and on both sides, if the stairs are very steep. It is also a good idea to have a white line painted on the edge of steps that are difficult to see – for instance in the garden or leading up to the front door.

It is perhaps stating the obvious to say that climbing on chairs and tables is dangerous – and yet we all do this. You should keep proper steps, preferably with a hand rail, to do high jobs in the house such as hanging curtains or reaching cupboards.

Floors can be another danger zone. Rugs and mats can slip on polished floors and should always be laid on some form of non-slip backing material. Stockinged feet are slippery on all but carpeted floors and new shoes should always have the soles scratched before you wear them. Remember also that spilt water or talcum powder on tiled or linoleum floors is a number one cause of accidents.

The **bathroom** is particularly hazardous for falls. Sensible precautionary measures include using a suction-type bath mat and putting handrails on the bath or alongside the shower. For older people who have difficulty in getting in and out of the bath, a bath seat can be helpful. Soap on a rope is safer in a shower, as it is less likely to slither out of your hands and make the floor slippery.

Regardless of age, you should make sure that all medicines are clearly labelled and throw away any prescribed drugs left over from a previous illness.

Fires can all too easily start in the home. If you have an open fire, you should always use a fireguard and sparkguard at night. The chimney should be regularly swept at least once a year and maybe more if you have a wood burning stove. Never place a clothes horse near an open fire or heater and be careful of inflammable objects that could fall from the mantelpiece.

Upholstered furniture is a particular fire hazard, especially when polyurethane foam has been used in its manufacture. If buying new furniture, make sure that it carries a red triangle label, indicating that it is resistant to smouldering cigarettes. Furniture which also passes the match ignition test carries a green label. Since March 1989, the use of polyurethane foam in furniture manufacture has been banned and 'combustion modified foam' which has passed the BS 5852 test now has to be used instead.

Portable heaters should be kept away from furniture and curtains and positioned where you cannot trip over them. Paraffin heaters should be handled particularly carefully and should never be filled while alight. Avoid leaving paraffin where it will be exposed to heat, including sunlight. If possible, it should be kept in a metal container outside the house.

Gas appliances should be regularly serviced by British Gas or other CORGI-registered installers. You should also ensure that there is adequate ventilation when using heaters. Never block up air vents: carbon monoxide fumes can kill.

British Gas publishes a free leaflet *Carbon Monoxide Awareness* which includes advice on how to recognise danger signs as well as how to use your gas appliances safely and effectively. A free safety check on gas appliances is available to any British Gas customer living alone who is over the age of 60 or registered disabled; or living with other people where everyone, like themselves, is either over 60 or registered disabled. If additional work needs to be done, you will receive an estimate and may be able to get help with the cost through your social security office or social services department. If you think you might qualify, you must get official approval before any work is started. You can arrange a check by contacting British Gas (the telephone number will be on your last bill or see telephone directory under 'Gas').

If you smell gas or notice anything you suspect could be dangerous, stop using the appliance immediately, open the doors and windows and call the Transco 24-hour emergency line on T:0800 111 999.

More than one in three fires in the home are due to accidents with **cookers**. Chip pans are a particular hazard: only fill the pan one-third full with oil and always dry the chips before putting them in the fat. Or better still, use oven-ready chips which you just pop into the oven to cook. Pan handles should be turned away from the heat and positioned so you cannot knock them off the stove. If called to the door or telephone, always take the pan off the ring and turn off the heat before you leave the kitchen.

Cigarettes left smouldering in an ashtray could be dangerous if the ashtray is full. Smoking in bed is a potential killer!

Faulty electric wiring is another frequent cause of fires, as are overloaded power points. The wiring in your home should be checked every five years and you should avoid using too many appliances off a single plug. Ask an electrician's advice what is the maximum safe number. Only use plugs that conform to the British Standard 1363 and it is a good idea to get into the habit of pulling the plug out of the wall socket when you have finished using an appliance, whether TV or toaster. All electrical equipment should be regularly checked for wear and tear and frayed or damaged flexes immediately replaced.

Wherever possible, have electric sockets moved to waist height to avoid unnecessary bending whenever you want to turn on the switch.

In particular, **electric blankets** should be routinely overhauled and checked in accordance with the manufacturer's instructions. It is dangerous to use both a hot water bottle and electric blanket – and never use an underblanket as an overblanket.

Electrical appliances are an increasing feature of labour-saving **gardening** but can be dangerous unless treated with respect. They should never be used when it is raining. Moreover, gardeners should always wear rubber soled shoes or boots and avoid floppy clothing that could get caught in the equipment.

As a general precaution, keep **fire extinguishers** handy and make sure they are maintained in working order. Small hand-held portable extinguishers are now available and easier to use but are only suitable for very small fires. All fire extinguishers above 1 kilo/1 litre need to conform to BS EN3; those made before 1996 should conform to BS 5423. Small hand-held aerosol extinguishers should conform to BS 6165. Many insurance companies now recommend that you install a smoke alarm as an effective and cheap early warning device. Prices start from about £5.

Useful reading

Keep Safe: ideas for older people and those with disabilities, a free booklet produced jointly by the Royal Society for the Prevention of Accidents (ROSPA) and Care & Repair; available from DTI Consumer Publications, Admail 528, London SW1W 8YT.

Safety in Your Home, Fire, Keep Out the Cold and *Security in Your Home*, free from the Information Department, Help the Aged, 207–221 Pentonville Road, London N1 9UZ.

Home security

Nine out of ten burglaries are spontaneous and take less than 10 minutes. However, there is much you can do to protect yourself. The Crime Prevention Officer at your local police station will advise you how to improve your security arrangements and will also tell you whether there is a Neighbourhood Watch Scheme and how you join it. This is a free service which the police are happy to provide.

The most vulnerable access points are doors and windows. Simple precautions such as fitting adequate locks and bolts can do much to deter the average burglar. Prices for a good door lock are about £55 to £80 plus VAT; and prices for window locks, about £12-£15 plus VAT, per window.

Doors should have secure bolts or a five-lever deadlock strengthened by metal plates on both sides, a door chain and a spyhole in the front door. Additionally, you might consider outside lights (ideally with infra-red sensor) to illuminate night-time visitors and an entry phone system requiring a caller to identify himself before you open the door.

Windows should also be properly secured with key-operated locks. Best advice is to fit locks to secure them when partially open. Install rack bolts or surface-mounted security pressbolts on french windows and draw your curtains at night, so potential intruders cannot see in. Louvre windows are especially vulnerable because the slats can easily be removed. A solution is to glue them in place with an epoxy resin and to fit a special louvre lock. An agile thief can get through any space larger than a human head, so even small windows such as skylights need properly fitted locks. Both double glazing and venetian blinds act as a further deterrent. If you are particularly worried, you could also have bars fitted to the windows or install old-fashioned internal shutters which can be closed at night. Alternatively, many DIY shops sell decorative wrought iron security grilles.

An obvious point is to ensure that the house is securely locked whenever you go out, even for five minutes. Insist that official callers such as meter men show their identity cards before you allow them inside. If you are going away, even for only a couple of days, remember to cancel the milk and the newspapers.

You might also like to take advantage of the Royal Mail's **Keepsafe** service. It will store your mail while you are away and so avoid it piling up and alerting potential burglars to your absence. There is a charge for the service which varies from £5.25 for up to two weeks to £15.75 for two months. A week's notice is necessary: application forms are obtainable from the post office or by calling the Royal Mail Enquiry Line on T:08457 740740 (all calls are charged at local rate).

If your home will be unoccupied for any length of time, it would be sensible to ask the local police to put it on their unattended-premises register. Finally, consider a time switch (cost around £15) which will turn the lights on and off when you are away and can be used to switch on the heating before your return.

If you want to know of a reputable locksmith, you should contact the Master Locksmiths Association who can either give you the name of an approved locksmith in your area over the telephone or will send you a list of their members, classified county by county. Their address is: **Master Locksmiths Association**, 5d Great Central Way, Woodford Halse, Daventry, Northants NN11 3PZ. Freephone: 0800 783 1498.

The Home Office issues a couple of useful booklets, *Your Practical Guide to Crime Prevention* and *Beat the Burglar*. Available free from your local police station or telephone T:0870 241 4680.

Burglar alarms and safes

More elaborate precautions such as a burglar alarm are one of the best ways of protecting your home. Although expensive – alarms cost from about £350 to well in excess of £1,000 for sophisticated systems – they could be worth every penny if, in the event of a break-in, you need to summon help or want the police to do what they can if you are away.

Many insurance companies will recommend suitable contractors to install burglar alarm equipment. Alternatively, contact: **NACOSS**, Queensgate House, 14 Cookham Road, Maidenhead, Berks SL6 8AJ, T:0870 205 0000; it will send a free list of their approved contractors in your locality who install burglar alarm systems to, among other, British Standard 4737. There are 700 recognised firms and some 1,000 branches. NACOSS will also investigate technical complaints.

If you keep valuables or money in the house, you should think about buying a concealed wall or floor safe. If you are going away, it is a good idea to inform your neighbours so that if your alarm goes off they will know something is wrong. Burglar alarms have an unfortunate habit of ringing for no reason (a mouse can trigger the mechanism) and many people ignore them as a result. It is advisable to give your neighbours a key so that they can turn off and reset the alarm should the occasion arise.

Insurance discounts

According to recent research seven out of ten householders are under-insured, some of them unknowingly but some intentionally to keep premiums lower. This could be dangerous because in the event of a mishap they could end up seriously out of pocket.

With recent increases in premiums, many readers may feel that this is hardly the moment to be discussing any reassessment of their policy. However, there are two good reasons why this could be sensible: firstly, because the number of burglaries has risen, so the risks are greater; but more particularly, because you may be able to obtain better value than you are getting at present. As you may know, a number of insurance companies now give discounts on house contents premiums if proper security precautions have been installed. These include: Cornhill Direct, Avon, Royal Sun Alliance and Direct Line.

Some insurance companies approach the problem differently and arrange discounts for their policyholders with manufacturers of security devices.

If you would welcome independent advice on choosing a policy, you might usefully contact the Institute of Insurance Brokers for details of local IIB brokers. Write to: **Institute of Insurance Brokers**, Higham Business Centre, Midland Road, Higham Ferrers, Northants NN10 8DW. T:01933 410003.

See also section headed 'Insurance' a little further along.

Personal safety

Older people who live on their own can be particularly at risk. A number of personal alarms are now available which are highly effective and can generally ease your peace of mind.

A sensible precaution is to carry a 'screamer alarm', sometimes known as a 'personal attack button'. These are readily available in department stores, electrical shops and alarm companies.

Age Concern Aid-Call provides a service which enables anyone living alone to call for help simply by pressing a button. The subscriber wears a small radio transmitter, worn as a pendant, which contacts a 24-hour monitoring centre. The centre alerts a list of nominated relatives and friends, or the emergency services, that something is wrong. There are two ways of paying for Aid-Call: option one consists of an installation and commissioning charge of £99 and a quarterly rental and monitoring charge of £37.05; option two, an installation and commissioning charge of £349 and a yearly rental and monitoring charge of £57.20. The firm operates a nationwide service and will arrange a demonstration through its head office. For a brochure, contact: **Age Concern Aid-Call**, Freepost (EX2356), Newton Abbott, Devon TQ13 7BR. Freephone: 0800 772266.

A telephone can also increase your sense of security. Some families come to an arrangement whereby they ring their older relatives at regular times to check that all is well.

Older people feel particularly vulnerable to mugging. While the dangers are often exaggerated, it must be sensible to take all normal precautions. The police are of the view that many muggings could be avoided if you are alert, think ahead and try to radiate confidence. In particular, don't hesitate to cross the street if you see a group of thugs ahead and, if you are followed, don't lead them to your home.

Insurance

As you near retirement, it is sensible to reassess your building and home contents policy. If the insurance was originally arranged through your building society it may cease when your mortgage is paid off, in which case it will be essential for you to arrange new cover direct. Similarly, when buying for cash – for instance when moving to a smaller house – it will be up to you to organise the insurance and to calculate the rebuilding value of your home. It is advisable to get a qualified valuer to do this for you.

Over the last twenty years the value of your home may have doubled or more and the chances are that the cost of replacing the fabric of your house, were it to burn down, would be significantly greater than the amount for which it is currently insured. Remember – you must insure for the full rebuilding cost: market value may be inadequate. Your policy should also provide money to meet architects' or surveyors' fees as well as alternative accommodation for you and your family if your home were completely destroyed.

If you are planning to move into accommodation which has been converted from one large house into several flats or maisonettes, check with the landlord or managing agent that the insurance on the structure of the total building is adequate. All too many people have found themselves homeless because each tenant only insured their own flat and the collective policies were not sufficient to replace the common parts.

If when buying a new property you decide to take out a new mortgage, contrary to what many people believe, you are under no obligation to insure your home with the particular company suggested by your building society – although this is not to recommend that you necessarily go elsewhere. The point is that, as with all insurance, policies vary and some are more competitive than others.

Many people are woefully under-insured with regard to the contents of their home. Insurance that simply covers the purchase price is normally grossly insufficient. Instead, you should assess their replacement cost and make sure you have a 'new for old' or 'replacement as new' policy.

Most insurance companies offer an automatic inflation proofing option for both building and contents policies. While it is obviously prudent to take advantage of this, many people unthinkingly sign on the dotted line quite forgetting to cancel items such as furniture or jewellery which they may have given away or sold – and so lumber themselves with higher charges than necessary. Equally, many forget to add new valuables they have bought or received as presents. In particular, do check that you are adequately covered for any home improvements you may have added such as an American style kitchen, new garage, conservatory, extra bathroom, swimming pool or other luxury.

Where antiques and jewellery are concerned, simple inflation proofing may not be enough. Values can rise and fall disproportionately to inflation and depend on current market trends. For a professional valuation, contact either **The British Antique Dealers' Association**, 20 Rutland Gate, London SW7 1BD, T:020 7589 4128; or

LAPADA, The Association of Art and Antique Dealers, 535 King's Road, London SW10 0SZ. T:020 7823 3511, for the name of a specialist.

Photographs of particularly valuable antiques can help in the assessment of premiums and settlement of claims as well as giving the police a greater chance of recovering the items in the case of theft. Property marking, for example with an ultra-violet marker, is another useful ploy as it will help the police trace your possessions should any be stolen.

People with disabilities often experience difficulty in obtaining suitable home insurance. An organisation that offers policies to meet the needs of people with all types of disability on a non-discriminatory basis and that also acts for over 5,000 UK charities is **MCIS Ltd.**, Church Court, Cox Street, St. Paul's Square, Birmingham B3 1RD. T:0121 233 2722.

The **Association of British Insurers**, 51 Gresham Street, London EC2V 7HQ, T:020 7600 3333, will send you information sheets on various aspects of household insurance and loss prevention including *Buildings Insurance for Home Owners* and *Home Contents Insurance* which describe what policies you need and advise on how to ensure you have the correct amount of cover.

The **British Insurance Brokers Association**, BIBA House, 14 Bevis Marks, London EC3A 7NT, T:020 7623 9043, can send you a list of registered insurance brokers in your area.

Some insurance companies offer home and contents policies for older people (age 50 and over) at substantially reduced rates. The rationale behind such schemes is that older people are less likely to leave their homes empty on a regular basis (i.e. 9 to 5) and are therefore less liable to be burgled. In some cases also, policies are geared to the fact that many retired people have either sold or given away many of their more valuable possessions and therefore only need to insure their homes up to a relatively low sum.

Such policies are arranged through: **Age Concern Insurance Services**, Freepost NWW 4865A, Lowthian House, Market Street, Preston, Lancs PR1 2ZZ. T:0845 606 5075; **Saga Services Ltd.**, The Saga Building, Middelburg Square, Folkestone, Kent CT20 1AZ. T:0800 414525; **Hill House Hammond Ltd.**, Freepost BS1162, Branch No 1, Hill House, Lewins Mead, Bristol BS1 2LL, T:0800 096 5855; **50plus Insurance Services**, Summit House, Glebe Way, West Wickham, Kent BR4 0RB. Freephone: 0800 195 6888; and through **Help the Aged Insurance Services**, T:0800 413180.

An increasing number of insurance companies, including Avon and Legal and General, offer generous no claims discounts. Another type of discount-linked policy that is becoming more popular is one that carries an excess, whereby the householder pays the first chunk of any claim – say, the first £100 or £250. Savings on premiums can be quite appreciable, so it is certainly worth asking your insurance company what terms they offer. If these are not very attractive, it could pay you to shop around for a better deal.

Raising money on your home

The problem for many retired people is that they are 'asset rich, cash poor', with their main asset being their home. As a result, many retired owner-occupiers have substantial amounts of money tied up in their homes while they struggle to make ends meet on reduced incomes.

One way round the dilemma is to sell up and move somewhere smaller in order to provide extra income. For those who prefer to stay put, however, there are a number of schemes that enable people to unlock capital without having to move. Generally known as home income or equity release plans, these usually fall into one of three categories: Reversion Schemes, Home Income Plans and Roll Up Loans.

While all have their attractions, no such scheme is without its drawbacks, so it is essential to make sure that you fully understand all the financial implications – including how the plan might affect your estate – before entering into any agreement.

A crucial point to check is that any plan you are considering carries an absolute guarantee of your being able to remain in your home for as long as you need or want to do so. In the past, many elderly people tragically lost their homes as a result of ill-advised and dangerous schemes. And while today it is extremely unlikely that you would be offered a high-risk plan (as most have now been banned by the regulators), where your home is concerned you cannot afford to take any chances.

In a welcome move to establish best practice and to give individuals greater protection, nine leading providers – Allchurches Life, BPT Bridgewater (Home Reversions) Ltd., Hodge Equity Release, Home & Capital Trust, Key Retirement Solutions, Northern Rock, Norwich Union, AMP Retirement Services and Legal & General Bank – have become a self-regulatory group, known as **SHIP (Safe Home Income Plans)**. All abide by a code of conduct and undertake to give a full and fair presentation of any plan offered, including what costs are involved and how the plan would affect the value of the person's estate. As a further safeguard, they will not finalise an arrangement without a certificate signed by the applicant's solicitor, confirming that they have fully explained the terms of the contract to their client.

SHIP advises that before signing anything, you seek clarification on any of the following points that are not already crystal clear:

- how the value of your estate would be affected
- what this could mean in terms of loss to your heirs
- whether the value of any plan benefits could be eroded by inflation
- how the rise or fall in property prices could affect you
- the setting up costs and/or other arrangement charges
- whether your state of health affects the plan in any way
- the position should you want to move
- whether the extra money would make sufficient difference to justify proceeding with the scheme

Though not essential, SHIP suggests that before finally committing yourself, it could be sensible to discuss the idea with close family.

Home reversion schemes

Home reversion schemes work as follows. You sell the ownership of all or part of your home to the reversion company for an agreed sum of money and additionally retain the right to live in the property for the rest of your life or until the plan comes to an end due to the need for long term care. You will not be charged any interest payments and normally the setting up costs are fairly low. However, the downside is that the money you receive from the sale will be substantially less than the current market value of your home, as the price paid reflects the fact that it could be a great many years before the reversion company can realise their investment. The longer you live, the more value you will get from the scheme. If your life expectancy is not that great, a particular point to query is whether there are any benefit guarantees in the event of early death.

Home reversion plans are offered by:

Hodge Equity Release, 30 Windsor Place, Cardiff CF10 3UR. Freephone: 0800 731 4076.

Home & Capital Trust Ltd., 31 Goldington Road, Bedford MK40 3LH. T:0800 253 657.

AMP Retirement Services, 30–36 Newport Road, Cardiff CF24 0DE. T:0800 707580.

BPT Bridgewater (Home Reversions) Ltd., Kings Lodge, 28 Church Street, Epsom KT17 4QB. T:01372 742741.

Key Retirement Solutions Ltd., Harbour House, Portway, Preston, Lancs PR2 2PR. T:0800 064 7075.

Home income plans

Home income plans work on the basis of a mortgage arrangement whereby the loan is used to purchase an annuity to provide a guaranteed income for life. The mortgage interest is fixed and is deducted from the annuity payment before you receive your share. While popular at one time, such plans have largely fallen out of favour due to the abolition of mortgage interest relief and worsening annuity rates. While still available, the view from SHIP is that few people would derive much value and that they should really only be considered by those well into their mid 80s. Home income plans are offered by just the one SHIP company:

Allchurches Life Assurance Ltd., Beaufort House, Brunswick Road, Gloucester GL1 1JZ. T:01452 334972.

Roll-up loans

Roll-up loans advance you a sum of money or regular income on which you pay no interest during your lifetime. Instead, the interest payments are added to the original loan at compound rates and are repaid from your estate on death. While attractive in that the recipient can spend the money safe in the knowledge that they will not have to make any repayments, the disadvantage is that compound interest can very quickly mount up leaving little or nothing for their heirs to inherit.

To reduce the risk, particular points to check are, firstly, that the interest is fixed rather than variable and, even more important, that the plan includes a guarantee (as all SHIP company plans do) that there is no danger to your estate of negative equity. Roll-up loans are offered by:

Norwich Union Equity Release Ltd., 2 Rougier Street, York YO90 1UU. T:0845 300 1622.

Northern Rock Plc., Northern Rock House, Gosforth, Newcastle-upon-Tyne NE3 4PL. T:0845 600 2220.

Hodge Equity Release, 30 Windsor Place, Cardiff CF10 3UR. Freephone: 0800 731 4076.

Legal & General Bank Ltd., Brunel House, Fitzalan Road, Cardiff CF24 0WJ. T: 0870 0100 338

Cashing in on the value of your home, while continuing to live there for the remainder of your life, has attractive advantages especially if the priority is to generate additional income or to provide you with a lump sum. However, despite the existence of SHIP and its stringent code of conduct, expert advice is essential. SHIP recommends that in addition to a discussion with a solicitor – which is an obligatory condition of sale for all SHIP companies before finalising a plan on a client's behalf – you should also consult an independent financial adviser (IFA) with expertise in equity release schemes.

For further information, contact specialist advisers **Hinton & Wild (Home Plans) Ltd.**, 1st Floor, Parker Court, Knapp Lane, Cheltenham GL50 3QJ. Freephone: 0800 328 8432.

Useful reading

Extra Capital and Income for Older Home Owners and *Safe Home Income Plans* leaflet*: Everything You Need to Know Before You Take Out a Plan*, free from Hinton & Wild (Home Plans) Ltd.

Raising Income or Capital from Your Home, free factsheet from Age Concern, Freepost (SWB 30375), Ashburton, Devon TQ13 7ZZ; or telephone free 0800 009966.

Letting rooms in your home

Rather than move, many people whose home has become too large are tempted by the idea of taking in tenants. For some, it is an ideal plan; for others, a disaster. At best, it could provide you with extra income and the possibility of pleasant company. At worst, you could be involved in a lengthy legal battle to regain possession of your property. Before either rushing off to put a card in the newsagent's window or rejecting the idea out of hand, it is helpful to understand the different options together with your various rights and responsibilities.

There are three broad choices: taking in paying guests or lodgers; letting part of your home as self-contained accommodation; or renting the whole house for a specified period of time. In all cases for your own protection it is essential to have a written agreement and to take up bank references, unless the let is a strictly temporary one where the money is paid in advance. Otherwise, rent should be collected quarterly and you should arrange a hefty deposit to cover any damage.

In a move to encourage more people to let out rooms in their home, the government allows you to earn up to £4,250 a year free of tax. Any excess rental income you receive over £4,250 will be assessed for tax in the normal way. For further information, see Inland Revenue booklet IR 87 *Letting and Your Home*, available from any tax office.

Finally, if you have a mortgage or are a tenant yourself (even with a very long lease), check with your building society or landlord that you are entitled to sublet.

Paying guests or lodgers. This is the most informal arrangement and will normally be either a casual holiday-type bed and breakfast let or a lodger who might be with you for a couple of years.

In either case, the visitor would be sharing part of your home, the accommodation would be fully furnished and you would be providing at least one full meal a day and possibly also basic cleaning services.

There are few legal formalities involved in these types of lettings and rent is entirely a matter for friendly agreement. As a resident owner you are also in a very strong position if you want your lodger to leave. Lodging arrangements can easily be ended, as your lodger has no legal rights to stay after the agreed period.

A wise precaution would be to check with your insurance company that your home contents policy would not be affected, since some insurers restrict cover to households with lodgers. Also, unless you make arrangements to the contrary, you should inform your lodger that his or her possessions are not covered by your policy.

N.B. If, as opposed to a lodger or the occasional summer paying guest, you offer regular B&B accommodation you could be liable to pay business rates. Although not new, it appears that in recent years the Valuation Office Agency has been enforcing the regulation more strictly against people running B&B establishments.

Holiday lets. It is a good idea to register with your Tourist Information Centre and to contact the Environmental Health Office at your local council for any help and advice.

Useful reading

Want to Rent A Room?, housing leaflet available from local libraries, Housing Advice Centres and Citizens' Advice Bureaux.

Letting Residential Property: A Practical Guide by Frances M Way, published by Kogan Page, £8.99.

Letting part of your home

You could convert a basement or part of your house as a self-contained flat and let this either furnished or unfurnished. Alternatively, you could let a single room or rooms.

As a general rule, provided you continue to live in the house your tenant/s would have little security of tenure and equally would not have the right to appeal against the rent. Whether you are letting part of the house as a flat, or simply a room to a lodger, you would be advised to check your home contents policy with your insurance company. For more details, see housing booklet *Letting Rooms in Your Home – A Guide for Residential Landlords.*

As a resident landlord, you have a guaranteed right to repossession of your property. If the letting was for a fixed term (e.g. six months or a year), the tenancy will automatically cease at the end of the fixed period. If the arrangement was on a more ad hoc basis with no specified leaving date, it may be legally necessary to give at least four weeks' notice in writing. The position over notices to quit will vary according to circumstances. For further information, see housing booklet *Notice That You Must Leave*. Should you encounter any difficulties, it is possible that you may need to apply to the courts for an eviction order.

Tax note. If you subsequently sell your home, you may not be able to claim exemption from capital gains tax on the increase in value of a flat if it is entirely self-contained. It is therefore a good idea to retain some means of access to the main house or flat, but take legal advice as to what will qualify.

Renting out your home on a temporary basis

If you are thinking of spending the winter in the sun or are considering buying a retirement home which you will not occupy for a year or two, you might be tempted by the idea of letting the whole house. In spite of the changes in the 1996 Housing Act, there are plenty of true horror stories of owners who cannot regain possession of their own property when they wish to return.

For your protection, you need to understand the assured shorthold tenancy rules. Unless notified in advance that you need the property back sooner (there are very few grounds on which you can make this notification) or unless earlier possession is sought because of the tenant's behaviour, your tenant would have the right to stay for at least six months and must be given two months' notice before you want the tenancy to end.

It is strongly advisable to ask a solicitor or letting agent to help you draw up the agreement. Although this provides for greater protection, you will probably still require a court possession order if your tenant will not leave after you have given the required amount of notice. The accelerated possession procedure may help in some cases to speed up the process.

In most circumstances, by far the safest solution if possible is to let your property to a company rather than to private individuals, since company tenants do not have the same security of tenure. However, it is important that the contract should make clear that your let is for residential, not business, purposes. Before entering into any agreement, you might find it useful to obtain a copy of booklet *Assured and Assured Shorthold Tenancies: a Guide for Landlords*, available from your local housing department; or from ODPM Free Literature, PO Box 236, Wetherby, West Yorkshire LS23 7NB. T:0870 122 6236. (N.B. The leaflet is about letting to individuals – not companies.)

Holiday lets

Buying a future retirement home in the country and renting it out as a holiday home in the summer months is another option worth considering. As well as providing you with a weekend cottage at other times of the year and the chance to establish yourself and make friends in the area, it can also prove a useful and profitable investment.

As long as certain conditions are met, income from furnished holiday lettings enjoys most – but not all – of the benefits that there would be if it were taxed as trading income rather than as investment income. In practical terms, this means that you can claim 25 per cent written down capital allowances on such items as carpets, curtains and furniture as well as fixtures and fittings, thereby reducing the initial cost of equipping the house. Or alternatively, you can claim an annual 10 per cent wear and tear allowance.

Running expenses of a holiday home, including maintenance, advertising, insurance cover and council tax (or business rates, see below) are all largely allowable for tax, excluding that element that relates to your own occupation of the property.

With the advent of independent taxation, it would be sensible for a married couple to consider whether the property should be held in the husband's name, the wife's name – or owned jointly. A solicitor or accountant would be able to advise you.

To qualify as furnished holiday accommodation, the property must be situated in the UK, be let on a commercial basis and be available for holiday letting for at least 140 days during the tax year and be actually let for at least 70 days. Moreover, for at least seven months a year, not necessarily continuous, the property must not normally be occupied by the same tenant for more than 31 consecutive days. This still leaves you with plenty of time to enjoy the property yourself as well.

The usual word of warning, however: there is always the danger that you might create an assured tenancy, so do take professional advice on drawing up the letting agreement. Similarly, if you decide to use one of the holiday rental agents to market your property, get a solicitor to check any contract you enter into with the company. The **Royal Institution of Chartered Surveyors**, 12 Great George Street, Parliament Square, London SW1P 3AD, T:0870 333 1600, has a useful set of guidelines for managing agents called *Code of Practice for Management of Residential Property*.

A further point to note is that tax inspectors are taking a tougher line as to what is 'commercial' and that loss-making ventures are being threatened with withdrawal of their tax advantages. To safeguard yourself, it is important to draw up a broad business plan before you start and to make a real effort to satisfy the minimum letting requirements.

Finally, property that is rented 'commercially' (i.e. 140 days or more a year) is normally liable for business rates, instead of the council tax you would otherwise pay. This could be more expensive, even though partially allowable against tax.

Useful reading

Housing Booklets, *Letting Rooms in Your Home* and *Notice That You Must Leave*. Available from local authority Housing Departments or ODPM Free Literature, T:0870 122 6236.

Housing benefit

Provided you have no more than £16,000 in savings, you may be able to get help with your rent from your local council. You may qualify for housing benefit whether you are a council or private tenant or live in a hotel or hostel.

Housing benefit is fairly complicated. The following outline is intended only as a very general guide. For more detailed advice about your own particular circumstances, contact your local authority; or your Citizens' Advice Bureau or Age Concern group.

The amount of benefit you get depends on five factors: the number of people in your household; your eligible rent (up to a prescribed maximum); your capital or savings; your income; and your 'applicable amount', which is the amount of money the government considers you need for basic living expenses. These are defined roughly as follows:

Eligible rent. This includes rent and some service charges related to the accommodation but excludes meals, water rates and, as a rule, fuel costs. An amount will generally also be deducted for any adult 'non dependant' (including an elderly relative) living in your household, based on a reasonable contribution on their part towards housing costs. This does not apply to commercial boarders or sub-tenants – but any income from a boarder or sub-tenant will be taken into account.

Capital. Any capital or savings up to £3,000 will be disregarded and will not affect your entitlement to benefit. People with savings or capital between £3,000 and £16,000 will receive some benefit but this will be on a sliding scale – with every £250 (or part of £250) over £3,000 assessed as being equivalent to an extra £1 a week of their income. (See para below, starting 'If your income is higher than your applicable amount ...'). This is called 'tariff income'. If you have savings of more than £16,000, you will not be eligible for housing benefit at all. 'Capital' generally includes all savings, bonds, stocks and shares and property other than your own home and personal possessions. The capital limits are the same for a couple as for a single person.

NB. If a person or their partner is aged 60 or over, any capital or savings of between £6,000 and £16,000 will be assessed on the same sliding scale as described above. Any savings below £6,000 will not affect entitlement to benefit.

Income. Income includes earnings, social security benefits, pension income and any other money you have coming in after tax and national insurance contributions have been paid. While most income counts when calculating your entitlement to housing benefit (N.B. a couple's income is added together), some income may be ignored, for example: all disability living allowance and attendance allowance; the first £5 of earnings (single person), £10 of earnings (couple) or £15 of earnings (if your 'applicable amount' includes a disability premium or carer's premium or, in special cases, the higher pensioner premium); war pensions are also ignored in part.

Applicable amount. Your 'applicable amount' will generally be the same as the amount of income support you would be eligible for and consists of your personal allowance, personal allowances for any younger children (i.e. normally those for whom you are receiving child benefit), plus any premiums (i.e. additional amounts for pensioners, the disabled and so on) to which you might be entitled. As an indication of the amounts involved, a single pensioner would be deemed to need an income of £98.15 a week; a married retired couple, £149.80 (2002/03 rates). Details of allowances and premium rates are contained in leaflet GL23 from any social security office.

If your income is less than your 'applicable amount' you will receive maximum housing benefit towards your eligible rent (less any non-dependant deduction), and you may be eligible for income support if your capital is less than £8,000; or less than £12,000, if aged 60 or over.

If your income is equal to your 'applicable amount' you will also receive maximum housing benefit.

If your income is higher than your 'applicable amount', a taper adjustment will be made and maximum housing benefit will be reduced by 65 per cent of the difference between your income and your 'applicable amount'. If this leaves you with Housing Benefit of less than 50p a week, it is not paid.

How to claim. If you think you are eligible for benefit (see leaflets GL16 and GL17 available from any Housing Benefit office), ask your council for an application form. They should let you know within 14 days of receiving your completed application whether you are entitled to benefit and will inform you of the amount.

Special accommodation. If you live in a mobile home or houseboat, you may be able to claim benefit for site fees or mooring charges. If you live in a private nursing or residential care home you will not normally be able to get housing benefit to help with the cost. However, you may be able to get help towards both the accommodation part of your fees and your living expenses through income support.

If you make a claim for income support you can claim housing benefit and council tax benefit at the same time. A claim form for these is included inside the income support claim form. When completed, the form is returned to your local authority.

Useful reading

Leaflet RR2 *A Guide to Housing Benefit and Council Tax Benefit*, free from your council.

Income Related Benefits: Income and Capital and *Housing Benefit and Council Tax Benefit*, free factsheets from Age Concern, Freepost (SWB 30375), Ashburton, Devon TQ13 7ZZ; or telephone free T:0800 009966.

Council tax

Council tax is based on the value of the dwelling in which you live (the property element) and also consists of a personal element – with discounts/exemptions applying to certain groups of people.

The property element

Most domestic properties are liable for council tax including rented property, mobile homes and house boats.

The value of the property is assessed according to a banding system, with eight different bands (A to H): ranging in England from property valued at up to £40,000 (band A) to property valued at over £320,000 (band H). In Wales, the bands run from up to £30,000 (band A) to over £240,000 (band H). In Scotland, the bands run from up to £27,000 (band A) to over £212,000 (band H).

The valuation of each property to determine in which band it falls is administered by the Inland Revenue Valuation Office. The ascribed value is based on prices applying at 1 April 1991. Small extensions/other improvements made after this date do not affect the valuation until the property changes hands.

New homes are banded as if they had already been built and sold on 1 April 1991, in order to be consistent.

Notification of the band is shown on the bill when it is sent out in April. If you think there has been a misunderstanding about the valuation (or your liability to pay the full amount) you may have the right of appeal (see 'Appeals' further along).

Liability

Not everyone pays council tax. The bill is normally sent to the resident owner, or joint owners, of the property; or in the case of rented accommodation, to the tenant or joint tenants. Married couples and people with a shared legal interest in the property are jointly liable for the bill.

In some cases, for example in hostels or multi-occupied property, a non-resident landlord or owner will be liable but may pass on a share of the bill to the tenants/residents which would probably be included as part of the rental charge.

The personal element

The valuation of each dwelling assumes that two adults will be resident. The charge does not increase if there are more adults. However if, as in many homes, there is a single adult, your council tax bill will be reduced by 25 per cent. Certain people are disregarded when determining the number of residents in a household.

There are also a number of other special discounts, or exemptions, as follows:

- People who are severely mentally impaired are disregarded; or, if they are the sole occupant of the dwelling, qualify for an exemption;
- Disabled people whose homes require adaptation may have their bill reduced to a lower band;

- People on income support should normally have nothing to pay, as their bill will be met in full by council tax benefit;
- Disabled people on higher rate attendance allowance need not count a full-time carer as an additional resident and therefore may continue to qualify for the 25 per cent single (adult) householder discount; exceptions are spouses/partners and parents of a disabled child under 18 who would normally be living with the disabled person and whose presence therefore would not be adding to the council tax;
- Young people over 18 but still at school are not counted when assessing the number of adults in a house;
- Students living in halls of residence, student hostels or similar are exempted; those living with a parent or other non-student adult are eligible for the 25 per cent personal discount;
- Service personnel living in barracks or married quarters will not receive any bill for council tax.

Discounts/exemptions applying to property

Certain property is either exempt from council tax or is eligible for a discount.

Discounts. Empty property (e.g. second homes) normally gets a 50 per cent discount. However, you should check on this, as some local authorities charge the full rate. There are some exceptions – see below – where empty property is exempt.

Exemptions. The most common cases of exemptions include:

- Property which has been unoccupied and unfurnished for less than six months;
- Home of a deceased person: the exemption lasts until six months after the grant of probate;
- Home that is empty because the occupier is absent in order to care for someone else;
- Home of a person who is/would be exempted from council tax due to moving to a residential home, hospital care or similar;
- Empty properties in need of major repairs or undergoing structural alteration can be exempt from council tax for up to 12 months. After 12 months, the standard 50 (or possibly 100) per cent charge for empty properties will apply.
- Granny flats that are part of another private domestic dwelling may be exempt but this depends on access and other conditions. To check, contact your local Valuation Office.

Business-cum-domestic property

Business-cum-domestic property is rated according to usage, with the business section assessed for business rates and the domestic section for council tax. For example, where there is a flat over a shop, the value of the shop would not be included in the valuation for council tax. Likewise, a room in a house used for business purposes would be subject to business rates and not to council tax.

Appeals

If you become the new person responsible for paying the council tax on a property (e.g. because you have recently moved or because someone else paid the tax before) that you feel has been wrongly banded, you have six months to appeal and can request that the valuation be reconsidered. Otherwise, there are only three other circumstances in which you can appeal. These are: (1) if there has been a material increase or reduction in the property's value (2) if you start, or stop, using part of the property for business or the balance between domestic and business use changes (3) if either of the latter two apply and the listing officer has altered the council tax list without giving you a chance to put your side.

If you have grounds for appeal, you should take up the matter with the valuation office (see local telephone directory). If the matter is not resolved, you can then appeal to an independent valuation tribunal. For advice and further information, contact your local Citizens' Advice Bureau.

Useful reading

- *Council Tax: A Guide to Your Bill*
- *Council Tax: A Guide to Valuation, Banding and Appeals*

Obtainable free from any council office or from ODPM Free Literature, PO Box 236, Wetherby, West Yorkshire LS23 7NB.

Council tax benefit. If you cannot afford your council tax because you have a low income, you may be able to obtain council tax benefit. The help is more generous than many people realise. For example, people on income support are entitled to rebates of up to 100 per cent. N.B. New claimants in bands F, G and H are only entitled to rebates up to a limit of the maximum available for property in band E.

Even if you are not receiving any other social security benefit, you may still qualify for some council tax benefit. The amount you get depends on: your income, savings, your personal circumstances, who else lives in your home (in particular whether they would be counted as a 'non-dependant') and on your net council tax bill, i.e. after any deductions which apply to your home. If you are not sure whether your income is low enough to entitle you to council tax benefit, it is worth claiming as you could be pleasantly surprised.

If you disagree with your council's decision, you can ask for this to be looked at again (a revision) or you can appeal to an independent appeal tribunal, administered by the Appeals Service. If you are still dissatisfied, you may apply for leave to appeal to the Social Security Commissioners, but only on a point of law. If you want a revision, you should get on with the matter as soon as possible, as if you delay your request may be out of time.

Apart from Council Tax Benefit for yourself, you may also be able to get help with your council tax if you share your home with someone who is on a low income. This is known as Second Adult Rebate; or Alternative Maximum Council Tax Benefit.

For further information, ask your local council for leaflet GL17 *Help With Your Council Tax*. As well as the English version, this is available in 11 other languages.

Useful organisations

The following should be able to provide general advice about housing and help with housing problems:

- Local authority Housing Departments
- Housing Advice or Housing Aid Centres
- Citizens' Advice Bureaux
- Local authority Social Service Departments if your problem is linked to disability
- Welfare Rights Centres if your problem, for example, concerns a landlord who does not keep the property properly maintained
- Local councillors and MPs

Other organisations that provide a helpful service are:

CHAS, The Catholic Housing Aid Society, 209 Old Marylebone Road, London NW1 5QT. T:020 7723 5928. CHAS serves anyone in acute housing need regardless of race or religion. It provides free information, advice and advocacy on housing, homelessness and welfare benefits issues.

Federation of Private Residents' Associations Ltd., 3rd Floor, Overseas House, 19–23 Ironmonger Row, London EC1V 3QN. T:020 7490 7073. This is a federation of associations of long leaseholders and tenants in private blocks of flats. It advises on setting up residents' associations and provides legal and other advice to its member associations. It issues quarterly newsletters and information sheets, publishes a pack on how to form a tenants'/residents' association (price £10 incl. p&p) and acts as a pressure group seeking to influence legislation regarding leasehold and management of flats in the private sector. FPRA also gives advice on buying the freehold and on management of collectively-owned blocks of flats.

Shelter, The National Campaign for Homeless People, 88 Old Street, London EC1V 9HU. T:020 7505 4699. Shelter provides advice to over 100,000 badly housed and homeless people every year through a national network of housing aid centres and a free 24-hour housing helpline T:0808 800 4444.

Useful reading

The Housing and Planning Year Book. This is published annually in the Longmans Community Information Guide series and will be found in most library reference sections. It lists, among others: all national and local government offices responsible for housing, all national advisory bodies, major house builders, housing associations, professional bodies and trade associations involved with house building. This is an invaluable book for anyone considering the options for retirement housing.

9 Leisure Activities

Whether you are looking forward to devoting more time to an existing interest, resuming an old hobby, studying for a degree or trying your hand at an entirely new pastime, the choice is enormous.

You can do anything from basket-weaving to bridge, archery to amateur dramatics. You can join a music-making group, a Scrabble club, a film society or become a beekeeper. There are any number of historic homes and beautiful gardens to visit, as well as museums, art galleries, abbeys and castles.

Almost every locality now has excellent sports facilities and there is scope for complete novices to take up bowls, golf, badminton, croquet and many others. Similarly, there are dancing and keep-fit classes, railway enthusiasts' clubs and groups devoted to researching their local history. Many of the organisations offer special concessionary rates to people of retirement age, as do a number of theatres and other places of entertainment.

This chapter should be read in conjunction with Chapter 14, Holidays, as many of the organisations listed there – such as the Field Studies Council – could apply equally well here. However to avoid repetition, most are only described once. Those that appear in the Holiday chapter tend in the main either to offer residential courses or would probably involve most people in spending a few days away from home to take advantage of the facilities.

While every effort has been made to ensure that prices are correct, these cannot be guaranteed and those quoted should, therefore, only be taken as a guide rather than gospel. The reason is that most organisations alter their charges from time to time and since there is no set date when this happens, it is impossible to keep track.

In addition to the suggestions contained in this chapter, your library, local authority recreation department and adult education institute will be able to signpost you to other activities in your area.

Given the immense variety of tantalising options on offer, it is perhaps no wonder that many retired people find that they have never been as busy in their lives.

Animals

If you are an animal lover, you will already know about such events as sheep dog trials, gymkhanas and the many wild life sanctuaries around the country. Our list is effectively limited to 'the birds and the bees' with just a couple of extra suggestions for fun.

British Beekeepers' Association, The National Beekeeping Centre, National Agricultural Centre, Stoneleigh, Warwickshire CV8 2LG. T:024 7669 6679. The

Association runs correspondence courses and practical demonstrations and will be glad to put you in touch with one of the 63 local organisations.

Our Dogs, 5 Oxford Road, Station Approach, Manchester M60 1SX. T:0161 237 1272. If you would enjoy showing a dog, the weekly newspaper *Our Dogs* gives details of local shows, rule and registration changes and also news and addresses of Canine and Breed Societies all over the country. There is an *Our Dogs* diary, which contains feeding and other hints, advice about the Kennel Club and much other useful information. For cat lovers, a similar magazine called *Our Cats* is available from the same publisher. Should you wish to receive a complimentary copy of either *Our Dogs* or *Cats*, please write, mentioning the *Good non-Retirement Guide* to Trina Shepherd at the *Our Dogs* address.

Wildfowl & Wetlands Trust (WWT), Slimbridge, Gloucestershire GL2 7BT. T:01453 890333. WWT works to conserve threatened wetland birds and their habitats. In addition to Slimbridge, there are visitor centres in Lancashire, Sussex, Tyne & Wear, Cambridgeshire/Norfolk Border, London, Dumfriesshire, South Wales and Northern Ireland. Membership, which costs £26 (£19 for senior citizens), gives you free entry to all WWT centres plus receipt of the quarterly magazine. Wheelchair access to all centres, grounds and many hides.

See also 'Animals', page 297, in the Voluntary Work chapter.

Adult education

Ever longed to take a degree, learn about computing, study philosophy or do a course in archaeology? Opportunities for education abound with these and scores of other subjects easily available to everyone, regardless of age or previous qualifications.

Adult Education Institutes

There is an Adult Education Institute in most areas of the country. Classes normally start in September and run through the academic year. Many AEIs allow concessionary fees for students over 60.

Choice of subjects is enormous and at one institute alone we counted over 50 options, ranging from Indian history, video production and creative writing to self defence, calligraphy, dressmaking and drama. Ask at your local library for details. Or in London, buy booklet *Floodlight* (£3.95), available from most bookstalls.

National Adult School Organisation (NASO), Riverton, 370 Humberstone Road, Leicester LE5 0SA. T:0116 253 8333. NASO promotes 'Conversation with a Purpose' through friendly discussion groups, meeting at places and times to suit their members. They follow either the NASO Handbook programme, topics of their own choice or a mixture of the two. Social activities and weekend conferences are organised nationally and regionally. Membership costs £11 a year. For information about your local group, write to the General Secretary at the above address.

National Extension College, The Michael Young Centre, Purbeck Road, Cambridge CB2 2HN. T:01223 400350. NEC is a non-profit-making educational trust established to provide high quality home study courses for adults, details of which are listed in their free *Guide to Courses*, available on request. Many of NEC's most able students are retired and are returning to study after many years. There is a choice of over 140 courses including: GCSE and 'A' level studies, IT skills, book-keeping, creative writing, interior and garden design, modern languages and many others. A student adviser can offer guidance on any aspect of your study plans and help you make an appropriate choice. Cost (2002) is £115 upwards depending on which course you select.

Open and Distance Learning Quality Council, 16 Park Crescent, London W1B 1AH. T:020 7612 7090. If you want to study at home by correspondence (or other open and distance learning methods), the Council will give you a list of colleges which teach your chosen subject, plus general advice on open and distance learning courses. Choice of subjects is enormous and, as well as academic and business subjects, includes such options as art, creative writing, graphology, needlework and sailing.

Open University, The Course Information and Advice Centre, PO Box 724, Walton Hall, Milton Keynes MK7 6ZS. T:01908 653231. Why not take a degree or other course through the Open University? Students are all ages – the oldest OU graduate was 92 – the majority of courses require no academic qualifications and there is a vast range of subjects from which to choose.

Courses normally involve a mix of: correspondence work, TV programmes, audio and video cassettes and contact with local tutors; in some cases, access to a computer is required. Some courses have a residential school. You can study at your own speed: on average people take up to six or eight years to acquire a degree. However, there is no long-term commitment and it is quite possible to sign on just for one course.

In addition to its degree studies, the Open University offers courses and study packs in areas of general community and vocational interest. Fees range from under £10 for a study pack up to £775 for a degree level course including the cost of residential school. (Other courses, designed for professional and technical audiences can be considerably more expensive.) Some local authorities will give financial assistance. Individuals who would otherwise find it difficult to pay the fees may be eligible for financial assistance from the Open University. There are also grants available to disabled students, to help with the extra costs of services and facilities needed for study because of their disability.

Television and radio

Both the BBC and Channel 4 are very active on the learning front.

BBC Education, BBC Television Centre, Wood Lane, London W12 7RJ. T:08700 100 222. Details of all educational programmes are available on request. Many have accompanying books as well as audio and video cassettes; there are also an increasing number of websites.

Channel 4 produces many booklets and leaflets in connection with their programmes, on a wide range of topics from history, the arts and sport to health, disability and politics. For a list of publications, write to: **Channel 4 Catalogue**, PO Box 4000, Manchester M60 3LL.

University extra-mural departments

Many universities have a Department of Extra-Mural Studies which arranges courses for adults, sometimes in the evening or during the vacation periods. For example, the University of London runs over 1,000 part-time courses through the Faculty of Continuing Education at Birkbeck, including such subjects as: music, philosophy, social studies and history. Classes meet about once weekly and students are encouraged to do reading and written work. Fees vary according to the length of the course and most offer concessions to those in receipt of State pension or government benefit. Birkbeck also runs one-week residential and non-residential summer schools. For further information, write to: **Birkbeck, University of London**, Faculty of Continuing Education, 26 Russell Square, London WC1B 5DQ. T:020 7631 6601. For other universities, enquire locally.

The Third Age Trust, University of the Third Age National Office, 26 Harrison Street, London WC1H 8JW. T:020 7837 8838. U3A is a self-help movement for people no longer in full-time employment, offering a wide range of educational, creative and leisure activities. It operates through a national network of local U3As, each of which determines its own courses and social programmes according to the interests of its members. There is also a national newspaper *U3A News* which is published three times a year. For a brochure, together with a list of names and addresses of all local U3As, contact the National Office enclosing sae.

Workers' Educational Association, Temple House, 17 Victoria Park Square, Bethnal Green, London E2 9PB. T:020 8983 1515. There are WEA branches in all parts of the country, offering a wide range of adult education courses including education for retirement. There is normally a choice of part-time, day or evening classes. Your library or education authority should be able to put you in touch with your local branch. Alternatively, contact the above address.

Arts

Enjoyment of the arts is certainly no longer confined to London. Whether you are interested in active participation or just appreciating the performance of others, there is an exhilarating choice of events including theatre, music, exhibitions, film-making and so on. Many entertainments offer concessionary prices to retired people.

Regional arts boards

For first-hand information about what is going on in your area, contact your regional arts board (see relevant address below); or in the case of those living in Scotland, Wales and Northern Ireland, the national arts council. Most areas arrange an immensely varied programme with musical events, drama, arts and craft exhibitions and sometimes more unusual functions, offering something of interest to just about everyone. Many regional arts boards produce regular newsletters with details of arts events in their area.

East England Arts, Eden House, 48–49 Bateman Street, Cambridge CB2 1LR. T:01223 454400. For Bedfordshire, Cambridgeshire, Essex, Hertfordshire, Norfolk and Suffolk and the non-metropolitan authorities of Luton, Peterborough, Southend, Thurrock.

East Midlands Arts, Mountfields House, Epinal Way, Loughborough, Leics LE11 0QE. T:01509 218292. For Derbyshire (including High Peak), Leicestershire, Lincolnshire, Northamptonshire and Nottinghamshire; and the unitary authorities of Derby, Leicester, Nottingham, Rutland.

London Arts, 2 Pear Tree Court, London EC1R 0DS. T:020 7608 6100. For Greater London.

Northern Arts, Central Square, Forth Street, Newcastle upon Tyne NE1 3PJ. T:0191 255 8500. For Durham, Northumberland and the metropolitan districts of Newcastle, Gateshead, North Tyneside, Sunderland and South Tyneside; and the non-metropolitan districts of Darlington, Hartlepool, Middlesborough, Redcar and Cleveland, Stockton.

North West Arts, Manchester House, 22 Bridge Street, Manchester M3 3AB. T:0161 834 6644. For Cheshire, Cumbria and Lancashire and the metropolitan districts of Bolton, Bury, Knowsley, Liverpool, Manchester, Oldham, Rochdale, St. Helens, Salford, Sefton, Stockport, Tameside, Trafford, Wigan and Wirral; and the non-metropolitan districts of Blackburn with Darwen, Blackpool, Halton and Warrington.

Southern and South East Arts, Winchester office: 13 St. Clement Street, Winchester, Hampshire SO23 9DQ. T: 01962 855099. Tunbridge Wells office: Union House, Eridge Road, Tunbridge Wells, Kent TN4 8HF. T: 01892 507200. For Bournemouth, Buckinghamshire, East Sussex, Hampshire, Isle of Wight, Kent, Oxfordshire, Surrey and West Sussex; and the non-metropolitan districts of Bracknell Forest, Brighton and Hove, the Medway Towns, Milton Keynes, Portsmouth, Reading, Slough, Southampton, Swindon, West Berkshire, Wiltshire, Windsor and Maidenhead and Wokingham.

From April 2003 Wiltshire, Swindon, Bournemouth, Poole and Christchurch will transfer to South West Arts.

South West Arts, Bradninch Place, Gandy Street, Exeter EX4 3LS. T:01392 218188. For Cornwall, Devon, Dorset (except borough of Christchurch), Gloucestershire and Somerset; and the non-metropolitan districts of Bath and North East Somerset, Bristol, North Somerset, Plymouth, South Gloucestershire, Torbay.

West Midlands Arts, 82 Granville Street, Birmingham B11 2LH. T:0121 631 3121. For the counties of Shropshire, Staffordshire, Warwickshire and Worcestershire; the metropolitan districts of Birmingham, Coventry, Dudley, Sandwell, Solihull, Walsall and Wolverhampton; and the non-metropolitan districts of Herefordshire, Stoke-on-Trent, Telford and Wrekin.

Yorkshire Arts, 21 Bond Street, Dewsbury, West Yorkshire WF13 1AX. T:01924 455555. For North Yorkshire and the metropolitan districts of Barnsley, Bradford, Calderdale, Doncaster, Kirklees, Leeds, Rotherham, Sheffield and Wakefield; and the non-metropolitan districts of East Riding, Kingston-upon-Hull, North East Lincolnshire, North Lincolnshire, York.

National arts councils

Arts Council of England, 14 Great Peter Street, London SW1P 3NQ. T:020 7973 6517.

Scottish Arts Council, 12 Manor Place, Edinburgh EH3 7DD. T:0131 226 6051.

Arts Council of Wales, 9 Museum Place, Cardiff CF10 3NX. T:029 2037 6500.

Arts Council of Northern Ireland, MacNiece House, 77 Malone Road, Belfast BT9 6AQ. T:028 9038 5200.

For those who wish to join in amateur arts activities, public libraries keep lists of choirs, drama clubs, painting clubs and similar activities in their locality.

Films

The cinema continues to flourish as an art form. If the only films showing in your area are the latest releases, you might like to think of joining a film society or perhaps taking a trip to the National Film Theatre to view some of the great performances of the past or to see some of the excellent foreign films that are rarely shown out of London.

British Federation of Film Societies, The Ritz Building, Mount Pleasant Campus, Swansea SA1 6ED. T:01792 481170. There are over 300 film societies throughout the UK. Addresses can be obtained from the British Federation. Most societies offer reduced rates for senior citizens. If, as a growing number of people are, you are interested in forming a local film society with a group of friends and neighbours, contact the BFFS at the above address for information on how to get started.

National Film Theatre, South Bank, London SE1 8XT. T:020 7928 3232. Some 2,000 films are shown a year at the NFT's three cinemas. Membership, which admits up to four guests and costs £20 annually (£13 for retired people), is available from the NFT or from the **British Film Institute**, 21 Stephen Street, London W1P 2LN, T:020 7255 1444.

Music and ballet

Scope ranges from becoming a Friend and supporting one of the famous 'Houses' such as Covent Garden to music-making in your own right.

Friends. If you live close enough to take advantage of the 'perks', subscribing as a Friend allows you a number of very attractive advantages including in all cases priority for bookings.

English National Opera, London Coliseum, St. Martin's Lane, London WC2N 4ES. T:020 7845 9420. As a Friend of ENO, you have the opportunity to apply for tickets for dress rehearsals and to gain an insight into the creation of opera through a variety of special lunch-time and evening events. You also receive advance programme information. Membership costs from £25 a year for senior citizens.

Friends of Covent Garden, Royal Opera House, Covent Garden, London WC2E 9DD. T:020 7212 9267. Friends receive regular mailings of news and information, free copies of the magazine *About the House* plus opportunities to attend talks, recitals, study days, master classes and 'open' rehearsals of ballet and opera. Annual membership is £60.

Friends of Sadler's Wells, Sadler's Wells Theatre, Rosebery Avenue, London EC1R 4TN. T:020 7863 8198. Sadler's Wells has an ever-changing programme of ballet, opera and contemporary dance. Friends receive discounts and free ticket offers and also occasional invitations to talks and other events. Annual membership is £36.

Music making

Just about every style of music is catered for, from bell-ringing to recorder playing. There is even an orchestra for retired people. Information about local societies and other groups is contained in the *British Music Education Year Book* and the *British Music Year Book*, both of which should be in the reference section of your library.

Handbell Ringers of Great Britain, 87 The Woodfields, Sanderstead, South Croydon, Surrey CR2 0HJ. T:020 8651 2663. The Society promotes the art of handbell tune ringing and supports handbell, handchime and belleplate players. Concerts, rallies, seminars and workshops are organised. To contact your local group, write to the above address or 'phone/fax the above number.

Making Music, 7–15 Rosebery Avenue, London EC1R 4SP. T:0870 872 3300. Making Music can provide you with addresses of some 1,950 affiliated choral societies, orchestras and music societies throughout the country. Most charge a nominal membership fee and standards range from the semi-professional to the unashamedly amateur.

National Association of Choirs, Fig Tree House, 9 The Green, Glinton, Peterborough PE6 7JN. T:01733 252464. The Association will put you in contact with an amateur choir in your area.

Society of Recorder Players, 15 Palliser Road, London W14 9EB. T:020 7385 7321. The Society has groups in many areas where members play together regularly. The branches welcome players of all standards and ages but do not provide tuition for beginners. There is an annual festival with massed playing, competitions and concerts. Annual subscription which includes a quarterly magazine is £14. Branch subscriptions may differ. Write to the Society, enclosing sae, for a list of addresses.

Poetry

Not so long ago, poetry was very much a minority interest. However, largely thanks to both the media and the Poetry Society, there has been a great upsurge in poetry readings in clubs, pubs and other places of entertainment. Your library should be able to tell you about any special local events.

The Poetry Society, 22 Betterton Street, London WC2H 9BX. T:020 7420 9880. Membership of the Society is open to anyone who enjoys reading, listening to or writing poetry. The Society runs a poetry criticism service where, for an agreed fee, you can have your work assessed. Each year the Society organises a National Poetry Competition with a first prize of £5,000. Additionally, members receive the Society's quarterly magazines *Poetry Review* and *Poetry News*. Annual subscription is £35; £25 for senior citizens. For further details, contact the Membership Manager.

Television and radio audiences

If you would like to be part of the invited studio audience for a radio or television programme, you can apply to the BBC through the relevant ticket unit for London-based programmes; or for outside London, through the appropriate regional centre. The ticket unit address for both radio and television is:

The Ticket Unit, **BBC Radio and Television Audience Services**, PO Box 3000, London W12 7RJ. T:020 8576 1227.

For independent television, audience participation in programmes is the responsibility of each programme maker and requests should be channelled to the appropriate contractor for the area. Addresses are as follows:

Anglia Television, Anglia House, Norwich NR1 3JG.

Border Television, The Broadcasting Centre, Carlisle CA1 3NT.

Carlton Television Ltd., 101 St. Martin's Lane, London WC2N 4AZ.

Central Independent Television, Central Court, Gas Street, Birmingham B1 2JT.

Channel Television, The Television Centre, St. Helier, Jersey, Channel Islands JE1 3ZD.

Grampian Television, Queen's Cross, Aberdeen AB9 2XJ.

Granada Television, Granada Television Centre, Quay Street, Manchester M60 9EA.

HTV Wales, The Television Centre, Culverhouse Cross, Cardiff CF5 6XJ.

HTV West, The Television Centre, Bath Road, Bristol BS4 3HG.

London Weekend Television (LWT), The London Television Centre, Upper Ground, London SE1 9LT.

Meridian Broadcasting Ltd., Television Centre, Southampton SO14 0PZ.

Scottish Television, Cowcaddens, Glasgow G2 3PR.

Tyne Tees Television, The Television Centre, City Road, Newcastle upon Tyne NE1 2AL.

Ulster Television, Havelock House, Ormeau Road, Belfast BT7 1EB.

Westcountry Television Ltd., Western Wood Way, Langage Science Park, Plymouth PL7 5BG.

Yorkshire Television, The Television Centre, Leeds LS3 1JS.

GMTV Ltd., The London Television Centre, Upper Ground, London SE1 9TT.

Channel 4 Television Corporation, 124 Horseferry Road, London SW1P 2TX.

Independent Television News (ITN), 200 Gray's Inn Road, London WC1X 8XZ.

The Network Centre ITV, 200 Gray's Inn Road, London WC1X 8HF.

Theatre

Details of current and forthcoming productions, as well as theatre reviews, are contained in the newspapers. As general wisdom, preview performances are invariably cheaper and there are often concessionary tickets for matinees. Listed here are one or two theatres and organisations that offer special facilities of interest, including priority booking and reduced price tickets. Also included is an association for enthusiasts of amateur dramatics.

Barbican Centre, Silk Street, London EC2Y 8DS. T:020 7638 4141 (for information). Box Office: 020 7638 8891. The Barbican Centre combines two theatres, concert hall, art gallery, concourse gallery, cinemas and library. There are frequent free live musical events in the foyers (including regular Sunday lunchtime jazz), free exhibitions and restaurant facilities. Reduced tickets for senior citizens are available for many concerts and theatre performances on a standby basis and are also given for the cinema and art gallery. For £10 a year, BarbicanCard holders receive a monthly guide and enjoy advance information and special offers for theatre, music and other events.

Royal National Theatre, South Bank, London SE1 9PX. T:020 7452 3400 (for information); Box Office: 020 7452 3000. The Royal National Theatre offers backstage tours, talks by theatre professionals, live foyer music before performances, free exhibitions and restaurant facilities as well as its three theatres. There are group price reductions and pensioners can buy matinee tickets (midweek and Saturday) at £16. The Royal National Theatre has a Mailing List Membership (£10 a year) which provides: advance information, priority booking and exclusive special offers. For details, contact **Royal National Theatre**, Mailing List, Freepost, London SE1 7BR; or ring 020 7452 3500 (10 a.m. to 6 p.m., Monday to Friday).

Society of London Theatre (SOLT), 32 Rose Street, London WC2E 9ET. T:020 7557 6700. Senior citizens can get substantial reductions for midweek matinee performances at many West End theatres. They can also receive concessionary prices for evening performances or weekend matinees on a standby basis with all listings showing the symbol 'S' in the *London Theatre Guide*. Standby tickets are available approximately an hour before the performance begins.

Concessions are subject to availability and it is always wise to check with the box office to make sure there are tickets before setting off for a performance. When buying tickets on a concessionary basis, you will need to present proof of your senior citizen status at the box office, for example, using a travel pass or pension book.

The Society presents the annual Laurence Olivier Awards. Members of the general public serve on the judging panels. If you would like to be considered for the Theatre, Opera or Dance panel, write to the Awards Office at the above address, enclosing sae, for application forms (available in the autumn). Members of the panels receive two complimentary tickets for all proposed productions during the judging period.

Theatre Tokens, which are welcome at over 190 theatres nationwide including all London West End theatres, are available from branches of WH Smith, Books Etc, Waterstones, Borders, Hammicks and James Thin or through **Tokenline** (24 hours) T:020 7240 8800.

Also extremely useful is the Society's *Disabled Access Guide to London West End Theatres* which provides information about special facilities, access for wheelchairs, transport advice and price concessions for disabled theatregoers. Available free from SOLT, T:020 7557 6751.

Scottish Community Drama Association, 5 York Place, Edinburgh EH1 3EB. T:0131 557 5552. The Association aims to develop amateur drama in the community by offering clubs and societies advice, encouragement and practical help. Individual membership (£15 a year, £10 concessionary price) gives access to the Association's libraries, training courses and script discounts. The Association also runs playwriting competitions and can put you in touch with local dramatic societies. Members receive regular copies of the house magazine *Scene*.

TKTS. The Booth sells tickets to many West End theatres at half-price on the day of performance. It is open to personal callers only, Monday to Saturday, from 10 a.m. to 7 p.m.; Sundays, from 12 noon to 3 p.m.; or in the case of matinees, until 1/2 hour before starting time. There is a service charge of £2.50 per ticket.

Late night trains. Late night trains run from many London stations. For details of services, enquire at your local station or ring National Rail Enquiries on T:08457 48 49 50.

Visual arts

If you enjoy attending exhibitions and lectures, membership of some of the arts societies offers you a number of delightful privileges.

Contemporary Art Society, 17 Bloomsbury Square, London WC1A 2NG. T:020 7831 7311. The aim of the Society is to promote the collecting of contemporary art and to acquire works by living artists for gift to public galleries. Members can take part in an extensive programme of events including: visits to artists' studios and private collections, previews and parties at special exhibitions, trips outside London and overseas. Membership benefits include a quarterly newsletter. The annual subscription is £40; £45 per couple.

National Art Collections Fund, Millais House, 7 Cromwell Place, London SW7 2JN. T:020 7225 4800. The National Art Collections Fund raises money to help museums, galleries and historic houses buy works of art to enrich their collections. The benefits of membership include: free entrance to over 200 museums and galleries; concessionary admission to many important exhibitions; a countrywide programme of lectures, concerts, private views and other special events including visits to houses not normally open to the public; *The Art Quarterly* magazine plus an illustrated review of the year's acquisitions. There are also art tours at home and abroad led by experts. Subscription is £31 per year; senior citizens, £23.

National Association of Decorative & Fine Arts Societies, NADFAS House, 8 Guilford Street, London WC1N 1DA. T:020 7430 0730. Member societies of NADFAS have programmes of monthly lectures, museum and gallery visits, as well as guided tours of historic houses. Events are usually held in the daytime (although some take place in the evening) and some societies may be able to help with transport.

Many societies have volunteer groups working in museums, libraries and historic houses and there are also church-recording groups which make detailed records of the interiors of churches. Details of your local society are available from NADFAS at the above address. Membership of a local society is about £30–£35 a year. It gives access to nationally run study courses, a quarterly magazine, reduced entry to some galleries plus the opportunity to join day events and tours organised both in the UK and abroad.

Royal Academy of Arts, Piccadilly, London W1J 0BD. T:020 7300 8000. Senior citizens enjoy reduced entrance charges to all exhibitions, including the big annual Summer Exhibition. You can become a Friend of the Royal Academy, which gives you free admission with an adult guest and four children under 16 and saves you queuing for tickets. Friends may also use the Friends' Rooms to meet for coffee and attend exhibition previews. Subscription (2002) is £50 a year.

Tate Britain, Millbank, London SW1P 4RG. T:020 7887 8000. Recorded Information: 020 7887 8008. **Tate Modern**, Bankside, London SE1 9TG. T:020 7887 8000. London now boasts two magnificent Tate galleries: Tate Britain at Millbank, which houses the most important collection of British art from 1500 to the present day; and the new Tate Modern gallery, on the site of the Bankside Power Station at Southwark, which contains international 20th and 21st century art including works by Giacometti, Picasso and Warhol. There are free weekly lectures and guided tours every day, except Sunday; also special tours for disabled people by prior arrangement. Friends of the Tate enjoy free admission to all exhibitions, receipt of *Tate: the Art Magazine* and access to the Members' Room including both those at the Tate Gallery, Liverpool and the Tate Gallery, St. Ives. Membership costs £61, which includes both member plus guest. For further information, ring T:020 7887 8752.

Painting as a hobby
If you are interested in improving your own painting technique, rather than simply viewing the works of great masters, contact your local Adult Education Institute for details of courses in your area. Your library may have information about local painting groups, clubs and societies.

Crafts

The vast majority of suggestions are contained in Chapter 14, Holidays, variously under 'Arts and crafts' and 'Special interest holidays', the reason being that most of the organisations concerned make a feature of arranging residential courses or of organising, for example, painting holidays. However, if you are interested in a particular form of craft work and want information or advice, many of the societies and others listed in Chapter 14 should be able to help you. Herewith one or two additional possibilities.

The Basketmakers' Association, Hon. Secretary: Mrs Isobel Edge, Highlanes Farm, Brockton, Eccleshall, Staffs ST21 6LY. T:01630 620363. The Association promotes better standards of design and technique in the art of basketmaking, chair seating and allied crafts. It arranges day schools, residential courses, demonstrations and exhibitions. There is a quarterly newsletter. Membership (2002) costs £15 (£22 family membership, two people).

Crafts Council, 44a Pentonville Road, Islington, London N1 9BY. T:020 7278 7700. As well as holding exhibitions, the Crafts Council runs an information centre and reference library which can give advice on almost everything you could possibly want to know: different craft courses throughout the country, addresses of craft guilds and societies, fact sheets on business practice for craftspeople as well as details of craft fairs and markets, galleries, shops and other outlets for work. Additionally, the Crafts Council has a slide and video library, publishes a bi-monthly magazine, *Crafts*, and maintains an index of craftspeople and the national register of makers. Admission to the Crafts Council Gallery is free: open Tuesday to Saturday, 11 a.m. to 6 p.m.; and Sunday, 2 to 6 p.m.

Embroiderers' Guild, Apartment 41, Hampton Court Palace, Surrey KT8 9AU. T:020 8943 1229. The Guild is an educational charity which aims to promote the craft of embroidery to the highest standards. Membership is open to all, beginners and experts, and members are offered a full programme of workshops, lectures, exhibitions and tours in the UK and abroad. They receive a newsletter three times a year with information about embroidery activities throughout the country and also a year book containing details of many special discounts. Members can also join one of the Guild's 230 local branches. Membership is £9. Branches have their own subscription rates.

Open College of the Arts, Unit 1B, Redbrook Business Park, Wilthorpe Road, Barnsley, South Yorkshire S75 1JN. T:01226 730495. The OCA, which is affiliated to both the University of Glamorgan and the Open University, offers courses for those wishing to acquire or improve their skills in creative digital arts, sculpture, textiles, photography, creative writing, garden and interior design, music and singing, art history and calligraphy. Course books are supplied and students have professional tutorial support. Course prices range from £299 to £439 for payment in advance.

Studio 1 D (Ceramic and Glass Restoration), 46B Stoneleigh Street, London W11 4DU. T:020 7460 3100. This china restoration studio runs two-week courses for beginners, which teach all the basic skills including use of tools and materials to enable you to restore china on your own. Cost is about £600 for two weeks (11 a.m. to 6 p.m. Monday to Friday). Consultations about restoring broken china are by appointment only.

Dance/keep fit

Clubs, classes and groups exist in all parts of the country, variously offering: ballroom, Old Tyme, Scottish, folk, ballet, disco dancing and others. Additionally, there are music and relaxation classes, aerobics and more gentle keep-fit sessions. Many of the relaxation and keep-fit classes in particular cater for all standards and some are specially designed for older people to tone up muscles and improve their circulation while making friends in an agreeable atmosphere. Best advice is to contact your adult education or sports centre, or alternatively the library, to find out what is available in your area. Listed here are some of the national organisations that can advise you and put you in touch with local groups. There are also some extra names in Chapter 13, Health, see 'Keep fit' section.

British Dance Council, Terpsichore House, 240 Merton Road, South Wimbledon, London SW19 1EQ. T:020 8545 0085. The Council, which is the governing body of ballroom dancing, can put you in touch with recognised dance schools in your area. Contact the Secretary at the above address, enclosing sae.

The Central Council of Physical Recreation, Francis House, Francis Street, London SW1P 1DE. T:020 7854 8500. The CCPR will provide information on all sporting activities e.g. badminton, swimming, bowls and offer advice to anyone wishing to become involved in a sport or recreation. The CCPR membership also includes 29 movement, dance and exercise organisations, many of which have special sessions for over-50s. For a free leaflet about the Movement and Dance Division, contact the Marketing and Promotions Manager for Movement and Dance at the above address.

English Folk Dance and Song Society, Cecil Sharp House, 2 Regent's Park Road, London NW1 7AY. T:020 7485 2206. There are some 570 clubs around the country which organise both regular and special events. In addition to ordinary folk dancing, programmes may include: country dancing, morris dancing, 'knees up', clog workshops, musician band sessions, sea shanties, lectures and concerts. Membership (2002), which includes journals and use of the library, costs £26; £37 joint membership; £13 and £21 respectively for members over 60. Contact the Society for details of your nearest branch.

Imperial Society of Teachers of Dancing, Imperial House, 22–26 Paul Street, London EC2A 4QE. T:020 7377 1577. Throughout the UK there are some 7,000 teachers offering instruction in virtually all forms of dancing. Many organise classes and events particularly for older people. The Society has lists of teachers in each geographic area. There is no standard charge but dance classes and social dancing tend to be an inexpensive activity.

Keep Fit Association, Astra House, Suite 105, Arklow Road, New Cross, London SE14 6EB. T:020 8692 9566. The Keep Fit Association offers 'Fitness through Movement, Exercise and Dance' classes, suitable for all ages and abilities. KFA teachers have special training in working with older people. Almost all adult education centres run classes in the daytime; many have special classes for keeping fit in retirement. (See also Extend, in Chapter 13, Health).

Royal Scottish Country Dance Society, 12 Coates Crescent, Edinburgh EH3 7AF. T:0131 225 3854. The Society has members from 16 to 80-plus in its many branches and groups all over the world. It publishes books, cassettes, CDs and videos and holds an annual summer school at St. Andrew's University. The branches offer instruction at all levels and members join in dance events. Information about your local branch/group can be obtained from the RSCDS Secretary.

For people with disabilities

Happily, there are increasingly fewer activities from which disabled people are debarred through lack of suitable facilities, as will be evident from many of the suggestions listed earlier in the chapter. This section, therefore only deals with one topic not covered elsewhere, namely enjoyment of books which for many blind or partially sighted people can be a special problem.

Calibre, Cassette Library, Aylesbury, Buckinghamshire HP22 5XQ. T:01296 432339. Calibre is a lending library of over 6,000 recorded books on ordinary standard cassettes. These are available to anyone who cannot read printed books because of poor sight or other difficulty. An official form is required certifying 'inability to read printed books in the normal way' – a photocopy of the Blind Registration is acceptable. Books include fiction and non-fiction and cover the full range of classifications. Members use their own cassette players. The library provides a free service although donations are welcomed.

Listening Books, 12 Lant Street, London SE1 1QH. T:020 7407 9417. The Library has books on cassette which it loans to people who have difficulty in reading due to disability. Members unable to use a normal machine can be provided with a specially adapted tape player and long-playing audio books. There is an annual membership fee of £50 which includes all postage costs.

National Library for the Blind, Far Cromwell Road, Bredbury, Stockport, Cheshire SK6 2SG. T:0161 355 2000. The Library lends books – and also music scores – in Braille and Moon free of charge to individual readers (post-free).

RNIB Talking Book Service, Falcon Park, Neasden Lane, London NW10 1TB. T:0845 7023 153. This is a library service for anyone who is registered as blind or partially sighted or whose vision is such that they cannot easily read normal print (certified on application form by opthalmologist, optician or GP).

Application for membership should be made to the local authority social services department or direct to Customer Services at the above number. The charge towards the cost of the service is normally paid by members' local authorities. Books, which are unabridged, are recorded on special cassettes which last about 12 hours and are played back on a special machine supplied on permanent loan. There are more than 13,000 titles from which to choose, covering all categories of books.

Games

Many local areas have their own bridge, chess, whist, dominoes, Scrabble and other groups who meet together regularly, either in a club, hall, pub or other social venue to enjoy friendly games. Competitions are organised and certainly in the case of bridge and chess, district and county teams are usually taken very seriously. Your library should know about any clubs or regular group meetings. Alternatively, you can contact the national organisations listed below.

British Chess Federation, The Watch Oak, Chain Lane, Battle, East Sussex TN33 0YD. T:01424 775222. Can provide information about chess clubs and tournaments.

English Bridge Union, Broadfields, Bicester Road, Aylesbury, Bucks HP19 8AZ. T:01296 317200. There are over 1,000 affiliated bridge clubs nationwide. Members receive a magazine six times a year which, among other features of interest, contains details of tournaments and bridge holidays at home and abroad. Annual membership costs £15 plus county fees (which range from £1 to £4).

Scrabble Clubs UK, Mattel House, Vanwall Business Park, Vanwall Road, Maidenhead, Berks SL6 4UB. T:01628 500283. There are over 300 Scrabble Clubs up and down the country. Some have their own premises and are highly competitive. Others meet in halls or members' houses for a friendly game. Many of them are involved in charitable work, such as raising money for people with disabilities or visiting the housebound. Many competitions are held, including a National Scrabble Championship and a big tournament for clubs. For details of your nearest Scrabble Club, contact Philip Nelkon at the above address.

Gardens and gardening

Courses, gardens to visit, special help for people with disabilities, how to run a gardening association … these and other interests are all catered for by the organisations listed.

The English Gardening School, at the Chelsea Physic Garden, 66 Royal Hospital Road, London SW3 4HS. T:020 7352 4347. The School teaches all aspects of gardening. Courses which range in length from a day to an academic year are held in the historic lecture room of the Chelsea Physic Garden, the centre for the study of horticulture for over 300 years. Topics include among others: the Small Garden, Garden Photography, Container Gardening, Pruning Roses, the Mixed Border and Botanical Illustration. Cost is from about £95 a day, including lunch.

Gardening for the Disabled Trust & Garden Club, Hayes Farmhouse, Hayes Lane, Peasmarsh, Nr. Rye, East Sussex TN31 6XR. The Trust provides practical and financial help to disabled people who want to garden actively. Their Garden Club publishes a quarterly newsletter, gives answers to horticultural questions and encourages gardeners with disabilities to meet. The annual subscription is £4.

HDRA, Ryton Organic Gardens, Coventry CV8 3LG.T:024 7630 3517. HDRA is Europe's largest organic gardening organisation. It encourages environmentally-friendly gardening and its centre is open to visitors throughout the year. Individuals can help by experimenting in their own gardens and joining a network of countrywide local groups. Members receive a quarterly magazine, a sales catalogue with discounts, gardening advice and free entry to ten gardens. Subscription is £21; £14 for senior citizens.

National Gardens Scheme, Hatchlands Park, East Clandon, Guildford GU4 7RT. T:01483 211535. (For England and Wales). The Scheme covers some 3,500, mostly private, gardens which open to the public a few days a year to raise money for a variety of charities including: Macmillan Cancer Relief, Marie Curie Cancer Care, the Queen's Nursing Institute and charities which care for retired gardeners and their dependants. Tea is often available, as are plants for sale. Entry fees average about £2. Further information plus directions are listed in the Scheme's Yellow Book, *Gardens of England and Wales Open for Charity* (£5.99 from bookshops or £7.75 including p&p from the address above). Practicality for wheelchairs is also indicated.

The Scheme is always looking for suitable new gardens. Should you wish to offer yours, however small, apply to the County Organiser whose address is in the handbook. Sometimes two or more gardens share a group opening, particularly on a village basis.

National Society of Allotment and Leisure Gardeners Ltd., O'Dell House, Hunters Road, Corby, Northants NN17 5JE. T:01536 266576. The Society encourages all forms of horticultural education and the forming of local allotment and gardening associations. It also acts as a national voice for allotment and leisure gardeners.

Annual membership costs £12.50; society membership, £1.25 per member. This gives you access to free help and advice, the right to attend the annual meeting plus receipt of the Society's bulletin. There is also a Seeds Scheme, offering special prices. Leaflets are available on growing vegetables, how to form a gardening association and the running of flower shows.

Royal Horticultural Society, PO Box 313, London SW1P 2PE. T:020 7821 3000. Members receive free entry to over 90 gardens and tickets discounts to RHS flower shows, including both Chelsea and Hampton Court Palace. They also receive a monthly copy of *The Garden* magazine plus free expert gardening advice. Membership costs £30 (plus a one-off enrolment fee of £7). For further information, telephone the Membership Department on the above number.

Scotland's Gardens Scheme, 22 Rutland Square, Edinburgh EH1 2BB. T:0131 229 1870. The Scheme supports retired Queen's Nurses, the Gardens Fund of the National Trust for Scotland and other charities through 360 gardens which are open to the public either on one day only or on a regular basis. The booklet giving opening times is £4 from bookshops (or £5 from the Scheme incl. p&p).

Thrive, The Geoffrey Udall Centre, Beech Hill, Reading RG7 2AT. T:0118 988 5688. Thrive offers support to those who no longer find gardening as easy as it once was. It will give advice over the telephone or by post including, for example, information about special tools and where these can be obtained. Thrive also runs four garden projects based in: Battersea Park, Hackney, Beech Hill, near Reading and Ryton, near Coventry.

Useful reading

Gardening Without Sight, £2.50; *Leisure for all – Opportunities for Blind and Partially Sighted People,* £3.50. Available from RNIB Customer Services, PO Box 173, Peterborough PE2 6WS. T:0845 702 3153.

History

People with an interest in the past have a truly glorious choice of activities to sample. You can visit historic monuments, including ancient castles and stately homes, in all parts of the country; explore the City of London; study genealogy; research the history of your local area; attend lectures and receptions.

Age Exchange Reminiscence Centre, 11 Blackheath Village, Blackheath, London SE3 9LA. T:020 8318 9105. The Centre features exhibitions recording the life-styles of the 1920s and 1930s. There are also publications depicting the period for visitors to enjoy plus a year-round programme of activities including, for example, reminiscence through the arts, music and drama. The Centre is open Monday to Saturday, between 10 a.m. and 5.30 p.m., and admission is free. There is sometimes a small charge for entrance to drama productions and similar. The Centre is fully equipped for disabled access.

Architectural Heritage Society of Scotland, The Glasite Meeting House, 33 Barony Street, Edinburgh EH3 6NX. T:0131 557 0019. The Society promotes the protection of Scottish architecture and encourages the study of Scottish buildings, their furniture and fittings, urban design and designed landscapes. There are six regional groups, covering all of Scotland, which arrange regular events including talks, visits and study trips. Members can also join case panels to assess Listed Building and Conservation Area Consent applications and planning applications. Annual membership, including the Society's publications, is £20; £30 for a family.

British Association for Local History, PO Box 1576, Salisbury, Wilts SP2 8SY. T:01722 332158. The Association exists to promote the study of local history. It will give advice and invite you to conferences and courses. Typical topics include introductory days at the Public Record Office, computers in local history and writing about your local area. Membership which includes copies of both *The Local Historian* and *Local History News* is £25.

Cadw: Welsh Historic Monuments, Crown Buildings, Cathays Park, Cardiff CF10 3NQ. T:029 2082 6185. Some 131 historic properties in Wales are maintained by Cadw. Most are open summer and winter. Season or single entry tickets can be purchased on site.

City of London Information Centre, St. Paul's Churchyard (South side), London EC4M 8BX. T:020 7332 1456. The City of London offers enough interest to occupy you for a year or longer. The Information Centre acts as a tourist office for the area, giving advice and guidance. Among the many attractions, all of which are open to the public at varying times, are: St. Paul's Cathedral, the Guildhall (open most of the year, Monday – Saturday, 10 a.m. to 4 p.m., free), Dr. Johnson's House, the Monument, the Barbican, the Central Criminal Court and several museums. Additionally, there are interesting examples of London's architecture. Many of the 43 churches give organ recitals and, in the summer, you can enjoy open air concerts. The Centre offers lots of free leaflets including the monthly events list.

English Heritage, (Membership Department), Freepost WD 214, PO Box 570, Swindon, Wilts SN2 2UR. T:0870 333 1181. English Heritage manages over 400 historic attractions throughout England. Members receive a colour handbook (see below) and map. They enjoy free admission to all English Heritage properties and are sent a quarterly magazine publicising events and developments of conservation interest. Annual subscription (2002) is £31.50, £21.50 for senior citizens, with reductions for couples. *The English Heritage Visitors' Handbook* indicates which sites have access for wheelchairs.

Federation of Family History Societies, PO Box 2425, Coventry CV5 6YX. T:07041 492032. An umbrella organisation for more than 200 societies throughout the world (160 in the UK) that provide assistance if you are interested in tracing your ancestors. Write to the administrator, Maggie Loughram, at the above address who will be glad to put you in contact with your local society, as well as provide some useful guidelines on how to get started. Please enclose (A4) sae.

Friends of Historic Scotland, Longmore House, Salisbury Place, Edinburgh EH9 1SH. T:0131 668 8999. Membership gives you free access to 330 of Scotland's historic buildings and ancient monuments, a free directory of the sites, special guided tours and a quarterly magazine to keep you up to date with new activities. Membership (2002) costs £30 a year; £23 for senior citizens over 60; £33 for retired couples.

Garden History Society, 70 Cowcross Street, London EC1M 6EJ. T:020 7608 2409. The Society is concerned with the enjoyment and conservation of historic parks and gardens. It organises visits and lectures for members. An annual summer conference and foreign tours are also arranged. There is a newsletter three times a year and a journal, *Garden History*. Subscriptions are £30 single; £38 joint.

Georgian Group, 6 Fitzroy Square, London W1T 5DX. T:020 7387 1720. The Group exists to preserve Georgian buildings and to stimulate public knowledge and appreciation of Georgian architecture and town planning. Activities include day visits and long weekends to buildings and gardens, private views of exhibitions and a programme of evening lectures in London. The Georgian Group also publishes advisory leaflets and holds study days on the history and conservation of Georgian buildings. Membership: £24 a year, £38 for couples.

Historical Association, 59a Kennington Park Road, London SE11 4JH. T:020 7735 3901. The Association brings together people of all ages and backgrounds who share an interest in and love for the past. Members receive *The Historian* (a fully illustrated quarterly magazine) and may join in a wide variety of activities such as lectures, outings, conferences and tours both at home and abroad conducted by expert lecturers. There are over 70 local branches nationwide offering a programme of social events and monthly talks by top historians. The Association also publishes a number of very useful historical pamphlets. Membership costs £35 a year; £22 for retired people.

Historic Houses Association, 2 Chester Street, London SWlX 7BB. T:020 7259 5688. Friends of the HHA enjoy free entrance during normal opening hours to nearly 300 HHA-member houses and gardens throughout the country, get the quarterly magazine *Historic House* and receive invitations to lectures, concerts, receptions and other events. Membership (HHA, PO Box 21, Heritage House, Baldock, Herts SG7 5SH): individual £30, double £44.

Monumental Brass Society, c/o Society of Antiquaries of London, Burlington House, Piccadilly, London W1V 0HS. The Society encourages the preservation and appreciation of monumental brasses. Members attend four meetings with lectures and discussions and receive three bulletins, the annual *Transactions*, and an invitation both to the annual excursion and conference. Subscription is £18 a year.

There are many brass rubbing centres around the country where facilities are provided for the craft.

National Trust, 36 Queen Anne's Gate, London SW1H 9AS. T:0870 458 4000. The National Trust exists to protect historic buildings and areas of great natural beauty in England, Wales and Northern Ireland. Membership gives you free entry to the Trust's many properties and to those of the National Trust for Scotland. You also receive three mailings with an annual handbook, magazines and details of activities in your own region. Thousands of special events are arranged each year, including guided house tours, pop and classical concerts, children's events and adult education activities. The Trust publishes a free annual booklet on facilities for visitors with disabilities; those requiring the help of a companion will be charged admission as normal but their companion will be admitted free of charge on request. The booklet is available on receipt of a stamped addressed adhesive label (minimum postage). Individual membership (2002) which includes a copy of the *Handbook* is £31.

National Trust for Scotland, 28 Charlotte Square, Edinburgh EH2 4ET. T:0131 243 9300. The National Trust for Scotland cares for over 100 properties and 183,000 acres of countryside. Members also enjoy free admission to any of the National Trust properties in England, Wales and Northern Ireland. Membership is £30 a year; senior citizens, £21.

Northern Ireland Tourist Board, St Anne's Court, 59 North Street, Belfast BT1 1NB. T:028 9023 1221. The Tourist Board issues a free information bulletin, *Stop and Visit*, listing historic sites and other places of interest together with opening hours and entrance fees. Many sites are free and others offer reduced rates for pensioners. Further discounts for those over 55 are listed in the *Holiday Breakaways* brochure. An *Events* leaflet describes a selection of the most important, interesting or new events in Northern Ireland each year, such as music festivals, sporting occasions, agricultural shows and art exhibitions.

Oral History Society, National Sound Archive, British Library, 96 Euston Road, London NW1 2DB. T:020 7412 7405. The Society offers support and advice to groups and individuals around the country who record the memories of older people, for projects in community history, schools, reminiscence groups and historical research. It publishes twice yearly journals and runs regular workshops and conferences. It welcomes the help of older people in all these activities. Individual membership is £15 a year.

Society of Genealogists, 14 Charterhouse Buildings, Goswell Road, London EC1M 7BA. T:020 7251 8799. The Society promotes the study of genealogy and heraldry. Lectures are arranged throughout the year and there are also a variety of courses, including day and weekend seminars. Members have access to the library and also receive a quarterly magazine. There is a joining fee of £7.50. Annual membership is £40 plus VAT. Non-members may use the library on payment of hourly, half-daily or daily fees.

Victorian Society, 1 Priory Gardens, Bedford Park, London W4 1TT. T:020 8994 1019. The Victorian Society campaigns to preserve fine Victorian and Edwardian buildings. It organises walks, tours, lectures and conferences through its national office and 11 regional groups. Membership: individual, £24; senior citizens, £15.

Hobbies

Whether your special enthusiasm is stamp collecting or model flying, most of the organisations listed organise events, answer queries and can put you in contact with kindred spirits.

The British Association of Numismatic Societies, Secretary: P H Mernick, c/o General Services, 42 Campbell Road, London E3 4DT. T:020 8980 5672. BANS is an umbrella organisation that helps to co-ordinate the activities of some 60 local clubs for those interested in the study or collection of coins, medals or similar. It organises two conferences a year, maintains a slide library and will be able to put you in touch with your nearest group.

British Jigsaw Puzzle Library, Clarendon, Parsonage Road, Herne Bay, Kent CT6 5TA. T:01227 742222. This is a lending library with puzzles usually exchanged by post. The puzzles are wooden and have no guide pictures. They vary in difficulty, style and size and the library tries to suit each member. Subscriptions range from £30 for three months to £75 for a year. Postal charges are extra.

British Model Flying Association, Chacksfield House, 31 St. Andrew's Road, Leicester LE2 8RE. T:0116 244 0028. The BMFA is responsible nationally for all types of model flying, now the world's most popular aviation sport. It organises competitions and fun fly meetings, provides advice and guidelines on model flying, offers third party insurance and can put you in touch with clubs in your area from its list of over 700 clubs. Many older members specialise in indoor free-flight or radio-controlled flying. Membership (2002) is £22 a year, which includes third party liability insurance cover.

Miniature Armoured Fighting Vehicle Association, 45 Balmoral Drive, Holmes Chapel, Cheshire CW4 7JQ. T:01477 535373. The MAFVA is an international society which provides advice and information on tanks and other military vehicles and equipment, issues a bi-monthly magazine *Tankette* and can put you in touch with a local branch or overseas members with similar interests. There are meetings, displays and competitions. Membership in the UK is £7 a year.

National Association of Flower Arrangement Societies, Osborne House, 12 Devonshire Square, London EC2M 4TE. T:020 7247 5567. NAFAS can put you in touch with local clubs and classes. It also organises weekend courses.

National Philatelic Society, 107 Charterhouse Street, London EC1M 6PT. T:020 7336 0882. The Society holds monthly Saturday afternoon meetings for stamp collectors at its premises. These normally consist of an auction and a display with questions to its exhibitor. Members receive a free bi-monthly journal *Stamp Lover* and have use of the Society's library. There is an exchange packet scheme and also an annual competition. Membership costs from £21 a year.

Radio Society of Great Britain, Lambda House, Cranborne Road, Potters Bar, Herts EN6 3JE. T:0870 904 7373. The Society provides advice on how to join the one-and-a-half million amateur radio operators around the world. The introduction of the Novice Licence has made it easier to participate in this hobby. Annual membership is £40.50; £31.50 for those over 65.

The Railway Correspondence & Travel Society, 365 Old Bath Road, Cheltenham, Glos GL53 9AH. T:01242 523917. The Society is among the leading railway enthusiast groups, with nearly 4,000 members all over the country. Members receive the monthly magazine, *The Railway Observer*, which includes the Society's fixtures. There are regular meetings at about 30 centres and the Society has a library with postal loan facility. Membership costs £18 a year.

Railway is a magazine for railway enthusiasts. It lists railway preservation events and gives information about local railway societies – including how to contact them. £3.05 monthly.

Museums

Most museums organise free lectures, guided tours, and sometimes slide shows, on aspects of their collection or special exhibitions. As with art galleries and theatres, an increasing trend is to form a group of 'Friends' who pay a membership subscription to support the museum and in return enjoy certain advantages, such as: access to private views, visits to places of interest, receptions and other social activities.

British Association of Friends of Museums, The Old Post Office, High Street, Butleigh, Glastonbury, Somerset BA6 8SU. T:01458 850520. BAFM is an umbrella organisation which acts as a national forum for Friends and volunteers who support museums around the UK. It shares news, provides advice on good practice, holds regional meetings and also produces a number of publications including a *Handbook* on setting up and running a Friends' organisation (£10). Many museums offer the opportunity, through membership of a Friends' group, of rewarding voluntary activity. If you like the idea, enquire locally or contact the Association to discover what scope exists in your area.

British Museum Friends, The British Museum, London WC1B 3DG. T:020 7323 8605. Members enjoy free entry to exhibitions and evening openings as well as information about lectures, study days and 'visits behind the scenes'. A mailing including the events programme and the *British Museum Magazine* is sent three times a year. Annual membership is £50.

Friends of the Fitzwilliam Museum, Fitzwilliam Museum, Trumpington Street, Cambridge CB2 1RB. T:01223 332933. Friends receive an annual programme listing exhibitions, concerts, lectures and preview parties. Lectures and tours are organised in the Museum and to galleries and historic houses further afield. The Friends welcome help from individual members. For membership details, please contact the Membership Secretary.

Friends of the National Maritime Museum, Greenwich, London SE10 9NF. T:020 8312 6678/6638. The Museum complex, housed in Greenwich Park, comprises the largest maritime museum in the world, Wren's Royal Observatory and Inigo Jones's Queen's House. Friends enjoy free entry to the buildings and exhibitions as well as: private views, lectures, astronomy and art clubs, sailing trips (for all abilities), visits to exhibitions and places of interest both in Britain and abroad plus regular newsletters and a yearbook. There are reciprocal free entry arrangements with many other maritime organisations. The subscription is £22 a year or £28 for a family or joint membership; £18 each for pensioners and disabled people.

Friends of the National Museums of Scotland, Development Office, Chambers Street, Edinburgh EH1 1JF. T:0131 247 4191. Members receive regular mailings and the *Explorer* magazine plus invitations to lectures and other events. There is also a UK and overseas travel programme. Annual membership (2002) is £16; £24 for couples.

Friends of the V & A, Victoria and Albert Museum, Cromwell Road, London SW7 2RL. T:020 7942 2270. Members enjoy free admission to all V & A exhibitions with a guest, an extensive programme of Friends' events, discounts in the V & A Shop and Restaurant and free subscription to *V & A Magazine*. Annual membership is £40; senior £35; double senior £50.

Nature and conservation

Many of the conservation organisations are very keen to recruit volunteers and are, therefore, listed in Chapter 12, Voluntary Work, rather than here. By the same token many of those concerned with field studies arrange courses and other special activity interests which, because there is usually a residential content, seem more appropriate in Chapter 14, Holidays. The potential list is enormous. To give you a flavour, herewith a short 'mixed bag', highlighting a range from canals to ecology.

Amenity organisations. If you are interested in conservation and the environment, you might like to join your local amenity society. You should be able to contact it through your public library.

British Ecological Society, 26 Blades Court, Deodar Road, Putney, London SW15 2NU. T:020 8871 9797. Membership is open to all who are genuinely interested in ecology. The BES holds general and special interest meetings and awards grants for ecological projects and expeditions. Membership costs £12, more if you wish to receive journals.

The Civic Trust, 17 Carlton House Terrace, London SW1Y 5AW. T:020 7930 0914. An environmental charity concerned about the quality of urban living that acts as an umbrella organisation for about 900 local amenity societies. Publishes a quarterly newsletter, *Civic Focus*, with articles on planning, conservation and transport issues. Annual subscription is £20.

Epping Forest Field Centre, High Beach, Loughton, Essex IG10 4AF. T:020 8508 7714. This Field Studies Council Day Centre promotes 'environmental understanding for all' through a wide-ranging programme of courses which take place both during the week and on many weekends of the year. Facilities include wheelchair access and a specially designed wheelchair path into the forest.

Forestry Commission, 231 Corstorphine Road, Edinburgh EH12 7AT. T:0131 334 0303. For information on Forestry Commission walks and trails, forest drives, picnic places and visitor centres contact your local Forestry Commission office or the Public Enquiries service at the above address (T:0845 367 3787).

Scottish Inland Waterways Association, Clifton Staithe, Newbridge EH28 8LQ. T:0131 333 1231. The Association co-ordinates the activities of local canal preservation societies and will put you in touch with your nearest group.

The Wildlife Trusts, The Kiln, Waterside, Mather Road, Newark NG24 1WT. T:01636 677711. There are 47 local Wildlife Trusts caring for 2,500 nature reserves and campaigning for the future of our threatened wildlife. If you would be interested in visiting the reserves, participating in some of the activities such as guided walks or joining a work party – which could mean taking part in anything from scrub bashing to otter surveys – contact your local Trust. Membership, which is optional, costs £20 and includes receipt of a magazine and events programmes. For further information, contact the UK National Office at the above address.

Pen-friends

Despite the telephone, pen-friendship is flourishing. It is an ideal activity for those who have difficulty in getting out and about and many life-long friendships develop this way. Among the organisations that promote pen-friend schemes are:

National Association of Widows Penclub, 48 Queen's Road, Coventry CV1 3EH. T:024 7663 4848. Many widows find great comfort in corresponding with others who can share and understand their feelings. Membership is free. For further information, write to the Penclub Organiser at the above address enclosing note of your interests and other basic details about yourself.

Saga Magazine Club, The Saga Building, Freepost CU250, Folkestone CT20 1AZ. T:01303 771526. Annual membership of the Club, which includes 12 issues of *Saga Magazine*, is £15.95.

Public library service

Britain's public library service is among the best in the world. It issues about 600 million books free a year, loans records and cassettes and is a source of an enormous amount of information about both local and national activities. Additionally, the reference sections contain newspapers and periodicals as well as a wide selection of reference books which might cover any subject from flower arranging to genealogy.

Many libraries have a mobile service which takes books into villages and/or to senior citizens' clubs, day centres and clinics for elderly and infirm people. Some libraries also have volunteer library visitors who deliver books and materials to housebound people. Among the many facilities on offer, large print books are available at most libraries as are musical scores, leaflets on State benefits, consumer information and details of local community activities. Larger libraries have access to computer databases and can provide specialised information from Europe and North America. Some also hold the International Genealogical Index with information on microfiche.

Additionally, all libraries act as a source of information. If the information you require is not available in the library itself, the trained staff will normally do their best to tell you where you might find it.

Sciences and other related subjects

If astronomy fascinates you or you would like to understand more about meteorology (who wouldn't, given our uncertain climate!), there are several societies and associations who would welcome you as a member.

British Astronomical Association, Burlington House, Piccadilly, London W1J 0DU. The Association is open to all people interested in astronomy. Members' work is co-ordinated in such sections as: Sun, Moon, Terrestrial Planets, Meteors, Jupiter, Asteroids, Historical, Telescope Making and so on. The Association holds meetings both in London and elsewhere and loans instruments to members who may also use the library. Membership costs £34 a year; £23 for those over 65.

Geologists' Association, Burlington House, London W1V 9AG. T:020 7434 9298. The Association organises lectures, field excursions and monthly meetings at Burlington House. There are varying levels of subscriptions, ranging from about £20 to £30. Local groups organise their own programmes. These exist in: Brent, Essex, Farnham, Guildford, Harrow, Ruislip, Oxford, Midlands, Lancashire, Staffordshire, South Wales, Avon, Kent, Cambridge and Mole Valley.

Royal Meteorological Society, 104 Oxford Road, Reading, Berkshire RG1 7LL. T:0118 956 8500. The Society, which includes among its membership both amateurs and professionals, exists to advance meteorological science. Members and others may attend scientific meetings and receive the monthly magazine *Weather*. Membership costs £48 a year; £28 for retired people.

Sport

Retirement is no excuse for giving up sport. On the contrary, it is an ideal time to get into trim. Facilities abound and, unlike people with a 9 to 5 job, you enjoy the great advantage of being able to book out of peak hours. To find out about opportunities in your area, contact your local authority recreational department or your sports/leisure centre.

Additionally, a useful organisation to know about is: **The Central Council of Physical Recreation**, Francis House, Francis Street, London SW1P 1DE. T:020 7854 8500. The CCPR will provide information on all sporting activities e.g. badminton, swimming, bowls and offer advice to anyone wishing to become involved in a sport or recreation.

Angling

The Angling Trades Association, Federation House, National Agricultural Centre, Stoneleigh Park, Warwickshire CV8 2RF. T:024 7641 4999. The Association promotes the interests of anglers and angling, including educational and environmental concerns. It can advise on where to find qualified tuition, local tackle dealers and similar information, as well as supply a number of useful leaflets.

Archery

Grand National Archery Society, Lilleshall National Sports Centre, Nr. Newport, Shropshire TF10 9AT. T:01952 677888. The Society is the governing body for archery in the UK. It will put you in touch with your nearest club of which there are over 1,000 around the country. Most clubs provide coaching at all levels including beginners' courses (covered by public liability insurance) for which they supply all equipment. The GNAS organises a full calendar of events and says many archers are still actively competing in their seventies, as the handicap system allows all abilities and disabled people to compete on equal terms. Club membership varies from approximately £30 to £100 a year, including affiliation fees.

Badminton

Badminton Association of England Ltd., National Badminton Centre, Bradwell Road, Milton Keynes MK8 9LA. T:01908 268400. Most sports and leisure centres have badminton courts and give instruction, as do many Adult Education Institutes. If you need advice, contact the Association. As well as offering information, it runs a number of short residential courses. Annual membership of the BAE (2002), which among other benefits includes physiotherapy insurance, costs £7.30 as a club member or £12.70 for non-club members.

Bowling

Over the past years, bowling has been growing in popularity. Your local authority may provide facilities. Alternatively contact:

English Bowling Association, Lyndhurst Road, Worthing, West Sussex BN11 2AZ. T:01903 820222. There are 2,600 local clubs, many of which provide instruction for beginners by qualified coaches. Some clubs have reduced rates for senior citizens. A national competition for 55-plus singles and pairs is organised through clubs each year. If you decide to take up bowls, you are advised not to buy your equipment without advice from the club coach.

English Indoor Bowling Association, Secretary, David N Brown, David Cornwell House, Bowling Green, Leicester Road, Melton Mowbray, Leics LE13 0DA. T:01664 481900. The EIBA is the governing body of indoor bowls for men in England. There are currently 340 clubs, many of which are open throughout the year. Some offer reduced rates for retired people. Coaching is available at most clubs and there are a number of national competitions for the over 50s and 60s.

English Women's Bowling Association, E.W.B.A. Office, Victoria Park, Archery Road, Leamington Spa, Warwickshire CV31 3PT. T:01926 430 686.

Clay pigeon shooting

Clay Pigeon Shooting Association, Bisley Camp, Brookwood, Woking, Surrey GU24 0NP. T:01483 485400. The CPSA is an association of individual shooters and a federation of clubs. As a member you have public liability insurance of £5 million, your scores are recorded in the national averages and you can compete in national events. The Association produces its own magazine *Pull!* which is distributed free of charge to all members. There are other specialist booklets available on most aspects of clay shooting. Individual membership (2002) is £42 per year; £32 for Veterans (60 and over).

Cricket

The AMP Oval, Surrey County Cricket Club, Kennington, London SE11 5SS. T:020 7582 6660. The AMP Oval is home to the Surrey County Cricket Club and one of the main venues for international and county cricket. There are special Club membership rates for pensioners entitling you to a number of benefits including free or reduced price tickets for the Members' Pavilion to watch international matches as well as county events.

Lord's Cricket Ground, St. John's Wood Road, London NW8 8QN. You can enjoy a conducted tour of Lord's which includes the Long Room, the new futuristic NatWest Media Centre and the MCC Museum, where the Ashes urn is on display. Price is £6.50 (£5 for pensioners) and tour times are normally at noon and 2 p.m. (plus 10 a.m. in summer). These times are subject to variation and you are advised to check before making a special visit on T:020 7432 1033.

Pensioners can attend county championship matches and the National League matches for half-price. There are no concessions, however, for major matches and early booking for these events is recommended. For details, T:020 7432 1066.

England and Wales Cricket Board, Lord's Cricket Ground, London NW8 8QZ. T:020 7432 1200. If you want to play, watch or help at cricket matches, contact your local club or send an sae to the above address. The ECB can put you in touch with your county cricket board. It also organises an over-50 County Cricket Championship.

Croquet

Croquet Association, Nigel Graves (Secretary), c/o Cheltenham Croquet Club, Old Bath Road, Cheltenham GL53 7DF. T:01242 242318. A growing number of local authorities as well as clubs now offer facilities for croquet enthusiasts. The Croquet Association runs coaching courses and can advise you about clubs, events, purchase of equipment and other information.

Cycling

Cyclists' Touring Club, 69 Meadrow, Godalming, Surrey GU7 3HS. T:0870 873 0060. CTC is the largest national cycling organisation. It offers members free third party insurance, free legal aid, a handbook, colour magazines, organised cycling holidays and introductions to 200 local cycling groups. There is also a veterans' section. Membership costs £28.50 a year; £17.50 for people over 65.

Darts

British Darts Organisation Ltd., 2 Pages Lane, Muswell Hill, London N10 1PS. T:020 8883 5544/5. Opportunities for playing darts can be found almost anywhere in clubs, pubs and sports centres. Contact the national body should you require further help.

Golf

English Golf Union, The National Golf Centre, The Broadway, Woodhall Spa, Lincs LN10 6PU. T:01526 354500.

Golfing Union of Ireland, Glencar House, 81 Eglinton Road, Donnybrook, Dublin 4. T:00 353 1 269 4111.

Scottish Golf Union, Scottish National Golf Centre, Drumoig, Leuchars, St Andrews, Fife KY16 0DW. T:01382 549500.

Welsh Golfing Union, Catsash, Newport, Gwent NP18 1JQ. T:01633 430830.

The National Golf Unions can provide information about municipal courses and private clubs, of which there are some 1,700 in England alone. Additionally many adult education institutes and sports centres run classes for beginners.

Rambling

Ramblers' Association, 2nd Floor, Camelford House, 87–90 Albert Embankment, London SE1 7TW. T:020 7339 8500. Rambling can be anything from a gentle stroll to an action-packed weekend trek with stout boots and a rucksack. The Ramblers have over 430 local groups throughout the country which, between them, organise hundreds of walks a week, all led by local experts. Membership (2002) is £20 a year; £11 for those of limited means.

Swimming

Amateur Swimming Association, Unit 1, Kingfisher Enterprise Park, 50 Arthur Street, Redditch, Worcs B98 8LG. T:01527 514 288. Coaching and 'Learn to Swim' classes are arranged by many authorities who also make the pool available at various times of the week for older people who prefer to swim quietly and unhindered. The Association offers an award scheme to encourage greater proficiency in swimming and as an incentive to swim regularly for fitness and health. Further details on request from the ASA.

Table tennis

English Table Tennis Association, 3rd Floor, Queensbury House, Havelock Road, Hastings, East Sussex TN34 1HF. T:01424 722525. Table tennis can be enjoyed by people of all ages and all levels of competence. It is played in community halls, church halls, clubs and many sports centres.

The Veterans English Table Tennis Society (VETTS) holds regional and national championships including singles and doubles events for over 40s, 50s, 60s and 70s. These attract increasing numbers of men and women who enjoy playing socially and competitively well into their retirement. Annual membership (2002) is £10; £5 for those over 65. For further information on VETTS contact: Mrs V Murdoch, Membership Secretary, Harwood House, 90 Broadway, Letchworth, Herts SG6 3PH. T:01462 671191.

Tennis

Lawn Tennis Association, The Queen's Club, West Kensington, London W14 9EG. T:020 7381 7111. As with swimming, facilities have been greatly improving and your local authority Recreation Department should be able to inform you. The LTA can give you information about anything to do with tennis, from advice on choosing a racket to obtaining tickets for major tournaments.

Veterans' Lawn Tennis Association of Great Britain, c/o Valerie Willoughby, 39 Molasses House, Plantation Wharf, London SW11 3TN. The Association promotes competitions for 'veterans' in various age groups. The VLTA *Handbook* (£2) lists affiliated clubs as well as tournaments in Great Britain and Europe, including national championships for all age levels, held on indoor, grass and clay courts.

Veteran rowing

Amateur Rowing Association, 6 Lower Mall, London W6 9DJ. T:020 8237 6700. Veteran rowing as a sport is fast growing in popularity. Enthusiasts range in age from 31 to well past 80. For those who enjoy a competitive edge, there are special races and regattas with types of boat including eights, fours, pairs as well as single and double sculling. Touring rowing is also on the increase and additionally, there is plenty of scope for those who simply want the exercise and a pleasant afternoon afloat. Nearly all clubs welcome novice veterans, both male and female, and usually the only qualification required is the ability to swim. Coaching is provided and membership is normally in the range of £60 to £180 a year. For information about clubs in your locality, contact the ARA at the above address.

Windsurfing

Seavets, The Senior & Veteran Windsurfers Association, 11 Keble Road, Maidenhead, Berkshire SL6 6BB. T:01628 412510. Seavets, which is affiliated to the Royal Yachting Association, aims to encourage the not-so-young of all abilities to enjoy the challenge of windsurfing. Events are organised throughout the country from March to October, providing recreational windsurfing and racing for Seniors (35+), Veterans (50+), Supervets (60+) and Megavets (70+). Additionally, Seavets raises money every year for the charity Research Into Ageing, which funds research into the disabilities of old age. Annual membership (2002) is £12.

Yachting

Royal Yachting Association, RYA House, Romsey Road, Eastleigh, Hampshire SO50 9YA. T:023 8062 7400. There are 1,600 clubs affiliated to the RYA and more than 1,500 recognised teaching establishments. The Association also provides comprehensive information services for boat owners and can give advice on everything from moorings to foreign cruising procedure. Membership costs £28 a year (£25 by direct debit).

Women's organisations

Although today women can participate in almost any activity on equal terms with men, women's clubs and organisations continue to enjoy enormous popularity. Among the best known are Women's Institutes, the Mothers' Union and Townswomen's Guilds.

Mothers' Union, 24 Tufton Street, London SW1P 3RB. T:020 7222 5533. The Mothers' Union (MU) is an Anglican organisation, with over a million members in seventy countries, which promotes the well-being of families. It is open to any member of the Christian churches who has been baptised and who declares their support for the Society's aims. Members can be involved in a wide range of projects within their local community and many attend branches for worship and fellowship.

National Association of Women's Clubs, 5 Vernon Rise, King's Cross Road, London WC1X 9EP. T:020 7837 1434. There are 212 Clubs with a membership of 7,250 throughout the country. They are open to women of all ages and interests. Each club is self-governing, choosing its own meeting times and programme. Typical activities include: crafts, drama, keep fit and talks from guest speakers covering a wide variety of subjects. There are outings to theatres and exhibitions and visits to places of interest and some clubs arrange holiday groups in Great Britain and abroad. Many do voluntary service in their communities for the sick and elderly. Membership is £7 a year to head office plus a small membership fee to the local club.

National Federation of Women's Institutes (NFWI), 104 New Kings Road, London SW6 4LY. T:020 7371 9300. WI is the largest national organisation for women with nearly 240,000 members and 8,000 local WIs nationwide. Through its community ties and wide-ranging activities, it offers women both friendship and the opportunity to develop their skills and talents. The WI has its own residential college, Denman College, and also publishes a monthly magazine *Home & Country*. Membership is £17.25 per annum.

Scottish Women's Rural Institutes, 42 Heriot Row, Edinburgh EH3 6ES. T:0131 225 1724. This is the Scottish counterpart of the Women's Institute movement. It has 29,000 members of all ages who enjoy social, recreational and educational activities. There are talks and demonstrations, classes in arts and crafts and discussions on matters of public interest. You can be put in touch with your local institute via the headquarters office.

If you live in Northern Ireland, contact the **Federation of Women's Institutes of Northern Ireland**, 209–211 Upper Lisburn Road, Belfast BT10 0LL, T:028 9030 1506/9060 1781.

National Women's Register, 3a Vulcan House, Vulcan Road North, Norwich, Norfolk NR6 6AQ. T:01603 406767. The NWR is an organisation of 'lively minded women' who meet informally in 500 local groups throughout the country to enjoy stimulating discussions. The groups choose their own topics and many also arrange a varied programme of social activities. Annual membership subscription is £12.

Townswomen's Guilds, Chamber of Commerce House, 75 Harborne Road, Edgbaston, Birmingham B15 3DA. T:0121 456 3435. The Townswomen's Guilds is an organisation committed to advancing the social awareness of all women, irrespective of race, creed or political affiliation. It has around 55,000 members in 1,600 Guilds across the UK who meet to exchange ideas, learn new skills and take part in a wide range of activities. Annual subscription is £13.

Public transport. One of the big gains of reaching retirement age is the availability of cheap travel. Most local authorities offer concessionary fares to senior citizens during the off-peak periods. Coaches too very often have special rates for older people and, as everyone knows, Senior Railcards, available to men and women over 60, offer wonderful savings. Details of these are given in Chapter 14, Holidays.

10 Starting Your Own Business

Running a small business can be one of the most satisfying retirement occupations. There are hundreds of success stories of those who took the plunge at 55-plus to build a company that provided involvement, fun and income plus a legacy for their children. However, a word of warning. For every success story there is a failure and your money will disappear fast if you set up in big company style. Small business is all about cutting costs, doing it yourself and driving second-hand cars until you are making profits with a positive cash flow. If you are married, your partner's attitude is probably crucial. Even if he or she is not directly involved they will have to accept the loss of a sitting room as an office, the out-of-hours phone calls and the suddenly cancelled social engagement.

If you have a skill to offer, the drive to sell it and the health to support your ambition, this chapter will give you the information you need to set up or buy into a small concern and join the ranks of other successful entrepreneurs.

Legal structure of business

If you are thinking of starting a business, you have three main choices as to the legal form it can take. You can operate as: a sole trader, a partnership, or a limited company.

Sole trader

This is the simplest form of trading, with virtually no start-up expenses and minimal bureaucracy involved. If you trade under your own name then, apart from informing the Inland Revenue, there are no legal formalities. If you use another name, you must indicate on documents such as letterheads that you are the owner (see 'Business names', page 223).

Even if you employ others, you will be treated as self-employed for both tax and national insurance purposes and will be liable to pay personal income tax on your profits, after deducting allowable expenses. You will also be required to pay national insurance contributions on your earnings.

Very small businesses, defined at time of writing as those with a total turnover from business and rental income of under £15,000, are spared the expense of supplying full accounts and instead are able to submit a three-line statement showing: income, expenses and profit. Proper records will nevertheless need to be kept in the event of a query or investigation by the tax office.

The main disadvantage of operating as a sole trader – and it is a major one – is that it carries unlimited liability so you would be personally liable for all business debts.

Should the business fail, your own assets as well as your business ones would be at the disposal of your creditors – and if the worst came to the worst, you could be made personally bankrupt.

Partnership

A partnership is a business with two or more proprietors. Similar to operating as a sole trader, a partnership can be formed without any legal formalities or documentation other than informing the Inland Revenue.

To avoid any possible future misunderstanding however, it is advisable to have a formal partnership agreement drawn up at the outset, covering such points as: distribution of profits (equal or unequal shares), voting rights, control of the bank account and arrangements for admitting new partners. While it is a simple matter to form a partnership, it can be very irksome to settle the affairs of one that has gone wrong. A few legal expenses at the beginning could prove a worthwhile investment.

As with sole traders, partners are treated as self-employed for both tax and national insurance purposes. Profits are divided and taxed as the personal income of individual partners. However, if one partner fails to pay his/her share the other partners will be called upon to meet the shortfall. Similarly, each partner carries unlimited liability for all the debts of the business.

An exception to this rule – although rare today – is that of a limited partnership. This has to be registered at Companies House and at least one partner has to incur unlimited liability. The limited partners (sometimes known as sleeping partners) cannot take part in the running of the business in any way and their liability is limited to their share of the partnership capital. Accounts need to be prepared at least once a year but they do not need to be published.

In common with sole traders, partnerships with a turnover limit of £15,000 (2002/03) can enter in their tax returns a three-line statement showing their income, expenses and profit instead of having to submit full accounts.

Limited company

A limited company is a legal entity in its own right. As its name implies, liability for the company's debts in the event of insolvency is limited to the amount invested in the business by each shareholder.

As a director of a limited company, you will be treated for tax and national insurance purposes as an employee of the business, paying income tax under the PAYE system. Corporation tax will also be payable on the profits of the company.

The main disadvantage of a limited company is the bureaucracy. The government has been reducing the red tape for small firms but not surprisingly there are still a number of legal requirements that must be fulfilled, both before and after trading starts. A limited company must be registered by Companies House (or, in Scotland, by the Registrar of Companies for Scotland): this involves the filing of both a Memorandum of Association and the Articles of Association (see below). The company's accounts have to be audited once a year by a firm of qualified accountants and a set showing, among other details, a profit and loss account must be filed annually with Companies House, together with basic information about the company and its directors, all of which are open to public inspection.

N.B. Small companies can take advantage of an abbreviated form of accounts for filing provided they can meet two of the following criteria: (1) fewer than fifty employees (2) turnover of less than £2.8 million (3) balance sheet total of less than £1.4 million.

Registering a limited company. Although you can register a limited company yourself, it is advisable to get a professional accountant, solicitor or company registration agent to do it for you. Charges vary considerably but are likely to start from around £80 upwards.

To register a limited company, you need to fill in: Form 10, *Notification of First Directors and Secretary and Location of Registered Office* and Form 12, *Declaration of Compliance*. These must be sent to the Registrar of Companies together with the *Memorandum of Association* (stating the company's name, registered office, share capital and nature and scope of the business arrangements, including the extent of liability) and the *Articles of Association* (stating the internal rules of the company).

All the necessary forms can be obtained either from law stationers or from Companies House at the Cardiff address (see below). Specimen memoranda and articles can only be obtained from law stationers.

Fees. There are two scale rates: the normal service, which costs £20 to register (plus an additional £15 per year, payable when the annual returns are sent in for public display); or the same-day incorporation service, which costs £80.

To take advantage of the same-day service, it is necessary to present the completed documents at Companies House by 3 p.m. If you use the standard service, registering a new company will take five working days from the receipt of correct documents at Companies House.

'Off the Shelf'. Another possibility, if you are not too fussy about the company name is to buy a previously registered company 'off the shelf' from a company registration agent. This will cost, on average, about £130 for all the documentation, including the company books. There will be a further charge of around £75 should you decide to change the name and a charge of around £25 to change the Articles of Association. If you simply need to change the name, which is not a difficult matter, you could do it direct with the Registrar. The cost in this case will be £10. For more information, contact the **Information and Enquiry Section**, Companies House, Crown Way, Cardiff CF14 3UZ. T:0870 333 3636; or **The Registrar of Companies for Scotland,** Companies House, 37 Castle Terrace, Edinburgh EH1 2EB. T:0870 333 3636. Forms, guidance notes and other information are available on the Companies House website.

Workers' co-operative

This is another possible form of business structure. Co-operatives are basically owned and controlled by the workers according to international co-operative principles – for instance, all members have equal voting rights irrespective of financial involvement, profits are distributed in proportion to members' participation in the activities of the business, and all workers qualify for membership after a suitable probationary period.

Co-operatives provide their members with limited liability, by registering either as limited companies (requiring a minimum of two founder members) or as Industrial and Provident Societies (requiring a minimum of three founder members).

Most new workers' co-operatives adopt Model Rules for registration. There are a number of different models available from the three national support bodies: ICOM (Industrial Common Ownership Movement), Wales Co-operative Centre Ltd. and Employee Ownership Scotland Ltd.

Registration will usually cost £270-£370 if Model Rules are used; alternatively ICOM provides a 'tailor-made' service where a group has special requirements, costing from £550. In addition, some areas of the country are now served by local Co-operative Development Agencies which can advise and assist on the establishment of a new co-operative venture; of these some also have loan funds available to provide start-up capital.

For more information, contact **Wales Co-Operative Centre Ltd.**, Llandaff Court, Fairwater Road, Cardiff CF5 2XP. T:029 2055 4955; **Employee Ownership Scotland Ltd.**, Robert Owen House, 87 Bath Street, Glasgow G2 2EE. T:0141 304 5465.

ICOM Legal and Registration Services, Co-operative Union incorporating ICOM, Holyoake House, Hanover Street, Manchester M60 0AS, T:0161 246 2900. ICOM publishes a number of useful books, including *A Guide to Co-operative* and *Community Business Legal Structures* (£5.50 incl. p&p).

Business names

It is no longer necessary to register a business name. However, where a sole trader uses a business name that is different from his real name, or where a partnership trades under a name that differs from those of all the partners, or a limited company trades other than under its full corporate name, then certain legal requirements have to be met. All business stationery – including letterheads, order forms, invoices and receipts – must contain the real name(s) of the sole trader, partner or company, together with the official address of the business. These details must also be prominently displayed on all business premises. Failure to do so is a criminal offence, punishable with a fine of up to £400.

There are also certain regulations governing the words that may be used in a business or company name 'without justification'. Prohibited words include: those considered offensive or those that imply connection with the Crown, the Government or a local authority, e.g. British, National, European.

Other prohibited categories are titles like Society or Institute which suggest a representative status or words which imply a specific function such as insurance or banking. In all such cases, approval must be sought from the appropriate government department or governing body that the use of such words is justified. The Registrar of Companies will also refuse to register a company name that is identical to one already on the register, even if it is your own name.

For more information see *Company Names* (GBF2) and *Business Names* (GBF3), available from Companies House. T:0870 333 3636.

Alternative ways of getting started

Rather than start a new business, you could buy into one that is already established or instead, consider franchising.

Buying a business

Buying an established business can be an attractive route to becoming your own boss, as it eliminates many of the problems of start-up. The enterprise is likely to come equipped with: stock, suppliers, an order book, premises and possibly employees. It is also likely to have debtors and creditors.

Take professional advice before buying any business, even one from friends. In particular, you should consider why the business is being sold. It may be for perfectly respectable reasons – for instance, a change of circumstances such as retirement. But equally, it may be that the market is saturated, that the rent is about to go sky high or that major competition has opened up nearby.

The value of the company's assets will be reflected in its purchase price, as will the 'good will' (or reputation) that it has established. For more information, contact **Christie & Co**., the agents specialising in small businesses, at 50 Victoria Street, London SW1H 0NW. T:020 7227 0700.

Before parting with your money, make sure that the assets are actually owned by the business and get the stock professionally valued. You should also ensure that the debts are collectable and that the same credit terms will apply from existing suppliers. Get an accountant to look at the figures for the last three years and have a chartered surveyor check the premises. It is also advisable to ask a solicitor to vet any legal documents, including staff contracts: you may automatically inherit existing employees. See DTI booklet PL 699 *Employment Rights on the Transfer of an Undertaking*, available from Jobcentres or by post from the DTI Publications Orderline, T:0870 150 2500.

Franchising

Franchising has become an increasingly popular form of distribution, with attractions for both franchisor and franchisee. The franchisor gains in that it enables an ambitious group to expand very quickly. The advantage to the franchisee is that there are normally fewer risks than starting a business from scratch.

A franchisee buys into an established business and builds up his own enterprise under its wing. In return for his investment plus regular royalty payments, he acquires the right to sell its products or services within a specified geographic area and enjoys the benefits of the organisation's reputation, buying power and marketing expertise. Examples of well-known franchises include Prontaprint, Budget Rent-a-Car and ServiceMaster.

As a franchisee you are effectively your own boss. You finance the business, employ the staff, and retain the profits after the franchisor has had his cut. You are usually expected to maintain certain standards and conform to the broad corporate approach of the organisation. In return, however, the franchisor should train you in the business, provide management support and give you access to a wide range of back-up services.

Cost. The amount of capital needed to buy a franchise varies enormously according to the type of business and can be anywhere between £3,000 and £500,000 or more. The franchisee is normally liable to pay:

- an initial fee, covering both the entry cost and the initial support services provided by the franchisor, such as advice about location, market research and so on. Advice should be taken as to whether the fee will be partially or wholly allowable for tax purposes;
- recurring fees or royalties, which are usually based on a percentage of gross sales (typically 10 per cent), exclusive of VAT. Sometimes, where the franchisor supplies his own exclusive products, he may derive his income from the usual mark-up on the sale of products to you.

Length of agreement. The length of the agreement will depend both on the type of business involved and the front end fee. Agreements can run from three to twenty years, with seven years being average. Many franchisors include an option to renew the agreement, which should be treated as a valuable asset.

Raising the finance. Franchising has now built up a good track record with a relatively low rate of business failures, so raising the money for a franchising venture is rarely a major difficulty. Most of the leading high street banks operate specialist franchise loan sections.

Franchisors may also be able to help in raising the money and can sometimes arrange more advantageous terms through their connections with financial institutions.

The British Franchise Association (BFA) represents 'the responsible face' of franchising and its members have to conform to a stringent code of practice. The BFA publishes a *Franchisee Guide* (£29) which provides comprehensive advice on buying a franchise together with a list of BFA member franchisors and affiliated advisers.

It is well worth visiting one of the four annual National Franchise Exhibitions, where you can see and compare the various franchise options on offer.

A good franchisor will provide a great deal of invaluable help. However, some franchisors are very casual in their approach, lacking in competence, or even being downright unethical. Points to look out for include overpricing of exclusive stock and lack of back-up services. Make careful enquiries before committing any money: as basic information, you should ask for a bank reference together with a copy of the previous year accounts. Also check with the BFA whether the franchisor in question is a member and talk to some of the other franchisees to find out what their experience has been. Before signing, seek advice from an accountant or solicitor.

For more information, contact **The British Franchise Association**, Thames View, Newtown Road, Henley-on-Thames, Oxon RG9 1HG. T:01491 578049.

Developing an invention

Inventors might usefully consider contacting Inventorlink, a London-based company which, for a fee, specialises in helping inventors find suitable manufacturers and distributors to market their idea. After strict vetting of projects only a fraction of those submitted are accepted. Financial rewards eventually depend on demand for the product. Manufacturers normally pay an upfront fee of between £5,000 and £25,000 and then pay a royalty on sales ranging from about 7.5 to 10 per cent. For more information, contact **Inventorlink**, 27–29 Vauxhall Grove, London SW8 1SY. T:020 7582 2333.

For information about patenting an invention, telephone the **Patent Office**, T:0845 950 0505.

Taxation

Taxation arrangements vary considerably according to whether you are operating as a sole trader, partnership or limited company. As you will know, tax rates, bands and allowances are revised annually and take effect at the beginning of the financial year in April. Figures quoted in this section apply to the 2002/03 financial year.

Sole trader or partnership

As soon as you start work on your own account, you should inform your local Inspector of Taxes. To do so, you should obtain Form CWF1 from your local Inland Revenue office (see telephone directory for address) and return it, when completed, together with your Form P45 which your employer will have given you when you left.

Income tax. As a sole trader or member of a partnership, you are treated as self-employed for tax purposes. Profits are aggregated with any other personal income and are taxed at the normal rates of income tax. After allowing for the 10 per cent rate on the first £1,920, the basic rate of 22 per cent extends to the first £29,900 of taxable income, with all income in excess of this subject to the higher rate of 40 per cent.

Not all your income is taxable. In common with everyone else, you get a personal tax allowance (currently £4,615); and if you qualify for the married couple's allowance, you will also receive the minimum £2,110 allowance (or more, if the husband's income is below the £17,900 income threshold).

Additionally, as a self-employed person (Schedule D), you are allowed certain other reliefs. As a general guideline, the following expenses and allowances are tax deductible:

- Business expenses: these must be incurred 'wholly and exclusively' for the purposes of the trade. Professional publications would probably qualify; however, your 'wages', national insurance contributions and any business entertaining would not. Bad debts are usually allowable. Certain expenses incurred in advance of getting the business started are also permitted, for example: necessary travelling, printing costs and telephoning.
- Partially allowable expenses: these mainly apply if you are working from home. They include such items as that part of your rent, heating, lighting and telephone usage that you devote to business purposes; also possibly, some of the running expenses on your car, if you use your car for your business.
- Spouse's wages: if you employ your partner in the business, his/her pay (provided this is reasonable) qualifies as a legitimate expense, in the same way as any other employee's, but must of course be accounted for through the PAYE system.
- Pension contributions: depending on your age, you are allowed to invest between 17.5 per cent and 40 per cent of your earnings in a pension plan, free of tax. However, for pension plans taken out after 1 June 1989, the relief only applies on earnings up to an Inland Revenue determined ceiling, currently (2002/03) £97,200.
- Capital allowances: a percentage of the cost of some items is 'allowed' for tax relief, for example, an annual allowance of 25 per cent (on the reducing balance) of the cost of plant and machinery, including office furniture, computer software and cars. N.B. Small and medium sized firms enjoy the benefit of more generous first year capital allowances. For most plant and machinery, this is 40 per cent. However, for a limited period between 1 April 2000 and 31 March 2003, small firms can claim 100 per cent first year capital allowance for investment in information and communications technology equipment including computers and software.
- Research and Development: 150 per cent relief is available for spending on qualifying R and D. This means that for every £100 a company spends on R and D, it can claim £150 against its taxable income. Companies not yet in profit can surrender their qualifying R and D losses to the Exchequer in exchange for a cash payment worth 24 per cent of their R and D expenditure. R and D tax credits are also available to companies that have not yet started to trade.
- Interest on loans: tax relief is given on money borrowed to invest in a small firm, in most normal circumstances.
- Tax losses: any tax losses in the first four years may enable you to recover PAYE from your last three years in employment. A tax loss made by the business can also be set against any other income the proprietor may have.

Because of these reliefs, being a sole trader or partner can offer substantial tax advantages. As a result, the Inland Revenue has become increasingly strict about the definition of self-employed. If you work as a consultant or freelance and most of your income derives from one employer, your Inspector of Taxes may argue that you are an employee of that firm – and not a self-employed person. For more information, see leaflet IR 56/NI 39 *Employed or Self-Employed?*, available from your local tax office.

Capital gains tax. Sole traders or partners are liable to capital gains tax at the normal 10, 20 or 40 per cent rate if they sell the business or any of its assets. Capital gains above the individual's annual tax-free allowance of £7,700 are taxed at the rate that would apply if they were treated as the 'top slice' of someone's income, so they could push a basic rate taxpayer into the higher tax bracket. Since the introduction of independent taxation, in the case of a married couple, both husband and wife are taxed independently on their capital gains and each enjoys his/her own separate annual exemption. Tax may not be payable if the proceeds are re-invested within three years in another business (or business assets). Assets bought the previous year might also qualify. This is normally referred to as roll-over relief.

Another valuable relief allows trading losses to be offset against capital gains tax. Proprietors of unincorporated businesses who make a loss (and do not have enough income in the year to offset that loss in full) can make a claim to set the unused loss against capital gains of the same year – with any excess of loss carried forward against capital gains of the following years.

If the owners want to give part of their business (or its assets) to their family, capital gains tax need not be payable until a sale to a third party occurs. This is called hold-over relief.

Another possibility is retirement relief, which could be an attractive solution if you were thinking of selling the business. However, you would need to act fast as retirement relief is in process of being phased out and will cease altogether after 5 April 2003.

Rather than rush into a sale prematurely, you might do better to take advantage of the taper relief on business assets, as the holding period for maximum taper relief has been reduced from four to two years for disposals made after 5 April 2002.

If you are selling a business before taper relief kicks in, you can take out a debenture or loan at the time of sale, enabling you to take advantage of the 10 per cent taper relief when the debenture is redeemed.

Also helpful is the new 'opt out' for incorporation relief which can reduce CGT in certain circumstances. Since there are both advantages and disadvantages in opting out, if you plan to sell a company or shares in a business that is not incorporated, it would be sensible to ask an accountant for advice.

Inheritance tax. Most small family-owned businesses can be passed on to the next generation free of inheritance tax. Although in recent years tax planning has become much easier for small business owners, you would nevertheless be strongly advised to speak to an accountant.

Preparation of accounts. Accounts must be submitted annually to the Inland Revenue. These are normally in two parts: the trading account and profit and loss account, which provide a summary of the year's trading transactions; and the balance sheet, which shows the assets and liabilities of the business at the end of the year.

The accounts of a sole trader or partnership do not have to be audited by an independent qualified accountant. However, whether you draw up the accounts yourself or engage professional help, full and accurate records must be kept from the start. While not essential, there is a very strong argument for having a qualified accountant to help you, since his/her advice is likely to prove invaluable in a whole range of matters. For assistance in finding a local accountant, contact: **The Enquiry Service of the Institute of Chartered Accountants in England and Wales**, T:020 7920 8597.

Very small businesses, i.e. those with a turnover of less than £15,000 a year, are no longer required to submit full accounts but are simply required to provide the Inland Revenue with the following information:

1. details of their total takings;
2. details of their expenses;
3. their profits.

Making a tax return. As an employee, you will have had income tax deducted from your gross pay automatically under the PAYE system. When you become self-employed, you become responsible for the payment of tax and are required by law to make a true return of your income each year.

Self-assessment

As an employer, self-assessment might affect you both personally and it might also affect some of your employees and/or co-directors. People who work for (or with) you who receive a tax return will require certain information from you – mainly about PAYE, benefits in kind and expenses payments. Details are contained in *Self-assessment – What it Will Mean for Employers*, obtainable free from tax offices.

There is no obligation on anyone to work out their tax liability themselves, as self-calculation is optional. However, regardless of whether you opt for self-calculation, both in your own capacity and as an employer you need to be aware of the requirements (including the need to keep records of all your sources of income and capital gains for at least 22 months; or 5 years and 10 months, in the case of a business).

Those choosing to calculate the tax themselves will have until 31 January following the end of the tax year to send in their tax return. Those wishing the Revenue to work out the amount of tax due and be notified in time to make any payment due by 31 January will need to submit their returns by the earlier date of 30 September. (The Revenue will always calculate the tax, if you wish, but returns received after 30 September cannot be guaranteed to have payment advice issued in time for the 31 January deadline). The dates are important, as there is an automatic penalty of £100 if your tax return arrives after 31 January.

For further information, see booklets SABK3, SABK4, SABK6, SABK7 and SABK8, all obtainable free from any tax office. You can also call the SA Orderline on T:0845 900 0444.

Useful reading

For more information about the tax position of sole traders and partnerships, see Inland Revenue booklet P/SE/1 *Thinking of Working for Yourself?* (obtainable from any tax office). Another helpful publication is *The Guide*, obtainable by calling the Newly Employed Helpline on T:08459 154515.

Limited company

The Inland Revenue will be automatically notified when a limited company is formed and will contact the directors in due course. However, to avoid delays it is sensible for you to contact the Revenue as soon as the company is incorporated.

Corporation tax. A company pays corporation tax on its taxable profits. At time of writing, the main rate of corporation tax (2002/03) is 30 per cent. This applies to companies with taxable profits over £1,500,000. A small companies' rate of only 19 per cent applies to companies with taxable profits of between £50,000 and £300,000 or less. There is marginal relief due if the profits are between £300,001 and £1,500,000.

Companies with taxable profits below £10,000 are no longer liable for any corporation tax. Those with taxable profits of between £10,000 and £50,000 get the benefit of marginal relief. Small businesses with taxable profits of over £50,000 pay the normal small companies' rate of 19 per cent.

As a director of a limited company, the business will pay your salary (which will be subject to PAYE) out of its trading income. Allowable expenses, similar to those for sole traders and partnerships, are also deductible before corporation tax is charged. Directors' expenses may however be disallowed, in whole or in part, if the Inland Revenue takes the view that these benefited directors personally – as opposed to being a legitimate business expense. Such expenses may be taxed as a personal benefit.

The Inland Revenue does not allow unlimited payments into pension schemes, particularly those designed to benefit directors. The limits depend, among other factors, on the age of the individuals concerned: it is advisable to discuss this with the company's accountants.

Relief for losses. If your company makes a loss, the directors cannot offset this against their personal taxable income. The losses can, however, be offset against both future and past profits made by the company – with trading losses carried back for up to one year.

Relief for pre-trading expenditure. The period for tax relief for expenditure incurred before the start of trading is seven years.

Preparation of accounts. Limited companies are required to file annual accounts, which have been audited by an independent qualified accountant, within twelve months of their year-end. These accounts will normally form the basis of the Revenue's tax assessment. As stated earlier however, small companies can take advantage of an abbreviated form of accounts for filing provided they can meet two of the following criteria: (1) fewer than fifty employees (2) turnover of less than £2.8 million (3) balance sheet total of less than £1.4 million.

Capital gains tax. When a company sells an asset at a profit, such as a building, it will pay corporation tax on the chargeable gain (currently 19 per cent for small firms). If the company itself is subsequently sold, the shareholders would have capital gains tax to pay on the gain realised from the sale of the shares.

Hold-over, roll-over or venture capital relief are available to individuals in certain circumstances.

Venture capital relief. Many entrepreneurs wishing to defer paying tax on gains arising from the sale of shares in their own companies used to think in terms of re-investment relief. Re-investment relief, as such, has been abolished and is now merged with the Enterprise Investment Scheme (EIS) to create a unified system of venture capital reliefs.

In practical terms, there is not a great deal of difference. Entrepreneurs (as well as other investors with gains) can defer paying CGT and in many cases can also obtain income tax relief at 20 per cent on investments of up to £150,000 a year, provided gains are re-invested in qualifying (i.e. with maximum gross assets of £15 million) unquoted companies within three years. An important change, however, is that under the new rules companies with property-backed assets, such as farming, hotels and nursing homes, no longer qualify as eligible trading companies. Any investment, therefore, would be relatively high risk.

A new taper relief designed to encourage serial entrepreneurs and others to invest in EIS companies was introduced in the 1999 Budget, enabling investors to move from one EIS investment to another, with the advantage of being able to defer the gain from their first investment (made after 5 April 1998) over the combined period of any subsequent investments – thus giving them the benefit of more generous taper relief in calculating their eventual liability for CGT.

Even more helpful perhaps is the new revised taper for business assets which reduces the CGT payable on disposals to an effective 10 per cent rate after a holding period of only two years. Prior to the change in April 2002, the holding period for maximum taper relief was four years.

Owner-managers engaged in running their own business are entitled to **retirement relief** on sale of the business, or their shares, when they retire. However, as explained earlier in the chapter (see page 228), retirement relief is being phased out and will cease altogether after 5 April 2003.

If you are planning to sell a major asset, you should consult your accountant to avoid the possibility of a double tax payment. A further point you might usefully discuss, particularly in view of the phasing out of retirement relief, is the optimum timing of any sale.

Tax offset. If your company makes a trading loss, this can be used as an offset against profits made on the sale of assets, provided the sale takes place in the same or previous year.

Inheritance tax. Since 1992 most small family-owned businesses have been taken out of the inheritance tax net and can be passed on to the next generation free of tax. In the 1995 Budget, the Chancellor went even further in protecting family-owned concerns from break-up by extending 100 per cent business relief to all shares in qualifying unquoted companies that have been held for at least two years.

There are certain cases, however, where inheritance tax could still be a factor, i.e.: where the controlling shares are in a fully quoted company; and where certain assets are owned by partners or by controlling shareholders and are used in their respective businesses. In such cases, there is tax relief of 50 per cent.

Although inheritance tax planning has now become much easier for small business owners, you would nevertheless be strongly advised to speak to an accountant.

New tax rules. If as many individuals do, you are thinking of setting up a limited company, charging your clients fees for your services and paying yourself a dividend at the end of the year according to what the company can afford, you should be aware that the Inland Revenue has tightened up the rules in order to clamp down on what it sees as the avoidance of PAYE and Class 1 national insurance contributions. If you are thinking of operating in an independent capacity – as opposed to becoming a bona fide employee – it would be sensible to discuss the tax implications with an accountant before determining whether you should operate as self-employed, a sole trader, partnership or limited company.

Value added tax (VAT)

Value added tax is imposed on most business transactions. The legal structure of the enterprise does not in general affect the issue.

Registration. Registration is required if your annual (2002/03) 'taxable turnover' exceeds £55,000. 'Taxable turnover' applies to the gross turnover of goods or services which are made or supplied by the business. You have 30 days to notify Customs and Excise if you become liable to register. Businesses may de-register from VAT, if they so choose, if their taxable turnover falls below £53,000.

Charging and paying VAT. You collect VAT from your customers by including it in, or adding it to, the price you charge (output tax). Similarly, you will be charged VAT by your suppliers on the goods and services you buy (input tax). When you receive a VAT return your input tax is subtracted from your output tax and the difference is paid to Customs and Excise. If the input tax is greater than the output tax, you can claim a refund on the difference.

Small businesses with a taxable turnover of up to £100,000 can opt to take advantage of a new flat rate scheme for calculating their VAT liability. Instead of keeping detailed records of the VAT charged on every purchase and sale, they can calculate the amount due by applying a flat rate percentage to their total turnover. The scheme which was introduced in April 2002 is planned to be extended to businesses with turnovers of up to £150,000 from April 2003.

Businesses with an annual turnover of less than £600,000 can opt to submit a VAT return once a year instead of quarterly. A condition is that they must make monthly payments by direct debit, based on estimates agreed with Customs and Excise – with a balancing adjustment made when the annual return is submitted.

Businesses with an annual turnover of less than £600,000 can opt for cash accounting for VAT, enabling them to delay paying the VAT on their sales to Customs and Excise until they have actually received payment for these. However, you cannot issue invoices in advance of supply or for sales where payment is not due for more than six months after the date of the invoice. The scheme should help the cash flow of small firms with tardy customers and provide automatic VAT relief for bad debts. Bad debts can be written off for the purpose of claiming VAT relief after six months. A debtor no longer has to be declared formally insolvent for relief to be allowed.

Taxable supplies and exempt supplies. Most transactions are liable to VAT at either the standard rate (currently 17.5 per cent) or the zero-rate (nil).

Zero-rated supplies include: most food (but not catering), books and newspapers, sales of new dwellings, young children's clothing and footwear, protective boots and helmets meeting EC safety standards, export of goods, dispensing of prescriptions and the supply of many aids for disabled persons, mobile homes and houseboats, water and sewage services. Zero-rated suppliers have to complete and return a VAT form, even though they are not liable to pay this tax.

Exempt supplies include: insurance, betting, gaming and lotteries, provisions of credit, certain education and training, services of doctors and other medical specialists, certain supplies by undertakers. Such suppliers do not have to complete regular VAT returns but must complete form VAT 1 when they apply for exemption. If you are granted exemption, you will not be able to reclaim the VAT you pay on goods and services for your business.

The 'de minimis' limit for partly exempt businesses is £7,500 a year. To qualify for partial exemption, VAT incurred on the exempt supplies must not exceed either £625 a month or 50 per cent of total input tax.

Below the VAT registration limit. If you are not registered for VAT, any expenditure which you incur which includes a charge for VAT should be entered in your records, inclusive of VAT. Even if you do not have to register at present, you may have to do so in the future if your taxable turnover increases. There could be an argument for early registration, as you would be able to offset the VAT the business has to pay to its suppliers. Another advantage is that VAT usually helps in establishing well kept accounts. For more information, see C & E booklet *Should I Be Registered for VAT?*, obtainable from any C & E office.

How to register. Fill in Form VAT 1 (or the Welsh equivalent Form VAT 20). If the business to be registered is a partnership you will also need Form VAT 2. If you have acquired a business as a going concern you may be able to have the registration number of the previous owner reallocated to you. See VAT leaflet *Selling or Transferring a Business as a Going Concern*.

N.B. Don't delay. If you do not notify within the 30-day limit once you are liable to be registered, you may have to account for tax which you have not collected, together with penalties for late registration. You should start keeping VAT records and charging VAT to your customers as soon as you know you are required to be registered. You will have to account for VAT from this date whether or not you have included VAT in your prices.

Planned reforms. The government is planning to introduce two helpful reforms in 2003 to make VAT simpler and less onerous for business. In the event of a bad debt, firms will no longer be required to notify their debtors in writing that they are claiming relief. Even more welcome, businesses with turnovers up to £150,000 that are late with their VAT payments will be offered help and advice rather than getting an automatic fine.

For further information, contact the Customs and Excise Advice Line on T:0845 010 9000 (8 a.m. – 8 p.m., Monday to Friday).

Benefits in kind

The rules affecting benefits in kind apply to all directors and to employees earning £8,500 or more a year (including the value of benefits in kind). Any tax payable is deducted via the PAYE system. A particular item of interest to many smaller businesses is company cars.

Company cars. As most company car owners will know, the tax system for company cars was changed in April 2002. Business mileage no longer counts. Instead, tax is now based on a percentage of the list price – varying from 15 to 35 per cent – according to the car's CO_2 emission level. Since a key aim is to cut pollution, larger gas – guzzling cars are charged more.

Cars registered before January 1998 are taxed according to their engine size as reliable emission data is not available for older vehicles. The maximum tax is slightly lower at 32 per cent.

For further information, see leaflet IR 172 *Income Tax and Company Cars*, obtainable from any tax office.

Free fuel is also treated as a benefit in kind for tax purposes. The scale charges for those with a company car who get free fuel for private motoring are unchanged from 2001/02.

Employers have to pay national insurance contributions on the provision of cars for private use by employees as well as on the fuel consumption they enjoy. (See leaflet CA 33 *Cars and Fuel – A Manual for Employers* and IR booklet 490 *Employee Travel – a Tax and National Insurance Contributions Guide for Employers*, available from the Employer's Stationery Orderline on T:08457 646646.)

Some companies are finding it a better and cheaper solution to give their employees a loan to buy their own car. (Beneficial loans up to £5,000 are not assessed as a taxable benefit).

Individuals using their own cars on company business are allowed tax-free payments of 40p a mile for up to 10,000 miles of business travel; 25p per additional mile over 10,000. The mileage rate system geared to a car's engine size has been abolished and since the start of the April 2002/03 tax year there is just a single rate for all cars and vans.

Individuals using their own motorcycles and bicycles are also allowed mileage payments. The table below shows the maximum exempt rates an employer can pay for 2002/03 without tax and NICs becoming due.

Motor cars and vans	
Up to 10,000 business miles	40p per mile
Over 10,000 business miles	25p per mile
Motorcycles	24p per mile
Bicycles	20p per mile

If you pay less than the above rates, employees can claim tax relief on the difference. If you pay more, tax will be payable on the excess.

IR booklet 125 *Using Your Own Car for Work* explains the tax position in detail for employees using their own car for business travel.

N.B. Businesses are able to recover VAT on cars bought wholly for business use.

If you have any queries about the new systems, contact the Employer's Helpline on T:08457 143143.

Useful reading

IR booklet 480 *Expenses and Benefits Tax Guide*, obtainable from any tax office.

National insurance

As with tax, your liability for national insurance contributions will depend on whether you are self-employed (sole trader or partner) or whether you are a director of a limited company.

Self-employed

If you are self-employed, you will have to pay flat rate Class 2 contributions – currently £2 a week – unless:

- you are over 65 for men; 60 for women (even if you have not retired from work)
- you are entitled to pay married women's or widow's reduced rate Class 1 contributions
- you have been granted 'a certificate of exception' because your (2002/03) earnings are likely to be less than £4,025 a year.

You must register to pay Class 2 contributions within three months of becoming self-employed or you risk incurring a £100 penalty.

If your annual taxable profits or profit share are above £4,615, you will also have to pay Class 4 contributions of 7 per cent on profits between £4,615 and £30,420, unless you are in one of the following categories:

- not resident for income tax purposes in the UK
- trustee, executor or administrator of wills and settlements (there are, however, exceptions)
- sleeping partner, taking a profit and supplying capital, but not active in the business

N.B. There is no additional NI liability on profits that exceed £30,420 and the maximum amount of Class 4 contribution payable (2002/03) is £1,806.35.

NIC rates 2003/04. Class 4 contributions are due to be increased from 7 to 8 per cent on earnings between £4,615 and £30,420 (i.e. the lower and upper profits limits). There will also be an extra 1 per cent to pay on all earnings above the upper limit of £30,420.

How to pay. Class 2 contributions can be paid either by direct debit from your bank or by the quarterly billing system which has replaced the traditional NI stamps. If you prefer quarterly billing, the National Insurance Contributions Office should automatically advise you of the amount owing for the previous quarter, which is payable through banks or at all post offices via Girobank.

Class 4 contributions are normally assessed and collected by the Inland Revenue, together with PAYE or Schedule D income tax. As they will be paid retrospectively, remember to keep the necessary cash ready and not spend it as part of your monthly salary.

Husband and wife. As with independent taxation, husband and wife are assessed separately for Class 4 contributions.

Further information about Schedule D tax assessments and related Class 4 national insurance contributions can be obtained from your local Inspector of Taxes. For help on deferment or refund of Class 4 contributions, contact: National Insurance Contributions Office, Deferment Group, **Inland Revenue**, Longbenton, Newcastle upon Tyne NE98 1YX.

Double income. If you are self-employed but also receive a salary you may have to pay NI contributions on both incomes. However, there is an overall limit of £2,628.80 (2002/03) above which contributions are not payable. If too much has been deducted in total you can reclaim the excess or ask for a reduction of Class 2 and/or Class 4 contributions.

Useful reading

Leaflet CWL 2 *National Insurance Contributions for Self-employed People, Class 2 and Class 4;* leaflet CA 04 *National Insurance Contributions Class 2 & Class 4: Direct Debit – the Easier Way to Pay*; and (for those liable for double income NI contributions) leaflet CA 01 *National Insurance for Employees*, available at all Inland Revenue (NI Contributions) offices.

Limited company

If you trade as a limited company, the company will pay employer's Class 1 contributions and you will suffer the same deductions from your salary as any other employee.

If you control the company, you will in effect be paying both the employer and the employee's share of NI contributions on your own account.

If you are a director of several companies, you may be liable for multiple NI contributions: see leaflet CA 44 *National Insurance for Company Directors*, available from Inland Revenue (NI Contributions) offices.

National insurance benefits

Different classes of contributions qualify you for different types of benefit.

Class 2 Contributions count for:

- incapacity benefit (leaflet IB 1)
- basic retirement pension (leaflet NP 46)
- bereavement benefits
- basic maternity benefit (leaflet NI 17A)

Class 1 Contributions entitle you to all the above and additionally to the jobseeker's allowance, should the need ever arise. They also count towards the additional state pension.

Class 3 Contributions. These may be paid voluntarily to help you qualify for, or improve your entitlement to, certain benefits. A flat rate of £6.85 a week is payable. See leaflet CA 08 *National Insurance Voluntary Contributions*, available from any Inland Revenue (NI Contributions) offices.

Pensions

Sole traders and partners are self-employed for pension as well as tax purposes and must make their own arrangements. Directors of limited companies are treated as employees and may be included in their company's pension scheme or may run their own self-administered pension schemes.

Self-employed pensions

Self-employed individuals can invest up to £3,600 a year in a personal pension or stakeholder pension and claim tax relief on the contributions at their top rate of tax. Those wishing to invest more can contribute between 17.5 per cent and 40 per cent of their earnings, depending on their age. In particular, for those between the ages of 51 and 55, the allowed amount is 30 per cent; for those aged between 56 and 60, 35 per cent; and for those aged 61 and over, 40 per cent.

If the full relief is not used in any one tax year, it may be possible to offset the pension premiums against either of the two previous years' earnings.

Loan-back facilities

Almost all old-style self-employment pension plans carry loan-back facilities which can provide a useful and tax-efficient line of credit for small businesses. Such loans can take one of two forms: either the self-employed can borrow up to the accumulated value of the pension fund; or the loan can be calculated as a multiple of the annual premiums paid.

In both cases, suitable security is required as collateral. You can usually delay the repayment of the loan (but not the interest) until you receive your tax-free lump sum on retirement. There are no restrictions on the purposes for which the loans can be used. However, under new rules which came into effect in July 1988 'loan-back' facilities are not allowed on new personal pensions.

Directors

Company pension schemes have limits on the maximum level of benefits they can provide: for instance, the maximum pension is limited to two-thirds of an employee's final salary. For anyone joining a new pension plan post-June 1989, the maximum pensionable final salary is £97,200. This figure is regularly adjusted to reflect changes in the RPI. However, unlimited contributions can be pumped into the fund by the company and written off against corporation tax so long as these maximum benefits are not exceeded. The employee (i.e. director) can make additional voluntary contributions up to a total of 15 per cent of his salary (provided these do not take him/her over the £97,200 cap) and offset the premiums against his top rate of tax. Members of an existing pension scheme, before the rule changes came into effect, are not affected by the £97,200 limit.

Company pension schemes can either be effected through an insurance company in much the same way as for self-employed schemes; or set up as a self-administered scheme, run mainly by its members and one independent 'pensioneer trustee'. The investment of the funds is almost entirely a matter for the trustees, subject to certain limitations imposed by the Inland Revenue to prevent abuse. Investments may include the company's own property, loans to the company and the company's own shares.

Company loan-back facilities

Loans by a company pension scheme to its members are not normally allowed. Small self-administered pension schemes however may loan money to the employer company. For the first two years of its existence, the scheme may loan up to 25 per cent of the fund (excluding transfers received from other schemes). After the fund has been in existence for two years, the amount allowed is increased to 50 per cent of the value of all the assets of the scheme. These limits on self-investment apply to the aggregate of loans to, and shares in, an employer company.

Such funds can therefore provide useful working or development capital in a tax-efficient way. Cash can be transferred into a tax-exempt fund and the contributions will qualify for tax relief. The company can then borrow back up to 25 per cent (50 per cent after the two years), and claim tax relief on the interest payments. The fund receives the interest net of tax and then claims the tax back from the Inland Revenue. The loans can only be used for the purpose of the business and must be for a fixed term and at a commercial rate of interest (i.e. not less than bank rate plus 3 per cent).

The agreement must also be in writing and have the approval of the independent pensioneer trustee.

Stakeholder Pensions

Since October 2001, all but the smallest employers without a company-wide occupational scheme are legally required to give their staff access to a stakeholder scheme. The only exceptions are: (1) businesses employing fewer than 5 people and (2) employers who offer a group PP and contribute at least 3 per cent of earnings. For further information, see *Stakeholder Pensions – a Guide for Employers*, available from the Employers' Orderline on T:08457 646 646. Or if you need advice, ring the Inland Revenue Employers' Helpline on T:08457 143143.

Your responsibilities as an employer

Many people starting a business wisely limit recruitment to the minimum in the early days, until they are sure that they can afford the cost of having permanent staff. Once you become an employer, you take on responsibilities. As well as paying the salaries, you will have to account for PAYE, keep national insurance records and conform with the multiple requirements of employment legislation.

While this may sound rather daunting, two recent measures should hopefully reduce much of the complexity. Firstly, the Contributions Agency has been transferred to the Inland Revenue, with the advantage that employers now only need to go through a single organisation to sort out tax and national insurance matters. Secondly, the government has launched a new service, staffed by new business advisers, to help small businesses employing staff for the first time get to grips with the tax and national insurance systems. For telephone advice or to arrange a visit by an adviser, ring the helpline on T:0845 607 0143.

If you are still worried or don't want the bother of doing the paperwork yourself, your bank and possibly your accountant are likely to offer a full payroll service which will cost you money but will take the burden off your shoulders.

PAYE

If you employ someone in your business (including your wife/husband) you are responsible for deducting income tax under the PAYE arrangements and accounting for it to the Collector of Taxes.

You will be provided with tax tables and working sheets. The tax office will then notify you of the various PAYE tax codes in respect of your employees and explain how to use the tax table to work out the deductions.

If an employee does not have an existing P45, you should ask him/her to complete a Starting Certificate Form P46, obtainable from the tax office.

An individual is liable for tax after deduction of their personal allowance and various reliefs. As a rough guide, for those only in receipt of the personal allowance (£4,615), this would be after earnings of £89 a week. Even if an employee's pay is less than £89, there could still be PAYE implications, as he/she may have other earnings. Employers whose average monthly payments of PAYE and NIC total less than £1,500 can make quarterly payments rather than monthly. The due dates for quarterly payments are: 19 July, 19 October, 19 January and 19 April. For more information, see Inland Revenue booklet NE 1 *First Steps as a New Employer*.

Tax Credits. At time of writing, there are two tax credits of possible concern to employers: Working Families Tax Credit (WFTC) and Disabled Person's Tax Credit (DPTC). Although both are funded by the government, employers are responsible for paying the credits through the payroll system and for keeping appropriate records. If applicable, the tax credit office will notify you and advise: whom to pay, what to pay and when to pay. This at least remains the situation up until the end of the 2002/03 tax year.

However, come April 2003, two new credits are being introduced and both the Working Families Tax Credit and Disabled Person's Tax Credit will cease.

There will be a new Child Tax Credit for families with children which will incorporate the existing children's tax credit with the child-related elements of income support and various other benefits. The good news is that Child Tax Credit will be paid by the Revenue direct to all families with children, so employers will not need to be involved.

The second new tax credit – called Working Tax Credit – will replace the adult-related elements of WFTC, DPTC and the New Deal 50+ Employment Credit and will also widen eligibility to more low income earners without children. It will normally be paid to employees through the payroll and the system will operate in much the same way as the existing scheme for WFTC and DPTC.

For further information, see IR 173 *Tax Credits: a Summary for Employers*, available from any tax office; or ring the Employers' Helpline on T:08457 143143.

National Insurance for employees

The national insurance threshold is £89 a week. With one or two exceptions, in particular persons over State retirement age, anyone earning over this amount will be liable for national insurance. You are responsible for the payment of both the employer's and employee's contributions but are entitled to deduct the employee's share from his/her earnings.

Happily, the NI system has been considerably simplified over the past couple of years. Whereas previously there were differing graduated rates in respect of both employees' and employers' contributions, these have now been abolished and replaced in each case by a single rate.

Employees now pay a standard rate of 10 per cent on weekly earnings between £89.01 and £585 (2002/03). However, those earning at least £75 a week (i.e. the lower earnings limit) will be treated as having paid a contribution, entitling them to the normal benefits. N.B. Employees earning less than £89 a week have nothing to pay. Likewise, those earning over £585 are not liable for extra contributions.

Employers now pay a standard contribution rate of 11.8 per cent on all earnings above the earnings threshold. In other words, during the current tax year (2002/03), employers are liable for contributions on all earnings above £89 a week.

Employees contracted out of the State earnings- related pension scheme pay a reduced NIC rate of 8.4 per cent (1.6 per cent less).

Employers who operate a contracted-out scheme also pay lower contributions. For salary-related schemes, the NICs payment is 8.3 per cent (3.5 per cent less); for money purchase schemes, payment is 10.8 per cent (1 per cent less).

Additionally in the case of COMPs, age-related rebates, ranging from 0.01 per cent for 17 year olds to 7.9 per cent for employees aged 50 and over, also apply.

Contact your local Inland Revenue office for leaflet CWG 2 *Employer's Further Guide to PAYE and National Insurance Contributions*. The staff will explain to you how the system works and answer any queries.

You will be sent a payslip booklet by the Collector of Taxes, together with official Deductions Working Sheets P.11 and P.14. Payments must be made within 14 days of the end of each income tax month.

NIC rates 2003/04. NIC rates are due to be increased by 1 per cent in April 2003. The change will affect both employers and employees on all earnings above the NIC threshold of £89. The additional contribution will mean that employers will pay 12.8 per cent on all earnings above the £89 threshold and employees will pay 11 per cent on all earnings between the £89 threshold and the 2003/04 upper earnings limit of £595. Employees will also have to pay an extra 1 per cent contribution on all earnings above the £595 upper earnings limit.

Statutory Sick Pay

Employers are responsible for paying Statutory Sick Pay (SSP) to their employees, including contract workers, for up to 28 weeks of sickness absence. The rate and earnings thresholds are subject to review annually. The current (2002/03) SSP rate is £63.25; it applies to employees with average weekly earnings of £75 or more. SSP is subject to deduction of income tax and NI contributions in the same way as ordinary pay. Employers are allowed to recover SSP costs in any month where these exceed 13 per cent of their NI liability for that month. The amount that can be reclaimed is the excess over 13 per cent. For further information, see CA 30 *Statutory Sick Pay Manual for Employers* and Help Book E14 *What to Do if Your Employee is Sick*.

Statutory Maternity Pay

Any woman with average weekly earnings of £75 and above (2002/03) who has been in the same job for 26 weeks by the qualifying week (15 weeks before the expected week of childbirth) is entitled to the following rates: 90 per cent of earnings for the first six weeks of maternity leave; a flat-rate payment of £75 for up to the remaining 12 weeks. In April 2003, the £75 flat-rate payment is being increased to £100 a week. At the same time, the payment period for maternity leave is being extended from 18 to 26 weeks. Small employers whose gross annual national insurance contributions (NICs) are £40,000 or less in the qualifying tax year are fully reimbursed and can claim 5 per cent compensation towards their extra costs. Those paying more than £40,000 a year in gross NICs can claim 92 per cent of SMP costs. For further information, see CA 29 *Statutory Maternity Pay Manual for Employers* and Help Book E15 *What to Do if Your Employee is Pregnant.*

N.B. Although a woman must have worked in the same job for 26 weeks to qualify for SMP, an employer can no longer request her to leave – however short a period she has been in a job (even one day) – on grounds of pregnancy.

Advice note. Most of what you need to know is contained in the CWG *Series of Guides to Pay as You Earn and National Insurance Contributions*, obtainable from Inland Revenue offices.

If you have queries about these or other benefit matters, you can telephone the Employers' Helpline, on T:08457 143143.

Paid paternity leave

Paid paternity leave is due to become a statutory right from April 2003. Provided they have been with their employer for at least 26 weeks, fathers will be entitled to two weeks paid leave, within 8 weeks of the child's birth, at the same rate as statutory maternity pay. Small employers will be fully reimbursed.

Adoption leave

Paid adoption leave is also due to become a statutory right from April 2003. Both the length of leave and the payment amounts are the same as for statutory maternity pay. Similarly small employers will be fully reimbursed and can also claim 5 per cent compensation towards their costs. The leave can be taken by either one of the parents and the other parent, whether father or mother, can claim paternity leave.

If you have any queries about paternity leave or adoption leave, telephone the Employers' Helpline on T: 08457 143 143.

Personnel records

Many businesses find it useful to keep personnel records, covering such information as national insurance numbers, tax codes, merit appraisal reports and so on. If you use either a computerised system or keep paper records, you would be advised to contact the Information Commissioner for advice about your obligations under the Data Protection Act. Write to or telephone **The Information Commissioner's Office**, Wycliffe House, Water Lane, Wilmslow, Cheshire SK9 5AF. Information Line T:01625 545745.

Employment legislation

As an employer, you have certain legal obligations in respect of your staff. The most important cover such issues as: health and safety at work, terms and conditions of employment and the provision of employee rights including, for example, parental leave, trade union activity and protection against unfair dismissal. Very small firms are exempted from some of the more onerous requirements and the government is taking steps to reduce more of the red tape. However, it is important that you understand in general terms what legislation could affect you.

Minimum wage. The minimum age rates were increased last year as follows: for workers aged 18 to 21, the minimum hourly rate is £3.60; for those aged 22 and above, the minimum is £4.20 an hour.

Health and safety at work. The Health and Safety at Work Act applies to everyone in a business whether employer, employee or the self-employed. It also protects the general public who may be affected by your business activity. The Health and Safety Executive publishes a number of useful free leaflets and also has a public enquiry point which is open between 8 a.m. and 6 p.m. Ring **Health and Safety Executive** Infoline on T:08701 545 500; Minicom: 029 208 085 537.

A model safety policy entitled *Writing Your Health and Safety Policy Statement*, with blank sections for an employer to fill in and step-by-step notes for guidance is available free from HSE Books, T:01787 881165; please quote order code number INDG 324.

Discrimination. An employer – however small his business – may not discriminate against someone on the grounds of sex, race or marital status. This applies to all aspects of employment, including training, promotion, recruitment, company benefits and facilities. If you have 15 or more employees, it is also unlawful to discriminate against someone who is disabled. Following the 1995 Disability Discrimination Act, there is a duty to make any necessary changes – known as 'reasonable adjustments' – to the workplace and employment arrangements, so that a disabled person is not at any substantial disadvantage. For more information, contact: **Equal Opportunities Commission**, Arndale House, Arndale Centre, Manchester M4 3EQ. Tel/Minicom: 0845 601 5901; the **Commission for Racial Equality**, Elliot House, 10–12 Allington Street, London SW1E 5EH. T:020 7828 7022; **Disability Rights Commission**, Arndale House, Arndale Centre, Manchester M4 3EQ. T:08457 622633.

The law against discrimination is due to be extended more widely. Both religion and sexual orientation are planned to be included in 2003 and, from October 2004, smaller businesses (i.e. with fewer than 15 employees) will no longer be exempted from the Disability Discrimination legislation. Also, which will please many readers, age discrimination is due to be made unlawful in 2006.

Contract of employment. A contract of employment is an agreement entered into between an employer and an employee under which they have certain mutual obligations. It comes into being as soon as an employee starts work, when it is taken that he/she accepts the job on the terms offered. Within two months of the job starting, the employer must normally give the employee a written statement highlighting the key terms and conditions of the job together with a general description of the duties.

The requirement for a contract of employment applies to all staff including part-timers and those working on fixed contracts. More specifically, the law requires them to be treated equally (i.e. as those working full time) in respect of training, holiday entitlement and benefits.

Useful booklets prepared by the DTI include, PL 700 *Written Statement of Employment Particulars*, PL 810 *Contracts of Employment* and PL 716 *Individual Rights of Employees*, available free from your local Jobcentre or from DTI Publications Orderline, Admail 528, London SW1W 8YT. T:0870 150 2500; Minicom: 0870 150 2100. Further information can also be obtained from Citizens' Advice Bureaux or a solicitor.

Parental leave. All parents, including adoptive parents, who have completed a year's service with their employer have the right in law to 13 weeks unpaid leave to look after a child born or adopted on or after 15 December 1999.

The leave would normally have to be taken in the first five years following the child's birth or placement for adoption. However, in the case of a disabled child, the right to parental leave is increased to 18 weeks and the take-up period is extended to the child's 18th birthday.

Parents of children born or adopted between 15 December 1994 and 14 December 1999 are also able to take 13 weeks parental leave but only if they have completed one year's continuous service with an employer between 15 December 1998 and 9 January 2002. They have until 31 March 2005 to take their entitlement (or, in the case of adoption, the child's 18th birthday if that is sooner).

Time off for dependants. Employees are entitled to a reasonable amount of time off to deal with an emergency (e.g. a childminder not turning up) affecting a member of the family or other dependant.

Useful reading

Parental Leave – a Guide for Employers and Employees (PL 509) and *Time-Off for Dependants – a Guide for Employers and Employees* (URN 99/1186), available from the DTI Publications Orderline on T:0870 150 2500 or from the DTI website.

Disputes

If you find yourself with a potential dispute on your hands, it is sensible to approach the Advisory, Conciliation and Arbitration Service (ACAS), which also operates an effective information and advisory service for employers and employees on a variety of workplace problems including employment legislation and industrial relations. To contact **ACAS**, see telephone directory for address of your local regional office.

Useful reading

Employing People: A Handbook for Small Firms. A useful guide which can be used as a quick reference to most problems of employment law such as industrial relations, health and safety, pay, trade union law and employment protection. Price £4.95, available from: ACAS Publications, PO Box 235, Hayes, Middx UB3 1HF.

Getting It Right: collection of 10 factsheets for small firms. Free from any ACAS office or £1.50 by post from the above address.

Trading regulations

Trading regulations laying down your obligations to your customers are contained in various Acts of Parliament, such as the Fair Trading Act, Trade Descriptions Act, Sale of Goods Act, Consumer Credit Act and the Consumer Protection Act. For free advisory literature, contact: **Office of Fair Trading**, Room 5C/05, Fleetbank House, 2–6 Salisbury Square, London EC4Y 8JX. T:020 7211 8887. Solicitors are also qualified to advise on such matters.

Licences

Certain types of business require a license or permit to trade, including: pubs, off-licences, nursing agencies, pet shops, kennels, mini-cabs or buses, driving instructors, betting shops, auction sale rooms, cinemas, hairdressers, street traders and, in some cases, travel agents and tour operators. You will also require a licence to import certain goods.

Your local authority Planning Office will advise you as to whether you require a licence and in many cases your council will be the licensing authority.

The Consumer Credit Act 1974 also imposes a licensing requirement on various types of business that offer credit and hire facilities. The Act is administered by the Office of Fair Trading (see above), which publishes a helpful booklet *Do You Need A Credit Licence?*.

Another useful source of information is the **Department of Trade and Industry Import Licensing Branch**, Queensway House, West Precinct, Billingham TS23 2NF. T:01642 364333.

Finding suitable premises

A few years ago, finding premises was often a real problem for small firms. Today, however, thanks to the relaxation of many planning regulations, together with an increase in small workshops, it has become very much easier. The sources to tap when you start looking include:

Newspapers. There are property pages in publications such as *Dalton's Weekly*, *Exchange & Mart* and the *Estates Gazette*. Evening and local newspapers also carry advertisements for industrial, commercial and retail property.

Estate agents. Ask for the department dealing with commercial premises. You will have to pay commission, which may be structured in various ways. Check carefully on the terms and conditions.

Local authorities. Councils often maintain a list of vacant properties including a register of small units. Many authorities own and manage workshop developments. If you are thinking of building your own premises, your District Council will also have information on sites earmarked for development and will be able to advise you on the planning implications. Contact the Industrial Development Officer.

Chambers of commerce. These are often an excellent source of information about vacant premises, as they have wide contacts with local businesses and others.

English Partnerships. English Partnerships can assist with finding building land in the 19 English new towns as well as a wide range of other locations. Contact: English Partnerships, Central Business Exchange, 414–428 Midsummer Boulevard, Central Milton Keynes MK9 2EA. T:01908 692692.

Enterprise Agencies. Again, a first class contact point. Some agencies run managed workshops. Their premises often provide shared facilities such as typing, fax and photocopying. For addresses of local enterprise agencies (enterprise trusts in Scotland), contact the **National Federation of Enterprise Agencies**, c/o NatWest Bank, Trinity Gardens, 9–11 Bromham Road, Bedford MK40 2UQ. T:01234 354055, who can put you in touch with your nearest EA/ET.

Spacia. Vacant railway arches, small shops, offices and other commercial property throughout England, Wales and Scotland are available to rent from: Spacia, The West Wing, The Hop Exchange, 26 Southwark Street, London SE1 1TU. T:0800 830840.

Enterprise Zones

Enterprise Zones have been set up in various parts of the country, with the intention of winning business to these areas. The major attraction is that EZs are exempt from industrial and commercial rates and are also largely free of planning controls, although the normal health and safety regulations apply. The rates holiday only lasts for 10 years. EZs are currently located in the following places: Lanarkshire (T:01698 745454), the three colliery closure areas of the East Midlands (T:01246 212685), Bassetlaw (T:01909 533190), Mansfield (T:01623 463463), Ashfield (T:01623 457352), Dearne Valley (T:01709 760207), East Durham (T:0191 586 3366), Tyneside North Shields (T:0191 200 6060) and Tyneside South Shields (T:0191 427 1717).

For further information, telephone relevant numbers above. For a free information pack on all current Enterprise Zones, call T:020 7944 3755.

Assisted Areas

A wide range of industrial and commercial property is available for rent or sale in the Assisted Areas. Premises can often be built or converted to suit your specific requirements. Many of the leases are very flexible, with short in-out options, to allow for the changing needs of expanding small firms.

In England, contact your local Regional Government Office (for addresses, see page 259).

For Wales and Scotland contact, as appropriate: **Welsh Development Agency** and **Highlands and Islands Enterprise**. See below for addresses.

Scotland

Highlands and Islands Enterprise, Cowan House, Inverness Retail and Business Park, Inverness IV2 7GF. T:01463 234171. HIE builds advance offices, factories and workshops for lease. Rents are competitive with other parts of the country.

Wales

Welsh Development Agency, Plas Glyndwr, Kingsway, Cardiff CF10 3AH. T:0845 777 5577 (English enquiry line); 0845 777 5566 (Welsh enquiry line). The WDA is one of the largest developers of industrial property in the UK and has a comprehensive range of business premises, varying in size from 1,000 to 50,000 sq.ft. It also offers a wide range of business services.

Get expert advice

However impeccable the organisation offering you property for lease or sale, you should always consult a solicitor before you sign a contract. If you are thinking of buying either a long lease or freehold, you are strongly advised to get a surveyor's report. Though you will have to pay for the service, it could save you a fortune if you otherwise later discovered dry rot, rising damp or worse.

Planning permission

If you intend to build or convert property, use a mobile shop or change the use of existing business premises, from say an office to a workshop, you will need to get planning permission from your local authority. This often used to take months and months but the procedure has now been greatly speeded up, especially where small businesses are concerned. Tempting as it is to take a chance or to install workmen before you have officially received the 'go-ahead', this is very unwise because in the event of permission not being granted, you could be ordered to restore the property to its original condition, which could be hugely expensive if you have knocked down the odd wall.

Advice from the former Rural Development Commission was that, before an application went to a planning committee, every effort should be made to sound out local opinion, explain the intention of the project and allay any fears.

As a further point, they recommended trying to obtain the blessing of the Parish Council, as this can often tip opinion in an application's favour. Although the RDC has now been merged with the Countryside Commission and can no longer be of assistance, the advice is still valid. In rural areas, the department to contact is the District Council Planning Office.

Other permissions

Depending on the nature of your business, other permissions may also need to be obtained, including those of the police, the environmental health department, licensing authorities and the fire prevention officer. In particular, there are special requirements concerning the sale of food and safety measures for hotels and guest houses. Your local authority will advise you what is necessary.

Working from home

Many people quietly 'set up shop' from home and there are no questions asked. There could, however, be trouble if in consequence of your business, there was an increase in traffic on your street, noise, smells or other inconvenience caused to your neighbours. Even more likely, unless you own the freehold of your home, you could have problems with your landlord if the tenancy agreement states that the accommodation is for domestic use only. If you simply use your home as a telephone base, this will probably not be an issue but if you have a stream of callers and a van parked outside, you could be accused of violating the lease. You may have to pay business rates (in addition to your council tax) on that part of your home you use as business premises.

Another possible down-side of working from home is that this could have capital gains tax implications should you ever want to sell the property.

As working out the various financial pros and cons has become rather a complex matter, before taking any decision you would be advised to take professional advice.

Useful reading

Planning Permission: a Guide for Business, booklet explaining the planning system, and giving clear guidance on working from home. Copies can be obtained from your local authority or ordered from: **ODPM Free Literature**, PO Box 236, Wetherby, West Yorkshire LS23 7NB.

Insurance

Insurance is more than just a wise precaution. It is essential if you employ staff, have business premises or use your car regularly for commercial purposes. Many insurance companies now offer 'package insurance' for small businesses that cover most of the main contingencies in a single policy. This usually works out more cheaply than buying a collection of individual policies. If you buy a package, check that it contains whichever of the following are relevant to your needs.

- **Employers' liability**. This is compulsory if you employ staff. It provides indemnity against liability for death or bodily injury to employees and sub-contractors, arising in connection with the business.
- **Product and public liability**. Insures the business and its products against claims by customers or the public. It could also cover legal expenses and the cost of complying with enforcements or judgements.
- **Professional indemnity**. Now essential for all businesses offering investment advice in whatever form. Also highly recommended for doctors, architects, consultants and other professionals who might be sued personally – or whose business might be sued – if a client suffered a mishap, loss or other damage in consequence of advice or services received. With the recent growth in litigation, many professional bodies are recommending that cover should continue after retirement in the event of an individual – or their estate – being sued for work done some years previously.

- **Material damage risk**. Covers against fire or other risk to the property, damage to equipment and theft. You can also be insured against loss of money or goods in transit.
- **Loss of profits or business interruption risk**. Insures the business against loss of profits in the event of your having to cease or curtail trading for a time, due to material damage. The two policies are normally linked. It should also cover the risk of break-down of a key item of machinery.
- **Motor risks**. Compulsory for all motor vehicles.
- **Life assurance**. Essential should you wish to provide for your own or key employees' families or to ensure that funds are available to pay off any debts or to enable the business to continue in the event of your death.
- **Permanent health insurance**. Otherwise known as 'income protection', it provides insurance against long-term loss of income as a result of severe illness or disability. Most income protection plans are pretty flexible and can be tailored to individual needs.
- **'Key man' insurance**. Applies to the loss of a key man or woman through prolonged illness as well as death. In small companies where the success or failure of the business is dependent upon the skills of two or three key executives, 'key man' insurance is increasingly being written into investment deals as part of the necessary security demanded by banks, financial institutions and private investors. Remember, however, that whereas life insurance benefits your family, key man insurance only benefits the company.
- **Jury service insurance**. Business people cannot seek automatic exemption from jury service even though prolonged absence from work could severely disrupt their business. Insuring against the risk of being called for jury service is therefore worth considering.

Insurance when working from home. If you are self-employed, you may need to extend your existing private policies to cover your commercial activities. A fire at home could destroy business products as well as your domestic possessions. Likewise your motor insurance may not be sufficient for business purposes, if the loss of your car could cause serious interruption to your trading. You should discuss these points with your insurance company or a broker.

Insurance Brokers. To find an insurance broker, contact: **British Insurance Brokers Association**, BIBA House, 14 Bevis Marks, London EC3A 7NT. T:020 7623 9043.

Useful reading

The Association of British Insurers, 51 Gresham Street, London EC2V 7HQ, publishes a useful free booklet: *Insurance Advice for Small Businesses*, available on the ABI website.

Marketing

Unless you were employed in sales or marketing, you may suspect that this is likely to be a weak point in your business plan. The essence of good marketing is very simple. Find out what the customer wants and then try to supply it rather than design a product or service and hope that buyers will come flocking to your door. You then also have to sell the sizzle as well as the sausage. The points you need to consider are:

- what kinds of individuals (or companies) are likely to be your customers, including their age group and sex
- whether you are competing with existing suppliers or are offering a genuinely new concept (including for example, a delivery service which other local shopkeepers do not supply)
- whether the market is expanding or contracting with particular emphasis on how many potential customers live close by
- finally, how you can inform the potential market that your new product or service is available.

This sort of preliminary thinking is essential. The following organisations may be able to help you formulate a realistic marketing plan.

Your local library will probably have trade directories and *Yellow Pages* from which you can see how many other organisations already offer a similar local service. It may also have copies of trade magazines relevant to the industry you plan to enter.

Your local council will have information on the population and demographic profile of the area and will be able to give you details of any development plans that could affect customer potential.

Your local Enterprise Agency and Business Link exist to help small businesses and should be able to offer valuable marketing advice.

Approved chambers of commerce should be able to offer practical advice and training in marketing techniques and may also be able to assist with useful contacts.

National organisations that may be helpful include:

The Chartered Institute of Marketing, Moor Hall, Cookham, Maidenhead, Berkshire SL6 9QH. T:01628 427500. Runs courses for non-members who need general marketing advice.

Office for National Statistics, Cardiff Road, Newport, Gwent NP10 8XG. T:01633 812973. Holds information on many aspects of the economy, including sales by UK manufacturers.

Chartered Management Institute, Management House, Cottingham Road, Corby, Northants NN17 1TT. T:01536 204222. Runs an extensive management information centre which non-members can visit with the agreement of the Institute.

Market Research Society, 15 Northburgh Street, London EC1V 0JR. T:020 7490 4911. The MRS can supply you with a copy of *The Research Buyer's Guide*, £40 (plus p&p),

which contains details of companies that could mount a research exercise on your behalf. Cost would normally be from about £2,000 and upwards depending on what is required.

BSI (British Standards Institution), 389 Chiswick High Road, London W4 4AL. T:020 8996 9000 (enquiries). Will provide technical help to ensure that products comply with standards laid down by the UK and EC governments.

Promotion

Once you have assessed where your market lies, you have to decide how to promote yourself. Methods of advertising your product (service) might include:

- direct mail shots and leaflet drops
- advertising in specialist publications or local newspapers with a potentially high readership among your target market
- a good website design that is user-friendly
- exhibitions and local displays at functions such as school prize givings, agricultural shows or local sporting events
- telephone sales, perhaps with the help of a small team
- editorial coverage in the press, on local radio programmes or TV.

You are likely to succeed better with any of these techniques if you discuss your plans with a professional consultancy. The names of local practitioners should be available from:

Institute of Public Relations, The Old Trading House, 15 Northburgh Street, London EC1V 0PR. T:020 7253 5151.

The Chartered Institute of Marketing, Moor Hall, Cookham, Maidenhead, Berkshire SL6 9QH. T:01628 427500.

Public Relations Consultants Association Ltd., Willow House, Willow Place, Victoria, London SW1P 1JH. T:020 7233 6026.

Competitors

It is useful to know who your competitors are and what they are doing. One way is to get copies of their annual reports, by writing to the companies concerned who will usually be glad to supply them free of charge; alternatively, these are available for a fee from the **Information and Enquiry Section**, Companies House, Crown Way, Cardiff CF14 3UZ. T:0870 333 3636. When writing, it would be helpful if you could quote the company number of those businesses whose annual reports you want. All companies should have this listed on their letterhead. It is also sensible to attend trade shows of the industries within which you are planning to compete. Your local library will probably hold a directory listing what shows are held each year.

Exports

Trade Partners UK, the government's network dedicated to building British business success in Europe and elsewhere, offers comprehensive information, advice and practical assistance to help you compete successfully. Assistance ranges from doing the groundwork of market research through to establishing a presence in the market. Facilities include free access to a comprehensive collection of foreign statistics and trade directories and also selective commercial databases held on CD-Rom and the Internet. For further information, telephone the general enquiry line on T:020 7215 5444.

Institute of Export, Export House, Minerva Business Park, Lynchwood, Peterborough PE2 6SF. T:01733 404400. The IOE offers technical help and advice on international trading matters and provides education and training through its short course programme. Fees and membership subscription details available on request.

Your local **chamber of commerce** should have first class information on some of the problems you might encounter and your **bank** will also have up-to-date information on the market conditions in most overseas countries, which it should supply free of charge.

Raising finance

Before you approach anyone for money, you must have a proper business plan. This means that you are bound to spend some time researching your business ideas and producing a realistic projection of cash flow needs. Your business plan should be brief and to the point but must contain the following items:

- a clear statement of what product or service you plan to offer
- sales and marketing projections, based if possible on some research or knowledge of the market
- your initial investment plus on-going cash flow requirements
- basic information concerning premises, staff, equipment and development plans
- profit and loss projections, showing when you expect the business to start making money.

It is a good idea to ask an accountant to vet your business plan. Some high street banks offer the same service for a fixed fee and may also offer other help, such as a period of free banking.

The different types of finance now available to small businesses through traditional sources such as banks and other institutions are more extensive than most people realise. They fall into four broad categories: overdrafts, commercial and bank loans, equity finance and government loans and grants.

Overdrafts

You will be familiar with overdrafts from your private banking arrangements. The bank allows you to borrow money up to a predetermined limit but only charges you interest on the amount outstanding. If you trade as a limited company the bank will almost certainly require a personal guarantee, which will make you liable for the overdraft if the company fails. Although overdrafts are theoretically repayable at a day's notice, in practice the banks will normally review the arrangement with you once a year. That said, over the past few years banks have been tightening up considerably and, if you think you might have a problem, the earlier you discuss this with your bank manager the more likely you are to avoid trouble. At very least, by putting your bank manager in the picture, you will know where you stand and may be able to buy extra time to make alternative arrangements, if necessary.

Interest on overdrafts fluctuates in line with bank base rate and you will usually have to pay a premium of between two per cent and five per cent over this level.

Loans

There are various types of loans including: bank loans for a fixed period; leasing and hire purchase arrangements; credit factoring and invoice discounting; stock financing; and the loan guarantee scheme.

In each case, your loan will be for a specific period but interest will normally fluctuate as it does with overdrafts. Most loans are made against the security of a specific asset, such as vans, office equipment, your debtors, or stock. Lenders may ask for a personal guarantee, which you should resist unless there is clearly no other way of obtaining the money.

Bank loans. Unlike an overdraft, the bank undertakes to lend you money for a fixed period, say, five years. You will be required to repay a percentage of the loan each year and before lending the bank will want to check your business plan to see that the agreed repayments are realistic. Quite apart from the interest charges, there may be an arrangement fee and the bank may also ask for a debenture which gives it security over all the assets of your business but does not involve you in pledging personal possessions such as your house.

Leasing and hire purchase. These are both methods of using equipment or vehicles and paying for them by instalments. Leasing is normally slightly cheaper, as the supplier owns the asset and benefits from the relevant tax allowances. As an alternative to negotiating an agreement with the supplier, it may be cheaper to ask your bank or other lender to arrange the necessary finance for you. Interest is usually fixed at the start and will remain at the same level throughout. This has the advantage that you know what your commitment is. However, such agreements tend to be expensive.

Bills of exchange, invoice discounting and credit factoring. Bills of exchange are possibly the simplest method of smoothing cash flow. The bill of exchange is sent by the supplier to the customer who signs indicating that it will be paid on maturity at some specific time in the future – say two months. The bill is then exchanged for cash in advance against the bill by a bank, minus a discount equivalent to an interest charge. The discount is usually lower than the interest charged on a bank loan or overdraft and therefore cheaper, but the bank will probably require you to 'back' your customer's bill giving recourse against you if the client does not pay.

Invoice discounting is somewhat similar but is only useful if you deal with prestigious companies whose credit is good. You sell selected invoices for about 75 per cent of their face value for immediate cash. You retain full responsibility for collecting the money and in the event of your customer defaulting have to repay the sum involved. In effect, you are paying a high premium for cash up front.

Credit factoring is a continuous financial arrangement whereby the trade debts of a business are sold to a factoring company as they arise. In return, you immediately receive about 80 per cent of the debt, less the factoring company's charges, and the balance of the money when your customer pays. A potentially useful aspect of factoring is the provision by the finance company of a full sales ledger, credit control, cash collection and bad debts service. Although this service sounds marvellous, it does not come cheap and can also be extremely complicated if your customers are not well known companies with good credit rating.

Both factoring and invoice discounting are offered by specialist companies within the major banking groups.

Stock financing. This is a means of helping small manufacturing businesses finance their stock of raw materials and finished products. The finance company purchases and sells back to the manufacturer, say, £30,000 of stock. The financier pays the manufacturer an immediate cheque, less his charges, and takes out a 90-day bill of exchange.

This can be a useful method of financing working capital if your high street bank will not lend you money against the security of your stock. Although more expensive than ordinary bank borrowing, it is less expensive than borrowing through a finance house.

Small Firms Loan Guarantee Scheme (SFLGS). The Loan Guarantee Scheme is a joint venture between the Small Business Service (SBS) and various financial institutions, including all the main high street banks, to help small businesses that were unable to obtain a conventional loan, because they lacked adequate security or a proven track record. The government provides a guarantee of 70 per cent of the money borrowed, up to a maximum of £100,000. For businesses that have been trading for two years or longer, the guarantee covers 85 per cent of the loan up to a maximum of £250,000. Loan terms can be between 2 and 10 years. There are simplified arrangements for agreeing loans up to £30,000 where certain banks and other lenders can grant the application without first referring it to the Small Business Service (SBS).

Lenders may charge an arrangement fee and additionally, there is a small premium, which is paid direct to the SBS. Loans are available to both start-up and established businesses. Certain types of businesses such as financial services, property development and retailing are excluded from the Scheme.

Although personal security cannot be taken for a Scheme loan the borrower may be required to pledge business assets as security for the guaranteed loan. Security taken by the lender in respect of guaranteed lending would always apply to the whole loan, as opposed to just the proportion not covered by the guarantee.

Applications should be made direct to one of the lenders involved in the Scheme. For further information and a list of participating lenders contact the Small Business

Service, Small Firms Loan Guarantee Scheme unit on T:0114 259 7308/09 (9 a.m. to 12 a.m. and 2 p.m. to 5 p.m.).

Help with late payment of debts. Many small firms are pushed into borrowing money because of cashflow problems, due to late payment of invoices. After years of active campaigning by small business, small firms now have the legal right to claim 8 per cent statutory interest on overdue debts owed by companies or public authorities.

Equity finance

With equity finance, as opposed to simply borrowing money, you are taking in a financial partner who will own part of your business. For this reason many small businessmen have been reluctant to accept equity investment. However, this is now changing as the value of venture capital as well as the practical contribution of investors are increasingly becoming appreciated. Unlike loans, equity investment is permanent capital. If a shareholder wishes to sell out, the proprietor is not bound to buy back his shares but sometimes has an option to do so.

The most likely sources of equity finance are friends or family, business angels or venture capital specialists. The Enterprise Investment Scheme offers another possibility.

Friends and family. You may know people who would like to back you when you are starting a business. It is important that both sides should understand the risks and commitments involved and be aware that these may affect your normal relationship. However close you are, it is sensible to ask an accountant or solicitor to advise you on a formal agreement. There are specific percentages of shareholdings, such as 25 per cent, that normally carry legal rights; it is important to understand what these are and to decide whether you wish them to apply. If an investor owns more than 10 per cent of your company, he/she would usually expect to be a director and maybe also play an active part in the business.

Business Angels. You may want to find an investor outside your circle of family and friends. This has become considerably easier than a few years ago, partly because the Enterprise Investment Scheme (see below) offers attractive tax relief to individuals investing in unquoted companies but also because several organisations run introductory services to put firms seeking funds in contact with potential investors – or business angels as they are often called.

One of the best known is the **National Business Angels Network (NBAN)**, which operates across the UK through approved practitioners to effect introductions between private investors and growth businesses seeking finance of between £20,000 and £3 million. As well as a website, there is also a monthly magazine of investment opportunities. For further information, contact: **NBAN**, 40–42 Cannon Street, London EC4N 6JJ. Hotline T:020 7329 4141.

Other sources of business angels include: **3i** (T:020 7928 3131); **Employee Ownership Scotland**, covering Scotland (T:0141 304 5465); **Capital Connections**, covering Kent, Surrey, Sussex, Hants and Isle of Wight (T:01273 833881); and **TechInvest**, covering the whole of the North West (T:01925 400 302).

Accountants are also worth approaching, as is your local Business Link.

Enterprise Investment Scheme. The EIS is designed to help small companies raise start-up and expansion finance by issuing shares to investors willing to back them. Particular attractions for individuals investing in unquoted companies include: 20 per cent tax relief on investments up to £150,000 in any tax year; exemption from capital gains tax on disposals of the EIS shares provided these are held for at least three years (five years for shares issued before 6 April 2000); deferral of capital gains arising on disposals of assets, where a re-investment is made in qualifying EIS shares in a period beginning one year before and ending three years after the disposal; relief against income tax or CGT on losses.

A further big plus, of particular appeal to many retired business angels, is that outside investors (i.e. not previously connected with the business) can play an active part as paid directors.

The previous requirement for the company raising the money to remain unquoted for at least three years if investors were not to lose their tax reliefs has been changed and now the only provision is that the company must be unquoted when the shares were actually issued and that no arrangements existed at the time for the company to cease being unquoted.

However, investment can only be in unquoted companies whose gross assets do not exceed £15 million before the shares are issued and do not exceed £16 million immediately afterwards. Additionally, companies with property-backed trades for example farming, hotels and retirement homes, are excluded from participation. Best bets for tracking likely investors are the same as for business angels plus also some venture capital companies. See Inland Revenue booklet IR 137.

Private Equity. There are over 150 private equity firms in the UK which make long-term investments in exchange for an equity stake in new and expanding businesses and in management buy-outs and management buy-ins. These firms will only invest in companies with a high growth potential with skilled, ambitious management. They may require a non-executive position on the board of the company, with the aim of helping the business to maximise its performance.

Sources of Private Equity. Private equity can be obtained from venture capital firms and business angels. The BVCA (British Venture Capital Association) produces a directory of members, available on their website, which includes UK venture capital firms' investment preferences and contact details, and lists experienced advisers. It also has a directory of non-member networks which aim to introduce companies looking for smaller amounts of private equity to business angels. *A Guide to Venture Capital* is also available from the BVCA. For further information, visit the **BVCA** website. Private equity firms can be approached directly, or your accountant or financial adviser may be able to arrange an introduction.

Although most private equity firms invest from £100,000 upwards, at time of writing the following were prepared to consider smaller investment amounts:

No Minimum	*Telephone*
The Manchester Technology Fund	0161 606 7235
Minimum £5,000	
Enterprise Ventures Ltd.	01772 819400
London Ventures (Fund Managers) Ltd.	020 7434 2425
Minimum £10,000	
Prelude Technology Investments Ltd.	01954 288090
WL Ventures Ltd.	01506 415144
Minimum £20,000	
Birmingham Technology (Venture Capital) Ltd.	0121 250 3500
BNFL Enterprise (Investment Management) Ltd.	01772 717577
ET Capital Ltd.	01223 422010
Midven Ltd.	0121 616 1133
UK Steel Enterprise Ltd.	0114 273 1612
Minimum £25,000	
Avlar Bioventures	01223 266799
Ferranti Ltd.	020 7835 1325
HSBC UK Enterprise for the South East	01273 835455
Industrial Technology Securities Ltd.	01483 457398
Northern Enterprise Ltd.	0191 442 4300
Transatlantic Capital Ltd.	020 7436 1216
Wales Fund Managers Ltd.	029 2054 6250
Minimum £30,000	
Gap Fund Managers Ltd.	0131 225 1302
Minimum £50,000	
3K Digital	020 7355 3322
Cambridge Research & Innovation Ltd.	01223 312856
Company Guides Ltd.	020 7247 6300
Derbyshire First Investments Ltd.	01246 207390
Equity Ventures Ltd.	020 7665 6611
Far Blue Ventures Ltd.	020 7481 8002
Seed Capital Ltd.	01865 784466
Strathdon Investments Ltd.	01962 870492

Venture Capital Trusts. These are investment vehicles (similar to investment trusts), aimed at encouraging more investment in smaller companies. To qualify as a VCT, at least 70 per cent of a Trust's investments must be in unlisted companies and the VCT itself must be quoted on the Stock Exchange. People investing in VCTs will be exempt both: from income tax on their dividends and from capital gains tax on disposal of their shares for investments of up to £100,000 a year provided the shares are held for at least three years (five years for shares issued before 6 April 2000). New subscribers will also receive roll-over relief on any gains used to invest in the VCT, as well as up-front income tax relief at 20 per cent. For a list of VCTs currently open, see the **BVCA** website. You might also like to see IR leaflet 169 *Venture Capital Trusts*.

Other useful organisations

Enterprise Boards. The Yorkshire and West Midlands Enterprise Boards, originally set up by local authorities in the early 1980's, have developed into important regional sources of venture and development capital, concentrating on equity investments in local small firms. Contact:

Yorkshire Enterprise Ltd., St Martins House, 210–212 Chapeltown Road, Leeds LS7 4HZ. T:0113 294 5000.

West Midlands Enterprise Ltd. (WME), Wellington House, 31–34 Waterloo Street, Birmingham B2 5TJ. T:0121 236 8855.

Useful reading

Venture Capital Report Business Angel Club publishes a monthly report in which they appraise companies which need equity capital investment and management expertise. VCR vets the companies to make sure that their claims and plans are realistic. The membership fee to join the club is £1,000 per year. Companies use VCR to raise sums from £250,000 to £1 million. It costs £1,000 (plus VAT) to be included in the VCR report plus a success fee of 5 per cent of the funds raised. VCR takes the option to purchase a small percentage of the equity. For further information, contact **VCR** at: 7 Old Park Lane, London W1K 1QR. T:020 7072 2410.

Government grants and loans

There is a vast range of public sector financial assistance, including in particular grants and loans, available from local authorities, government sources and the EC. Most major firms of accountants and also the banks produce comprehensive publications listing all such resources currently available.

The types of funds listed below are among the most potentially useful to smaller firms.

Local authority assistance. Local authorities are now playing a much fuller role in co-ordinating the advice and financial resources available to small companies in their area. Many have developed their own loan and grant schemes. In particular, councils can offer generous mortgages to buy or improve land or buildings and can provide rent and/or rates relief. With government agreement, they can sell land below market value, provide improvement grants, build advance factories and give employment subsidies. Contact your local authority Planning Department or alternatively, where appropriate, the Industrial Development Department.

Grants in Assisted Areas. Firms in selected areas of Britain may be eligible for a Regional Selective Assistance Grant or possibly for a grant from EC structural funds.

Regional Selective Assistance Grants may be available to both manufacturing and some service companies in the Assisted Areas. To qualify for assistance, the project must be commercially viable, create or safeguard employment, demonstrate a need for assistance and offer national or regional benefits.

The new map of Assisted Areas was approved by the Commission in July 2000 and will operate until 2006. For further information, contact the relevant government office in England, the Scottish Executive or the National Assembly for Wales.

EC structural funds. Some areas have regeneration programmes partly funded by EC structural funds which may include schemes for assisting small to medium-sized enterprises. To find out details of any such grants in your area, contact your local Business Link or Regional Government office.

Enterprise Grants. A new scheme was introduced in England in January 2000 to offer assistance to high growth small and medium sized enterprises with fewer than 250 employees. The scheme offers assistance up to a maximum of £75,000. For further information, contact your regional government office. N.B. Wales and Scotland have responsibility for their own schemes.

Regional Government Offices. The government has established nine regional offices which bring together under one roof the former local departments for Trade and Industry, Employment, Transport and the Environment. Two particular benefits of this reorganisation are that services can be tailored in a more integrated fashion to the needs of the community and that business people now have a single port of call for all enquiries. Addresses are:

Eastern Region: Building A, Westbrook Centre, Milton Road, Cambridge CB4 1YG. T:01223 346700.

East Midlands: The Belgrave Centre, Stanley Place, Talbot Street, Nottingham NG1 5GG. T:0115 971 9971.

London: Riverwalk House, 157–161 Millbank, London SW1P 4RR. T:020 7217 3456.

North East: Wellbar House, Gallowgate, Newcastle upon Tyne NE1 4TD. T:0191 201 3300.

North West: Sunley Tower, Piccadilly Plaza, Manchester M1 4BE. T:0161 952 4000.

South East: Bridge House, 1 Walnut Tree Close, Guildford, Surrey GU1 4GA. T:01483 882255.

South West: 4th Floor, The Pithay, Bristol BS1 2PB. T:0117 900 1700.

West Midlands: 77 Paradise Circus, Queensway, Birmingham B1 2DT. T:0121 212 5000.

Yorkshire and Humberside: PO Box 213, City House, Leeds LS1 4US. T:0113 280 0600.

The main offices for small business enquiries in Scotland and Wales are:

Scottish Executive, Meridien Court, 5 Cadogan Street, Glasgow G2 6AT. T:0141 248 4774.

National Assembly for Wales, Cathays Park, Cardiff CF10 3NQ. T:029 2082 3976.

Regional Agencies. If you are planning to start a business in Scotland or Wales, these agencies (or in the case of Wales, the Industry and Training Division) offer financial facilities that may be of assistance to you. All finance is discretionary and to be eligible, your business would almost certainly either have to increase job opportunities, offer export potential, reduce the need for imports or hold promise of significant expansion.

Depending on the area, priority may be given to enterprises involved in: tourism, manufacturing, new technology and, in the Highlands and Islands, viable use of natural resources. In the main, retailing is unlikely to receive assistance. For further information, contact the appropriate agency:

Scottish Enterprise, 150 Broomielew, Atlantic Quay, Glasgow G2 8LU. T:0845 607 8787.

Highlands & Islands Enterprise, Cowan House, Inverness Retail and Business Park, Inverness IV2 7GF. T:01463 234171.

Loans from the European Investment Bank. The European Investment Bank has arranged credit facilities for most UK banks and financial institutions to help promote financing for capital investment by small and medium-sized businesses (those with fewer than 500 employees, net fixed assets of less than £60 million and with capital investment projects of up to £20 million).

Loans are available direct from the EIB for capital investment projects of £20 million and over in industry and related services, infrastructure, communications, environmental protection, energy and meeting European Union priorities. The EIB may finance up to half the gross investment cost. For further information contact: **European Investment Bank**, Headquarters, 100 Boulevard Konrad Adenauer, L-2950 Luxembourg, T:00 352 4379–1.

Advice and training

Never has small business been so well served when it comes to general help and training. A number of organisations offer free advice and low cost consultancy, as well as a variety of training schemes ranging from general information on setting up and developing a business to more specialised courses.

Business Links

A network of 45 Business Links exists throughout England to provide small businesses with access to the full range of advisory and support services in their area.

They can provide help and guidance across a wide range of topics including: business planning, financial management, employment issues, marketing and e-commerce.

For further information, contact your local Business Link through the National Contact Centre, T:0845 600 9006.

Adult Education Centres

Short courses in specific business skills are run by business schools, polytechnics and colleges of higher and further education. Various trade and professional associations also run courses. Enquire through your local education authority (see telephone directory).

Regional Agencies

These organisations are designed to assist the development of industrial activity in their areas and all have small business divisions that will be only too glad to offer any assistance they can.

Scottish Enterprise. Scottish Enterprise operates through a network of 12 Local Enterprise Companies, in lowland Scotland, offering a wide range of services to start-up and expanding businesses. For further information, telephone the Network helpline on T:0845 607 8787 who will put you in touch with your nearest regional office.

Highlands and Islands Enterprise. The HIE network covers the Northern and Western parts of Scotland, as well as the Scottish Islands. It offers a free counselling service to small firms and to those considering setting up in these areas. Financial assistance may be given to meet start-up and training expenses. For further information, contact: Highlands and Islands Enterprise, Cowan House, Inverness Retail and Business Park, Inverness IV2 7GF. T:01463 234171.

For list of addresses in England, see page 259.

Other Regional Agencies

Various other regional agencies, usually established as partnerships between the public and private sectors, now operate in different parts of the country.

Part development agency, part enterprise agency and part enterprise board, they generally offer a wide range of help for businesses in the region. Some useful addresses include:

Advantage West Midlands, 3 Priestley Wharf, Holt Street, Aston Science Park, Birmingham B7 4BN. T:0121 380 3500.

Lancashire Enterprises Plc., Lancaster House, Centurion Way, Leyland, Preston PR26 6TX. T:01772 819400.

One Base North East, Great North House, Sandyford Road, Newcastle upon Tyne NE1 8ND, T:0191 261 2000.

Non-government sources of advice and training

Many enterprise agencies, chambers of commerce, business institutes and small business clubs, scattered around the country, provide counselling services, together with, in some cases, more formal training.

Enterprise Agencies (Enterprise Trusts in Scotland)
These are partnerships between local businesses, the professions, approved chambers of commerce, local authorities and others, designed to stimulate the start-up and expansion of small businesses by providing advice and counselling.

There are more than 300 LEAs/ETs now operating in the U.K., offering varying facilities which often include: free business advice, provision and management of small business workshops, enterprise training and the facilities of a small business club.

For further information and address of your nearest EA, contact: the **National Federation of Enterprise Agencies**, c/o NatWest Bank, Trinity Gardens, 9–11 Bromham Road, Bedford MK40 2UQ. T:01234 354055.

One London. An example of a comprehensive service is provided by One London. This Enterprise Agency offers:

- a loan scheme for start-up and early-stage growth businesses
- free business counselling for loan fund recipients, as and when their business needs it
- access to specialist consultancy services including, for example, marketing and computer information
- a 'marriage bureau' service for introducing investors to companies seeking funds.

For further information, contact: **One London**, 28 Park Street, London SE1 9EQ, T:020 7940 1528.

Chambers of Commerce. Approved chambers specialise in providing on-going help, general business advice and training. Examples of regular courses, offered by many, include telephone sales and data preparation for computers. Costs vary but average £60 a day for non-member companies. Chambers provide informal networks of contacts with other business people who may well need the products/services you plan to offer. Addresses are listed in the local telephone directory. Alternatively, contact: **British Chambers of Commerce**, Manning House, 22 Carlisle Place, London SW1P 1JA. T:020 7565 2000.

Institute of Business Advisers. IBA is a non-profit making professional institute with over 2,000 members nationwide who offer advice based on practical business experience. Topics covered include accounting, marketing, production, taxation and exporting. Initial advice for a new business can usually be arranged free of charge through your local Business Link or Enterprise Agency. If you are unable to locate a suitable business advisory service locally, write to: Mike Horner, Chief Executive, **Institute of Business Advisers**, Response House, Queen Street North, Chesterfield S41 9AB. T: 01246 453322.

Institute of Directors Business Information and Advisory Services (IAS). Staffed by experienced people, IAS gives information, advice and counselling on the more complicated problems of business life from whether a redundancy settlement is fair to advice on raising finance, export marketing or operating a group of companies. General information on such things as the Retail Prices Index can also be supplied, often over the telephone. Each of the advisers specialises in certain areas, including: finance, tax and small businesses; personnel management, retirement, redeployment and conditions of service; exports and marketing; company secretarial practice and company commercial and employment law. The service, which is exclusive to members, is free. Contact **IAS, Institute of Directors**, 116 Pall Mall, London SW1Y 5ED. T:020 7451 3100 for an appointment; or to discuss your problem over the telephone with an adviser.

Lawyers for Your Business, Law Society, Freepost WC2576, London WC2A 1BR. T:020 7405 9075. A legal advisory service set up by the Law Society with the aim of encouraging smaller businesses to seek the advice of a solicitor at an early stage in the hope of avoiding future problems. Applicants are offered an initial free 1/2 hour consultation at which they can discuss – and may often resolve – any queries. Further consultations, if these are required, are charged at normal rates. For leaflets giving further information and a list of participating solicitors, telephone the above number.

Trade Associations

Virtually all industries have a trade association that provides advice and other services to members. If you are considering purchasing or starting a business in a particular trade sector, ask at your local library for the name and address of the relevant trade body. Examples are: National Federation of Retail Newsagents, British Institute of Interior Design, the Institute of Employment Consultants and the Booksellers Association.

Tourist boards

There are many opportunities for mature people to start tourism-related businesses, especially if they live or plan to retire to one of the major tourist areas. Advice about the development and marketing of tourist attractions and amenities is available from the tourist boards, as follows:

Wales Tourist Board, Brunel House, 2 Fitzalan Road, Cardiff CF24 0UY. T:029 2049 9909.

Visit Scotland, 23 Ravelston Terrace, Edinburgh EH4 3TP. T:0131 332 2433.

Northern Ireland Tourist Board, St. Anne's Court, 59 North Street, Belfast BT1 1NB. T:028 9023 1221.

English Tourism Council, Thames Tower, Black's Road, London W6 9EL. T:020 8563 3000. The English Tourism Council publishes a selection of guides for people branching out in a tourism-related business. Titles include: *First Steps in Tourism* (free), *How to Obtain Planning Approval* (£5) and *The Pink Booklet*, explaining the laws which affect accommodation businesses (£6); p&p charges normally come to about £3.50. Available from Mail Order Services at the above address.

Local authorities are closely involved in the development of tourism in their area. Contact the Tourism Development Officer at your County or District Council.

Useful organisations

The following are the key organisations representing small business interests. Some act as pressure groups, conduct research and also provide a service to their members:

Federation of Small Businesses, Sir Frank Whittle Way, Blackpool Business Park, Blackpool FY4 2FE. T:01253 336000.

Forum of Private Business, Ruskin Chambers, Drury Lane, Knutsford, Cheshire WA16 6HA. T:01565 634467.

Institute of Directors, 116 Pall Mall, London SW1Y 5ED. T:020 7839 1233.

The CBI, Small & Medium Enterprise Council, Centre Point, 103 New Oxford Street, London WC1A 1DU. T:020 7395 8100.

Useful reading

A list of books for small and start-up businesses published by Kogan Page is available from 120 Pentonville Road, London N1 9JN. T:020 7278 0433.

11 Looking for Paid Work

Far from thinking of putting your feet up when you retire from your present job, perhaps like many other people today one of your ambitions is to continue working in some form of paid employment. If so, the encouraging news is that, prospects are improving all the time as more and more employers are actively seeking to recruit older people. However, before dashing off a shoal of application letters, it helps to think through some of the practicalities. Start by asking yourself a few basic questions.

Firstly, what is your main motive in wanting to work? The wish to supplement your income? The companionship? Fear of boredom? The desire for mental stimulation? The need to have a sense of purpose? Or the lurking suspicion that without a job, friends and social acquaintances will be less interested in hearing your views?

The answer may well be a combination of factors but you should at least try to pinpoint your priorities to avoid drifting into a job that does not satisfy your main aims. The stories are legion of people whose prime reason for seeking work was to get out of the house to make new friends and who then plumped for a solitary occupation working from home. Likewise, one frequently hears of those whose real purpose was financial but who somehow signed on instead for unpaid voluntary work.

Another fundamental consideration is how many hours you are thinking of committing per week. A full Monday to Friday? Or just a couple of half-days? And while on the subject of time, is working a long-term goal or simply a pleasant occupation to fill in the next year or so?

What about distance? Would you be prepared to commute or are you aiming for a job that is strictly local? Was there anything, for example the travel, that you particularly disliked about your previous employment and that you are determined to avoid in your future job?

Also very much to the point, are you planning to seek an opening in a similar field, where your experience and contacts would come in useful? Or do you want to do something entirely different? And if so, were this to help, would you be willing to do a training course?

Moreover, have you considered the important economic questions? It may sound stupid when you have been working most of your life but factors such as your age, your total weekly earnings, your pension and other income, as well, of course as any out-of-pocket expenses you incur, could mean that at the end of the day the sums look rather different from what you had supposed.

Financial considerations

Until the late eighties one of the big flies in the ointment was a provision known as the Earnings Rule, whereby any man between the ages of 65 and 69 and any woman between the ages of 60 and 64 who was earning more than £75 a week had their State pension reduced. Happily the earnings rule has been abolished; so today, regardless of your age or how much you earn, there is no longer any forfeit to your State pension, although of course you may have to pay tax on your additional income.

In the past as a means of getting round the earnings rule, we used to recommend that consideration be given to deferring your State pension. Although the earnings rule no longer applies as a reason for this, if you are working close to a full-time week and/or have enough money to live on, there could still be an advantage in asking the DWP to defer your pension as this will entitle you to a bigger pension in the future. Your local Social Security office could advise whether this would be worthwhile. Each year of deferral earns an increment of about 7.5 per cent of the pension.

Decisions concerning your occupational pension could also arise, particularly if you are not so much looking for a retirement job, as a last big move before you retire. Most (though not all) pension schemes apply actuarial reductions for early retirement and joining a new pension scheme in late middle age, though not impossible, can present difficulties or impose certain limitations, especially for very high earners who could be affected by the £97,200 earnings cap on entitlement for tax relief. For further information, see section 'Early leavers' in the Pensions chapter.

National Insurance is another consideration. Unless you are over State retirement age or have earnings of £89 a week or less (2002/03), in which case you can forget about NI contributions, you will be liable for the normal Class 1 contributions. If, as many early retirers do, you work for two or more different employers you will have to pay Class 1 in respect of each. The maximum you would have to contribute is £2,628.80 (2002/3). To avoid being billed for more, fill in the form attached to leaflet CA 01 *National Insurance for Employees*, available from Inland Revenue (NI Contributions) offices.

If you obtain work through an agency (e.g. catering, nursing, exhibition work), you are usually regarded as an employee of the agency for national insurance purposes and the agency is responsible for the payment of Class 1 contributions on your behalf. However, this does not apply if: you do the work from home; are not subject to anyone's direct supervision; or are in the entertainment business. See leaflet CA25 *National Insurance for Agencies and People Working for Agencies*.

If you are over retirement age and have a job, the only requirement is that you obtain an exemption card to give to your employer. See Form CF 384 (Certificate of Exception).

If you do freelance or other assignment work (unless virtually all your earnings come from one employer, in which case the Inland Revenue would argue that you are an employee of the organisation), you are officially considered to be self-employed for both national insurance and taxation purposes (see Chapter 10, Starting Your Own Business). For further information, you might find it helpful to read leaflet IR56/NI39 *Employed or Self-Employed?* available from any tax office.

New Tax Rules. The Inland Revenue has tightened up the rules in order to clamp down on what it sees as the avoidance of PAYE and Class 1 national insurance contributions in respect of the provision of services, including for example consultancy and contract work. Those most likely to be affected are individuals in small limited companies who either work over a period of time for a sole organisation and those who work for a client/s who have the right to control and supervise how the work is performed, as opposed to leaving the initiative to the individual concerned. If you are thinking of operating in an independent capacity – as opposed to becoming a bona fide employee – it would be sensible to discuss the tax implications with an accountant before determining whether you should operate as self-employed, a sole trader, partnership or limited company.

Jobseeker's Allowance (JSA). You can claim JSA provided that:

- you are under State pension age
- are unemployed or working less than an average 16 hours a week
- have paid, or been credited with, sufficient class 1 national insurance contributions **or** have a low income.

To qualify however, you must be both available for and actively seeking work and must abide by a Jobseeker's Agreement arranged with your local Jobcentre. The essence of the agreement is an action programme worked out with an adviser to help maximise your chances of finding a job. You will receive help and advice and there is also a fortnightly jobsearch review to give you and your adviser an opportunity to assess your progress and to discuss any potential openings that might be suitable.

Claimants are not allowed to turn down a job offered to them via their jobcentre without good reason. Lower pay would not normally be accepted as a reason although, that said, there is a 'permitted period' up to a maximum of 13 weeks when individuals are allowed to restrict their job search to openings that take advantage of their skills, experience and reasonable salary expectations.

The rules also allow 'employment on trial', when you can try out a job for between 4 and 12 weeks (provided you have been unemployed for at least 13 weeks) without risking disqualification for receiving jobseeker's allowance if you decide to leave.

A particularly welcome feature of JSA is that it makes it much more worthwhile for recipients to do part-time work. Firstly, everyone receiving the allowance gets national insurance credits. And secondly, claimants who have been entitled to JSA for 3 months can start building up a back-to-work bonus, enabling them to receive a maximum lump sum of £1,000 when they move off the allowance; if they receive income-based JSA, their partner's earnings can also contribute to the bonus.

The current (2002/03) rate of jobseeker's allowance for people over 25 is £53.95. For low income couples (who previously would have received income support), the amount is £84.65. Those moving into full-time work after a year or more on jobseeker's allowance, income support, incapacity benefit or severe disablement allowance also receive a tax-free £100 job grant.

For further details, see leaflet JSA L5 *Jobseeker's Allowance: Helping You Back to Work*, available from any social security office or jobcentre.

Tax Credits. If you have a job but are not earning very much, there are two tax credits that could be helpful. The one is **Working Families Tax Credit** (WFTC); the other, **Disabled Person's Tax Credit** (DPTC). Both are payments given to individuals who despite working at least 16 hours a week only have a modest income and limited savings.

An essential condition to receive the Working Families Tax Credit is that the family, or lone parent, must have at least one child in full-time education, aged under 19, living with them.

The Disabled Person's Tax Credit is only given to individuals on low income with an illness or disability to help them return to work.

Each credit consists of a basic credit plus a number of possible extras, variously for children and also a further supplement if the earner works at least a 30-hour week. However, because the credits are means-tested, the amount actually payable depends on the family's, or disabled person's, net income.

Most recipients get the money in their pay packet. However the self-employed and also, in the case of WFTC if a couple so chooses, a non-earning partner receive the payment direct from the Inland Revenue.

Come April 2003, both tax credits are due to go in their present form and will be replaced by a single **Working Tax Credit** (WTC). No existing recipient is likely to miss out. Indeed, the major change is that more people will benefit as WTC will extend support to those aged 25 plus, who work at least 30 hours a week, irrespective of whether they have children or a disability.

If you are currently in receipt of Working Families Tax Credit or Disabled Person's Tax Credit, you should have had a letter from the Inland Revenue inviting you to apply for the new Working Tax Credit and possibly also for Child Tax Credit, which will be replacing the existing Children's Tax Credit (see page 74).

If to date, you have not been getting any work-related tax credit but believe you might now be eligible, you should be able to pick up an application form from any Inland Revenue Enquiry Centre. Or for information, ring the WTC helpline: 0845 609 5000.

Redundancy. If you have just been made redundant, or fear this is a possibility, see information in the 'Money in General' chapter, page 17.

Special measures to assist disabled people to work

The government has launched a package of measures to make it easier and more financially worthwhile for people with disabilities to get a job.

As well as the Disabled Person's Tax Credit, described above, there have been a number of helpful changes to the benefit rules: (1) the former rule limiting unpaid voluntary work to 16 hours a week for those on incapacity benefits has now been abolished (2) recipients of incapacity benefits who need to ease back slowly can work up to 16 hours a week, for a period of 6 months to a year, and earn up to £66 a week (2002/03) without loss of benefit; thereafter they can earn up to a maximum of £20 a week while remaining on benefit; and (3) former claimants of incapacity benefits who start a job and then need to give up – either because the work was temporary or because of illness/disability – can reclaim benefit almost immediately, should this be necessary.

Other measures include a job broker service to assist disabled people in their quest for work and to advise them about any benefits and other support which might be helpful. Also those who have been on benefit for 12 months or longer will, on their return to work, be eligible for a £100 job grant.

If you have any queries, or would welcome one-to-one help from a job broker, call Freephone: 0800 137 177 (7 a.m. to 11 p.m., 7 days a week).

New Deal 50-plus Programme

The government has extended the New Deal for help in getting a job to include people aged 50-plus. It is applicable to individuals who have been in receipt of jobseeker's allowance, income support, incapacity benefit or severe disablement allowance for six months and who need practical help in order to get started again, either in a self-employed capacity or paid work.

There is no age limit and the New Deal is also applicable to dependent partners of people in receipt of any of the above benefits. In either case, eligibility is restricted to claimants with a maximum personal income of £15,000.

The package offered consists of individual advice plus two types of financial assistance: a £1,500 training grant and a cash top-up (known as an employment credit) to make returning to work financially viable for low earners. Amounts for the cash top-up, which is tax-free, are £60 a week for full-time work and £40 for part-time (i.e. between 16 and 30 hours). For further information, obtain leaflet NDL54 *Put Yourself in the Picture*, obtainable from Jobcentres. Or ring the New Deal Helpline T:0845 606 2626.

Assessing your abilities

Some people know exactly what they want to do. They have planned their action campaign for months, done their research, prepared a CV, followed up selective openings and are just waiting for their present employment to come to an end before embarking on a new career. But for most of us, it is not like that. Having merrily announced our intention to find a job, there comes a moment of truth when the big question is what?

Knowing what you have to offer is an essential first step. Make a list of everything you have done, both in your formal career and ordinary life, including your outside interests such as: local politics, Rotary, hobbies, voluntary work and even jobs around the home – decorating, gardening, carpentry or cooking. In particular, consider any practical or other skills, knowledge or contacts that you have acquired through these activities which may now prove useful, for example: public speaking, fund-raising, committee work, conference organisation, production know-how, computer knowledge or fluency in a foreign language.

As a result of writing everything down, most people find that they have far more to offer than they originally realised.

Add too your personal attributes and any special assets you can offer an employer. The list might include: health, organising ability, a good telephone manner, communication skills, the ability to work well with other people, use of a car and willingness to do flexible hours.

Maturity can also be a positive asset. Many employers prefer older people as being more reliable and less likely to be preoccupied with family and social demands. Also, in many small firms in particular, a senior person's accumulated experience is often rated as especially valuable.

By dint of looking at yourself afresh in this fashion, you may get a clearer idea of the sort of job that would suit you. Although there is an argument for keeping a fairly open mind and not limiting your applications too narrowly, the worst mistake you can make is to answer scores of advertisements indiscriminately – and inevitably end up with a sackload of rejections.

Of course, offers do sometimes turn up out of the blue; and in some cases in a field that it would never have occurred to you to look. But as a general rule when job-hunting, it helps to know at least in broad terms what you are seeking before you start.

Many people find this extraordinarily difficult. After years of working in one occupation, it takes quite a leap in imagination to picture yourself in another role – even if it is in the same or a related area. If you intend to do something completely different, it will be harder still, as your knowledge of what the job entails will probably be second-hand. Also quite apart from deciding what you would enjoy, in many parts of the country the issue may be more a matter of what is available.

Talking to other people helps. Friends, family, work colleagues or business acquaintances may have useful information and moreover will quite likely be able to appraise your abilities more objectively than you can yourself. It could also be sensible to consult outside experts, who specialise in adult career counselling and whose advice may be more realistic than that of friends in the context of current employment opportunities.

Job counselling

This is usually a mixture of helping you to identify your talents in a vocational sense combined with practical advice on successful job-hunting techniques. Counsellors can assist with such essentials as writing a curriculum vitae, preparing for an interview and locating job vacancies. They can also advise you of suitable training courses. Counselling is offered both by government agencies and private firms.

Jobcentre Plus

Jobcentres are in process of being changed into organisations known as Jobcentre Plus. They are combining the Benefits Agency and Employment Service to provide a one-stop shop where jobseekers can get help and advice about work, training opportunities and also about any benefits they would be able to claim. Jobcentre Plus is planned to be available nationwide by 2006. In the meantime, there are several services that could be helpful to adult jobseekers. In all cases, contact your local jobcentre (see telephone directory).

Programme Centres. Programme Centres operate over most of Great Britain. They have replaced traditional job search courses with a modular approach that addresses the needs of individual jobseekers. Areas without a programme centre provide help through Jobclubs or Resource Departments in Jobcentres.

Work Trials. These give jobseekers who have been unemployed for six months or more the chance to try out a job for a maximum of fifteen working days and prove their suitability to an employer while remaining on JSA.

Travel to Interview Scheme. Provides financial assistance in meeting travel costs to long-distance interviews. The scheme is available to people who have been unemployed and receiving Jobseeker's Allowance (JSA) or National Insurance contributions.

Jobseeker Direct. Jobseekers can ring a national number T:0845 606 0234, charged at a local rate, to gain access to details of job vacancies nationwide. There is also a textphone on T:0845 605 5255.

Jobcentre Plus Website. The website at www.jobscentreplus.gov.uk lists details of all job vacancies (around 250,000 at any time) held by Jobcentres, as well as general information about their services.

Jobcentres. As well as being the place to go for further information about any of the above services, Jobcentres can give general advice about local employers, training opportunities and other openings. Some have an Information Centre with details of a wide range of courses available locally, as well as useful reading material including tips on self-employment and addresses of other agencies that could be helpful. Jobcentres are open daily during normal office hours. You can simply call in without making an appointment.

Private counselling

Job counselling has become a growth industry in the private sector. Some people find it extremely helpful; others, an expensive waste of time. Best advice is to obtain brochures from a variety of agencies and study the literature carefully to see exactly what you are being offered. You could ask for a list of former clients and then speak to one or two of them direct, to find out whether they found the service useful. Some of the better known organisations include:

Career Counselling Services, 46 Ferry Road, London SW13 9PW. T:020 8741 0335. Individual counselling is staged over a number of sessions, lasting 12–14 hours in all. The service includes various tests and questionnaires which are used as a basis for discussion. A tape recording of this discussion is given to you. Price is £450 plus VAT. A service to help with job-hunting is also available.

Career and Educational Guidance, 4 Cadogan Lane, London SW1X 9EB. T:020 7631 1209. Offers a combination of tests with a detailed follow-up interview and a written report. Price is £375 incl. VAT.

Those living out of London should look in the *Yellow Pages* under the word 'Career' or 'Vocational'.

Training opportunities

Knowing what you want to do is one thing. But before starting in a new job, you may want to brush up existing skills or possibly acquire new ones. Most professional bodies have a full programme of training events, ranging from one-day seminars to proper courses lasting a week or longer. Additionally, adult education institutes run a vast range of courses or, if you are still in a present job, a more practical solution might be to investigate open and flexible learning.

Open and flexible learning. Open and flexible learning is successfully helping to provide a greater range and flexibility of vocational education and training opportunities for individuals of all ages. In particular, it is designed to increase the scope for participants to learn at a time, place and pace best suited to their own particular circumstances. For further information on the full range of open learning opportunities, contact **Learn Direct** on Freephone: 0800 100 900.

See also Adult Education, pages 181 to 190.

Help with finding a job

The ideal is to find a job for your retirement while you are still at work. Quite apart from it being more difficult to summon the energy to start looking around after a period of being idle, employers tend to give preference to those they see as being busy and involved, rather than those whom they suspect as having got out of the habit of the normal disciplines of work.

However, whether you leave it a while or start hunting well in advance, this will not affect the approach you probably adopt. The only extra tip if you have been retired for some time is to consider doing some voluntary work, or a short course, so you have a convincing answer to the inevitable question: what have you been doing?

There are four basic ways of finding a job: through contacts; by following up advertisements; by applying to an agency for suitable introductions; or by direct approaches to suitable employers. As general wisdom, the more irons you have in the fire, the better.

Make sure all your friends and acquaintances know that you are in the market for work – and include on the list your present employer. Some firms actually encourage consultancy links with former executives, or at least are prepared to respond to a good idea. A greater number are more than happy to take on previous employees over a rush period or during the holiday season.

Another obvious move, if you are a member of a professional institute, is to inform them of your availability. Many institutes keep a register of members wanting work and, the encouraging part is, receive a fair number of enquiries from firms seeking qualified people for projects, part-time or temporary work, or sometimes even for permanent employment.

A further source of very useful contacts is the local Chamber of Commerce, CBI or Institute of Directors. Likewise, if you are a member of a Rotary Club, it can only be useful to spread the word; and the same applies to, say, a golf club, political association where you are active, any committee you sit on or other group with which you are involved. Often the most unlikely person turns out to be the one who helps you most.

If you intend to follow up advertisements, selectivity is the name of the game. Rather than write around to all and sundry, limit your applications to those that sound genuinely promising. You will save yourself a lot of stationery, not to mention disappointments when another 'sorry' letter arrives – or you fail to hear anything at all. As well as national and local newspapers, remember that the trade press often offers the best bet of all. Some local radio programmes broadcast a regular weekly 'job spot'; it could be useful to check when this is scheduled.

Agencies will invariably have more applicants than vacancies, except where skill shortages exist. However, most of them clearly place a fair number of people (or they would be out of business) and, as with other endeavours, keenness counts. People who simply register their name and then sit back and wait tend to be forgotten. The moral is telephone frequently to enquire what opportunities have arrived; or if you live close-by, pop into the office from time to time. Being on the spot at the right time is nine-tenths of success. A selection of agencies that specialise in appointments for people aged 50-plus is listed at the end of the chapter.

A direct approach to likely employers is another option. Study the business press and talk to your colleagues for ideas of firms that might be interested in employing someone with your abilities. Always find out who the appropriate person is to whom you should be writing – a properly addressed letter is far more likely to get noticed than one merely marked 'For the attention of the Personnel Manager'.

Regardless of whether you use contacts, advertisements or agencies – or preferably all three – a prime requirement will be to have a well presented CV.

CV writing

This is your personal sales document. It should contain:

- your name
- address
- telephone number
- a summary of your work experience including: dates, employers, job titles and outline of responsibilities

- age (optional)
- brief details of your education
- other achievements
- key outside interests

Ideally, it should not be longer than two pages of A4 and it must be typed.

There are a number of firms that specialise in providing assistance with the writing of CVs, who advertise their services regularly in *The Times* and other serious newspapers. While some are highly professional, a common fault tends to be the production of over-lengthy CVs, which can be definitely counter-productive. An all-purpose CV can also put off employers. Wherever possible, you should try to gear your CV specifically to the job on offer, emphasising those elements of your experience and skills that are relevant. If you are thinking of using a specialist service, check the price first as charges can be on the hefty side. As with other purchases, you should do a bit of price comparison before making a decision. The price will normally include a batch of immaculately typed copies of your CV, ready for you to distribute.

A far cheaper option is to take advantage of the government work preparation courses, which are run by Jobcentre staff or other agencies on the government's behalf to assist those who have been out of work for six months or more (people with disabilities can apply as soon as they wish). As part of the service, help is given with CV preparation and free facilities are provided including telephone, typewriter and photocopying equipment. Contact your Jobcentre for details.

Women's Job Change, operating as part of the charity Birmingham Settlement, offers a similar wide-ranging and free service to unemployed women. Help and advice can be obtained on matters relating to finding a job, education and retraining opportunities. Among other facilities, there are a range of IT courses from introductory to advanced. Further information from: **Women's Job Change**, Birmingham Settlement, 318 Summer Lane, Newtown, Birmingham B19 3RL. T:0121 248 3000.

Interview technique

If you have worked for the same employer for a number of years, your interview skills are liable to be a little rusty. It is a good idea to list all the questions you expect to be asked, (including those you hope won't be brought up) and then get a good friend to rehearse you in your answers.

In addition to questions about your previous job, be prepared for some or all of the following: what you have done since leaving employment; why, if you are now seeking a job, you retired earlier than you might have done; whether your health is good – this may take the form of a polite enquiry as to whether you would not find the hours or travelling too much of a strain; why you are particularly interested in working for them as an employer; and given the job requirements, what you think you have of special value to offer. You may also be asked what you know about the organisation. If the answer is likely to be 'very little', it could pay you to do a bit of research – such as obtaining a copy of the annual report.

Obvious mistakes to avoid are: claiming skills/knowledge that you do not possess; giving the impression that you have a series of stock answers to problems; criticising your former employer; or by contrast, drawing comparisons which could be interpreted as being faintly disparaging of the organisation where you are attending for interview.

Possibly the most difficult subject of all to come up may be the question, how much money would you expect? As a sad generalisation, most jobs for retired people – including early retirers – pay less than their previous employment, so you may have to strike a balance between what you want and the risk of pricing yourself out of the market.

Part-time openings

Another reason why the pay may appear low is that the work is part-time. For some people, of course, this is the ideal arrangement. Others may regard it as very second best. However, do not sniff at part-time work if the opportunity is available. Firstly, it is a way back into the market and many part-time or temporary assignments develop into full-time jobs in due course. This is especially true in small firms, which may of necessity be cautious about recruitment while the business is in the early development stage.

Additionally, far-reaching changes have been happening in the job market, with temporary, or project-based, professional and executive assignments becoming increasingly common. For example, freelance accountants are in growing demand, as are supply teachers, nurses, IT staff and personnel specialists with particular knowledge of, say, pensions or performance pay. Proficient temporary secretaries are again high on the 'wanted list'. Likewise, there are a growing number of part-time and other openings for older people to work in supermarkets, chain stores, hotels, conference centres and other outlets connected with the tourist industry.

Furthermore, according to recent research, it is estimated that over a fifth of all new jobs are now on a contract basis – the average being for six months or a year – and while the downside is an obvious lack of security for younger people seeking permanent employment, mature candidates have everything to gain. Firstly, because there is greater turnover of jobs – so more vacancies; and secondly, because the stock excuses for not employing older applicants, which mainly revolve around the fact that they won't be 'developing' with the company or that it is not worth training them for just a short time, are now patently nonsensical. Moreover, any such excuses will soon become illegal as the government is pledged to introduce legislation to outlaw age discrimination by 2006.

Part-time or freelance work can to all intents and purposes become a full-time occupation in its own right. Ask any retired businessman who has taken on half a dozen such appointments and the likelihood is that he will tell you that he is working harder than he has ever done in his life.

Employment ideas

Going the established routes – agencies and so forth – while obviously recommended, may not suffice. Many of the best jobs are never advertised, either because people obtain them through personal recommendation or because – and this is becoming more frequent – individuals have been partially instrumental in creating their own opportunities.

One clear-cut way of doing so is to use a bit of initiative when spreading the word of your availability, by actually suggesting work you could usefully perform. Consultancy is very much a case in point.

Consultancy

Many retired executives make a tidy income by hiring themselves back to their former employer in a consultancy guise. As opposed to being paid a regular salary and working full time, they undertake specific projects for which they are paid a fee. This may be structured as a lump sum, for example £5,000 for devising and helping implement a merit appraisal scheme; or as many consultants do, they may negotiate a day-rate.

Consultancy, by definition, is not limited to a single client. By using your contacts judiciously plus a bit of marketing nous, it is quite possible to build up a steady list of assignments on the basis of your particular expertise.

Marketing skills are always in demand, as is computer knowledge, experience in pensions, and personnel-related subjects and, increasingly today, public relations know-how.

Small firms are often a good bet for consultants, as they cannot afford to employ specialists full-time, so normally buy in expertise, as and when it is required. Any contacts with the chamber of commerce or similar could prove fruitful avenues for promoting your services.

Many established consultancies retain a list of associates – a sort of freelance register – whom they call on, on a horses-for-courses basis, to handle suitable assignments. The Institute of Management Consultancy (IMC) might be able to assist if you are looking for consultant firms to contact. If you are serious about consulting, the Institute will also be able to offer you plenty of guidance including details of the standards required to qualify for membership. The address is: **Institute of Management Consultancy**, 3rd Floor, 17–18 Hayward's Place, London EC1R 0EQ. T:020 7566 5220.

A useful organisation to know about is the Institute of Business Advisers which, with a membership of over 2,000 and 20 branches nationwide, has contact with all Business Advice Centres, Enterprise Agencies and similar organisations seeking business men and women qualified to advise small, start-up and medium-sized businesses. A code of conduct and professional standards of competence and personal development have been established and substantial business experience is a prerequisite of membership.

There is a registration fee of £50 and annual subscriptions (2002/03) are as follows: Associate (AIBA), £79; Member (MIBA) £110; Fellow (FIBA) £130. A low cost professional indemnity insurance scheme is available for members. For further information, contact: Membership Department, **Institute of Business Advisers**, Response House, Queen Street North, Chesterfield, S41 9AB. T:01246 453322.

Interim management

Interim management has been one of the biggest growth areas in recruitment over the past few years.

The term covers an enormously wide range, from a temporary manager engaged to cover in an emergency or to handle a specific job such as the closure of a plant, to an outside specialist recruited short-term to implement a particular assignment – for example, a marketing campaign or the installation of a new computer system.

The growth is largely due to two factors: the down-sizing of personnel by large organisations and the requirement of many small companies for specialist skills that they cannot afford to employ full-time. Either way, what it means is an upsurge in temporary job opportunities for experienced managers and/or those with particular expertise to offer – with many of the plum jobs going to those who have recently taken early retirement or been made redundant.

Most of the organisations that specialise in such placements have more candidates on their books than vacancies but all agree that this is a growth industry with opportunities set to increase.

As in consultancy, fees vary enormously. While the going rate for senior people is around £400 to £700 a day, some managers command double or even more. However, as with any temporary or freelance situation, there will inevitably be days when you will not be working and, in contrast to a permanent job, very few interim assignments offer the normal executive perks. Typical assignments last between six and nine months and may be full-time or simply involve one or two days' work a week.

There is now an organisation representing those engaged in interim management, known as the **Interim Management Association**, 36–38 Mortimer Street, London W1N 7RG, T:020 7636 7166. Member organisations are:

Archer Mathieson, Thames Court, 1 Victoria Street, Berkshire SL4 1YB. T:**01753 752 323.**

Armadillo Executive Resourcing, King's Court, Parsonage Lane, Bath BA1 1ER. T:01225 443077.

Ashton Penney Partnership Ltd., 4th Floor, Marcol House, 289–293 Regent Street, London W1R 7PD. T:020 7659 0600.

Atlan Executive Resourcing, 10 Fleet Road, Fleet, Hampshire GU51 4BL. T:01252 816 816.

Barnes Kavelle Ltd., Cavendish House, Littlewood Court, Bradford, West Yorkshire BD19 4TE. T:01274 854200.

BIE Interim Management, 22 Queen Anne's Gate, London SW1H 9AA. T:020 7222 1010.

Boyden Interim Management Ltd., 24 Queen Anne's Gate, London SW1H 9AA. T:020 7222 9033.

Calibre One, 38 Welbeck Street, London W1G 8DP. T:020 7070 3000.

Charter Interim Management, Victoria Court, Penny Street, Lancaster LA1 1XN. T:01524 846847.

Chiumento, 8 Elm Place, Eynsham, Oxford OX29 4BD. T:01865 882100.

Executive Support Group Ltd., 97 West Street, Faversham, Kent ME13 7JQ. T:01795 530830.

Global Executives Ltd., 18 Stoneleigh Court, Frimley, Surrey GU16 8XH. T:01276 671535.

Hogg Robinson Skillbase, 19 Picton House, Westside View, Waterlooville, Hampshire PO7 7SQ. T:023 9223 1040.

IEL, Kings Road House, 2 Kings Road, Windsor, Berkshire SL4 2AG. T:01753 836 280.

Impact Executives, 13 Bruton Street, London W1X 7AH. T:020 7314 2000.

IMS Interim Management, 33 Throgmorton Street, London EC2N 2BR. T:020 7861 9670.

Inbucon Interim Management, 34 Paradise Road, Richmond upon Thames, Surrey TW9 1SE. T:020 8334 5767.

Interregna Interim Solutions, 28 Friars Stile Road, Richmond, Surrey TW10 6NE. T:020 8940 8078.

KPMG Interim Management, 1–2 Dorset Rise, London EC4Y 8AE. T:020 7694 2333.

Nexus Interim Management Ltd., 212 Piccadilly, London W1V 9LD. T:020 7917 2789.

Norman Broadbent, 20 Regent Street, London SW1Y 4PM. T:020 7484 0048.

Odgers Interim, 11 Hanover Square, London W1S 1JJ. T:020 7529 1084.

Ortus Interim Solutions, (Associate member), 33 Sloane Street, London SW1X 4NR. T:020 7556 2980.

Penna Interim, Gladstone House, Lawnswood Park, Leeds LS16 6QY. T:0113 274 1809.

Praxis Executive Taskforce Ltd., Norfolk House, The Courtyard, Gorsey Lane, Coleshill, Birmingham B46 1JA. T:01675 466812.

Resources Connection, 117 Houndsditch, London EC3A 7BT. T:020 7422 7780.

RHI Management Resources, Rex House, 10 Regent Street, London SW1Y APE. T:023 8023 3131.

Russam GMS Ltd., 48 High Street, Dunstable, Bedfordshire LU6 1LA. T:01582 666 970.

Veredus Executive Resourcing, Plumtree Court, London EC4A 4HT. T:020 7212 3862.

Other firms (not members of the Interim Management Association) that could be worth contacting are:

Albemarle Interim Management Services Plc., 26–28 Great Portland Street, London W1W 8QT. T:020 7079 3737.

Barton International Ltd., Bere Barton, Bere Ferrers, Yelverton, Devon PL20 7JL. T:01822 840220.

EIM, 39 St. James's Street, London SW1A 1JD. T:020 7629 2832.

Executives on Assignment Ltd., Norfolk House, The Courtyard, Gorsey Lane, Coleshill, Warwickshire. T:01675 430 330.

Triple-A International, 18 Lawrence Avenue, New Malden, Surrey KT3 5LY. T:020 8335 3135.

W & S Transition Management Ltd., Regent House, 22 Nutford Place, Edgware Road, London W1H 5YN. T:020 7725 7119.

Openings via a company or other reference

Just as your company could turn out to be your best customer for consultancy services, it could also open other doors. If you are still a couple of years off retirement, you could broach your employer about seconding you to an enterprise agency or charity, where you would be helping small businesses or a worthwhile voluntary organisation in your local community. Secondment can be part-time for a few hours a week or full-time for anything from a few weeks to two years. It can also often lead to a new career.

Normally only larger employers are willing to consider the idea since, as a rule, the company will continue to pay your salary and other benefits during the period of secondment. If you work for a smaller firm it could still be worth discussing the suggestion, as employers benefit from the favourable publicity the company attracts by being seen to support the local community.

The major organisation specialising in co-ordinating secondments is Business in the Community. It is the leading consultant to companies on secondment policies and practice, as well as the main agency arranging all forms of secondment to community organisations. For further information, contact: **Business in the Community**, T:0870 600 2482.

Public appointments

Opportunities regularly arise for individuals to be appointed to a wide range of public bodies, such as tribunals, commissions and consumer consultative councils. Many appointments are to local and regional bodies throughout the country, including Scotland, Wales and Northern Ireland. Some are paid but many offer an opportunity to contribute to the community and gain valuable experience of working in the public sector on a part-time expenses-only basis.

An information pack which includes a self-nomination form is available from: **The Public Appointments Unit**, Cabinet Office, 70 Whitehall, London SW1A 2AS. T:0845 0000 040.

The Public Appointments Unit does not itself make appointments but puts forward names of candidates in response to requests by departments. Registration with the unit is, of course, no guarantee of appointment.

The Unit is not the only gateway to nomination and those with particular interests may also wish to make their availability known to the relevant government department or public body. Further information is available from the Unit at the above address.

Additionally, both the TUC and CBI are consulted on some appointments. If you are active on either, there is nothing to lose by letting it be known that you could be interested in a public appointment.

Non-executive directorships

Many retiring executives see this as the ideal. The problem, whichever way you look at it, is: either that more executives want appointments than there are directorships available; or that not enough companies have yet recognised the merits of having outside directors on their board.

The old idea that such appointments are a pleasant sinecure is distinctly out of date. In the past few years a more exacting business climate has developed, coupled with more onerous demands made on all company directors by recent legislation. If you are able, committed and have the necessary experience a couple of organisations to which you might apply are:

The 3i Independent Directors Programme, 91 Waterloo Road, London SE1 8XP. T:020 7928 3131. Essentially interested in candidates who run, or have run, their own business or have served on the main board of another business.

The Non Executive Register, Wrest House, Wrest Park, Silsoe, Beds MK45 4HS. T:01525 862234. Interested in being contacted by any executives with demonstrable boardroom experience.

Traditionally the two best routes for obtaining a non-executive directorship were via headhunters and the old boy network. However, while both are still useful, increasingly today openings are being advertised in the recruitment pages of the national press. You have nothing to lose by looking.

Another route to becoming a part-time director which might appeal is to join the growing number of business angels by taking a stake in one or several smaller companies. For further information, see Chapter 10, page 255.

Market research

In addition to the normal consultancy openings in marketing, there is also scope for those with knowledge of market research techniques. The work covers a very broad spectrum, from street or telephone interviewing to data processing, designing questionnaires, statistical analysis and sample group selection.

Some market research agencies employ researchers and analysts on a freelance basis. However, as with other fields, supply exceeds demand so there is a certain amount of luck involved, as well of course as ability, in finding regular work. Although not essential, IT skills are increasingly an asset.

For a list of market research companies, see *The Research Buyer's Guide*, price £40 (plus p+p), obtainable from: **Market Research Society**, 15 Northburgh Street, London EC1V 0JR. T:020 7490 4911.

Survey interviewing

No experience is necessary to become a freelance interviewer for the National Centre for Social Research. At the present time, they are looking to recruit people nationwide to ask members of the public for their views on such topics as education, health, housing and similar. The work consists of interviewing people in their own homes and recording their answers on a laptop computer or paper questionnaire.

A minimum of 3 days a week is required, which will usually include a certain amount of evening and weekend work. Applicants need to have use of a car and telephone and be computer literate. There are two days paid training at the start, after which new interviewers can expect to earn about £10 for an hour-long interview; about £15 in London. For further information, contact: Penny De Geus, **National Centre for Social Research**, 100 Kings Road, Brentwood, Essex CM14 4LX. T:01277 200600.

Paid work for charities

Although charities rely to a very large extent on voluntary workers, most charitable organisations of any size have a number of paid appointments. Other than social workers and other specialists that particular charities may require for their work, the majority of openings are for general managers/administrators, fundraisers and for those with financial skills. Secretarial vacancies also exist from time to time.

Salaries have been improving but in general are still considerably below the commercial market rate. A further point is that, unlike the big company world, managers cannot expect to find a battery of support staff and must be willing to turn their hand to the more menial jobs such as adding up the petty cash and fixing the photo-copier – as well as handling meetings, building up good media relations and sustaining the enthusiasm of volunteers and paid staff alike.

It is essential therefore that anyone thinking of applying for a job in a charity must be in sympathy with its aims and style. Agencies specialising in charity recruitment advise that it is a good idea to do a stint as a volunteer before seeking a paid appointment, as not only will this provide useful experience but will help you to decide whether you would find the work satisfying.

Most of the serious newspapers carry charity job advertisements: the *Guardian*, *Times* and the *Sunday Times* are especially fertile hunting grounds. Other possibilities are to approach a charity direct or to register with one of the agencies below.

Charity and Fundraising Appointments, Lloyds Court, 1 Goodman's Yard, London E1 8AT. T:020 7953 1190. Helps charities fill their key jobs – for example, chief executive, finance director and fundraiser – and also finds trustees who are unpaid.

Charity Recruitment, 40 Rosebery Avenue, London EC1R 4RX. T:020 7833 0770. An appointments service specialising in recruiting senior and middle managers for charities and other non-profit organisations. It advises regretfully that it is more difficult to place candidates over 60. CR also helps charities to find trustees who can offer skills and experience on a voluntary basis. CVs will be treated in confidence.

Sales

If you are a whizz salesperson, you will hardly be reading this chapter. You will have already used your contacts and flair to talk yourself into a dozen jobs, with the only problem being which one to choose. Almost every commercial firm in the country is crying out for people with that particular brand of authority, charm and persuasiveness to win extra orders.

Many people who have never thought of sales could be excellent in the job, because of their specialist knowledge in a particular field combined with their enthusiasm for the subject. Educational and children's book publishers for example are often keen to recruit ex-teachers to market their books to schools and libraries.

There is an almost insatiable demand for people to sell advertising space and if you are an avid reader of a particular publication, for example a specialist motoring or gardening magazine, you might find the work fun and be very successful.

Another possibility where star performers can do exceptionally well is insurance selling. Standards have been considerably tightened up since the furore over personal pensions with the result, which can only be a good thing, that far more attention is now being given to training. Another gain is that earnings are becoming less commission-dependent – with instead proper basic salaries being paid by a growing number of companies.

Selling today is not just standing in a shop or trudging the rounds of sceptical customers. Over the past few years telephone selling has caught on in a big way and, like mail order, is used by a vast array of very different businesses; so if you have a good telephone voice, this could be for you.

Additionally, many firms employ demonstrators in shops or at exhibitions for special promotions. The work is usually temporary or freelance by definition; and while pay is normally good, the big drawback is that you could be standing on your feet for long periods of the day.

The big 'beware' are firms that pay on a commission-only basis. Far from merely earning a pittance, you could end up distinctly out of pocket.

If the idea of selling appeals, either study the newspaper advertisements or, better still, approach firms direct that you reckon could make genuine use of your special knowledge. If the idea makes you quail, the likelihood is that selling is not for you. If it fires you with enthusiasm, you could actually find yourself making more money in your retirement than ever before.

Sales distributor

Some companies employ softer-sell methods, using distributor agents who call on their neighbours with a catalogue or arrange parties at which it is possible to buy a range of merchandise.

Betterware which recruits several thousand distributors a year – including many retirees – says the essence is building up friendly relationships, noting down orders and delivering the goods a few days later. There is no financial outlay, the hours are totally flexible and most agents can reckon on earning about £50 – £200 a week, depending on the number of hours they work. The minimum requirement is 10 hours a week.

Other big name companies employing freelance distributors include Avon, Tupperware and Amway and, while their terms and conditions all vary slightly (e.g. some encourage distributors to purchase samples or charge them a nominal amount for catalogues), all have frequent openings for both permanent and temporary work.

For further information, contact the companies direct or write to the Direct Selling Association, requesting a list of all member companies together with their advice sheet, listing points to check before signing on as a distributor. Addresses are:

Direct Selling Association, 29 Floral Street, London WC2E 9DP. T:020 7497 1234.

Amway (UK) Ltd., Snowdon Drive, Winterhill, Milton Keynes MK6 1AR. T:01908 298 005.

Avon Cosmetics Ltd., Nunn Mills Road, Northampton NN1 5PA. T:01604 232425.

Betterware UK Ltd., Stanley House, Park Lane, Castle Vale, Birmingham B35 6LJ. T:0845 129 4500.

Tupperware UK & Ireland, Keaton House, Widewater Place, Moorhall Road, Harefield, Uxbridge, Middx UB9 6NS. T:01895 826400.

Tourist guide

An extrovert personality is also needed for tourist guide work. Happily age is no longer a factor – there are a growing number of tourist guides well into their sixties and older. However, fitness is essential as it is a job that requires bags of stamina as well as a real liking for people.

You must also be prepared to put in some fairly concentrated study. While there are various possible qualifications (some easier than others), training for the coveted *Blue Badge* takes 15 months and the exam itself is considered to be equivalent in standard to a first degree.

Even the Blue Badge is no guarantee of steady work as openings are largely seasonal, most tourist guides are self-employed and the field is highly competitive. Perhaps not surprisingly, opportunities are greatest in London especially for those with fluency in one or more foreign languages.

If despite the challenges you would like to know more, contact **The Institute of Tourist Guiding**, Lloyd's Court, 1 Goodman's Yard, London E1 8AT. T:020 7953 1257.

For more information about the London Blue Badge course, contact **Training Professional Guides**, 31 Sterndale Road, London W14 0HT T:020 7603 9844.

Another possibility is to sign on as a lecturer with one of the growing number of travel companies offering special interest holidays. To be eligible you need real expertise in a subject, the ability to make it interesting and an easy manner with people. Pay is usually fairly minimal, although you may receive tips plus of course the bonus of a free holiday.

While the number of openings is fairly limited, two of my own friends have got on the circuit – the one lecturing on tours around India, the other running painting classes in Italy. The Holiday chapter gives names of operators that make a feature of special interest programmes. The travel pages of most newspapers should also give you plenty of ideas.

Other tourist work

You might like to consider courier work. Holiday firms are increasingly looking to recruit people in their fifties and early sixties, in part due to the decline in the number of available students but equally because they are finding that their clients often prefer having more mature people in charge.

Some jobs take you overseas, others not. Either way, it is demanding work that calls for a calm, unflappable personality. If the idea appeals, watch the classified columns for vacancies or, if there is a travel company you particularly admire, you might try approaching them direct.

If you live in a popular tourist area, there is a whole variety of seasonal work, including: jobs in hotels, restaurants, shops and local places of interest. Depending on the locality, the list might also include: deckchair attendants, play leaders for children, caravan site staff, extra coach drivers and many others.

Teaching and training skills

If you have been a teacher at any stage of your career, there are a number of part-time possibilities:

Coaching

With examinations becoming more competitive, demand has been increasing for ex-teachers with knowledge of the public examination system to coach youngsters in preparation for 'A' level, GCSE and common entrance. Contact local schools or a specialist educational consultancy such as **Gabbitas Educational Consultants Ltd.**, Carrington House, 126–130 Regent Street, London W1B 5EE. T:020 7734 0161. Gabbitas provides a wide range of recruitment and consultancy services to independent schools in Great Britain and for English-speaking schools overseas. It also maintains an extensive register of teachers seeking appointments, as well as a register for tutors.

It is also worth looking in the *Yellow Pages* under 'Coaching', 'Tutoring' and 'Education'.

Specialist subjects

Teachers are in demand for mathematics, physics, chemistry, technology and modern languages. People with relevant work experience and qualifications may be able to teach or give tuition in these subjects. A formal teaching qualification is, however, required to teach in state maintained schools.

The **Teacher Training Agency**, Communication Centre, PO Box 3210, Chelmsford, Essex CM1 3WA, T:0845 600 0991, has a range of publications about entry into teaching. It also operates an information and advice line.

English as a foreign language

Over the past decade, there has been a mini-explosion of new schools teaching English to foreign students. These tend to be concentrated in London and the major academic cities such as Oxford, Cambridge, Bath and York. The basic requirement for people entering the profession is the Cambridge Certificate in English Language Teaching to Adults (CELTA); or for those interested in English Language Teaching to Young Learners in language schools, the relevant certificate is the CELTYL. Both can be studied either part-time or full-time. A list of UK, also overseas, centres offering the course can be obtained from: The **EFL Helpdesk**, UCLES, 1 Hills Road, Cambridge CB1 2EU. T:01223 553355.

Other. Adult Education Institutes and Colleges of Further Education may sometimes have part-time vacancies.

Working in the third world

There are various opportunities for suitably qualified people to work in the developing countries of Africa, Asia, the Caribbean and the Pacific on a semi-voluntary basis.

Skills most in demand include: civil engineering; mechanical engineering; water engineering; architecture; urban, rural and regional planning; agriculture; forestry; medicine; teaching English as a foreign language; maths and physics training; and economics. All air fares, accommodation costs and insurance are usually covered by the organising agency and pay is limited to a 'living allowance' based on local levels. As a general rule, there is an upper age limit of 65 and you must be willing to work for a minimum of two years. The following are the major agencies involved in this kind of work. Fuller details are contained in the chapter on Voluntary Work.

VSO (Voluntary Service Overseas), 317 Putney Bridge Road, Putney, London SW15 2PN. T:020 8780 7500. Minicom: 020 8780 7440.

Skillshare International, People and Organisation Development Unit, 126 New Walk, Leicester LE1 7JA. T:0116 254 1862.

International Co-operation for Development, Unit 3, Canonbury Yard, 190a New North Road, London N1 7BJ. T:020 7354 0883.

International Service, Suite 3a, Hunter House, 57 Goodramgate, York YO1 7FX. T:01904 647799.

Publishing

Publishers are increasingly using freelance staff with appropriate experience for: proof-reading, copy-editing, design, typography, indexing and similar work as well as for writing specialist copy. For a list of firms that could be interested, your local reference library should have a copy of *Directory of Publishing* which catalogues businesses by the type of publishing they do. Alternatively, *The Bookseller* (available through newsagents) carries classified advertisement columns, useful for advertising your own skills as well as for finding work.

Freelance journalism

This is a highly competitive field with very limited scope and, other than for professionals, should really be included in the hobbies section. Best bet if you remain undaunted is to approach specialist magazines direct, where you have a real knowledge of the subject. It is normally a waste of time sending articles 'on spec'. Instead, telephone the editor with a list of suggestions – and find out exactly what the magazine wants, including number of words and so on.

Caring for other people

There are a number of opportunities for paid work in this field. Mature women or couples are often preferred.

Fostering elderly people

An increasing number of local authorities run fostering schemes, whereby an elderly person either lives with a family as an ordinary member of the household, receiving whatever care and special assistance is necessary; or receives day-time support at a neighbour or in their own home. As with child fostering, enormous trouble is taken by social workers in matching families with their foster guest. Pay varies from one area to another but averages around: £5 an hour for day-time support and between £200 to £250 a week for every elderly person fostered on a live-in basis.

Since April 1993, anyone providing personal care for a non-relative who is living in their home, is required to register with their local authority.

Ask at your Social Services Department whether there is a fostering or adult placement scheme to which you could contribute. Alternatively contact the **National Association of Adult Placement Services**, 72 Rodney Street, Liverpool L1 9AF. T:0151 709 1200.

Domestic work

A number of private domestic agencies specialise in finding temporary or permanent companions, housekeepers, caretakers, emergency mothers and extra care help for elderly and disabled people or for those who are convalescent. Many of these jobs are particularly suitable for retired people or couples and, with ever-growing demand especially for carers, finding work is probably easier than it has ever been. Pay generally starts at around £295 a week plus travelling expenses (£100 a week for caretakers). Daily rates, depending on what is required, start from about £42 plus fares. Agencies worth contacting include:

Anchor Care Alternatives Ltd., 7th Floor, Chancery House, St Nicholas Way, Sutton, Surrey SM1 1JB. T:020 8652 1900.

Consultus Services Agency Ltd., 17 London Road, Tonbridge, Kent TN10 3AB. T:01732 355231.

Country Cousins (Horsham) Ltd., 10a Market Square, Horsham, West Sussex RH12 1EX, T:0845 601 4003.

Universal Aunts Ltd; PO Box 304, London SW4 0NN. T:020 7738 8937.

Local agencies will be listed in *Yellow Pages* under 'Domestic', 'Employment' or 'Care Agencies'.

Home helps

Local authorities sometimes have vacancies for home helps, to assist disabled or elderly people in their own home by giving a hand with the cleaning, light cooking and other chores. Ask at your local Social Services Department.

Childminding

If you already look after a grandchild during the day, you might consider caring for an additional couple of youngsters. You will need to be registered with the local Social Services Department who will explain all the requirements.

Nursing

Qualified nurses are in great demand in most parts of the country and stand an excellent chance of finding work at their local hospital or alternatively through one of the many nursing agencies. See *Yellow Pages*. Family Planning clinics could also be worth approaching.

Those with suitable experience although not necessarily a formal nursing qualification could apply to become a Care Worker for the charity Crossroads, which provides regular short-term relief for carers of sick or disabled people in their own homes. For information on local schemes, contact: **Crossroads,** Caring for Carers, 10 Regent Place, Rugby CV21 2PN. T:01788 573653.

Homesitting

Homesitting means taking care of someone else's home while they are away on holiday or business trips. Mature, responsible people, usually non-smokers with no children or pets, are in demand for this type of work. More like a paid holiday, you could expect to receive anything from about £65 to £130 a week (extra if care of pets is involved), depending on the responsibilities and on the size of house or flat. Food and travelling expenses are normally also paid. It is useful to have your own car. Firms specialising in this type of work include:

Absentia, Little London, Berden, Bishops Stortford, Herts CM23 1BE. T:01279 777412.

Home and Pet Care Ltd., Nether Row Hall, Hesket-New-Market, Wigton, Cumbria CA7 8LA. T:016974 78515.

Homesitters Ltd., Buckland Wharf, Buckland, Aylesbury, Bucks HP22 5LQ. T:01296 630730.

Universal Aunts, PO Box 304, London SW4 0NN. T:020 7738 8937.

Cashing in on your home interests

Cooking, gardening, home decorating, dressmaking and DIY skills can all be turned into modest money-spinners.

Cooking

Scope includes: catering other people's dinner parties, selling home-made goodies to local shops and cooking for directors' lunches. Other than top class culinary skills, requirements are: a large deep-freeze, a car (you will normally be required to do all the necessary shopping) and plenty of stamina.

Notify your friends, advertise your services through the local newspapers, chamber of commerce or local businessmen's club or, if you are really serious about it, enrol with one of the specialist catering agencies. See *Yellow Pages*.

Gardening

Small shopkeepers and florists sometimes purchase flowers or plants direct from local gardeners, in preference to going to the market. Alternatively, you might consider dried flower arrangements or herbs for which there has been a growing increase in demand. However, before spending any money, check around to find out what the sales possibilities are. If you are willing to tend someone else's garden, the likelihood is that you will be inundated with enquiries. Spread the word among friends, acquaintances, local shops and in the pub.

Dressmaking and home decorating

If you are happy to do alterations, the chances are that you could be kept busy from dawn to dusk. Many shops are desperate for seamstresses. Likewise, many individuals and families would love to know of someone who could alter clothes, as well as dressmake properly. Perhaps to a slightly lesser extent, the same goes for curtains, chair covers and other soft furnishings. Often a good move is to approach firms selling materials for the home, who may be only too glad to put work out to you. Alternatively, put up a card in newsagents' shops or run a small advertisement in the local paper.

DIY

Competition is more intense, as many small builders offer this service. However, elderly people often require small jobs, as do women who do not have a handy-man around the house. Advice for getting your services known is the same as for gardening.

Pubs and paying guests

Many people dream of running a pub in their retirement – and many people live to regret it. A less strenuous option which others may prefer is offering bed and breakfast accommodation in their own home.

Running a pub

Running a pub is more a way of life than a job and one that requires a great deal of stamina. Anything less like a quiet retirement would be hard to imagine. You are on your feet for most of the day, the hours are long and when you are not pulling pints or preparing bar snacks, you will be dealing with the paperwork plus all the other day-to-day business requirements.

You can either buy your own 'free' house outright or become the tenant or lessee of a brewery or pub-owning company. Prices vary according to the length of lease, location and so on but, as a rough guide, you would need at least £20,000 in order to get started as a tenant; and between £60,000 and £250,000 – or even more – for a 'free house'. Big free houses in London can fetch over £1 million today. On top of all this, as with any other business, you will need to budget for operating capital.

Tenancy packages vary and may include the range of products you sell as well as repairs and decorations. As a self-employed business person, a tenant or leaseholder has responsibility for the hiring and firing of any staff, compliance with the fire regulations and with the other laws of the land. As a licensee, he is also required to know and enforce the licensing laws.

If you are over 50, some experience of self-employment or the leisure industry is vital in order to be considered for a tenancy or long-term lease and even then, you may need to convince the company that you are not making the mistake of imagining that running a pub is a congenial way of easing into retirement. The British Institute of Innkeeping advises that anyone thinking of running a pub should try working in one first and only then, if after a fair trial you are still enthusiastic, to begin looking at the options seriously.

Information on training courses and qualifications can be obtained from the **British Institute of Innkeeping**, Wessex House, 80 Park Street, Camberley, Surrey GU15 3PT. T:01276 684449. Details of tenancies and pubs for sale are contained in *The Licensee and Morning Advertiser* and in *The Publican* (available from newsagents).

Useful reading

Successful Pubs and Inns by Michael Sargent and Tony Lyle, Butterworth Heinemann, £16.99.

Handbook for the National Certificate for Licencees, obtainable from the British Institute of Innkeeping; £8.25 incl. p&p.

Pub Industry Handbook; price £75 incl. p&p; available from Quantum Publishing, T:020 8565 4200.

Bed & breakfast

Tourist areas, in particular, offer scope for taking in bed and breakfast visitors. However, unless you want to make a regular business of it, it is advisable to limit the number of guests to a maximum of five otherwise you will be subject to stringent fire regulation precautions requiring special doors and other expensive paraphernalia. To be on the safe side, contact the local Environmental Health Officer (see telephone directory or enquire at the town hall) who will advise you of anything necessary you should do. You should also register with your local Tourist Information Centre. See the section headed 'Letting rooms in your home' in Chapter 8, Your Home.

Agencies and other useful organisations

Jobhunting through agencies is very much a question of luck. People can be on their books for months and months and not be sent to a single interview. Someone else can walk through the door and within 48 hours be fixed up with an ideal job.

Applicants normally greatly exceed vacancies and the majority of jobs, especially for the over-60s, tend to be on the modest side: clerical, security work, gardening, domestic services and similar. However, more challenging opportunities are sometimes registered and one or two of the organisations listed below specialise in executive appointments. Retired accountants in particular are almost always in demand, as are individuals with fund-raising skills.

A positive attitude – with agencies as well as with prospective employers – unquestionably helps. People are often their own worst enemy when it comes to job-hunting and sadly this is especially true of older people, who may give the impression of half expecting to be turned down on the grounds of age. While you may be asked to state your date of birth (in which case it is usually better to be honest), there is no need to volunteer the information unless requested – least of all at the start of an interview.

Equally, there is no need to limit your applications to agencies that specialise in placing older candidates. If you are serious about finding work, you need to cast your net as widely as possible. So check the *Yellow Pages* and keep an eye on the local papers for other agencies in your area. Depending on what you are looking for, several of the following organisations may be able to help.

Jobcentres. It is easy to forget the obvious. Jobcentres have changed their image considerably over the last few years and now carry a wide range of vacancies for all levels of ability. In particular, many small firms use them for recruitment in preference to the more expensive private employment agencies. There are around 1,000 Jobcentres throughout Great Britain which, between them, handle about 2.5 million vacancies a year. They also act as a gateway to many of the training courses and advisory services. See local telephone directory for address.

Other organisations

Corps of Commissionaires, Market House, 85 Cowcross Street, London EC1M 6PF. T:020 7566 0500. Offers full or part-time work to ex-servicemen and women, police, prison officers, members of the emergency services and similar. Jobs cover a fairly broad range of security, reception and facilities support posts that require the wearing of the Corps' blazer or uniform, for example: commissionaires, security staff, ushers at sporting or official events. Age is unlikely to be a barrier provided candidates are sufficiently fit for the job. All applicants are invited to an interview and are required to provide well-documented references.

Executive Stand-By Ltd., 6 Commonhall Street, Chester CH1 2BJ. T:01244 323600. Specialises in placing executives of proven competence in management or similar posts in industry, commerce and voluntary organisations. These are mainly temporary or part-time but can lead to permanent positions. There are also occasional openings abroad. In almost all cases, there is an upper age limit of 65.

Extend, 22 Maltings Drive, Wheathampstead, Herts AL4 8QJ. T:01582 832760. Extend runs recreational exercise-to-music classes for the over-sixties and for people with disabilities of all ages. The organisation is constantly looking for potential group teachers. Training courses last approximately 12 days spread over several weeks and cost about £450. There are written and practical assessments on completion. At the present time, eight training teams operate in different parts of the UK and Ireland. Details can be obtained from the above address, on enclosure of sae.

HERA, 232 Great Guildford Business Square, 30 Great Guildford Street, London SE1 0HS. T:020 7928 6141. Applicants receive a weekly magazine listing of vacancies in the field of housing with jobs throughout the country, ranging from senior management to administration. HERA also offers careers counselling relevant to jobs in housing.

Manpower Plc., International House, 66 Chiltern Street, London W1U 4JT. T:020 7224 6688. Manpower is a major supplier of temporary, contract and permanent staff. Skills in particular demand include: hotel and restaurant staff; secretarial and clerical experience; driving and assembly/manufacturing. Additionally, at the present time, one of the fastest growing areas of demand is for telephone call centre staff.

Officers' Association, Employment Department, 48 Pall Mall, London SW1Y 5JY. T:020 7930 0125. The Association provides a job-finding service for managerial, professional and senior technical people, aged under 65, who are either leaving the armed services or who, having served as an officer, are currently unemployed. A wide range of vacancies is handled in all sectors. There is also an office in Edinburgh, T:0131 556 5266.

Resourcing Solutions – Parity, Orchard Fields, Maylands Avenue, Hemel Hempstead, Herts HP2 7DF. T:01442 240761. Specialises in all types of IT contract and permanent work with openings nationwide for among others, senior project managers, analysts, programmers and network/software engineers.

Part-Time Careers Ltd., 10 Golden Square, London W1R 3AF. T:020 7437 3103. Specialises in permanent part-time secretarial jobs as well as accountancy, book-keeping and reception work.

Quality Assurance Design Services Ltd., 69 Nantwich Road, Crewe, Cheshire CW2 6AW. T:01270 250 055. Caters for both permanent and interim (part and full-time) personnel, specialising in the engineering, quality and construction sectors. Assignments cover both the UK and overseas.

Wrinklies Direct, Treasure House, 19–21 Hatton Garden, London EC1A 8LG. T:0870 600 1921. Wrinklies Direct is a network of recruitment agencies around the country which specialise in finding work for older people. Vacancies handled vary across a very broad range and could be anything from night portering to a senior management job. To be put in touch with your nearest local agency, call the central number above.

Campaign Against Age Discrimination in Employment (CAADE), 395 Barlow Road, Altrincham, Cheshire WA14 5HW. T:0845 345 8654. This is a lobby organisation which, as its name implies, was set up to campaign against age discrimination in matters affecting employment. CAADE publishes a number of books and other literature, as well as a fortnightly online newsletter.

Third Age Challenge, 39 Hawkins Street, Rodbourne, Swindon SN2 2AQ. T:01793 533370. TAC is a not-for-profit company committed to tackling age discrimination and to helping older people find work. Among other practical help, it runs local job search and IT training courses and can provide addresses of specialist organisations for 50-plus jobseekers in many parts of the country.

Local job-finding agencies. A number of selective recruitment agencies, concentrating on the over-40s or 50s have recently been springing up in different parts of the country to assist unemployed people in their middle years back into work. Most concentrate on fairly local vacancies – with range of jobs very much a question of what is needed in the area. Enquire at your library or jobcentre for any useful names and addresses. Your local chamber of commerce may also have information.

Useful reading

Welcome to Jobcentre Plus, free Government booklet, available from Jobcentres, containing details of programmes and services for unemployed people. Also obtainable in large print, audio and braille versions.

12 Voluntary Work

There are probably as many different kinds of voluntary work that need to be done, as there are organisations that need your help. The range of tasks and the variety of groups are both enormous. Perhaps this is one reason why some people simply steer clear of the whole area, fearing that the commitment may get out of control and that they may find themselves involved to a greater extent than they wish. Though this may be true in a few cases there are probably many thousands more who, starting in a small way, find themselves caught up in the enthusiasm for their cause and immensely rewarded by the contribution they feel able to make and by the new friends this has brought them.

Very broadly, voluntary help falls into four main categories: clerical/ administrative, fund-raising, committee work, and direct work with the public.

Clerical. Any active group is likely to need basic administrative help from typing and stuffing envelopes to answering the telephone and organising committees. This may involve a day or so a week or simply occasional assistance at peak times.

Fund-raising. Every voluntary organisation needs more money and their ingenuity in raising it seems boundless. Jumble sales, coffee mornings and flag days are probably still the most common, but sponsored events of all kinds are hugely growing in popularity and negotiating contributions from local or national businesses may test anyone's diplomatic skill.

Committee work. This can cover anything from very occasional help to virtually full-time commitment as branch treasurer or secretary. People with business skills or financial or legal backgrounds are likely to be especially valuable.

Direct work. Driving, delivering 'meals on wheels', doing counselling work, visiting the housebound, working in a charity shop, helping with a playgroup, giving the mother of a sick child a chance to get out of the house for an hour or so ... the list is endless and the value of the work incalculable.

While certain qualifications and experience – financial, legal, nursing, social work – have particular value in some circumstances, there is also a multitude of interesting and useful jobs for those without special training or with relatively ordinary abilities like driving or computer skills.

Similarly, the time commitment can be varied to suit both helper and organisation. It is far better to give just one morning a month and be reliable than to promise more time than you can spare and end up always being late or having to cancel at the last minute. Equally, as with a paid job, before you start you should be absolutely clear about all the terms and conditions.

- What sort of work is involved?
- Who will be working with you?
- What is expected?
- When will you be needed?
- Are expenses paid? What for? How much? (See tax note.)

If you straighten all this out in the beginning there will be less chance of any misunderstandings and you will find that voluntary work is not only very rewarding in its own right but also allows you to make a real contribution to the community.

Tax note. Volunteer drivers who receive a motor mileage allowance and who make a small profit, in that the allowance exceeds their actual incurred expenses (i.e. petrol and maintenance), are taxed on any profit they make. For further information, see leaflet IR 122 *Volunteer Drivers*, obtainable from any tax office.

Choosing the right voluntary work

It is one thing to decide that you would like to do some kind of voluntary work; quite another to discover what is available in your area and what particular outlet would suit you. For this reason we have included a list of organisations, arranged in broad categories of interest, indicating the types of activities for which they are seeking volunteers. But no such list can be complete – there are literally thousands of voluntary groups, national and local, which need help in some way or other. For further information on needs and opportunities in this sector there are several other major sources to which you can turn:

REACH, 89 Albert Embankment, London SE1 7TP. T:020 7582 6543. REACH was set up over 20 years ago to place men and women with management or other professional skills in voluntary organisations, throughout the UK. It finds only part-time, voluntary roles, but with out-of-pocket expenses paid. REACH is itself a registered charity and makes no charge to either the volunteer or voluntary organisation. Many openings are waiting to be filled so there is a good chance of finding an opening that makes real use of your particular talents.

Trustee Register, 2nd Floor, 6 Sloane Street, London SW1X 9WD. T:01753 830861. The Register acts as an introductory service in finding trustees and committee members for established charities. Interested candidates are asked to complete a short form, giving information about themselves and any strong preferences they may have regarding type of charity to which their name may be forwarded. Commitment varies but averages about a day a month. Travel expenses may sometimes be paid.

Volunteer Bureaux. Most towns have a body of this kind which seeks to match up volunteers with local organisations seeking help. For local addresses, see the *Volunteer*

Bureaux Directory which is available at most libraries or can be obtained direct from **The National Association of Volunteer Bureaux**, 16 Waterloo Street, Birmingham B2 5UG, T:0121 633 4555. Price of the 2003 Directory is expected to be about £13 incl. p&p. The Association is happy to put enquirers in contact with their nearest local Bureau.

Volunteer Development Scotland, Stirling Enterprise Park, Stirling FK7 2RP. T:01786 479593. Can help you find out about volunteering opportunities anywhere in Scotland by putting you in touch with a local organisation.

Wales Council for Voluntary Action, Baltic House, Mount Stuart Square, Cardiff Bay CF10 5FH. T:029 2043 1700. This is the umbrella body for voluntary activity in Wales. If you are interested in volunteering, it would be glad to put you in contact with an organisation that would welcome your help.

Citizens' Advice Bureau. Your local CAB will also have information on local needs and groups to contact.

General

The scope of the work of the British Red Cross, WRVS and Citizens' Advice Bureau is so broad that they almost justify a category to themselves.

British Red Cross (BRCS), 9 Grosvenor Crescent, London SW1X 7EJ. T:020 7235 5027. The Red Cross is the world's largest humanitarian organisation. It needs volunteer help from men and women for first aid, manning medical loan depots, fire victim support and vital community services. Training is always provided. Contact the local branch (under 'British' or 'Red Cross' in the telephone book) or write to the Volunteering Unit at the national headquarters above.

WRVS (Women's Royal Voluntary Service), Milton Hill House, Milton Hill, Steventon, Abingdon, Oxon OX13 6AD. T:01235 442900. The WRVS works in partnership with many organisations including local authorities and hospitals to cover a wide range of needs in the community. It particularly welcomes offers of help from men and women with time during the working day. Activities are too numerous to list but include: meals on wheels, home support for older people, providing transport in rural areas, helping in hospital shops and assisting with catering and welfare services in emergencies. No special qualifications are required, as training is given.

Citizens' Advice Bureau (See telephone book for your local branch.) First founded in 1939, the service has continued giving invaluable help and advice for over 60 years. Throughout the country, it deals with over 6 million enquiries a year. Apart from being an excellent source of information on other voluntary organisations needing help, the CAB itself has over 22,000 volunteer helpers working in its 700 or so branches throughout the country.

The work involves interviewing and advising clients on a wide range of questions from welfare benefits and legal rights to local events and community schemes. No formal qualifications are required and training is given. As well as general advisers, the CAB is also looking for volunteers to assist with IT, social policy work or with general administrative support. Language skills are also urgently needed to help local people for whom English is a second language. For further information contact your nearest CAB.

Another well known organisation which functions across a more general spectrum is: **Community Service Volunteers (CSV)**, 237 Pentonville Road, London N1 9NJ. T:020 7643 1385. CSV operates a UK-wide programme called the Retired and Senior Volunteer Programme (RSVP) for people aged 50 and over who want to be involved in their community. Each local group plans its own activities which include befriending frail older people, helping children with reading and numeracy in schools or working with health centres on primary care projects. For further details, contact Denise Murphy, Director of RSVP.

There is also **Toc H**, 1 Forest Close, Wendover, Aylesbury, Bucks HP22 6BT. T:01296 623911. Toc H has branches in all parts of the country involved in a wide range of good neighbour schemes within their local community. Volunteers are needed for such activities as hospital visiting, giving a day out to children in inner cities and providing a helping hand to people with disabilities. There is no special commitment – just whatever time you can spare. For further information, contact Toc H at the above address.

Animals

Cinnamon Trust, Foundry House, Foundry Square, Hayle, Cornwall TR27 4HH. T:01736 757900. The Cinnamon Trust is a registered charity which seeks to relieve the problems of elderly pet owners who, owing to illness or some other emergency, are temporarily unable to care for their pets. It also offers a long-term haven to animals whose owners have died.

Animal lovers throughout the country assist in a voluntary capacity, either by fostering a pet in their own home or helping out on a daily basis, for example walking a dog, feeding it, cleaning out a bird cage or similar. Likewise, long-term homes are required for pets who have lost their owners. For further details, write to Mrs. Averil Jarvis at the above address (enclosing sae).

Pet Fostering Service Scotland, PO Box 6, Callander FK17 8ZU. T:01383 730005. The service provides short-term foster care for the pets of elderly people who, owing to some emergency such as going into hospital, are temporarily unable to manage. Volunteers may either look after a pet in their own home until the owner is able to take it back or provide some other caring service, such as walking a dog. Food, cat litter and any vet's fees that may be incurred are paid for by the owner. If you live in Scotland, have a love of pets and would like to help out in a crisis, telephone the above number.

Pets As Therapy, 17 Ambrook Road, Reading, Berks RG2 8SL. T:01189 212 467. Pets as Therapy is a national charity which originated the PAT visiting scheme to give those in hospitals and residential care homes the important contact with animals that many may miss. It is essential that the dogs/cats are well behaved and fully vaccinated. At present, there are over 4,000 volunteers throughout the country making regular visits. If you would like to join them, contact the above address. Annual membership is from £11.

Royal Society for the Prevention of Cruelty to Animals, Wilberforce Way, Southwater, Horsham, West Sussex RH13 7WN. T:0870 010 1181. The RSPCA works to promote kindness and to prevent cruelty to animals. Operating through its team of 328 inspectors, it is concerned with the welfare of all animals and with education of the general public – especially children – by campaigning in the media and through its wide range of promotional material. It also works for the cause of animal welfare abroad. Volunteers are needed to help with fund-raising at local level. Contact headquarters for the address of your nearest branch.

Wildfowl & Wetlands Trust (WWT), Slimbridge, Gloucestershire GL2 7BT. T:01453 890333. WWT works to conserve threatened wetland birds and their habitats. As well as Slimbridge, there are visitor centres in: Lancashire, Sussex, Tyne & Wear, Cambridge/Norfolk Border, London, Dumfriesshire, South Wales and Northern Ireland. All have a network of volunteers who give valuable help, variously: attending the information desk, dealing with visitor enquiries, conducting guided tours and assisting staff with administrative work. There is no minimum commitment but most volunteers come in for a few hours or one day a week. For further information, contact Anna Weekes at the above address.

Bereavement

Cruse Bereavement Care, Cruse House, 126 Sheen Road, Richmond, Surrey TW9 1UR. T:020 8939 9530. Cruse, which has 178 branches throughout the UK, is the national organisation for people who have been bereaved. It provides support, counselling and practical help and also runs both friendship groups and drop-in centres. Volunteers are needed in the branches to help with all these services. Training for counselling is given. For further information, contact your local branch (see telephone directory) or write to the above address.

Children and young people

Action for Sick Children, National Children's Bureau, 8 Wakley Street, London EC1V 7QE. T:020 7843 6444. The Charity supports sick children and their families and advocates that health services be planned to cater for their special needs. Local branches give practical help to parents and professionals in the hospitals.

Work is organised through local branches which can be contacted through the London headquarters. Although different branches may operate slightly different schemes, most will welcome voluntary help, for example:

- Help with transport. Either driving, where a mileage charge is payable, or accompanying mothers with young children.

- Help with volunteer play schemes, on wards or in out-patients' departments.
- Help with fund-raising for more parents' and children's facilities in hospital.
- Administrative assistance at the London HQ.

Barnardo's, Tanners Lane, Barkingside, Ilford, Essex IG6 1QG. T:020 8550 8822. Barnardo's provides services for children who face disability or disadvantage. Projects throughout the country include work with families, day care centres, community projects, playgroups, play buses and holiday schemes. Two major areas require help:

- Fund-raising. Thousands of people work as voluntary fund-raisers for Barnardo's. Activities may include helping in a charity shop or with local flag-days and events. Write to the National Volunteer Development Manager at the above address who will pass on your application to your regional branch.
- Child Care Programme. This could involve helping a child with its reading or befriending a young person with a disability, to give the mother a much-needed break. Write to the Information Officer at the above address.

Save the Children UK, 17 Grove Lane, London SE5 8RD. T:020 7703 5400. Save the Children UK is an international charity working to create a better future for children. Volunteers are very much welcomed to assist with administrative tasks at Head Office and in particular for fund-raising via one of the 580 local branches or groups. For further information, contact your local Area Manager (see telephone directory) or call the Volunteer Actionline on T:0845 606 4027.

Scout Association, Gilwell Park, Bury Road, Chingford, London E4 7QW. T:0845 300 1818. The Scout Association provides an enjoyable programme of activities for young people aged 6 to 20. Volunteers are needed in many roles, for example: as leaders running weekly meetings or as commissioners, overseeing several different groups. Other openings include becoming an Administrator or Fellowship member who, among other aspects of the Association's work, help with managing the property, organise fund-raising, contribute to training (e.g. vehicle maintenance, map reading, first aid) and edit newsletters.

Sea Cadet Corps, 202 Lambeth Road, London SE1 7JF. T:020 7928 8978. The Sea Cadet Corps is a youth organisation which offers boys and girls aged 10–18 challenging new experiences and adventure. Emphasis is placed on waterborne activities, with encouragement given to those who wish to pursue a career at sea. Units exist throughout the UK and welcome volunteer help either as administrators or specialist instructors. Details may be obtained by contacting the national headquarters above.

The Children's Society, Edward Rudolf House, Margery Street, London WC1X 0JL. T:020 7841 4400. The Children's Society runs over 90 projects for highly vulnerable children and young people in England including providing refuges for runaways and help for those leaving care, excluded from school or in trouble with the law. Every local branch would be grateful for more fund-raisers. There are also more than 150 charity shops, run entirely by volunteers. Contact may be made either through the London headquarters or the local office, which may be listed in the telephone book.

Volunteer Reading Help, Charity House, 14–15 Perseverance Works, 38 Kingsland Road, London E2 8DD. T: 020 7729 4087. VRH recruits and trains volunteers to work with children who find reading difficult. They then work in a primary school with the same three children every week, helping them to improve their literacy skills and increase their confidence. No formal qualifications are needed but you would be asked to give three hours a week during term time for at least a year. For further information, contact the National Office above.

Community focused activities

If you have a good idea for a new voluntary project or would like to help in developing one, the following organisations would be interested in hearing from you.

New Horizons Trust, Bronzeoak House, Stafford Road, Caterham, Surrey CR3 6JG. T:01883 332634. New Horizons Trust is a registered charity offering grants of up to £5,000 to groups of retired people who wish to start a new voluntary project drawing on their own knowledge and experience for the benefit of their local community. To qualify, there must be at least 10 people in the group, half of whom must be over the age of 60. Schemes may improve local amenities or fill identified gaps in social services. Examples of projects around the country which have been helped by the Trust include: an out-of-hours school club, church bells, a workshop for refurbishing old furniture for those in need, another workshop where retired craftsmen can pass on their skills to young people, 'Domesday' books recording villages and towns and the creation of several memorial gardens.

Another idea which might appeal is to become an 'Active Citizen' under the **Help the Aged Millennium Awards** scheme and run a project in your local community. Awards are available for carrying out the projects which, to qualify, would need to contribute in some way to the quality of life in your local area. For example, this could be a project for improving the environment or one aimed at improving the inclusiveness of the community.

The scheme is for people aged over 55 and support and training are available throughout to assist participants in completing their project. For further information, call the Millennium Awards Hotline on T:0870 770 3280.

Conservation

Architectural Heritage Society of Scotland, The Glasite Meeting House, 33 Barony Street, Edinburgh EH3 6NX. T:0131 557 0019. The Society promotes the study and protection of Scottish architecture. As well as enjoying events such as talks and visits, members can join case panels for which volunteers are always needed. The work involves visiting and assessing listed building and conservation and planning applications. Annual membership, including the Society's publications, is £20; £30 for families.

BTCV, 36 St. Mary's Street, Wallingford, Oxfordshire OX10 0EU. T:01491 821600. BTCV plays a leading role in encouraging volunteers from both town and country to improve the environment. Over 500 working holidays are organised nationally and over 2,500 local groups run community projects at weekends and during the week. Typical projects include planting trees, cleaning ponds, restoring footpaths, protecting valuable habitats for wildlife, creating urban nature areas and assisting with woodland management. Not all of them involve heavy work but a reasonable degree of fitness is required. Volunteers are also needed to help the local offices with administration, fund-raising and publicity.

CPRE (Council for the Protection of Rural England), 128 Southwark Street, London SE1 0SW. T:020 7981 2800. CPRE works to protect and enhance the countryside. Voluntary helpers act as local watchdogs within CPRE's county branches, assessing and reporting unsightly development projects and threats to the environment and sometimes representing CPRE at enquiries. There is also a need for help with fund-raising which is carried out by local groups.

Friends of the Earth, 26–28 Underwood Street, London N1 7JQ. T:020 7490 1555. Friends of the Earth is one of the leading environmental pressure organisations in the UK, aiming to conserve and protect the resources of the earth. Over 200 groups run local campaigns and fund-raising projects. These can be contacted through the London office which can also use help with the administration and with answering enquiries. Travel and lunch expenses are reimbursed.

Greenpeace, Canonbury Villas, London N1 2PN. T:020 7865 8100. An international environmental pressure group which campaigns to protect the natural environment. Volunteers are needed both to help in the London office and also for campaigning by local groups across the country.

Ramblers' Association, 2nd Floor, Camelford House, 87–90 Albert Embankment, London SE1 7TW. T:020 7339 8500. The Ramblers' aims are to encourage walking, to keep footpaths open and to protect the beauty of the countryside. Nearly all the work is carried out by volunteers, who keep an eye on footpaths, check maps of access areas, campaign on countryside matters, compile guidebooks, organise walks, help with administration and many other tasks. The time involved is whatever you can manage.

The Royal Society for the Protection of Birds, The Lodge, Sandy, Bedfordshire SG19 2DL. T:01767 680551. The RSPB is Europe's largest wildlife conservation charity with over 1,000,000 members and 158 nature reserves around the UK. Volunteers have a valuable contribution to make and are regularly needed to undertake biological surveys, assist with management work on nature reserves, help with visitors and young people or carry out administrative tasks in regional offices around the country. Volunteer opportunities range from a few days to a few weeks. No particular expertise is required nor, if you would like to help, is it necessary to become a member. For those who would like to join, annual membership (2002) costs £27 single, £36 joint.

The elderly

Abbeyfield Society, 53 Victoria Street, St. Albans, Herts AL1 3UW. T:01727 857536. Local volunteers acquire or build houses to provide independent accommodation for older people who are on their own. The aim is to achieve a friendly atmosphere and to support the independence of each resident. There are also registered residential care houses for older people who need a high degree of support. Voluntary help needed may vary from befriending residents, gardening, committee work or organising fund-raising events to giving specialist financial, management and legal advice. There are about 550 local Abbeyfield Societies nationwide involving over 10,000 volunteers.

Age Concern England, Astral House, 1268 London Road, London SW16 4ER, T:020 8765 7200; **Age Concern Scotland**, 113 Rose Street, Edinburgh EH2 3DT, T:0131 220 3345; **Age Concern Cymru**, 4th Floor, 1 Cathedral Road, Cardiff CF11 9SD, T:029 2037 1566; **Age Concern Northern Ireland**, 3 Lower Crescent, Belfast BT7 1NR. T:028 9024 5729. The aim of Age Concern is to promote the welfare of older people. It does this by campaigning on their behalf and by organising services to meet their needs. Local groups, using volunteer helpers, operate all over the country and services include day care, lunch clubs, home visiting, over-60's clubs and, in some areas, specialist services for physically and mentally frail elderly people. Fund-raising activities in all their variety are also organised locally. For further details, contact the national organisations above.

Carers UK, 20–25 Glasshouse Yard, London EC1A 4JT. T:020 7490 8818. Carers UK is a mine of information for family, partners or friends who need help because they look after an ill, frail or disabled person at home. With over 120 local self-help groups, it provides information and advice through a CarersLine and campaigns for a better deal for carers. Administrative help is needed at head office and at carers' groups, who meet to discuss mutual problems. Contact the above address for further details.

Contact the Elderly, 15 Henrietta Street, Covent Garden, London WC2E 8QG. Freephone: 0800 716543. Contact the Elderly offers a way of making new friends while at the same time providing much needed companionship for lonely elderly people living nearby. Contact volunteers keep a personal link with isolated elderly people by taking them on one Sunday afternoon each month to have tea in the home of a volunteer host. Help is needed with driving (one Sunday a month) and/or hosting a tea-party for about 10 elderly visitors once or twice a year. No expenses are paid.

There are Contact groups nationwide. The name and address of the nearest local organiser can be got from the above address.

Help the Aged, 207–221 Pentonville Road, London N1 9UZ. T:020 7278 1114. Help the Aged aims to improve the quality of life for elderly people here and overseas. In the UK, it provides funds for day centres, community transport, home safety devices, emergency alarm systems and sheltered housing. It also produces a range of advice leaflets and operates a freephone advice line on T:0808 800 6565. Overseas, it advises on social policy for older people and supports projects in combating destitution and ill-health. Help the Aged is a major fund-raising charity. Volunteer help is needed to staff charity shops and to assist local fundraising committees. Contact the Volunteer Co-ordinator at the above address for further details.

The Princess Royal Trust for Carers, 142 Minories, London EC3N 1LB. T:020 7480 7788. The PRTC is establishing Carers Centres in all parts of the UK to give those caring for a dependent relative or friend information, advice and practical support in times of need. Volunteers are especially wanted to assist with respite sitting, in order to give carers a short break, or to run aromatherapy and relaxation sessions. Help is also needed to provide telephone/administrative help in the centres. There are also openings for people with accountancy, fundraising and other business skills to serve on their local management committee. For further information, contact the above address.

The family

Family Service Units, 207 Old Marylebone Road, London NW1 5QP. T:020 7402 5175. Twenty local Units work to prevent the breakdown of family and community life by running services for disadvantaged communities, deprived families and children. They carry out welfare counselling, community work and social work with families. The Units, which are professionally staffed, are managed by voluntary committees and help is needed on these as well as with administration and fund-raising. From time to time local Units need to recruit honorary treasurers.

Marriage Care, Clitherow House, 1 Blythe Mews, Blythe Road, London W14 0NW. T:020 7371 1341. MC runs pre-marriage courses and also provides a professional counselling service for anyone with relationship problems. Help is required in running and administering its 64 centres. New potential counsellors are also sought. For local addresses, contact the headquarters above.

Relate, Herbert Gray College, Little Church Street, Rugby, Warwickshire CV21 3AP. T:01788 573241. Relate works to support marriage and family life. There are about 103 local Relate centres which offer counselling to anyone with relationship problems; some also undertake education work in schools. Volunteers who would like to become counsellors receive training. There are also openings to serve on committees and help in the office. The work is most likely to appeal to people who have been previously involved with social or community activity of some kind.

SSAFA Forces Help, 19 Queen Elizabeth Street, London SE1 2LP. T:020 7403 8783. SSAFA Forces Help provides a welfare and advisory service for the families of service and ex-servicemen and women. There are 7,500 volunteers in branches throughout the UK and overseas, as well as professionals wherever service families are stationed. Case workers deal with every kind of problem – domestic, financial, legal and compassionate. Training is given and although there is no minimum time commitment it is obviously critical to see a case through to the end. Help is particularly needed in inner cities. There is also a requirement for assistance in the counties as chairman, treasurer, administrative helper and publicity and fundraising officer. A service background is not necessary.

Health

BackCare, 16 Elmtree Road, Teddington, Middlesex TW11 8ST. T:020 8977 5474. BackCare funds research into the causes and treatment of back pain. It teaches children and adults how to use their bodies sensibly and runs a network of local self-help branches. BackCare needs volunteers to start local branches and to provide practical help for back pain sufferers. Particular activities include: organising exercise and hydrotherapy classes, arranging talks and demonstrations and running social and fund-raising events. For further information, contact the Branches Officer at the above address.

British Heart Foundation (BHF), 14 Fitzhardinge Street, London W1H 6DH. T:020 7935 0185. The British Heart Foundation funds research into the causes, prevention, diagnosis and treatment of heart disease. Its educational role includes: promoting training in simple life-saving skills, informing the medical and scientific community about the results of its research and making the information known to the general public. BHF also provides life-saving cardiac care equipment to hospitals and other health providers and helps support rehabilitation courses and heart support groups.

With a national network of over 400 branches BHF helps fund this vital work through a wide variety of fund-raising schemes. For details of your local branch please contact head office or look in *Yellow Pages*.

British Ski Club for the Disabled, Springmount, Berwick S. John, Shaftesbury, Dorset SP7 0HQ. T:01747 828 515. The aim of the Club is to encourage people with a disability to learn or continue to enjoy the fun of skiing and the self-confidence gained from participating in an exhilarating sport. Volunteers, who must be competent skiers, are needed to act as guides both on artificial slopes around the country and skiing holidays abroad. The Club runs its own guide courses. Small subsidies are available for guides on authorised holiday parties.

Calibre, Cassette Library, Aylesbury, Bucks HP22 5XQ. T:01296 432339. Calibre is a national lending library of recorded books on ordinary standard cassette tapes for use by 'anyone unable to read'. Volunteers are needed to help run the library, which is maintained entirely from donations. Publicity and fund-raising help are also required. Contact the Volunteer Co-ordinator, Sue Hawkes.

Cancer Research UK, 10 Cambridge Terrace, London NW1 4JL. T:020 7009 8675. The aim of Cancer Research UK is to bring hope to all those touched by cancer through pioneering research into the prevention, treatment and cure of the disease. It is almost entirely dependent on the generosity of the general public and your support, whether helping to raise funds or sparing a few hours of your time, will contribute towards the work of their scientists in their efforts to conquer cancer. Thousands of volunteers organise local fundraising events, help in Cancer Research UK's shops (sorting, serving, pricing, ironing) or assist with general work in their office. For more information, contact the above address.

Leonard Cheshire, 30 Millbank, London SW1P 4QD. T:020 7802 8200. Leonard Cheshire, one of the leading disability care charities, works with people affected by a wide range of disabilities, helping them to live their lives as they choose. Its many services throughout the UK are supported by local people, who make an enormous contribution. There are endless practical ways in which you can lend a hand. This might include driving, gardening, painting and decorating, shopping and writing letters. Or you might help with local fund-raising events. Contact the London office above for the address of your nearest Cheshire service.

Mental Health Foundation, 7th Floor, 83 Victoria Street, London SW1H 0HW. T:020 7802 0300. The Mental Health Foundation plays a vital role in pioneering new approaches to the prevention, treatment and care of mental illness and in helping people with learning disabilities. Its work includes: allocating grants for research and community projects, contributing to public debate, educating healthcare professionals and striving to reduce the stigma attached to mental illness. Volunteers are needed for organising fund-raising in their local area. For further information, please write to the Director at the above address.

Mind (The Mental Health Charity), Granta House, 15–19 Broadway, London E15 4BQ. T:020 8519 2122. Mind works for a better life for people with experience of mental distress. It has offices in England and Wales and more than 200 local associations. While these vary in size and the scope of their work, all raise their own funds and provide information and practical support. Their activities include running social clubs, day centres, befriending schemes, an advocacy service and self-help groups. If you would like to help, contact your local association (see telephone directory); or ring Mind's national Infoline on: T:0845 766 0163.

National Association of Hospital and Community Friends, 2nd Floor, Fairfax House, Causton Road, Colchester, Essex CO1 1RJ. T:01206 761227. The Association is the representative body for Leagues of Friends throughout the UK. Each League is autonomous and all work to improve the comfort and dignity of patients in both hospitals and the community.

Volunteers, of whatever age, are always welcomed. Opportunities for voluntary work vary but all Leagues are concerned with both service to patients and fund-raising. The National Association can put new volunteers in touch with their local League.

Riding for the Disabled Association, Avenue R, National Agricultural Centre, Kenilworth, Warwickshire CV8 2LY. T:024 7669 6510. The Association aims to help provide opportunities for riding for disabled children and adults. You do not have to be horsey to help in one of the 650 local groups. Legal and financial knowledge is particularly valuable in connection with the opening of new groups and with keeping the accounts. For those with experience of horses (which may be supplemented by training courses) the main jobs are leading or walking beside the ponies while they are being ridden and accompanying parties on riding holidays. Write to the head office above for the address of your nearest group.

Royal National Institute for the Blind (RNIB), 105 Judd Street, London WC1H 9NE. T:08457 669999. RNIB aims to help blind and partially sighted people lead full and independent lives. Among many other initiatives, it runs schools for blind children, provides careers advice, offers training and assists with finding suitable employment. It also manages two rehabilitation centres and special homes; has a welfare advisory service; sells specially designed or adapted goods to make life easier and safer for blind or partially sighted people; publishes books and magazines in Braille and Moon and runs the Talking Book Library.

Help is mostly required with fund-raising: by lending a hand on flag days; or by placing and emptying RNIB collecting tins. Additionally, volunteers are needed all over the country to service talking book players on a regular basis, two or three times a month. London office will put you in touch with your nearest local group.

Scope, Olympus House, Britannia Road, Patchway, Bristol BS34 5TA. T:0117 906 6309. Scope works to create housing, leisure, education and employment opportunities for people with cerebral palsy and related disabilities. There are also over 250 local groups and a helpline (T:0808 800 3333) which offers free information, confidential counselling and advice.

Volunteers are particularly needed for helping in Scope shops, supporting local groups and running fund-raising events. Help is also needed with street collections and office work.

St. John Ambulance, 27 St. John's Lane, London EC1M 4BU. T:08700 104950. Best known for their first aid role at public events, St. John Ambulance volunteers also carry out care within the community. Volunteers receive a special induction training, tailored to their needs according to their chosen activity, which could variously be: care, transport, communications, work in charity shops, library service or first aid.

Scope for volunteers is hugely varied and includes such activities as vehicle maintenance, fund-raising, public relations and community care as well, of course, as first aid. For further information contact your county office or the national headquarters at the above address.

Heritage and the arts

There is scope for becoming involved in the arts in a volunteer capacity through community arts projects, arts centres, local arts councils and other arts activities associated with special groups such as, for example, the youth services or people with disabilities. All kinds of abilities are needed from painting and other creative skills to accounting and clerical know-how. For addresses and other information about local arts organisations, contact your local authority or library.

Council for British Archaeology, Bowes Morrell House, 111 Walmgate, York YO1 9WA. T:01904 671417. Various archaeological excavations take place throughout the UK, mainly from March to September. The work will probably involve lifting, stooping and wheeling barrows so is not suitable for people with bad backs. No training is necessary. A two-week stay is the average. Accommodation will vary according to the site but may be pretty basic. Information on the various digs is given in *British Archaeology* (£27 annual membership subscription, from the above address). The Council will also supply the address of the nearest local Archaeological Society (enclose sae).

National Trust, 33 Sheep Street, Cirencester, Glos GL7 1RQ. T:0870 609 5383. The National Trust involves volunteers in many aspects of the work of conservation in the great houses open to the public and on 248,000 hectares of coast and countryside properties. Inevitably, the needs will vary according to the location and time of the year. However last year over 40,000 volunteers worked alongside Trust staff in the regions. If you are interested, contact the Volunteers Office at the address above.

There is also a separate programme of working holidays in outdoor conservation, including a series of projects especially for the over-50s. To obtain a brochure, telephone T:0870 429 2428.

Society for the Protection of Ancient Buildings (SPAB), 37 Spital Square, London E1 6DY. T:020 7377 1644. SPAB promotes the sensitive repair of old buildings. Volunteers are needed in London and around the country to help with organising events, administration and with cataloguing the archive. SPAB would also very much like to hear from qualified architects, building surveyors and structural engineers to assist with specific projects. For further information, contact the head office above.

The needy

Alexandra Rose Day, 2a Ferry Road, London SW13 9RX. T:020 8748 4824. Founded in 1912, Alexandra Rose Day is an umbrella organisation that helps over 1,000 local charities dedicated to supporting the needy raise funds for themselves through participation in the flag day. ARD is actively seeking volunteer county co-ordinators to work with charities in their area in preparing for flag days. This is a year-round job, with summer invariably the busiest time. Qualified accountants are also required to check and certify official returns. For further details, contact the National Director at the above address.

Elizabeth Finn Trust, 1 Derry Street, London W8 5HY. T:020 7396 6700. The Elizabeth Finn Trust assists people from professional or similar backgrounds either financially or with nursing and care in a number of homes. There is a network of county committees as well as committees based on each home. Work involves general fund-raising and also visiting residents and helping to organise outings and entertainments for them.

International Voluntary Service (IVS), Castlehill House, 21 Otley Road, Headingley, Leeds LS6 3AA. T:0113 230 4600. IVS runs international projects in Britain, Europe, the former Soviet Union, USA, Australia, North Africa and Japan. Assignments normally last from two to four weeks and involve work such as helping in a psychiatric hospital, assisting with holidays for handicapped children, running children's playschemes and working with minority groups. There are also environmental and conservation work projects. No experience is needed – but motivation is. The summer project list which comes out in April is obtainable from the above address (price £4.66 incl. postage).

OXFAM, Oxfam House, 274 Banbury Road, Oxford OX2 7DZ. T:0845 300 0311. Oxfam works with others to overcome poverty and suffering. Over 22,000 volunteers are involved in all parts of Great Britain. One of the main areas of need is help with the running of Oxfam shops: activities range from the day-to-day management to sorting and pricing, serving customers and arranging shop windows. Help is also needed to organise fund-raising events, give administrative help and support the educational and campaigning aspects of Oxfam's work. Reasonable travel and meal expenses can be reimbursed. For further information, contact your local Oxfam shop or office (see telephone directory); or write to the above address.

Royal British Legion, Poppy Appeal, Aylesford, Kent ME20 7NX. T:01622 717172. The Royal British Legion was founded to help needy ex-service men and women and also their dependants. Today, with over 4,000 branches in the UK, it runs convalescence and care homes; maintains sheltered workshops for the disabled; gives pension counselling; provides training for jobseekers; offers advice and friendship, and through its welfare service, gives financial help. It also organises pilgrimages to war graves overseas and has a small business advice service.

The Royal British Legion's most important fund-raising activity for all this work is the Poppy Appeal, which takes place during the fortnight leading up to Remembrance Day on the second Sunday in November. Its most pressing need is to recruit more voluntary organisers and helpers to assist with the Appeal by sparing a few hours for street or house-to-house collections. If you would like to help with this worthy job, please write to – or telephone – the Head of the Poppy Appeal at the above address. If you would like to help in other ways, ring T:0845 7725 725.

The Samaritans, The Upper Mill, Kingston Road, Ewell, Surrey KT17 2AF. T:020 8394 8300. The Samaritans aims to offer 24-hour emotional support to the suicidal and the despairing. Much of the work is done on the telephone and, while no special qualifications are required, an unshockable disposition and complete reliability are essential qualities in a volunteer. Training is given – often at weekends – and those who are selected will be expected to attend further courses from time to time. The minimum time commitment is about 4 hours a week plus one night duty a month. Apart from this work, there is need for fund-raising help from anyone with a little time and a lot of enthusiasm.

Offenders and the victims of crime

Nacro, 169 Clapham Road, London SW9 0PU. T:020 7582 6500. Nacro strives to make society safer by finding practical solutions to reducing crime. It provides housing, training and resettlement services for prisoners and ex-offenders; supports disadvantaged families and communities and steers young people away from crime. Opportunities for voluntary work, which are organised on a local basis, are limited to a small number of projects such as running activities for young people. For further information, contact the Resettlement Plus Helpline on T:020 7540 6464.

Society of Voluntary Associates (SOVA), 1st Floor, Chichester House, 37 Brixton Road, London SW9 6DZ. T:020 7793 0404. SOVA trains volunteers from local communities to work, alongside the Probation Service and other agencies, with offenders, their families and young people in need of support. The work may be with children, in the adult literacy scheme, prison visiting or helping ex-offenders.

New Bridge, 27a Medway Street, London SW1P 2BD. T:020 7976 0779. New Bridge offers friendship and support to people in prison, and on their release, with the aim of giving them the encouragement and practical skills to lead responsible and law-abiding lives in the future. It achieves this by running vocational and parenting courses, giving assistance with finding employment and managing a befrienders' scheme involving hundreds of volunteers who visit offenders in prison and keep in touch through letter-writing. Volunteers devote as much or as little time as they can spare. However, all are required to do an initial weekend training and to attend a local monthly group meeting. If you could be interested in participating in this valuable work, contact the Director at the above address.

Work after work

British Chambers of Commerce, Manning House, 22 Carlisle Place, London SW1P 1JA. T:020 7565 2000. Chambers of commerce, the organisations representing the local business community, are highly active in a wide range of projects to promote local economic development and renewal in the wider community. Many chambers, for example, take the lead in initiatives for inner city regeneration, crime prevention, industry/education links, training schemes and similar and very much welcome input from retired business people to contribute to their special working parties. There are also opportunities for involvement in the representational role of chambers on behalf of business, as a committee or panel member looking into such areas as transport, the environment and industrial affairs. For further information, contact your local chamber direct (see telephone directory) or get in touch with the BCC at the above address.

National Federation of Enterprise Agencies, c/o NatWest Bank, Trinity Gardens, 9/11 Bromham Road, Bedford MK40 2UQ. T:01234 354055. For executives and managers who would like to continue to work in business after retirement, an enterprise agency may be the answer. Set up as a partnership between government, employers, trade unions and the voluntary sector it aims to encourage the greater local involvement of businesses in the communities in which they operate. In practice the work will involve advising and helping new small firms at the start-up stage and as they further develop. Time involved is likely to be of the order of one day a week. Expenses are paid. Contact can be made through your nearest local Enterprise Agency (listed in the telephone book), via the head office above or, for Enterprise Trusts (as they are known in Scotland), through **SBC**, 30 Hanover Street, Edinburgh EH2 2DR, T:0131 220 3001.

Politics

You may not immediately think of political parties in the context of voluntary work but all of them use vast numbers of volunteer helpers. Between elections the help is mostly required with fund-raising, committee work and staffing the constituency offices. At election time activity is obviously intense: delivering literature, addressing and stuffing envelopes, recording canvas returns, driving elderly and disabled people to the polls, and, for the politically informed, canvassing. Contact your constituency office which will be listed in the telephone book or, if you have difficulty in finding it, contact the national party headquarters. The addresses of the major parties are:

Conservative Central Office, 32 Smith Square, Westminster, London SW1P 3HH. T:020 7222 9000.

Labour Party Headquarters, 16–18 Old Queen Street, London SW1H 9HP. T:020 7802 1000.

Liberal Democrats, 4 Cowley Street, London SW1P 3NB. T:020 7222 7999.

Plaid Cymru, 18 Park Grove, Cardiff CF10 3BN. T:029 2064 6000.

Scottish National Party, 107 McDonald Road, Edinburgh EH7 4NW. T:0131 525 8900.

Green Party, 1a Waterlow Road, London N19 5NJ. T:020 7272 4474.

Social Democratic and Labour Party (SDLP), 121 Ormeau Road, Belfast BT7 1SH. T:028 9024 7700.

Ulster Unionist Party, 49 Hollywood Road, Belfast BT4 2LN. T:028 90 765 500.

Long-term volunteering

If you are thinking of a long-term, probably residential, commitment there are a number of organisations both in the UK and abroad in need of voluntary help for a wide variety of projects. Some require specialist skills, such as engineering or medicine; others essentially need people with practical qualities, common-sense and enthusiasm.

As an indication of the kinds of opportunities that exist, we have listed below some of the main bodies in the sector.

Overseas

There are four major groups all of which require a two-year minimum period of service. General conditions are similar for all of them, i.e. travel is paid plus a living allowance/salary which is based on local levels rather than on expatriate rates; couples without dependent children are welcome as long as both have the necessary skills; national insurance contributions are provided and a resettlement grant is paid on completion of the tour.

VSO (Voluntary Service Overseas), 317 Putney Bridge Road, Putney, London SW15 2PN. T:020 8780 7500. VSO places nearly a thousand volunteers a year to work in developing countries in Africa, Asia, the Pacific and Eastern Europe in order to help local people acquire more skills. It is particularly keen to recruit retired men and women with a professional or practical background in education, health, agriculture, technical trades and engineering, business and social development. For further information, contact the Enquiries Unit at the above address.

Skillshare International, People and Organisation Development Unit, 126 New Walk, Leicester LE1 7JA. T:0116 254 1862. Skillshare International co-ordinates volunteers to work on a variety of projects in partnership with the people and communities of Southern Africa, Tanzania, Uganda and India. You must be qualified with at least two years' relevant experience. The range of jobs to be done is very diverse and technical, educational, medical, agricultural, business, community based and environmental work skills are all required. All applicants are required to pass a medical examination.

International Co-operation for Development, Unit 3, Canonbury Yard, 190a New North Road, London N1 7BJ. T:020 7354 0883. ICD (a programme of CIIR) provides technical assistance for community projects which tackle the causes of poverty. It operates in the Caribbean, Latin America, Africa and the Yemen. The programme is open to professionally qualified and technical people with several years' experience. ICD has frequent vacancies in the field of health, agriculture and small business training. Most jobs involve training local people in new skills and some knowledge of Spanish or Arabic would be useful. A preliminary orientation course is arranged with training sessions and thorough briefings.

International Service, Suite 3a, Hunter House, 57 Goodramgate, York YO1 7FX. T:01904 647799. International Service is a voluntary body which sends skilled personnel to work in the Third World (West Africa, Latin America, Palestine) on projects aiming to achieve a fundamental change in the distribution of wealth and power. It is essential to have overseas experience and also either knowledge of the local language or the ability and willingness to learn. Recent vacancies have been for people with a wide range of skills from nurses and agronomists to water engineers and community development workers. There is a one-month orientation course plus language training as necessary.

An organisation which operates on a rather different, less long-term basis is **BESO (British Executive Service Overseas)**, 164 Vauxhall Bridge Road, London SW1V 2RB. T:020 7630 0644. BESO is an independent charity whose objectives are to aid development, trade and employment in developing and emerging economies abroad, with help mainly focused on small and medium sized enterprises.

Mature volunteers with a skill or professional qualification are particularly sought to help on projects in over 140 countries. Assignments vary in length from two weeks to six months. Volunteers receive neither salary nor fee but travel, insurance and incidentals are met by BESO. Accommodation, subsistence and local transport – and sometimes airfare – are paid for by the requesting organisation.

In UK

Although the groups which we have listed in this section are primarily concerned with schemes requiring volunteer help for between two weeks and six months, many of them also need shorter term help with administration and fund-raising.

Children's Country Holidays Fund, 1st Floor, 42–43 Lower Marsh, Tanswell Street, London SE1 7RG. T:020 7928 6522. Contact: The Chief Executive. The purpose of this charity is to give disadvantaged London children aged between five and twelve a country or seaside summer holiday, either in private homes or camps, with or without their families. Suitable host families are needed as are country representatives who undertake to find local hostesses willing to welcome one or two children into their home. There are also opportunities for: London organisers; camp supervisors; train marshals to escort parties of youngsters to and from holidays; people to co-ordinate the travel arrangements at stations; volunteer office helpers and fund-raisers.

Sue Ryder Care, 114–118 Southampton Row, London WC1B 5AA. T:020 7400 0440. Sue Ryder Care Centres cater for the sick and disabled. They are run as far as possible as family homes in the true sense of the word. Volunteers are needed for work in a variety of jobs including the general running of the care centres and with help in the Sue Ryder Care charity shops.

The Winged Fellowship Trust, Angel House, 20–32 Pentonville Road, London N1 9XD. T:020 7833 2594. Volunteers of all ages are needed most times of the year at the five holiday centres run by the Trust for disabled people and their carers. No formal qualifications are required. The work involves supporting and providing companionship for guests. Stay is for one or two weeks. Board and lodging are free and fares are refunded for travel within the UK.

13 Health

How often have you enviously commented when meeting a recently retired friend: 'Goodness, he looks a different man. Fit, relaxed, contented – retirement must suit him.' And why not? Perhaps more than any other period since your twenties, retirement is a time for positive good health! You have more chance to be out in the fresh air and take up a favourite sport again. You won't have to rush your meals so much and, without the need for business lunches or sandwiches day after day, will probably knock off a few pounds without any effort at dieting. At the same time, there will be less temptation to pop into the pub on the way home so you will feel brighter and more alert at the start of the evening.

A major gain is that there will be no more fighting your way to work on buses and trains, jam-packed with people all coughing and sneezing; or sitting in traffic, raising your blood pressure. Also, once free of the strains and pressures that are part of any job, you will feel less harassed, look better, maybe cut down on smoking and, best of all, have the energy to devote to new interests and activities.

People can get aches and pains of course as they become older but, as any doctor will tell you, this is far less likely if you remain physically and mentally active. In other words, the days for putting out the carpet slippers and equating retirement with the onset of old age are definitely attitudes of the past.

Today's retirement brigade – younger in age, looks and behaviour than any previous generation – can legitimately look forward to many healthy years ahead.

As with anything else, however, bodies do require a modicum of care and attention if they are to function at their best and, just as cars need regular servicing, routine checks such as eye testing and dental appointments are obviously sensible.

Also moderation, middle-aged as it may sound, is generally a wiser policy than excess. Don't get it wrong! This has nothing to do with treating yourself as a premature geriatric – quite the reverse. It means enjoying small vices without paying the penalty for over-indulgence, keeping trim instead of getting out of shape and looking good when you take exercise rather than puffing like the proverbial grampus.

Keeping fit

Exercise plays an important part in keeping you healthy. It tones up muscles, improves the circulation, reduces flab, helps ward off illnesses such as heart disease and, above all, can be a great deal of fun.

The experts' motto is: little and often. For those not accustomed to regular exercise, it is essential to build up gradually. If you are planning to run a marathon, win the local tennis competition, start playing your son at squash or recapture the sporting feats of your youth, do check with your doctor before jumping into your track suit.

Training in a whole range of sports is available around the country, with beginners in their fifties and older especially welcome. Details of some of the many facilities, together with other keep-fit options, are listed in Chapter 9, Leisure Activities.

In addition to some of the more exotic choices, swimming has long been recognised as one of the best forms of exercise. Some swear that there is nothing to beat a good brisk walk. Gardening is also recommended. With the explosion of sports clubs, leisure centres and adult keep fit classes run by local authorities, opportunities have never been better for athletes of all ability levels – and none.

At the plush end of the market, there are de luxe health clubs located in hotels, sports clubs and other commercial organisations where, in addition to facilities such as a fitness centre, swimming pool, massage and beauty salon, qualified staff advise on – and supervise – personal fitness programmes. However, at a fraction of the price, many local authority leisure centres offer a marvellous range of sports as well as regular classes in everything from self-defence to badminton.

Equally, emphasis on more leisurely keep fit is also on the increase and a welcome innovation is the growing number of opportunities for older people as well as for those with disabilities. The town hall should be able to tell you what local provision exists. Additionally, the following organisations may be able to help you.

Extend, 22 Maltings Drive, Wheathampstead, Herts AL4 8QJ. T:01582 832760. Extend aims to enhance the quality of life for over-sixties and disabled people of all ages by providing structured recreational movement sessions to music. Write to the above address for information about classes in your area. (Please enclose stamps to the value of £2.)

The Fitness League, 52 London Street, Chertsey, Surrey KT16 8AJ. T:01932 564567. A national organisation whose aim is to promote fitness in an atmosphere of 'happy informality'. Emphasis is on exercise and movement to music with special regard to individual ability. There are classes suitable for all ages with some participants in their seventies and older. Membership (including joining fee) is around £10. Classes cost from about £3 to £5.

Medau Movement, 8b Robson House, East Street, Epsom, Surrey KT17 1HH. T:01372 729056. Medau Rhythmic Movement was evolved in Germany at the beginning of the century. Recreational movement classes aim to provide enjoyable lessons which improve posture and muscle tone, while developing suppleness, strength and stamina. There are also special breathing exercises, influenced by yoga, which are designed to aid respiration and stimulate the circulation. Classes are held all over the country. For further information, send large sae to the address above.

Yoga

The number of yoga enthusiasts is increasing year by year and it is estimated that over half a million people in Britain regularly practise yoga as a means of improving fitness and helping relaxation. Classes are provided by a great many local authorities. There are also a number of specialist organisations. Three which arrange courses in many parts of the country are:

British Wheel of Yoga, 25 Jermyn Street, Sleaford, Lincs NG34 7RU. T:01529 306851. The British Wheel of Yoga, which is the governing body for yoga in Great Britain, runs classes suitable for all levels of ability. Fees vary according to class size and area of the country but average about £25 to £30 a term. Some classes have special rates for retired people. For further details, write to the above address.

Iyengar Yoga Institute, 223a Randolph Avenue, London W9 1NL. T:020 7624 3080. The Institute runs classes at all levels, including remedial for those with medical conditions. Of special interest is the 59-plus class for people who would like to start gently. Fees begin at £4; membership is £30 a year. For further information and addresses for local classes contact the Institute's headquarters above.

Yoga for Health Foundation, Ickwell Bury, Biggleswade, Bedfordshire SG18 9EF. T:01767 627271. This is a registered charity with clubs and teachers around the country. Additionally, residential programmes are provided at the Foundation's headquarters near Biggleswade. Cost includes full board and for five days would be around £250. There are also special courses for the over-50s. National membership is £16.50 a year (£22 for couples), which includes a quarterly journal.

Sensible eating

A trim, well kept body is one of the secrets of a youthful appearance, whereas being fat and out-of-condition adds years to anyone's age. Regular exercise is one-half of the equation, sensible eating the other. Not to put too fine a point on it, more than one in five adults in Britain is obese – in other words, overweight. No one is going to fuss about two or three pounds but half a stone or more, as well as looking unsightly, starts to become a health risk. In middle-aged men in particular, it increases the possibility of a heart attack, can lead to other illnesses, makes operations more difficult – and, in older people, is one of the causes of restricted mobility.

No one should go on a serious diet without first consulting their doctor. However, medical advice is not necessary for knocking off: sweets, cakes, sticky buns, deep-fried foods, alcohol and rich sauces. Healthy foods which most people (except of course those on a special doctor's diet) can eat in almost unlimited quantities are: fruit, salad, vegetables, fish and white meat such as chicken.

Excessive cholesterol (fatty deposits that collect in the arteries) is another concern and, whereas it often goes with overweight, slimmer people can also be affected. The basic health message is: eat more of the foods listed above; include plenty of roughage such as wholemeal bread in the diet; cut down on dishes with a high sugar, salt and animal fat content – including cream, butter and too much red meat.

As every health magazine advises, crash diets are no solution for long-term fitness – not least because, unless individuals re-educate their eating habits, the weight creeps back on; or more frequently, gallops back within a few days.

However, most of us need a boost to get ourselves started. One increasingly popular method is sponsored dieting for charity. Another possibility, which some people swear by and others rubbish, is going to a health farm. As opposed to starvation, the emphasis today is on a few days' general fitness eating (but usually enough to avoid being hungry). If nothing else, the experience is very relaxing, albeit expensive, with average costs being in the region of £150 to £235 a day. Magazines such as *Vogue* carry regular advertisements.

Cheaper and arguably more successful for long-term slimmers are Weight Watchers' meetings, of which there are now over 6,000 a week across the British Isles. The aim of Weight Watchers is to help members establish a permanent way of healthy eating so that they 'lose weight without feeling hungry by eating three balanced meals a day, giving a lower calorie intake and being nutritionally sound'.

Undoubtedly part of Weight Watchers' success is the help and encouragement members receive by belonging to a group where everyone else is trying to shed a few pounds. More important than the initial weight loss, the organisation sets store by teaching members how to maintain their desired weight. Initial registration is £9; £7.50 for over 60s. There is also a fee for local meetings. For further information and the addresses of local meetings, ring T:08457 123000.

As an initiative to help those unable (or unwilling) to attend meetings, Weight Watchers have introduced Weight Watchers 'At Home'. Participants follow an eight-week programme and, as well as the material which includes a food plan and helpful advice, they have access to a helpline facility where a consultant will answer any queries as they go along. For further details, telephone 01628 418500; or write to **Weight Watchers At Home**, Freepost (SL2467), Maidenhead, Berkshire SL6 7YE.

Of particular interest to women, the Women's Nutritional Advisory Service maintains that many of the problems associated with the menopause can be alleviated without recourse to hormone replacement therapy (HRT) by healthy eating and exercise. The organisation runs clinics in London and Sussex (initial consultation about £80, subsequent visits £48) and also has a three-month postal course which costs £128. For further information and a free explanatory leaflet, write enclosing sae plus four first class stamps to the **Women's Nutritional Advisory Service**, Menopause, PO Box 268, Lewes, East Sussex BN7 1QN. T:01273 487366.

As a rule chubby people tend to be those who enjoy rather too many good meals in the company of others. People living on their own, however, sometimes also get weight problems: either because they cannot be bothered to cook for themselves, so snack off the wrong kinds of food such as jam sandwiches and chocolate biscuits; or because they neglect themselves and do not take enough nourishment.

Elderly ladies, in particular, sometimes quite literally hardly eat enough to keep a bird alive and, in consequence, not only undermine their health but because of their general frailty are more susceptible to falls and broken bones. Two excellent stocking fillers for anyone living alone or for couples whose family has flown the nest are: *More Easy Cooking for One or Two* by Louise Davies. Penguin, £5.99 and *Cooking for One* by Molly Perham. Foulsham, £4.99.

Self-help to avoid trouble is one thing. But anyone who suspects that they could have something wrong should not hesitate to consult a doctor.

Food safety

No discussion about food would be complete without a word or two on the subject of food safety. As most readers will know it is inadvisable for anyone to eat raw eggs, whether consumed steak tartare fashion or used in uncooked dishes such as mayonnaise and mousses. To be on the safe side, elderly people as well as the very young should probably also avoid lightly cooked eggs. Likewise, if as was the case several summers ago, there is an official warning about certain seafood, then it is only common sense to refrain from eating the items in question.

However, when it comes to food poisoning, eggs and seafood are far from being the only culprits. A recent survey revealed that two-thirds of us shop only once a week for perishable food, so are running the risk of eating items that are no longer as fresh as they should be. 'Cook-chill' foods in particular, including ready-cooked chickens and pork pies, are a breeding ground for bacteria especially in the summer, when many foods – even vegetables – are liable to deteriorate more quickly.

Storage and cooking also play a major part in warding off the dangers of food poisoning. The government leaflet *Food Safety* recommends the following basic advice:

- Keep all parts of your kitchen clean
- Aim to keep your refrigerator temperature at a maximum of 5°C
- Keep raw and cooked foods separate and use within the recommended dates
- Cook foods thoroughly
- Do not reheat food more than once and don't keep cooked food longer than two days.

Drink

Most doctors cheerfully maintain that 'a little bit of what you fancy does you good'. The majority of healthy adults can enjoy a drink at a party or a glass of wine with dinner without any ill effects and retirement is no reason for giving up these pleasures. Moreover, in small quantities, it can be a very effective nightcap and can also help to stimulate a sluggish appetite. However, where problems begin is when people fancy more than is good for them. Alcoholism is the third great killer after heart disease and cancer.

The condition is far more likely among those who are bored or depressed and who, perhaps almost without realising it, drift into the habit of having a drink to cheer themselves up or to pass the time when they have nothing else to do. The trouble is the habit can become insidious and, though at the beginning it does not feel that way, individuals can quite quickly start becoming dependent on drink. Because the early symptoms appear fairly innocuous, the danger signs are apt to be ignored but these include: needing a drink as a confidence boost; having 'just one more' out of misplaced conviviality at the end of a party; drinking in the morning to cure a hangover; drinking on your own; keeping a spare bottle 'just in case'; and having sneak drinks when you think no-one is noticing.

Whereas most people are sensible enough to be able to control the habit themselves, others may need help. The family doctor will of course be the first person to check with for medical advice. But additionally, for those who need moral support, the following self-help groups may be the answer.

Alcoholics Anonymous, PO Box 1, Stonebow House, Stonebow, York YO1 7NJ. T:01904 644026. Helpline: 0845 769 7555. AA has over 3,000 autonomous groups all over the country, designed to help those with a serious alcohol problem learn how to stay sober. Through friendship and mutual support, sufferers assist each other in coping which is made easier by meeting others with the same problem. Meetings take two forms. Some are for members only; others are open to relatives and friends. Membership is free, although a collection is taken towards the cost of renting meeting rooms. For addresses of local groups, see telephone directory or contact the above helpline.

Al-Anon Family Groups UK & Eire, 61 Great Dover Street, London SE1 4YF. T:020 7403 0888 (confidential helpline open 10 a.m. – 10 p.m. every day). Al-Anon Family Groups offer support and understanding where a relative or friend's drinking is causing concern. Of possible interest to worried grandparents, Alateen, a part of Al-Anon, is specifically for teenagers aged 12–20 whose lives are or have been affected as a result of someone else's drinking. There are over 900 groups throughout the UK and Eire. Write or telephone for details of local meetings.

Alcohol Concern, Waterbridge House, 32–36 Loman Street, London SE1 0EE. T:020 7928 7377. Alcohol Concern is a charity which aims to promote better understanding of alcohol-related problems and to improve services for those in need of help. It publishes a quarterly magazine, has a library and a small bookshop and can supply addresses of local advice and information centres.

Smoking

Any age is a good one to cut back on smoking or preferably to give up altogether. The gruesome facts are that smokers are 20 times more likely to contract lung cancer. They are at more serious risk of suffering from heart disease, particularly coronary thrombosis; and additionally are more liable to chronic bronchitis as well as various other ailments.

Most people agree that is easier to give up completely than attempt to cut back since, as every smoker knows, after the first cigarette of the day you can always think of a thousand excuses for lighting another. Aids to will-power include: requesting a non-smoking table in restaurants; leaving your cigarettes behind when you go out; not buying cigarettes for guests to smoke in your home, which they leave but you take; and refusing as a personal point of honour to cadge off friends. Many hardened smokers also swear by nicotine patches, available from most chemists.

Working out how much money you could save in a year and promising yourself a holiday or other reward on the proceeds could help. Thinking about your health in years to come should be an even more convincing argument.

Dozens of organisations concerned with health publish leaflets giving the facts, including the harm you can do to non-smokers. To list just a couple, you can obtain literature from:

Quitline, Ground Floor, 211 Old Street, London EC1V 9NR. T:0800 002200. Offers information, advice and counselling for smokers and ex-smokers alike. Lines are open from 1 p.m. to 9 p.m., daily.

Smokeline (Scotland only), T:0800 848484. Offers free advice, counselling and encouragement to those wishing to give up smoking. Available noon to midnight, seven days weekly.

There is now also an **NHS Smoking Helpline**, T: 0800 169 9 169. Offers help and advice to smokers who want to quit and can give information about local cessation services which include: nicotine replacement therapy, one-to-one counselling and group support.

Accident prevention

One of the most common causes of mishap is accidents in the home including, in particular, falls and incidents due to faulty electrical wiring. The vast majority could be avoided by taking normal common-sense precautions, such as repairing worn carpets and installing better lighting near staircases. For a list of practical suggestions, see 'Safety in the home', in Chapter 8, Your Home.

If you are unlucky enough to be injured in an accident, whether in the street or elsewhere, the Law Society offers a free service called **The Accident Line** to help you decide whether you can make a claim. You will be entitled to a free consultation with a local solicitor specialising in personal injury claims who will inform you whether you have a good case, how to go about claiming and how much you might claim. Should you decide to pursue the matter, you are under no obligation to ask the same solicitor to act for you. To arrange a free consultation, telephone Freephone: 0800 192939.

A similar service is offered by **The National Accident Helpline**, T:0800 556 557.

Aches, pains and other abnormalities

There is nothing about becoming 50, 60 or even 70 that makes aches and pains an inevitability. Age in itself has nothing to do with the vast majority of ailments.

However, a big problem is that many people ignore the warning signs when something is wrong, on the basis that this symptom or that is only to be expected as one becomes older. More often than not, treatment when a condition is still in its infancy can either cure it altogether or at least help to delay its advance.

The following should always be investigated by a doctor, to be on the safe side:

- any pain which lasts more than a few days
- lumps, however small
- dizziness or fainting
- chest pains, shortness of breath or palpitations
- persistent cough or hoarseness
- unusual bleeding from anywhere
- unnatural tiredness or headaches
- frequent indigestion
- unexplained weight loss.

Health insurance

An increasing number of people are covered by private health insurance or provident schemes during their working lives. If you wish to continue this benefit, and you are unable to remain in your company scheme after retirement, you will normally be welcomed as an individual client by most of the main groups provided you are under the age of 70 (or in some cases, even older). You can then renew your membership when you do reach 70.

Even if you have not previously been insured, it is not too late to consider doing so. Although obviously this will be an extra expense, should you be unfortunate enough to fall ill or need an operation and want to be treated as a private patient, insurance will save you a great deal of worry and expense.

Terms and conditions of the different schemes offered by health insurance groups vary to some extent but all the major ones offer to pay all or the greatest part of the costs of in-patient accommodation, treatment and medical fees as well as out-patient charges for specialists, X-rays and similar services. They do not normally cover GPs' costs.

Subscription levels largely depend on area and on the type of hospital to which you choose to be admitted. The top figure is usually based on charges in private hospitals in London; the next is based on private hospitals outside London; and the lowest rate is based on charges in NHS paybeds and some private hospitals.

Other factors that can substantially affect the price are: your age, the extent of the cover offered and the various restrictions – or exclusions – that may apply. Many insurers have recently introduced a range of budget policies which, while they have the advantage of being less costly, are naturally also less comprehensive. For example, some policies confine cover to surgery or only cover certain specified procedures. Particular illnesses, or conditions, may be excluded as may out-patient treatment.

There may be an annual cash limit or the policy may include an excess – i.e. the subscriber pays a fixed amount of every claim, typically between £100 and £500. Another popular saving are policies which restrict private care to cases where the wait for NHS treatment would exceed six (sometimes twelve) weeks. As with all types of insurance the small print matters, so look carefully at all the plans available before selecting the scheme that best suits your needs.

Although the NHS has an excellent record in dealing with urgent conditions and accidents, it sometimes has a lengthy waiting list for the less urgent and more routine operations such as hip replacements and hernias. By using health insurance to pay for private medical care you will probably get faster treatment as well as greater comfort and privacy in hospital. The major organisations are:

BUPA, T:0800 600 500. BUPA is the largest of the provident associations and offers two medical insurance schemes for individuals:

BUPA Heartbeat. Customers are given a personalised price, with the flexibility to choose which benefits they would like included from a wide range of options. This can be either on an annual basis or alternatively there is the option to fix subscriptions for five to ten years.

For further information and quote tailored to your requirements, call T:0800 600 500.

BUPA Local HospitalCare – provides cover for prompt, private treatment at around 170 specially selected BUPA Partnership Network Hospitals. It covers specialist treatment of acute diseases, illness and injuries, related consultations after a hospital stay and any diagnostic tests recommended by a consultant. The cost of seeing a consultant privately before going into hospital is not covered.

Example of subscription costs (May 2002) shown below all include insurance premium tax at 5 per cent.

	£/month
Single person aged 60	65.26
Single person aged 65	79.68
Single person aged 70	99.48
Single person aged 75, subject to medical report	121.84

Subscriptions to both policies can be reduced by electing to take an excess option, where you pay the first part of any claims you make in a year. There are five levels of excess: £100, £150, £200, £250 and £500. You pay this excess only once in the subscription year, not every time you make a claim.

For more information on BUPA Local HospitalCare, call the telephone number above.

PPP healthcare, Phillips House, Crescent Road, Tunbridge Wells, Kent TN1 2PL. T:0800 335555. PPP healthcare offers a range of personal healthcare products to meet the cost of private treatment. All include access to the PPP healthcare Health Information Line – a confidential 24-hour service staffed by nurses and pharmacists with whom customers can discuss any health issues that concern them. Benefits and monthly subscriptions (April 2002) are shown below. Customers who pay by single annual premium receive a 5 per cent discount.

PPP healthcare Key Plan. Provides full cover for in-patient care, day care, outpatient surgical procedures, CT and MRI scans, chemotherapy and radiology. It also provides £300 worth of cover for out-patient consultations and practitioner charges that relate to in-patient treatment. Private ambulance cover is also included.

Age	*Band 1*	*Band 2*
	£	£
60	88.28	74.80
65	107.21	89.03
70	136.20	110.88
80-plus	227.45	181.99

PPP healthcare Ideal. Provides all the same benefits as Key Plan with £700 worth of care for out-patient consultations, diagnostic and practitioner charges.

Age	*Band 1*	*Band 2*
	£	£
60	176.56	107.21
65	234.87	138.96
70	288.50	173.91
80-plus	355.80	214.43

PPP healthcare Classic. Provides all the same cover as Key Plan but with the following extras: £900 worth of care for out-patient consultations, diagnostic and practitioner charges; home nursing care; and international travel insurance including emergency repatriation cover.

Age	*Band 1*	*Band 2*
	£	£
60	200.34	126.29
65	266.58	163.74
70	327.45	204.82
80-plus	403.87	252.61

All three policies have an optional excess of £100, £200 and £500 that reduce monthly premiums.

Exeter Friendly Society, Lakeside House, Emperor Way, Exeter EX1 3FD. T:08080 556 575. Exeter is an old established non-profit making friendly society with subscribers throughout the UK. Its private health insurance scheme has three major distinguishing features that may make it particularly attractive to people of retiring age:

- it accepts new subscribers of any age up to 79

- it does not increase subscription rates on account of age, which is a big advantage if income is tight in retirement
- the subscription rates for older people are considerably lower than for most other schemes.

Examples of monthly starter rates (April 2002) for those aged 60 and over, are:

Low Cost Plan:

	Level 1	*Level 2*
	£	£
Single aged 60	86.92	57.92
Couple both aged 60	173.84	115.84
Couple 65 and 60 years	180.44	120.26
Couple 70 and 63 years	204.71	136.57

Preferred Plan:

	Level 1	*Level 2*
	£	£
Single aged 60	138.34	92.16
Couple both aged 60	276.68	184.32
Couple 65 and 60 years	293.01	195.02
Couple 70 and 63 years	327.26	218.00

Although some benefits are marginally smaller, cover in general is very comparable with the other main schemes and the substantially lower annual subscription may more than compensate for any differences.

Other groups that offer health insurance plans relevant to people over retirement age include:

Abbey National Healthcare. Details from any Abbey National branch or call T:0800 222399.

BCWA Healthcare, James Tudor House, 90 Victoria Street, Bristol BS1 6DF. T:0117 929 5555.

Legal & General Healthcare, Freepost, PO Box 2344, Hove, East Sussex BN3 1BR. T:0500 669966.

Norwich Union Healthcare Ltd., Chilworth House, Hampshire Corporate Park, Templars Way, Eastleigh, Hants SO5 3RY. T:0800 142142.

Saga Services Ltd., The Saga Building, Middelburg Square, Folkestone, Kent CT20 1AZ. T: 0800 857 857.

Help with choosing a scheme

With so many plans on the market, selecting the one that best suits your needs can be quite a problem. If you would welcome advice, you can either ask an independent financial adviser for help or approach a specialist insurance broker.

Health and Group Bristol operates a telephone advice line and will send you, free of charge, details of plans that are most likely to suit your personal circumstances. T:0117 988 7533 (Mon – Fri, 9 a.m. to 5 p.m.). Or you could contact **The Private Health Partnership** who will send you a questionnaire and then help you match your key requirements to the most suitable scheme. Charge is £10 (plus VAT). For further information, telephone helpline: 01943 851133. Although there is no obligation, both services will arrange the purchase of the policy for you.

Private patients – without insurance cover

If you do not have private medical insurance but want to go into hospital as a private patient, there is of course nothing to stop you doing so provided your doctor is willing and you are able to pay the bills. The choice is between the private wings of NHS hospitals, hospitals run by charitable or non-profit-making organisations (such as the Nuffield Hospitals) and those run for profit by private companies. If you cannot pay immediately, Nuffield Hospitals may be able to arrange an interest-free loan (for repayment within 12 months) for treatment at any one of their 43 hospitals. For further information call freephone: 0800 688 699.

Long-term care insurance

An emergency operation is one thing; long term care because an individual can no longer cope unaided, quite another. Over the past few years, a number of insurance companies have launched policies designed to help meet the costs in the event of a person needing to stay long-term in a nursing home or requiring a carer to look after them in their own home.

The days when the welfare state automatically picked up the bill no longer exist. Anyone with total assets of more than £11,750 will be expected to contribute according to their means, while those with capital of over £19,000 including the value of their home will not qualify for assistance and will need to support themselves from their savings. (N.B. A married couple would not be forced into selling their home if the other partner were still living there.)

With average nursing home fees costing £18,200 to £26,000 a year and care in your own home, if you were ever to become seriously incapacitated, likely to be at least as expensive, some provision against long term care must be worth considering.

The big advantages of insurance cover are that it buys peace of mind and would help safeguard your savings should care ever become a necessity in the future. An additional plus point is that benefits paid out to a policyholder are tax-free.

However, although a godsend in case of need, none of the policies is exactly cheap and in most cases the criteria for paying out are pretty stringent. Cover normally only applies if an illness is diagnosed after joining and while some plans cover a wide range of eventualities, others specifically exclude some of the critical illnesses such as cancer.

The premiums which can be paid on a regular annual basis or as a lump sum vary considerably, as of course does the amount of financial assistance given. In all cases, the charges are largely determined by the subscriber's age at time of first joining and, as you would expect, are very much cheaper at 55 than 75.

To avoid wrangles over eligibility for benefit, most of the schemes have adopted a system, known as Activities of Daily Living (ADLs). ADLs typically include: bathing/washing; dressing; feeding; going to the lavatory; getting in and out of a bed/chair. The higher the number of these an individual is unable to manage on their own, the greater their benefit entitlement. In some policies, Alzheimer's Disease is specifically covered.

Although pre-funded insurance is the cheapest way of buying care cover, a disadvantage is that if you never claim you lose all the money you have paid over the years.

Some policies link the insurance with an investment, with a pay-out on death if no claim has been made. Though initially more expensive, you can take your money out of the plan at any time. However, if the investment growth is poor you could lose some of your capital.

Companies offering long term care policies include: Scottish Widows, BUPA, PPP Lifetime Care, Eagle Star, Norwich Union, Scottish Provident and Pensions Annuity Friendly Society.

A possible alternative to a conventional long-term care policy is **critical illness insurance** which pays a lump sum if you are unfortunate enough to be struck by one of a specified number of dread diseases, such as cancer or a stroke.

Another possibility advocated by some financial advisers is to invest in a lump sum immediate care plan, if and when the need for long term care arises. In effect these are annuity plans which pay an income for life. The income is usually considerably higher than normal annuity rates but with no return of capital to benefit your successors (capital protection is available with higher contributions). An advantage, however, is that you would only buy a care plan at such time as it would actually be useful. A further plus point is that all money paid by the policyholder direct to the care provider, including a home nursing agency, is free of tax.

Deciding on your best option is not easy, since quite apart from the cost, all such policies – although becoming more flexible – are restrictive in one way or another. You are strongly advised to shop around and to read the small print extremely carefully before signing. If, as may be suggested, you are thinking of investing some of your lump sum to pay for the policy, it would be sensible to ask a lawyer or financial adviser to check the policy for any hidden drawbacks. Alternatively, and this might be the best idea, you could ask an independent financial adviser (IFA) to recommend what would be your best choice. An organisation worth contacting if you would like names of local IFAs with specialist knowledge of long term care is: **IFACare Administration**, Bridge House, Severn Bridge, Bewdley, Worcs DY12 1AB. T:01299 406040.

You might also usefully speak to the **Nursing Home Fees Agency** which runs a free advice service and has a wealth of experience in advising on financial planning for long term care. The address to contact is NHFA, St. Leonards House, Mill Street, Eynsham, Oxford OX29 4JX. Freephone: 0800 998833.

Permanent Health Insurance

PHI should not be confused with other types of health insurance. It is a replacement of earnings policy for people who are still in work and who, because of illness, are unable to continue with their normal occupation for a prolonged period and in consequence suffer loss of earnings. While highly recommended for the self-employed, many employees have some protection under an employer's policy. Either way, if you are close to retirement, PHI would be unlikely to feature on your priority list.

Health screening

Prevention is better than cure and most of the provident associations offer a diagnostic screening service to check general health and to provide advice on diet, drinking and smoking if these are problem areas. These tests show that roughly a quarter of patients aged over 55 have an unsuspected problem which can often be treated quickly and easily.

Screening services normally recommend a check-up every two years and centres are usually available to members of insurance schemes and others alike.

BUPA. There is a network of BUPA Wellness Centres up and down the country, offering a range of health assessments. In most cases, same-day results can be provided so you can discuss the findings with your health adviser and doctor there and then. Prices range from £95 for a breast health assessment to £475 for the BUPA Premier Health Assessment.

The Wellness Centres are located in: Aberdeen, Belfast, Birmingham, Blackpool, Brentwood, Bristol, Cambridge, Cardiff, Edinburgh, Farnham, Gatwick, Glasgow, Harpenden, Hythe, Leeds, Leicester, London (7 centres), Manchester, Norwich, Nottingham, Portsmouth, Reading, Southampton, Southend, Walderslade, Warrington and Wirral. For further details, call BUPA on T:0800 616029.

BMI Health Services Ltd., part of General Healthcare Group Ltd., has screening centres in: Basingstoke, Bath, Beckenham, Bedford, Blackburn, Buckingham, Canterbury, Cheadle, Chertsey, Crewe, Croydon, Dorset, Droitwich, Dyfed, Eastbourne, Edgbaston, Edinburgh, Enfield, Glasgow, Harrow, Leeds, London, Lostock, Maidstone, Milton Keynes, Norfolk, Nottingham, Nuneaton, Poole, Rochdale, Sheffield, Swindon, Winchester, Windsor. Screening programmes, known as Personal Health Profiles, cost £495 for women aged 60 to 69 and £395 for women aged 70 plus. For men, prices are respectively £435 and £325. For further information contact: The Medical Centre, BMI Health Services, 46 Wimpole Street, London W1M 7DG. T:0800 004600.

National Health Service. The NHS offers several different screening services of particular relevance to those aged 50-plus. Two are especially for women and the others are more general. Firstly, all adults who have not been seen by a GP over the last three years can request an appointment for an assessment of their general health. This will include a few simple tests, such as checking your blood pressure, and the opportunity to discuss any health problems that could be worrying you, as well as discussion of factors to do with your lifestyle that could be affecting your health. All patients over 75 should be offered an annual health check by their GP, which could be arranged in their own home if they prefer. As well as their general state of health, the check will cover such matters as eyesight, hearing, possible mobility problems, worries that might be causing depression, use of medicines and similar.

The special women's tests are to screen for cancer of the breast and cervical abnormalities. These are now available in all parts of the country. All women between 20 and 64 years will be offered a smear test at least every five years; and all women between 50 and 64 years will be invited for screening by breast X-ray every three years. The age for breast screening is in process of being raised to 70 and, by 2004, women nationwide should automatically continue to receive invitations to attend if they are registered with a GP. In the meantime, women over 64 can request a breast X-ray every three years.

If for some reason you have not been receiving invitations for screening, you should ask your GP for details or enquire at your local Primary Care Trust.

For further information, see leaflets *NHS Cervical Screening – The Facts* and *NHS Breast Screening – The Facts*, both obtainable from GPs and Primary Care Trusts.

Hospital care cash plans

These schemes provide a cash sum for every night the insured person spends in hospital. Premiums start from £1 a week, giving a payment of about £18 a day. All benefits are tax-free and are available to anyone joining before age 65. A number of schemes cater for individuals aged over 65.

About 28 organisations offer such schemes as well as a wide range of other health insurance including cover for optical and dental treatment. A list can be obtained from: **British Health Care Association**, 24a Main Street, Garforth, Leeds LS25 1AA. T:0113 232 0903.

National Health Service

Most readers will need no introduction to the National Health Service. However, there are one or two scraps of information that you may not know – or possibly have forgotten – that may come in useful around retirement.

One area is the range of professionals, including district nurses and occupational therapists, who can provide invaluable support if you are caring for an elderly relative or if a member of the household requires to go into hospital. Most of what you need to know is described in Chapter 15, Caring for Elderly Parents.

Choosing a GP

If you move to a new area, you will need to find a new doctor. The best way is normally by recommendation but if you do not know whom to ask you can write to, or call into, your local **Strategic Health Authority (StHA)** or Primary Care Trust, see telephone directory for address.

You could ask to consult the local medical directory, where you will find details of GPs' qualifications and special areas of knowledge. This could be useful if someone in the household has a particular health problem and you would feel happier with a doctor who has more specialised experience.

Additional points you may want to consider are: how close the doctor is to your home; whether there is an appointments system; whether it is a group practice and, if so, how this is organised. All GPs must now have practice leaflets, available at their premises, with details about the service. The information should include: names, addresses, sex, year of qualification and type of qualifications along with essential practice information such as surgery hours, services provided and arrangements for emergencies and night calls.

Having selected a doctor, you should take your medical card to the receptionist in order to have your name registered. This is not automatic as, firstly, there is a limit to the number of patients any one doctor can accept. Also, some doctors prefer to meet potential patients before accepting them on their list. If you do not have a medical card, you will need to fill in a simple form.

If you want to change your GP, you go about it in exactly the same way. If you know of a doctor whose list you would like to be on, you can simply turn up at his/her surgery and ask to be registered; or you can ask the Strategic Health Authority or Primary Care Trust, or Health Board in Scotland, to give you a copy of their directory before making a choice. You do not need to give a reason for wanting to change and you do not need to ask anyone's permission. Two useful publications to read are:

- *The NHS Reforms and You*
- *You and Your GP*

Available free from libraries, Strategic Health Authorities and doctors' surgeries.

NHS Direct. If you need medical advice when you are on holiday or at some other time when it may not be possible to contact your doctor, you could ring NHS Direct which offers a 24-hour free health advice service, staffed by trained nurses. The number to call is T:0845 46 47.

Help with NHS Costs

If you or your partner are in receipt of income support or income-based jobseeker's allowance, you are both entitled to free: NHS prescriptions, NHS dental treatment, NHS wigs and fabric supports and an NHS sight test. You are both equally entitled to the maximum value of an optical voucher to help towards cost of glasses or contact lenses and payment of travel costs to and from hospital for NHS treatment. You may be entitled to help if you and/or your partner are in receipt of the Working Families Tax Credit (WFTC), Disabled Person's Tax Credit (DPTC) or, from April 2003, Working Tax Credit and are named on a current tax credit NHS exemption certificate.

Even if you are not automatically entitled to help with the above costs, you and your partner may be entitled to some help on the grounds of low income. To find out, fill in claim form HC1 – obtainable from any social security office as well as many NHS hospitals, dentists, opticians and GPs – and send it to the Health Benefits Division in the prepaid envelope provided with the form.

If you are eligible for help, you will be sent a certificate which is valid for up to 12 months according to your circumstances. Depending on your income, you may receive an HC2 certificate, which entitles you to full help with NHS costs; or alternatively, an HC3 certificate which will entitle you to partial help.

For more details see leaflet HC 11 *Are You Entitled to Help with Health Costs*, available from social security offices, main post office and NHS hospitals. Or ring the Health Literature line on T: 0800 555 777.

Benefits

If you are on income support and have a disability, you may be entitled to certain premiums on top of your ordinary income support allowance. There are four rates: £23 (single); £32.80 (couple) for the generally disabled; £42.25 for the severely disabled; £84.50 if both partners qualify as severely disabled.

Various social security benefits are also available to those with special problems because of illness. These include:

- *Attendance Allowance,* see leaflet DS 702
- *Disability Living Allowance,* see leaflet DS 704
- *Incapacity Benefit,* see leaflet IB 1

Incapacity Benefit

Sickness and Invalidity Benefit were abolished in April 1995 and have been replaced by Incapacity Benefit.

People who cannot work because of an illness or disability and were receiving either sickness or invalidity benefit immediately before 13 April 1995 receive incapacity benefit instead – at the same rate as their previous benefit – providing they continue to remain unfit for work. An important change, however, is that an individual claiming benefit would normally be expected to have what is known as a 'personal capability assessment' medical test to assess whether they would be capable of doing any type of job and, if so, what kind they might realistically manage.

The situation for people first claiming after April 1995 is as follows. There are three basic levels of payment: two for short-term incapacity – a lower and higher rate; and one for long-term incapacity. Benefit payments quoted below are for 2002/03. There are also certain additions, for example for age, which might entitle you to extra.

The lower rate short-term payment is for people (including the self-employed and those temporarily without a job) who are unable to get Statutory Sick Pay from an employer, who are sick for more than four days in a row and who are unable to do their normal job. A doctor's certificate, confirming their unfitness for work, is required. People without a regular occupation will additionally be asked to have a 'a personal capability assessment'. The benefit is £53.50 a week and is payable for up to 28 weeks of sickness.

The higher short-term rate is for people who are still unable to work after the first 28 weeks. The test is more stringent and applies, not just to your normal occupation, but to a wider range of jobs. You will be sent a questionnaire and may also be requested to have a medical examination. This higher rate is payable from week 29 to the remainder of the year (week 52). Payment is £63.25 a week.

Long-term incapacity benefit is for those who, due to an illness/disability, are still unable to work after a year. Individuals receiving the highest rate component of Disability Living Allowance and those who are terminally ill may be entitled to benefit paid at the long-term rate after only 28 weeks, instead of having to wait for a year. Payment is £70.95 a week.

In all cases, eligibility for Incapacity Benefit is restricted to people under State pension age or to those whose illness began before ages 65 (men) or 60 (women). People in this latter category who have since reached pension age may be able to get the short-term benefit – paid at the retirement pension rate – for up to a year of incapacity.

Another important point to note is that, other than short-term benefit paid for the first 28 weeks, Incapacity Benefit is normally taxable. N.B. People receiving Invalidity Benefit before 13 April 1995 are not liable for tax on their Incapacity Benefit.

For further information, including the special concessions for voluntary and therapeutic work, see leaflet IB 1 *A Guide to Incapacity Benefit – Information for New Customers*, available from any social security office.

Prescriptions

Men – as well as women – aged 60 and over are now entitled to free NHS prescriptions. Additionally certain other groups, including those on low income (see 'Help with NHS costs', page 332) and people who suffer from a specified medical condition, are also entitled to free prescriptions. If you are not sure if you qualify, you should pay and ask the pharmacist for an NHS receipt form FP57, which tells you how to claim a refund. For further information, see leaflet HC 11 *Are You Entitled to Help with Health Costs?*, obtainable from social security offices, main post offices and NHS hospitals.

People who do not qualify but who require a lot of prescriptions could save money by purchasing a prescription pre-payment certificate. This costs £32.40 for four months; or £89 for a year. A pre-payment certificate will work out cheaper if you are likely to need more than 5 prescription items in four months, or more than 14 items in twelve months. Obtain Application Form FP95 (EC95 in Scotland) from a post office or pharmacy.

Going into hospital

Stories abound of people who wait months and months for an operation because of shortage of beds. But while waiting lists for a hernia or hip replacement may be depressingly long in one area, hospitals in another part of the country may have spare capacity. Many patients are unaware that they can ask their GP to refer them to a consultant at a different NHS Trust or even, in certain cases, help make arrangements for them to be treated overseas.

Finding out which hospitals have beds has become very easy. The **College of Health** operates a telephone helpline service to advise which hospitals have the shortest waiting lists for particular operations. The list includes: general surgery, orthopaedic, ear, nose and throat, gynaecology, ophthalmology, oral surgery, urology, cardiac surgery, neurosurgery and plastic surgery. Either you or your doctor can telephone the National Waiting List Helpline, which is open Monday to Thursday, between 11 a.m. and 7 p.m.; and Friday, 11 a.m. to 5 p.m. The number to ring is T:020 8983 1133.

Before you can become a patient at another hospital, your GP will of course need to agree to your being referred. A major consideration will be whether the treatment would be as clinically effective as you would receive locally.

A further useful point to know is that the government has promised that by the start of April 2003 the maximum waiting time for admission to hospital will be reduced from 15 months to 12 months and that by the end of 2005 this will be further reduced to 6 months. Equally, by the end of 2005, the maximum waiting time for a first outpatient appointment following GP referral will be cut from 6 months to 3 months.

In the meantime, if you are on a waiting list for treatment and your condition has deteriorated and become more urgent, you should speak to your GP who may be able to arrange with the hospital for your appointment to be brought forward. See also 'Complaints', below.

Those likely to need help on leaving hospital should speak to the Hospital Social Worker, who will help make any necessary arrangements.

Help is sometimes available to assist patients with their travel costs to and from hospital. If you receive income support or income-based jobseeker's allowance, you can ask for repayment of 'necessary travel costs' (if you are not sure what would qualify, you can check with the hospital before you travel). If you have a war or MOD disablement pension, you may get help with travel costs for treatment of your pensionable disability. There are special schemes for people who live in the Isles of Scilly or the former Scottish Highlands and Islands Development Board area; enquire at your local health centre (Scilly) or ask your GP (Scotland). Claims for help can also be made on the grounds of low income. For detailed information, see leaflet HC 11 *Are you Entitled to Help with Health Costs?*

If you go into hospital, you will continue to receive your State pension as normal for six weeks. After that, it will be reduced. Certain social security benefits are also affected if you or a dependant have to go into hospital. NB. From April 2003, your pension plus other benefits will only start to be reduced if you stay in hospital for thirteen weeks or longer. For further information, see leaflet GL12 *Going Into Hospital?*, obtainable from any social security office.

If you have any complaints while in hospital, you should speak to someone close to the cause of the complaint or to the Complaints Manager within the hospital; or if the matter is more serious, you should write to the Chief Executive of the hospital. See also information below.

Complaints

The NHS has a complaints procedure if you are unhappy about the treatment you have received.

In the first instance, you should speak to someone close to the cause of the problem, e.g. the doctor, nurse, receptionist or practice manager. If, for whatever reason, you would prefer to speak to someone who was not involved in your care, you can speak to the 'Complaints Manager' at your local NHS Trust or Strategic Health Authority (StHA) instead; addresses will be in the telephone directory. In jargon terms, this first stage is known as **Local Resolution**.

If you are not satisfied with the reply you receive, you can ask the NHS Trust or StHA for an **Independent Review**. The Complaints Manager will be able to tell you whom to contact about arranging this.

If you are still dissatisfied after the Independent Review, then the Health Service Ombudsman (known formally as the Health Service Commissioner) might be able to help. The Ombudsman is independent of both Government and the NHS. He investigates complaints of failure or maladministration across the whole range of services provided by, or for, the NHS including pharmacists, opticians and dentists, as well as private hospitals and nursing homes if these are paid for by the NHS. He cannot, however, take up legal causes on a patient's behalf. Addresses to write to are:

Health Service Ombudsman for England, Millbank Tower, Millbank, London SW1P 4QP. T:0845 015 4033.

Health Service Ombudsman for Wales, 5th Floor, Capital Tower, Greyfriars Road, Cardiff CF10 3AG. T:0845 601 0987.

Health Service Ombudsman for Scotland, 28 Thistle Street, Edinburgh EH2 1EN. T:0845 601 0456. (Likely to be moving during 2003).

If you have a complaint, you should get on to the matter fairly speedily or your complaint may be dismissed on grounds of being 'out of time'. Time limits require you to register complaints within twelve months of the incident or within twelve months of your realising that you have reason for complaint. These time limits may be waived if you have a very good reason why you could not complain sooner.

If you need further advice on the complaints procedure, contact your local Community Health Council or CAB. N.B. Community Health Councils are due to be scrapped during 2003. If there is no longer a CHC in your area, contact the Patient Advice and Liaison Service at your local Primary Care Trust or NHS hospital trust; or alternatively, the Independent Complaints Advocacy Service, available via your GP or NHS trust.

Rather than proceed through the formal channels described above, an alternative approach – which of course does not prevent you from also applying to the Ombudsman or to anyone else – is to get in touch with **The Patients Association**, PO Box 935, Harrow, Middx HA1 3YJ. Helpline: 0845 608 4455. This is an independent advice centre which offers guidance to patients in the event of a problem with the health service. The Association also publishes a selection of useful leaflets, a directory of self-help groups and a quarterly magazine – *Patient Voice*.

Useful reading. *Your Guide to the NHS*, obtainable from the NHS Health Literature Line on T:0800 555777.

Alternative medicine

Alternative medicine remains a very controversial subject. Some doctors dismiss it out of hand. Many patients claim that it is of great benefit. We list here some of the better known organisations.

British Acupuncture Council, 63 Jeddo Road, London W12 9HQ. T:020 8735 0400. Treatment, using fine needles, is claimed to be effective for a wide range of illnesses including: migraine, lumbago, arthritis and high blood pressure. The Council can provide you with a list of professionally qualified acupuncture practitioners in your local area.

British Chiropractic Association, Blagrave House, 17 Blagrave Street, Reading RG1 1QB. T:0118 950 5950. Practitioners specialise in mechanical disorders of the spine and joints and the effects on the nervous system. Treatment is mainly by specific manipulation without drugs or surgery. For a list of members in your area, write to the Association enclosing a 9" x 6" sae. A full national register is available at £6.

British Homeopathic Association, 15 Clerkenwell Close, London EC1R 0AA. T:020 7566 7800. Homeopathy is essentially natural healing which follows the principle of looking at the whole person rather than just the illness. Homeopathy is available on the NHS but as yet not many doctors are trained in this branch of medicine. The Association can supply a list of practising GPs as well as the names and addresses of pharmacies that stock homeopathic medicines.

Patients wanting NHS treatment can only apply to GPs in their catchment area or get a letter of referral to one of the homeopathic hospitals or to a GP able to take NHS referrals. Otherwise, patients can be treated anywhere by doctors on a private basis. Membership of the BHA costs £15 a year and includes 4 issues of their magazine and use of their extensive library.

British Hypnotherapy Association, 67 Upper Berkeley Street, London W1H 7QX. T:020 7723 4443. Hypnotherapy may help people with phobias, emotional problems, anxiety, migraine or relationship difficulties. For details of the nearest registered trained hypnotherapist, including qualifications and fees, contact the

Association indicating what the problem is. You will also be sent a pamphlet answering common questions about hypnotherapy.

Incorporated Society of Registered Naturopaths, Kingston Coach House, 70 Kingston Avenue, Edinburgh EH16 5SW. T:0131 664 3435. Naturopaths are concerned about the underlying conditions that may cause illness including, for example: diet, general fitness, posture, stress and the patient's mental outlook on life. The Society can put you in touch with your nearest practitioner.

National Institute of Medical Herbalists, 56 Longbrook Street, Exeter, Devon EX4 6AH. T:01392 426022. The practice of herbal medicine aims to offer the sufferer not just relief from symptoms but an improved standard of general health and vitality. For further information and a register of practitioners, write to the above address enclosing large sae.

Osteopathic Information Service, Osteopathy House, 176 Tower Bridge Road, London SE1 3LU. T:020 7357 6655. Osteopathic treatment is often appropriate for those with back problems or with muscle or joint disorders. It can also provide pain relief from arthritis. Advice and leaflets are available on request (please send sae); or you can telephone for a list of osteopaths in your area.

Wessex Healthy Living Foundation, Beekay House, 6c St. Catherine's Road, Southbourne, Bournemouth BH6 4AA. T:01202 422087. The Foundation is a non-profit-making registered charity which, as well as having an educative purpose, runs a clinic where all natural therapies are available under one roof. Annual membership of the Foundation is £15; £20 for families. Members enjoy the benefit of reduced clinic fees and also receive a bi-annual newsletter and information leaflets. For further details, write enclosing sae.

Eyes

It is advisable to have your eyes checked at least every two years. Eye tests are now free for all men, as well as women, aged 60 and over. If you are not yet 60, you can only get a free NHS sight test if: you are registered blind or partially sighted; are prescribed complex lenses; are diagnosed as having diabetes or glaucoma; if you are over 40 and are a close relative of someone with glaucoma; (i.e. parent, brother, sister, son or daughter); or if you are a patient of the hospital eye service or have been referred by them to an optometrist. You are also entitled to a free sight test if you or your partner are getting income support or income-based jobseeker's allowance. You may also be entitled to some help if you are in receipt of the Working Families Tax Credit, the Disabled Person's Tax Credit or, from April 2003, Working Tax Credit; for details, see leaflet HC11.

Even if you do not belong to any of these groups but are on a low income, you may be entitled to a free, or reduced cost, sight test. To find out if you qualify for help, you should fill out claim form HC1 which you can get from social security offices, NHS hospitals and opticians, together with a stamped envelope addressed to the Health Benefits Division (HBD) in Newcastle. The HBD will either send you a full help HC2 certificate; or an HC3 certificate which will state whether you are entitled to partial help (in which case, it will show the amount you have to contribute yourself) – or whether you will have to pay the full cost.

People with mobility problems can ask for a domiciliary visit to have their eyes examined at home. This is free for those with an HC2 certificate or who are in receipt of one of the benefits listed above. People with a (partial help) HC3 certificate can use this towards the cost of a private home visit by their optician.

The going rate for private sight tests if you do have to pay is about £19. Many opticians, however, charge less for people who are retired or run special promotions at various times of the year. Even if this is not advertised in the window, you have nothing to lose by asking before booking an appointment.

As you probably know, you do not need a doctor's referral to have your eyes tested. Simply book an appointment with a registered optometrist or ophthalmic medical practitioner. If you qualify for help with the cost, remember to take your HC2 or HC3 certificate with you to show to the optician. The sight test should establish whether or not spectacles are required and should also include an eye examination to check for signs of injury, disease or abnormality.

Whether you have to pay or not, the optician must either give you a prescription identifying what type of glasses you require or alternatively give you a statement confirming that you have no need of spectacles. The prescription is valid for two years. If you do not use it straight away, you should keep it carefully so that it is handy when you need to use it. When you do decide to buy spectacles or contact lenses, you are under no obligation to obtain them from the optician who tested your eyes but can buy them where you like.

There is a voucher system for helping with the purchase of glasses or contact lenses. If you or your partner are in receipt of income support or income-based jobseeker's allowance, you will receive an optical voucher, with a cash value (April 2002/03) of between £30.50 and £157. The amount you get will depend on your optical prescription. If you do not get any of the above benefits but are on a low income, you may still be entitled to help. To find out fill in claim form HC1, as explained above.

The voucher might be sufficient to pay for your contact lenses or spectacles outright or it may only make a small contribution towards the cost. Part of the equation will depend on the frames you choose. You will not be tied to any particular glasses: you can choose specs that cost more than the value of the voucher and pay the difference yourself. For further details, see leaflets HC 11 *Are You Entitled to Help with Health Costs?* (available in large print size) and HC 12 *NHS Charges and Optical Voucher Values*, obtainable from main post offices, social security offices and many opticians. People who are registered blind are entitled to a special tax allowance of £1,480 a year.

A great deal of practical help can be obtained by contacting the Royal National Institute for the Blind. In addition to giving general advice and information it can supply a range of special equipment, details of which are listed in a free catalogue. There are also a number of leaflets relating to blindness. For information, contact the **Royal National Institute for the Blind (RNIB)**, 105 Judd Street, London WC1H 9NE. T: 0845 766 9999.

Many elderly people with failing sight suffer from macular degeneration which affects their ability to distinguish detail. Although there is no known cure individuals can be helped to make the most effective use of their sight by special magnifiers and other aids, such as clip-on lenses that fit over normal spectacles.

For further information contact: **The Partially Sighted Society Sight Centre**, PO Box 322, Doncaster DN1 2XA. T:01392 210656. There are also centres in London and Doncaster.

Another helpful organisation is the National Library for the Blind, which lends books and music scores in Braille and Moon free of charge, and post-free, to any blind reader who registers with the service. For information, contact: **National Library for the Blind**, Far Cromwell Road, Bredbury, Stockport, Cheshire SK6 2SG, T:0161 355 2000.

Another special library is the **Talking Book Service**, Falcon Park, Neasden Lane, London NW10 1TB, T:0845 7023 153.

A regular tape of a local newspaper is available free from Talking Newspaper Groups, of which there are now 540 around the country. Also, for an annual membership fee – from £30 – listeners can enjoy national newspapers and magazines on cassette tapes, computer disk, CD-ROM or e-mail. For further information, contact: Tim McDonald, **Talking Newspaper Association of the United Kingdom (TNAUK)**, National Recording Centre, Heathfield, East Sussex TN21 8DB. T:01435 866102.

Yet another useful resource for those with limited vision is the special range of radio/radio cassette equipment provided by British Wireless for the Blind Fund. For further information, contact **BWBF Direct** on T:01634 832501.

For gardening enthusiasts, there is *Come Gardening*, a quarterly magazine available on audiotape and in Braille, and the **Cassette Library for Blind Gardeners** which is offered as an auxiliary service to subscribers. There are also residential courses for blind gardeners. Inclusive annual subscription is £5. For further information, contact: **Thrive**, The Geoffrey Udall Centre, Beech Hill, Reading RG7 2AT. T:0118 988 5688.

Also worth knowing, all the main banks will provide statements in Braille; and Barclaycard now also issues credit card statements in Braille, on request. Additionally, several institutions offer large print cheque books or templates for cheque books as well as other facilities, such as a taped version of their annual report. There is no extra charge for these services.

Finally, BT has introduced a free directory enquiry service for blind and disabled customers. To use the service you first need to register with BT who will issue you with a personal identification number. For an application form and other information, call the free Linkline on T:0800 800195.

Feet

Many people forget about their feet until they begin to give trouble. Corns and bunions if neglected can become extremely painful and ideally everyone, especially women who wear high heels, should have chiropody treatment from early middle age or even younger.

One of the problems of which chiropodists complain is that because many women wear uncomfortable shoes they become used to having painful feet and do not notice when something is more seriously wrong. The result can sometimes be ingrowing toenails or infections.

Chiropody is available on the National Health Service without referral from a doctor being necessary but facilities tend to be very over-subscribed, so in many areas it is only the very elderly or those with a real problem who can get appointments.

Private state registered chiropodists are listed in the *Yellow Pages*. Alternatively, you can write to the Society of Chiropodists and Podiatrists which is the professional association for state registered chiropodists, asking for some local names off their list. In addition to keeping a list of members, the Society can supply a number of free leaflets on foot health. The address to contact is: **Society of Chiropodists and Podiatrists**, 1 Fellmongers Path, Tower Bridge Road, London SE1 3LY. T:020 7234 8620.

Help the Aged has produced a helpful leaflet called *Fitter Feet* which advises on how to avoid problems, gives tips on buying shoes and provides information on where to go for further help and treatment. Available free from: The Information Department, Help the Aged, 207–221 Pentonville Road, London N1 9UZ.

Hearing

As they grow older, a great many people suffer some deterioration in their sense of hearing. Should you begin to have difficulty in hearing people speak clearly or find that you are having to turn up the television, it is probably worth having a word with your doctor.

Your GP may well refer you to a consultant who will advise whether a hearing aid would be helpful; or alternatively may refer you direct to a hearing aid centre for examination and fitting.

You can either obtain a hearing aid and batteries free on the NHS or you can buy them privately. Either way, you may like to read a booklet entitled *How to Use Your Hearing Aid* (HAG 2), available free from Department of Health, PO Box 777, London SE1 6XH.

There are many other aids on the market that can make life easier. BT, for example, has a variety of special equipment from louder bell tones to flashing light systems. You can either try out the gadgets at one of BT's Aids Centres or, for further information, dial BT free on T:0800 800150.

There are also a number of specialist organisations that can give you a lot of help, both as regards hearing aids and other matters.

Hearing Concern, 7–11 Armstrong Road, London W3 7JL. T:020 8743 1110; Helpline: 0845 0744 600; Text: 020 8742 9151. Hearing Concern runs an advisory service, publishes a selection of practical leaflets and offers information for the family on communication with hard of hearing people. It also publishes a quarterly magazine, free to members, and has local social clubs throughout the UK. Membership is £12.50 a year.

RNID, 19–23 Featherstone Street, London EC1Y 8SL. T:0808 808 0123; 0808 808 9000 (textphone). RNID publishes a comprehensive range of free leaflets and fact-sheets for deaf and hard-of-hearing people. Titles include: *All About Hearing Aids*; *Age-related Hearing Loss*; *Ears and Ear Problems* and *Equipment for Deaf People*. Membership including bi-monthly magazine is £17.99 a year; £10.99 for retired people.

British Tinnitus Association, Ground Floor, Unit 5 Acorn Business Park, Woodseats Close, Sheffield S8 0TB. Freephone: 0800 018 0527. Tinnitus is a condition that produces a sensation of noise, for example hissing or ringing, in the ears or head. The BTA helps to form self-help groups and provides information through its quarterly journal *Quiet*.

British Deaf Association, 1–3 Worship Street, London EC2A 2AB. Textphone: 0800 6522 965; T:0870 770 3300. The BDA works to protect the interests of deaf people and also provides an advice and advocacy service.

Friends and family can do a great deal to help those who are deaf or hard of hearing. One of the essentials is not to shout but to speak slowly and distinctly. You should always face the person, so they can see your lips and avoid speaking with your hand over your mouth or when smoking. It could also be helpful if you, as well of course as deaf people themselves, were to learn British Sign Language. In case of real difficulty, you can always write down your message.

Teeth

Everyone knows the importance of having regular dental check-ups. Many adults, however, slip out of the habit which could result in their having more trouble with their teeth as they become older.

Dentistry is one of the treatments for which you have to pay under the NHS, unless you have a low income. Charges are based on 80 per cent of the cost up to a current maximum (April 2002/03) of £366. If you or your partner are in receipt of income support or income-based jobseeker's allowance, you are entitled to free NHS dental treatment. You may also receive some help if you are in receipt of the working families tax credit or the disabled person's tax credit; for details, see leaflet HC11.

Even if you do not belong to any of these groups, you may still get some help if you have a low income. To find out if you qualify fill in claim form HC1 (obtainable from social security offices, main post offices and NHS dentists). To avoid any nasty surprises when the bill comes along, it is important to confirm with your dentist before he treats you whether you are being treated under the NHS. This also applies to the hygienist should you need to see one. Best advice is to ask in advance what the cost of your treatment is likely to be.

Denplan. For those who like to be able to budget ahead for any dental bills, a scheme called Denplan Care could be of interest. Described as 'a low cost preventive dental healthcare plan for dental health', the idea is that you pay a fixed amount each month which entitles you to normal treatment as and when required.

Among other benefits, membership of Denplan entitles you to emergency treatment worldwide up to £690 per claim; insurance cover of up to £10,000 per claim for accidental damage and access to a 24-hour UK helpline. Fees are calculated according to your dental history and the state of your teeth and gums at time of joining, with £14.45 a month being about average. Registration must of course be with a Denplan member dentist but as over a third of dentists in the UK participate this should not be a problem.

For further information, contact: **Denplan Ltd.**, Denplan Court, Victoria Road, Winchester, Hampshire S023 7RG. T:0800 401 402.

Another company offering a similar scheme but with, as yet, fewer dentists on its books is: **CDC**, 115 Station Road, Hayes, Middx UB3 4BX. T:020 8848 1028.

A number of other companies offer insurance cover for dental treatment, including: Cigna (T:0800 515 876) and Boots (T:0845 840 1111). If you would welcome advice on helping you to select the scheme that best suits your needs, you might like to contact **The Private Health Partnership**, T:01943 851133.

Prevention is always better than cure. The British Dental Health Foundation's dental helpline, Word of Mouth, provides free, independent and impartial advice on all aspects of oral health. Free literature is available on a wide range of topics including patients' rights, finding a dentist and dental care for older people. The service can be contacted Monday to Friday, from 9 a.m. to 5 p.m., on T:0870 333 1188. Or write enclosing sae to: **British Dental Health Foundation**, 2 East Union Street, Rugby CV22 6AJ.

Another useful free factsheet is: *Dental Care and Older People* from Age Concern, Freepost (SWB 30375), Ashburton, Devon TQ13 7ZZ. Freephone: 0800 009966.

Personal relationships

Retirement is a bit like getting married again. It involves a new life style, fresh opportunities and inevitably, as with marriage, a few adjustments for both husband and wife to make. He will have to accustom himself to no longer going to a regular job. She will have to start thinking about another meal to prepare and may possibly feel that she will have to reorganise her domestic or working routine. Alternatively, of course, it may be the other way round with the wife giving up her job and the husband, who has long acted as household chef, sighing at the prospect of a regular gourmet lunch to produce.

After years of perhaps hardly seeing each other for more than a few hours a week except for weekends, suddenly almost the whole of every day can be spent together. He may feel hurt that she does not appear more delighted. She may feel guilty about wanting to pursue her normal activities especially if, as more and more women are, she is still working after her husband has retired. Even in the most loving marriages, the first weeks of retirement – for either partner – can produce tensions, which may even affect their sex life, that neither had anticipated.

Normally with good will and understanding on both sides any difficulties are quickly resolved and an even deeper, more satisfying relationship develops. However, for some couples it does not work out so easily and it may be helpful to seek skilled guidance.

Relate, Herbert Gray College, Little Church Street, Rugby, Warwickshire CV21 3AP. T:01788 573241. Relate offers a counselling service to people who are experiencing difficulties in their marriage or other personal relationships. Their clients are all ages. Some have been married twice or even three times. Many are in the throes of actually seeking a divorce but are trying to prevent the bitterness that can develop. Some come for advice because of upsets with their stepchildren. Others may have sexual problems.

Sometimes couples come together. Sometimes, either the husband or wife comes alone. Often, the emphasis is not on a particular crisis but instead because couples are seeking to make their marriage more positively enjoyable, as at retirement.

Relate offers counselling through 103 centres around the country. You can either find the address in the local telephone directory under 'Relate' or 'Marriage Guidance' or by contacting the national headquarters above. Each counselling session costs about £25 and at the initial interview counsellors will discuss with clients what they can reasonably contribute. However, no-one is turned away if they cannot afford to make a contribution.

The address of the equivalent organisation in Scotland is: **Couple Counselling Scotland**, 18 York Place, Edinburgh EH1 3EP. T:0131 558 9669.

Marriage Care offers a similar service, plus also a confidential telephone helpline, for those who are having problems with their marriage or other close personal relationship. Contact: **Marriage Care**, Clitherow House, 1 Blythe Mews, Blythe Road, London W14 0NW. T:020 7371 1341. Helpline: 0845 660 6000 (open Monday to Friday 10 a.m. – 4 p.m.).

Other helpful organisations include:

Scottish Marriage Care, 196 Clyde Street, Glasgow G1 4JY. T:0141 204 1239.

Accord, Central Office, Columba Centre, Maynooth, Co. Kildare. T: 00 353 1 505 3112.

Two other organisations that may be of interest are:

Albany Trust, Counselling, Psychotherapy & Consultancy Services, 280 Balham High Road, London SW17 7AL. T:020 8767 1827. Offers counselling for people with difficulties in relationships, depression or psychosexual problems. Cost is £40 per session (£55 for couples). After the initial consultation, fees are negotiable for those on low income.

SPOD, 286 Camden Road, London N7 0BJ. T:020 7607 8851. SPOD is a registered charity, partly funded by the Department of Health, that offers a telephone counselling service to people with a disability (or whose partner has a disability) who are experiencing sexual or relationship problems. In particular, it can usually put individuals in touch with a professional counsellor in their area and also publishes a wide range of leaflets. The telephone line above is open Tuesdays and Thursdays, 11 a.m. to 2 p.m.

Help for grandparents

A sad result of today's divorce statistics is the risk to grandparents of losing contact with their grandchildren. While some divorcing parents lean over backwards to avoid this happening, others – maybe through force of circumstance or hurt feelings – deny grandparents access or even sever the relationship completely.

Until 1989 grandparents had very few rights. However, following the introduction of the Children Act, grandparents may, with the leave of the court, seek an order for contact with the child or for residence so that the child may live with them. Generally, a fee is payable to the court for the making of such applications unless the grandparent is in receipt of community legal service funding (formerly legal aid).

In reaching a decision the paramount consideration for the court must be what action, if any, is in the best interest of the child. If the court feels that the child is of sufficient age and understanding it will take into account his or her views in reaching a decision.

Recourse to the law is never a step to be taken lightly and should obviously be avoided if there is the possibility that a more conciliatory approach could be successful. An organisation with considerable experience of advising grandparents is: **Grandparents' Federation**, Moot House, The Stow, Harlow, Essex CM20 3AG. T:01279 428 040. Advice Line, T:01279 444964.

Depression

Depression can be first cousin to marriage and other relationship problems. It is fairly common after bereavement, can be caused by worries or may occur after an operation. Sometimes too, as a number of retired people find, it develops as a result of loneliness, boredom or general lack of purpose. Usually people come out of it of their own accord: either as time heals sorrow or the scars of a relationship that has gone wrong; or in the case of those who are temporarily bored and fed up, as they find new interests and outlets for their talents.

If the condition persists for more than a few days, a doctor should always be consulted as depression can create sleeping difficulties as well as affect the appetite and lead to an overall feeling of physical malaise. The sufferer can be caught in a vicious circle of being too listless to enjoy anything, yet not having done enough during the day to be able to sleep at the proper time.

Another reason for consulting a doctor is that depression may be due to being physically run down, as after 'flu, and all that is required is a good tonic – or perhaps a holiday.

Sometimes, however, depression persists and it may be that rather than medicines or the stimulus of a new activity, individuals may feel they need to talk to someone outside the family circle who has a deeper understanding of what they are experiencing. There are several organisations that may be able to help.

Depression Alliance, 35 Westminster Bridge Road, London SE1 7JB. T:020 7633 0557. This is a self-help organisation which offers assistance both to anyone suffering from depression and also to the carers of sufferers. As well as a nationwide network of groups where individuals can meet to provide mutual support, there is a penfriend scheme and a written advisory service for members. Depression Alliance also produces a quarterly newsletter and a wide range of booklets. For further information, write to the headquarters enclosing 9" x 7" sae or 'phone the above number for information pack.

The Samaritans, The Upper Mill, Kingston Road, Ewell, Surrey KT17 2AF. T:020 8394 8300. The Samaritans are available at any time of the day or night, every single day of the year. They are there to talk or listen for as long as an individual needs or wants to be able to speak to another person. Although most people think of The Samaritans as being a telephone service for those who feel they may be in danger of taking their own lives, anyone who would like to can visit their local branch. You do not need to feel positively suicidal before contacting The Samaritans; if you are simply depressed, they will equally welcome your call. The service is free and completely confidential. To find your local branch, look in the telephone directory under 'S'.

Mind (The Mental Health Charity), Granta House, 15–19 Broadway, London E15 4BQ. T:020 8519 2122. Mind works for a better life for people with experience of mental distress. It has offices in England and Wales and more than 200 local associations which offer a wide range of special facilities and services, including: housing with care, day centres, social clubs, advocacy and self-help groups. Mind also runs a national information line and produces a variety of publications including a bi-monthly magazine. For further information ring the Mind Infoline on T: 0845 766 0163; or contact your local association (see telephone directory).

Sane, 40 Adler Street, London E1 1EE. T:020 7375 1002. Sane is a mental health charity which, in addition to initiating and funding research, operates a helpline to give individuals in need of emotional support or practical information the help they require. It can provide information about: local and national mental health services, mental health law and the rights of both service users and carers. SANELINE is open every day, from 12 noon to 2 a.m., T:0845 767 8000; all calls are charged at local rates.

Some common afflictions

Quite probably you will be one of the lucky ones and the rest of this chapter will be of no further interest to you. It deals with some of the more common afflictions, such as back pain and heart disease, as well as with disability. However, if you are unfortunate enough to be affected, or have a member of your family who is, then knowing which organisations can provide support could make all the difference in helping you to cope.

Arthritis and rheumatism

Although arthritis is often thought of as an older person's complaint, it accounts for the loss of an estimated 70 million working days a year in Britain.

Arthritis Care, 18 Stephenson Way, London NW1 2HD. T:020 7380 6500. Arthritis Care is a registered charity and national welfare organisation working with, and for, people with arthritis. It encourages self-help and has over 600 local branches offering practical support including transport and social activities. Arthritis Care also provides specially adapted holiday centres and publishes various leaflets and booklets. Publications subscription, including membership and *Arthritis News* six times a year, is £18. For address of local branch, contact the regional office or the UK office above.

Arthritis Research Campaign, Copeman House, St. Mary's Court, St. Mary's Gate, Chesterfield S41 7TD. T:0870 850 5000. In addition to funding a major research programme, **arc** publishes a large number of free booklets on understanding and coping with arthritis and also produces a quarterly magazine *Arthritis Today*, which is available to supporters paying a £15 annual donation.

Back pain

Four out of five people suffer from back pain at some stage of their lives. While there are many different causes, doctors agree that much of the trouble could be avoided through correct posture, care in lifting heavy articles, a firm mattress and chairs that provide support in the right places. Whether you have problems or are hoping to prevent them, the following two organisations could be helpful.

The Back Shop, 14 New Cavendish Street, London W1G 8UW. T:020 7935 9120. A shop and mail order business that sells medically approved products that help prevent back trouble or may provide relief for those who suffer. The shop is staffed by assistants with specialised knowledge of back pain and related problems. A free mail order catalogue is available on request.

BackCare, 16 Elmtree Road, Teddington, Middlesex TW11 8ST. T:020 8977 5474. BackCare is a registered charity that funds research into the causes and treatment of back pain and also publishes a range of leaflets and fact sheets to help back pain sufferers. BackCare has local branches around the country which organise talks, lectures and exercise classes as well as social activities and fund-raising events. Membership which includes copies of the quarterly magazine, *Talkback*, is £17.50. Information packs are available at £4.

Cancer

One of the really excellent trends in recent years is a far greater willingness to talk about cancer. Quite apart from the fact that discussing the subject openly has removed some of the dread, increasingly one hears stories of people who have made a complete recovery. Early diagnosis can make a vital difference. Doctors recommend that all women should undergo regular screening for cervical cancer and women over 40 are advised to have a routine mammography to screen for breast cancer at least once every three years. Computerised cervical screening systems for women aged 20 to 64 and breast cancer screening units for women aged 50 to 64 are available nationwide. Anyone with a lump or swelling, however small, should waste no time in having it investigated by a doctor.

There are a number of excellent support groups for cancer sufferers. Rather than list them all, we have only included two as CancerBACUP, as well as its own services, can act as an information service about other local cancer support groups.

CancerBACUP, 3 Bath Place, Rivington Street, London EC2A 3JR. Offers a free and confidential telephone information service to help people affected by cancer. Calls are answered by a qualified nurse who has the time, knowledge and understanding to answer your questions and listen to how you may be feeling. Call Freephone: 0808 800 1234. The information service is open from 9 a.m. to 7 p.m., Monday to Friday.

There are regional centres in Nottingham (T:0115 840 2650), Glasgow (T:0141 553 1553), Manchester (T:0161 446 8100), Coventry (T:02476 535 099) plus three in London. CancerBACUP also produces many booklets and factsheets on different types of cancer and their treatment. A publications list is available on request.

Breast Cancer Care, Kiln House, 210 New King's Road, London SW6 4NZ. Helpline: 0808 800 6000. Offers practical advice, information and emotional support to women who have, or fear they have, breast cancer or benign breast disease. Its services include helplines, free leaflets, a prosthesis fitting service and one-to-one support from volunteers who have themselves experienced breast cancer, or whose partner has been affected.

Chest and heart diseases

The earlier sections on smoking, diet, drink and exercise list some of the most pertinent 'dos and don'ts' that can help prevent heart disease. The advice is not to be taken lightly.

Latest statistics reveal that UK death rates from coronary heart disease are among the highest in the world, killing over 125,000 people a year and responsible for one in five of all deaths. Although people tend to think of heart attacks as particularly affecting men, over four times as many women die from heart disease as from breast cancer.

In an effort to reduce the casualty rate, the British Heart Foundation publishes a range of 'help yourself' booklets, designed to create greater awareness of how heart disease can best be prevented through healthy living. For further information, ring BHF's Heart Healthline on T:0870 600 6566 or write to: the **British Heart Foundation**, 14 Fitzhardinge Street, London W1H 6DH.

Diabetes

Diabetes is caused by there being more glucose in the blood than the body is able to use properly. It can sometimes be treated by diet alone; sometimes pills or insulin may also be needed. Diabetes can be diagnosed at any age, although it is common in the elderly and especially among individuals who are overweight.

Diabetes UK, 10 Parkway, London NW1 7AA. T:020 7424 1000. Careline: 020 7424 1030. Diabetes UK aims to improve the lives of people with diabetes. It offers information and support to affected individuals, their families and friends. There are around 430 local groups throughout the UK which hold regular meetings and social activities. Membership which includes a regular magazine *Balance* costs £20 a year. For details, contact the above address.

Migraine

Migraine affects over 6 million people in the UK. It can involve severe head pains, nausea, vomiting, visual disturbances and in some cases temporary paralysis.

The Migraine Trust, 45 Great Ormond Street, London WC1N 3HZ. T:020 7831 4818. The Trust funds and promotes research, holds international symposia and runs an extensive support service which includes a helpline, free information pack, factsheets and a regular newsletter.

Osteoporosis and menopause problems

Osteoporosis is a disease affecting bones, which become so fragile that they can break very easily, with injuries most common in the spine, hip and wrist. It affects one in three women (also one in twelve men) and often develops following the menopause when body levels of oestrogen naturally decrease.

National Osteoporosis Society, Camerton, Bath BA2 0PJ. T:01761 471771. The Society offers help, support and advice on all aspects of osteoporosis. There is a medical helpline staffed by specialist nurses, a range of leaflets and booklets and also a network of over 130 local support groups throughout the UK. Membership, which is optional but which would entitle you to free newsletters and publications, is £10 (£15 for non-sufferers). All donations gratefully received. For further information and list of publications, contact the above address.

Women's Health Concern (WHC), PO Box 2126, Marlow, Bucks SL7 2NB. T:01628 488065. Helpline: 01628 483612. WHC is a national charity, founded in 1972 to offer professional advice and counselling to women with gynaecological and hormonal disturbance problems, in particular with the menopause and proper use of HRT. As well as distributing literature to some 70,000 women a year, it runs a telephone counselling service and also sees patients face-to-face at its centres in Newcastle, Surbiton, Blandford Forum, Birmingham and London. As a charity, WHC charges no fee but donations are very much appreciated. For further information, contact the above address.

The Menopause Exchange, PO Box 205, Bushey, Herts WD23 1ZS. T:020 8420 7245. Produces a quarterly newsletter with the aim of providing reliable and easily understood information about the menopause and other health issues of concern to women in midlife. Annual subscription is £15.

Stroke

Over 130,000 people in the UK suffer a stroke each year. Stroke is like a heart attack in the brain. It is unpredictable in its effects which may include muscular paralysis or weakness on one side, loss of speech or loss of understanding or language, visual problems or incontinence. Prevention is similar to the prevention of heart disease.

The Stroke Association, Stroke House, Whitecross Street, London EC1Y 8JJ. T:0845 303 3100. The Stroke Association works to prevent stroke illness and helps stroke patients and their families. It produces a wide range of publications and provides advice and welfare grants to individuals through its London office and regional centres. Its Community Services, Dysphasia Support and Family Support help stroke sufferers through home visits and over 400 stroke clubs provide social and therapeutic support. A free information pack and details of local groups are available from the London office above.

AIDS

If you are concerned about the possibility of Aids and do not feel able to consult your doctor, there are a number of helpful organisations to which you can turn for advice. Among those with telephone helplines are:

National Aids Helpline. T:0800 567123. Free service, available 24 hours a day.

Terrence Higgins Trust Helpline. T:020 7242 1010. Hours are 12 noon to 10 p.m. every day.

London Friend. T:020 7837 3337. This is a befriending and counselling agency for gay and bi-sexual men and women. The helpline is open every evening between 7.30 p.m. and 10 p.m. London Friend also runs a number of social support groups and offers face-to-face counselling where requested.

'Health-Lines' or **'Aids-Lines'**, as they are sometimes called, have been set up in a number of local areas. Ask telephone directory enquiries for the number of your nearest centre.

GUM Clinics. Genito-urinary-medicine clinics exist in all NHS Hospitals. You can get telephone numbers from your strategic health authority. Or look in the telephone directory under 'Venereal' or 'Sexually transmitted diseases'.

Disability

Disability is mainly covered in Chapter 15, Caring for Elderly Parents, so if you or someone in your family has a problem, you may find the answer you need there. In this section, we list some of the key organisations that can help you and include one or two other points that may be useful for younger people.

Local authority services

Social Services Departments (Social Work Department in Scotland) provide many of the services which people with disabilities may need, including:

- practical help in the home, perhaps with the support of a home help
- adaptations to your home, such as a ramp for a wheelchair or other special equipment for your safety
- meals on wheels
- provision of day centres, clubs and similar
- issue of orange badges for cars driven or used by people with a disability (in some authorities this is handled by the Works Department or by the Residents' Parking Department)
- advice about other transport services or concessions that may be available locally.

In most instances, you should speak to a social worker who will either be able to make the arrangements or signpost you in the right direction. He/she will also be able to tell you of any special facilities or other help provided by the authority.

Occupational therapists, who can advise about special equipment and help teach someone with a disability through training and exercise how best to manage, also come within the orbit of the Social Services Department.

Health care

Services are normally arranged either through a GP or the local authority health centre. Key professional staff include:

- health visitors: qualified nurses who, rather like social workers, will be able to put you in touch with whatever specialised services are required
- district nurses: will visit patients in their home
- physiotherapists: use exercise and massage to help improve mobility, for example after an operation
- medical social workers: employed at hospitals and will help with any arrangements before a patient is discharged.

Employment

The Disablement Resettlement Officer helps and advises people looking for work and can also give information about any available grants, for example towards the cost of fares to work and for special equipment that may make work life easier. Ask at your nearest Jobcentre.

Council tax

If someone in your family has a disability, you may be able to claim a reduction on your council tax. If you have an orange badge on your car, you may get a rebate for a garage. You would normally apply to the Housing Benefits Officer but different councils employ different officers to deal with this. Either ask a councillor or enquire at the town hall whom you should approach.

Equipment

If you have temporary need of, say, a wheelchair, you will normally be able to borrow this from the hospital or your local British Red Cross branch. If you want equipment including aids for the home on a more permanent basis, the best source of information is the Disabled Living Foundation Equipment Centre where all sorts of equipment can be seen and tried out by visitors. Information advisers are on hand to demonstrate the material and to give advice. Contact: **Disabled Living Foundation**, 380–384 Harrow Road, London W9 2HU. To check opening hours, which vary, T:020 7289 6111. For advice and information about equipment for daily living, telephone the Helpline on T:0845 130 9177.

If it is not possible for you to come to London, the **Disabled Living Centres Council** (T:0161 834 1044) will be able to recommend a centre nearer your home.

Another extremely useful organisation to contact for advice on equipment and home adaptations is RADAR – see 'Helpful Organisations' below.

Finally, BT supplies more than 70 aids to enable people with disabilities to use the telephone more easily. These are illustrated in a booklet entitled *BT Guide for People Who Are Disabled or Elderly*. For further information, dial BT free on 0800 800150.

Helpful organisations

Fount of all knowledge on almost every topic to do with disability is: **Royal Association for Disability and Rehabilitation (RADAR)**, 12 City Forum, 250 City Road, London EC1V 8AF. T:020 7250 3222; Minicom: 020 7250 4119.

RADAR can give help and advice across a very wide spectrum including: statutory and voluntary services, mobility issues, holidays, employment, civil rights and housing. It publishes a monthly bulletin with sections on legislation and other helpful information for people with disabilities.

RADAR also helps with the National Key Scheme for Toilets for Disabled People. About 400 local authorities throughout the country have fitted standard locks to their loos – and issue keys to disabled people – so that the facilities can be used by them, even when these would normally be locked against vandalism. RADAR supplies keys at a charge of £3.50 incl. p&p for those who are unable to obtain an NKS key in their own locality. Applicants must state their name and address together with a declaration of disability. For all further information and RADAR's publications list, contact the above address.

Age Concern England runs the Ageing Well UK Programme. Over 160 local projects recruit volunteer 'senior health mentors' to encourage people of their own generation to improve and maintain their health. For further information, contact ActivAge Unit, Age Concern England, Astral House, 1268 London Road, London SW16 4ER. T: 020 8765 7321.

Disability Alliance, Universal House, 88–94 Wentworth Street, London E1 7SA. T:020 7247 8776; Rights Advice Line: 020 7247 8763 (both Minicom access). Provides advice over the telephone on social security benefit issues. Also publishes a number of guides including the annual *Disability Rights Handbook* which is packed with information about benefits and services both for people with disabilities and their families. Price is £13.50 (post-free); £9.50 for customers in receipt of any benefit.

Health Education Board for Scotland, Woodburn House, Canaan Lane, Edinburgh EH10 4SG. T:0131 536 5500. The HEBS has an excellent library and can provide leaflets and information on all aspects of positive health.

Disability Wales/Anabledd Cymru, Wernddu Court, Caerphilly Business Park, Van Road, Caerphilly CF83 3ED. T:029 2088 7325. Disability Wales works to promote the rights, recognition, inclusion and support of disabled people in Wales.

Greater London Action on Disability, 336 Brixton Road, London SW9 7AA. T:020 7346 5800; Minicom: 020 7326 4554. GLAD provides information on non-medical disability issues. Among other material, it produces a monthly newsletter (price, £8 a year).

DIAL UK (National Association of Disablement Information and Advice Lines), St Catherines, Tickhill Road, Doncaster DN4 8QN. T:01302 310123. Offers free independent advice on all aspects of disability through a network of some 140 disability advice centres. Contact DIAL UK for details of your local centre.

Help the Hospices, 34–44 Britannia Street, London WC1X 9JG. T:020 7520 8200. Help the Hospices is a national charity dedicated to the support of hospices, their special day centres and home care teams and other providers of palliative care for terminally ill people and their families. For a list of independent charitable hospices, which are free to patients, and other information contact the above address.

Mobility Advice and Vehicle Information Service (MAVIS), O'Wing Macadam Avenue, Old Wokingham Road, Crowthorne, Berkshire RG45 6XD. T:01344 661000. MAVIS is an information service run by the government which advises on all aspects of mobility – in particular, problems associated with driving. Its services include assessment of older motorists wishing to return to driving after a stroke or other disabling illness and advice on car adaptations to relieve the pain of arthritic joints or other conditions that make driving uncomfortable. While general information is free, charges for more specialised services are as follows: driving ability assessment for individuals who have suffered a disability, £60; advice on car adaptations including test driving, £40; vehicle familiarisation session, £15.

Motability, Customer Information Services, Goodman House, Station Approach, Harlow, Essex CM20 2ET. T:01279 635666. Motability is a registered charity set up to assist recipients of the higher rate mobility component of disability living allowance to use their allowance to lease, or buy, a car or a powered wheelchair or scooter. Motability's charitable fund can help those unable to afford the advance payment on some lease vehicles – or necessary adaptations to the vehicle. Grants are available for the least expensive option to meet individuals' basic mobility needs.

Wellbeing. A free health information service, essentially for people in Scotland. Answers calls 24 hours a day and can put individuals in touch with over 1,600 organisations. T:0141 248 1899.

Useful reading

Health and Well-Being: A Guide for Older People (HB6/96). Department of Health booklet, obtainable by writing to Department of Health, PO Box 777, London SE1 6XH.

14 Holidays

Holidays can be even better when you retire! You do not have to plan months ahead in order to fit in with colleagues. You can avoid the peak periods which are almost invariably more expensive and crowded. You can also enjoy real flexibility, in a way that is usually not possible when you are working, by taking several mini breaks when you feel like it or going away for an extended period.

Additionally, one of the great things about retirement is the availability of concessionary prices, including in particular the possibility of cheaper fares and reduced charges for hotel accommodation.

Apart from these benefits, the fact of being retired makes very little difference. You can ride an elephant in India, take a caravan around Europe, sail on the Norfolk Broads, go bird-watching in Scotland, combine a holiday with a special interest such as painting or music, enrol for summer school, exchange homes with someone in another country or sign on for a working holiday, such as voluntary conservation activity or home-sitting, for which you get paid.

The choice is literally enormous. The list of suggestions which follows is by no means exhaustive. You can go to any travel agent and collect further ideas by the dozen. However, the two main criteria we adopted in deciding which, among the thousands of possibilities, to include, were: variety and holidays which, one way or another, offer some special attraction or specifically cater for those aged 50 and above.

Some of the options verge on the exotic, with prices to match; others are extremely reasonable in cost. There are suggestions which are only suitable for the really fit and active; at the other extreme, there are a number of inclusions which would only be of interest to individuals in need of special care. Some of the choices may strike you as mad, risky, humdrum, too demanding – or simply not your style. But retirement is a time for experimentation and trying something entirely different is half the fun.

For ease of reference, entries are listed under such headings as 'arts and crafts', 'sport', 'self-catering holidays' and so on. Inevitably, some organisations criss-cross several sections but to avoid repetition, the majority are only featured once in what, hopefully, is the most logical place.

At the end of the chapter, there is a general information section with brief details about insurance, concessionary fares and other travel tips.

Prices and some of the other detailed information, while accurate at the time of writing, may be slightly out of date as programmes change (sometimes at very short notice) and it is impossible to keep track. The intention is to provide an indication of fairly typical events together with an idea of price bracket.

Art appreciation

The choice ranges from visiting some of the famous sights of Egypt to exploring Jordan or Minoan Crete. It also includes the music and drama festivals held in many parts of the country, as well as some of the famous festivals overseas.

National Association of Decorative & Fine Arts Societies, NADFAS House, 8 Guilford Street, London WC1N 1DA. T:020 7430 0730. NADFAS is an organisation of over 300 UK societies. It organises tours abroad, through Cox and Kings, to places of interest to its members. Recent examples have been Jordan – Castles, Caravans and Cities (7 days, £1,050) and Minoan Crete (8 days, £1,025). There is a single room supplement. For information about your local Society, write to NADFAS at the above address.

Specialtours, 2 Chester Row, London SW1W 9JH. T:020 7730 2297. Specialtours arranges holidays in many countries of the world for tour groups from the National Art Collections Fund and other prestigious societies. Destinations planned for 2003 include: The Czech Republic, Italy, Spain, Libya, Jordan, Butrint, Austria, France, Moscow, Germany, Sweden, Slovakia, Samarkand, the Netherlands, Ethiopia and the USA. The costs include flight, hotels, usually meals, travel within the country, guides and entrance fees. Prices start from about £900. Non-members are welcome but are required to pay the subscription fee to the sponsoring society before the tour begins.

The British Museum Traveller, 46 Bloomsbury Street, London WC1B 3QQ. T:020 7436 7575. The British Museum organises cultural tours, accompanied by their own specialist lecturers, to visit the sites of some of the great civilisations of the past. Parties are limited to a maximum of 25 people and hotels are of good standard. The 2002 programme included: Egypt: The Story of the Nile (14 days, £1,895); Discover Lebanon (8 days, £1,198); Christmas in Petra (7 days, £1,275) and many more.

Festivals

A veritable feast of music, drama and the arts. The most famous are those held at Edinburgh and Aldeburgh. Over the years the number of festivals has been growing and these are now a regular feature in many parts of the country. To find out what is going on where, you should contact the Arts Council or your Regional Arts Association. **The British Federation of Festivals** publishes a *Year Book*, which should be in your local reference library, listing festivals around the country. The major events, especially at the bigger festivals, tend to get booked well in advance, so early application for tickets is advisable.

Aldeburgh Productions, Snape Maltings Concert Hall, Snape, Saxmundham, Suffolk IP17 1SP. T:01728 687100. Box Office: 01728 687110. The Aldeburgh Festival of Music and the Arts is held annually during June (Fifty-sixth Festival 6–22 June 2003). A varied programme of classical and contemporary music and opera at Snape Maltings Concert Hall, Jubilee Hall and other local venues is complemented by exhibitions, talks, walks and films. There are also three other festivals, variously at Easter, during August and in October. In addition there is a year-round programme of concerts and master classes which are open to the public. For further details contact Aldeburgh Productions at the above address.

Edinburgh International Festival, The Hub, Edinburgh's Festival Centre, Castlehill, Royal Mile, Edinburgh EH1 2NE. T:0131 473 2000. The 2003 Edinburgh International Festival runs from 10th – 30th August. A free brochure giving details of music, theatre, dance, opera and other events is available from late March. For further information, contact the above address.

Arts and crafts

The focus here is on taking courses or just participating for the pleasure, rather than viewing the works of others. The choice includes wood carving and other crafts, painting and music. Further suggestions are also given in Chapter 9, Leisure Activities.

Benslow Music Trust, Little Benslow Hills, Hitchin, Herts SG4 9RB. T:01462 459446. Benslow Music Trust provides opportunities for the study and practice of music, with a year-round programme of weekend and other courses for amateur players and singers of all standards. The programme includes chamber music, choral and solo singing, music appreciation, Alexander Technique, jazz, solo wind, orchestras, brass ensembles and early music. The fee for a weekend or two-day course averages £155 with full board or £130 non-resident.

Crafts Council, 44a Pentonville Road, Islington, London N1 9BY. T:020 7278 7700. The Council keeps a list of organisations that run their own short craft courses or that can provide information on where similar courses are being held.

West Dean College, West Dean, Chichester, West Sussex PO18 0QZ. T:01243 811301. West Dean College, housed in a beautiful mansion surrounded by landscaped gardens and parkland, organises short residential courses in contemporary and traditional crafts, the visual arts, photography, music and gardening – variously lasting a weekend, five or seven days. A typical programme includes: stained glass, calligraphy, textile design, woodcarving, picture framing, music appreciation, blacksmithing, sculpture, drawing and painting, jewellery, cane and rush seating and many more. Prices, which include full board, range from about £180 for a weekend to £425 for a five-day course.

There are full-time one/two-year Diploma programmes in the conservation and restoration of antiques, run in conjunction with the British Antique Dealers' Association, as well as tapestry weaving and musical instrument making, all of which are validated by the University of Sussex.

Coach holidays

Some of the coach companies organise holidays proper, as distinct from simply offering a mode of transport. Advice note from other holidaymakers: before embarking on a lengthy coach tour, try a few shorter excursions to see how you cope with the journey. Some people swear by the comfort, others find coach travel very exhausting.

Frames Rickards Coach Tours, 4 Fountain Square, 123–151 Buckingham Palace Road, London SW1W 9SH. T: 020 7233 6668. Frames Rickards operate a comprehensive range of coach tours in the UK. Prices cover: travel in reclining-seat coach; full breakfast and dinner; rooms with private bath or shower and all sightseeing. Year 2002 examples included: Devon and Cornwall, three days from £240; Welsh Wonderland, four days from £340; Quick Look at Britain, from £340.

National Express, T:08705 808080. Provides a scheduled coach network to over 1,200 destinations across England, Scotland and Wales and also a wide choice of short-break holidays. An attractive example is a London short break from about £45, including return travel and one night's accommodation with breakfast. Overseas breaks include: Paris, Amsterdam, Brussels and Dublin.

Field studies

The number and variety of courses arranged by National Parks and Field Centres almost deserves a special publication of its own. In addition to wildlife studies, the choice, which varies from one centre to another includes: archaeology, photography, painting and drawing, ecology, crafts, rambling and many others.

National Parks are located in Northumberland, Lake District, Yorkshire Dales, North York Moors, Peak District, Snowdonia, Pembrokeshire Coast, Brecon Beacons, Exmoor, Dartmoor and the Norfolk and Suffolk Broads. To give you a flavour of the varied programmes that are on offer in the parks, a mini description of typical events in the Peak District follows.

Peak District National Park Centre, Losehill Hall, Castleton, Derbyshire S33 8WB. T:01433 620373. Weekend and week-long special interest breaks include: painting and illustration, natural history, bird watching, navigation and rambling. All courses are led by experts. Losehill Hall is set in beautiful countryside with comfortable single and twin-bedded en-suite accommodation. Prices start from £160 for a weekend and are fully inclusive of meals, accommodation, transport and tuition.

Field Studies Council (FSC), Head Office, Montford Bridge, Shrewsbury SY4 1HW. T:01743 852100. The FSC offers over 600 leisure and special interest courses at its 15 centres in England, Wales and Northern Ireland. The courses cover a wide variety of subjects including: Walking, Cycling and Outdoor Pursuits; Natural History; Ecology and Conservation; Botany; Birds and Animals; History and Archaeology; Painting and Drawing; Photography; Crafts and Traditional Skills and many other general interest activities.

The Centres are based in: the Lake District, Yorkshire Dales, Snowdonia, Shropshire, Pembrokeshire, Exmoor, South Devon, Suffolk, the North Downs, Epping Forest and County Fermanagh.

The courses vary in length from a weekend to a week. The cost (2002) which includes full board, accommodation, tuition, and transport during excursions is around £118 for a weekend; £260 for a full week.

The FSC also organises natural history and art holidays overseas. Planned destinations for 2003 include: New Zealand, the Canadian Rockies and the Hidden Parts of Catalonia.

Free brochures are obtainable from the above address. Membership of the FSC, which is optional, costs £10 a year and entitles members to a reduction in course fees.

Scottish Field Studies Association, Kindrogan Field Centre, Enochdhu, Blairgowrie, Perth PH10 7PG. T:01250 881286. The Centre runs a wide range of residential courses in natural history and the countryside covering most aspects of the environment. Examples include: Mountain Flowers, Fungi, Birds, Identifying Mosses and Walking. Cost is about £335 for a week including tuition, board and lodging. An annual programme can be obtained from the centre.

Historical holidays

Holidays with a particular focus on history are becoming increasingly popular. The choice includes: battlefield tours, exploring famous archaeological sites of Britain and the highly imaginative 'production' at Kentwell Hall.

Holts' Tours – Battlefields & History, The Plough, High Street, Eastry, Kent CT13 0HF. T:01304 612248. Holts' offer a choice of over 200 battlefield, historical and archaeological tours to some 80 countries worldwide. All are accompanied by a specialist guide-lecturer and local experts are also used. Highlights of the 2002 programme included: World War One (four-day introductory tour, £395); Waterloo (four days, £495); The Anglo-Zulu War (11 days, £2,595).

Most tours are half board in good standard hotels with private facilities. Every effort is made to cater for single travellers, many of whom are ladies. Special group tours can be arranged.

Kentwell Hall, Long Melford, Suffolk CO10 9BA. T:01787 310207. Every summer Kentwell Hall recreates a living panorama of what life was like during the Tudor period. Participants are required to provide their own costumes and to enter into the role of a character living at the time: for example, this could be a 16th-century cook or hay-maker. You are expected to prepare yourself by reading and there are Open Days at Kentwell with briefing sessions. The event lasts for three weeks and participants can stay for one, two or three complete weeks. The only cost involved is the provision of a suitable costume. All meals are free and there is camping space available. Those requiring more comfort can book into one of the many local bed and breakfast hotels.

Middlebrook-Hodgson Battlefield Tours, Lancaster Farm, Tumby Woodside, Nr Boston, Lincolnshire PE22 7SP. T:01526 342249. Military historians, Martin Middlebrook and Michael Hodgson, organise coach tours for small groups (about 26 people) to visit World War One and Two battlefields. Recent tours (variously between three and five nights) were to the Somme, Ypres, Loos, Verdun, Gallipoli, Normandy and Arnhem. The cost is from about £250 for all travel, bed and meals, local tours and guiding.

Should you wish to visit a particular grave, the **Commonwealth War Graves Commission**, 2 Marlow Road, Maidenhead, Berkshire SL6 7DX, T:01628 634221, will help you identify the exact location.

People interested in visiting war cemeteries, battlefields or where they were stationed should contact **Remembrance Travel**, The Royal British Legion Village, Aylesford, Kent ME20 7NX, T:01622 716729/716182. Remembrance Travel is the recognised authority in this field and each year visits are organised to about 20 different countries in the Far East, Africa and Europe. Approximate prices, which include all travel, half-board, accommodation in a good standard hotel and some excursions (including a non-denominational Service of Remembrance in one of the Commonwealth War Cemeteries) range from £99 for a two-day pilgrimage to France/Belgium; £640 for an eight-day visit to Italy; and £1,570 for a ten-day pilgrimage to Burma. A brochure is obtainable from the above address.

Under the Government's War Widows Grant-in-Aid Scheme, run by the Legion, war widows can apply for a government grant to cover seven-eighths of the cost of one visit.

Language courses

If you are hoping to travel more when you retire, being able to speak the language when abroad will greatly add to your enjoyment. Quickest and easiest way to learn is in the country itself. There are attractive opportunities for improving your French, German, Italian, Spanish and even Japanese.

The British Institute of Florence, Piazza Strozzi 2, 50123 Florence, Italy. T:(from England) 00 39 055 2677 8200. The Institute, a joint Anglo-Italian institute of over 80 years' standing, runs two-to-four week graded Italian language courses throughout the year for learners of all ages and levels. There are also courses in history of art, drawing, opera, watercolour painting, wine appreciation and cooking. Various events such as lectures and concerts are arranged by the Institute for students and local people. Summer courses are available near the Tuscan coast.

Accommodation can be arranged in local homes, *pensioni* and hotels: cost is from about £14 a day. Tuition fees vary according to the length and intensity of the course you choose: for example, a four week Italian course costs (2002) £280. A week's intensive Art in Florence course (in English) costs £275.

En Famille (Overseas), 4 St. Helena Road, Colchester CO3 3BA. T:01206 546741. The Agency arranges short or long stays with host families for people who want an insider's view of a European country. There is a registration fee of £35 plus a selection and booking fee of £30. You pay travel costs and about £190-£270 a week full board; or £165-£240 demi-pension. En Famille matches your background and interests to the families on their register (a majority are in France) and sends you details of a selection of host families from which to choose. The Agency also runs some homestays combined with language courses in France and Spain.

Eurocentres, 26 Dean Park Road, Bournemouth BH1 1HZ. T:01202 554426. Eurocentres run language learning courses in France, Italy, Japan, Switzerland, Spain, Germany and Russia for adults of all levels. The courses last from a couple of weeks to about six months and are set in the life and culture of the host country. Most people live with families but Eurocentres will also arrange hotels.

A 4-week French course in Paris with accommodation (single room) and half board costs about £4,500; a two-week course in Florence with half board costs about £650. In all cases, fares are additional.

Goethe-Institut Inter Nationes, Helene-Weber Allee 1, Postfach: 190419, D80637 München, Germany. T:00 49 89 159 21 200. For German courses in Britain: **Goethe Institut**, 50 Princes Gate, Exhibition Road, London SW7 2PH. T:020 7596 4004. The Goethe Institut offers one, two, four or eight-week German language courses, for beginners to examination level, at 15 centres in Germany. The instruction is designed so that you can follow from one level to another in all centres. Price of a four-week course in Germany averages Euro 900. Accommodation costs about Euro 400 for the whole month. Course fees include such items as excursions and cultural events as well as the help of course assistants.

Instituto Cervantes, 102 Eaton Square, London SW1W 9AN. T:020 7245 0621. Can provide details of Spanish language and culture courses for adults, throughout Spain.

Other people's homes

Living in someone else's home for free is one of the cheapest ways of enjoying a holiday. There are two ways of arranging this. You can exchange your home with another person, in this country or abroad. The onus is on you to select a suitable property and to decide whether the person with whom you are swapping is likely to care for your home properly. The alternative is to become a homesitter and, for a modest payment, mind someone else's property while they are away.

Home exchange

Unless you are lucky enough to hear about someone through personal recommendation, probably the easiest method of finding a swap (and of advertising your own home) is through a specialised directory or website listing. In most cases, this is not an introduction service as such. The exchanges are normally arranged direct between the two parties concerned, who agree the terms between themselves. Some people even exchange their cars and pets.

Home Base Holidays, 7 Park Avenue, London N13 5PG. T:020 8886 8752. Home Base Holidays operates an international home exchange agency. Accommodation varies from small city apartments to large country homes complete with swimming pool. Annual registration costs from £29 for access to listings on their website. Your own exchange offer is also included on the website. Home Base Holidays does not get involved in the actual arrangements but is happy to give advice. Information pack, including sample listings, sent on request.

Homelink International, Linfield House, Gorse Hill Road, Virginia Water, Surrey GU25 4AS. T:01344 842642. Publishes five directories a year, containing in the region of 12,000 listings, covering 50 countries throughout the world. Annual membership which costs £95 includes internet listing and entitles members to feature their home in one of the directories (December, February, April, May or June) but to receive all five books if they wish to do so. There is a supplement of £10 for inclusion of a photograph of the property.

Intervac International Home Exchange, Coxes Hill Barn, North Wraxall, Chippenham, Wiltshire SN14 7AD. T:01225 892011. Can provide information about some 12,000 properties, ranging from bedsitters to mansions, across 50 countries worldwide. Detailed hints are provided on points to check before agreeing an exchange and discounts are available on holiday insurance. To use the service, there is a membership fee of £99.

Homesitting

Retired people are generally considered ideal. Homesitting means that you provide a caretaking service and get paid for doing so. Duties variously involve: light housework, plant watering, care of pets and sometimes tending the garden. First class references are naturally required.

Absentia, Little London, Berden, Bishops Stortford, Herts CM23 1BE. T:01279 777412. Absentia sitters variously: offer a holiday care service, provide long-term specialised care (as, for example, if a property is vacant during probate) or will care for a home and any pets if the owner has to go into hospital. They will also visit the patient, take in mail and generally keep them in touch with domestic events during their absence. Pay, depending on duties, averages from £147 a week.

Home and Pet Care Ltd., Nether Row Hall, Hesket-New-Market, Wigton, Cumbria CA7 8LA. T:01697 478515. Although Home and Pet Care get some requests for simply caring for a property while the owners are away, they specialise in offering pet care as part of the service. Predictably, most requests are for dogs and cats. However, they cheerfully accept any type of pet from a baby alligator to a mynah bird. Pay varies according to the species of the pet in question but averages about £115 a week.

Homesitters, Buckland Wharf, Buckland, Aylesbury, Bucks HP22 5LQ. T:01296 630730. Homesitters are looking for mature, responsible people, non-smokers with no children or pets. Assignments may be for short or long periods. It is useful to have your own car. Pay is from £56.00 a week depending on responsibilities, plus a food allowance of £42 per week and travel expenses. With agreement, a Homesitter can take their partner. The houses can be anything from a city centre apartment to an isolated country mansion.

Universal Aunts, PO Box 304, London SW4 0NN. T:020 7738 8937. Universal Aunts organise a home and pet sitting service for absent owners and recruit single or pairs of mature, responsible people for this work. Payment is £32 a day plus travelling expenses (whether you go alone or with a partner). All applicants for the home sitters panel are interviewed before acceptance on the list.

Overseas travel

Many of the big tour operators make a feature of offering special holidays, designed for the over 55s. For fun, we have also included companies that specialise in arranging cruises and packaged motoring holidays; and also information about time-sharing. For up-to-date details, you should check the brochures.

Explore Worldwide Ltd., 1 Frederick Street, Aldershot, Hants GU11 1LQ. T:01252 760100. Explore Worldwide arranges more than 300 tours to over 100 countries. Examples of recent tours include: Cruising the Greek Islands (8 days from £565); Discovering Wildlife on the Galapagos Islands (12 days from £1,949); Experiencing the Wonders of India (10 days from £925); The Highlights of China (11 days from £1,395) and Safaris in Tanzania (11 days from £1,045). Accommodation varies from camping to modest hotels and rustic lodges. Prices quoted are per person and include return air flights from the UK.

Relais de Silence. These are a French group of independently owned hotels with a network of about 300 hotels throughout Europe and about 15 in Britain. They offer tranquil, rural settings in 2, 3 and 4-star comfort at reasonable prices with good food and a family-like atmosphere. For more information, contact the **French Government Tourist Office**, 178 Piccadilly, London W1J 9AL. T:09068 244123 (60p a minute).

Saga Holidays Ltd., The Saga Building, Freepost (F049), Folkestone, Kent CT20 3ZH. T:0800 056 5880. Saga holidays are exclusively for people aged 50 and over. There is a large range of options worldwide including, among others: ocean and river cruising (including Saga's own cruise ship, Saga Rose) safaris, short and long stay resort holidays and multi-centre tours. There is also a selection of special interest holidays including, for example, gardens, music, walking and computer studies.

Saga Holidays are sold direct and not through a travel agent. For further information and brochures, telephone the above number.

Thomson Young at Heart, Greater London House, Hampstead Road, London NW1 7SD. T:0870 550 2555. Short and long-stay winter sunshine holidays in hotels and apartments for people over 55, with special Young at Heart Representatives. The resorts are in: Mainland Spain, the Algarve, Canary Islands, Majorca, Madeira, Malta, Tunisia, Greece, Cyprus, Egypt and Italy. Special interest holidays include walking, dancing, bowls and natural relaxation. There are entertainments at all hotels. Many feature a variety of special offers and some do not charge single room supplement.

Cruises

Cruises seem to become more exotic by the year. Among the programmes that we particularly liked are those arranged by:

Fred. Olsen Cruise Lines, Fred. Olsen House, White House Road, Ipswich, Suffolk IP1 5LL. T:01473 742424. Operates three ships, with departures mostly from Dover or Southampton year round, as well as a wide range of fly/cruise options. Destinations include: Europe, the Arctic and Scandinavia, Baltic, Africa, Caribbean, South America, Canada and North America. Prices range from £395 (per person, inside cabin, twin occupancy) for a four-night cruise to Guernsey and Rouen to £9,860 (per person, outside cabin, twin occupancy) for 72 nights around South America. Suites and single occupancy cost proportionately more.

Norwegian Cruise Line, 1 Derry Street, Kensington, London W8 5NN. T:0800 181 560. Fly-cruise and stay holidays in the Caribbean, Alaska, New England and Canada, Bermuda, South America, Panama Canal, Hawaii, Mexico, the Mediterranean and Scandinavia. Nine nights Caribbean Cruise, from £999 per person; 9 nights Alaskan Cruise with hotel stay, from £1,759.

P&O Cruises, Richmond House, Terminus Terrace, Southampton, Hants SO14 3PN. T: 0870 5726 726. P&O Princess has three separate cruising programmes:

P&O Cruises (T: 0845 3555 333) offer a wide range of destinations including two Round World Cruises, the Mediterranean, Atlantic Isles, Scandinavia and the Caribbean;

Princess Cruises (T: 0845 3550 800) has ten ships cruising to Alaska, the Far East and Australia, the Caribbean, Panama Canal, Mexico, South America, Hawaii and the South Pacific, New England, the Mediterranean and Scandinavia;

Swan Hellenic Cruises (T: 0845 3555 111) runs East and West Mediterranean, Baltic and British Isles, Red Sea and Black Sea, Gulf, India and Far East cruises for lovers of art and archaeology; also river cruises on the Rhine and Danube.

Cargo Ship Cruises. If price is one of the main considerations and you don't mind sacrificing the dressing-up and organised activity, a happy solution could be to travel via cargo ship. Accommodation and facilities (there is often a swimming pool) vary according to the size and type of vessel, which could be a roll-on, roll-off container or a banana boat going to South America and back. Two of the best known operators offering a wide range of choices are: **Strand Voyages** (T:020 7836 6363) and **Cargo Ship Voyages** (T:01473 736265).

Page & Moy Ltd., PO Box 155, Leicester LE1 9GZ. T:0870 010 6444. Choosing the cruise most likely to offer what you want no longer entails elaborate detective work thanks to a comprehensive listing published by travel agents Page & Moy. Discounts are offered on every booking and there are also many exclusive special offers. Cruise specialists are available seven days a week to give assistance.

Motoring holidays abroad

A number of organisations – including in particular some ferry operators – offer 'packages' for the motorist which include ferry crossings, accommodation and insurance. While these often provide very good value, some people prefer to make all their own arrangements in order to give them exactly what they want. Whatever your preference, if a main concern is carefree motoring, maybe one of the options suggested below could provide a happy solution.

Brittany Ferries offer short-break holidays in France and Spain including accommodation, breakfast and return car ferry crossings. The 2002 choice included: four nights' bed and breakfast in Normandy from £152 per person; four nights in the Loire Valley, in two-star hotel, from £163; and a five-night bed and breakfast break in Spain from £347 per person. All the above are based on holidays in September with two people travelling together. There is also a selection of gites holidays in France. For further details, contact your local travel agent or call Brittany Ferries direct on T:08705 360360.

Automobile Association, Fanum House, Basingstoke, Hants RG21 4EA. The AA offers several helpful products and services for motoring at home and abroad including: route planning, maps, AA Five Star Europe Breakdown Assistance and travel guides.

RAC Motoring Services, Travel Services, PO Box 1500, Bristol BS99 2LH. As well as motoring breakdown cover for Europe, RAC offers a range of overseas single trip or annual travel insurance, plus international driving permits, camping cards and other essential documents. For further details, call free on T:0800 550055.

Tips when motoring abroad. All basic common-sense but, given the tales of woe one hears, many holiday-makers forget the obvious precautions:

- have your car thoroughly serviced before you go;
- take the following with you: a tool kit, manual for your car, a rented spares kit, a gallon can, a mechanic's light which plugs into the cigarette lighter socket and at least one extra set of keys;
- always lock your car and park it in a secure place overnight (nearly 75 per cent of luggage thefts abroad are from cars).

Unless you are taking one of the packages which include insurance, you should contact your insurance company or broker well ahead of time to arrange special insurance cover. ABI information sheet *Holiday Insurance and Motoring Abroad* summarises the essentials you need to know when taking your car overseas. Obtainable free from the **Association of British Insurers**, 51 Gresham Street, London EC2V 7HQ. A further possibility is to contact either the AA or RAC overseas travel department. Both have facilities for helping you if you become stranded and welcome non-members.

Two other recommended organisations are: **Europ Assistance**, Sussex House, Perrymount Road, Haywards Heath, West Sussex RH16 1DN. T:01444 442211; **Green Flag**, Cote Lane, Leeds LS28 5GF. Freephone: 0800 400638.

Advice from seasoned travellers is to have information about garages, spare parts and the legal rules of the country, or countries, through which you are driving. The requirements – and documents you need to carry – are not the same for all European countries and failure to produce the right bond or special permit could mean a fine, or even imprisonment.

If your main purpose in taking your car is to enjoy the freedom it offers when you reach your destination, rather than the journey itself, it is worth looking at the Motorail facilities to Southern France and Italy and the long range ferries to Spain and Portugal which save on wear and tear and may be no more expensive than the extra cost of petrol plus overnight stays.

If instead of taking your own car, you plan to hire a car or motor scooter overseas, you will probably have to buy special insurance at time of hiring the vehicle. Make sure that this is properly comprehensive (check for any excesses or exclusions) and that at very least it gives you adequate third party cover. If in any doubt, you would be recommended to seek advice from the local motoring organisation as to the essential requirements – including any foreign words or terms you particularly need to understand before signing.

Short breaks

A very large number of organisations offer short break holidays all year round with special bargain prices in spring and autumn. Many British hotels have winter breaks from November to April when full board can be considerably cheaper than the normal rates. Likewise, many overseas travel operators slash prices during the off-peak seasons. While the brochures contain plenty of suggestions, including some glorious city breaks, for very best value (and often all the more fun for being unplanned) see the newspapers and Internet for last minute bargains.

Timesharing

Timesharing is an investment in long-term holidays and, as with other investments, should not be undertaken lightly. The idea is that you buy the use of a property for a week or longer, either for an agreed term or in perpetuity. Your timeshare can be lent to other people, sub-let or left eventually in your will. Most timeshare schemes allow you to swap your week(s) for one in other developments throughout the world for your annual holiday.

A week's timeshare will cost from under £3,500 to more than £15,000 depending on the location, the size of the property, the time of year and the facilities of the resort. The average is around £6,500 for one bedroom (peak season). Maintenance charges could cost another £180 or so a week and you should always check that these are linked to some form of cost of living index such as the RPI and ascertain – item by item – precisely what the charges cover. Another useful point to check is that there is an owners' association linked to the property.

While the great majority of people enjoy very happy experiences, stories about unscrupulous operators still occur. You should be on your guard against dubious selling practices which, despite efforts by industry watchdogs, have not been entirely stamped out. In particular, you should beware timeshare scratchcards and likewise be wary of enticing promotional gifts such as a 'free' holiday flight to visit the property. Above all, do not be stampeded into signing any commitment until you have had the validity of all aspects of a proposed contract thoroughly vetted by a solicitor. You might also like to check whether the operator is a member of the OTE (Organisation for Timeshare in Europe), formerly the Timeshare Council.

For some years, buyers signing contracts in the UK have had a 14-day cooling-off period. Now, thanks to the 1994 Timeshare Directive, all EU member countries must provide a 10-day minimum cooling-off period and a full prospectus to EU member country residents in their own language. In the UK, there is now also a ban on timeshare providers taking a deposit during the cooling-off period. However, this may not apply to deposits signed outside the UK and buyers who are asked to give a deposit to a third party, such as a trustee, should check carefully before parting with their money.

Among the terms you need to be specially careful about are the future management/maintenance charges (these have been known to sky-rocket within a year or so of purchase) and the potential resale value of a property – or its timeshare weeks/timeshare points – which sometimes has been found to be very substantially below the initial purchase price. Also timeshare owners in Spain could be liable for a property tax.

Although you cannot be too careful, there are hopeful signs that the industry is tightening itself up by the imposition of more regulation and stricter vetting procedures.

The OTE is the regulatory body dedicated to promoting the interests of all with a legitimate involvement in the industry. It offers potential buyers free advice and information. Contact: **OTE**, Rue Defacqz 78–80, 4th Floor, 1060 Brussels, Belgium. T:00 32 2 533 3069 (please enclose sae).

Most reputable companies also belong to one of two worldwide exchange organisations:

RCI Europe, Kettering Parkway, Kettering, Northants NN15 6EY. T:0870 6090 141.

Interval International Ltd., Coombe Hill House, Beverley Way, London SW20 0AR. T:020 8336 9300.

Existing owners wishing to sell their property should be on their guard against unknown resale agents contacting them 'on spec' and offering, in exchange for a registration fee, to act on their behalf. While some may be legitimate, the OTE has received complaints about so-called 'agents' taking money and doing nothing further. A telephone call to OTE will establish whether the company is a member body. If not, leave well alone. If you are actually seeking an agent, OTE can provide you with a list of reputable resale companies (please enclose sae).

Retreats

Some people want to have no more than peace and quiet for a few days. If you would welcome the idea of a retreat you might like to contact:

The Retreat Association, The Central Hall, 256 Bermondsey Street, London SE1 3UJ. T:020 7357 7736. The Association's annual journal *Retreats* gives details of 240 retreat centres in Britain and Ireland, together with their programmes.

Another publication listing more than 300 retreats in the UK, Ireland, France and Spain is *The Good Retreat Guide* by Stafford Whiteaker (Rider, £12.99).

Self-catering and other low budget holidays

If you cannot quite manage to survive on a tenner a day, some of the suggestions in this section need hardly cost you very much more. This applies especially if you are camping, caravanning or renting very simple accommodation with friends. The list includes: farm cottages, hostels, university accommodation, forest cabins and other rentals of varying degrees of sparseness or comfort.

Camping & Caravanning Club, Greenfields House, Westwood Way, Coventry CV4 8JH. T:024 7669 4995. Operates a national network of over 90 full facility club sites, most of which are open to non-members. There are, however, many advantages in joining the Club. Members receive several free publications including a monthly magazine *Camping and Caravanning* and the *Big Sites Book* which lists details of over 3,500 UK camp sites. The Club also offers members a wide range of services including an RAC-operated breakdown and recovery service, insurance and a full foreign touring service including ferry bookings and overseas site reservations. Members aged over 55 normally pay reduced fees on Club sites. Membership costs £27.50 plus £5 joining fee.

Venuemasters, The Workstation, Paternoster Row, Sheffield S1 2BX. T:0114 249 3090. Venuemasters is a consortium of university and college centres that let residential accommodation in the vacation periods. Some of the centres let rooms throughout the year and others have self-catering flats. Charges start from about £22 for bed and breakfast; £52 per person, per week, for a self-catering apartment.

English Country Cottages, Stoney Bank, Earby, Barnoldswick BB94 0AA. T:0870 585 1111 (brochures). T: 0870 585 1155 (bookings – England and Wales).

Country Cottages in Scotland. T: 0870 585 1133 (brochures). T:0870 444 1133 (bookings).

Country Cottages in Ireland. T: 0870 585 1166 (brochures). T: 0870 585 1177 (bookings).

The 'cottages' range enormously in size, style and location and are variously capable of sleeping between 2 and 22. Many are available for long or short breaks all year round, with low out-of-season prices from November to March. Apply for a free brochure which gives full details and photographs of properties.

Farm Stay UK Ltd., National Agricultural Centre, Stoneleigh Park, Warwickshire CV8 2LZ. T:024 7669 6909. Many farms take paying guests, let holiday cottages or run sites for tents or caravans. Farm Stay members offer a range of high quality accommodation, all Tourist Board inspected, plus a glimpse of life on a farm. The Farm Stay Holiday Guide *Stay on a Farm* contains information on over 1,000 good value farm holidays all over Great Britain and Northern Ireland. Bed and breakfast facilities are normally from about £18 upwards. Many farms provide an evening meal, if required. Self-catering cottages start at around £150. The Guide is available free from the address above.

Forestry Commission, 231 Corstorphine Road, Edinburgh EH12 7AT. T:0131 314 6100. The Forestry Commission lets fully equipped log cabins in Scotland, Yorkshire and Cornwall. These sleep up to six people and cost from £149 a week per cabin. The Commission also runs 24 camping and caravanning sites throughout Britain.

Individual Travellers Company Ltd., Manor Courtyard, Bignor, Pulborough, West Sussex RH20 1QD. T:08700 771 771. Offers a large range of self-catering holidays in France, Corsica, Italy, Sicily, Spain, Portugal and New England (USA). Properties vary widely in price, size and amenities, from chateaux complete with swimming pool to modest but comfortable apartments. Some in Spain and Southern France are suitable for short or long winter booking. Many of the rentals include car hire and flights; other travel can be arranged.

Landmark Trust, Shottesbrooke, Maidenhead, Berkshire SL6 3SW. T:01628 825925. The Trust owns 170 buildings of special architectural interest, which out of peak season can be rented for less than a week. Sample prices (2002) are: £1,109 per week for a castle in Wales, sleeping six, in October; from £394 for a three-night weekend in November, for a tower in Kent, sleeping two; £344 for a mid-week stay, February-March, for a folly in Scotland, sleeping four people. The Trust has a fully illustrated Handbook, price £9.50 (refunded on first booking) from the above address.

Lee Abbey, Lynton, North Devon EX35 6JJ. T:01598 752621. Lee Abbey is a holiday, retreat and conference centre, run by a Christian community. Set in a 275-acre coastal estate, accommodation is either in the house or in self-catering units. Depending on the time of the year, visitors can stay for either a short break weekend or up to a fortnight. There is a Christian content to the holidays and guests can be involved as much or as little as they please. Costs vary according to season, starting from about £42 per night full board. There are reductions for clergy and their families.

M P Associates, 306 Wellingborough Road, Northampton NN1 4EP. T:01604 230505. Specialises in low-cost, long winter holidays (three or four months) in Spain, Portugal and Tenerife. Accommodation varies from one-bed apartments to four-bed villas. Rents are reasonably nominal but in exchange visitors are expected to maintain the properties as they would their own homes. For further details, send large sae (57p).

National Trust Holiday Cottages. The National Trust has a wide variety of holiday cottages and flats in many areas of England, Wales and Northern Ireland with varying accommodation for 2 to 14 people. Although very popular in the high holiday seasons, there are usually plenty of vacancies at other times of year. A brochure, including information as to suitability for people with disabilities, is available from major National Trust Shops or by writing to PO Box 536, National Trust Enterprises, Melksham, Wilts SN12 8SX. T:0870 458 4411. Please enclose £2 to cover p&p costs.

For holiday accommodation in Scotland brochure, information on cruises, free copy of *Information About Trust Properties for Disabled Visitors* and annual handbook, contact **The National Trust for Scotland**, 28 Charlotte Square, Edinburgh EH2 4ET.

Scottish Farmhouse Holidays, Renton Terrace, Eyemouth, Berwickshire TD14 5RE. Over 100 farms and crofts in all areas of Scotland, plus a few farm houses in England, which take guests for two nights or longer. The cost is from £24 per night for dinner, bed and breakfast or from £20 per night bed and breakfast. SFH can offer help with car rental and ferry crossings. Free brochure available.

Venuemasters Scotland, PO Box 808, Edinburgh EH14 4AS. T:0131 449 4034. Provides holiday letting in ten of Scotland's leading universities. Between them, they offer over 10,000 beds in: Aberdeen, Dundee, Edinburgh, Glasgow, Heriot-Watt, Napier, Queen Margaret University College, St. Andrews, Stirling and Strathclyde. Choices range from secluded chalets to stylish apartments. Cost of bed and breakfast starts from about £26.

YHA (England and Wales) Ltd., Trevelyan House, Dimple Road, Matlock, Derbyshire DE4 3YH. T:0870 870 8808. Despite the name, YHA welcomes people of all ages. Membership (2002) costs £13 a year. This gives you access to over 200 youth hostels in England and Wales and over 4,500 worldwide.

Most hostels provide meals, self-catering facilities, cycle storage and local tourist information. The accommodation ranges from dormitories to twin rooms, some with en-suite facilities. Overnight charges vary according to the amenities and location of the centre: prices range from £9.50 to £24 in a London hostel.

P.S. Watch the Sunday newspapers. From about early January, the classified section begins to fill up with advertisements for rentals both in this country and overseas. Later in the season, this is the column to watch for slashed prices and other last minute bargains.

Special interest

This is the longest section – and a real mixed bag. It includes weekend courses and more formal summer schools, between them offering a huge range of subjects including: crafts, cooking, computer studies, drama, video techniques, wildlife, creative writing and many others. It also includes holidays in the more conventional sense, both in Britain and abroad, but with the accent on a hobby such as: bridge, folk dancing, yoga, photography, antiques and other pastimes. There are one or two pre-retirement courses included in the holiday programme.

They are impossible to categorise other than alphabetically because many of the organisations offer a veritable bran-tub of choices.

Centre for Alternative Technology, Machynlleth, Powys, Wales SY20 9AZ. T:01654 705950. Set in magnificent scenery in the mountains of Mid-Wales, the Centre is a working exhibition of the possibilities of alternative technology with displays of wind, solar and water power, organic gardens and high-insulation houses. The Centre is open daily to the public throughout the year, except Christmas and mid-January. Short residential courses are held frequently, ranging from two to five days, and subjects covered include renewable energy systems, organic gardening, vegetarian cookery, crafts and many others. Accommodation is in simple but comfortable two- to six-person bedrooms; there are also a few single rooms. Fees range from £125 to £800, including full board and all tuition fees. Pensioners and those on low incomes are charged less.

Opportunities also exist for voluntary work. For a week or fortnight volunteers live and work as members of staff, helping with all the tasks of running a busy, experimental visitor centre. Volunteers pay about £5 a day towards bed and board.

Countrywide Holidays, Miry Lane, Wigan, Lancs WN3 4AG. T:01942 823 456. Countrywide Holidays aims to provide warm hospitality, comfortable accommodation and sensible prices for holidays throughout the year. Many include walking or offer other activities, such as: folk dancing, bridge, photography, literature, singing and many more. The cost varies from about £275 per week in winter and from about £309 in summer including full board. There are special Vintage Holidays for people who enjoy more gentle walking and excursions, as well as traditional house parties over Christmas and New Year costing from £321 for five nights at Christmas and from £262 for four nights over the New Year.

Denman College (National Federation of Women's Institutes), Marcham, Abingdon, Oxfordshire OX13 6NW. T:01865 391991. Denman College is the WI's residential adult education college. It runs over 500 short courses (2, 3 and 4 nights) each year for WI members, their families and friends. These cost between £159 for a

2-night course and £299 for a 4-night course, including full board and tuition. Most of the accommodation is in single rooms, many with en-suite bathrooms. Courses cover such subjects as: antiques, IT, dance, drama, literature, crafts, aromatherapy and many others. For a programme, telephone the number above.

Earnley Concourse, Earnley, Chichester, Sussex P020 7JL. T:01243 670392. A residential centre near Chichester which holds weekend and week-long courses throughout the year on such subjects as: arts and crafts, music, wildlife, computer studies, cookery, keep fit, yoga and others. Charges are from £173 for a weekend.

HF Holidays Ltd., Imperial House, Edgware Road, London NW9 5AL. T:020 8905 9558; for brochures, T:020 8905 9388. HF Holidays offers walking and special interest holidays in a wide range of locations throughout Britain and abroad. The choice of activities includes, among others: golf, bridge, bowls, ballroom dancing, yoga, egg decorating, painting, photography, music making and birdwatching. There are also discovery coach tours and holidays, with gentle rambles and excursions, for those who want a more leisurely break. Prices start from £164 for three nights full board. The walking holidays range from easy walking to rock scrambling. A week's guided walking in Devon costs from £321 full board. A week in Austria costs from £399 half-board, including flight. Other overseas destinations include: France, Majorca, Malta, Switzerland, Italy, Canada, USA and New Zealand.

Mercian Travel Centre Ltd., 109 Worcester Road, West Hagley, Worcs DY9 0NG. T:01562 883795. Specialises in arranging bridge and bowling holidays in both England and overseas with choice of destinations including Spain, China, Egypt and many others. Fourteen nights in Tunisia is from £565; fourteen nights in Spain, from £580; fourteen nights in Croatia, from £385. All prices quoted are for half-board in twin-bedded room, inclusive of flights.

City & Guilds, 1 Giltspur Street, London EC1A 9DD. T:020 7294 2850. Special interest day, weekend and summer school courses are offered by many colleges and universities throughout the country. Choice of subjects is enormous ranging from yoga to astronomy, creative writing to video techniques. Prices vary very roughly from about £25 to £35 a night, including full board and tuition. Probably the easiest way to find out what is available is to obtain a copy of *Time to Learn*, published twice a year by City & Guilds. Price £4.95 plus p&p.

Old Rectory, Fittleworth, Pulborough, West Sussex RH20 1HU. T:01798 865306. The programme is tilted at those nearing retirement with the aim of stimulating new interests and opportunities. Typical courses, which last 3 to 7 days, include: painting, crafts, music and singing, bridge, writing, theatre, complementary therapies and many others. Prices start at £148 for a weekend residential course.

Pontin's, Sagar House, Eccleston, Chorley, Lancs PR7 5PH. T:0870 533 1199. Organise Special Event Holidays at the majority of their locations. These include such activities as: darts, snooker, bowling, line dancing and salsa. Year 2002 prices were from £99 per person for 4 nights, full board; and from £34 per person for a weekend self-catering break.

Summer Academy, Keynes College, The University of Kent, Canterbury, Kent CT2 7NP. T:01227 470402/823473. Offers summer study courses at 10 British universities. Prices start at £495 and cover full board for seven nights, tuition fees, course-related excursions and some social activities. Study topics include: heritage, archaeology, literature, creative writing, art history, natural history, computing and music. Accommodation is in single rooms with private bathrooms in university halls of residence.

Vegi-Ventures, Castle Cottage, Castle Square, Castle Acre, Norfolk PE32 2AJ. T:01760 755888. A holiday tour company that specialises in catering for vegetarians, offering an attractive range of destinations in Britain, Europe and wider afield. Accommodation is chosen very much with the food in mind and is variously in hotels, special guest houses and retreat centres with own cook. A flavour of this year's holidays includes: house parties (two nights, from £79); a week's walking and sightseeing in the Lake District including half board and guided walks (seven nights, £279); three weeks 'journey of a lifetime' in Peru with tour guide and half board (£1,300). Flights are willingly arranged but are not included in prices quoted above.

Sport

Holidays with on-site or nearby sporting facilities exist all over the country. However, if sport is the main objective of the holiday, it is often more difficult to know where to apply. The list that follows is limited to organisations that can advise you about organised residential courses or can offer facilities, rather than simply put you in touch with, say, your nearest tennis club. For wider information, see Chapter 9, Leisure Activities, which lists some of the many national sports associations.

Sportscotland, Caledonia House, South Gyle, Edinburgh EH12 9DQ. T:0131 317 7200. Sportscotland runs three national sports centres which offer courses for all levels in sports such as golf, hill-walking, skiing and sailing. Contact the above address for further information.

Boating

One or two ideas for holidays afloat are included as well as organisations that offer serious sailing instruction.

Royal Yachting Association, RYA House, Romsey Road, Eastleigh, Hants SO50 9YA. T:023 8062 7400. The RYA can supply you with a list of recognised schools which offer approved courses in sailing, windsurfing, motor cruising and power boating.

Blakes Holiday Boating, Spring Mill, Garby, Barnoldswick BB94 0AA. T:0870 2200 577. Blakes offer holiday boating throughout all the main waterways of Britain, and also in France, Ireland and Holland. Basic boating tuition is provided for novices. Costs vary according to season, size and type of accommodation. For example, a weekend boating on the Norfolk Broads during the spring and autumn months costs around £254 a couple. Boats for two to four people in France start at about £600 a week, including Dover-Calais ferry crossing. Pets are normally allowed on British holidays. For holidays abroad, Blakes will quote an inclusive price with travel arrangements.

French Government Tourist Office, 178 Piccadilly, London W1J 9AL. T:09068 244123 (60p a minute). Can provide information about houseboats and other craft for hire in France.

Hoseasons Boating Holidays, Lowestoft, Suffolk NR32 2LW. T:01502 501010 (UK holidays); 01502 500555 (overseas boating holidays). Hoseasons arrange boating holidays on the Norfolk Broads, the Cambridgeshire Waterways, the Thames, the canals of England, Scotland and Wales as well as boating holidays in France, Belgium and Germany. A July ferry-inclusive package to France, based on a party of four, costs (2002) around £250 per person per week. Prices for a week's holiday for four people on the Norfolk Broads start from about £100 per person during the low season.

Cycling

Cycling for Softies, Susi Madron's Cycling Holidays Ltd., 2 & 4 Birch Polygon, Rusholme, Manchester M14 5HX. T:0161 248 8282. Offers over 50 holiday options in ten regions of France from 7 to 14 nights, cycling between a network of small country hotels, with terrain varying from very easy to quite a few hills. The cost (2002) which included hotel, dinner, bed and breakfast, bicycles, equipment and information packs ranged between £694 and £1,360. Travel, which is extra, can be arranged.

Cyclists' Touring Club, 69 Meadrow, Godalming, Surrey GU7 3HS. T:0870 873 0060. CTC organises cycling tours in Britain and overseas and can also provide a great deal of extremely helpful information for cyclists wishing to organise their own holiday, including advice on accommodation and scenic routes. Organised UK cycle tours cost from about £175 a week with hostel accommodation or £300 a week bed and breakfast with evening meal. Overseas tours vary from about £300 for a fortnight's camping in Southern France to about £1,000 for three weeks in South Africa. CTC also offers members: free third-party insurance, free legal aid, a handbook and introductions to local cycling groups. Membership costs £28.50 a year; £17.50 for people aged 65 plus.

Railways. Cycles are normally allowed on trains, although some have strict limits as to the number they will accept especially during rush hours when they may be completely prohibited. On most services, advance reservation is required and there is usually a small charge. Around South-East England, long distance trains still carry cycles for free. For further details, ring National Rail Enquiries on T:08457 48 49 50.

Golf

Many clubs will allow non-members to play on weekdays when the course is less busy, on payment of a green fee. (A telephone call to the Secretary before arrival is normally advisable). Better still, if you can spare the time, many hotels around the country offer special golfing weekends and short-break holidays. If you fancy a golfing holiday overseas, **BA Holidays** (T:0870 242 4249) offers a wide choice, with favourite destinations including Florida, Spain and the Algarve in Portugal. The travel ads in newspapers and golfing magazines should also give you plenty of ideas. See also the Tourist Board activity booklets.

Rambling

Rambling features on many special interest and other programmes as one of the options on offer. Three organisations that specialise in rambling holidays are described below.

ATG Oxford, 69–71 Banbury Road, Oxford OX2 6PJ. T:01865 315678. Forget staying in cheap hostels and lugging around a rucksack with all your possessions for a week. Walking ATG Oxford style means staying in the most comfortable hotels in the area, having your luggage transported and enjoying the option of a ride on days when you feel like taking it easy. The emphasis is on visiting places of historical or artistic interest, exploring the scenic highlights and dining out on the best local cuisine.

Groups are limited to a maximum of 16 and most holidays last between 8 and 11 days, with Italy a favourite destination. Other choices include France, Sicily, Portugal, Spain, Greece, the Czech Republic and many others.

Prices exclusive of flight, range from £695 to £4,750. There are also tailor-made walking and cycling holidays (from £285) for those who prefer to travel more independently yet who welcome the services of a local representative including having their luggage transported.

Ramblers Holidays Ltd., PO Box 43, Welwyn Garden, Herts AL8 6PQ. T:01707 331133. Ramblers Holidays, in conjunction with the Ramblers' Association, organise guided walking tours at home and abroad, ranging in choice from just four or five hours a day relatively gentle exercise to maybe nine hours a day hard mountain trekking. Some trips focus on a special interest such as bird-watching or flowers or make a particular feature of visiting places of cultural interest. There is a huge choice of destinations including New Zealand, North America, China, South Africa, the Far East and most of Europe. Prices start from £220 for a week in Britain inclusive of all meals and VAT; and from about £380 for a week in Europe including flights and half board.

Waymark Holidays, 44 Windsor Road, Slough SL1 2EJ. T:01753 516477. Choice of graded walking holidays in Europe (from about 4 hours a day) throughout the year. Accommodation is in hotels and guesthouses. Cost for half board is from about £400 for seven nights, depending on the country and time of year. Cross-country skiing holidays are also offered during the winter.

Skiing

Ski Club of Great Britain, The White House, 57–63 Church Road, London SW19 5SB. T:020 8410 2000. The Ski Club runs skiing holidays in Austria, France, Italy,

Switzerland, Canada and the USA for over-50s who have some skiing experience. The cost is from about £750 a week for half board, travel and qualified leaders who accompany each group and will ski with you and offer advice, if wanted. Two weeks are also available.

A disability, including blindness or even an amputated leg need no longer be a bar to skiing, thanks both to the availability of special equipment and to the efforts of the British Ski Club for the Disabled who have specially trained guides to assist.

Also, many artificial slopes in England and Wales have reserved sessions with specialist guides for people with disabilities. A list can be obtained from the **British Ski Club for the Disabled**, Springmount, Berwick St. John, Shaftesbury, Dorset SP7 0HQ. T:01747 828 515.

Tennis

The Lawn Tennis Association, The Queen's Club, West Kensington, London W14 9EG. T:020 7381 7111. The LTA can provide details of residential courses at home and abroad.

For **other sporting holidays** see 'Tourist Boards' (page 380). Their publications list scores of suggestions for golfing, sailing and fishing holidays, pony trekking in Wales, skiing in Scotland and many others.

Wine tasting

Wine-tasting holidays are becoming more popular every year. The best guided tours ensure plenty of variety with a mix of visits, talks, convivial meals, free time for exploring and memorable tastings.

Arblaster & Clarke Wine Tours, Clarke House, Farnham Road, West Liss, Nr Petersfield, Hants GU33 6JQ. T:01730 893344. Operates tours to: France, Spain, Portugal, Italy, California, Australia, Hungary, Chile and South Africa. Most of the chosen regions are places of interest in their own right, famous for their historic buildings or picturesque scenery. Guides accompany every tour and though groups can be as large as 36, every effort is made to give personal attention and to create a friendly, informal atmosphere. A flavour of year 2002 visits included: champagne weekends (from £249); Swiss wine and jazz (five days, £799); week-long vineyard walks (from £949). Supplementary charge for single rooms.

Winetrails, Greenways, Vann Lake, Ockley, Dorking RH5 5NT. T:01306 712111. Wine-tasting holidays, combined with walking or cycling, in France, Italy, Spain, Portugal, Hungary and many others. Most last between 6 and 12 days and groups are limited to a maximum of twelve people. The average cost, inclusive of full board (excluding ferry or flight) is £90 – £140 per day. Trips for independent travellers and private groups can also be arranged.

Working holidays

There is scope for volunteers who would like to engage in a worthwhile project during their holidays. Activities vary from, for example, helping run play schemes to conservation work. In order to avoid repetition, only a couple of suggestions are listed here. For more information and ideas, see Chapter 12, Voluntary Work.

BTCV, 36 St. Mary's Street, Wallingford, Oxfordshire OX10 0EU. T:01491 821600. Anyone who would like a working holiday can become a conservation volunteer. BTCV organises over 500 conservation holidays each year throughout the UK. Projects usually last either a week or weekend and the work can vary from hedge-laying to repairing dry stone walls. No experience is necessary, only plenty of enthusiasm plus reasonable fitness. Prices start from £30 for a weekend, and £50 for a week, which includes food and accommodation. There are also over 70 international BTCV holidays, with projects ranging from protecting turtles in Thailand to building footpaths in Iceland.

BTCV Scotland, Balallan House, 24 Allan Park, Stirling FK8 2QG. T:01786 479697. BTCV Scotland offers training in conservation skills and opportunities to work as a conservation volunteer for as much or as little time as you can spare. There are 7 to 10-day conservation projects called 'Action Breaks' as well as weekend and single day events across Scotland. Type of work varies from conservation proper – drystone dyking, fencing, footpath conservation, historic building restoration and habitat management – to office jobs in BTCV Scotland's local centres. Cost of Action Breaks start at £50 for a week.

The National Trust Working Holidays, Wroxham, Norwich NR12 8DH. Brochureline T:0870 429 2428. The NT organises over 450 week and weekend outdoor conservation projects each year on Trust properties in England, Wales and Northern Ireland. Full guidance and instruction is given by Trust wardens and many of the projects are suitable for the reasonably fit and active of all ages, from 35 to 70. Cost is £29 per weekend; £54 per week.

Toc H, 1 Forest Close, Wendover, Aylesbury, Bucks HP22 6BT. T:01296 623911. Toc H organises short residential events throughout the year, normally lasting between a weekend and three weeks. Scope for volunteers includes running play schemes, activities with disabled people, conservation and manual work. There is a registration fee of between £10 and £30, depending on length of stay; accommodation and food, however, are usually free. For a copy of the Events Programme, contact the address above.

Holidays for singles

Many people would rather not go on holiday if it means travelling alone. Until recently single people, especially women over 50, were virtually ignored by the holiday industry. For a start, tour operators arranging group parties would often impose an age limit with the aim of keeping the sexes roughly in balance. There was (and still is) almost invariably a supplement for single rooms. And worst of all was the prospect of dining alone or of receiving unwanted attentions which could become embarrassing.

Over the past few years however, the outlook has been improving considerably. Many of the 'special interest holidays' listed on pages 371 to 373 are ideal for those without a partner, as are some of the 'working holidays' – see section above and also in Chapter 12, Voluntary Work. Additionally, one or two organisations are now springing up that cater specifically for solo holidaymakers. A couple that have been in existence for a number of years and are not essentially biased towards the under-35s (as many are) include:

Solo's Holidays, 54–58 High Street, Edgware, Middx HA8 7EJ. T:08700 746453. Specialises in arranging holidays for single people including a good selection for those aged 45 to 69. A vast choice of special interests is catered for including opera, golf, trekking in Nepal, cruises and many others. All tours are escorted 24 hours a day and most hotels are 4-star without single room supplement.

Travel Companions, 2 Coxhill Cottages, Boldre, Lymington, Hants SO41 8PS. T:01590 683005. An organisation for individuals aged 25 to 75 seeking a congenial companion with whom to go on holiday. All applicants complete a form listing their special interests, the type of destination they have in mind, as well as other requirements, and Travel Companions will then put them in contact with like-minded people. All personal information is handled in strict confidence. Travel Companions emphasises that it is not a dating service and makes the point that people often prefer to travel with someone of their own sex. Cost is £63.

Single Travellers Action Group, Church Lane, Sharnbrook, Bedford MK44 1HR. Founded in 1994 with the aim of fighting to get a better deal over the single room supplement, STAG now produces three newsletters a year giving details of supplement-free holidays and hotels both at home and abroad. It also arranges its own Christmas and other one or two-week holidays for single travellers aged 50 plus. Membership is £10 a year.

Holidays for those needing special care

Over the past few years, facilities for infirm and disabled people have at last been improving. More hotels are providing wheelchairs and other essential equipment. Transport has become easier. Specially designed self-catering units are more plentiful and of a higher standard. Also, an increasing number of trains and coaches are installing accessible loos. As a result of these improvements, many people with disabilities can now travel perfectly normally, stay where they please and participate in the entertainment and sightseeing without disadvantage. This section lists general sources of advice plus one or two organisations that arrange special care holidays.

Travel and other information

If you need help getting on and off a train or plane, inform your travel agent in advance. Arrangements can be made to have staff and, if necessary, a wheelchair available to help you at both departure and arrival points. If you are travelling independently, you should ring the airline and/or local station: explain what assistance you require, together with details of your journey in order that facilities can be arranged at any interim points, for example if you need to change trains.

A useful free leaflet is *Rail Travel for Disabled Passengers*, available from mainline stations.

A couple of other helpful publications are: *The Disabled Travellers' Guide*, £4.99 (free to AA members) obtainable by calling the AA Disability Helpline on 0800 262050; *Holidays in Britain and Ireland*, £8, available from: Royal Association for Disability and Rehabilitation, 12 City Forum, 250 City Road, London EC1V 8AF.

A useful organisation to contact could be: **Holiday Care**, 2nd Floor, Imperial Buildings, Victoria Road, Horley, Surrey RH6 7PZ. T:01293 774535; Minicom: 01293 776943. This is a central information and advice service on holiday opportunities in the UK and abroad for elderly and disabled people and their companions. The service is free. Details are available on transport and attractions, together with a range of leaflets (one for each region) listing inspected hotels with accessible accommodation.

If rather than simply point you in the right direction you are looking for an agency that can make all the practical arrangements, get on to ATS Travel which specialises in organising tailor-made holidays for people with disabilities. Among other services, they will arrange the journey from door-to-door, book suitable accommodation according to your requirements, organise the provision of special equipment and generally take care of any other details to make your holiday as enjoyable and trouble-free as possible. For further information, contact **ATS Travel**, 1 Tank Lane, Purfleet, Essex RM19 1TA. T:01708 863198.

Many local Age Concern groups are a mine of information. They can often put individuals in touch with organisations that assist with, say, transport; or that organise special care holidays, as do a number of Age Concern groups themselves. Age Concern England also publishes a free fact sheet *Holidays for Older People*, available from **Age Concern**, Freepost (SWB 30375), Ashburton, Devon TQ13 7ZZ; or telephone free T:0800 009966.

Another source to contact is your local Social Services department. Some local authorities arrange holidays or give financial help to those in real need.

Examples of special holidays

John Grooms, PO Box 36, Cowbridge CF71 7GB. T:01446 771311. Provides a variety of accessible holiday accommodation including three award winning hotels and a number of self-catering flats, bungalows and chalets.

Winged Fellowship Trust, Angel House, 20–32 Pentonville Road, London N1 9XD. T:0845 345 1970. Provides holidays for people with physical disabilities and their carers, in five purpose-built centres. There are plenty of activities in which to take part including theatre outings and other excursions. The Trust also organises holidays abroad. Cost is from about £370 per week. For a brochure, ring the above number.

Many voluntary organisations and others provide special holidays for those with a particular disability.

Arthritis Care, 18 Stephenson Way, London NW1 2HD. T:020 7380 6500. Runs four holiday centres specially adapted for people with arthritis. Price is £150–£275 a week, depending on the time of year. Specialist holidays include painting weeks, whist, Scrabble and birdwatching. Family weeks are also a feature.

Diabetes UK, 10 Parkway, London NW1 7AA. T:020 7424 1000. Provides information for holidaymakers who want to manage their diabetes confidently.

Royal National Institute for the Blind (RNIB), 105 Judd Street, London WC1H 9NE. T:0845 766 9999. Has two hotels, specially catering for blind and partially sighted people. Additionally, RNIB can provide advice about suitable hotels, self-catering holidays, accommodation in London, outdoor activity and educational holidays.

Multiple Sclerosis Society of Great Britain & Northern Ireland, MS National Centre, 372 Edgware Road, London NW2 6ND. T:020 8438 0700. Runs several respite care and holiday homes throughout the UK. Additionally, some local branches have adapted self-catering accommodation for family holidays.

Parkinson's Disease Society, 215 Vauxhall Bridge Road, London SW1V 1EJ. T:020 7931 8080.

Tourist boards

England's Regional Tourist Boards and the Scottish and Wales Tourist Boards are the main sources of information for all aspects of holidays in their areas. They can advise about: accommodation, transport, highlights to see, special events and festivals, sporting facilities, special interest holidays – in short, almost everything you could possibly want to know. All produce excellent leaflets and guide books.

There are also 560 Tourist Information Centres in England which can give impartial advice and information about accommodation, days out and places to eat. Call **Scoot** on T:09002 192 192 for details of your nearest centre.

Visit Scotland, 23 Ravelston Terrace, Edinburgh EH4 3TP. T:0131 332 2433. Free brochure: *Scotland: The Main Guide for 2003*. There are also guides to hotels and guest houses, bed and breakfast, self-catering accommodation and camping and caravanning sites.

Wales Tourist Board, Brunel House, 2 Fitzalan Road, Cardiff CF24 0UY. T:029 2049 9909. *A View of Wales* (free).

Regional Tourist Boards. Addresses of England's 10 regional tourist boards are:

Cumbria Tourist Board, Ashleigh, Holly Road, Windermere, Cumbria LA23 2AQ. T:015394 44444.

East of England Tourist Board, Toppesfield Hall, Hadleigh, Suffolk IP7 5DN. T:01473 822922. Covering Cambridgeshire, Essex, Norfolk, Suffolk, Hertfordshire, Lincolnshire and Bedfordshire.

Heart of England Tourist Board, Woodside, Larkhill Road, Worcester WR5 2EF. T:01905 761100. Covering Derbyshire, Gloucestershire, Leicestershire, Northamptonshire, Nottinghamshire, Shropshire, Staffordshire, Warwickshire, West Midlands, Hereford and Worcester, Rutland and representing the districts of Cherwell and West Oxfordshire.

London Tourist Board, 1 Warwick Row, London SW1E 5ER. T:020 7932 2000.

Northumbria Tourist Board, Aykley Heads, Durham DH1 5UX. T:0191 375 3000. Covering the Tees Valley, Durham, Northumberland and Tyne & Wear.

North West Tourist Board, Swan House, Swan Meadow Road, Wigan Pier, Wigan, Lancashire WN3 5BB. T: 0845 600 6040. Covering Cheshire, Greater Manchester, Lancashire, Merseyside and High Peak District of Derbyshire.

South East England Tourist Board, The Old Brew House, Warwick Park, Tunbridge Wells, Kent TN2 5TU. T:01892 540766. Covering East and West Sussex, Kent and Surrey.

Southern Tourist Board, 40 Chamberlayne Road, Eastleigh, Hampshire SO50 5JH. T:023 8062 5400. Covering Hampshire, East and North Dorset, Isle of Wight, Berkshire, Buckinghamshire and Oxfordshire.

South West Tourism, Woodwater Park, Pynes Hill, Rydon Lane, Exeter EX2 5WY. T: 0870 4420 830. Covering Bath, Bristol, Cornwall, Devon, Somerset, Dorset, Wiltshire and Isles of Scilly.

Yorkshire Tourist Board, 312 Tadcaster Road, York, North Yorkshire YO24 1GS. T:01904 707961. Covering Yorkshire and North East Lincolnshire.

Long-haul travel

The two specialist organisations below can offer a great deal of practical information and help, as well as assist in obtaining low cost fares, if you are planning to travel independently. Round-the-world air tickets are an excellent buy. Most airlines offer their own fares or travel agents can put together routes using various carriers.

Trailfinders Travel Centre, 194 Kensington High Street, London W8 7RG. Long-haul flights: 020 7938 3939. European and Transatlantic flights: 020 7937 5400. First and business class flights: 020 7938 3444. Will work out an itinerary for you to any destination worldwide, obtain the necessary visas and arrange comprehensive travel insurance. Trailfinders has a reference library and information centre, medical advisory and immunisation centre, a map and bookshop and also a bureau de change.

WEXAS International, 45 Brompton Road, London SW3 1DE. T:020 7589 3315. As well as provide a comprehensive travel service for independent holidaymakers, WEXAS also offers a variety of trips to long-haul destinations including such places as the Antarctic, China and the Nile Valley. Members enjoy flight, hotel and car hire discounts and receive the *Traveller* magazine. There is a special (lower) introductory membership rate of £22 for *Good non-Retirement Guide* readers.

Insurance

Even the best laid holiday plans can go wrong. It is therefore only sensible to take out proper insurance cover before you depart.

Many tour operators try to insist that, as a condition of booking, you either buy their inclusive insurance package; or alternatively, make private arrangements which are at least as good. While this suggests that they are demanding very high standards, terms and conditions vary greatly; so before signing on the dotted line, you should read the small print carefully to ensure that the package you are being offered meets all the eventualities and provides you with adequate cover should you make a claim. If for any reason, you are unable to see an actual copy of the policy, ask any questions that you think might be relevant, including in particular any special conditions you would have to satisfy in making a claim (e.g. under medical or possibly sporting/other activities) that the policy would not cover.

If you are travelling independently, if anything it is even more important to be properly insured, since you will not be protected by the normal compensation that the reputable tour operators provide for claims for which they could be held liable in the event of a mishap.

Holiday insurance should cover you for:

- Medical expenses including: hospital treatment, cost of ambulance, air ambulance, emergency dental treatment plus expenses for a companion, who may have to remain overseas with you should you become ill (see 'Medical Insurance' page 384)
- Personal liability cover, should you cause injury to another person or property
- Personal accident leading to injury or death: check the small print as some policies have reduced level cover for older travellers
- Additional hotel and repatriation costs resulting from injury or illness
- Loss of deposit or cancellation: check what emergencies or contingencies this covers
- Cost of having to curtail your holiday, including extra travel expenses, because of serious illness in the family
- Compensation for inconvenience caused by flight cancellations or other travel delays

- Cover for baggage and personal effects and for emergency purchases should your baggage be delayed
- Cover for loss of personal money and documents.

If you are planning to take your car abroad (see earlier 'Motoring abroad' page 365), you will need to check your existing car insurance to ensure that you are properly covered. Alternatively, if you are planning to hire a car or motor scooter overseas, you will need to take out fully comprehensive insurance cover (which you may need to purchase while on holiday).

Before lashing out on new insurance, check whether any of the above items are already covered under an existing policy. This might well apply to your personal possessions and to medical insurance. Even if the policy is not sufficiently comprehensive for travel purposes, it will be better and cheaper in the long run to pay a small supplement to give you the extra cover you need than to buy a holiday insurance package from a tour operator. This could be especially true if you are over 65, as many travel agents load premiums against older holiday-makers on the basis of more costly medical insurance. A cost-effective plan may be to extend any existing medical insurance to cover you while abroad and then to take out a separate policy (without medical insurance) to cover you for the rest of your travel needs.

Although many travel agents would like you to believe otherwise, **you are under no obligation to buy insurance from a travel company**. Thanks to a new law that came into effect in November 1998, travel companies can no longer oblige customers to buy their insurance as a condition of obtaining a special deal or discount.

When assessing holiday insurance, and especially inclusive packages, it pays to do a bit of mental arithmetic. Although at first glance the sums look enormous, the likelihood is that should you have to claim you will end up being out of pocket. A sum of £750 or even £1,000 in respect of lost baggage might well be insufficient if, as well as your clothes, you had to replace your watch, camera and other valuables.

The Association of British Insurers suggests the following guidelines in respect of the amount of cover holidaymakers should be looking for in their policy:

Cancellation or curtailment of holiday: the full cost of your holiday, as well as the deposit and any other charges paid in advance; plus cover for any extra costs, should you be forced to return early.

Money and travel documents: £500.

Luggage/belongings: minimum £1,500. (N.B. check the limit on single articles).

Delayed baggage: £75 for emergency purchases in case luggage is lost en route and arrives late.

Delayed departure: £20 per hour after the first 12 hours; and full cost of your holiday if you cancel after the first full 24 hours' delay.

Personal liability: up to £1 million (£2 million for the USA).

It is essential that you take copies of the insurance documents with you, as losses or other claims must normally be reported immediately. You will also be required to quote reference number and/or other details, given on the docket. Additionally, there may be particular guidelines laid down by the policy, e.g. you may have to ring a helpline before incurring medical expenses. Failure to report a claim within the specified time limit could nullify your right to compensation. Best advice is to check that you have the 24-hour helpline number and to keep it with you at all times.

Be sure to get a receipt for any special expenses you incur – extra hotel bills, medical treatment, long-distance phone calls and so on. You may not get all the costs reimbursed but if your insurance covers some or all of these contingencies, you will need to produce evidence of your expenditure.

The **Association of British Insurers** (51 Gresham Street, London EC2V 7HQ, T:020 7600 3333) publishes a free information sheet on holiday insurance and motoring abroad, explaining the key points you should know in simple language.

The **Association of British Travel Agents** (68–71 Newman Street, London W1T 3AH, T:020 7637 2444) operates a code of conduct for all travel agents and tour operators who are members of ABTA and also runs a consumer advisory service for holidaymakers on how to seek redress if they are dissatisfied with their travel company.

Also useful to know about is the **Denied Boarding Regulation**, which entitles passengers who cannot travel because their flight is overbooked to some immediate cash payment, even if the airline puts them up in a hotel or books them on to an alternative flight a few hours later. To qualify, passengers must have a confirmed reservation and have checked in on time. Also, the airport where they were 'bumped off' must be in an EU country. (It may sometimes also be possible to get compensation in the States.) Charter flights are excluded.

Compensation for short-haul flights varies between about £50 and £100 depending on the length of delay; and for long-haul flights, between about £100 and £200. Not all airlines volunteer the information – so if you want the compensation, it may be up to you to ask!

For further information, or if you have trouble in obtaining your compensation, contact the **Air Transport Users' Council** on T:020 7240 6061.

Medical insurance

This is one area where you should never skimp on insurance. Although many countries now have reciprocal arrangements with the UK for emergency medical treatment, these vary greatly both in quality and generosity. Some treatments are free, as they are on the National Health Service; others, even in some EC countries, may be charged for as if you were a private patient.

Department of Health leaflet *Health Advice for Travellers* (T6) explains what is entailed and what forms you should obtain. In particular you should get a Form E111 which is a certificate entitling you to free or reduced-cost emergency treatment throughout the European Economic Area. An application form is contained in the T6 leaflet. You can pick up a copy at any main post office which will process the paperwork and stamp your Form E111 for you on the spot.

However, even the very best reciprocal arrangements may not be adequate in the event of a real emergency; and they certainly will not cover you for any additional expenses you may incur, such as: the cost of having to prolong your stay; extra hotel bills if a companion has to remain with you; special transport home, should you require it, and so on. Additionally, since in an emergency you may need or want private treatment, you would be advised to insure for this – even if you are going to a country where good reciprocal arrangements exist.

In America the cost of medical treatment is astronomic. For peace of mind, most experts recommend cover of £1 million for anywhere in the world. Some policies offer higher, or even unlimited, cover.

Most insurance companies impose various terms and let-out clauses as a condition of payment. You should read these very carefully because, whereas some are obviously sensible, others may be very restrictive or, for whatever reason, you may not be able to satisfy the requirements: for example, if you have a chronic heart condition. Even though this may result in your having to pay a higher premium, you should declare any pre-existing illnesses or conditions. Failure to do so could nullify your claim if you had to make one.

Although there is no upper age limit if you want to take out medical insurance, many companies request a note from a qualified medical practitioner stating that you are fit to travel if you are over 75; or require you to confirm that you are not travelling against medical advice.

Another common requirement is that the insured person should undertake not to indulge in any dangerous pursuits, which is fine in theory but in practice (depending on the company's interpretation of 'dangerous') could debar you from any activity that qualifies as 'strenuous'.

Book through a reputable operator. Many of the sad tales of woe one hears, could have been avoided, or at least softened by compensation, had holidaymakers checked to ensure that their travel agent or tour operator was affiliated to either ABTA or to the Association of Tour Operators (ATO). Both organisations have strict regulations which all member companies must follow and both run an arbitration scheme in the event of complaints. No-one can guarantee you against every mishap but a recognised travel company plus adequate insurance should go a long way towards giving you at least some measure of protection.

Travel and other concessions

Buses, coaches, some airline companies and especially the railways offer valuable concessions to people of retirement age. Some of the best-value savings which are available to anyone aged 60 and over are provided by train companies. These include:

Senior Railcard. This costs £18 and entitles you to one-third off most fares including: Cheap Day singles and returns; Savers and SuperSavers returns and most Rail

Rover tickets; first class single and return tickets; and all-zone one-day Travelcards subject to a minimum fare. Discounts are also available on some ferry services.

Family Railcard. This costs £20 and entitles up to four adults to one-third off most fares including Cheap Day singles and returns, Savers and SuperSavers. Children aged between 5 and 15 get 60 per cent off the normal child fare (subject to a minimum fare of £1). Under 5's go free.

Disabled Persons Railcard. This costs £14 and entitles the holder and one accompanying adult to reduced train fares. Details and conditions should be available from your local staffed station.

Network Railcard. This costs £20 and is only available in South-East England. It gives a one-third reduction on most Standard Class fares after 10 a.m., Monday to Friday, subject to a £10 minimum fare. The same reduction applies at week-ends and bank holidays, when happily there is no minimum fare; also passengers can travel at any time, as opposed to only after 10 a.m. Up to four adults (including the cardholder) can travel at a discount and up to four children aged 5 to 15 will get 60 per cent off the normal child fare (subject to a minimum fare of £1). Under 5's travel free.

Details of all Railcards are available from **National Rail Enquiries**, T:08457 48 49 50.

Railplus Cards. Available to persons from age 60 who are also British Senior Railcard holders. They cost £12 and entitle you to savings of up to 25 per cent on 1st and standard/2nd Class full fares on cross-border journeys within Europe.

Reductions on Cross Channel Seacats and ships are only allowed if these services are part of rail/sea combined tickets to or from the Continent. The cards also allow you to purchase discounted international tickets for cross-border travel on the Continent.

Railplus Cards can be obtained from: selected railway stations; Connex and Rail Europe appointed travel agencies; the Rail Europe Travel Shop Centre at 179 Piccadilly, London W1J 9BA (telephone enquiries and sales: 08705 848848).

Although there is no special 'senior age' fare on Eurostar, the Leisure Apex 7 and Leisure Apex 14 fares offer good discounts for early booking.

Buses and coaches

There are often reduced rates for senior citizens on long-distance buses and coaches. For example, discounts of 33 per cent apply on National Coaches on both ordinary and Rapide services. If you are planning to travel by coach, *Good non-Retirement Guide* readers have advised that it is worth shopping around to find out what bargains are available.

Airlines

Several of the airlines offer attractive discounts to older travellers. The terms and conditions vary, with some carriers offering across-the-board savings and others limiting them to selected destinations. Likewise, in some cases the qualifying age is 60; in others, it is a couple of years older. A particular bonus is that concessions are often extended to include a companion travelling at the same time.

These discounts are not particularly widely advertised and may well not be suggested by airline staff, often because they do not know a passenger's age. Best advice is to ask your travel agent at time of booking what special discounts, if any, are offered.

Overseas

Many countries offer travel and other reductions to retired holidaymakers including, for example, discounts for: entry to museums and galleries, day excursions, sporting events and other entertainment. As in Britain, provisions are liable to change and for up-to-date information probably the best source to contact is the national tourist office of the country to which you are travelling. Herewith, however, a flavour of reductions current at time of writing. The rail discounts are available in each case to holders of a Railplus Card purchasing international rail travel tickets and are applicable to both first and second class travel.

All EC countries – as well as Norway, Hungary, the Czech Republic, Slovakia and most lines in Switzerland – give 25 per cent reductions on international rail fares. Additionally, extra concessions apply in the following countries:

Austria: most museums and galleries are free at weekends.

Denmark: most museums offer pensioner discounts.

Eire: CIE Rambler Tickets give unlimited travel by rail and bus at discounted prices. Most museums are free and most entertainments offer concessionary prices to people of retirement age.

Finland: there are 30 per cent reductions on internal weekday Finnish airline flights and also on coaches for people over 65. Additionally, many museums offer reduced entrance charges.

France: there are lower entrance charges at most museums as well as at some theatres and cinemas.

Luxembourg: discounts up to 30 per cent on coaches and buses.

Netherlands: reduced prices on internal KLM flights; also cheaper entrance charges at museums.

Sweden: 30 per cent reductions on some coaches; off-peak flat rate fare for internal flights; concessionary entry to museums and entertainment.

Switzerland: for a full list of concessions, see *Season for Seniors* – information from the Swiss National Tourist Office.

N.B. As in the UK, concessions in overseas countries sometimes change. To be certain of what is on offer when you go on holiday, ask your travel agent or check with the particular country's national tourist office.

If you are expecting to travel extensively by train while abroad, it could be worth considering a Euro-Domino ticket or an Inter-Rail 26+ ticket. Explanatory leaflets about each are available from most main line stations, or by contacting Rail Europe (T:08705 848848).

Air Travel Advisory Bureau. T:020 7636 5000. Advises on travel insurance and low cost fares to all parts of the world. If you are looking for good value fares, it is well worth giving them a ring rather than shopping around.

Health tips for travellers

Most are plain common sense – but worth repeating for all that.

- Remember to pack any regular medicines you require: even familiar branded products can be difficult to obtain in some countries.
- Take a mini first aid kit, including: plaster, disinfectant, tummy pills and so on.
- If you are going to any developing country, consult your doctor as to what pills (and any special precautions) you should take.
- One of the most common ailments among British travellers abroad is an overdose of sun. In some countries, it really burns, so take it easy, wear a hat and apply plenty of protective lotion.
- The other big travellers' woe is 'Delhi belly', which unhappily can apply in most hot countries, including Italy and Spain. Beware the water, ice, salads, seafood, ice cream and any fruit which you do not peel yourself. Department of Health advice is only to eat freshly cooked food which is thoroughly cooked and still piping hot.
- Always wash your hands before eating or handling food, particularly if you are camping or caravanning.
- Travelling is tiring and a sudden change of climate more debilitating than most of us admit: allow plenty of time during the first couple of days to acclimatise before embarking on an activity programme that would exhaust a 17-year-old.
- Have any inoculations or vaccinations well in advance of your departure date.
- When flying, wear loose clothes and above all comfortable shoes as feet and ankles tend to swell in the air.
- To avoid risk of deep vein thrombosis, which can be fatal, medical advice is to do foot exercises and walk around the plane from time to time; and for long-haul travel especially, to wear compression stockings which can be bought at most chemists. Unless advised otherwise by your doctor, taking an aspirin before flying is also recommended.
- On long journeys, it helps to drink plenty of fruit juice and remember the warning that 'an alcoholic drink in the air is worth two on the ground'. If you have a special diet, inform whoever makes your booking: most airlines, especially on long-distance journeys, serve vegetarian food.
- Department of Health leaflet T6, *Health Advice for Travellers* contains essential information and advice on what precautions to take when you travel abroad, how to

cope in an emergency and what vaccinations may be required. Available from any post office or by ringing T:0800 555777 (call free). Prestel 50063 or CEEFAX (pages 460–464) has updated information.

- Should some disaster befall you, there are air-ambulance services which will fly you home with a doctor and nurse in attendance. One such is **Heathrow Air Ambulance**, PO Box 279, Iver, Bucks SL0 0BQ, T:020 8897 618544.
- Finally, the old favourite, don't drink and drive.

Keep fit and have a wonderful holiday!

15 Caring for Elderly Parents

Most of us sooner or later have some responsibility for the care of elderly parents. Although an increasing number of people live well into their eighties and beyond, the vast majority manage with a little help to remain in their own homes rather than go into residential care. While there is no hiding the fact that with a very elderly person this can impose strains, most families cope exceedingly well. Moreover, since the evidence shows that this is the undoubted preference of most older people themselves, the main bias of this chapter is towards helping aged parents remain as independent as possible.

Knowing what facilities are available, what precautions you can take against a mishap occurring and whom you can turn to in an emergency can make all the difference, both to you and to parents who may fear becoming a burden. Over the last few years provision has enormously improved and ranges from simple gadgets such as alarm systems which can buy peace of mind to full-scale nursing care, should this become necessary.

A basic choice for many families is whether parents should move in with them or continue to live on their own. While the decision will depend on individual circumstances, in the early days at least the majority choice on all sides is generally in favour of 'staying put'. Although later in the chapter we cover sheltered housing, which some people see as the best of all worlds, an alternative solution to any move may be simply to adapt the home to make it safer and more convenient.

Ways of adapting a home

Many even quite elderly people will not require anything more complicated than a few general improvements, such as: better lighting, especially near staircases; a non-slip mat and grab-rail in the bathroom; safe heating arrangements; and perhaps the lowering of some kitchen and other units to place them within easy reach.

Another sensible plan worth considering is to convert a downstairs room into a bedroom and bathroom, in case managing the stairs should later become a difficulty. These and other common-sense measures are covered in more detail in Chapter 8, Your Home.

For some people, however, such arrangements are not really sufficient. In the case of a physically handicapped or disabled person, more radical improvements will usually be required. Far from presenting a major problem as used to be the case, today these are normally fairly easy to organise.

Local authority help

Local authorities have a legal duty to help people with disabilities and, depending on what is required and the individual's ability to pay, may assist with the cost.

Your parents can either approach their GP or contact the Social Services Department direct. A sympathetic doctor will be able to: advise what is needed; supply any prescriptions such as for a medical hoist; suggest which unit or department to approach; and can make a recommendation to the Housing Department, should rehousing be desirable.

The social services department may be able to supply kitchen, bathroom and other aids for the home, arrange an appointment with an occupational therapist and support an application for a housing grant, should major adaptations be required.

If only relatively small changes are necessary, e.g. a hand-rail on the stairs or ramp for a wheelchair, the occupational therapist may arrange for these to be done by the local authority. This can take months however, so if your parents cannot wait and want the work done privately, the Occupational Therapist will give you names of local firms.

Home improvement agencies

HIAs are voluntary and/or local authority organisations, set up to help older or disabled home owners repair and adapt their homes. They help to assess your needs, get a builder, supervise the work, raise the finance, verify the estimate and check the completed job.

Housing grants

There are several grants available, in the event of more substantial adaptations being required. The three most likely to be of interest are: renovation grant, disabled facilities grant and home repair assistance. All are either means-tested or, in the case of home repair assistance, specifically intended to help those on low incomes. Most types of work for which grant is given are at the discretion of the council, so it is very important not to commence any work until your grant application has been approved. The Council will not pay for any work started prior to their approval.

More detailed information as to the criteria for eligibility and other points is given in Chapter 8, Your Home (see section headed 'Improvement and repair grants', page 161). Also, it could be useful to contact your local Home Improvement Agency as HIA's help elderly people, individuals with disabilities and those on low incomes to carry out repairs and improvements to their home. They can usually assist with selecting a reputable builder, applying for a grant or other source of finance and with supervising the builder's work. The service is normally free of charge.

To find out if there is an HIA operating in your area, contact Foundations, the national co-ordinating body for HIA's at the following address: **Foundations**, Bleaklow House, Howard Town Mills, Glossop SK13 8HT. T: 01457 891909.

If there is no HIA in your area, you might usefully try contacting your local Citizens' Advice Bureau or Age Concern Group.

Renovation grant. There are seven main eventualities where application for a grant might be successful: (1) to bring a property up to a standard of fitness for human habitation; (2) for works to comply with a statutory repairs notice served on the owner;

(3) to replace or repair rotten or defective parts of the structure including, for example, doors, windows, walls, an ineffective damp-proof course or unsatisfactory wiring; (4) for home insulation or other energy-saving works; (5) to provide heating facilities; (6) for the provision of satisfactory internal arrangements such as improvement of a very steep or winding staircase; (7) for conversions, such as the creation of a granny flat.

Disabled facilities grant. This is designed to adapt or provide facilities for a home (including the common parts where applicable) to make it more suitable for occupation by a disabled person. It can cover a wide range of improvements to enable them to manage more independently including, for example: work to facilitate access either to the property itself or to the main rooms; the provision of suitable bathroom or kitchen facilities; the adaptation of heating or lighting controls; improvement of the heating system; plus various other works where these would make a home safe for a disabled person.

Home repair assistance. HRA can help pay for small but essential works of repair, improvement or adaptation to your home, including works to make it suitable for an older, or disabled, person to come to live with you permanently.

Payment of the grant is at the discretion of your local council. Eligibility is restricted to those who are elderly, infirm or disabled or who are in receipt of one of the following benefits: income support, housing benefit, income-based jobseeker's allowance, council tax benefit, disabled person's tax credit or working families tax credit (working tax credit from 2003); or to those needing to adapt their home to enable an older or disabled person to live with them and be cared for. Additionally, applicants must normally either be an owner occupier or private sector tenant (this includes tenants of housing associations) and the property itself (which could be a mobile home or houseboat) must be their only, or main, residence.

Maximum grant is £5,000 per application.

How to apply

Contact the Home Improvement Section or Environmental Health Department of your local council for an application form. At the same time, it could be useful to request the latest government booklets on grants. All are available in large print editions.

Other sources of help

DEMAND (Design & Manufacture for Disability), The Old Chapel, Mallard Road, Abbots Langley, Herts WD5 0DQ. T:01923 681800. Can design and make individual items of furniture and equipment, or modify existing products, for people with particular needs where there is nothing suitable available elsewhere.

The Disabled Living Foundation, 380–384 Harrow Road, London W9 2HU. Helpline: 0845 130 9177; Minicom: 0870 603 9176. DLF is a charity concerned with the practical daily living problems of disability. As well as run a telephone enquiry service, DLF has an Equipment Centre where gadgets of all kinds can be demonstrated and tried out by visitors. The range includes: special equipment for the bathroom, kitchen, bedroom and living room; hoists, wheelchairs and gadgets to assist reading and writing. None of the items is for sale but the Centre can provide information on suppliers and prices.

The Centre is staffed by information advisers who show visitors round and discuss individual needs. For details of opening hours, which vary, T:020 7289 6111.

The Royal Association for Disability and Rehabilitation (RADAR), 12 City Forum, 250 City Road, London EC1V 8AF. T:020 7250 3222; Minicom: 020 7250 4119. RADAR can help and give advice across a very wide spectrum, including: statutory and voluntary services, mobility issues, holidays, employment, civil rights and housing. It publishes a useful monthly bulletin and can supply names and addresses of the many Disabled Living Centres (as can the co-ordinating body for the DLC, i.e. the **Disabled Living Centres Council**, Redbank House, 4 St. Chad's Street, Manchester M8 8QA, T:0161 834 1044) which are now being established throughout the country. These exist in: Aylesbury, Belfast, Birmingham, Bristol, Eastbourne, Leeds, Leicester, Liverpool, Macclesfield, Manchester, Middlesbrough, Stockport, Welwyn Garden City and many other places.

Both the **British Red Cross** and **Age Concern** (see local telephone directory) can loan equipment in the short term and may also be able to advise on local stockists. Larger branches of Boots, for example, sell a wide range of special items for people with disabilities, including: bath aids, wheelchairs and crutches.

Keep Able, Sterling Park, Pedmore Road, Brierley Hill, West Midlands DY5 1TB. A chain of specialist shops in the Midlands, South East and South West, which stock a wide range of gadgets and equipment to make life easier for elderly and less able people. Professional advice is available in all the shops and home visits can be arranged without obligation. A free mail-order catalogue is available. For further information and address of your nearest branch, telephone the National Helpline on T:08705 202122.

REMAP, Hazeldene, Ightham, Sevenoaks, Kent TN15 9AD. T:0845 1300 456. Can often help design or adapt goods to suit individuals, where there is no commercially available product to meet their particular needs.

The **Centre for Accessible Environments**, Nutmeg House, 60 Gainsford Street, London SE1 2NY. T:020 7357 8182. Runs an architectural advisory service and can recommend local architects with experience of designing for people with disabilities. When writing, you should give broad details of the type of work required. The Centre also offers an information service on accessible design and additionally will check architects' drawings to confirm their suitability for a proposed project. Cost for the checking service is about £75 an hour but could prove invaluable for people planning to adapt their home either for their own retirement or for, say, a parent coming to live with them. A publications list is available on request.

BT supplies some 70 devices to assist those with hearing difficulties, visual handicap, impaired mobility and other problems that make using a telephone more difficult. For details see the *BT Guide for People who are Disabled or Elderly*, available from local BT offices. A home visit can sometimes be arranged for those who are housebound. For further information, dial BT free on T:0800 800 150.

Another useful body to know about is **OFTEL** which operates a complaints line for consumers who have a complaint about their telecom company, which they are unable to resolve with the company direct. T:0845 714 5000.

Other helpful sources of advice include:

Disability Wales/Anabledd Cymru, Wernddu Court, Caerphilly Business Park, Van Road, Caerphilly CF83 3ED. T:029 2088 7325.

DIAL UK (National Association of Disablement Information and Advice Lines), St. Catherines, Tickhill Road, Doncaster DN4 8QN. T:01302 310123.

Useful reading

A series of 13 books with information about a wide range of available equipment and self-help devices for those with a disability or who are no longer as active as they once were are available from: **FAST** (Foundation for Assistive Technology), Mary Marlborough Centre, Windmill Road, Headington, Oxford OX3 7LD, T:01865 227599. Prices are between £3.50 and £11. The books are also stocked by many public libraries.

Electrical Controls by Tessa Palfreyman contains advice on the safe location of switches and controls for use by elderly and disabled people plus information on specialist equipment such as visual door bells and smoke alarms; price £2.50. Obtainable from the **Centre for Accessible Environments**, at the address above.

Alarm systems

Alarm systems have become very much more widespread in recent years. The knowledge that help can be summoned very quickly in the event of an emergency is not only reassuring in its own right but in practical terms can enable many elderly people to remain independent far longer than would otherwise be sensible. Some local authorities have alarm systems that now allow people living in their own homes to be linked to a central control. Types of alarm vary greatly. Some have a telephone link, enabling personal contact to be made; others simply signal that something is wrong. In other areas, a relative or friend who has been nominated will be alerted; or sometimes, the police. To find out whether your parents' local authority operates such a system, contact the social services department.

Commercial firms

A number of firms install and operate alarm systems. Price, installation cost and reliability can vary quite considerably. For advice on choosing an alarm plus a list of suppliers, telephone **Disabled Living Foundation** on Helpline: 0845 130 9177.

Community alarms

Telephone alarm systems operated on the public telephone network can be used by anyone with a direct telephone line. The systems link into a 24-hour monitoring centre and have a pendant which enables help to be called even when the owner is some distance from the telephone. Grants may be available in some cases to meet the costs. One of the most widely used systems is SeniorLink, run by Help the Aged. For further information, contact **SeniorLink Response Centre**, 1 Centurion Business Park, Bessemer Way, Rotherham S60 1FB. T:01709 389388.

Age Concern Aid-Call

This is another highly recommended alarm system. The subscriber wears a small radio transmitter which contacts a 24-hour monitoring service. The centre then alerts a list of nominated relatives or friends, or the emergency services, that something is wrong and help can be on its way in a matter of minutes. (See Chapter 8, Your Home, for details of costs). Contact: **Age Concern Aid-Call**, Freepost (EX 2356), Newton Abbott, Devon TQ13 7BR. T:0800 772266.

Main local authority services

Quite apart from any assistance with housing, local authorities supply a number of services which can prove invaluable to an elderly person. The two most important are meals on wheels and home helps. Additionally, there are social workers and various specialists concerned with aspects of health.

Since the introduction of Community Care, local authority social services departments have taken over all responsibility for helping to assess and co-ordinate the best arrangements for individuals according to their particular requirements.

Meals on wheels

The meals on wheels service is sometimes run by local authorities direct and sometimes by voluntary organisations, such as the Women's Royal Voluntary Service (WRVS), acting as their agents. As you will know, the purpose is to deliver a hot lunch (or batch of frozen lunches) to individuals in their own home. Different arrangements apply in different areas and schemes variously operate from two to seven days a week; or possibly less frequently when frozen meals are supplied. Cost also varies: from about £1.50 to £3 a day, with the norm being about £2. For further information, contact the social services department.

The WRVS also runs a private frozen meals scheme, Home Choice Meals, for people who do not qualify for Meals on Wheels but who would welcome having healthy meals delivered to their home. Price of a 3-course meal ranges from £4.35 to £5.50. For further information, call T:0845 602 1123.

Home helps

Local authorities have a legal obligation to run a home help service to help frail and housebound elderly people with such basic household chores as shopping, tidying up, a little light cooking and so on. In many areas the service is overstretched, so the amount of help actually available varies considerably, as does the method of charging. Different local authorities have different policies and while some may charge nothing or just a small weekly amount, as a rule people are means-tested according to their ability to pay. If your parents could afford to do so, this could mean paying the full cost. Apply through the social services department. Some of the larger authorities have a special telephone number which may be listed either as 'Home Help Services' or 'Domiciliary Services'.

Specialist helpers

Local authorities employ a number of specialist helpers, variously based in the Social Services Department or Health Centre, who are there to assist.

Social workers. Normally the first people to contact if you have a problem. They can put you in touch with the right person, if you require a home help, meals on wheels, have a housing difficulty or other query and are not sure whom to approach. Often, even if ultimately it is the responsibility of another department, a social worker may come and discuss the matter with you – or with your parents direct. You should ring the Social Services Department; in Scotland, this is normally referred to as the Social Work Department.

Occupational therapists. Have a wide knowledge of disability and can assist individuals via training, exercise, or access to aids, equipment or adaptations to the home. Ring the Social Services Department.

Health visitors. Qualified nurses with broad knowledge both of health matters and of the various services available through the local authority. Rather like social workers, health visitors can put you in touch with whatever specialised facilities are required. Contact through the local Health Centre.

District nurses. Fully qualified nurses who will visit a patient in the home: change dressings, attend to other routine nursing matters, monitor progress and help with the arrangements if more specialised care is required. Contact through the Health Centre.

Physiotherapists. Use exercise and massage to help improve mobility and strengthen muscles, for example after an operation or to alleviate a crippling condition. Normally available at both hospitals and health centres.

Medical social workers. In the old days, used to be known as almoners. Are available to consult, if patients have any problems – whether practical or emotional – on leaving hospital. MSWs can advise on coping with a disablement, as well as such practical matters as transport, after-care and other immediate arrangements. Work in hospitals and an appointment should be made before the patient is discharged.

Good neighbour schemes

A number of local authorities have an organised system of good neighbour schemes. In essence, these consist of individuals contracting with the authority to act as good neighbours to one or several elderly people living close by. Depending on what is required, they may simply pop in on a daily basis to check that everything is alright; or they may give more sustained assistance such as providing help with dressing, bathing, shopping or preparing a light meal. In some authorities, the service may largely be run by volunteer organisations. In others 'good neighbours' are paid by the authority, according to the number of hours they commit. To find out whether such a scheme exists locally, enquire at the social services department.

Key voluntary organisations

Voluntary organisations complement the services provided by statutory health and social services in making life easier for elderly people living at home. The range of provision varies from area to area but can include:

- Lunch clubs
- Day centres and clubs
- Aids such as wheelchairs
- Transport
- Good neighbour schemes
- Advice and information
- Holidays and short-term placements
- Friendly visiting
- Odd jobs and decorating
- Gardening
- Prescription collection
- Family support schemes.

The particular organisation providing these services depends on where you live but the Citizens' Advice Bureau will be able to advise you whom to contact. The following are the key agencies:

Age Concern may provide any or all of the voluntary services listed above in your local area. Most local groups recruit volunteers to do practical jobs and provide friendship. They also give advice and information and when necessary refer enquirers to a more appropriate agency. Their addresses and telephone numbers are in the local phone book. Alternatively you can contact the **Age Concern Information Line** on T: 0800 009966 for referral to a local Age Concern organisation.

National organisations in Scotland, Wales and Northern Ireland are:

Age Concern Scotland, 113 Rose Street, Edinburgh EH2 3DT. T:0131 220 3345.

Age Concern Cymru, 4th Floor, 1 Cathedral Road, Cardiff CF11 9SD. T:029 2037 1566.

Age Concern Northern Ireland, 3 Lower Crescent, Belfast BT7 1NR. T:028 9024 5729.

Women's Royal Voluntary Service runs many local projects:

- Books-on-wheels
- Meals on wheels
- Lunch clubs
- Darby and Joan clubs
- Social transport
- Good neighbour schemes
- Meal delivery service for those not qualifying for meals on wheels

Contact **WRVS** head office: Milton Hill House, Milton Hill, Steventon, Abingdon, Oxon OX13 6AD. T:01235 442900.

British Red Cross supplies some important services to elderly people. The principal ones available from many branches include:

- Helping sick, disabled or frail people make essential journeys
- Loaning medical equipment for short-term use at home and on holiday
- Providing home-from-hospital support: easing the transition of patients to their own home after discharge and giving support to both them and their carers
- Respite for carers, such as for a planned short break or in an emergency
- 'Signposting' vulnerable people towards the statutory or voluntary services from which their needs may best be met.

To contact your local British Red Cross branch, see telephone directory, or write to: **British Red Cross (BRCS)**, 9 Grosvenor Crescent, London SW1X 7EJ. T:020 7235 5027.

St. John Ambulance has over 45,000 volunteers who provide first aid and care services. They help in hospitals and will also come to people's homes to assist with various practical tasks such as shopping, collecting pensions, staying with an elderly person for a few hours or providing transport to and from hospital. It is emphasised, however, that the kind of help which the volunteers can provide (if any) varies enormously from county to county and depends on the local resources available. In some areas loan of equipment such as wheelchairs, can be arranged.

St. John gives advice on caring and runs courses locally for carers looking after elderly people. Anyone wishing to enlist the help of St. John Ambulance Volunteers should contact the national headquarters: **St. John Ambulance**, 27 St. John's Lane, London EC1M 4BU. T:08700 104950.

Other sources of help and advice

Counsel & Care, Twyman House, 16 Bonny Street, London NW1 9PG. Advice Line T:0845 300 7585 (10 a.m. – 12.30 p.m. and 2 p.m. – 4 p.m., local rate); Administration and Appeals: 020 7241 8555. Provides a free confidential advisory service, which is used by thousands of elderly people and their relatives each year. Advice workers liaise with all the statutory services, private and voluntary organisations as well as with charities and benevolent funds in order to inform you of the various options. There is a range of factsheets. Limited funds are also available to help with an exceptional needs payment.

Jewish Care, 221 Golders Green Road, London NW11 9DQ. Provides services for elderly Jewish people in London and the South East. Principal facilities include:

Day centres, of which there are five in the London area for elderly or disabled Jewish people and one in Southend. Individuals are sometimes referred by a hospital but can apply direct and will be invited to be a guest for one or two days. Charges range from £4.50 to £7.50 a day.

Other services include domiciliary care, hostels and a day care centre for those recovering from mental illness. There are also 12 residential homes in London and the South East.

There is also a Kosher meals service in many areas of London. Enquire through the local authority social services department.

For services outside London, contact:

Leeds Jewish Welfare Board, 311 Stonegate Road, Leeds LS17 6AZ. T:0113 268 4211.

Manchester Jewish Community Care, 85 Middleton Road, Crumpsall, Manchester M8 4JY. T:0161 740 0111.

Brighton & Hove Jewish Welfare Board, 76 Marmion Road, Hove, East Sussex BN3 5FT. T:01273 722523.

Merseyside Jewish Community Care, Shifrin House, 433 Smithdown Road, Liverpool 15. T:0151 733 2292.

A *Directory of Jewish Social Services*, listing facilities throughout the UK, is published by the Board of Deputies of British Jews, Commonwealth House, 6 Bloomsbury Square, London WC1A 2LP. T:020 7543 5400. Price (2002) is £7.50 incl. p&p.

Help the Aged, 207–221 Pentonville Road, London N1 9UZ. T:020 7278 1114. Runs SeniorLine, a free advice and information service, available throughout the UK for older people and their carers. Trained advice workers can help with enquiries about welfare/disability benefits, community/residential care and housing options. Call free for England, Scotland and Wales on T:0808 800 6565. For Northern Ireland call on T:0808 808 7575. Lines are open 9 a.m. – 4 p.m., Monday to Friday.

Civil Service Retirement Fellowship, 1b Deals Gateway, Blackheath Road, London SE10 8BW. T:020 8691 7411. The Fellowship runs a home visiting service for those who are housebound or living alone and has an extensive network of branches and local groups throughout the country which offer a wide range of social activities for retired civil servants and their partners.

Disability Alliance, Universal House, 88–94 Wentworth Street, London E1 7SA. T:020 7247 8776; Rights Advice Line: 020 7247 8763. Gives advice over the telephone on social security benefit issues. Also publishes an annual *Disability Rights Handbook* which is packed with information on benefits and services for all people with disabilities and their families. Price £13.50 post-free (£9.50 for customers in receipt of any benefit).

Transport

The difficulty of getting around is often a major problem for elderly and disabled people. In addition to the facilities run by voluntary organisations already mentioned, there are several other very useful services.

Tripscope. Lists details of hundreds of transport schemes around the country and abroad, helpful to elderly and/or disabled people, including those needing to use a wheelchair. For further information, T:0845 758 5641 (voice and minicom).

London Taxi Card Service. A scheme whereby disabled people can incur taxi fares up to £10.80 but only pay about £1.50. Normal extras, however, such as weekend charges and additional passengers, are payable by the cardholder. The fleet includes taxis capable of accommodating wheelchairs. Leaflets and application forms are obtainable from local authority social services departments or The Association of London Government Taxi Card (T:020 7484 2929). The prices quoted above are a general London average but vary to some extent according to the borough in which the user is resident.

Mobility Advice and Vehicle Information Service (MAVIS), O'Wing Macadam Avenue, Old Wokingham Road, Crowthorne, Berkshire RG45 6XD T:01344 661000. MAVIS is an information service which advises on all aspects of mobility – in particular, problems associated with driving. Its services include assessment of older motorists wishing to return to driving after a stroke or other disabling illness and advice on car adaptations to relieve the pain of arthritic joints or other conditions that make driving uncomfortable. While general information is free, charges for the more specialised services are as follows: driving ability assessment for individuals who have a disability, £60; advice on car adaptations, including test driving, £40; vehicle familiarisation session, £15.

Driving licence renewal at age 70

All drivers aged 70 are sent a licence renewal form and have to pay a £6 fee to have their licence renewed. The licence has to be renewed (and £6 paid) at least every three years. Depending on the individual's health, including in particular their eyesight, the driver might be sent a new form to complete after only one or two years. If this applies, the form must be completed honestly but no extra charge will be made.

If you have any queries or if, after three weeks of returning the form, your new licence has not arrived, contact: Customer Enquiries – Drivers, DVLA, Swansea SA6 7JL. T: 0870 240 0009. Minicom: 01792 782787.

Holidays

Many people in their late seventies and older travel across the world, go on activity holidays, see the great sights in this country and abroad without any more difficulty than anyone else. They will find ideas galore in Chapter 14, including information about how to obtain assistance at airports and railway stations. However, some elderly people, especially those who are in any way disabled, need special facilities if a stay away from home is to be possible. A number of organisations can help.

ATS Travel, 1 Tank Lane, Purfleet, Essex RM19 1TA. T:01708 863198. ATS Travel specialises in arranging holidays for people with disabilities, whether travelling alone, with a companion or in a group. It will fix all the necessary arrangements to make travel, whether in the UK or overseas, as easy as possible, including: organising the journey, booking suitable accommodation, ensuring the availability of special diets, arranging for the provision of aids or equipment that may be needed together with any other requirements.

Holiday Care, 2nd Floor, Imperial Buildings, Victoria Road, Horley, Surrey RH6 7PZ. T:01293 774535; Minicom: 01293 776943. Runs an information service providing details of holiday facilities, both in the UK and abroad, for people with special needs including the frail elderly and those with disabilities. The service is free.

John Grooms, PO Box 36, Cowbridge CF71 7GB. T:01446 771311. Manages a variety of accessible holiday accommodation including self-catering chalets, flats and three award-winning hotels, one of which in South Glamorgan offers 24-hour care.

A number of the specialist voluntary organisations run holiday centres or provide specially adapted self-catering accommodation. In some cases, outings and entertainment are offered; in others, individuals plan their own activities and amusement. Guests requiring assistance usually need to be accompanied by a companion, although in a few instances care arrangements are inclusive. Most of the organisations can advise about the possibility of obtaining a grant or other financial assistance. For further details, contact the following:

Arthritis Care, 18 Stephenson Way, London NW1 2HD. T:020 7380 6500.

Multiple Sclerosis Society, MS National Centre, 372 Edgware Road, London NW2 6ND. T:020 8438 0700. Helpline: 0808 800 8000 (9 a.m. – 9 p.m., Monday – Friday).

Royal National Institute for the Blind (RNIB), 105 Judd Street, London WC1H 9NE. T: 0845 766 9999.

Parkinson's Disease Society, 215 Vauxhall Bridge Road, London SW1V 1EJ. T:020 7931 8080.

Winged Fellowship Trust, Angel House, 20–32 Pentonville Road, London N1 9XD. T:0845 345 1970. Provides holidays for people with disabilities. Care is provided and guests can come alone or with their carer. A number of weeks are kept specially for people with Alzheimer's Disease.

There are also a couple of useful publications, listing a wide choice of holiday venues, where disabled travellers can go in the normal way but with the advantage of having special facilities provided.

The Disabled Travellers' Guide, by the AA, gives information on holiday accommodation suitable for disabled individuals and their families, together with advice on travelling in Europe. £4.99 (free to AA members) by calling the AA Disability Helpline on T:0800 262050.

Holidays in Britain and Ireland, £8, available from RADAR.

Finally, a number of organisations provide rent-assisted (or sometimes, free) holidays for the financially needy. Local Citizens' Advice Bureaux, Age Concern groups and county branches of the British Red Cross will often know what, if anything, is available to residents in the area.

Power of attorney

Around the late-60s, many perfectly fit men and women wonder whether it might be sensible to give power of attorney to someone they trust. This involves authorising another person to take business and other financial decisions on their behalf, on the basis that any such decisions would reflect the action that they themselves would have taken. Until a few years ago, the power could only be used where the individual was unwilling rather than incapable of acting for him/herself. So in effect just at the time when the power was most needed it ceased to exist. However, thanks to a law known as the Enduring Powers of Attorney Act 1985, an enduring power is not automatically revoked by any subsequent mental incapacity but can now continue, regardless of any decline, throughout the individual's life. (N.B. An ordinary power of attorney would be revoked by subsequent mental incapacity.)

To protect the donor and the nominated attorney, the Act clearly lays down certain principles which must be observed, with both sides signing a declaration that they understand the various rights and duties involved. The Act furthermore calls for the power to be formally registered with the Public Trust Office in the event of the donor being, or becoming, mentally incapable.

As any lawyer would explain, the right time to give power of attorney is when the individual is in full command of his or her faculties, so that potential situations that would require decisions can be properly discussed and the donor's wishes made clear. For the enduring power of attorney to be valid, the donor must in any event be capable of understanding what he/she is agreeing to at the time of making the power.

There are two ways of drawing up an enduring power of attorney: either through a solicitor or by buying a standard form published by OyezStraker Business Services Ltd. (ref. Con 36E), available by phone from **OyezStraker Group Ltd** on T: 0870 737 7370 or from any OyezStraker shop. It is sensible for people without a legal background to consult a solicitor.

Temporary living-in help

Elderly people living alone can be more vulnerable to 'flu and other winter ailments. They may have a fall; or, for no apparent reason, may go through a period of being forgetful and neglecting themselves. Equally, as they become older, they may not be able to cope as well with managing their home or caring for themselves. In the event of an emergency or if you have reason for concern – perhaps because you are going on holiday and will not be around to keep a watchful eye – engaging living-in help can be a godsend. Most agencies tend inevitably to be on the expensive side, although in the event of a real problem often represent excellent value for money. A more unusual and interesting longer-term possibility is to recruit the help of a Community Service Volunteer.

Community Service Volunteers, 237 Pentonville Road, London N1 9NJ. T:020 7278 6601. The Volunteers are young people, aged over 16, involved in community service through a range of nationwide projects. CSV's Independent Living Projects match full-time helpers with individuals and families who need a high degree of support. The volunteers are untrained and work for periods of 4 to 12 months away from home.

They take their instructions from the people for whom they are working but are not of course substitutes for professional carers. In general they provide practical assistance in the home including, for example: shopping, light cooking, tidying up, attending to the garden and sometimes also decorating jobs. They also offer companionship.

Usually a care scheme is set up through a social worker, who supervises how the arrangement is working out. Volunteers are placed on a one month's trial basis. There is an annual retainer of £2,160 that can be paid in monthly instalments (in case of real financial need, the social worker would assess whether the local authority could pay the costs). Other charges include: fares; accommodation; full board or a weekly food allowance of £33.50; pocket money of £27 a week; plus one week's break with allowances, after four months. Contact your parents' local social services department; or approach CSV direct, at the address given above.

Agencies

The agencies listed specialise in providing temporary help, rather than permanent staff. Charges vary, but in addition to the weekly payment to helpers, there is normally an agency booking fee. As a rule payment is gross, so your parents will not be involved in having to work out tax or national insurance.

Consultus Services Agency Ltd., 17 London Road, Tonbridge, Kent TN10 3AB. T:01732 355231.

Country Cousins (Horsham) Ltd., 10a Market Square, Horsham, West Sussex RH12 1EX. T:0845 601 4003.

Universal Aunts Ltd., PO Box 304, London SW4 0NN. T:020 7738 8937.

For a further list of agencies, see *Yellow Pages* under heading 'Employment' or 'Care' agencies.

Nursing care

If one of your parents needs regular nursing care, their doctor may be able to arrange for a community or district nurse to visit them at home. This will not, of course, be a sleeping-in arrangement but simply involves a qualified nurse calling round when necessary.

If you want more concentrated home nursing you will have to go through a private agency. Consultus can sometimes supply trained nurses. Additionally, there are many specialist agencies, which can arrange hourly, daily or live-in nurses on a temporary or longer term basis.

Terms of employment vary considerably. Some nurses will literally undertake nursing duties only – and nothing else; and may even expect to have their meals provided. Others will do light housework and act as nurse-companions. Fees vary throughout the country, with London inevitably being most expensive. Private health insurance can sometimes be claimed against part of the cost but this is generally only in respect of qualified nurses.

Your local Health Centre or Social Services Department should be able to give you names and addresses of local agencies. Or look in the *Yellow Pages* under 'Nursing Agencies'.

Permanent living-in help

There may come a time when you feel that it is no longer safe to allow one of your parents to live entirely on their own. One possibility is to engage a companion or housekeeper on a permanent basis but such arrangements are normally very expensive: the going rate for housekeepers in London is anything between £295 and £400 a week clear. However, if you want to investigate the idea further, many domestic agencies (see the *Yellow Pages*) supply housekeeper-companions. Alternatively, you might consider advertising in *The Lady*, which is probably the most widely read publication for these kinds of posts.

Permanent help can also sometimes be provided by agencies (such as those listed under 'Temporary living-in-help'), who will supply continuous four-weekly placements. This is an expensive option and the lack of continuity can at times be distressing for elderly people, particularly at the change-over point. But it can also lead to a happier atmosphere as the housekeeper comes fresh to the job and neither party has time to start getting on each other's nerves.

Au pairs are cheaper: roughly £50 to £65 a week with full board and lodging. A drawback, however, is that most au pairs speak inadequate English (at least when they first arrive); and, as they are technically students living 'en famille', they must by law be given plenty of free time to attend school and study. An alternative solution for some families is to engage a reliable daily woman who, in the event of illness or other problem, would be prepared to stay overnight.

Flexible care arrangements

One of the problems for many elderly people is that the amount of care they need is liable to vary according to the state of their health and other factors including, for example, the availability of neighbours and family. Whereas after an operation the requirement may be for someone with basic nursing skills, a few weeks later the only need may be for someone to act as a companion – or simply to pop in for the odd hour during the day to cook a hot meal and check all is well. Few agencies cater for all the complex permutations that may be necessary in caring for an elderly person in their own home but two that aim to offer a genuinely flexible service are Anchor Care Alternatives and Cura Domi – Care at Home. Equally worth knowing about is the United Kingdom Home Care Association.

Anchor Care Alternatives, 7th Floor, Chancery House, St. Nicholas Way, Sutton, Surrey SM1 1JB. T:020 8652 1900. Care workers can be engaged by the hour, or nightly, for temporary or longer periods; or also on a more permanent residential basis. All staff are personally interviewed; their references are taken up and training is given. There is also a 24-hour emergency helpline.

Prices vary according to the area and duties required. To give you an idea: hourly daytime rates, for example, are £9.86 in London, £8.17 in Wolverhampton and £8 in Bolton.

Cura Domi – Care at Home, Guardian House, Borough Road, Godalming, Surrey GU7 2AE. T: 01483 420055. Carers undertake all or any of the tasks traditionally managed by a reliable housekeeper-companion: shopping, cooking, attending to the chores around the home, helping an elderly person bath or dress, reading aloud and generally providing whatever assistance may be needed. Where appropriate, carers can also provide all personal care and help needed with such problems as incontinence and dementia. Depending on what is required, they will come in for the hour or live in full-time for a few days, few weeks or longer. Great care is taken to try to match clients with a carer who possesses the right skills and temperament and all carers are backed by a team of RGN care managers on 24-hour call, seven days a week.

There is a once-only non-returnable registration/assessment fee with a list of varying prices according to whether the job is weekday, weekend, day-time, night-time or live-in. For example: hourly rates are from £9.96 weekdays, £13.44 weekends; overnight hourly sleep-in charges are from £4.30 weekdays, £5.30 weekends. Live-in fees vary according to the requirements, from £577.92 to £655.20 for a seven day week. Other than travel costs, all prices quoted are inclusive. At the present time daily care is only available in the Surrey and Hampshire areas. Live-in care, however, can be arranged anywhere in the country.

United Kingdom Home Care Association, 42b Banstead Road, Carshalton Beeches, Surrey SM5 3NW. T:020 8288 1551. Represents over 1,000 member branches throughout the country that specialise in providing care for elderly and/or disabled people in their own home. All requirements are catered for including temporary and permanent posts, residential, daily, overnight and hourly work. UKHCA runs a Helpline which can refer enquirers to local members committed to upholding the Association's Code of Practice.

Although any of these suggestions can work extremely well, many families find them either too expensive or haphazard – or both. So, sooner or later the decision may come down to a choice between residential care and inviting a parent to live with you.

Most families, to their credit, choose to care for an elderly parent in their own home; or sometimes, particularly in the case of a daughter, to move into their parents' home.

Emergency care for pets

For many elderly people a pet is a most important part of their lives, providing companionship and fun as well as stimulating them into taking regular outdoor exercise. But in the event of the owner having to go into hospital or due to some other emergency being temporarily unable to care for their pet, there can be real problems including concern for the welfare of the animal and considerable distress to the owner.

To overcome these problems, two highly imaginative schemes have been set up, one operating throughout the UK and the other just in Scotland. Depending on what is required, volunteers will either simply feed or exercise the animal or will care for it in their own home until the owner can manage again.

Cinnamon Trust, Foundry House, Foundry Square, Hayle, Cornwall TR27 4HH. T:01736 757900. As well as the above services, Cinnamon also offers permanent care for pets whose owners have died. Some animals stay at the Trust's havens in Cornwall and Devon. Others are found alternative loving homes with a new owner. Either way, every effort is made to help pets adjust. Familiar possessions, such as the animal's basket or favourite toy, are very much encouraged and as far as possible 'families' of pets are kept together to avoid the further distress of separating them from their companions. Emergency services can be called 24 hours a day. The Trust makes no charge but donations, or a bequest, are very much appreciated.

Pet Fostering Service Scotland. T:01877 331 496. The focus is on temporary care. The only charges are the cost of pet's food, litter – in the case of cats – and any veterinary fees that may be incurred during fostering. In the main the service caters for dogs, cats and birds but some volunteers are willing to care for more exotic species such as rodents. If help is needed telephone the above number.

Another organisation that could be useful to know about is Home and Pet Care which, as well as providing a home-sitting service, specialises in caring for any household pets. Average charges are about £140 a week. Contact: **Home and Pet Care Ltd.**, Nether Row Hall, Hesket-New-Market, Wigton, Cumbria CA7 8LA. T:016974 78515.

Practical help for carers

If your parent is still fairly active – visits friends, does his/her own shopping, enjoys some hobby which gets him/her out and about – the strains and difficulties may be fairly minimal. This applies particularly if your home lends itself to creating a granny flat, so everyone can retain some privacy and your parent can continue to enjoy maximum independence. However, this is not always possible and in the case of an ill or very frail person far more intensive care may be required.

If you have to go out to work, need time to attend to other responsibilities or quite understandably feel that if you are to remain human you must have time for your own interests, it is important to know what help is available and how to obtain it.

The many services provided by local authorities and voluntary agencies, described earlier in the chapter, apply for the most part equally to an elderly person living with their family as to one living alone. If there is nothing in the list that solves a particular problem you may have, it is sensible to talk to the Citizens' Advice Bureau and Social Services Department, as there may be some special local facility that could provide the solution.

In particular, you might ask about **day centres and clubs**. Activities and surroundings vary, so you might wish to investigate. However, a responsible person will always be in charge and transport, to and from the venue, is often provided.

You could also ask the local Age Concern group and WRVS. Age Concern will also be able to tell you about the possibility of **voluntary sitters**: people who come in and stay with an elderly person for a few hours (or sometimes overnight), to prevent them being on their own. Other sources to try include: the local branch of the British Red Cross, St. John Ambulance and the Volunteer Bureau (see local telephone directory).

In response to the government's Community Care scheme, most areas now have, or are planning, **respite care facilities** to enable carers to take a break from their dependants from time to time. Depending on the circumstances, this could be for just the odd day or possibly for a week or two to enable carers who need it to have a real rest. A particularly welcome aspect of respite care is that many schemes specially cater for, among others, elderly people with dementia. For further information, contact your local Health or Social Services Department.

Another service well worth knowing about is Crossroads which arranges for helpers to care for very frail or disabled people in their own home, while the regular carer is away. They will come in during the day, or stay overnight, and provide whatever practical help is required. Arrangements are planned very much on an individual basis and are tailored to meet particular family circumstances. Demand for the service is very high, so priority is given according to the strain imposed on the carer.

Both the Citizens' Advice Bureau and Social Services Department should be able to give you the address of the local branch. Alternatively, you could contact Crossroads direct: **Crossroads**, Caring for Carers, 10 Regent Place, Rugby, Warwickshire CV21 2PN. T:01788 573653.

More help should be on the way. The Princess Royal Trust for Carers is aiming to help set up one Carers Centre in every social services area in the UK in order to give carers advice, information and support. Centres in over 100 places – including Scotland, Wales and Northern Ireland – have already been established with more due to open during 2003. For further information, ask at your social services department; or contact **The Princess Royal Trust for Carers** on T:020 7480 7788.

Holiday breaks for carers

There are various schemes to enable families with an elderly relative to go on holiday alone or simply to enjoy a respite from their caring responsibilities.

A number of local authorities run **fostering schemes**, on similar lines to child fostering. Elderly people are invited to stay in a neighbour's home and live in the household as an ordinary family member. Lasting relationships often develop. There may be a charge or the service may be run on a voluntary basis (or be paid for by the local authority). Schemes are patchy around the country. The Citizens' Advice Bureau and Social Services Department will advise you if anything exists.

Some voluntary organisations, including Age Concern groups and sometimes the Mothers' Union, organise **holidays for older people** to give relatives a break. Different charities take responsibility according to the area where you live: the CAB, Volunteer Bureau or the Social Services Department should know whom you should approach. As with most types of provision, priority is given to families in greatest need.

You might also usefully contact Holiday Care which, as well as advising on holidays for elderly and disabled people, can also advise carers who need a holiday about suitable provision for their dependent relative while they are away. Write to or telephone **Holiday Care**, 2nd Floor, Imperial Buildings, Victoria Road, Horley, Surrey RH6 7PZ. T:01293 774535.

Another solution is a **short stay home**, which is residential accommodation variously run by local authorities, voluntary organisations or by private individuals which caters specifically for elderly people. Style and facilities vary from the very luxurious to the frankly decrepit. The different types of home are described in more detail under the heading 'Residential care' further in the chapter. For information about local authority provision, ask the Social Services Department.

If, as opposed to general care, proper medical attention is necessary, you should consult your parent's GP. Many **hospitals and nursing homes** offer short-stay care arrangements as a means of relieving relatives and a doctor should be able to help organise this for you.

Fount of almost all knowledge on anything to do with caring is:

Carers UK, 20–25 Glasshouse Yard, London EC1A 4JT. T:020 7490 8818 (general); 0808 808 7777 (CarersLine, Mon – Fri, 10 a.m. – noon; 2 p.m. – 4 p.m.). Carers UK, which was set up to support and campaign for those caring for an ill, frail or disabled relative at home, has over 120 self-help branches which are run for and by carers. Annual membership is £8 and all members receive the magazine *Caring*.

Jewish Care, 221 Golders Green Road, London NW11 9DQ. T:020 8922 2000. Runs a number of carers' groups, mostly in London.

Useful reading

Caring for Someone? (SD4), available free from social security offices.

Benefits and allowances

There are a number of benefits/allowances available to those with responsibility for the care of an elderly person and/or to elderly people themselves.

Entitlements for carers

Home responsibilities protection. A means of protecting your State pension if you are unable to work because of the necessity to care for an elderly person. For further details, see under 'State pensions' at the start of Chapter 3 or ask for form CF 411 at any social security office.

Invalid Care Allowance. Men and women who spend at least 35 hours a week looking after a severely disabled person (i.e. someone who gets Attendance Allowance, Constant Attendance Allowance or, the two higher care components of Disability Living Allowance) may qualify for ICA. You do not need to be related to the person; nor do you need to live at the same address. Current ICA payment (2002/03) is £42.45 a week and counts as taxable income. Carers who receive income support, housing benefit or council tax benefit are entitled to a special £24.80 premium. If caring ceases, for whatever reason, the carer premium continues to be paid for a further eight weeks.

Claimants may earn up to £75 a week after deduction of allowable expenses without loss of benefit.

NB: An important change is that the previous age limit for entitlement to ICA has been removed and carers aged 65 and over are now equally eligible to claim the allowance. From April 2003, the name is also being changed to Carer's Allowance. For further details, enquire at your social security office.

Entitlements for elderly/disabled people

Higher Personal Allowance. People over 65 receive a higher personal allowance – £6,100 for those aged 65–74 and £6,370 for those aged 75 and over – compared with the basic personal allowance of £4,615 (2002/03). The full amount is only given to people whose income does not exceed £17,900. People with higher incomes will have the age-related element of their personal allowance reduced by £1 for every £2 of income above the income limit. For further information, see Inland Revenue leaflet IR 121 *Income Tax and Pensioners*, available from any tax office.

Higher Married Couple's Allowance. A higher married couple's allowance is similarly available to those couples where the elder partner is over 75. The current amount is £5,535 compared with the normal minimum of £2,110. Less well off couples aged between 65 (i.e. before 6 April 2000) and 74 receive £5,465. However, as with higher rate personal allowance (see above), the full amount is only given to those whose income does not exceed £17,900. All married couples allowances are restricted to 10 per cent tax relief.

Attendance Allowance. This is paid to people aged 65 or over who are severely disabled, either mentally or physically, and have needed almost constant care for at least six months. (They may be able to get the Allowance even if no-one has actually given them that help). An exception to the six months' qualifying period is made in the case of those who are terminally ill, who can receive the allowance without having to wait.

There are two rates of allowance: £56.25 a week for those needing 24-hour care; and £37.65 for those needing intensive day or night-time care. The allowance is tax free and is generally paid regardless of income (although payment might be affected by entering residential care). For further details, together with a claim form, obtain leaflet DS 702 from your social security office.

Disability Living Allowance (DLA). This benefit is paid to people up to the age of 65 inclusive who become disabled. It has two components – a mobility component and a care component. A person can be entitled to either one or to both components.

The level of benefit depends on the person's care and/or mobility needs. There are two rates for the mobility component and three rates for the care component.

The higher rate mobility component, i.e. for people who are unable or virtually unable to walk, is £39.30 a week; the lower rate, i.e. for those who due to physical or mental disability need guidance or supervision in getting around, is £14.90.

The three rates for the care component are: higher rate, £56.25; middle rate, £37.65; lower rate, £14.90.

Disability Living Allowance is tax free and is generally paid regardless of income (although payment might be affected by entering residential care).

Except in the case of people who are terminally ill who can receive the higher rate care component of DLA immediately, there is a normal qualifying period of three months.

For further information see leaflet DS 704, obtainable from any post office, Citizens' Advice Bureau or Social Security office. The leaflet contains a reply slip, which you should complete and return as soon as possible in order to obtain the necessary claim pack. The pack includes a questionnaire with space for you to explain how the disability is making your life more difficult.

Cold weather payments. These are designed to give particularly vulnerable people extra help with heating costs during very cold weather. Anyone aged 60 and over who is in receipt of income support, or income-based jobseeker's allowance, qualifies automatically. The payment is made by post as soon as the temperature in an area is forecast to drop – or actually drops – to zero degrees celsius (or below) for seven consecutive days, so people can turn up their heating secure in the knowledge that they will be receiving extra cash help. The amount paid is £8.50 a week and those eligible should receive it without having to claim. In the event of a problem, contact your social security office.

Winter fuel payments. This is a special annual tax-free payment of £200 given to all households with a resident aged 60 or older. Until very recently the payment only applied to households where someone had reached actual pension age. However, because the law has now been changed men who missed out as a result of being under 65 may be able to claim a back payment for up to three years. To be able to claim for the full three years they would need to have been born by at latest 11 January 1938. The payments have been altered several times, so claims could only be for the amount that was payable at the time, namely: £20 for 1997 and 1998 and £100 for 1999. Men who were aged 60 or more in 1997 when the payments first started and who think they might have a claim should ring the helpline on T:08459 151515 for further information.

A number of women aged 60 or older may also have missed out on receiving the payment, most usually because they were not in receipt of a State pension. They too are advised to call the above helpline.

Free TV licence. People aged 75 and older no longer have to pay for their TV licence.

Financial assistance

A number of charities give financial assistance to elderly people in need. These include:

Counsel & Care, Twyman House, 16 Bonny Street, London NW1 9PG. T:0845 300 7585 (10 a.m. – 12.30 p.m. and 2 p.m. – 4 p.m.). Advice can be given to those in need of nursing care who wish to remain in their own homes. Single needs payments are sometimes available to help towards holidays, special equipment, telephone installations and other priority items.

Elizabeth Finn Trust, 1 Derry Street, London W8 5HY. T:020 7396 6700. Provides grants to enable people to remain in their own home or in the care home of their choice. Also runs its own care homes.

Guild of Aid for Gentle People, 10 St. Christopher's Place, London W1U 1HZ. T:020 7935 0641. Can assist those 'of gentle birth or good education' who want to stay in their own home and who cannot call on any professional/trade body. The Guild will also consider long-term help with fees in residential and nursing homes.

Independent Living 93 Fund, PO Box 183, Nottingham NG8 3RD. T:0115 942 8191. This is a trust fund set up with government backing to assist people – aged 16 to 65 – with severe disabilities, pay for domestic or personal care to enable them to remain in their own homes.

To become eligible, applicants must first approach their local authority for assistance under the community care scheme and be successful in obtaining care services to the value of about £200 a week. The Trust may top this up by up to an extra £395, provided: (1) they are living on their own or with someone who is unable to provide all the care they need (2) they are receiving income support (or have a similar level of income once care has been paid) (3) they have savings of under £18,500 and (4) they receive the highest rate care component of Disability Living Allowance.

Motability, Customer Information Services, Goodman House, Station Approach, Harlow, Essex CM20 2ET. T:01279 635666. This is a registered charity set up to assist recipients of the higher rate mobility component of DLA to use their allowance to lease, or buy, a car or a powered wheelchair or scooter. Motability's charitable fund can help those unable to afford the advance payment on some lease vehicles – or necessary adaptations to the vehicle. Grants are available for the least expensive option to meet individuals' basic mobility needs.

Royal United Kingdom Beneficent Association (RUKBA), 6 Avonmore Road, London W14 8RL. T:020 7605 4200. Provides life-time annuities to older persons in need. Also publishes a free advice guide for the over 60's, entitled '60-Wise'.

SSAFA Forces Help, 19 Queen Elizabeth Street, London SE1 2LP. T:020 7403 8783. Assistance is restricted to those who have served in the armed forces and their families. Grants can be made to meet immediate need including rent, wheelchairs and similar essentials. Contact via the local branch is preferred (see local telephone directory for address or ask at Citizens' Advice Bureau).

The Royal Agricultural Benevolent Institution, Shaw House, 27 West Way, Oxford OX2 0QH. General enquiries T:01865 724931; Emergency helpline T:01865 727888. Supports retired disabled or disadvantaged members of the farming community and their families, in England, Wales and Northern Ireland. Assistance includes a range of grants, help towards fees in residential and nursing homes and advice on other available support. RABI has two residential care homes and also sheltered flats available at Bury St. Edmunds and Burnham-on-Sea and nomination rights to other homes across England and Wales.

Wireless for the Bedridden Society, 159a High Street, Hornchurch, Essex RM11 3YB. T:01708 621101. Freephone: 0800 018 2137. Loans on a permanent basis radios and televisions to elderly housebound people who cannot afford sets. Application should be made through a health visitor, social worker or officer of a recognised organisation.

Useful reading

For other sources of financial help, ask your library for: *A Guide to Grants for Individuals in Need*, published by the Directory of Social Change; also *The Charities Digest*, published by Waterlow Professional Publishing.

Helpful guidance

For many people one of the main barriers to getting help is knowing which of the many thousands of charities to approach.

Charity Search exists to help elderly people in need overcome the problem by putting them in contact with those charities most likely to be able to assist. Write to: The Secretary, **Charity Search**, 25 Portview Road, Avonmouth, Bristol BS11 9LD. T:0117 982 4060.

Special accommodation

Retired people who need particular support, assistance or care may choose or need to move to accommodation where special services are provided. This can either be sheltered housing or a residential home. Both terms cover an enormous spectrum, so anyone considering either of these options should make a point of investigating the market before reaching a decision.

An all too common mistake is for people to anticipate old age long before it arrives and to move into accommodation that is either too small or quite unnecessarily 'sheltered', years before they have need of the facilities. By the same token, some individuals buy or rent sheltered housing with a minimum of support services, only to have to move a few months later because they need rather more help than is available.

Choosing the right accommodation is critically important, as it can make all the difference to independence, life style and general well-being. It can also of course lift a great burden off families' shoulders to know that their parents are happy, comfortable, in congenial surroundings and with help on tap, should this be necessary.

Sheltered housing

As a general description, sheltered housing is usually a development of independent, purpose-designed bungalows or flats within easy access of shops and public transport. They generally have a warden, an alarm system for emergencies and often some common facilities, such as: a garden, possibly a launderette, a sitting room and a dining room with meals provided for residents, on an optional basis, either once a day or several days a week.

Residents normally have access to all the usual range of services – home helps, meals on wheels – in the same way as any other elderly person.

Sheltered housing is available for sale or rental, variously through private developers, housing associations or local authorities. It is occasionally also provided through gifted housing schemes; or on a shared ownership basis.

Sheltered housing for sale

During the early part of the nineties, anyone looking to purchase sheltered accommodation was very much in a buyers' market. Not only was there a wide choice of property but due to the recession prices actually dropped.

While there were bargains to be had, the downside was that some developers went into receivership. Many others either froze all new work or cut back dramatically on the number of new properties they were planning.

The result is that, with sales now once again on the increase, there are fears of a shortage with some buyers having to go on a waiting list. Although this is emphatically not a reason for rushing into a decision you might regret, if you were hoping to move in the fairly near future it could be as well to start looking sooner rather than later.

There are around 30 companies offering sheltered housing for sale – with standards and facilities varying enormously. Some also provide residential and nursing care as an adjunct to their retirement home schemes.

Flats and houses are usually sold on long leases (99 years or more) for a capital sum, with a weekly or monthly service charge to cover maintenance and resident care services.

Should a resident decide to move, the property can usually be sold on the open market, either through an estate agent, or through the developer, provided the prospective buyer is over 55 years of age. Most developers impose a levy of 1 per cent of the sale price for checking the credentials of incoming residents, irrespective of whether the property is sold through them. Look carefully at any schemes that enable you to buy the property at a discount as many such schemes entitle the developer to retain a proportion of the equity on resale.

Occupiers normally have to enter into a management agreement with the housebuilder and it is important to establish exactly what the commitment is likely to be before buying into such schemes. Factors that should be considered include: who the managing agent is; the warden's duties; what the service charge covers; the ground rent; the arrangements for any repairs that might prove necessary; whether there is a residents' association; whether pets are allowed; what the conditions are with regard to reselling the property – and the tenant's rights in the matter.

Although the rights of sheltered housing residents have been strengthened over the years, you would nevertheless be strongly recommended to get any contract, or agreement, vetted by a solicitor before proceeding.

Prices. The range of prices is very wide – between approximately £50,000 and £600,000 – depending on size, location and type of property. Weekly service charges vary between roughly £35 and £55, with around £40 being the norm. Additionally, there is normally an annual ground rental.

The service charge usually covers: the cost of the warden, alarm system, maintenance, repair and renewal of any communal facilities (external and internal) and sometimes the heating and lighting costs. It may also cover insurance on the building (but not the contents). A particular point to watch is that the service charge tends to rise annually, sometimes well above the inflation level. Be wary of service charges that seem uncommonly reasonable in the sales literature, as these are often increased sharply following purchase. Owners of sheltered accommodation have the same rights as other leaseholders and charges can therefore be challenged by appeal to a leasehold valuation tribunal.

A further safeguard is the Sheltered Housing Code operated by the **National House Building Council** (Chiltern Avenue, Amersham, Bucks HP6 5AP. T:01494 434477), which is mandatory for all registered housebuilders selling sheltered homes. The Code, which applies to all new sheltered dwellings in England and Wales registered on or after 1st April 1990, has two main requirements: (a) that every prospective purchaser should be given a Purchasers Information Pack (PIP), clearly outlining all essential information that they will need to enable them to decide whether or not to buy; (b) that the builder and management organisation enter into a formal legal agreement giving purchasers the benefit of the legal rights specified in the Code. An independent advice service is run in association with Age Concern.

For those on lowish incomes, it may also be possible to get housing benefit to meet some or all of the service charge. The local authority Housing Department will advise on this.

The following organisations can provide information about sheltered housing for sale:

Elderly Accommodation Counsel, 3rd Floor, 89 Albert Embankment, London SE1 7TP. T:020 7820 1343. Maintains a nationwide database of all types of accommodation for elderly people and gives advice and detailed information to help enquirers choose the accommodation most suited to their needs.

AIMS, Astral House, 1268 London Road, London SW16 4ER. T:020 8765 7465. AIMS, a part of Age Concern, offers information, legal advice and a mediation service to residents of both rented sheltered housing and private retirement housing.

Useful reading
A Buyer's Guide to Retirement Housing, published by Age Concern England/National Housing and Town Planning Council, price £6.99 (plus £1.95 p&p). An excellent guide to the sort of questions you should ask before committing yourself. Also useful information on the financial aspects of buying a sheltered home. Available from Age Concern Books, PO Box 232, Newton Abbot, Devon TQ12 4XQ. T:0870 442 2044.

Private companies with sheltered housing for sale
New developments are constantly under construction. Properties tend to be sold quickly soon after completion, so it pays to find out about future developments and to get on any waiting lists well in advance of a prospective purchase. Firms specialising in this type of property include:

Beechcroft Developments, 1 Church Lane, Wallingford, Oxfordshire OX10 0DX. T:01491 825522. Two and three-bedroom cottages and apartments situated in market towns in: Berkshire, Buckinghamshire, Oxfordshire, Wiltshire, Hampshire, Gloucestershire, Surrey and Dorset. Prices range from £245,000 to £600,000. Brochures available on request.

Bovis Homes Retirement Living, The Manor House, North Ash Road, New Ash Green, Longfield, Kent DA3 8HQ. T:01474 876363. One and two-bedroom apartments – in Dorset, Lincoln, Eastbourne, the Wirral, Essex, Surrey and the West Midlands – with prices ranging from £105,000 to £450,000.

English Courtyard, 8 Holland Street, London W8 4LT. Freephone: 0800 220858. Architecturally award-winning 'courtyard-style' schemes throughout England. Two and three-bedroom houses, cottages and flats for sale on 150-year leases. Prices range from £330,000 to £505,000.

Home Housing Association, Ridley House, Regent Centre, Gosforth, Newcastle upon Tyne NE3 3JE. T:0191 285 0311. Sites throughout the country with varying levels of independence/management. Prices up to £80,000.

McCarthy & Stone (Developments) Ltd., Homelife House, 26–32 Oxford Road, Bournemouth, Dorset BH8 8EZ. T:01202 292480. Builds over 1,500 new retirement apartments a year in all parts of the country including Scotland and Wales. Prices start at around £60,000.

Retirement Care Group Ltd., 43–45 High Road, Bushey Heath, Herts WD23 1EE. T:020 8901 0300. A major management company with retirement estates in all parts of England and Wales. Resale properties available, including studios, flats, cottages and bungalows, at prices from £50,000 – £250,000.

Also of interest: **Country Houses Association**, Suite 10, Aynhoe Park, Aynho, Banbury, Oxon OX17 3BQ. T:01869 812800. CHA provides one-to three-room fully serviced apartments in historic country houses across the south of England. Residents pay a deposit for their apartment which is refunded in full when they leave. Additionally, there is a monthly charge which covers all meals, heating, cleaning and maintenance. Deposits range from £45,000 to £100,000, and monthly charges from £1,200 per person. CHA also offers short holiday breaks and a membership scheme for those interested in visiting the houses.

Housing associations with sheltered housing for sale

Housing associations build sheltered housing for sale and also manage sheltered housing developments on behalf of private construction companies.

Guardian Retirement Housing, Milestone Place, 100 Bolton Road, Bradford, Yorks BD1 4DH. T:01274 381 600. Flats and bungalows are available on long leases at prices ranging from £30,000 to £300,000.

Retirement Lease Housing Association, 2nd Floor, 1 Pickford Street, Aldershot, Hants GU11 1TY. T:01252 356 000. Bungalows and flats on 99-year leases from around £80,000 and upwards in the South East. Shared ownership purchase available in some cases.

Rented sheltered housing

This is normally provided by local authorities, housing associations and certain benevolent societies. As with accommodation to buy, quality varies.

Local authorities. This is usually only available to people who have resided in the area for some time. There is often an upper and lower age limit for admission and prospective tenants may have to undergo a medical examination, since as a rule only those who are physically fit are accepted. Should a resident become infirm or frail, alternative accommodation will be found. Apply to the local Housing or Social Services Department or via a Housing Advice Centre.

Housing associations. Housing associations supply much of the newly built sheltered housing. Both rent and services charges vary around the country, with the average rent being £40 to £65 a week and service charge, depending on the facilities on offer, averaging between £10 and £25 a week. The **National Housing Federation** expects the combined weekly rent/service charge to average £65 during 2003. In case of need, income support or housing benefit may be obtained to help with the cost.

Before signing an agreement, a point you should be aware of is that some charitable housing associations, including the Abbeyfield Society, offer a licensee arrangement which does not provide the same security of tenure as some other tenancy agreements. Where this is the case, you are strongly advised to have the proposed contract checked by a lawyer to ensure you properly understand your rights – and those on the other side.

Citizens' Advice Bureaux and Housing Departments often keep a list of local housing associations. You can look in the *Yellow Pages* telephone directory. Or alternatively, you can contact the Housing Corporation, at the following address:

Housing Corporation, 149 Tottenham Court Road, London W1T 7BN. T:020 7393 2000. Will send you a list of their local offices who will be able to supply you with addresses of housing associations in their area.

For Scotland, Wales and Northern Ireland, contact:

Scottish Homes, Thistle House, 91 Haymarket Terrace, Edinburgh EH12 5HE. T:0131 313 0044.

The National Assembly for Wales, Cathay Park, Cardiff CF10 3NQ. T:029 2082 5111.

Northern Ireland Housing Executive, The Housing Centre, 2 Adelaide Street, Belfast BT2 8PB. T:028 9024 0588.

A few of the very many housing associations include:

The Abbeyfield Society, 53 Victoria Street, St. Albans, Herts AL1 3UW. T:01727 857536. Abbeyfield has over 800 very sheltered houses nationwide providing independent accommodation, a resident house-manager and main meals of the day. Also 82 houses providing 24-hour registered residential care facilities.

Anchor Trust, Fountain Court, Oxford Spires Business Park, Kidlington, Oxon OX5 1NZ. T:01865 854000. Provides over 24,000 flats for older people whose existing housing is inappropriate and who for pressing social, health and financial reasons need the security and support of sheltered housing. The flats are all over England and most schemes have a guest room and laundry. There are also a number of special retirement schemes for frail people who need more help with everyday living.

BNAI BRITH JBG Housing Association Ltd., Harmony Close, Princes Park Avenue, London NW11 0JJ. T:020 8381 4901. Some 600 sheltered flats primarily for Jewish people in housing need. Properties are located in London, Hemel Hempstead and Margate.

Central and Cecil Housing Trust, 2 Priory Road, Kew, Richmond, Surrey TW9 3DG. T:020 8940 9828. Provides a range of sheltered housing and residential care homes throughout London. Priority is given to those in greatest need with a local connection. Current charges for sheltered accommodation range from £83 a week for a bedsit to £102 for a one-bedroom flat. Residential care charges range from £340 to £480.

Habinteg Housing Association, 1 Pemberton Row, Fetter Lane, London EC4A 3PQ. T:020 7822 8700. Habinteg builds houses and bungalows for rent across England. All are fully accessible for wheelchair users and most of the schemes have an on-site community assistant to offer support if needed.

Hanover Housing Association, Hanover House, 1 Bridge Close, Staines TW18 4TB. T:01784 446000. Manages over 15,000 retirement properties for rent and sale throughout England. There are also 20 extra care housing estates where care is available 24 hours a day. Applications are encouraged from people over 60.

James Butcher Housing Association, James Butcher House, 39 High Street, Theale, Reading RG7 5AH. T:0118 931 7200. Provides sheltered and non-sheltered housing schemes, and also retirement leasehold apartments and bungalows, in Central Southern England. There are regional offices in Portsmouth, Polegate, Marlborough, Chobham and Theale.

Servite Houses, 2 Bridge Avenue, London W6 9JP. T:020 8307 3300. Some seventy sheltered housing schemes with resident warden in and around London, West Sussex, the West Midlands and Merseyside. Rent (incl. service charges) is about £65 per week. There are also nine residential care homes, two nursing homes and a day centre in the London region; three residential care homes in the West Midlands; and a day centre in Merseyside.

Benevolent societies. These all cater for specific professional and other groups.

Housing 21, The Triangle, Baring Road, Beaconsfield, Bucks HP9 2NA. T:01494 685200. A charitable care provider and housing association with over 14,000 properties in 400 sheltered housing schemes throughout England.

Royal Alfred Seafarers' Society, SBC House, Restmor Way, Wallington, Surrey SM6 7AH. T:020 8401 2889. Residential homes in Banstead and Eastbourne for retired mariners, their widows and those closely connected with the sea. Nursing care is provided at Banstead, as is sheltered housing under assured tenancy terms. For further details, contact the General Secretary at the above address.

SSAFA Forces Help, 19 Queen Elizabeth Street, London SE1 2LP. T:020 7403 8783. Works with the Abbeyfield Society to provide sheltered accommodation for retired ex-service people.

Alternative ways of buying sheltered accommodation

For those who cannot afford either to buy into sheltered housing outright or through a mortgage, there are a variety of alternative payment methods:

Shared ownership and 'Sundowner' schemes. Part-ownership schemes are now offered by a number of developers. Would-be residents who must be over 55 years part-buy/part-rent, with the amount of rent varying according to the size of the initial lump sum. Residents can sell at any time but they only recoup that percentage of the sale price which is proportionate to their original capital investment, with no allowance for any rental payments made over the intervening period.

'Investment' and gifted housing schemes. Some charities and housing associations operate these schemes, for which a capital sum is required to obtain sheltered accommodation. They work as follows. The buyer puts in the larger share of the capital, usually 50 to 80 per cent, and the housing association puts in the remainder. The buyer pays rent on the housing association's share of the accommodation and also service charges for the communal facilities.

Gifted housing schemes differ in that an individual donates his/her property to a registered charity, in return for being housed and cared for in their own home. The attraction is that the owner can remain in his or her own property with none of the burden of its upkeep. For further information, you might like to contact: **Help the Aged**, Community Services Division, 207–221 Pentonville Road, London N1 9UZ. T:020 7278 1114. However, it is advisable to consult a solicitor before signing anything, because such schemes have the big negative of reducing the value of the owner's estate with consequent loss for any beneficiaries.

Almshouses

The term 'almshouse' describes sheltered housing for elderly people of reduced means, which is administered by a charitable trust. There are now over 2,500 groups of almshouses providing about 30,000 dwellings. Although many are of considerable age, most of these have been modernised, and new ones are being built. Rents are not charged but there may be a maintenance contribution towards upkeep and heating.

A point you should be aware of is that, similar to Abbeyfield and some other charitable housing associations, almshouses do not provide the same security of tenure as some other tenancies. You would be well advised to have the proposed agreement checked by a lawyer or other expert to ensure you understand exactly what your rights are.

There is no standard way to apply for an almshouse since each charity has its own qualifications for residence. Some housing departments and advice centres keep lists of local almshouses; or write to: **The Almshouse Association**, Billingbear Lodge, Wokingham, Berkshire RG40 5RU. T:01344 452922.

Granny flats

A granny flat or annexe is a self-contained unit attached to a family house. A large house can be converted or extended for this purpose, but planning permission is needed. Enquire at your local authority planning department. Some councils have houses to rent with granny flats, particularly New Towns.

Housing for ethnic groups

ASRA Greater London Housing Association Ltd., 1 Long Lane, London SE1

4PG. T:020 7940 6600. Provides sheltered and residential care accommodation for Asian elders and single Asian women. There are also general family homes.

ASRA Midlands Housing Association, 78 Burleys Way, Leicester LE1 3BD. T:0116 253 6646. Offers a similar service to the above, together with an Emergency Call Centre and a Meals on Wheels service.

Salvation Army homes

The Salvation Army has 19 homes for elderly people in various parts of the UK, offering residential care for men and women unable to manage in their own homes. Christian caring is given within a family atmosphere, in pleasant surroundings, but the homes are not nursing homes. Fees are determined by negotiation with local authority social services. For more information contact: **The Salvation Army Social Services Department**, 101 Newington Causeway, London SE1 6BN. T:020 7367 4500.

Very sheltered schemes

A number of organisations which provide sheltered accommodation also have extra care sheltered housing, designed for those who can no longer look after themselves without assistance. Cost ranges from about £150 to £330 a week. Although expensive, it is cheaper than most private residential homes and often more appropriate than full-scale nursing care. A possible problem is that tenants of some of these schemes do not have security of tenure and could therefore be asked to leave if more intensive care were required.

Among the housing associations that provide these facilities are: Housing 21, Hanover, Anchor, Abbeyfield and Servite Houses. Additional names should be obtainable from the various local offices of the **Housing Corporation**, 149 Tottenham Court Road, London W1T 7BN.

Community Care

Since the start of Community Care in April 1993, anyone needing help in arranging suitable care for an elderly person should contact their social services department.

Before making suggestions, the department will assess what type of provision would best meet the needs of the individual concerned. This could be either services or special equipment to enable them to stay in their own home; residential home accommodation; or a nursing home. If residential or nursing home care is necessary, the department will arrange a place – either in a local authority or other home – pay the charge and seek re-imbursement from the individual according to their means. (See 'Financial Assistance for Residential and Nursing Home Care', page 423).

The general range of choices is the same as for an individual making their own private arrangements, which of course anyone – providing they can afford it – is free to do.

Residential care homes

There may come a time when it is no longer possible for an elderly person to manage without being in proper residential care. Sometimes known as rest homes, the accommodation usually consists of a bedroom plus communal dining rooms, lounges and gardens. All meals are provided, rooms are cleaned and staff are at hand to give whatever help is needed. Most homes are fully furnished, though it is usually possible to take small items of furniture. Except in some of the more expensive private homes, bathrooms are normally shared. Intensive nursing care is not usually included.

Homes are run by private individuals (or companies), voluntary organisations and local authorities. All private and voluntary homes must be registered with the Social Services to ensure minimum standards. Any unregistered home should not be considered!

No home should ever be accepted 'on spec'. It is very important that the individual should have a proper chance to visit it and ask any questions. Before reaching a final decision, it is a good idea to arrange a short stay to see whether the facilities are suitable and pleasant.

It could also be sensible to enquire what long-term plans there are for the home. Over the past couple of years, many private and voluntary rest homes have been closing due to the increasing expense of running them. While in the event, a move may turn out to be a blessing in disguise, equally it can be a highly distressing experience for an elderly person who has become attached to the staff and made friends among the other residents. Though a move can never be totally ruled out, awareness of whether the home is likely to remain a going concern could be a deciding factor when making a choice. Possible clues could include whether the place is short-staffed or in need of decoration – or, if run by a company or charity, you could request to see their latest accounts.

Private homes. Private rest homes tend either to be converted houses, taking up to about 30 people; or, as more companies move into the market, purpose-built accommodation which may include heated swimming pool and luxury facilities. The degree of care varies. If a resident becomes increasingly infirm, a rest home will normally continue to look after them if possible although it may be necessary at some point to arrange transfer to a nursing home or hospital. Fees cover an enormous range: from about £275 a week to over £750. The average is about £350.

Voluntary rest homes. These are run by charities, religious bodies or other voluntary organisations. Eligibility may be determined by age, background or occupation, depending on the criteria of the managing organisation. Income may be a factor, as may general fitness and individuals may be invited to a personal interview before acceptance onto the waiting list. Priority tends to be given to those in greatest need. Homes are often in large converted houses, with accommodation for under 10 people or up to 100. Fees normally start at around the £275 mark with top charges, about £550 – and even higher for Greater London.

Local authority homes. These are sometimes referred to as 'Part III Accommodation' and admission would invariably be arranged by the social services department. If someone does not like the particular accommodation suggested, they can turn it down and ask the department what other offers might be available. Weekly charges vary around the country, starting from about £268. In practice, however, individuals are only charged according to their means.

Nursing homes

Nursing homes provide medical supervision and fully qualified nurses, 24 hours a day. Most are privately run with the remainder being supported by voluntary organisations. All nursing homes must be registered with the local Strategic Health Authority which keeps a list of what homes are available in the area.

Private. They normally accommodate between 15 and 100 patients. Average fees are between £385 and £600 a week; in London, they start at around £450 – rising in some of the plusher nursing homes to over £1,000 weekly; in many other parts of the country, charges can reach £600 or even more if intensive nursing is required. For information about nursing homes in the UK, contact the following: **Elderly Accommodation Counsel**, 3rd Floor, 89 Albert Embankment, London SE1 7TP. T:020 7820 1343; **The Registered Nursing Home Association**, 15 Highfield Road, Edgbaston, Birmingham B15 3DU. T:0121 454 2511.

Voluntary organisations. There are normally very long waiting lists and beds are often reserved for those who have been in the charity's rest home. Charges in Greater London start at around £385 but are calculated according to means. Voluntary organisations which run care homes include:

Crossways Trust Ltd., 1st Floor, 19 Parkfield Road, West Worthing, West Sussex BN13 1EN.

Elizabeth Finn Trust, 1 Derry Street, London W8 5HY.

Friends of the Elderly, 40–42 Ebury Street, London SW1W 0LZ.

Jewish Care, 221 Golders Green Road, London NW11 9DQ.

Royal United Kingdom Beneficent Association, 6 Avonmore Road, London W14 8RL.

Catholic Old People's Homes are listed in the *Catholic Directory*, available in libraries.

Free nursing care

Since October 2001, the nursing costs of being in a home have been made free to all patients. This does not include the personal care costs (e.g. help with bathing, dressing or eating) nor the accommodation costs, both of which individuals will continue to be assessed for under the rules, described below. In Scotland exceptionally, the personal care costs are also free.

Financial assistance for residential and nursing home care

Under the Community Care arrangements people needing to go into a residential or nursing home may receive help from their local authority social services department.

As explained earlier, the department will make the arrangements direct with the home following their assessment procedure and will seek reimbursement from the person towards the cost, according to set means-testing rules.

People who were already in a residential or nursing home before April 1993 used to receive special levels of income support. This arrangement, known as 'preserved rights', ended in April 2002 and instead the full cost of residential care is now met by the individual's local authority.

People who had been or are currently paying for themselves but can no longer afford to do so may have the right to claim help, now or in the future, if they qualify on grounds of financial need – for example if their savings fall to £19,000. People with assets below £11,750 will not have to pay anything.

For more information, see leaflet GL15*: Help if you Live in Residential Care or Nursing Home* from your social security office.

Age Concern also publishes a useful factsheet: *Local Authority Charging Procedures for Care Homes;* available from Age Concern, Freepost (SWB 30375), Ashburton, Devon TQ13 7ZZ. A separate Scottish version is also available.

A little extra help. A major worry for many people going into residential care is the requirement to sell their home to cover the costs. While this may still eventually be necessary, the rules have been made slightly more flexible to allow a short breathing space for making decisions. Under the new rules introduced in April 2001, the value of a person's home is disregarded from the means-testing procedure in assessing their ability to pay for the first three months of their going into residential care.

Also, instead of selling, you may be able to borrow the money (secured against your home) from the local council, who will eventually reclaim the loan at a later stage or from your estate.

Further information

Key sources of information about voluntary and private homes are: the *Charities Digest* (available in libraries, Housing Aid Centres and Citizens Advice Bureaux) and the *Directory of Independent Hospitals and Health Services* (available in libraries).

Help the Aged runs a Care Fees Advisory Service, offering free financial advice on how to meet the costs of ongoing care. Recommendations, tailored according to individual circumstances, cover the full range of possibilities from help with claiming benefits to choosing a suitable savings plan for long term care. Depending on the enquiry, advice can be given over the telephone or in face-to-face discussion with an adviser. For further details, call T:0500 767476.

Elderly Accommodation Counsel, 3rd Floor, 89 Albert Embankment, London SE1 7TP. T:020 7820 1343. Has a nationwide database with details of all types of accommodation suitable to meet the needs of retired or elderly people including sheltered housing for sale or rent, residential care and nursing homes.

The Relatives and Residents Association, 4 Tavistock Place, London WC1H 9SN. Offers a support service to families and friends of older people in, or considering, long-term care. There are local groups around the country where relatives can meet and discuss any practical or emotional worries they may have about opting for residential care and there is also a helpline (T:020 7916 6055, Monday to Friday, from 10 a.m. – 12.30 p.m. and 1.30 p.m. – 5 p.m.), which can give advice on most questions from finding a home to concerns about the standard of care. Membership is £12 a year, though any extra would be very much appreciated.

Cinnamon Trust, Foundry House, Foundry Square, Hayle, Cornwall TR27 4HH. T:01736 757900. Maintains a register of residential and care homes that allow pets to be kept.

Social services departments keep lists of both voluntary and private homes.

Useful reading

Finding Residential and Nursing Home Accommodation. Free factsheet obtainable from Age Concern, Freepost (SWB 30375), Ashburton, Devon TQ13 7ZZ.

Home from Home, £6.58 incl. p&p. From Kings Fund Bookshop, 11–13 Cavendish Square, London W1G 0AN.

Some special problems

A minority of people, as they become older, suffer from special problems which can cause great distress. Because families do not like to talk about them, they may be unaware of what services are available so may be missing out both on practical help and sometimes also on financial assistance.

Hypothermia

Elderly people tend to be more vulnerable to the cold. If the body drops below a certain temperature, it can be dangerous because one of the symptoms of hypothermia is that sufferers no longer actually feel cold. Instead, they may lose their appetite and vitality and may become mentally confused. Instead of doing all the sensible things like getting a hot drink and putting on an extra sweater, they are liable to neglect themselves further and can put themselves at real risk.

Although heating costs are often blamed, quite wealthy people can also be victims by allowing their home to become too cold or not wearing sufficient clothing. For this reason, during a cold snap it is very important to check up regularly on an elderly person living alone.

British Gas, Electricity Companies and the Solid Fuel Association are all willing to give advice on how heating systems can be used more efficiently and economically. (See telephone directory for nearest branch or ask at the Citizens' Advice Bureau).

Insulation can also play a very large part in keeping a home warmer and cheaper to heat. There are various grants available to assist with this. See heating and insulation sections in Chapter 8, Your Home.

Additionally, elderly and disabled people in receipt of income support may receive a cold weather payment to help with heating costs during a particularly cold spell, i.e. when the temperature is forecast to drop to zero degrees celsius (or below) for seven consecutive days. The amount paid is £8.50 a week. Those eligible should receive the money automatically. In the event of any problem, ask at your social security office. In the event of any emergency, such as a power cut, contact the Citizens' Advice Bureau or local Age Concern group.

Finally, every household with someone aged 60 or older will get an annual tax-free winter fuel payment of £200. For further information, telephone the Winter Fuel Payment Helpline on T:08459 151515.

Incontinence

Bladder or bowel problems can cause deep embarrassment to sufferers as well as inconvenience to relatives. The problem can occur in an elderly person for all sorts of reasons and a doctor should always be consulted, as it can often be cured or at least alleviated by proper treatment. To assist with the practical problems, some local authorities operate a laundry service which collects soiled linen, sometimes several times a week. The person to talk to is the Health Visitor or District Nurse (telephone your local Health Centre) who will be able to advise about this and other facilities.

Incontinence Information Helpline. T:0845 345 0165. Operates Monday to Friday from 9.30 a.m. to 1.00 p.m. and is staffed by nurses with a special understanding of bladder and bowel problems.

Useful reading

Free booklets on continence care are available from Coloplast Ltd., Peterborough Business Park, Peterborough, Cambs PE2 6FX.

Dementia

Sometimes an elderly person can become confused, forgetful, suffer severe loss of memory or can have violent mood swings and at times be abnormally aggressive. It is important to consult a doctor as soon as possible as the cause may be due to depression, stress or even vitamin deficiency, all of which can be treated and often completely cured. If dementia is diagnosed, there are ways of helping a sufferer to cope better with acute forgetfulness and other symptoms. As well as a doctor, it is usually a very good idea to talk to the Health Visitor, as she will know about any helpful facilities that may be available locally and can also arrange appointments with other professionals, such as the Community Psychiatric Nurse and Occupational Therapist.

The charity, Mind, can often also help. Addresses to contact are:

Mind (The Mental Health Charity), Granta House, 15–19 Broadway, London E15 4BQ, T:020 8519 2122; for Wales, **Mind Cymru**, 3rd Floor, Quebec House, Castlebridge, Cowbridge Road East, Cardiff CF11 9AB. T:029 2039 5123.

Scottish Association for Mental Health, Cumbrae House, 15 Carlton Court, Glasgow G5 9JP. T:0141 568 7000.

Northern Ireland Association for Mental Health, Beacon House, 80 University Street, Belfast BT7 1HE. T:028 9032 8474.

Two other helpful organisations giving support to people with dementia and their carers are:

Alzheimer's Society, for England and Wales and Northern Ireland, Gordon House, 10 Greencoat Place, London SW1P 1PH. T:020 7306 0606. Helpline, open 8.30 a.m. to 6.30 p.m. Monday to Friday, T:0845 300 0336.

Alzheimer Scotland – Action on Dementia, 22 Drumsheugh Gardens, Edinburgh EH3 7RN. T:0808 808 3000 (24-hour helpline). The Society has local services throughout Scotland; for addresses and other information, call the Helpline on the above number.

Useful reading

Caring for the Person with Dementia, published by the Alzheimer's Society, £6.50 incl. p&p.

Understanding Dementia, £1, available from Mind Mail Order Service, at the address listed above.

16 No One is Immortal

In Bali death is celebrated with glorious processions, merry-making and days of feasting. In Western society, we go to the other extreme. Many couples never even discuss death or the financial practicalities, in the subconscious belief perhaps that to do so would be tempting fate. For the same reason, many people put off making a will or rationalise that it does not really matter, since in any case their possessions will eventually go to their family. However, as every widows' organisation would testify, a great deal of heartbreak and real financial worry could be avoided if husbands and wives were more open with each other.

Wills

Anyone who is married, has children or is over the age of 35 should make a will. At very least, should anything happen, this will ensure that their wishes are known and properly executed. But also very important, it will spare their family the legal complications that arise when someone dies intestate. A very major problem if someone dies without leaving a will is that the surviving husband or wife will usually have to wait very much longer for badly needed cash, as the legal formalities are more complex. There will be no executor. Also, the individual's assets will be distributed according to a rigid formula, which may be a far cry from what he or she had intended and may perversely result in their partner's security being quite unnecessarily jeopardised.

Laws of intestacy

The rules if you die without leaving a will are as follows:

- If there is **a surviving spouse but no surviving children, parents, brothers, sisters or direct nephews or nieces** of the deceased, the widow/widower inherits the whole of the estate.
- If there are **children but no surviving spouse**, the estate is divided equally among the children. If one child has died, his/her share would go to his/her own children.
- If there is a **spouse and children**, the partner receives: all personal possessions, £125,000, plus a life interest in half of the remainder. The other half goes to the children.
- If there are **no children** but other close members of the family still living (parents, brothers, sisters, direct nephews or nieces), the surviving spouse receives: all personal possessions, £200,000, plus half of the remainder of the estate. The other half is divided between the rest of the family.

- **Non-married partners** do not inherit automatically; they have to make a court application.
- If a **couple are separated**, but not divorced, they are still legally married and, therefore, the separated partner could be a major beneficiary.

Making a will

You have three choices: you can do it yourself; you can ask your bank to help you; or you can use a solicitor.

Doing it yourself

Homemade wills are not generally recommended. People often use ambiguous wording, which while perfectly clear to the individual who has written it, may be less patently obvious to others. This could result in the donor's wishes being misinterpreted and could also cause considerable delay in settling the estate.

You can buy forms from W.H. Smith and other stationers which, while helpful, are not perfect and still leave considerable margin for error.

For individuals with sight problems, RNIB has produced a comprehensive guide to making or changing a will which is available in large print size, Braille and on tape, as well as in standard print size. This is obtainable free by contacting the Donor Development department at **RNIB**, 105 Judd Street, London WC1H 9NE. T:0845 766 9999.

Two witnesses are needed and an essential point to remember is that beneficiaries cannot witness a will; nor can the spouses of any beneficiaries. In certain circumstances, a will can be rendered invalid. A sensible precaution for anyone doing it themselves is to have it checked by a solicitor or by a legal expert from the Citizens' Advice Bureau.

Banks

Advice on wills and the administration of estates is carried out by the trustee companies of most of the major high street banks.

In particular, the services they offer are: to provide general guidance, to act as executor and to administer the estate. They will also introduce clients to a solicitor and keep a copy of the will – plus other important documents – in their safe, to avoid the risk of their being mislaid. Additionally, banks (as solicitors) can give tax planning and other financial guidance, including advice on inheritance tax. Some banks will draw up a will for you.

Solicitors

Solicitors may offer to: draw up a will, act as executors and administer the estate. Like banks, they will also of course keep a copy of your will in safe keeping (most will not charge for storing a will). If you do not know a solicitor, you can look in the *Yellow* Pages or ask the Citizens' Advice Bureau.

Charges

These can vary enormously, depending on the size and complexity of the will. A basic will could cost around £60 or, if your affairs are more complicated, the cost could run into many hundreds of pounds. Always ask for an estimate before proceeding. Remember too that professional fees normally carry 17.5 per cent VAT. Some solicitors charge according to the time they spend on a job, so although the actual work may not take very long, if you spend hours discussing your will, or changing it every few months, the costs can escalate very considerably. However nowadays, many solicitors will give you a fixed-fee estimate for a will, so you should have a good idea from the outset what it would cost.

Community Legal Service Funding

Civil Legal Aid has been replaced by the Community Legal Service Fund. Financial assistance for legal help and advice is available to certain groups of people for making a will. These include, among one or two other categories: people aged over 70; disabled people; and a parent of a disabled person whom they wish to provide for in their will. Additionally, to qualify, they will need to satisfy the financial criteria. For further information enquire at your CAB or other advice centre.

Executors

You will need to appoint at least one executor to administer your will. An executor can be a beneficiary under the estate and can be a member of your family or a friend whom you trust to act impartially, always provided of course that he/she is willing to accept the responsibility. Or, and this is generally advisable for larger estates, you could appoint your solicitor or bank.

The fees will be additional. They are not paid at the time of making the will but instead come out of the estate. Pretty significant sums could be involved, so the advice on obtaining an estimate is, if anything, even more relevant. In certain instances, banks can be more expensive; in others, solicitors. The only way to discover is to get an estimate from each.

Banks publish a tariff of their charges. Solicitors render bills according to the time involved; so, although it is impossible for them to be precise, they should nevertheless be able to give a pretty accurate assessment – at least at the time of quoting. Both banks' and solicitors' fees may increase during the interval between their being appointed and fulfilling their duties as executor.

Other points

Wills should always be kept in a safe place – and their whereabouts known. The most sensible arrangement is for the solicitor to keep the original and for both you and the bank to have a copy.

A helpful initiative devised by the Law Society is a mini-form, known as a **Personal Assets Log**. This is for individuals drawing up a will to give to their executor or close relatives. It is, quite simply, a four-sided leaflet with space to record the essential information: name and address of solicitor; where the will and other important documents – for example, share certificates and insurance policies – are kept; the date of any codicils and so on. Logs should be obtainable from most solicitors.

Wills may need updating in the event of an important change of circumstances, for example: a divorce, remarriage or the birth of a grandchild. An existing will becomes invalid in the event of marriage or remarriage and should be revised. Any changes must be by codicil (for minor alterations) or by a new will, and must be properly witnessed.

Partners who wish to leave all their possessions to each other should consider including 'a survivorship clause' in their wills, as an insurance against the intestacy rules being applied were they both to be involved in the same fatal accident.

If you have views about your funeral, it is sensible to write a letter to your executors explaining your wishes and to lodge it with your will. If you have any pets, you may equally wish to leave a letter filed with your will explaining what arrangements you have made for their immediate/long term welfare. The charity Pro Dogs provides special cards for this purpose for owners to complete, obtainable from: **Pro Dogs**, Rocky Bank, 6 New Road, Ditton, Maidstone, Kent ME20 6AD. T:01732 872222.

Increasingly, over the years, we have been receiving enquiries about living wills. For those who would like information, the Voluntary Euthanasia Society supplies free leaflets plus, for £5, a set of living wills. Contact the **Voluntary Euthanasia Society**, 13 Prince of Wales Terrace, London W8 5PG. T:020 7937 7770.

If you would be willing to donate an organ which might help save someone else's life, you could indicate this in your will or alternatively obtain an organ donor card. These are available from most hospitals, chemists and social security offices as well as some charities.

Useful reading

Making Your Will. Free factsheet from **Age Concern**, Freepost (SWB 30375), Ashburton, Devon TQ13 7ZZ; or telephone free: 0800 009966. A separate Scottish version is available.

Will Information Pack. Free from Wills and Legacies Department, **Help the Aged**, 207–221 Pentonville Road, London N1 9UZ.

Provision for dependent adult children

A particular concern for parents with a physically or mentally dependent son or daughter is what plans they can make to ensure his, or her, care when they are no longer in a position to manage. There is no single right answer as each case is individual depending on the severity of the disability or illness, the range of helpful voluntary or statutory local facilities and the extent to which they, as parents, can provide for their child's financial security long-term.

While Social Services may be able to advise, parents thinking ahead might do better to consult a specialist organisation, experienced in helping carers in this situation explore the possible options available to them. Useful addresses are: **Carers UK**, 20–25 Glasshouse Yard, London EC1A 4JT. T:020 7490 8818; **The Princess Royal Trust for Carers**, 142 Minories, London EC3N 1LB. T:020 7480 7788.

Parents concerned about financial matters such as setting up a trust or making alternative provision in their will would also be advised to consult a solicitor or accountant.

Money worries – and how to minimise them

Most people say that the first time they really think about death, in terms of what would happen to their nearest and dearest, is after the birth of their first baby. As children grow up, requirements change but key points that any family man or woman should consider – and review from time to time – include life insurance and mortgage protection relief.

Both husbands and wives should have **life insurance cover**. If either were to die, not only would their partner lose the benefit of their earnings, they would also lose the value of their services: home decorating, gardening, cooking and so forth.

Most banks and building societies urge homeowners to take out **mortgage protection schemes**. If you die, the loan is paid off automatically and the family home will not be repossessed.

Banks also offer **insurance to cover any personal or other loans**. This could be a vital safeguard to avoid leaving the family with debts.

Many people worry about **funeral costs**. Burial services can vary, according to different parts of the country, from about £1,490 to £3,930 or even more depending on the choice of coffin and other arrangements. Although you may well hear of cheaper estimates, these are normally exclusive of disbursements which include minister's fees, cremation fees, medical certificate fees and other items.

While cremations are cheaper, prices have increased by more than 10 per cent over the past few years – with £1,325 being a rough average. But here again, costs can vary significantly according to both area and how grand, or simple, the arrangements are.

As a way of helping, a number of insurance companies offer policies to cover funeral costs and while these could be sensible, a drawback is that you are budgeting today against an unknown cost in the future. Over the past three or four years, funeral costs have soared by over 20 per cent, so there would be no guarantee even with the best policies that the eventual pay-out would be sufficient to cover the expenses.

A rather different type of scheme, which overcomes the uncertainties and is growing in popularity, is the pre-paid funeral plan which is designed so you pay all the costs in advance, at present day prices. In other words, if you join today, the funeral is paid at today's price: whenever the service is actually required; and whatever the prices are at the time.

One such scheme is **Dignity Funeral Plans** (Freepost MID 30011, Sutton Coldfield, B72 1BR. T:0800 387717) which offers a varied range of choices to suit different requirements, with in all cases the option of paying in a single payment or by monthly instalments.

Additionally, both **Age Concern Funeral Plan** (Freepost SEA3369, London SE21 8BR, T:0800 387718) and **Help the Aged Funeral Plan** (Freephone: 0800 169 1112) offer pre-arranged, pre-paid funeral plans, as do several regional insurance companies.

Alternatively you might like to investigate the Perfect Choice pre-paid funeral plan – offered by the National Association of Funeral Directors – which is a 'bespoke' scheme, as opposed to a package, so enabling you to choose all the details you want. For further information, contact: **National Association of Funeral Directors**, 618 Warwick Road, Solihull, West Midlands B91 1AA. T:0121 709 0019.

Another organisation that, as well as a selection of standard plans, offers a personalised service that allows you to specify every detail including the choice of funeral director is **Golden Charter** (Freepost Golden Charter, T:0800 833800).

The company, a founder member of the Funeral Planning Council, requires that the funeral director concerned guarantees that the price is fully inclusive of all selected arrangements and that your family will never be asked to pay any extra.

Funeralcare, part of the Co-operative Group, a nationwide network of more than 600 funeral homes and founder member of the Funeral Planning Council, likewise offers the choice of pre-paid tailor-made arrangements or a selection of funeral plan packages. For details contact **FPP Customer Services**, Freepost (NW 3091A), Manchester M60 5SH. Freephone: 0800 289120.

If you are thinking of giving the idea serious consideration, as with any other important purchase, it is sensible to compare the different plans on the market to ensure that you are choosing the one that best suits your requirements.

While most pre-paid funeral schemes are problem-free, as an **Office of Fair Trading** report warned, there can be pitfalls – including the risk of losing your money, if the company which sold you the plan should go out of business.

Happily this is far less likely today, as the government has recently introduced new regulations designed to ensure that customers' money is properly safeguarded and will be available to pay for the funeral when the time comes.

Another welcome new development is the setting up of the Funeral Planning Authority, a self-regulatory organisation which monitors members' compliance procedures and has rules and a code of practice, laying down strict professional standards which all funeral providers registered with the Authority are expected to observe. For further details and a list of approved funeral companies, contact: **Funeral Planning Authority**, Harelands, 22 Bentsbrook Park, North Holmwood, Dorking, Surrey RH5 4JN. T:01306 740 878.

Helpful as these new measures are, before making any advance payment you would still be wise to investigate the following points: (1) whether your money will be paid into a trust administered by independent trustees (2) what fees are deducted from the investment (3) what exact expenses the plan covers and (4) if you cancel the plan, can you get all your money back – or only a part?

If you have a complaint about a funeral, the Ombudsman Scheme might be able to help. The Ombudsman has power to award compensation but cannot assist unless the complainant has first tried to resolve the matter with the funeral company concerned. Also the company itself must be a member of the scheme. For further information, contact: **The Funeral Ombudsman**, Richmond House, Old Brewery Court, 156 Sandyford Road, Newcastle upon Tyne, NE2 1XG. T:0191 230 5554.

Those in receipt of income support, housing benefit or council tax benefit may qualify for a payment from the Social Fund to help with funeral costs. For details of eligibility and how you claim, see Leaflet D 49, *What To Do After A Death*, obtainable from any social security office. If the matter is urgent, make a point of asking for Form SF 200.

A very real crisis for some families is the need for immediate money while waiting for the estate to be settled. At least part of the problem can be overcome by couples having a **joint bank account**, with both partners having drawing rights without the signature of the other being required. Sole-name bank accounts and joint accounts requiring both signatures are frozen.

For the same reason, it may also be a good idea for any savings or investments to be held in the joint name of the couple. However, couples who have recently made any changes – or were planning to do so – as a result of independent taxation could be advised to discuss this point with a solicitor or qualified financial adviser.

Additionally, an essential practical point for all couples is that any financial and other **important documents should be discussed together** and understood by the wife as well as by the husband. Even today, an all too common saga is for widows to come across insurance policies and other papers, which they have never seen before and do not understand – often causing quite unnecessary anxiety. A further common-sense 'must' is for both partners to **know where important papers are kept**. Best idea is either to lock them, filed together, in a home safe; or to give them to the bank to look after.

If someone dies, **the bank manager should be notified as soon as possible**, so he can assist with the problems of unpaid bills and help work out a solution until the estate is settled. The same goes for the **suppliers of essential services**: gas, electricity, telephone and so on. Unless they know the situation, there is a risk of services being cut off if there is a delay in paying the bill. Add too any credit card companies, where if bills lie neglected, the additional interest could mount up alarmingly.

Useful reading

What to Do After a Death. Free booklet from any social security office.

Arranging A Funeral, free factsheet from **Age Concern**, Freepost (SWB 30375), Ashburton, Devon TQ13 7ZZ; or telephone free T:0800 009966. A separate Scottish version is available.

State benefits, tax and other money points

Several extra financial benefits are given to widowed persons. Most take the form of a cash payment. However, there are one or two tax and other points that it may be useful to know.

Benefits paid in cash form

There are three important cash benefits to which widowed people may be entitled: bereavement benefit, bereavement allowance and widowed parent's allowance. These have replaced the former widows' benefits as all benefits are now payable on equal terms to men and women alike.

To claim the benefits, fill in Form BB 1, obtainable from any social security office. You will also be given a questionnaire (BD 8) by the Registrar. It is important that you complete this, as it acts as a trigger to speed up payment of your benefits. For more information, see leaflet *The New Bereavement Benefits*, obtainable by ringing the Pensions Info-line on T:0845 731 3233.

Bereavement benefit. This has replaced what used to be known as widow's payment. It is a tax-free lump sum of £2,000, paid as soon as an individual is widowed provided that: (1) their spouse had paid sufficient NI contributions (2) they personally are under State retirement age or (3) if over State retirement age, their husband/wife had not been entitled to retirement pension.

Bereavement allowance. This has replaced the widow's pension. Women already in receipt of widow's pension before 6 April 2001 are not affected and will continue to receive their widow's pension as normal.

The new bereavement allowance is for those aged between 45 and State pension age who do not receive widowed parent's allowance. It is payable for 52 weeks and, as with widow's pension before, there are various levels of payment: the full rate and age-related bereavement allowance. Receipt in all cases is dependent on sufficient NI contributions having been paid.

Full-rate bereavement allowance is paid to widowed persons between the ages of 55 and 59 inclusive. The weekly amount is £75.50, which is the same as the current pension for a single person.

Age-related bereavement allowance is for younger widows/widowers, who do not qualify for the full rate. It is payable to those who are aged between 45 and 54 inclusive when their partner dies. Rates depend on age and vary from £22.65 for 45 year olds to £70.22 for those aged 54.

Bereavement allowance is normally paid automatically once you have sent off your completed form BB 1, so if for any reason you do not receive it you should enquire at your social security office. In the event of your being ineligible, due to insufficient NI contributions having been paid, you may still be entitled to receive income support, housing benefit or a grant or loan from the social fund. Your social security office will advise you.

Widowed parent's allowance. This is paid to widowed parents with at least one child for whom they receive child benefit. The current value (2002/03) is £75.50 a week. The allowance is usually paid automatically. If for some reason, although eligible, you do not receive the money, you should inform your social security office.

Retirement pension. Once a widowed person reaches State retirement age, they should receive a State pension in the normal way. An important point to remember is that a widow/widower may be able to use their late spouse's NI contributions to boost the amount they receive. See leaflets NP 46 *A Guide to Retirement Pensions* and RM1 *Retirement*.

Problems. Both pension payments and the new bereavement benefits are dependent on sufficient NI contributions having been paid. Your social security office will inform you if you are not eligible. If this should turn out to be the case, you may still be entitled to receive income support, housing benefit, council tax benefit or a grant or loan from the Social Fund – so ask. If you are unsure of your position or have difficulties, ask at your Citizens' Advice Bureau who will at least be able to help you work out the sums and inform you of your rights.

Particular points to note

- Most widowed persons' benefits are taxable. However, the £2,000 bereavement benefit is tax-free, as are pensions paid to the widow/widowers of Armed Forces personnel.
- Widowed persons will normally be able to inherit their spouse's additional pension rights, if he/she contributed to SERPS (see N.B. below); or at least half their guaranteed minimum pension, if they were in a contracted-out scheme. Additionally, where applicable, all widowed persons are entitled on retirement to half the graduated pension earned by their husband/wife.

N.B. SERPS benefits paid to surviving spouses are due to be halved over the coming years. The cuts are gradually being phased in between October 2002 and October 2010. Anyone over State pension age before 6 October 2002 will be exempt from any cuts and will keep the right to pass on their SERPS pension in full to a bereaved spouse. Equally, any younger widow or widower who had already inherited their late spouse's SERPS entitlement before 6 October 2002 will not be affected and will continue to receive the full amount.

- Women in receipt of widow's pension who remarry, or live with a man as his wife, lose their entitlement to the payment unless, that is, the cohabitation ends in which case they can claim it again. If aged over 60, the fact that a woman may be living with a man will not affect her entitlement to a retirement pension based on her late husband's contribution record.
- Thanks to a recent change in the law, widows/widowers of Armed Forces personnel whose deaths were a direct result of their service are now entitled to keep their Armed Forces attributable pension for life, regardless of whether they remarry or cohabit.

Tax allowances

At time of writing, widows and widowers receive the normal single person's tax allowance of £4,615 a year and, if in receipt of married couple's allowance, are also entitled to any unused portion of the allowance in the year of their partner's death. Those aged 65 and older may be entitled to a higher personal allowance, (see page 70).

Useful Inland Revenue leaflets. These are available from any tax office.
IR 45: *What to do About Tax When Someone Dies*
IR 90: *Tax Allowances and Reliefs*
IHT 3: *An Introduction to Inheritance Tax*.

Advice. Many people have difficulty in working out exactly what they are entitled to – and how to claim it. The Citizens' Advice Bureau is always very helpful. Additionally, Cruse and the National Association of Widows (see below) can assist you.

Organisations that can help

Problems vary. For some, the hardest thing to bear is the loneliness of returning to an empty house. For others, money problems seem to dominate everything else. For many older women in particular, who have not got a job, widowhood creates a great gulf where for a while there is no real sense of purpose. Many widowed men and women go through a spell of feeling enraged against their partner for dying. Most are baffled and hurt by the seeming indifference of friends, who appear more embarrassed than sympathetic.

In time, all these feelings soften, problems diminish and individuals are able to recapture their joy for living with all its many pleasures. Talking to other people who know the difficulties from their own experience can be a tremendous help. The following organisations not only offer opportunities for companionship but also provide an advisory and support service.

Cruse Bereavement Care, Cruse House, 126 Sheen Road, Richmond, Surrey TW9 1UR. Helpline T:0870 167 1677 (9.30 a.m. – 5 p.m.). Cruse offers free help to anyone who has been bereaved by providing both one-to-one and group counselling through its 178 local branches throughout the UK. Practical advice can be given and there are also drop-in centres and friendship groups. A list of publications and a newsletter are available. For further information, contact your local branch (see telephone directory) or the headquarters address above.

National Association of Widows, 48 Queen's Road, Coventry CV1 3EH. T:024 7663 4848. The Association is a national voluntary organisation. Its many branches provide a supportive social network for widows throughout the country. Membership is £8 a year.

Many professional and other groups offer a range of services for widows and widowers associated with them. These include:

Civil Service Retirement Fellowship, 1b Deals Gateway, Blackheath Road, London SE10 8BW. T:020 8691 7411.

The War Widows' Association of Great Britain, c/o 48 Pall Mall, London SW1Y 5JY. T:0870 241 1305.

Lesbian and Gay Bereavement Project, c/o HGLC, 40 Borough High Street, London SE1 1XW. T:020 7407 3550; Helpline: 020 7403 5969 (7 p.m. – 10.30 p.m. Monday – Friday). Offers telephone or face-to-face counselling for those affected by bereavement. A free will pack is available on request.

Many local Age Concern groups offer a counselling service. Trade unions are often particularly supportive, as are Rotary Clubs, all the armed forces organisations and most benevolent societies.

Classified advertisements

Appeals/Donations

CAF, Kings Hill, West Malling, Kent ME19 4TA. Tel: 01732 520 050. Fax: 01732 520 001.

Giving Made Easy. A CAF Charity Account is the ideal way to support your favourite charities and manage your giving tax-free.

Carers UK, Department GR-03 (Fundraising), 20–25 Glasshouse Yard, London EC1A 4JT. Tel: 020 7566 7634.

Carers UK is the leading charity for carers, our commitment is to get them a better deal. Help us to care for the carers.

Greenpeace, Canonbury Villas, London N1 2PN. Tel: 020 7865 8100. Fax: 020 7865 8201.

Greenpeace promotes solutions to environmental problems internationally to change things for the better. We rely entirely on support from individuals.

Relate, Herbert Gray College, Little Church Street, Rugby CV21 3AP. Tel: 0845 456 1310. Fax: 01788 535 007.

Relate is the UK's leading relationship counselling organisation. We provide expert, impartial advice and support to people experiencing difficulties in their relationships.

The Relatives & Residents Association, 4 Tavistock Place, London WC1H 9SN. Tel: 020 7916 6055 (Advice Line). Fax: 020 7916 6093.

Supports relatives of older people in long-term care. Helpline, Publications, Training etc. Depends on donations to maintain and expand services.

Courses

City & Guilds, Publication Sales, 1 Giltspur Street, London EC1A 9DD. Tel: 020 7294 2850.

Time to Learn – directory of residential learning breaks and day schools, published twice a year, price £4.95 (plus £1 p&p). Also on-line at www.timetolearn.org.uk

Holidays

Absentia, Little London, Berden, Bishops Stortford CM23 1BE. Tel: 01279 777412. Fax: 01279 777049.

Retired? Bored? Would you like to care for our clients' homes and pets? Remuneration is modest, the lifestyle is fun.

En Famille Overseas, 4 St. Helena Road, Colchester CO3 3BA. Tel: 01206 546741. Fax: 01206 546740. E-mail: marylou_toms@btinternet.com

Well-established Agency tailor-makes holidays and language study in the homes of delightful host families in France, Spain, Italy.

FSC (Field Studies Council), Head Office, Preston Montford, Montford Bridge, Shrewsbury SY4 1HW. Tel: 01743 852100. Fax: 01743 852101.

Wildlife, walking, photography and painting – over 700 courses at our centres in the UK and study tours further afield. Contact us for our free brochure.

Scottish Field Studies Association, Kindrogan, Enochdu, Blairgowrie, PH10 7PG. Tel: 01250 881286. Fax: 01250 881433. E-mail: kindrogan@btinternet.com

Fascinating informative courses and holidays, Highland Glen. Plants, birds, art, craft, walking. Direct London train. Telephone Ros Bromley to find out more.

Page & Moy Ltd., PO Box 155, Leicester LE1 9GZ. Tel: 0870 010 6444. Website: www.1st4cruising.com

Working closely with the cruise lines to bring you the very best offers. Visit www.1st4cruising.com for the latest deals or call our knowledgeable consultants to book.

STAG, Church Lane, Sharnbrook, Bedfordshire MK44 1HR.

Details of supplement-free hotels and holidays at home and abroad etc. Subscription £10 p.a.

Home Improvement & Equipment

Association of Plumbing & Heating Contractors, 14/15 Ensign House, Ensign Business Centre, Westwood Way, Coventry CV4 8JA. Tel: 024 7647 0626. Fax: 024 7647 0942.

Upgrade your heating for greater comfort and reduced running costs! For your local installer contact APHC on 024 7647 0626.

Investments/Savings

British Insurance Brokers' Association, 14 Bevis Marks, London EC3A 7NT. Tel: 020 7623 9043. Fax: 020 7626 9676.

BIBA is the UK's leading independent broker and intermediary organisation, offering expertise and professionalism to brokers and their customer.

Leisure

Centre for Alternative Technology, Machynlleth, Powys, Wales SY20 9AZ. Tel: 01654 705950. Fax: 01654 702782.

Europe's leading Eco-centre combines amazing views of Snowdonia with interactive displays and organic gardens, Britain's greenest shop and wholefood café.

Croquet Association, c/o Cheltenham Croquet Club, Old Bath Road, Cheltenham GL53 7DF. Tel: 01242 242318. Fax: 01242 243573.
E-mail: caoffice@croquet.org.uk

Croquet is the ideal sport for those whose athleticism is waning, but whose competitive instinct is undimmed.

CTC – the national cyclists' organisation, 69 Meadrow, Godalming, Surrey GU7 3HS. Tel: 0870 873 0060. Fax: 0870 873 0064. E-mail: cycling@ctc.org.uk

CTC can provide you with free routes, travel information, friendly advice, membership benefits and local people to cycle with.

Historic Houses Association, Membership Department, Heritage House, PO Box 21, Baldock SG7 5SH. Tel: 01462 896688. Fax: 01462 896677.

HHA friends have free access to nearly 300 historic houses and gardens throughout England, Scotland and Wales.

The Keep Fit Association, Suite 1.05, Astra House, Arklow Road, London SE14 6EB. Tel: 020 8692 9566. Fax: 020 8692 8383.

Fitness – it's never too late to get fit through movement, exercise and dance. Classes nationwide. Call for details today.

The Wildlife Trusts – Charity No. 207238, The Kiln, Waterside, Mather Road, Newark, Notts NG24 1WT. Tel: 0870 036 7711. Fax: 0870 036 0101.
E-mail: info@wildlife-trusts.cix.co.uk

The Wildlife Trusts protect wildlife for the future. Contact us for information on reserves, events and ways to help from membership to volunteering.

Property

Home Housing Association Ltd., Ridley House, Regent Centre, Gosforth, Newcastle upon Tyne NE3 1NZ. Tel: 0191 202 8741. Fax: 0191 202 8795.

We develop and manage shared ownership housing specifically aimed at the retirement market, mainly in the north of England.

SOS Help

Aid-Call Ltd., Linhay House, Linhay Business Park, Ashburton, Devon TQ13 7BR. Tel: 0800 772266. Fax: 01364 654111. E-mail: info@aidcall.co.uk

Since 1980 Aid-Call emergency response alarm has helped thousands of people throughout the UK to maintain independent lives, secure in the knowledge that help is always at hand.

Association of Plumbing & Heating Contractors, 14/15 Ensign House, Ensign Business Centre, Westwood Way, Coventry CV4 8JA. Tel: 024 7647 0626. Fax: 024 7647 0942.

Beware of Cowboys! For a local plumber you can trust, ensure you contact APHC first on 024 7647 0626. Work guaranteed.

Rukba, 6 Avonmore Road, London W14 8RL. Tel: 020 7605 4200. Fax: 020 7605 4201. E-mail: charity@rukba.org.uk

Rukba helps older people in need retain their independence by providing life-long financial support and the friendship of dedicated volunteers.

Volunteers

International Voluntary Service, IVS South (Registered Office), Old Hall, East Bergholt, Colchester CO7 6TQ. Tel: 01206 298215. IVS North (Tel: 0113 230 4600). IVS Scotland (Tel: 0131 226 6722). Please contact your regional office.

Sends volunteers to take part in diverse, short term (2–3week) International Voluntary Projects in over 40 countries, including GB.

The Keep Fit Association, Suite 1.05, Astra House, Arklow Road, London SE14 6EB. Tel: 020 8692 9566. Fax: 020 8692 8383.

It's never too late to learn! Gain/maintain your fitness through teaching fitness classes. Call for courses in your area.

The National Trust, The Dairy House, Ickworth, Bury St Edmunds, Suffolk IP29 5QE. Tel: 01284 736008. Fax: 01284 736006. E-mail: avotdc@smtp.ntrust.org.uk

Pre-retirement packs designed for employers and trainers to distribute information on volunteering opportunities within The National Trust. Available free.

Winged Fellowship Trust, Angel House, 20–32 Pentonville Road, London N1 9XD. Tel: 020 7833 2594. Fax: 020 7278 0370.

Provides holidays for disabled people and breaks for carers at five UK centres in Essex, Cornwall, Hampshire, Nottinghamshire and Merseyside.

Website Index

The Abbeyfield Society	www.abbeyfield.com
Absentia	www.home-and-pets.co.uk
Action for Sick Children	www.actionforsickchildren.org
Aid-Call Ltd.	www.aidcall.co.uk
AITC (Association of Investment Trust Companies)	www.aitc.co.uk
Alzheimer's Society	www.alzheimers.org.uk
Alzheimer Scotland – Action on Dementia	www.alzscot.org
AMP Retirement Services	www.amp.com.au
Annuity Bureau	www.annuity-bureau.co.uk
Annuity Direct	www.annuitydirect.co.uk
APCIMS	www.apcims.co.uk
APHC (Association of Plumbing & Heating Contractors)	www.licensedplumber.co.uk
The Association of Policy Market Makers	www.apmm.org
ARP/O50 (Association of Retired and Persons Over 50)	www.arp.org.uk
Beale Dobie & Co Ltd.	www.bealedobie.co.uk
Benslow Music Trust	www.benslow.org
BIBA (British Insurance Brokers' Association)	www.biba.org.uk
Bovis Homes Retirement Living	www.bovishomes.co.uk
Breast Cancer Care	www.breastcancercare.org.uk
British Bankers Association	www.bba.org.uk
British Institute of Florence	www.britishinstitute.it
British Model Flying Association	www.bmfa.org
The British Museum Traveller	www.britishmuseumtraveller.co.uk
British Wireless for the Blind Fund	www.blind.org.uk
BUPA	www.bupa.co.uk
BVCA (British Venture Capital Association)	www.bvca.co.uk
BWPDA (British Wood Preserving and Damp-Proofing Association)	www.bwpda.co.uk
CAF	www.allaboutgiving.org
Calibre	www.calibre.org.uk
The Camping and Caravanning Club	www.campingandcaravanningclub.co.uk
Carers UK	www.carersuk.demon.co.uk
Centre for Alternative Technology	www.cat.org.uk
Chase de Vere Investments Plc	www.chasedevere.co.uk
City & Guilds	www.timetolearn.org.uk
Civil Service Retirement Fellowship	www.csrf.co.uk
Companies House	www.companieshouse.gov.uk
Consultus Services Agency Ltd.	www.consultusagency.co.uk

The Continence Foundation	www.continence-foundation.org.uk
CPRE (The Council for the Protection of Rural England)	www.greenchannel.com/cpre
The Croquet Association	www.croquet.org.uk
Crown Equity Release Ltd.	www.crownequityrelease.com
CSV-RSVP (Retired Senior Volunteer Programme)	www.csv-rsvp.org.uk
Cycling for Softies	www.cycling-for-softies.co.uk
CTC (Cyclists' Touring Club)	www.ctc.org.uk
The Donkey Sanctuary	www.thedonkeysanctuary.org.uk
The Elisabeth Svendson Trust	www.thedonkeysanctuary.org.uk
Embroiderers' Guild	www.embroiderersguild.com
En Famille Overseas	www.enfamilleoverseas.co.uk
English Courtyard	www.englishcourtyard.co.uk
Eurocentres	www.eurocentres.com
Explore Worldwide	www.exploreworldwide.com
50*plus* Insurance Services	www.50plusinsurance.co.uk
The Fitness League	www.thefitnessleague.com
Friends of the Earth	www.foe.co.uk
Forestry Commission	www.forestry.gov.uk
FSC (Field Studies Council)	www.field-studies-council.org
Funeral Planning Authority Ltd.	www.funeralplanningauthority.com
Glass and Glazing Federation	www.ggf.org.uk
Goethe-Institut	www.goethe.de/london
Golden Charter	www.golden-charter.co.uk
Grandparents' Federation	www.grandparents-federation.org.uk
Greenpeace	www.greenpeace.org.uk
Handbell Ringers of Great Britain	www.hrgb.org.uk
Hanover Housing Association	www.hanover.org.uk
Hearing Concern	www.hearingconcern.org.uk
Hinton & Wild (Home Plans) Ltd.	www.hinton-wild.co.uk
Historic Houses Association	www.hha.org.uk
Historical Association	www.history.org.uk
Hodge Equity Release	www.HodgeEquityRelease.com
Home & Capital Trust	www.homecapital.co.uk
Home Base Holidays	www.homebase-hols.com
Home Housing Association	www.homehousing.org.uk
International Voluntary Service	www.ivs-gb.org.uk
James Butcher Housing Association	www.jbha.co.uk
The Keep Fit Association	www.keepfit.org.uk
Landmark Trust	www.landmarktrust.co.uk
LEASE (The Leasehold Advisory Service)	www.lease-advice.org
League Against Cruel Sports	www.league.uk.com

Mental Health Foundation	www.mentalhealth.org.uk
Mothers Union	www.themothersunion.org
National Adult School Organisation	www.naso.org.uk
National Association of Hospital & Community Friends	www.hc-friends.org.uk
National Business Angels Network	www.bestmatch.co.uk
National Centre for Social Research	www.natcen.ac.uk
The National Trust	www.nationaltrust.org.uk/volunteers
The National Trust	www.nationaltrust.org.uk
The National Trust for Scotland	www.nts.org.uk
Nursing Home Fees Agency	www.nhfa.co.uk
Occupational Pensions Regulatory Authority (OPRA)	www.opra.gov.uk
Open and Distance Learning Quality Council	www.odlqc.org.uk
Open College of the Arts	www.oca-uk.com
Oral History Society	www.oralhistory.org.uk
OTE	www.ote-info.com
Page & Moy Ltd.	www.1st4cruising.com
Relate	www.relate.org.uk
Relatives & Residents Association	www.relres.org.uk
REMAP	www.remap.org.uk
Remembrance Travel	www.remembrancetravel.com
Royal Agricultural Benevolent Institution	www.rabi.org.uk
The Royal British Legion	www.britishlegion.org.uk
RSPB (Royal Society for the Protection of Birds)	www.rspb.org.uk
RUKBA (Royal United Kingdom Beneficent Association)	www.rukba.org.uk
The Salvation Army	www.salvationarmy.org.uk
The Samaritans	www.samaritans.org
Scottish Field Studies Association	www.kindrogan.com
Scottish Pre-Retirement Council	www.sprc.org.uk
Skillshare International	www.skillshare.org
SOVA	www.sova.org.uk
SSAFA Forces Help	www.ssafa.org.uk
Toc H	www.toch.org.uk
Training Professional Guides Ltd.	www.guidetraining.co.uk
Vegi Ventures	www.vegiventures.com
The Voluntary Euthanasia Society	www.ves.org.uk
Walter Segal Self Build Trust	www.segalselfbuild.co.uk
West Dean College	www.westdean.org.uk
The Wildfowl & Wetlands Trust	www.wwt.org.uk
The Wildlife Trusts	www.wildlifetrusts.org
Winged Fellowship Trust	www.wft.org.uk
WEA (Workers' Educational Association)	www.wea.org.uk
WRVS (Women's Royal Voluntary Service)	www.wrvs.org.uk

Index

Index of Advertisers